The Duty of Medical Practitioners and CAM/TCM Practitioners to Inform Competent Adult Patients about Alternatives

Xiju Zhao

The Duty of Medical Practitioners and CAM/TCM Practitioners to Inform Competent Adult Patients about Alternatives

Springer

Xiju Zhao
Department of Law
College of Social Science and Humanities
Shandong University of Traditional Chinese Medicine
Jinan, P.R. China

ISBN 978-3-642-31646-3 ISBN 978-3-642-31647-0 (eBook)
DOI 10.1007/978-3-642-31647-0
Springer Heidelberg New York Dordrecht London

Library of Congress Control Number: 2012948638

Printed on acid-free paper

Springer is part of Springer Science+Business Media (www.springer.com)

To my mom and my sister

Acknowledgments

This book is based on a thesis that I wrote for the degree of Doctor of Philosophy at the University of Otago, New Zealand. I would like to begin by thanking Prof. Mark Henaghan and Prof. Peter Skegg who supervised my Ph.D. Mark has always been available to provide guidance, encouragement and endless support. Peter gave high priority to reading my writings and devoted so much time in his busy periods, even sacrificed his weekends and vacations, to read my thesis draft, word by word, and make detailed comments and suggestions about it, including presentation. Those comments are very helpful and constructive. They are greatly appreciated.

I also benefited from discussing the issues with Prof. Colin Gavaghan, Prof. John Dawson and Prof. Nicola Peart. The input they gave me is valuable. Despite many other commitments, John agreed to proofread Chaps. 1 and 11 of my thesis. His insightful comments and focus on detail are very much appreciated.

My thanks also go to three anonymous examiners of my Ph.D. thesis. Now I have the honour to know who they are. They are Prof. Erwin Deutsch (Germany), Prof. J. A. Devereux (Australia), and Prof. Grant Gillett (New Zealand). Their comments are very constructive and helpful for my amending the thesis. I appreciate very much their time in reading my thesis and writing the reports on it.

Furthermore, I want to extend my thanks to anyone who has helped me, in one way or another, during my Ph.D. journey. They include many other staff members at the Law Faculty and the Law Library of the University of Otago.

Finally, I would like to dedicate my thesis to my mother, my sister, my wife and my son. In 2009, both my mother and sister were diagnosed with lung cancer. It shocked me. They passed away during my graduation period. I am sorry that I did not spend much of my time with them. I am also sorry that I did not give much of my time to my son. My wife, as a working mother, devoted so much of her time to take care of and look after our son, while I was living many thousands of miles away from them, working on this thesis. I thank them sincerely for their understanding and tolerance.

I am responsible for the arguments presented in this thesis, and for any errors.

Contents

Chapter 1
Introduction

Abstract Informed consent literatures have prospered in the past decades. However, they have centred mainly on disclosure of *risks* of one particular treatment/procedure proposed by a doctor. There is a need to explore the topic of the duty to inform patients of *alternatives*. In the common law world, there are significant differences between jurisdictions with regard to whether a doctor has a *legal* duty to inform about alternatives, and what kinds of alternatives fall within a doctor's duty to inform. This book covers the law of a wide range of jurisdictions, including England, the USA, Canada, Australia, New Zealand, Japan and China. The first few chapters (Chaps. 2, 3, 4, 5, 6, 7 and 8) examine the collective wisdom and experience of a few common law jurisdictions. Chapters 9 and 10 examine the New Zealand context and the Chinese context. To highlight the uniqueness of the New Zealand context, in Chap. 9 distinctions are drawn between New Zealand and the three common law jurisdictions with which it is most commonly compared (England, Canada and Australia).

Informed consent literatures have prospered in the past decades. However, mirroring the focus of case law, they have centred mainly on disclosure of *risks of one particular treatment/procedure proposed by a doctor*. The topic of the duty to inform patients of *alternatives* remains almost untouched. This book concentrates on the duty to inform of alternatives. As the title of the book indicates, it has two inclusions and exclusions. First, it focuses on *medical practitioners (doctors) and Complementary and Alternative Medicine (CAM), including Traditional Chinese Medicine (TCM), practitioners*, excluding involvement of other health practitioners, such as nurses. Second, it is confined to *competent adult patients*, thereby avoiding the need to deal with issues of competency and also proxy consent.

In the common law world, although there are many similarities in a doctor's duty to inform of risks of a procedure among jurisdictions, there are significant differences between jurisdictions with regard to whether a doctor has a *legal* duty to inform about alternatives, and what kinds of alternatives fall within a doctor's duty to inform.

X. Zhao, *The Duty of Medical Practitioners and CAM/TCM Practitioners to Inform Competent Adult Patients about Alternatives*,
DOI 10.1007/978-3-642-31647-0_1,

This book covers the law of a wide range of jurisdictions, including England, the USA, Canada, Australia, New Zealand, Japan and China. In the first few chapters (Chaps. 2, 3, 4, 5, 6, 7 and 8), I do not draw many distinctions between jurisdictions. They are the result of examining the collective wisdom and experience of many common law jurisdictions. In these chapters, my tasks are (1) to highlight the distinctive nature of information disclosure; (2) to construct a model concerning the drawing of distinctions between the disclosure of alternatives and other aspects of health care, thereby putting the issue of "disclosure" of alternatives in a clear context; (3) to identify the circumstances and factors that may broaden or narrow a doctor's duty to inform of alternatives; (4) to categorize "alternatives"; and (5) to explore some topical, debateable and complex issues, such as a health care practitioner's duty to inform of emerging treatment options, financially unavailable treatment options and Complementary and Alternative Medicine (CAM) therapies. I devote the last two chapters (Chaps. 9 and 10) to examining the New Zealand context and the Chinese context. To highlight the uniqueness of the New Zealand context, in Chap. 9 I draw distinctions between New Zealand and the three common law jurisdictions with which it is most commonly compared (England, Canada and Australia).

Chapter 2 provides some background knowledge about a doctor's duty to inform. Its aim is to draw readers' attention to the distinctive profiles of information disclosure. It highlights the inappropriateness of uncritically applying the *Bolam* test to every aspect of health care, including information disclosure.

There is a group of leading and landmark informed consent cases in the common law world, such as the USA's *Canterbury v. Spence*, Canada's *Reibl v. Hughes*, Australia's *Rogers v. Whitaker*, and England's *Sidaway*. Although these cases have many things in common, there are still differences in their approaches to a doctor's duty of information disclosure, which I highlight at the beginning of Chap. 2. I trace these legal developments in Commonwealth jurisdictions. Because of its increasing popularity in many jurisdictions, I single out for special attention the "materiality" test, which was formulated for disclosure of "risks", and try to figure out the ways in which it can be translated into clinical practice, especially with respect to the disclosure, or non-disclosure, of information about alternatives.

To illustrate that health care is divisible and information disclosure is distinctive, I highlight three distinctions that have been made in the law: between a doctor-oriented standard and a patient-oriented standard, between "medical judgment" and "layperson's knowledge", and between "information" and "materiality". I conclude that, in a patient-oriented jurisdiction, while appreciation and knowledge of medical information, such as risks of proposed treatments and alternative treatment options, may still depend on medical judgment, whether a patient would attach importance to some piece of information is a question that falls primarily within lay knowledge.

The purpose of Chap. 2 is to set a basic tone for the next chapters. Drawing distinctions between diagnosis/treatment and information disclosure justifies my effort to draw further distinctions, in Chap. 3, and in the context of disclosure of *alternatives*, between "disclosure", "selection", "recommendation", and "performance" of treatments. It also justifies legal authorities adopting a more interventionist approach in the realm of information disclosure and promoting information integration between different schools of medical opinion.

It seems to me that some courts and scholars have a tendency to confuse "disclosure of alternatives" with recommendation of treatments and other aspects of health care. In Chap. 3, I endeavour to construct a model for interpreting different aspects of health care, distinguished by the concepts of "unbiased/balanced disclosure", "genuine selection", "personalised recommendation", and "performance" of treatment. That helps to put the issue of *the duty to inform about alternatives* in a clear context. Before drawing distinctions between these four aspects of health care, I critically examine the conventional or conservative wisdom of only subjecting *recommended* procedures to the duty to inform.

To construct my model, I collect support from the case law of different jurisdictions, such as England and the USA's wisdom regarding "selection" of treatment options, Australia's wisdom regarding "recommendations", and Canada and New Zealand's wisdom concerning "disclosure" of alternatives. As far as "disclosure" of alternatives is concerned, a basic theme is that, while doctors have latitude and liberty in "selecting" treatments between different "schools" of thought, they should overcome their preferences or "school", and present patients with unbiased and balanced information about divergent "schools" of thought, when it comes to disclosure.

In Chap. 4, I examine four elements that have the effect of narrowing a doctor's duty to inform. They are "medical knowledge", "the patient's condition", "materiality" and "causation". I also examine the circumstances which create the potential for broadening a doctor's duty to inform about alternatives. These three circumstances are where procedures have an "elective" or "experimental" nature, or where the patient delivers an inquiry.

In Chap. 5, I categorize "alternatives". I adopt the view that the term "alternatives" does not just mean "alternative treatment options". It also embraces "alternatives not readily available legally, financially and geographically" and "CAM therapies". "Alternative" may also encompass the "option of having another practitioner perform the proposed procedure" (alternative provider). Some important, complex, and frequently-raised issues, such as whether or not a doctor has a duty to inform patients of "emerging" treatments options, financially unavailable treatment options, and CAM therapies, are explored in separate chapters that follow.

In exploring the duty to inform about "emerging" treatment options, financially unavailable treatment options and choices between conventional medicine treatments and CAM therapies, I always draw distinctions between *provision or delivery* of treatments and *disclosure* about treatment options. That reflects my adherence to my arguments in Chaps. 2 and 3, where I highlight the distinctive aspects of information disclosure and make (unbiased, balanced, and contextualised) information disclosure distinct from (preference-allowed) selection and (personalised) recommendation of treatment options. Therefore, Chap. 6 (emerging treatment options), Chap. 7 (financially unavailable treatment options) and Chap. 8 (CAM and alternatives) share the same structure: the context of information *disclosure* is considered alongside the distinct context of the *adoption or provision* of treatment. The layout will provide readers with a clear sense of the different aspects of the issues.

In Chap. 6, I raise the concern that the law is convention-reinforcing in that it gives overwhelming weight and priority to conventional treatment options in formulating legal rules and chills efforts to adopt and disclose emerging treatment options. First,

I raise the issue of whether it is appropriate to apply the "two schools of thought" theory or the *Bolam* test, which is popular in the context of diagnosis and treatment, in the context of disclosure of treatment options. After highlighting the differences between the two contexts, I form the view that the threshold for a treatment option falling within a doctor's duty to inform may be lower than the threshold established by rules of law based on the concepts of "a school of thought" or "a responsible body of opinion". The information disclosure context is a place to cultivate a patient-need-oriented culture, rather than one for reinforcing orthodoxy and the personal preferences of the health practitioner. Emerging, minority and experimental treatment options may fall within a doctor's duty to inform.

In proposing that a doctor's duty to inform encompasses disclosure of emerging, minority and experimental treatment options, I sense the difficulty of defining the threshold for those options falling within a doctor's duty to inform. My view is that we should keep the door open. Whether or not a doctor needs to inform about an emerging treatment will depend on the needs of a particular patient and the circumstances of the particular case. It seems that the major reason why a doctor may not mention "minority" treatment options is that he prefers and recommends a "majority" treatment option and fails to place his recommendation in the context of divergent medical opinions. Again, my argument for drawing a distinction between preference-oriented selection/recommendation of treatment and contextualised information disclosure applies.

In Chap. 6, I also raise the inappropriateness of categorizing a treatment option as simply either "conventional" or "experimental". The all-or-nothing approach of drawing the experimental-conventional dichotomy does not correctly reflect the reality that, in clinical care, treatment options exist on a spectrum rather than falling on one or other side of a bright-line distinction between standard and experimental treatment. My suggestion is that, when presenting treatment options, more attention should be focused on the "merits" of treatment options rather than their conventional or experimental "nature" or label. Alternatively, a more graduated approach of categorising treatment options may alleviate the problems that a mere conventional-experimental dichotomy will create.

In Chap. 7, I try to answer the question of whether or not a doctor should inform patients of treatment options not available in the publicly-funded health care system due to limited resources in that system. When we talk about a doctor's duty to inform of alternatives, that is one of the questions frequently raised by thinkers. That is also a real, important but unresolved issue produced by a cost-containment culture, which is prevailing not only in publicly-funded health care systems but also in private health care systems. Because there is little case law to inform my thinking about a doctor's duty to inform about financially unavailable treatment options, I cite many academic contributions, including surveys published in medical journals and medical ethics journals. I know academic arguments are not, strictly speaking, sources of law. However, they are useful in proposing and forming legal arguments. I confine Chap. 7 to the context of publicly-funded heath care, although arguments there are also applicable to private health care. The key issue is not whether health care is publicly-funded or privately-funded, but whether health care is cost-contained and resource-conscious.

Chapter 7 follows and reinforces a distinction between the "provision" of care and information disclosure. I propose three questions: (1) Should the provision of treatments be resource-conscious? (2) Should the scope of information disclosure, especially the question of disclosure of treatment options not readily available in publicly-funded health care, be equally qualified by resource constraints? (3) What are the implications of resource-blind information disclosure, for example, disclosure of financially unavailable treatments? Or, do its negative consequences outweigh its benefits?

Chapter 7 acknowledges and answers many concerns raised about disclosing treatment options not available in publicly-funded health care, such as the distress and discomfort this may cause patients and doctors, and how it may disrupt rationing, and be time-consuming. I cite the English case law (as an example) and much survey data (from medical journals) to show that these concerns are substantially unfounded. I also critically examine an approach which is popular among doctors when revealing treatments not readily available in publicly-funded health care, i.e. tailoring the extent of disclosure based on whether the patient is "inquisitive", "well-informed", "well-educated" and has the ability to afford the treatments. This approach is discriminatory in nature and may cause further social inequities. All of these arguments point towards recognising a duty for doctors to honestly and proactively present full information. A sensitive approach to disclosure should be dependant on patients' preferences rather than patients' social status.

My task in Chap. 7 is to establish that a doctor has a duty to inform patients of treatment options that are not available in publicly-funded health care. That is made in the bigger context of drawing distinctions between provision of services (diagnosis and treatment) and information disclosure. On the one hand, in a cost-containment culture, the law needs to stand with resource-conscious initiatives and honour and promote a cost-effective body of medical opinion or practice. The reality of resource restrictions or resource constraint should be allowed for in defining the standard of care for doctors. Doctors have a duty to take reasonable account of resource restrictions. On the other hand, in an effort to reconcile the conflict between resource limitations and patients' freedom of choice, the profession-oriented, community-regarding, and resource-conscious rule concerning the "provision" of health care should be complemented by a patient-oriented, autonomy-regarding and resource-blind rule concerning information disclosure. Doctors need to offer information not only about cost-effective treatment options, but also about effective, but expensive, treatment options.

In Chap. 8, I explore the issue of informing patients of choices between conventional medicine and Complementary and Alternative Medicine (CAM). Because there is little case law to inform this issue, this chapter involves many academic arguments. In this chapter, I categorize practitioners into three types: orthodox (conventional) medicine practitioners, dual practitioners and CAM practitioners. Following the adoption-disclosure distinction, the position of each type of practitioner is considered in two contexts: adoption/delivery of service and information disclosure.

I devote specific attention to the fact that the evidence base for CAMs and conventional medicine practitioners' knowledge base about CAMs is increasing. That strengthens the argument that the duty to inform about alternatives imposed on orthodox medicine practitioners may be extended to cover CAM therapies. In contrast with TCM practitioners in China who have a strong knowledge base about conventional medicine and enjoy a wide scope of practice, CAM practitioners in "Western" or conventional-medicine-dominated jurisdictions are only allowed a narrow scope of practice and have a weak knowledge base about conventional medicine. That weakens the force of the argument that the scope of CAM practitioners' duty to inform may encompass conventional medicine treatments. I invest hope in rigorous CAM regulation to change the situation.

I conclude Chap. 8 with my call for both conventional medicine practitioners and CAM practitioners to provide their patients with unbiased and contextualised information that overcomes the boundaries of their "schools" of medicine. As where only conventional medicine is involved, in a context involving both conventional medicine and CAM, an "integrated" model, where all practitioners provide patients with contextualised information about divergent schools of thought, is better than a "fragmented" model, where every practitioner presents patients with information only about his "school" of thought, leaving patients to search for information about other "schools" of thought themselves. I maintain that, while health care practitioners are given some allowance and latitude in adopting and delivering treatments they favour, patients are entitled to have full information about a range of treatments to make an informed decision.

In Chap. 9, I concentrate on the New Zealand context. To highlight the uniqueness of the approach to information disclosure in New Zealand's Code, I begin the chapter by drawing distinctions between jurisdictions, mainly England, Australia and Canada. There I highlight that, although they share similarly rigorous *professional and ethical* principles regarding information disclosure, England, Australia, Canada and New Zealand differ from each other on the *legal* principles regarding a doctor's duty to inform about alternatives.

Australia is still at the stage of *academically* arguing for expanding the duty to inform to include disclosure of alternative treatments. Australian common law and civil liability legislation are still narrowly focusing on disclosure of "risks" of proposed treatments, although it has a very encompassing test for materiality of "risks". The English law offers some hints that a doctor should contemplate disclosing divergent procedures as a legal duty. However, because its focus is still on the "risks" aspect of information disclosure, i.e. the "risks" of the proposed procedure and the "comparative risks" of a different procedure, it is still unclear how far English law will go with regard to disclosure of alternative treatment options. Canadian courts have proactively translated academic arguments for disclosure of alternatives into legal principles. Canada supports a very embracing duty of information disclosure for medical practitioners. But the Canadian expansive approach is adopted within a tort law framework. That dictates that an encompassing duty to inform will inevitably be constrained by some hurdles, such as causation.

The middle and the majority of Chap. 9 is devoted to New Zealand law, especially its Code of Patients' Rights. The Code and the jurisdiction of the Health and Disability Commissioner (HDC) is a unique legal scheme. The Code has been consistently interpreted by the HDC to support a very encompassing duty to inform for health practitioners. For example, alternatives that may fall within a medical practitioner's duty to inform under the Code include: (1) conventional treatment options (alternatives to new/experimental treatments); (2) non-recommended treatment options (alternatives to proposed or recommended treatments); (3) minority treatment options (alternatives to the treatments favoured by a majority of practitioners); (4) treatment options not available in publicly-funded health care (or the option of seeking private treatments, which may include financially unavailable treatment options); (5) treatment options not available in New Zealand but available overseas (geographically unavailable treatment options); and (6) the option of having the treatment performed by another medical practitioner or provider (alternative providers). The ready availability of HDC jurisdiction is matched by low level remedies.

I then examine New Zealand law with regard to CAM. In contrast with the active call for balanced and contextualised disclosure in a context involving only conventional medical treatment options, New Zealand's approach of dealing with disclosure of alternatives in the context of conventional medicine and CAM is basically conventional-medicine-reinforcing. CAM and dual practitioners are required to present patients with balanced information about alternatives, such as conventional medical treatment options. But in practice there is no comparable duty for conventional medicine practitioners to disclose CAM options.

In the Conclusion part of the chapter, I draw further distinctions between common law jurisdictions and compare the Code approach with the tort law approach. Under the Tort approach which other common law jurisdictions have adopted, a seemingly liberal duty to inform is always constrained by considerations of "causation". By comparison, I illustrate the encompassing nature of the New Zealand's Code approach in responding to the issue of disclosure of alternatives.

China has different legal and medical landscapes. China is a civil law country. Traditional Chinese Medicine (TCM) is China's native medicine. In Chap. 10, I examine China's legal context, medical context and law relating to TCM. In the legal context, China demonstrates that a jurisdiction can, through statutory intervention or legislation, expand the scope of a doctor's duty to inform to cover the disclosure of *alternatives*. It also further illustrates that the Tort approach is not always the best way to honour a patient's right to be informed. Medical negligence law, which is basically medical-profession-oriented and is fraught with hurdles and restrictions, is not consistent with the rationales of the doctrine of informed consent. Although claiming and highlighting the distinctiveness of information disclosure could alleviate the problem, once the informed consent rule is captured within the Tort law context, following general Tort principles is unavoidable.

In the medical context, China presents an "integrative" medical culture, which is unique and not readily transferable worldwide. Following the misguided policy to "modernise" TCM, China's integration of TCM and Western medicine is Western-medicine-oriented. Almost all norms and rules are formulated according to a Western medical model, but are then applied to TCM. TCM education has a significant component of Western medicine education and TCM practitioners are allowed to practise Western medicine. Behind the facade of TCM's flourishing and equal status to Western medicine, TCM's uniqueness has actually been diluted by the Western-medicine-oriented approach of integration.

Although I doubt the wisdom of according practitioners freedom to practise both TCM and Western medicine, because of the irreconcilability of the two medical cultures, the "integrative" approach is consistent with my thesis that health care practitioners would better possess and present patients with contextualised information that transcends the boundaries of the different "schools of thought". Like conventional medical practitioners in other jurisdictions, TCM practitioners in China enjoy wide latitude in choosing practices and have a wide scope of practice. They also have a strong knowledge base about Western medicine. All of these point to expectations that TCM practitioners in China should have more awareness of the limitations of their "school of thought" and the availability of conventional medical therapies than their counterparts in other jurisdictions. Arguably conventional medical treatment options would fall within the ambit of a TCM practitioner's duty to disclose in China more readily than the case for CAM practitioners in other jurisdictions.

Finally I have two notes. The first is about the use of "physician" and "doctor". I find that American and Canadian law and scholars prefer to use the word "physician", while UK, Australian and New Zealand law and scholars prefer "doctor". Because the book covers a wide range of jurisdictions, both the terms "physician" and "doctor" are used. They are interchangeable. Second, when I mention a patient or a doctor in a general sense, I simply use "he". It means "he or she". In the same way, "his" means "his or her". They should be read as neutral.

Chapter 2
Information Disclosure: A Distinctive Profile

Abstract This chapter provides some background knowledge about a doctor's duty to inform. It highlights the inappropriateness of uncritically applying the *Bolam* test to every aspect of health care, including information disclosure. To illustrate that health care is divisible and information disclosure is distinctive, three distinctions have been made in the law: between a doctor-oriented standard and a patient-oriented standard, between "medical judgment" and "layperson's knowledge", and between "information" and "materiality". Under the patient-oriented standard of information disclosure and the "materiality" test, the "information" prong, such as that concerning the gravity, likelihood of the potential risks of treatments, and existence/availability of treatment options, is subject to medical judgment, but the "materiality" prong, i.e. whether or not a reasonable person in the patient's position would attach significance to the undisclosed information, falls within human/layperson knowledge. The information/materiality dichotomy dictates that the judiciary can ask healthcare professionals to transcend the boundaries of professional opinion and give more patient-centred information.

2.1 Introduction

The USA-originating phrase "informed consent", condemned as having confusing and misleading effects, has not won much popularity in major Commonwealth countries.[1] However, this "oft-used and somewhat amorphous

[1]*Reibl v. Hughes* (1980) 114 D.L.R. (3d) 1, 8–9 (S.C.C.) (Supreme Court of Canada preferring to "abandon" the term because it "tends to confuse battery and negligence"); *Rogers v. Whitaker* (1992) 175 C.L.R. 479, 490 (HCA) (High Court of Australia sharing the view that the "somewhat amorphous" phrase of "informed consent" is "apt to mislead as it suggests a test of the validity of a patient's consent");

X. Zhao, *The Duty of Medical Practitioners and CAM/TCM Practitioners to Inform Competent Adult Patients about Alternatives*,
DOI 10.1007/978-3-642-31647-0_2,

phrase"[2] at least reminds readers that the doctrine of informed consent has a historical origin traced back to battery. The seeds of the doctrine of informed consent and the rationale underlying the doctrine were planted in a battery case.[3] Although battery provides more fertile soil for the flourishing of a patient's right self-determination,[4] it is not a doctor-friendly legal framework.[5] Shifting the issue of "informed consent" out of the battery framework to the negligence domain is, in effect, a doctors-protective move.

As far as the scope of information disclosure is concerned, there is no surprise that the earlier informed consent cases echoed traditional rules of medical negligence

---

Rosenberg v. Percival 2001 205 CLR 434, 440 (High Court of Australia Gleeson CJ warned against uncritical use of the American concepts, such as "patient's right of self-determination" and "informed consent", "which ought to be valuable currency, but which are susceptible to rhetorical inflation"). Despite these criticisms, the phrase "informed consent" has many academic and judicial supporters. It was acknowledged that the concept "informed consent" has been "a well accepted legal term that describes an area of law" with precision and honesty. *See*, Don Chalmers and Robert Schwartz (1993), 149. One commentator had embraced the idea that "once the law imposes a duty on the doctor to disclose to his patient information relating not only to the general nature and purpose of the proposed treatment, but also to the risks and dangers inherent therein, then, ... it can be said that a single doctrine of informed consent exists." *See*, Gerald Robertson (1981), 103. Kirby J. from High Court of Australia acknowledged that what the *Rogers* rule targeted are "the concerns that are commonly dealt with ... as relevant to securing the 'informed consent' of a patient to invasive treatment", and kept an open mind towards "legal and medical literature" on "informed consent" to support his reconsideration of the *Rogers* test. *See, Rosenberg v. Percival* 2001 205 CLR 434, 477. In the House of Lords case *Chester v. Afshar*, Lord Hope frequently utilised the concept "informed consent" when restating the English case law history on the issue of "the duty to warn". *See, Chester v. Afshar* 2004 4 All ER 587, 601–604.

[2]*Rogers v. Whitaker* (1992) 175 C.L.R. 479, 490 (HCA) (Mason CJ, Brennan, Dawson, Toohey and McHugh JJ).

[3]*Schloendorff v. The Society of New York Hospital*, 105 N.E. 92, 93 (1914) (Justice Cardozo giving these frequently-quoted words: "Every human being of adult years and sound mind has a right to determine what shall be done with his own body; and a surgeon who performs an operation without his patient's consent commits an assault, for which he is liable in damages.").

[4]Marjorie Maguire Shultz (1985), 224 (noting that, under the battery analysis, "the patient's wishes take priority over even the fully competent recommendation of a doctor", and "the right to be secure against unconsented touching is close to absolute"); Harvey Teff (1993), 216 (noting that "an action for battery grounded in the right to bodily inviolability suggests the clearest possible repudiation of paternalism and vindication of patient choice").

[5]First, the importance and weight of medical experts testimony and medical judgment is significantly reduced in the battery suits. In a battery suit, "the doctor normally may not invoke professional judgment or the exercise of a 'therapeutic privilege'" (*see*, Harvey Teff 1993, 217). Second, battery does not require proof of causation. Third, battery is actionable per se, rendering proof of damage unnecessary. Fourth, battery "casts upon the defendant the burden of proving consent to what was done" (*see, Reibl v. Hughes* (1980) 114 D.L.R. (3d) 1, 9 (S.C.C.)). Moreover, the anti-social and culpable flavour inherent in battery makes common law battery a poor fit for most informed consent cases which involve a context of doctor-physician relationship. *See, Natanson v. Kline*, 350 P.2d 1093, 1100 (Kan. 1960); *Howard v. University of Medicine*, 800 A.2d 73,78 (N.J. 2002); *Trogun v. Fruchtman*, 207 N.W. 2d 297, 313; *Sidaway v. Bethlem Royal Hospital Governors* 1985 1 All ER 643, 650; John A Harrington (1996), 352; Gerald Robertson (1981), 124.

and favoured a physician-oriented standard.[6] Although subsuming information disclosure into ordinary negligence rules was intended to "balance legitimate patient autonomy expectations with legitimate practitioner expectations of independence in medical judgment" (McNichols 1995, 716), ordinary professional negligence theory is obviously not a good place to accommodate and promote a patient's dignity and autonomy.[7] That led to a legal landscape that "[t]he battery law notion of a right to bodily integrity remained, but was commonly administered through the more flexible standards of negligence law: standard of care, higher causation threshold, and emphasis on reasonableness." (Gatter 1999, 952–953) It was against this background that the distinctive aspects of information disclosure, as opposed to traditional medical context of diagnosis and treatment, emerged.

English and American courts historically diverged in the perspectives of viewing the information disclosure. Most American courts have given considerable weight to the patient's right of self-determination, running the risk of re-invoking the battery principles and, thus, confusing the negligence and battery theories. English courts have insistently focused on the doctor's duty/obligation to take reasonable care in informing patients, making the issue of the duty to warn safely fall within the logic of negligence but sacrificing its uniqueness. As case law illustrated, English law and its followers adhered to the "unitary and comprehensive duty" argument. Their pro-patient standard of information disclosure was established by the contour of redefining the functions of courts and medical experts, and highlighting a treatment/information distinction, not by direct acknowledgement of a patient's right, especially a patient's right of self-determination.[8]

In this chapter, I first highlight the difference of the approaches, between the Commonwealth jurisdictions and some USA jurisdictions, to the issue of information disclosure in the medical law context. Both approaches acknowledge the distinctive profiles of information disclosure. I then pay special attention to the materiality test, which is popular in jurisdictions where the patient-oriented standard

[6]For example, the *Natanson* case is a landmark case in the United States in the sense that it marked the transition in courts from the battery analysis to the negligence analysis. In the new context of information disclosure, the court still followed the logic of traditional professional negligence, i.e. "medical judgment – expert medical testimony – professional standard", to support its physician-oriented holding. *See, Natanson v. Kline*, 350 P.2d 1093, 1106 (Kan. 1960).

[7]Alan Meisel (1977), 92 ("[t]he effect of the assimilation of informed consent to the negligence form of action was to transfer some of the old barriers to compensation to the informed-consent doctrine"); Harvey Teff (1993), 214 (there is a "lack of fit between rights-based analysis and the underlying theory of liability for negligence").

[8]*Rogers v. Whitaker* (1992) 175 C.L.R. 479, 490 (HCA) (noting that "nothing is to be gained by reiterating the expressions used in American authorities, such as "the patient's right of self-determination" .... The right of self-determination is an expression which is, perhaps, suitable to cases where the issue is whether a person has agreed to the general surgical procedure or treatment, but is of little assistance in the balancing process that is involved in the determination of whether there has been a breach of the duty of disclosure"; adding that "the consent necessary to negative the offence of battery is satisfied by the patient being advised in broad terms of the nature of the procedure to be performed").

of information disclosure has been adopted. Analysis of the materiality test motivates me to further make dichotomies between "information" and "materiality", and between "medical judgement" and "lay knowledge". Those dichotomies help to further establish the distinctive aspects of information disclosure. Both the USA law and Australian law regarding the standard and the scope of information disclosure support the information – materiality distinction and the medical judgment – lay knowledge distinction. Although they differ in their ways of interpreting a doctor's duty to inform, the USA law and the Commonwealth law have some thinking in common. That encourages me, at the end of the chapter, to propose that, while legal authorities, such as the judiciary, have reasons to adopt a more non-interventionist approach towards medical practice, to allow technical commitments shown by health practitioners and to tolerate health care fragmentation, in the context of diagnosis and treatment where medical judgment is heavily involved, they can show confidence in scrutinising medical practice and promoting informational integration in the realm of information disclosure because the latter context engages lay knowledge.

2.2 The Commonwealth Approach

In the Commonwealth countries, the orthodox test for establishing professional negligence is the *Bolam* test.[9] It is a medical-profession-oriented test. It shows high deference to the medical profession's opinions. The test was born in a hybrid treatment and warning case. Although having attracted some negative comments,[10] in the traditional area of diagnosis and treatment, the *Bolam* test has been applauded as "[having] stood the test of time"[11] and having "the enormous advantage of clarity" (Mason and Brodie 2005, 299). The big question posed is, however, whether the *Bolam* test fits comfortably with the context of information disclosure.

The first attempt to depart from the traditional *Bolam* test in the context of the duty to inform occurred in the *Sidaway* case,[12] but failed. It needs to be firstly noted that the majority opinion of the case distinguished the situation of "volunteering

---

[9] *Bolam v. Friern Hospital Management Committee* 1957 2 All ER 118, 122, per McNair J. ("A doctor is not guilty of negligence if he has acted in accordance with a practice accepted as proper by a responsible body of medical men skilled in that particular art. … Putting it the other way round, a doctor is not negligent, if he acting in accordance with such a practice, merely because there is a body of opinion that takes a contrary view.").

[10] John Keown (1994), 16–19 (criticising the *Bolam* test as having a "corrosive effect on the development of English medical law"); *Anasson v. Koziol* unreported, ACTSC, BC9606317, 20 December 1996, Miles CJ, at [20] ("Some might regard *Bolam* as a case decided on its facts. It was not considered important enough to be published in the authorised reports.").

[11] *Shaw v. Doctor Diarmuid De Burca* 2008 NIQB 151, at [25]; *Haughey v. Newry & Mourne Health & Social Care Trust* [2009] NIQB 53, at [53].

[12] *Sidaway v. Bethlem Royal Hospital Governors* 1985 1 All ER 643, (1985) AC 871.

unsought information" from the scenario of "responding to patient's specific questions", confining their pro-*Bolam* stance only to the former situation.[13] Although their Lordships' opinions were divided on the question of whether the *Bolam* test should be unreservedly followed in the context of information disclosure,[14] the "single comprehensive duty" theory prevailed.[15]

In *Sidaway*, with the notable exception of Lord Scarman, their Lordships confirmed a traditional judicial deference to the views of medical profession in standard-setting. While this stance may be more reasonable "in respect of technical proficiency in diagnosis and treatment", "it is less defensible in the context of disclosure, where considerations other than those calling for a purely clinical judgment are often relevant" (Teff 1985, 432).

The "single comprehensive duty" theory also dominated another English information disclosure case – the *Gold* case[16] – where the Court of Appeal not only did

---

[13]*Sidaway v. Bethlem Royal Hospital Governors* 1985 1 All ER 643, 659 (Lord Diplock), 661 (Lord Bridge), 664 (Lord Templeman).

[14]As far as the possibility of departure from tradition in the duty-to-warn cases is concerned, their Lordships' attitudes had actually formed an ascending hierarchy – Lord Diplock, Lord Bridge of Harwich, Lord Templeman and Lord Scarman – with Lord Diplock almost unconditionally standing with the *Bolam* test and Lord Scarman extensively embracing the newly-developed, patients-oriented rules and drawing a clear, categorical distinction between diagnosis and treatment, on the one hand, and advice, on the other. Although the *Sidaway* case can be generally viewed as the House of Lord's ultimate retention of the *Bolam* doctrine in the failure-to-disclose cases, only one Lord unreservedly stood with the *Bolam* test. *See, Sidaway v. Bethlem Royal Hospital Governors* 1985 1 All ER 643, 657–658 (Lord Diplock).

[15]The Court held that,

> In English jurisprudence the doctor's relationship with his patient which gives rise to the normal duty of care to exercise his skill and judgment to improve the patient's health in any particular respect in which the patient has sought his aid has hitherto been treated as *a single comprehensive duty* covering all the ways in which a doctor is called on *to exercise his skill and judgment in the improvement of the physical or mental condition of the patient* for which his services either as a general practitioner or as a specialist have been engaged. This general duty is *not subject to dissection into a number of component parts to which different criteria of what satisfy the duty of care apply*, such as diagnosis, treatment and advice (including warning of any risks of something going wrong however skillfully the treatment advised is carried out). … In modern medicine and surgery such dissection of the various things has to do in the exercise of his whole duty of care owed to his patient is neither meaningful nor medically practicable. … (emphasis added)

It was added,

> To decide what risks the existence of which a patient should be voluntarily warned and the terms in which such warning, if any, should be given, having regard to the effect that the warning may have, is as much *an exercise of professional skill and judgment* as any other part of the doctor's comprehensive duty of care to the individual patient, and *expert medical evidence* on this matter should be treated in just the same way. (emphasis added)

See, Sidaway v. Bethlem Royal Hospital Governors 1985 1 All ER 643, 657–659, per Lord Diplock.

[16]*Gold v. Haringey Health Authority* 1988 1 QB 481 (involving nondisclosure of both "risks" and "alternatives").

not allow the distinction between diagnosis/treatment and advice to be drawn, but also opposed the effort of distinguishing advice or warning in a "therapeutic" context from that in a "contraceptive" context.[17]

It is widely accepted that the Australian case of *Rogers v. Whitaker*[18] marked a real departure from the *Bolam* test.[19] Thanks to this nondisclosure case involving an *inquisitive* patient, the High Court of Australia followed the Canadian landmark informed consent case *Reibl v. Hughes*,[20] made it more explicit that medical opinions are not determinative of setting standards. That effect was achieved and vividly demonstrated by the court's highlighting the distinct face of the context of information disclosure.[21] Although acknowledging that the duty of a medical practitioner to exercise reasonable care and skill in the provision of professional advice and treatment is "a single comprehensive duty", [22] the majority opinion immediately pointed out that

> the factors according to which a court determines whether a medical practitioner is in breach of the requisite standard of care will *vary according to whether it is a case involving diagnosis, treatment or the provision of information or advice*; the different cases raise varying difficulties which require consideration of different factors. (emphasis added)[23]

---

[17]*Gold v. Haringey Health Authority* 1988 1 QB 481, 488–490 (observing that "[t]o dissect a doctor's advice into that given in a therapeutic context and that given in a contraceptive context would be to go against the whole thrust of the decision of the majority of the House of Lords in that case").

[18]*Rogers v. Whitaker* (1992) 175 C.L.R. 479 (HCA).

[19]*Johnson v. Biggs* [2000] NSWCA 338 (24 November 2000, unreported, BC200007233), at [52] ("[u]nlike the United Kingdom, the standard of care in fulfilling that duty to warn is not determined solely or even primarily by reference to the practice followed or supported by a responsible body of opinion in the medical profession, though it is a useful guide. Rather this question is ultimately for the court to determine"); *King v. South Eastern Area Health Service* [2005] NSWSC 305 (Newman J., 8 April 2005, unreported, BC200505896), at [36]–[39] ("As far as the scope of the extent of the duty owed by a medical practitioner to a patient is concerned the common law in Australia has departed from that which pertains in England").

[20]*Reibl v. Hughes* (1980) 114 D.L.R. (3d) 1, 13 (S.C.C.) ("To allow expert medical evidence to determine what risks are material and, hence, should be disclosed and, correlatively, what risks are not material is to hand over to the medical profession the entire question of the scope of the duty of disclosure, including the question whether there has been a breach of that duty. Expert medical evidence is, of course, relevant to findings as to the risks that reside in or are a result of recommended surgery or other treatment. It will also have a bearing on their materiality but this is not a question that is to be concluded on the basis of the expert medical evidence alone.").

[21]*Rogers v. Whitaker* (1992) 175 C.L.R. 479, 489–490 (HCA) ("*Whether* a medical practitioner a medical practitioner carries out a particular form of treatment in accordance with the appropriate standard of care is a question in the resolution of which responsible professional opinion will have an influential, often a decisive, role to play; *whether* the patient has been given all the relevant information to choose between undergoing and not undergoing the treatment is a question of a different order. Generally speaking, it is not a question the answer to which depends upon medical standards or practices. Except in those cases where there is a particular danger that the provision of all relevant information will harm an unusually nervous, disturbed or volatile patient, no special medical skill is involved in disclosing the information, including the risks attending the proposed treatment. (footnote omitted)").

[22]*Rogers v. Whitaker* (1992) 175 C.L.R. 479, 489 (HCA).

[23]*Rogers v. Whitaker* (1992) 175 C.L.R. 479, 489 (HCA).

In the opinion of the majority, there was fundamental difference between these two spheres.[24] Justice Gaudron, in giving her separate opinion, also raised "the considerable conceptual and practical differences between diagnosis and treatment, on the one hand, and the provision of information and advice, on the other",[25] noting that, in the latter context, "[t]he duty takes its precise content, ... from the *needs, concerns and circumstances of the patient*", and, thus, "there is simply no occasion to consider the practice or practices of medical practitioners in determining what information should be supplied."[26]

Although the *Rogers* principles[27] arose out of a case involving distinct information disclosure, the Australian case law seemed to give them (especially the principles concerning the determination of the standard of care) general application.[28] It was emphasised that what *Rogers* involved was "*the sharing of as much of the medical expertise* of the medical specialist with the patient or his carers as was necessary to discharge the duty of care imposed by the law".[29] If *Rogers*'s contribution to the law is confined only to allocation of functions between courts and medical opinions in setting standard of care, the *Rogers* principles are destined to make little difference in defining the scope of a doctor's duty to inform.[30] The traditional line of

---

[24] *Rogers v. Whitaker* (1992) 175 C.L.R. 479, 489 (HCA) ("In diagnosis and treatment, the patient's contribution is limited to the narration of symptoms and relevant history; the medical practitioner provides diagnosis and treatment according to his or her level of skill. However, except in cases of emergency or necessity, all medical treatment is preceded by the patient's choice to undergo it. ... But the choice is, in reality, meaningless unless it is made on the basis of relevant information and advice. Because the choice to be made calls for a decision by the patient on information known to the medical practitioner but not to the patient, it would be illogical to hold that the amount of information to be provided by the medical practitioner can be determined from the perspective of the practitioner alone or, for that matter, of the medical profession.")

[25] *Rogers v. Whitaker* (1992) 175 C.L.R. 479, 492 (HCA).

[26] *Rogers v. Whitaker* (1992) 175 C.L.R. 479, 493 (HCA) (emphasis added).

[27] *Schiller v. Connah* [2002] NSWSC 1264 (Taylor AJ, 11 June 2002, unreported, BC200208286), at [114], [115] (identifying four *Rogers* principles: (1) "a single comprehensive duty" theory; (2) all medical treatment is preceded by the patient's "informed" choice; (3) medical standards or practices have less or no say in the context of information disclosure; (4) defining the "materiality" of a risk).

[28] *Walker v. Sydney West Area Health Service* [2007] NSWSC 526 (Simpson J, 25 May 2007, unreported, BC200703982), at [89]; *Lowns v. Woods; Procopis v. Woods*, NSWCA, unreported, 5 February 1996, BC9600091, Kirby P, Mahoney and Cole, JJA, at [16], per Kirby P (deeming the *Rogers* principle to be "one of general application, governing the relevant communications between a medical practitioner and a patient").

[29] *Lowns v. Woods; Procopis v. Woods*, NSWCA, unreported, 5 February 1996, BC9600091, Kirby P, Mahoney and Cole, JJA, at [17] (emphasis added), per Kirby P.

[30] *Lowns v. Woods; Procopis v. Woods*, NSWCA, unreported, 5 February 1996, BC9600091, Kirby P, Mahoney and Cole, JJA (involving an allegation that the physician failed to inform parents of a child with a history of epileptic seizures of the availability and advisability of rectal diazepam (Valium) to control the seizure in exigencies; Kirby P, applying two different standards (the *Bolam-Sidaway* rule and the *Rogers* rule), reached the same conclusion; Mahoney JA, who reached the same pro-physician conclusion as Kirby P did, devoted most of his reasoning to a court's respect for "a clinical decision"). *See also* José Miola (2009), 103 (observing that "the majority in *Sidaway*, despite following *Bolam*, was asserting what is essentially the same as the objective strand of the *Rogers* test – that while medical evidence is relevant to the determination of the duty to disclose, it is not decisive").

the *Bolam-Sidaway* authorities, if appropriately interpreted, can competently serve the same functions as *Rogers* did. If *Rogers* is read as a case only involving reallocating roles of courts and medical opinions in medical malpractice cases, *Rogers*'s force, weight and distinctive nature can be easily diluted by the way of reframing a doctor's conduct as involving medical judgment.[31] In Australia, it seems that the two contexts of diagnosis/treatment and information disclosure, although different, are "logically interwoven".[32]

The dichotomy suggested in *Rogers* between the context of giving warning or providing information and the context of diagnosis and treatment was maintained in some states' statutory provisions in Australia. Responding to the concern that "the pendulum has swung too far in the opposite direction" (David Ipp 2007a, 460), the Australian nationwide negligence law reform[33] witnessed the law's shift back towards the *Bolam* test in the context of defining the standard of care for professionals. The civil liability legislation in many states of Australia[34] favoured and modified the *Bolam* rule.[35]

---

[31]*Johnson v. Biggs* [2000] NSWCA 338 (24 November 2000, unreported, BC200007233), at [53] ("It is important to put the duty to warn in its *therapeutic context*."); *Darley v. Shale* NSW (Common Law Division), Wood, J., 23 October 1992, unreported, BC9202762, at [20], per Wood J (involving "*aspects of clinical judgment* in relation to the inquiry made by the defendant and in relation to the decision to proceed to laparoscopy *in preference to* laparotomy"); *Crisp v. Keng* NSW (Common Law Division), Wood J, 2 December 1992, unreported, BC9201449, at [103], per Wood J (the instance case "involves *aspects of clinical judgment* in relation to the defendants' *decision to opt for conservative treatment* of the haematoma and infection", warranting the judicial respect for clinical judgment) (emphasis added).

[32]*Howarth v. Adey* [1996] 2 VR 535, at [31], [32], [37], [38] (On the one hand, the scope and content of the duty to inform about risks "depends upon principles which are not co-extensive with the principles which govern and inform a decision of negligent treatment and management". On the other hand, the nature of informed consent claim "was *logically interwoven* with the [treatment] claim, the denial of the right to present it carried with it, … the prospect of no being able to present the case *in a coherent fashion*".) (emphasis added).

[33]As a legislative response to "insurance crisis", the reform aims to "limit[] liability and quantum of damages arising from personal injury and death", by different ways, including reformulating the test for the standard of care. The reform also responded to the concern that "it has become too easy for plaintiffs in personal injury cases to establish liability for negligence on the part of defendants". *See*, Commonwealth of Australia (2002), pages 9 and 25. As to Australian pre-reform and post-reform legal climate, *please see* David Ipp AO. 2007a. The politics, purpose and reform of the law of negligence. *Australian Law Journal* 81:456–464, at 456; David Ipp AO. 2007b. Themes in the law of Torts. *ALJ* 81:609.

[34]Not all Australian jurisdictions have enacted a Civil Liability Act. The Commonwealth and the state governments rejected uniform tort law reform. The states and territories in Australia chose to individually legislate to introduce some of the Ipp Committee's recommendations, either by amending existing legislation or by introducing new legislation. The state civil liability legislation include: Australian Capital Territory: *Civil Law (Wrongs) Act 2002*; New South Wales: *Civil Liability Act 2002*; Queensland: *Civil Liability Act 2003*; South Australia: *Civil Liability Act 1936*; Tasmania: *Civil Liability Act 2002*; Victoria: *Wrongs Act 1958*; Western Australia: *Civil Liability Act 2002*.

[35]*Civil Liability Act 2003* (Qld), s 22(1) (2) (3) (4); *Civil Liability Act 2002* (Tas), s 22; *Civil Liability Act 2002* (WA), s 5PB; *Civil Liability Act 1936* (SA), s 41; *Civil Liability Act 2002* (NSW), s 5O.

The new formulation[36] provides a professional with a defence to negligence liability if a professional opinion is "widely accepted by a significant number of respected practitioners". That stands even if there exists another different professional opinion also widely accepted by a significant number of respected practitioners. It would not be for the court to adjudicate between the opinions. There are only "very exceptional cases", where the professional opinion is considered to be irrational, that the court would show more willingness to intervene. The modified *Bolam* rule applies to all professions, not just medical profession. However, most of recent Australian civil liability legislation expressly denied the application of the re-formulated *Bolam* test into the context of giving of information.[37]

Rogers has been cited by New Zealand case law on several occasions.[38] In the New Zealand case of *B v Medical Council*, [39] the High Court emphasised that

> usual professional practice, while significant, may not always be determinative: the reasonableness of the standards applied must ultimately be for the Court to determine, taking into account all the circumstances including not only usual practice but also patient interests and community expectations, including the expectation that professional standards are not to be permitted to lag.[40]

---

[36]For example, *Civil Liability Act 2003* (Qld), s 22(1) (2) (3) (4) stipulates that: "(1) A professional does not breach a duty arising from the provision of a professional service if it is established that the professional acted in a way that (at the time the service was provided) was widely accepted by peer professional opinion by a significant number of respected practitioners in the field as competent professional practice. (2) However, peer professional opinion can not be relied on for the purposes of this section if the court considers that the opinion is irrational or contrary to a written law. (3) The fact that there are differing peer professional opinions widely accepted by a significant number of respected practitioners in the field concerning a matter does not prevent any 1 or more (or all) of the opinions being relied on for the purposes of this section. (4) Peer professional opinion does not have to be universally accepted to be considered widely accepted."

[37]*Civil Liability Act 2003* (Qld), s 22(5), *Civil Liability Act 2002* (NSW), s 5P; *Civil Liability Act 1936* (SA), s 41(5); *Civil Liability Act 2002* (Tas), s 22 (5). For example, *Civil Liability Act 2003* (Qld), s 22(5) points out that the Section 22 "Standard of Care for Professionals" "does not apply to liability arising in connection with the giving of (or the failure to give) a warning, advice or other information, in relation to the risk of harm to a person, that is associated with the provision by a professional of a professional service". Section 21(1) of *Civil Liability Act 2003* (Qld) separately stipulates that "[a] doctor does not breach a duty owed to a patient to warn of risk, before the patient undergoes any medical treatment (or at the time of being given medical advice) that will involve a risk of personal injury to the patient, unless the doctor at that time fails to give or arrange to be given to the patient the following information about the risk – (a) information that a reasonable person in the patient's position would, in the circumstances, require to enable the person to make a reasonably informed decision about whether to undergo the treatment or follow the advice; (b) information that the doctor knows or ought reasonably to know the patient wants to be given before making the decision about whether to undergo the treatment or follow the advice".

[38]*Doyle v. Accident Compensation Corporation* [1997] 3 NZLR 160 (HC), 165, per Fisher J. (in the context of "medical misadventure"); *B v. Medical Council of NZ* (Note) [2005] 3 NZLR 810 (involving professional conduct for disciplinary purposes).

[39]*B v. Medical Council of NZ* 8/7/96, Elias J, HC Auckland HC 11/96, noted at [2005] 3 NZLR 810.

[40]*B v. Medical Council of NZ* (Note) [2005] 3 NZLR 810, 811.

Elias J added that "[p]atient and community interests and expectations may be *particularly important* in the case of the provision of advice and information".[41] New Zealand's Code of Patients' Rights[42] also maintain a dichotomy between Right 4 (Right to Services of An Appropriate Standard) and Right 6 (Right to be Fully Informed).[43]

As far as the applicability of the *Bolam* test to the context of information disclosure is concerned, I prefer the scope of the *Bolam* test to be confined to "the realm of diagnosis and treatment".[44] The *Bolam* test, with its inherent paternalism, is antithetical to patient autonomy (Amirthalingam 2003, 123).The *Sidaway* case is full of robust criticisms, insistent deviations and soft qualifications of the *Bolam* test. Erosion or dilution of the old principle in the new context of information disclosure is apparent (Mason and Brodie 2005, 300). The *Bolam* test was almost forgotten in the English non-disclosure case of *Chester v. Afshar*,[45] where the House of Lords was more attracted to the patient's right to autonomy. English courts continue to affirm *Bolam*, but may in a restricted manner be watering down its application (Amirthalingam 2003, 128). More and more Commonwealth jurisdictions denied the *Bolam* approach in favour of the *Rogers* approach (Shuaib 2000). Australian experience demonstrates that, even in an environment where the voice of "limiting liability" through restoring the authority to the medical profession is very strong, there is still a need to confine the *Bolam* test to the traditional realm of diagnosis and treatment.

Several arguments, all of which are based on the treatment/disclosure distinction, can explain why the *Bolam* test is not appropriate in the realm of provision of information. First, even in the sphere of diagnosis and treatment, "the heartland of the skilled medical practitioner", the *Bolam* principle has not always been applied.[46] In this traditional realm, the judiciary still can draw a distinction between matters which require technical skill and expertise, and therefore fall within the exclusive professional competence of doctors, and conduct which does not involve medical expertise, and which a layman is therefore in a position to evaluate.[47]

---

[41] *B v. Medical Council of NZ* (Note) [2005] 3 NZLR 810, 811 (emphasis added).

[42] Health and Disability Commissioner (Code of Health and Disability Services Consumers' Rights) Regulation 1996, Schedule.

[43] Right 4 of the Code of Rights, which is profession-oriented, is mostly suitable to be used in a context involving clinical judgment, such as diagnosis and treatment. Right 6 of the Code of Rights is a statutory acknowledgment of the distinctive aspects of information disclosure. Unlike Right 4, it is formulated in the consumers' (patients') perspective.

[44] *Bolam v. Friern Hospital Management Committee* [1957] 2 All ER 118, 121 ("[i]n the realm of diagnosis and treatment [involving medical expertise] there is ample scope for genuine difference of opinion") (quoting Scottish case *Hunter v. Hanley* [1955] S.L.T. 213, 217).

[45] *Chester v. Afshar* [2004] 4 All ER 587, [2004] UKHL 41; [2005] 1 AC 32.

[46] *Rogers v. Whitaker* (1992) 175 C.L.R. 479, 487 (HCA) (citations omitted). In Australia, although legislation have kept a modified version of the *Bolam* test alive, the test was judicially abolished not only in an unusual non-disclosure case (*Rogers*), but also in a diagnosis and treatment case (*Naxakis v. Western General Hospital*, [1999] HCA 22; (1999) 162 ALR 540).

[47] Lord Woolf (2001), 8; *ter Neuzen v. Korn*, [1995] 3 S.C.R. 674; (1993) 103 D.L.R. (4th) 473; aff'd (1995) 127 D.L.R. (4th) 577 (SCC).

Second, even if the *Bolam* test or a modified version retains great force in the realm of diagnosis and treatment, it has very limited role or application in the field of providing information. The rationale for attaching great weight to medical opinions in the realm of diagnosis and treatment is that non-medically qualified judges or jury members normally lack medical expertise in second-guessing the medical opinion. However, when the scenario shifts to the realm of information disclosure, where "attempting to analyse whether or not the doctors' justification for non-disclosure is logical and rational will not be a task bedevilled by too much technical or scientific detail",[48] and where more ordinary knowledge rather than medical skills is engaged, or more radically, where, quoting *Rogers v. Whitaker*, "no special medical skill is involved",[49] the non-professionals will feel "less disadvantaged by a lack of medical training" (Manning 2007, 404), and will show more confidence and competency to have their own say.[50]

Third, even the advocates of universal application of the *Bolam* test in the realms of both treatment and information disclosure have admitted that their arguments are only confined to the context of physicians' providing information *on their own initiative*, without ambitiously touching on the context of a physician providing information as a response to *a patient's inquiries*.[51] This exclusion deeply undermines the basis and all-embracing power of the *Bolam* test. This line of qualification also reflects awareness that, in the situation of patients' questioning, the inadequacies and shortcomings of the traditional *Bolam* test will be vividly demonstrated.[52] Furthermore, singling out the patient's questioning as the one context in which common medical practice can be challenged will deteriorate into further drawing arbitrary distinctions, such as the "general enquiry/specific enquiry" distinction,[53] further demonstrating vividly "the dangers of applying the *Bolam* principle in the area of advice and information".[54]

---

[48]Margaret Brazier and José Miola (2000), 108; John Keown (1994), 16 ("[j]udicial deference to medical opinion is especially objectionable when the issue in question falls outwith clinical competence").

[49]*Rogers v. Whitaker* (1992) 175 C.L.R. 479, 490 (HCA).

[50]*F. v. R.* (1983) 33 S.A.S.R 189, 205 (The medical practice is "least likely to be decisive" when the allegation is of a failure to warn and where no information about the method of procedure or basis of diagnosis is required.).

[51]*Sidaway v. Bethlem Royal Hospital Governors* [1985] 1 All ER 643, 661, 664, per Lord Diplock, Lord Templeman.

[52]*Rogers v. Whitaker* (1992) 175 C.L.R. 479, 486–487 (HCA) (noting that if the law allows the *Bolam* principle to play a decisive role in the realm of providing information, the express desire of a particular patient for information "would logically be of little or no significance" since it is medical opinion that determines whether the risk should be disclosed).

[53]Karen Tickner (1995), 117 (highlighting the case *Blyth v. Bloomsbury Health Authority* [1993] 4 Med LR 151, where the Court found that "the question of what a plaintiff should be told in answer to a general enquiry cannot be divorced from the *Bolam* test any more than when no such enquiry is made.").

[54]*Rogers v. Whitaker* (1992) 175 C.L.R. 479, 486–491(HCA) (In this case, although the patient incessantly questioned about the possible complications and expressed a keen interest in the outcome of the suggested procedure, the court encountered a body of opinion which held that an inquiry should have elicited a reply dealing with sympathetic ophthalmia only if it specifically directed to the possibility of the left eye being affected by the operation on the right eye.)

Fourth, if the parameters of the *Bolam* test encompass information disclosure, even where the plaintiff's claims can be supported by a responsible body of professional opinion, which indicates that they would have disclosed the information, the existence of *another contrary responsible professional view* advocating non-disclosure of the information would produce a disastrous result for the plaintiff. The application of the *Bolam* test in the non-disclosure cases would be more hazardous than in the treatment cases. Professional judgments regarding information disclosure are perhaps more inherently variable and individualised than in relation to diagnosis and treatment, putting a plaintiff in a more difficult position to establish negligence (Jones 1999, 111). Furthermore, the possibility of identifying a common practice in the context of information disclosure has been deeply doubted.[55]

2.3 The USA Approach

Unlike English cases which "have tended to place the emphasis on the [best interests/beneficence] value and in consequence to formulate the test of negligence, largely, and sometimes exclusively, in terms of the extent of disclosure required by the *practice prevailing in the medical profession*",[56] some jurisdictions in the United States tend to "place greater weight on the patient's right" – "the right of self determination".[57] Under the USA law, especially in jurisdictions adopting the patient-oriented standard of information disclosure, the distinctiveness of information disclosure mainly comes from two aspects: (1) respect for the patient's right of self-determination, and (2) more involvement of non-medical judgment. Information disclosure involves more human knowledge rather than medical judgment/technical skills.[58]

[55]Michael A. Jones (1999), 112 (noting that "[t]here is evidence that individual doctors find it difficult to identify a common practice in relation to information disclosure, even within a speciality and even for relatively common procedures"); *Canterbury v. Spence*, 464 F.2d 772, 783–784 (1972) (deeply suspecting the existence of custom in the realm of information disclosure: "the reality of any discernible custom reflecting a professional consensus [sic] on communication of option and risk information to patients is open to serious doubt").

[56]*F. v. R.* (1983) 33 S.A.S.R 189, 191, per King C.J. (emphasis added).

[57]*F. v. R.* (1983) 33 S.A.S.R 189, 191, per King C.J.. *See, Schloendorff v. The Society of New York Hospital*, 105 N.E. 92, 93 (1914); *Natanson v. Kline*, 350 P.2d 1093, 1104 (Kan. 1960) ("each man is considered to be master of his own body, and he may, if he be of sound mind, expressly prohibit the performance of life-saving surgery, or other medical treatment. A doctor might well believe that an operation or form of treatment is desirable or necessary but the law does not permit him to substitute his own judgment for that of the patient by any form of artifice or deception.").

[58]*Canterbury v. Spence*, 464 F.2d 772, 785 (1972) (in nondisclosure cases, "the governing standard is much more largely divorced from professional considerations" and "the factfinder is not invariably functioning in an area of such technical complexity that it must be bound to medical custom as an inexorable application of the community standard of reasonable care"); *Cobbs v. Grant*, 502 P.2d 1, 10 (1972) ("[t]he weighing of these risks against the individual subjective fears and hopes of the patient" does not involve expert skill); *Wilkinson v. Vessey*, 295 A.2d 676, 688 (R.I. 1972) ("[t]he decision as to what is or is not material is a human judgment, … which does not necessarily require the assistance of the medical profession. The patient's right to make up his mind should not be delegated to a local medical group – many of whom have no idea as to his informational needs.").

Under the reasonable patient standard and the materiality test, there is an information/materiality dichotomy. Assessing the materiality of a risk involves a two-pronged analysis: (1) the information prong – an examination of the existence and nature of the risk and the probability of its occurrence; (2) the materiality prong – a determination of whether a reasonable person in the plaintiff's position would attach significance to the specific risk.[59] Medical judgment is confined to (1) *appreciation of information* about the merits and demerits of the proposed treatments and alternatives, and (2) invocation of "therapeutic privilege".[60] The significant task of determining the *materiality* of relevant information involves human/non-medical knowledge and is reserved to laypersons. The trier of fact can, without expert assistance, determine what a reasonable person in the plaintiff's position would consider significant within the context of a particular set of facts.[61] Therefore, in the context of informed consent, medical judgment and expert medical testimony play a lesser role than in the realm of diagnosis and treatment. While there is still a necessity of expert testimony to establish the first information prong,[62] there is less or no reason to let the medical experts to decide the second materiality prong.[63]

2.4 The Materiality Test

As mentioned before, as far as the scope of information disclosure is concerned, there is now a dichotomy between the physician-oriented/professional standard and the patient-oriented standard/the materiality test. The physician-oriented standard mirrors what one would expect in a typical professional negligence action. It asserts that the duty of a doctor to make adequate disclosure is, as in other cases of medical malpractice, measured by the standard of the reasonable medical practitioner under the same or similar circumstances.[64] Paying more attention to the distinctive profiles

---

[59] *Jaskoviak v. Gruver*, 638 N.W. 2d 1, 8–9 (N.D. 2002).

[60] *Cobbs v. Grant*, 502 P.2d 1, 10 (1972); *Aiken v. Clary*, 396 S.W.2d 668, 674 (Mo. 1965); *Woolley v. Henderson*, 418 A.2d 1123, 1130 (Me. 1980).

[61] *Bey v. Sacks*, 789 A.2d 232, 238 (Pa. Super. 2001); *Jaskoviak v. Gruver*, 638 N.W. 2d 1, 9 (N.D. 2002).

[62] *Canterbury v. Spence*, 464 F.2d 772, 791–792 (1972) (medical experts are ordinarily indispensable "to identify and elucidate for the factfinder the risks of therapy and the consequences of leaving existing maladies untreated").

[63] *Reibl v. Hughes* (1980) 114 D.L.R. (3d) 1, 13 (S.C.C.); *Korman v. Mallin*, 858 P.2d 1145, 1149 (Alaska 1993); *Canterbury v. Spence*, 464 F.2d 772, 792(1972); *Jaskoviak v. Gruver*, 638 N.W. 2d 1, 8–9 (N.D. 2002); *Bey v. Sacks*, 789 A.2d 232, 238–239(Pa. Super. 2001).

[64] *Natanson v. Kline*, 350 P.2d 1093, 1106 (Kan. 1960) ("The duty of the physician to disclose, … is limited to those disclosure which a reasonable medical practitioner would make under the same or similar circumstances. How the physician may best discharge his obligation to the patient in this difficult situation involves primarily a question of medical judgment."); *Aiken v. Clary*, 396 S.W.2d 668, 674 (Mo. 1965) (holding that the question of what disclosure of risks should be made in a particular situation is a question of "whether defendant doctor in that particular situation failed to adhere to a standard of reasonable care", and expert medical evidence on what a reasonably prudent practitioner would disclose is necessary);

of information disclosure, such as respect for a patient's right of self-determination, less involvement of medical judgment, and less significance of medical expert opinions, would inevitably point towards favouring a different standard of information disclosure – the patient-oriented standard/the materiality test. The patient-oriented standard of disclosure holds that, because a doctor's obligation to disclose therapeutic risks and alternatives arises from the patient's right of self-determination, the disclosure duty should be measured by the patient's need for information.[65] Under this rule, doctors have a legal obligation to disclose information about risks and options that is *material* to the patient's decision to undergo treatment.[66]

The patient-oriented standard is reflecting a growing national trend in the United States of America.[67] It has been adopted in many other major common law jurisdictions, including Canada,[68] Australia,[69] New Zealand[70] and Ireland.[71]

Under the patient-oriented standard, the question of what risk is a material one and therefore falls within a doctor's duty to inform needs to be answered. The issue of "materiality" of risks is a non-medical matter and is subject to lay knowledge. It is intimately related to the patient-oriented standard. The "materiality" test does not fit comfortably with the doctor-oriented standard of information disclosure,

---

Woolley v. Henderson, 418 A.2d 1123, 1131 (Me. 1980) (holding that "the scope of a physician's duty to disclose is measured by those communications a reasonable medical practitioner in that branch of medicine would make under the same or similar circumstances and that the plaintiff must ordinarily establish this standard by expert medical evidence").

[65]*Canterbury v. Spence*, 464 F.2d 772, 786 (1972); *Cobbs v. Grant*, 502 P.2d 1, 10 (1972); *Woolley v. Henderson*, 418 A.2d 1123, 1129 (Me. 1980).

[66]*Canterbury v. Spence*, 464 F.2d 772, 786–787 (1972) ("the test for determining whether a particular peril must be divulged is its materiality to the patient's decision: all risks potentially affecting the decision must be unmasked"; "[a] risk is … material when a reasonable person, in what the physician knows or should know to be the patient's position, would be likely to attach significance to the risk or cluster of risks in deciding whether or not to forgo the proposed therapy"); *Woolley v. Henderson*, 418 A.2d 1123, 1129 (Me. 1980).

[67]Annotation, Modern Status of Views As to General Measure of Physician's Duty to Inform Patient of Risks of Proposed Treatment, 88 A.L.R 3d 1008, §§3, 6–7 (1979 and Supp. 1995).

[68]*Reibl v. Hughes* [1980] 2 SCR 880, (1980) 114 D.L.R. (3d) 1 (S.C.C.) (declining to allow expert medical testimony to have a determinative or conclusive say in determining the materiality of certain risks).

[69]*Rogers v. Whitaker* (1992) 175 C.L.R. 479 (HCA).

[70]Health and Disability Commissioner (Code of Health and Disability Services Consumers' Rights) Regulation 1996, Schedule, Right 6.

[71]*Geoghegan v. Harris* [2000] 3 IR 536, 549, per Kearns J. ("The application of the reasonable patient test seems more logical in respect of disclosure. This would establish the proposition that, as a general principle, the patient has the right to know and the practitioner a duty to advise of all material risks associated with a proposed form of treatment."); *Fitzpatrick v. White* [2008] 3 IR 551, 563–564, at [33], [35] per Kearns J.("the patient centred test is preferable, and ultimately more satisfactory from the point of view of both doctor and patient alike, than any 'doctor centred' approach…").

although arguably materiality can be found in the mind of doctors, not patients.[72] The "materiality" test should answer the question of in whose eyes, *the patients' or the doctors'*, the risk should be judged as material. It has nothing to do with the allocation of functions between *courts and medical profession*, or the issue of relevance or decisiveness of medical evidence.[73] As to the "materiality" of "risks", Australia offered a two-prong *Rogers* test:

> The law should recognize that a doctor has a duty to warn a patient of a material risk inherent in the proposed treatment; a risk is material if, in the circumstances of the particular case, *a reasonable person in the patient's position*, if warned of the risk, would be likely to attach significance to it or if the medical practitioner is or should reasonably be aware that *the particular patient*, if warned of the risk, would be likely to attach significance to it. (emphasis added)[74]

The objective ("a reasonable person in the patient's position") limb (the proactive duty to inform) explores "if, in the circumstances of the particular case, a reasonable person in the patient's position, if warned of the risk, would be likely to attach significance to it". It requires a medical practitioner to give information regardless of whether the practitioner knows or ought to know that the patient wants to be given the information. The word "a reasonable person in the patient's position" has both an objective element ("a reasonable person") and a subjective element ("in the patient's position"). The objective limb is actually a mixture of objectivity and subjectivity.

The second, or subjective, limb (the reactive duty to inform) recognises that a particular patient may not a "reasonable" one,[75] he may have a number of "unreasonable" concerns peculiar to him, he may ask questions or communicate in other ways concerns that "should have enlivened an appreciation" on the part of doctors of the requirement to communicate particular information.[76] These particular concerns should be given full weight if the medical practitioner was or should have been aware of them.[77] This means that "the more inquisitive, or demanding, or less or more sophisticated perhaps, or obsessive, or suspicious, or hypochondriacal the

[72] James A. Bulen (2003), 336 (but holding that physician-oriented disclosure is problematic because it creates a circular, potentially biased process in which medical community norms shape disclosure standards designed to protect individuals who typically are not members of that community). *See also*, José Miola (2009), 76–108 (talking about "material risks" in the context of doctor-oriented *Bolam-Sidaway* line of authorities).

[73] *Compare*, José Miola (2009), 105 (claiming that there is little difference between the *Rogers* test and 'new' *Bolam* approach because both just abandon the decisiveness of medical evidence and do not make medical evidence irrelevant); Sara Fovargue and José Miola (2010), 13–14 (reinterpreting *Sidaway* and formulating three approaches of deciding whether a risk is material: by courts, by medical profession, and by patients).

[74] *Rogers v. Whitaker* (1992) 175 C.L.R. 479, 490 (HCA) (ending with the qualification that "[t]his duty is subject to the therapeutic privilege").

[75] *Rosenberg v. Percival* [2001] 205 CLR 434, 459 per Gummow J; 500, per Callinan J.

[76] *Rosenberg v. Percival* [2001] 205 CLR 434, 482–483, per Kirby J.

[77] *Rosenberg v. Percival* [2001] 205 CLR 434, 459 per Gummow J.

patient may be, the greater the need for identification of and elaboration upon the slightest risks because such a patient may be likely to attach significance to them."[78]

One way of satisfying the subjective limb, thus triggering the doctor's awareness, is by a patient's asking questions, but that is not the only means of indicating or revealing particular concerns.[79] There are "a multitude of potential circumstances" in which a court might find that a medical practitioner should have known of a particular concern.[80] The reactive duty to inform may target particular patients and particular information, thus adding more subjectivity to the test.

Information disclosure does not depend on a patient asking questions. The objective limb is a "universal" test for a hypothetical reasonable person in the patient's position.[81] But, under the subjective limb, the needs of a reasonable person in the patient's position may be "enlarged" in the case of particular patients.[82]

The *Rogers* test not only abandoned the *Bolam* principle but also established a "rigorous legal obligation".[83] It caused some alarm among the medical profession in Australia. Ten years later, the High Court of Australia got its opportunity to revisit the *Rogers* test.[84] The *Rogers* test survived the review.[85] Although *Rosenberg* may be read

[78] *Rosenberg v. Percival* [2001] 205 CLR 434, 500, per Callinan J.

[79] *Rosenberg v. Percival* [2001] 205 CLR 434, 459 per Gummow J.

[80] *Rosenberg v. Percival* [2001] 205 CLR 434, 459 per Gummow J.

[81] *Rosenberg v. Percival* [2001] 205 CLR 434, 500, per Callinan J.

[82] *Rosenberg v. Percival* [2001] 205 CLR 434, 478, per Kirby J.

[83] *Chappel v. Hart* (1998) 195 CLR 232, 272, per Kirby J.

[84] *Rosenberg v. Percival* [2001] 205 CLR 434.

[85] In *Rosenberg v. Percival*, Kirby J. admitted that the *Rogers* rule is "undoubtedly strict one", and was open-minded towards any suggestion of reconsidering the ambit of the rule. His Honour highlighted some considerations that may support arguments suggesting confining the *Rogers* rule. These considerations include: (1) some patients' wish of not being unsettled by unnecessary disclosure; (2) patient's imperfect understanding of risks; (3) time constraints on doctors to do the disclosure task; (4) the cost-effectiveness of disclosure; (5) the disclosure rule being simplified as "a single instance of warning" rather than being viewed as "a continuous dialogue"; (5) the increase in malpractice litigation and the emergence of defensive medicine. His Honour admitted that such considerations may contribute to thinking that the content of the duty to warn should be "realistic and achievable". However, his Honour concluded that "[n]o reason has been shown to reformulate [the *Rogers* test] more narrowly". To the contrary, his Honour highlighted the following considerations that are supportive of the view that stringency of the *Rogers* test deserves to be unshaken: (1) a recognition of individual autonomy and a wider appreciation of basic human rights and human dignity; (2) defects of communication between doctors and patients; (3) conflicts of interests which a health provider may face; (4) the value of the symbolism which legal principles may afford; (5) the fact that giving sufficient warning is actually likely to diminish recriminations and litigation following disappointment after treatment. *See, Rosenberg v. Percival* [2001] 205 CLR 434, 476–481. *Also see, Rosenberg v. Percival* [2001] 205 CLR 434, 501 (Callinan J.: "The decision in *Rogers v. Whitaker* has been received with some consternation by the medical profession…. The common law does however evolve, albeit usually incrementally, with the result that practices and conduct may have to be changed to accord with it. ").

as indicative of "tightening up" of the application of the *Rogers* test (Amirthalingam 2003, 128), it has been argued that "[t]he distinctions made in *Rogers* between disclosure cases and diagnosis/treatment cases, and the relevant standards to be applied to each category, are … not eroded by *Rosenberg*" (Parker 2003, 159).

In formulating a standard of information disclosure, England seems to lag behind other common law jurisdictions. In the *Sidaway* case, most of the Lordships only required doctors to respond positively to patients' questioning. What the *Bolam-Sidaway* authorities established is a "doctor centred" approach.[86] There are some hints that English law has begun to prefer the patient-oriented test or the materiality test as a better yardstick for assessing the scope of the duty to warn. A notable example of this is that, in *Pearce v. United Bristol Healthcare NHS Trust,*[87] Lord Woolf MR, after uncritically quoted at length the majority opinion of the *Sidaway* case and the *Bolitho* case, held that:

> if there is a *significant risk* which would affect the judgment of *the reasonable patient*, then in the normal course it is the responsibility of a doctor to inform the patient of that *significant risk*, if the information is needed so that the patient can determine for him or herself as to what course he or she should adopt. (emphasis added) [88]

Although the author of this "significant risk" formulation deems it as just a product of reinterpretation of *Sidaway* in light of *Bolitho* (Woolf 2001, 11), the above-quoted passage appears to introduce a new reasonable patient standard into English traditional doctor-oriented thinking (Mason and Brodie 2005, 301) – "a significant risk affecting the judgment of a reasonable patient places the onus upon the doctor to disclose that significant risk by virtue of the *Bolam* test", via "the court's assessment of what a reasonable doctor ought to disclose" (Jones 1999, 118).

Lord Woolf MR's "significant risk" formula was quoted with approval by Lord Steyn who formed part of the majority in the House of Lords case *Chester v. Afshar*.[89] It was interpreted as a development of a trilogy of decisions (*Bolam*, *Sidaway* and *Bolitho*).[90] It was cited to support his Lordship's "patient's rights, correlatively surgeon's duty" reasoning,[91] ending with the observation that "[i]n modern law

[86]This line of categorisation was used in *Fitzpatrick v. White* [2008] 3 IR 551, 560 at [25] per Kearns J.(the *Bolam-Sidaway* authorities "established that a medical practitioner's duty to warn was to be assessed *in accordance with the practice accepted at the time as proper by a responsible body of medical opinion*. While the decision as to what risks should be disclosed to the particular patient to enable him to make a rational choice whether to undergo the particular treatment was *primarily a matter of clinical judgment*, the disclosure of a particular risk of serious adverse consequences might, in a given case, be *so obviously necessary* for the patient to make an informed choice that *no reasonably prudent doctor* could fail to disclose the risk, and if there was such a failure, the medical practitioner could be found in breach of the duty to disclose" (emphasis added)).

[87]*Pearce v. United Bristol Healthcare NHS Trust* (1999) 48 BMLR 118; [1999] PIQR 53.

[88]*Pearce v. United Bristol Healthcare NHS Trust* (1998) 48 BMLR 118, 124; [1999] PIQR 53, 59.

[89]*Chester v. Afshar* [2004] 4 All ER 587, [2004] UKHL 41; [2005] 1 AC 32.

[90]*Chester v. Afshar* [2004] 4 All ER 587, 593–594, paras. 15, 16.

[91]*Chester v. Afshar* [2004] 4 All ER 587, 593–594, para. 14.

medical paternalism no longer rules and a patient has a prima facie right to be informed by a surgeon of a small, but well established, risk of serious injury as a result of surgery". Lord Woolf MR's "significant risk" formulation was also cited in a recent English High Court case involving disclosure of alternatives, with an observation that "[t]he obvious rationale [underlying Lord Woof MR's statement of the law and Lord Steyn's words] is patient autonomy and respect for the reality that it is the patient who must bear any consequences if a risk transforms itself into a reality".[92] It was also optimistically viewed as a step to move to "a version of the 'reasonable patient' test"[93] and was applauded as "more reasonable" by the Supreme Court of Ireland.[94]

Lord Woolf MR's "significant risk" formulation has a potential for being developed into a patient-oriented/materiality standard, as witnessed by the Irish law which adopted the "proactive" limb of the *Rogers* test:

> [the test outlined by Lord Woolf] is still an onerous test and not dissimilar from the requirement enunciated in *Rogers v. Whitaker*, and in this context I would regard the words *"significant risk" and "material risk" as interchangeable*. In *Geoghegan v. Harris* I suggested that any consideration of "materiality" would involve consideration of both (a) the severity of the consequences and (b) the statistical frequency of the risk. Putting it another way, *a risk may be seen as material if, in the circumstances of the particular case, a reasonable person in the patient's position, if warned of the risk, would be likely to attach significance to it*. I am leaving to one side here considerations of those cases where the medical practitioner may be *aware* that *the particular patient*, if warned of the risk, would be likely to attach significance to it where another patient might not. (emphasis added) [95]

"Materiality" usually means the *significance* a reasonable person in the patient's position would attach to the undisclosed information in deciding whether to submit or not to submit to treatment.[96] The material information which should be discussed with the patient is that information which would be considered by a reasonable person in the patient's position as *significant* when evaluating whether to proceed with the treatment. Framed in another way, a risk is considered to be material when a reasonable person in the patient's position would likely attach significance to the potential risk in deciding whether or not to forego the treatment.

As I will clarify in Chap. 4, materiality is different from causation. In a *negligence* cause of action, in addition to the issue of "*materiality*" (a physician failed to disclose a material risk of the therapy undertaken or reasonable alternatives to it), a plaintiff must also show that (1) the patient would have chosen against the recommended

---

[92] *Birch v. University College Hospitals NHS Trust* [2008] EWHC 2237 (QB), at [72].

[93] *Fitzpatrick v. White* [2008] 3 IR 551, 560 at [26] per Kearns J.

[94] *Fitzpatrick v. White* [2008] 3 IR 551, 564 at [35] per Kearns J. ("I would see as more reasonable for those cases the test outlined by Lord Woolf, namely, that if there is a significant risk which would affect the judgment of a reasonable patient, then in the normal course it is the responsibility of a doctor to inform the patient of that significant risk.").

[95] *Fitzpatrick v. White* [2008] 3 IR 551, 564 at [35] per Kearns J.

[96] *Wilkinson v. Vessey*, 295 A.2d 676, 689 (R.I. 1972) (but confining to information about "risk or risks"). *See also*, *Rogers v. Whitaker* (1992) 175 C.L.R. 479, 490 (HCA); *Fitzpatrick v. White* [2008] 3 IR 551, 564 at [35] per Kearns J.

therapy (*decision-causation*); and (2) as a result of the therapeutic intervention the plaintiff suffered injury (*injury-causation*).[97] Common law jurisdictions differ in adopting a *subjective* test of causation or an *objective* approach to causation.[98]

In order to prove a case in negligence, a party must be able to prove both factual causation and legal causation. The conventional test to determine *factual* causation is the "*but for*" test and "balance of probability".[99] In circumstances where the basic "but-for" test is unworkable and leads to clear injustice, alternatives are developed. For example, under the *material contribution* test,[100] the conduct of a defendant is regarded as a cause-in-fact if it materially contributed to the loss. If the defendant's act materially contributed to the plaintiff's injury, the "but for" test is deemed to be satisfied. In determining *legal* causation, one of the key considerations is the *remoteness* of the person's *damage* from the negligence of the other. Moreover, there may exist intervening acts or causes which break the chain of causation. A person's negligence is deemed to be too remote or not a "proximate cause" of another's damages if a reasonable person would never *reasonably foresee* it happening. The distinction between factual causation and legal causation is based on the notion that negligence damages should not be awarded in events where no one could foresee something bad happening and therefore take the necessary steps to avoid it. Factual and legal causation are said to be distinguished from each other in an effort to avert the danger of defendants being exposed to "liability in an indeterminate amount for an indeterminate time to an indeterminate class."[101]

People may have different ways of phrasing the issue of remoteness of damage or the foreseeability of damage. The remoteness or foreseeability issue may be phrased either in terms of proximate cause, or in terms of duty of care. For example, in the leading USA case of *Palsgraf v. Long Island Rail Road Co.*,[102] Judge Cardozo

[97] *Canterbury v. Spence*, 464 F.2d 772, 787–791 (USA, non-disclosure of risks); *Sicard v. Sendziak*, 2008 ABQB 690, at [116] (Court of Queen's Bench of Alberta) (Canada, non-disclosure of alternative treatments).

[98] England and Australia favour a subjective test of causation, i.e. whether the particular patient (i.e., the plaintiff) would have consented to the procedure after being informed of the risk. *See*, **England**: *Chatterton v. Gerson*, (1981) 1 QB 432; *Hills v. Potter*, (1984) 1 WLR(4). **Australia**: *Rogers v. Whitaker* (1992) 175 C.L.R. 479, 490 (HCA); *Chappel v. Hart* (1998) 195 CLR 232, 272; *Ellis v. Wallsend District Hospital* [1989] 17 NSWLR 553 (C.A.); *Civil Liability Act 2003* (Qld) s 11(3); *Civil Liability Act 2002* (NSW) s 5D (3); *Civil Liability Act 2002* (Tas) s 13(3); *Civil Liability Act 2002* (WA) s 5C(3). Canada has adopted an objective or a modified objective approach to causation in informed consent cases. The objective test is one which determines whether a reasonable or prudent person in the patient's position would have consented to the treatment had the information been disclosed. *See*, *Reibl v. Hughes* (1980) 114 D.L.R. (3d) 1, 17 (S.C.C.); *Arndt v. Smith* (1997), 148 D.L.R. (4th) 48, 51(S.C.C.).

[99] *Barnett v. Chelsea & Kensington Hospital Management Committee* [1969] 1 QB 428.

[100] *Bonnington Castings Ltd v. Wardlaw* [1956] AC 613.

[101] *Ultramares Corp. v. Touche* (1931) 255 N. Y. 170, 174 N. E. 441 (In the words of Cardozo, J.).

[102] *Palsgraf v. Long Island Rail Road Co.*, 248 N.Y. 339, 162 N.E.99 (N.Y. 1928). The plaintiff, Palsgraf, was hit by scales that fell on her as she waited on a train platform. The scales fell because of a far-away commotion. A train conductor had run to help a man into a departing train. The man was carrying a package as he jogged to jump in the train door. The package had fireworks in it.

opined that, because a *duty* was owed only to *foreseeable* plaintiffs, the defendant owed "no duty" of care to the plaintiff. Without any perception that one's actions could harm someone, there could be no duty towards that person, and therefore no negligence for which to impose liability. However, the three-judge dissent, written by Judge Andrews, saw the case as a matter of *proximate cause*, arguing that the defendant owed a duty to the plaintiff, regardless of foreseeability, because all people owe one another a duty not to act negligently.

Although there are some subtle differences in formulations of the materiality test amongst jurisdictions opting for the patient-oriented standard of information disclosure, almost all formulations have one thing in common: the information to which "*a reasonable person in the patient's position*" would be likely to *attach significance* falls within a doctor's duty to inform. How can this test be translated into clinical practice? Here are some hints and rules which, although formulated in the context of disclosure of *risks*, may be applicable to both disclosure of risks and disclosure of alternatives:

- **The *content* of the disclosure**: (1) The *content* of the disclosure rests in the first place with the physician.[103] (2) The physician, with knowledge of, or ability to learn, his patient's background and current condition, is in a superior position to *identify* particular dangers and make a judgment as to whether and to what extent disclosure to the patient is called for.[104]
- **The *scope* of the disclosure**: (1) The scope of the physician's communications to the patient must be measured by the patient's need.[105] What patients need is the information material to their decision.[106] (2) The scope of the standard is objective with due regard for *the patient's informational needs* and with suitable leeway for *the physician's situation*.[107] (3) Australian law indicates that the *content and scope* of the duty to inform should not be looked at solely from the point of view of the patient, that the duty to inform is part of the law of negligence, and accordingly the nature of the duty is "a duty to take reasonable care to inform", and that considerations should be given to the *situation of the practitioner*.[108]

The conductor mishandled the passenger or his package, causing the package to fall. The fireworks slipped and exploded on the ground causing shockwaves to travel through the platform. As a consequence, the scales fell. Because Palsgraf was hurt by the falling scales, she sued the train company who employed the conductor for negligence.

[103] *Canterbury v. Spence*, 464 F.2d 772, 787 (1972).

[104] *Canterbury v. Spence*, 464 F.2d 772, 787 (1972).

[105] *Canterbury v. Spence*, 464 F.2d 772, 786 (1972).

[106] *Canterbury v. Spence*, 464 F.2d 772, 786 (1972).

[107] *Canterbury v. Spence*, 464 F.2d 772, 787 (1972).

[108] Commonwealth of Australia (2002), p. 47, para. 3.44. Some legislation in Australia followed the Panel's recommendations. For example, Section 50 of *Wrongs Act 1958 (Vic)* provides that "[a] person (the defendant) who owes a duty of care to another person (the plaintiff) to give a warning or other information to the plaintiff in respect of a risk or other matter, satisfies that duty of care if the defendant takes *reasonable care* in giving that warning or other information" (emphasis added).

This refinement may help to reassure doctors that the law does not require of them *unrealistic* standards of behaviour.[109]

- **"Significance" and "materiality"**: (1) The materiality test would summon the physician to *second-guess the patient*, whose ideas on materiality could *hardly be known to the physician*, and that would produce an undue demand upon medical practitioners.[110] (2) Although a physician cannot know with complete exactitude what the patient would consider important to his decision, he, on the basis of his medical training and experience, can *sense* how the average, reasonable patient expectably would react.[111] (3) There is no bright line separating the significant from the insignificant.[112] (4) Australian law indicates that, in determining whether a reasonable patient or the particular patient would be "likely to attach significance to" a risk, the nature of the matter to be disclosed and the nature of the treatment may need to be considered.[113] Among the factors that need to be considered, "the extent or severity of the potential injury" and "the likelihood of the injury actually occurring" are two matters that are of great importance in cases of failure to warn.[114] They should be considered together.[115] They need to be weighed against the circumstances of the patient. The circumstances may include: (a) the patient's need for the operation;[116] (b) the existence of reasonably available and satisfactory alternative treatments;[117] (c) whether the procedure is elective rather than life saving.[118] (5) Similarly, the USA law indicates that the *factors contributing significance* to the dangerousness of a medical technique are, of course, the incidence of injury and the degree of the harm threatened.[119]
- **"Knowledge" (actual knowledge + constructive knowledge)**: Consonantly with orthodox negligence doctrine, the issue on nondisclosure must be approached from the viewpoint of the *reasonableness* of the physician's disclosure in terms of what he *knows or should know* to be the patient's informational needs.[120] The law needs to assess the reasonableness of the doctor's conduct *in the light of his knowledge, including constructive knowledge, of the needs* of a reasonable person with certain salient characteristics of the patient (Teff 1985, 441–442).

---

[109] Commonwealth of Australia (2002), p. 47, para. 3.46.

[110] *Canterbury v. Spence*, 464 F.2d 772, 787 (1972).

[111] *Canterbury v. Spence*, 464 F.2d 772, 787 (1972).

[112] *Canterbury v. Spence*, 464 F.2d 772, 788 (1972).

[113] *F. v. R.* (1983) 33 S.A.S.R 189, 192–193, per King C.J.

[114] *Rosenberg v. Percival* [2001] 205 CLR 434, 458, per Gummow J.

[115] *Rosenberg v. Percival* [2001] 205 CLR 434, 458, per Gummow J.

[116] *Rosenberg v. Percival* [2001] 205 CLR 434, 458, per Gummow J.

[117] *Rosenberg v. Percival* [2001] 205 CLR 434, 458–459, per Gummow J.

[118] *Rosenberg v. Percival* [2001] 205 CLR 434, 459, per Gummow J.

[119] *Canterbury v. Spence*, 464 F.2d 772, 788 (1972).

[120] *Canterbury v. Spence*, 464 F.2d 772, 787 (1972).

- **"Information"**: The *information* that demands a communication may include "the inherent and potential hazards of the proposed treatment, the alternatives to that treatment, if any, and the results likely if the patient remains untreated".[121]

These points I summarised from the USA and Australian case law and legislation not only give some hints on how a test can be translated into clinical practice, but also support several notions, some of which I will explain more clearly in the following part of this chapter. Among other things, these notions include: (1) There is a distinction between the "content" of the disclosure and the "scope" of the disclosure. The content of the disclosure depends on knowledge, including constructive knowledge, of doctors. The scope of the disclosure is, however, driven by a patient's needs. (2) There is a distinction between "information" and "materiality". The scope of "information" available relies on the knowledge base of the medical profession. The "significance" and "materiality" of a piece of information is, however, gauged in a patient's perspective.

2.5 Making Health Care Divisible

As far as the relationship between legal authorities and heath care practice is concerned, Professor Jonathan Montgomery identified two models – a less deferential model (or a more "legalistic" approach) and a more deferential model (or an "integrated" model) (Montgomery 2006, 185–210). The less deferential model prefers to see healthcare as equivalent to other enterprises. Under this model, the judiciary would show more readiness to formulate and refine legal principles rather than just referring to the more general test of "best interests" (Montgomery 2006, 204). The healthcare law becomes more like law and less like an extension of professional ethics (Montgomery 2006, 204).

The more deferential model endorses the *Sidaway* approach of refusing to subdivide the health care into different aspects and subject them to different tests. This approach subjects all aspects of medical practice to one single test – the *Bolam* test – which is medical-profession-oriented. Making the *Bolam* test universally applicable and keeping the professional duties of doctors indivisible is a key feature of what was described as an "integrated" model of incorporating the moral dimension into professional practice in dealing with the relationship between technical skill and moral reasoning. On this model, moral reasoning is seen as an essential part of the practice of healthcare. Based on the assumption that professional practice already takes into account the moral dimension and approaches its regulation on that basis, reinforcing prevailing professional standards through universally applying the profession-oriented *Bolam* test is deemed as also reinforcing moral practice.

[121] *Canterbury v. Spence*, 464 F.2d 772, 787–788 (1972).

The *Bolam* test demonstrates the judicial deference to medical opinions or decisions (even just the decision-makers – doctors), and the judicial reluctance to scrutinise the substantive dimension of the decision. There was an argument that what *could* be done and what *should* be done should not be separated (Montgomery 2006, 201). In this view, using the *Bolam* test as a benchmark of acceptable practice does not mean abandoning normative judgment. It reinforces the values of the health profession. The non-interventionist approach, which is enshrined in the *Bolam* philosophy, is built on the faith that delivering healthcare – highly skilled, dedicated and altruistic staff applying uncertain but technical knowledge for the benefit of patients – is "an altruistic vocation, not a commercial enterprise tainted by sordid financial pressures" (Montgomery 2006, 201).

Echoing that argument, the more deferential or "integrated" approach would advocate judicial non-intervention in medical practice. "[T]he law supported medicine, looked favourably on its claims to the moral high ground and presented little threat to the autonomy of the professions or the hegemony of medicine" (Montgomery 2006, 201). Medical professionals are freed from detailed legal scrutiny. When faced with difficult cases, the judiciary would be reluctant to codify legal principles, preferring to use the concept of best interests as a way to resolve individual disputes without articulating precise legal rules (Montgomery 2006, 202). The legal purpose of consent was construed narrowly and instrumentally, deeming that consent provides the doctor with a defence against being sued and serves to build faith in, and cooperation with, the treatment (Montgomery 2006, 202).

The "integrated" model has attractiveness. It does not create a confrontational environment. It creates a legal context in which professional morality could flourish (Montgomery 2006, 209). However, the realisation of the model is conditional on formation of an ideal context: doctors are always trustful, moral, always altruistically formulating best interest judgments for their patients.[122] It needs "reclaiming the moral basis of health care practice and restoring trust in medicine and the other health professions" (Montgomery 2006, 209). It is beautiful, but it does not have much preparedness for bad situations.[123] It only reinforces the instrumental value of

[122] *Please see, Burke, R (on the application of) v. General Medical Council & Ors* [2005] EWCA Civ 1003, [2006] QB 273, [2005] 3 WLR 1132, para. [83]. Although the Court of Appeal refused a more interventionist approach towards medical practice and professional Guidance and preferred a more deferential approach, it noted that: "It is in our view of the utmost importance that the Guidance should be understood and implemented at every level throughout the National Health Service and throughout the medical profession. *People in the unhappy position of [the patients] are entitled to have confidence that they will be treated properly and in accordance with good practice, and that they will not be ignored or patronised because of their disability.* Having produced the Guidance, the task of the GMC, it seems to us, is to ensure that it is vigorously promulgated, taught, understood and implemented at every level and in every hospital"(emphasis added).

[123] Jonathan Montgomery (2006), 207 (highlighting that a series of scandals undermined the trust and shattered the illusion that the regulation of healthcare does not require the same legal scrutiny as other spheres of activity).

the doctrine of informed consent. It is confident that doctors can claim competency in deciding both medical/technical issues and non-technical/moral/social matters. It is also confident that the medical profession has competency in allocating resources. It would prefer implicit rationing.[124]

Although admitting that the "integrated" model has many merits, at least within the realm of information disclosure, I still doubt the wisdom of applying the medical-profession-oriented *Bolam* test universally to every aspect of health care. There is a need to differentiate information disclosure from diagnosis/treatment. While the judiciary could show more deference to doctors' expertise and technical commitments in the area of diagnosis and treatment, it has expertise to promote informational integration in the area of information disclosure.

I prefer Sir Ian Kennedy's observation that doctors' "unique competence" or "specific competence" lies in formulating diagnosis, prognosis and available treatment options (Kennedy 1988, 19–31). Doctors have to "make too many hard decisions which it is not really their job to make".[125] The diagnosis, prognosis, and range of available treatments are technical-medical matters.[126] As Sir Ian Kennedy elaborated,

> [A] doctor's special competence lies in, first the *knowledge* which allows him to make a *diagnosis and prognosis* of what is generally accepted as being ill health; second, *the knowledge of what therapies, if any, are available* in the context of a particular condition of ill health; third, the *judgment of which therapy or response to adopt* so as to produce, to the best of his ability, an end result deemed appropriate not by him but by the patient, one approved by society at large. No more, no less. (emphasis added) (Kennedy 1988, 30)

Sir Ian Kennedy further noted that, when formulating what should be done with a patient's condition, judgment should be made "in light of his patient's wishes and general moral principles as to what ought to be done" (Kennedy 1988, 30). A doctor's particular values, though relevant, are not decisive (Kennedy 1988, 30).

Although appreciation of treatment options falls within doctors' expertise, it is beyond their competency to figure out which treatment option their patients would attach importance to. While information and knowledge about treatment options is subject to medical judgment, the question of whether one piece of information is material to a patient's decision is best left to patients to make.

The indivisibility of the health care is the key feature of the "integrated" model. The "integrated" model involves wide issues. Here I will focus on the question of whether it is desirable to keep the health care indivisible and apply the *Bolam* test to the context of information disclosure. I have observed the inappropriateness of applying the *Bolam* test to the realm of information disclosure before. Here, to highlight the distinctive nature of information disclosure, I will present three

---

[124] Jonathan Montgomery (2006), 198 (acknowledging that the moral problems of rationing are masked under the guise of clinical judgment).

[125] Ian Kennedy (1988), 24 (contending that as the concepts of health and ill health have been expanded enormously without rigorous intellectual examination, the sphere of alleged unique competence of the doctor has correspondingly expanded).

[126] Ian Kennedy (1988), 24 (noting that there are countless decisions taken by doctors which are not medical, but rather involve economic analysis, political judgments, philosophical thinking and moral theory).

dichotomies – (1) the doctor-oriented standard v. the patient-oriented standard of information disclosure, (2) medical judgment v. layperson knowledge, (3) information v. materiality. That would reinforce the argument that the *Bolam* test or similar version of a physician-oriented test (such as the doctrine of "two schools of thought") does not sit comfortably with the distinctive nature of information disclosure. The cases and literatures cited are not confined to England.

2.5.1 The Doctor-Oriented Standard v. The Patient-Oriented Standard

As far as the scope of information disclosure is concerned, the patient-centred standard is not universally accepted. There are still some jurisdictions which favoured the physician-oriented standard.[127] In England, the landmark *Bolam*[128] and *Sidaway*[129] cases, by according greater deference to medical profession, actually established a doctor-oriented approach to the standard of information disclosure.[130] English law measures the doctor's duty to warn "by applying the standard of competent professional opinion".[131]

The doctor-oriented standard is an ordinary product of the general rules of torts. It "closely paralleled the rules of liability in medical negligence cases generally" in that what is customary in the profession will dominate standards (Meisel 1977, 93). It stems from a misconceived perception that medical judgment and expert testimony is just as necessary to establish negligence in failing adequately to disclose as it is to prove negligence in diagnosis or treatment. The physician-oriented standard seems to "perpetuate medical paternalism by giving the profession sweeping authority to decide unilaterally what is in the patient's best interests".[132]

The patient-oriented standard of information disclosure honours the patient's right of self-determination[133] and the distinctions drawn between "medical judgment"

---

[127] *Natanson v. Kline*, 350 P.2d 1093, 1106 (Kan. 1960); *Aiken v. Clary*, 396 S.W.2d 668, 674 (Mo. 1965); *Woolley v. Henderson*, 418 A.2d 1123, 1131 (Me. 1980).

[128] *Bolam v. Friern Hospital Management Committee* [1957] 2 All ER 118, [1957] 1 WLR 582.

[129] *Sidaway v. Bethlem Royal Hospital Governors* [1985] 1 All ER 643, (1985) AC 871.

[130] *Chester v. Afshar* [2004] 4 All ER 587, 603, para. 57, per Lord Hope of Craighead (indicating that English *Bolam* test is a reasonable doctor standard).

[131] *Chester v. Afshar* [2004] 4 All ER 587, 601, para. 52, per Lord Hope of Craighead.

[132] *Scott v. Bradford*, 606 P.2d 554, 557 (Okla. 1979) (citing Katz, Informed Consent – A fairy Tale? 39 U. Pitt. L. Rev. 137, 143 (1977)).

[133] *Canterbury v. Spence*, 464 F.2d 772, 784–786 (1972); *Largey v. Rothman*, 540 A.2d 504, 508 (N.J. 1988); *Wilkinson v. Vessey*, 295 A.2d 676, 687 (R.I. 1972) (the physician-oriented standard "relegates the patient's right to make an informed election to a position of secondary importance because it measures that right entirely in terms of standards adopted by those whose obligation is to inform"; "[t]he keystone of [the] doctrine [of informed consent] is every competent adult's right to forego treatment, or even cure, if it entails what for him are intolerable consequences or risks however unwise his sense of values may be in the eyes of the medical profession, or even the community.").

and "layperson knowledge", and between knowledge of "information" and "materiality" of information. I will highlight those distinctions in the following parts of this chapter.

2.5.2 *Medical Judgment v. Layperson Knowledge*

2.5.2.1 Diagnosis and Treatment: Medical Judgment

Traditionally, there is a heavy deference paid by the courts towards a recognized and respectable practice in the medical profession. The medical profession as a whole is "assumed" to have acted "in the best interests of patients and are not inherently negligent".[134] The reason for such deference is that courts do not ordinarily have the *expertise* to tell medical professionals that they are not behaving appropriately in their field.[135] Courts should not involve themselves in resolving *scientific* disputes which require the expertise of the profession.[136] Courts and juries do not have the necessary expertise to assess *technical* matters relating to the diagnosis or treatment of patients.[137]

2.5.2.2 Information Disclosure: Medical Judgment and Lay Knowledge

(a) Medical judgment
In jurisdictions where the physician-oriented standard of disclosure is adopted, the question of what disclosure of risks incidental to the proposed treatment should be made in a particular situation is regarded as involving medical judgment.[138] The medical judgment argument is always coupled with the "best interests"

---

[134] *ter Neuzen v. Korn*, (1993) 103 D.L.R. (4th) 473; aff'd (1995) 127 D.L.R. (4th) 577, 590 (SCC).

[135] *ter Neuzen v. Korn*, (1993) 103 D.L.R. (4th) 473; aff'd (1995) 127 D.L.R. (4th) 577, 590 (SCC).

[136] *ter Neuzen v. Korn*, (1993) 103 D.L.R. (4th) 473; aff'd (1995) 127 D.L.R. (4th) 577, 592 (SCC).

[137] *ter Neuzen v. Korn*, (1993) 103 D.L.R. (4th) 473; aff'd (1995) 127 D.L.R. (4th) 577, 592 (SCC).

[138] *See, Aiken v. Clary*, 396 S.W.2d 668, 674 (Mo. 1965); *Natanson v. Kline*, 350 P.2d 1093, 1106 (Kan. 1960) ("The duty of the physician to disclose, ... is limited to those disclosures which a reasonable medical practitioner would make under the same or similar circumstances. How the physician may best discharge his obligation to the patient in this difficult situation *involves primarily a question of medical judgment*. So long as the disclosure is sufficient to assure an informed consent, the physician's choice of plausible courses should not be called into question if it appears, all circumstances considered, that the physician was motivated only by the patient's *best therapeutic interests* and he proceeded as competent medical men would have done in a similar situation. "(emphasis added)); *Smith v. Auckland Hospital Board*, [1964] NZLR 241, 248 (declining to distinguish between "the realm of diagnosis or technique" and "the area of advice"; being reversed in *Smith v. Auckland Hospital Board*, [1965] NZLR 191 where the Court of Appeal shifted the emphasis to a particular, special or somewhat exceptional/uncommon circumstance – the patient's specific inquiry).

rationale, the notion of "beneficence" and a paternalistic tenor. Actually, in the context of information disclosure, medical judgment is not applicable to every area. It is reserved to: (1) appreciation of the risks and benefits of the proposed treatment and alternatives;[139] (2) exercise of "therapeutic privilege".[140]

(b) Lay knowledge

In *Sidaway* case, Lord Scarman expressed deep doubt on the rightfulness and competency of medical judgment in determining the scope of the duty to warn,[141] noting that "in very many cases factors other than the purely medical will play a significant part" in a patient's decision-making process.[142] In the Australian "high-water mark" decision, *Rogers v. Whitaker*, it was indicated that, generally speaking, "no special medical skill is involved in disclosing the information".[143] In *Cobbs v. Grant*,[144] the Supreme Court of California divided the informed consent process into two parts. The first is "appreciat[ing] the risks inherent in the procedure [a doctor] is prescribing, the risks of a decision not to undergo the treatment, and the probability of a successful outcome of the treatment".[145] This part involves the doctor's expert function. The second part is, once the relevant information has been disclosed, "[t]he weighing of these risks against the individual subjective fears and hopes of the patient".[146] Such evaluation and decision does not involve expert skill, and is a non-medical judgment, and thus should be reserved to the patient alone.[147] In *Wilkinson v. Vesey*,[148] the Supreme Court of

---

[139] *Cobbs v. Grant*, 502 P.2d 1, 10 (1972); *Woolley v. Henderson*, 418 A.2d 1123, 1130 (Me. 1980) ("[w]hether the physician has acted unreasonably is often a question of *professional judgment*. In determining whether and how much he should disclose, the physician must consider *the probable impact of disclosure on the patient*, taking into account his peculiar knowledge of *the patient's psychological, emotional and physical condition*, and must evaluate the *magnitude of the risk, the frequency of its occurrence and the viability of alternative therapeutic measures*." (emphasis added)); *Woolley v. Henderson*, 418 A.2d 1123, 1130 (Me. 1980) (noting that medical evidence is necessary to *identify the known risks of treatment, the nature of available alternatives and the cause of any injury* suffered by the plaintiff).

[140] *Aiken v. Clary*, 396 S.W.2d 668, 674 (Mo. 1965) ("[t]his determination involves medical judgment as to whether disclosure of possible risks may have such an adverse effect on the patient as to jeopardize success of the proposed therapy, no matter how expertly performed."); *Largey v. Rothman*, 540 A.2d 504, 507 (N.J. 1988) (alleging that only a physician can effectively *estimate both the psychological and physical consequences* that a risk inherent in a medical procedure might produce in a patient); *Rogers v. Whitaker* (1992) 175 C.L.R. 479, 490 (HCA).

[141] *Sidaway v. Bethlem Royal Hospital Governors* [1985] 1 All ER 643, 649, per Lord Scarman (dissenting).

[142] *Sidaway v. Bethlem Royal Hospital Governors* [1985] 1 All ER 643, 652, per Lord Scarman (dissenting).

[143] *Rogers v. Whitaker* (1992) 175 C.L.R. 479, 490 (HCA). However, the Court acknowledged the necessity of a physician's skills in communicating information.

[144] *Cobbs v. Grant*, 8 Cal. 3d 229, 502 P.2d 1, 104 Cal. Rptr. 505 (1972).

[145] *Cobbs v. Grant*, 502 P.2d 1, 10 (1972).

[146] *Cobbs v. Grant*, 502 P.2d 1, 10 (1972).

[147] *Cobbs v. Grant*, 502 P.2d 1, 10 (1972).

[148] *Wilkinson v. Vessey*, 295 A.2d 676 (R.I. 1972).

Rhode Island made it clear that "[t]he decision as to *what is or is not material is a human judgment*", and it does "not necessarily require the assistance of the medical profession".[149]

It is fair to say that "[a]lthough *knowledge of the risks and alternatives* requires medical expertise, *deciding whether to disclose such knowledge* does not" (Morris 2002, 326, emphasis added). Some scenarios involve patients' very "intensely personal decisions".[150] A patient may well have in mind circumstances, objectives, and values which he may reasonably not make known to the doctor but which may lead him to a different decision from that suggested by a purely medical opinion.[151] The doctor's duty is "to provide his patient with the information needed to enable the patient to consider and balance the medical advantages and risks *alongside other relevant matters*, such as, for example, his family, business or social responsibilities *of which the doctor may be only partially, if at all, informed*."[152]

2.5.3 *Information v. Materiality*

Under the reasonable patient standard, a physician must disclose information *material* to the patient's decision.[153] As mentioned above, assessing the materiality of a risk involves a two-pronged analysis: (1) the information prong; (2) the materiality

---

[149] *Wilkinson v. Vessey*, 295 A.2d 676, 688 (R.I. 1972) (emphasis added). *See also*, *Canterbury v. Spence*, 464 F.2d 772, 785 (1972) (noting that, in nondisclosure cases, "the governing standard is much more largely divorced from professional considerations" and "the factfinder is not invariably functioning in an area of such technical complexity that it must be bound to medical custom as an inexorable application of the community standard of reasonable care").

[150] *Burke, R (on the application of) v. The General Medical Council Rev 1* [2004] 2 FLR 1121, [2005] 2 WLR 431, [2004] EWHC 1879 (Admin), [2005] QB 424, para. [97] (citing an example involving one treatment (chemotherapy) and two patients (one is anxious to prolong his life as long as possible, irrespective of the quality of his life, because he is desperate to live long enough to see his daughter married or his first grandchild born; the other is determined to complete some project – a book, perhaps, or a work of art – for which he needs a clear mind free of the unpleasant side effects); noting that doctors are "not qualified to" take the ultimate decision about whether to undergo treatment).

[151] *Sidaway v. Bethlem Royal Hospital Governors* (1985) AC 871, 884 (per Lord Scarman).

[152] *Sidaway v. Bethlem Royal Hospital Governors* (1985) AC 871, 884 (per Lord Scarman) (emphasis added).

[153] **USA:** *Canterbury v. Spence*, 464 F.2d 772, 786–788 (1972) ("the test for determining whether a particular peril must be divulged is its materiality to the patient's decision: all risks potentially affecting the decision must be unmasked"; "[a] risk is … material when a reasonable person, in what the physician knows or should know to be the patient's position, would be likely to attach significance to the risk or cluster of risks in deciding whether or not to forgo the proposed therapy"; the information that demands a communication may include "the inherent and potential hazards of

prong.[154] Expert medical evidence or medical judgment is, of course, relevant to findings as to the *risks* that reside in or are a result of recommended surgery or other treatment.[155] It will also have a bearing on their *materiality* but this is not a question that is to be concluded on the basis of the expert medical evidence alone.[156] The giving of information "involves wider issues about the relationship between medical practitioners and patients and the right of individuals to decide their own fate".[157] Because the risks of the proposed treatment and its alternatives are intimately related, I would argue that the "information" that falls within the first prong not only include the "risks" of the proposed treatment, but also encompass information about its "alternatives".

Expert medical testimony and medical judgment are generally necessary to identify and define the relevant information, such as "the risks of treatment, their gravity, likelihood of occurrence, and reasonable alternatives".[158] However, there is no or less need for such testimony to establish the materiality of information.[159] The information/materiality distinction illustrates and reinforces the notion that "medical facts are for medical experts and other facts are for any witness – expert or not – having sufficient knowledge and capacity to testify to them" (Fig. 2.1).[160]

Although my formulation regarding the information/materiality distinction, to some extent, benefits from the wisdom of the USA law, the Commonwealth law does not lack the same wisdom. For example, in determining whether the risk should be disclosed, the Supreme Court of South Australia, in the 1983 case of *F* v. *R*,[161] formulated five factors that need to be taken into account: (1) the nature of the matter to be disclosed; (2) the nature of the treatment; (3) the desire of the patient

the proposed treatment, the alternatives to that treatment, if any, and the results likely if the patient remains untreated"); *Wilkinson v. Vessey*, 295 A.2d 676, 689 (R.I. 1972) (materiality may be said to be "the significance a reasonable person, in what the physician knows or should know is his patient's position, would attach to the disclosed risk or risks in deciding whether to submit or not to submit to surgery or treatment"). **Australia**: *Rogers v. Whitaker* (1992) 175 C.L.R. 479, 490 (HCA) ("a doctor has a duty to warn a patient of a material risk inherent in the proposed treatment; a risk is material if, in the circumstances of the particular case, a reasonable person in the patient's position, if warned of the risk, would be likely to attach significance to it or if the medical practitioner is or should reasonably be aware that the particular patient, if warned of the risk, would be likely to attach significance to it."). **Ireland**: *Fitzpatrick v. White* [2008] 3 IR 551, 564 at [35] per Kearns J ("a risk may be seen as material if, in the circumstances of the particular case, a reasonable person in the patient's position, if warned of the risk, would be likely to attach significance to it").

[154] *Jaskoviak v. Gruver*, 638 N.W. 2d 1, 8–9 (N.D. 2002).

[155] *Reibl v. Hughes* (1980) 114 D.L.R. (3d) 1, 13 (S.C.C.).

[156] *Reibl v. Hughes* (1980) 114 D.L.R. (3d) 1, 13 (S.C.C.).

[157] Commonwealth of Australia 2002, p. 45, para. 3.37.

[158] *Jaskoviak v. Gruver*, 638 N.W. 2d 1, 9 (N.D. 2002) (quoting *Winkjer v. Herr*, 277 N.W.2d 579, 588 (N.D. 1979)).

[159] *Bey v. Sacks*, 789 A.2d 232, 238 (Pa. Super. 2001).

[160] *Canterbury v. Spence*, 464 F.2d 772, 792(1972) (citations omitted).

[161] *F. v. R.* (1983) 33 S.A.S.R 189.

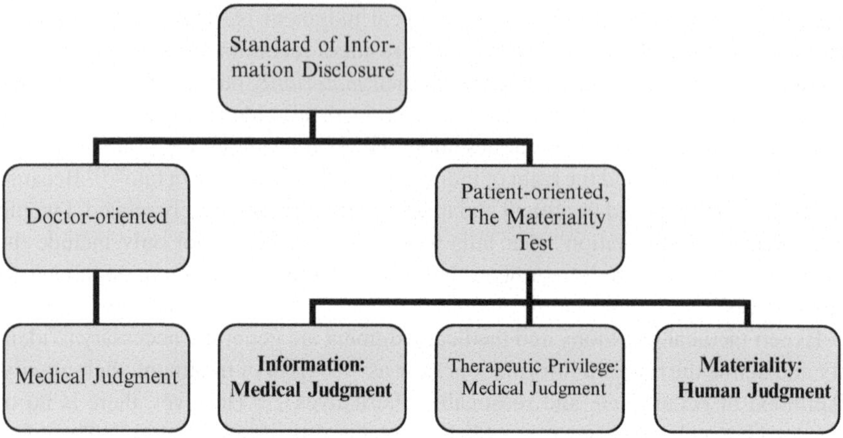

Fig. 2.1 Standard of information disclosure and the information/materiality distinction

for information; (4) the temperament and health of the patient; (5) the general surrounding circumstances.[162]

The first is the "nature of the matter to be disclosed",[163] the likelihood and seriousness of the potential harm. A doctor's duty to disclose extends only to "matters which *might influence* the decisions of a reasonable person in the situation of the patient", so that the patient could make an informed choice about whether to undergo the treatment.[164] Formulated in the *Rogers* way, an ordinary person is more likely to *attach significance* to a risk that is relatively likely to occur, or that has serious consequences (Skene 2008, 182).

The second factor is the nature of the proposed treatment.[165] For *major* surgery or *complex* interventions, more information, such as information about the risks inherent in the proposed treatment and information regarding alternative treatment options, may be needed.[166] For procedures classified as not clinically necessary, such as cosmetic surgery, more information should be given (Skene 2008, 184). Conversely, common risks in minor procedures need not be disclosed because an ordinary person is unlikely to attach importance to them.

---

[162] *F. v. R.* (1983) 33 S.A.S.R 189, 192–193, per King C. J. Echoing the five factors, Gummow J., in the *Rosenberg v. Percival* case, observed that: (1) Among the factors that need to be considered, "the extent or severity of the potential injury" and "the likelihood of the injury actually occurring" are two matters that are of great importance in cases of failure to warn. They should be considered together. (2) They need to be weighed against the circumstances of the patient. (3) The circumstances may include: (a) the patient's need for the operation; (b) the existence of reasonably available and satisfactory alternative treatments; (c) whether the procedure is elective rather than life saving. *See, Rosenberg v. Percival* [2001] 205 CLR 434, 458–459, per Gummow J.

[163] *F. v. R.* (1983) 33 S.A.S.R 189, 192.

[164] *F. v. R.* (1983) 33 S.A.S.R 189, 192, per King C.J. (emphasis added).

[165] *F. v. R.* (1983) 33 S.A.S.R 189, 192.

[166] *F. v. R.* (1983) 33 S.A.S.R 189, 192.

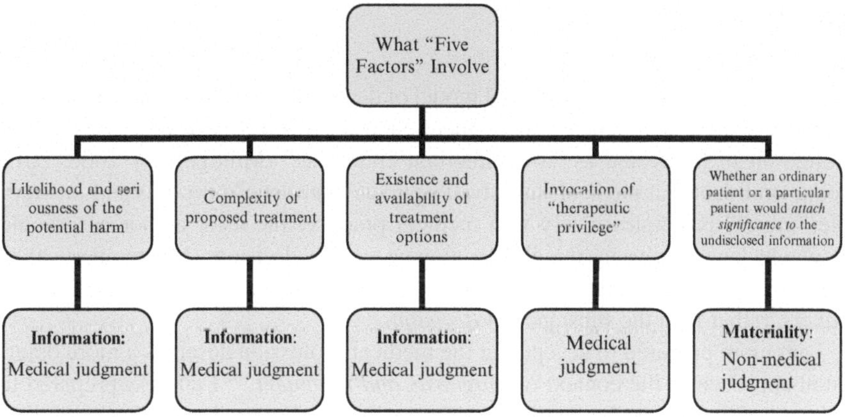

Fig. 2.2 Australia: "Five Factors" and the information-materiality distinction

The third factor, "the desire of the patient for information", highlights the importance of the patient's questions in defining the scope of information disclosure. If the patient asks questions, the questions should be answered honestly and directly. Asking questions makes the doctor "aware" of matters to which the patient attaches importance. This line of legal principles was inherited and reinforced by the subjective or "particular patient" limb of the *Rogers* test.

The fourth factor, "the temperament and health of the patient", provides doctors some room to invoke the exception of "therapeutic privilege". If it is reasonably believed that the patient's mental or physical health might be damaged by the information, or that "the patient's temperament or emotional state is such that he would be unable to make the information a basis for a rational decision",[167] that might justify withholding information about risks from patients.

The fifth factor, "general surrounding circumstances", envisages that the extent of the duty to advise might be limited by situations such as emergencies or the absence of opportunity "for detached reflection".[168]

The "five factors" involve considerations of (1) the likelihood and seriousness of the potential harm; (2) the complexity of interventions or proposed treatment; (3) the existence and availability of treatment options; (4) invocation of "therapeutic privilege"; (5) a particular patient's concerns, and (6) judgment of whether the patient would attach significance to, or would be influenced by, the information. Medical evidence is relevant, even crucial, to the first four considerations (Miola 2009, 101 102). The issue of whether an ordinary patient or a particular patient would have attached significance to the undisclosed information does not involve medical judgment (Fig. 2.2).

[167] *F. v. R.* (1983) 33 S.A.S.R 189, 192.

[168] *F. v. R.* (1983) 33 S.A.S.R 189, 192.

2.6 Proposal

The "integrated" or more deferential model of dealing with the relationship between the law and medical practice, which I mentioned above, does not want to see medical profession to be treated as "a commercial enterprise" (Montgomery 2006, 201). Being confident that medical staff always pursue "altruistic" purposes and incorporate "moral" principles nicely into medical practice, the legal authorities should show reluctance to give meaningful scrutiny on medical decisions (Montgomery 2006, 201). The judicial scrutiny is procedural in nature. It only goes to the *decision-makers*, rather than the substance of *decision*.

I am more prepared to accept that the medical profession deserves a more deferential approach in the context of *diagnosis and treatment*.[169] I am less prepared to share the view that, in the context of information disclosure, doctors know the best for their patients and the courts should adopt a non-interventionist approach towards medical practice.

The judiciary's non-interventionist approach towards medical practice has more persuasive power in the context of diagnosis and treatment rather than in the realm of information disclosure. It is built on the courts' acknowledgement that they lack expertise in making medical judgment and the courts' confidence that medical professionals will practice medicine altruistically and honestly adhere to nice ethical principles.

Following several distinctions I highlighted above, I would like to see the law make health care divisible. A general distinction can be drawn between the realm of diagnosis and treatment and the context of information disclosure. The big difference between the two contexts is that the former involves medical expertise and medical judgment, while the latter engages less medical judgment and more lay expectation. In the next chapter, I would further divide health care into four parts, each having its own focuses and rules.

As far as the relationship between the legal authorities and the medical authorities is concerned, I recommend that the judicial deference to medical judgment is confined to medical/technical matters. The judiciary could show more confidence in making judgments on non-technical or non-medical issues. Legal authorities can tolerate health care fragmentation and give more deference to *technical commitments* shown by health care practitioners. However, in the realm of information disclosure, the legal authorities can do more to promote *informational integration*. To answer the question of what information, including that about alternative treatment options, should fall within the scope of a doctor's duty to disclose, a distinction needs to be drawn between technical commitments and informational commitments.

[169] It needs to be noted that many civil liability legislation in Australia have re-formulated the rules of "professional negligence" along the line of the *Bolam* test and the *Bolitho* rule. It applies to all professions, not just doctors. *See, Civil Liability Act 2003* (Qld), s 22(1) (2) (3) (4); *Civil Liability Act 2002* (Tas), s 22; *Civil Liability Act 2002* (WA), s 5PB; *Civil Liability Act 1936* (SA), s 41; *Civil Liability Act 2002* (NSW), s 5O.

References

Amirthalingam, Kumaralingam. 2003. Anglo-Australian law of medical negligence – Towards convergence? *Torts Law Journal* 11: 117–135.

Brazier, Margaret, and José Miola. 2000. Bye-bye *Bolam*: A medical litigation revolution? *Medial Law Review* 8: 85–114.

Bulen, James A. 2003. Complementary and alternative medicine: Ethical and legal aspects of informed consent to treatment. *The Journal of Legal Medicine* 24: 331–358.

Chalmers, Don, and Robert Schwartz. 1993. *Rogers v.* Whitaker and informed consent in Australia: A fair dinkum duty of disclosure. *Medical Law Review* 1: 139–159.

Commonwealth of Australia. 2002. *Review of the law of negligence: Final report*. http://revofneg.treasury.gov.au/content/review2.asp. Accessed 22 July 2008.

David Ipp, A.O. 2007a. The politics, purpose and reform of the law of negligence. *Australian Law Journal* 81: 456–464.

David Ipp, A.O. 2007b. Themes in the law of Torts. *ALJ* 81: 609.

Fovargue, Sara, and José Miola. 2010. How much information is "enough"? *Clinical Ethics* 5: 13–15.

Gatter, Ken Marcus. 1999. Protecting patient-doctor discourse: Informed consent and deliberative autonomy. *Oregon Law Review* 78: 941–993.

Harrington, John A. 1996. Privileging the medical norm: Liberalism, self-determination and refusal of treatment. *Legal Studies* 16: 348–367.

Jones, Michael A. 1999. Informed consent and other fairy stories. *Medical Law Review* 7: 103–134.

Kennedy, Ian. 1988. *Treat me right: Essays in medical law and ethics*. Oxford: Clarendon.

Keown, John. 1994. Burying *Bolam*: Informed consent down under. *Cambridge Law Journal* 53: 16–19.

Manning, Joanna. 2007. The standard of care and expert evidence of accepted practice in medical negligence. *JLM* 15: 394–407.

Mason, Kenyon, and Douglas Brodie. 2005. *Bolam, Bolam* – Wherefore art Thou *Bolam*? *Edinburgh Law Review* 9: 298–306.

McNichols, William J. 1995. Informed consent liability in a 'material information' jurisdiction: What does the future portend? *Oklahoma Law Review* 48: 711–753.

Meisel, Alan. 1977. The expansion of liability for medical accidents: From negligence to strict liability by way of informed consent. *Nebraska Law Review* 56: 51–152.

Miola, José. 2009. On the materiality of risk: Paper tigers and panaceas. *Medical Law Review* 17: 76–108.

Montgomery, Jonathan. 2006. Law and the demoralisation of medicine. *Legal Studies* 26: 185–210.

Morris, Grant H. 2002. Dissing disclosure: Just what the doctor ordered. *Arizona Law Review* 44: 313–370.

Parker, Malcolm. 2003. Reforming the law of medical negligence: Solutions in search of a problem. *Torts Law Journal* 11: 136–164.

Robertson, Gerald. 1981. Informed consent to medical treatment. *The Law Quarterly Review* 97: 102–126.

Shuaib, Farid Sufian. 2000. *Rogers v. Whitaker*: The end of the *Bolam*'s saga in medical negligence cases in Malaysia? *Professional Negligence* 16: 25–30.

Shultz, Marjorie Maguire. 1985. From informed consent to patient choice: A new protected interest. *The Yale Law Journal* 95: 219–299.

Skene, Loane. 2008. *Law and medical practice: Rights, duties, claims and defences*, 3rd ed. Chatswood: LexisNexis Butterworths.

Teff, Harvey. 1985. Consent to medical procedures: Paternalism, self-determination or therapeutic alliance? *The Law Quarterly Review* 101: 432–453.

Teff, Harvey. 1993. Medical models and legal categories: An English perspective. *Journal of Contemporary Health Law and Policy* 9: 211–232.

Tickner, Karen. 1995. *Rogers v. Whitaker* – Giving patients a meaningful choice. *Oxford Journal of Legal Studies* 15: 109–118.

Woolf, Lord. 2001. Are the courts excessively deferential to the medical profession? *Medical Law Review* 9: 1–16.

Chapter 3
Disclosure of Alternatives: In a Wide Context

Abstract Some courts and scholars have a tendency to confuse "disclosure of alternatives" with recommendation of treatments and other aspects of health care. There is a need to put the issue of the duty to inform about alternatives in a clear context. This chapter endeavours to construct a model for interpreting different aspects of health care, distinguished by the concepts of "unbiased/balanced disclosure", "genuine selection", "personalised recommendation", and "performance" of treatment. As far as "disclosure" of alternatives is concerned, a basic theme is that, while doctors have latitude and liberty in "selecting" treatments between different "schools" of thought, they should overcome their preferences or "school", and present patients with unbiased and balanced information about divergent "schools" of thought, when it comes to disclosure. The conventional or conservative wisdom of only subjecting *recommended* procedures to the duty to inform confuses the context of selection/recommendation of the proposed treatment with that of disclosure of treatment options.

3.1 Introduction

"Disclosure" of alternative treatment options is frequently confused with "selection" and "recommendation" of treatments. This chapter will put the analysis of disclosing alternatives within a wider context. Being aware that there is no single jurisdiction that is strong enough to support the whole arguments proposed, this chapter chooses to present collective wisdom. Rather than focusing only on one individual jurisdiction, it has adopted an integrated approach, attempting to weave together the good laws from various common law jurisdictions.

As case citations illustrate, the jurisdictional scope of this chapter mainly covers some major common law countries, such as England, the USA, Canada, Australia and New Zealand. Despite that, the author prefers diversity rather than uniformity. The author acknowledges that, although they share common law tradition, all these jurisdictions have their own legal landscapes, which are tailored to their unique

X. Zhao, *The Duty of Medical Practitioners and CAM/TCM Practitioners to Inform Competent Adult Patients about Alternatives*,
DOI 10.1007/978-3-642-31647-0_3,

contexts. By combining them together, this chapter intends to offer wider and more coherent perspectives that may help to inform debate and decision of every jurisdiction in this field.

This chapter begins by highlighting traditional thought on the duty to disclose alternatives, observing that the traditional approach of requiring doctors to disclose only information regarding recommended procedures blurred the selection/recommendation – disclosure distinction. After briefly highlighting the distinction drawn between selection/recommendation/performance of treatment and disclosure of treatment options, the chapter draws further distinctions among selection, recommendation, and disclosure of treatments. This leads to the conclusion that, compared with conventional wisdom where a medical practitioner's duty to disclose only attaches to recommended/proposed procedures, an integrated model, where unbiased/balanced/contextualised disclosure is accompanied by genuine selection and personalised recommendation of treatment options, would better serve the needs of both according considerable respect for medical judgment and, at the same time, honouring the rationale and the distinctive aspects of the informed consent rule.

3.2 From Disclosure of Risks to Disclosure of Alternatives

Medical negligence – the dominant basis for legal actions based on inadequate disclosure – is predicated on *harm*. Legal proceedings normally followed after a *risk* inherent in a procedure *materialised* and a patient sustained harm. The requirement to provide information preceding any operation has inevitably focused on the *risks* inherent in treatment (Heywood et al. 2010, 171). The development of the law has undoubtedly encouraged prominence to be attached to this component of information disclosure. Therefore, it is not surprising that most of traditional landmark informed consent cases involved the issue of disclosure of risks attaching a proposed procedure.[1] A particular procedure was proposed and recommended first by a doctor. The doctor's duty to inform surrounded disclosing the merits and demerits, especially the negative aspects, of this particular procedure. What a patient was accorded seemed to be only a veto power – undergoing or forgoing the proposed procedure.

However, if the real rationale behind a doctor's duty to inform is that patients are entitled to make their own decisions and to be given sufficient information to make an informed choice, there is no reason to confine the duty of disclosure only to information about risks.

[1]For example, what the *Rogers* test offered is about the materiality of "risks". The Australian civil liability legislation followed the focus on "risks". For example, Section 21(1) of *Civil Liability Act 2003* (Qld) ("A doctor does not breach a duty owed to a patient to warn of *risk*, before the patient undergoes any medical treatment (or at the time of being given medical advice) that will involve a *risk* of personal injury to the patient, unless the doctor at that time fails to give or arrange to be given to the patient the following information about the *risk*..." (emphasis added)).

Although the earlier landmark informed consent cases concentrated on a doctor's duty to inform about risks, in formulating legal principles, the courts and judges had envisaged that the information that falls within a doctor's duty to disclose was not confined to *risks*, and it might encompass information about *alternatives* to the proposed treatment. I will cite some examples from England, USA and Australia case law to support this. First, the following paragraph was quoted from the England's *Sidaway* case:

> In a medical negligence case where the issue is as to the *advice and information* given to the patient as to *the treatment proposed, the available options and the risk*, the court is concerned primarily with a patient's right. The doctor's duty arises from his patient's rights. If one considers the scope of the doctor's duty by beginning with the right of the patient to make his own decision whether he will or will not undergo the treatment proposed, the right to be informed of significant risk and the doctor's corresponding duty are easy to understand, for the proper implementation of the right requires that the doctor be under a duty to inform his patient of the material risk inherent in the treatment. (emphasis added)[2]

Second, the *Canterbury* Court in the USA also contemplated that a physician's duty to inform may encompass both the risks as to the proposed treatment and its alternatives:

> Where that is the situation, professional custom hardly furnishes the legal criterion for measuring the physician's responsibility to reasonably inform his patient of the *options* and the *hazards* as to treatment. (emphasis added)[3]

Third, the *Rogers* Court in Australia also hinted that the information that needs to be disclosed is not confined to the risks inherent in the proposed treatment:

> Except in those cases where there is a particular danger that the provision of all relevant information will harm an unusually nervous, disturbed or volatile patient, no special medical skill is involved in disclosing the *information, including the risks attending the proposed treatment*. (emphasis added)[4]

Furthermore, in the Australian case of *Rosenberg v. Percival*, Kirby J said that health professionals have a duty

> to inform patients contemplating invasive procedures (such as surgery) of the material risks … and *any available alternatives*. Any "choice" by the patient, in respect of such procedures, without the provision of such information, is meaningless. (emphasis added)[5]

Some Canadian, Australian and New Zealand commentators also favour an expansive approach to the duty to disclose.[6] The duty to advise patients of alternatives

---

[2] *Sidaway v. Bethlem Royal Hospital Governors* [1985] 1 All ER 643, 654.

[3] *Canterbury v. Spence*, 464 F.2d 772, 784–785(1972).

[4] *Rogers v. Whitaker* (1992) 175 C.L.R. 479, 489–490 (HCA).

[5] *Rosenberg v. Percival* [2001] 205 CLR 434, 465.

[6] *See*, **Canada**: *Seney v. Crooks* (1998), 166 D.L.R. (4th) 337, 352, at [55] (Alta. C.A.) (citing Picard J. A. and Robertson *Legal Liability of Doctors and Hospitals in Canada*, 3rd ed. (Scarborough: Carswell, 1996), pp. 129–130). **Australia**: (1) Loane Skene. 2008. *Law and Medical Practice: Rights, Duties, Claims and Defences* (3 ed.). Australia: LexisNexis Butterworths. 190; (2) Michael Weir. 2003. Obligation to advise of options for treatment – Medical doctors and Complementary and Alternative Medicine practitioners. *JLM* 10:296–307. 297;

to the proposed treatment should be an intrinsic element of the duty to disclose.[7] As observed by Joanna Manning, "[k]nowledge of the alternatives may be as significant as knowledge of risks, since a patient may need information about alternative treatments, including the option of non-treatment, so as to compare the risks and benefits of those options with those of the recommended treatment" (Manning 2004, 195).

There is a close relationship between disclosure of risks and disclosure of alternatives. Firstly, factors, such as the availability of alternative treatments and their nature, may have some impact on the necessity of disclosure of some risks and the materiality of risks. A failure to advise of reasonable treatment alternatives is "an important consideration" in determining whether a physician has complied with the duty to advise of material and/or special or unusual risks.[8] In determining whether a reasonable patient or the particular patient would be "likely to attach significance to" a risk, "the extent or severity of the potential injury" and "the likelihood of the injury actually occurring" need to be weighed against the existence of reasonably available and satisfactory alternative treatments.[9] The more alternatives available to a patient and the less risk that the alternative treatment will entail, the more likely that a patient will attach significance to the risks of one treatment.[10] Even a small risk should be disclosed "given that alternative nonsurgical treatment was available, with lack of risk, a significant chance of success, and the paucity of evidence that the condition disabled [a patient] significantly".[11]

Secondly, one cannot make an informed decision to undertake a risk without knowing the alternatives to the option of undergoing the risk.[12] It was not really possible for a doctor to explain the advantages and disadvantages of the procedure which he favoured, without making specific reference to the other available procedures.[13] Risks disclosure and alternatives disclosure are intimately related. Failure

(3) Elizabeth Brophy. 2003. Does a doctor have a duty to provide information and advice about complementary and alternative medicine? *JLM* 10:271–284. 276. **New Zealand**: Joanna Manning. 2004. Informed consent to medical treatment: The common law and New Zealand's Code of Patients' Rights. *Medical Law Review* 12:181–216, 194–195.

[7] Joanna Manning (2004), 194–195 (citing I. Kennedy and A. Grubb, *Medical Law* (3rd edn.) (2000) at 712).

[8] *Thibault v. Fewer,* [2002] 1 W.W.R. 204, 216 at [57].

[9] *Rosenberg v. Percival* [2001] 205 CLR 434, 458–459, per Gummow J.

[10] Thomas Addison (2003), 177. However, there is also some evidence to show that courts have found risks to be material, even if the treatment involved is essential or inevitable at some point in time. *See*, *Chappel v. Hart* [1998] HCA 55; (1998) 195 CLR 232; 156 ALR 517; (1998) 72 ALJR 1344 (HC of A). It is submitted that the availability of alternative treatments, including alternative procedures entailing comparable risks, is most appropriately considered at the causation stage rather than at the materiality stage. *See*, Thomas Addison (2003), 177–178.

[11] *Haughian v. Paine* (1987), 37 D.L.R. (4th) 624, 643.

[12] *Haughian v. Paine* (1987), 37 D.L.R. (4th) 624, 644.

[13] *Richards v. Rahilly* [2005] NSWSC 352, at [229].

to warn of risks and failure to advise of alternatives should not be considered independently of, and in isolation from, each other.[14] These two elements of informed consent may have a strong bearing on each other.[15]

The legal move from *risks* disclosure to *alternatives* disclosure is achievable. There are at least three approaches to achieve that. A more conservative approach to embrace alternatives disclosure under the duty to inform is, while focusing on traditional risks disclosure, to argue that a genuine appreciation of the *risks of a proposed procedure* depends on or needs awareness of *comparative risks of its alternatives*. For example, in the English case of *Birch v. University College Hospitals NHS Trust*, the court entertained that

> there will be *circumstances* where … the duty to inform a patient of the *significant risks* will not be discharged unless she is made aware that *fewer, or no risks*, are associated with *another procedure*. In other words, unless the patient is informed of the *comparative risks of different procedures* she will *not be in a position* to give her fully informed consent to one procedure rather than another. (emphasis added)[16]

A moderate way of extending the ambit of the duty to inform is simply to accord risks disclosure and alternatives disclosure an equal significance. "The duty to disclose *similarly attaches to* recognized possible alternative forms of treatment and to the anticipated results of the treatment proposed and administered."[17] For example, when expressing "a cause of action for medical malpractice due to negligent nondisclosure", the Supreme Court of Minnesota always had both "risks" and "alternatives" in mind:

> We first recognized a cause of action for medical malpractice due to negligent nondisclosure of *a significant risk of treatment or alternative treatment plan* in deciding the prior appeal of this case. To make out such a claim, a plaintiff must establish a duty on the part of the physician to know of *a risk or alternate treatment program*. He must also show a duty to disclose the *risk or alternate treatment plan* by evidence establishing that a reasonable person in what the physician knows or should have known to be the patient's position would likely attach significance to that *risk or alternative* in formulating his decision to consent to treatment. He further must show breach of that duty, causation, and damage. (emphasis added)[18]

A more ambitious approach to accommodate alternatives disclosure is to adopt more encompassing phrases, such as "material facts",[19] "material

---

[14] *Haughian v. Paine* (1987), 37 D.L.R. (4th) 624, 644.

[15] *Haughian v. Paine* (1987), 37 D.L.R. (4th) 624, 644.

[16] *Birch v. University College Hospitals NHS Trust* [2008] EWHC 2237 (QB), at [74].

[17] *Adams v. Richland Clinic, Inc., P.S.*, 681 P.2d 1305, 1309–1310 (Wash.App. 1984) (emphasis added).

[18] *Cornfeldt v. Tongen*, 295 N.W.2d 638, 640 (Minn. 1980).

[19] *Adams v. Richland Clinic, Inc., P.S.*, 681 P.2d 1305, 1310 (Wash. App. 1984), footnote 4 (talking about statutory provisions (RCW 7.70.050(2) (3); "a fact is defined as or considered to be a material fact, if a reasonably prudent person in the position of the patient or his representative would attach significance to it deciding whether or not to submit to the proposed treatment"; material facts include "the recognized possible alternative forms of treatment, including nontreatment").

information",[20] or "material data".[21] For example, in the USA case of *Sard v. Hardy*,[22] by employing more embracing words, such as "material" "data", the court applied the materiality test smoothly to the context of alternatives disclosure.[23]

There is no need to debate the appropriateness of extending the ambit of a doctor's duty to inform to cover information about treatment options since the medical professions themselves have embraced the notion that the information that needs to be disclosed includes not only the risks-benefits of the proposed treatment but also the alternatives.[24] There is no doubt that the notion will be translated into medical practice.

However, a professional and ethical duty is different from a *legal* duty. Therefore, I still hope that those jurisdictions which have not recognised a legal duty to inform

---

[20]The Committee on California Civil Jury Instructions, *California Civil Jury Instructions* (*BAJI*) (Spring 2009 Edition) 6.11 ("a physician has a duty to disclose to the patient *all material information* to enable the patient to make an informed decision regarding the proposed operation or treatment" (emphasis added); "[m]aterial information is information which the physician knows or should know would be regarded as significant by a reasonable person in the patient's position when deciding to accept or reject a recommended medical procedure"); *Mathis v. Morrissey,* 13 Cal. Rptr.2d 819, 827 (Cal. App. 3 Dist. 1992) ("A plaintiff is free to present expert evidence and argument that, as a factual matter, the existence of an opposing school of thought was material information that should have been disclosed.").

[21]*Sard v. Hardy*, 379 A.2d 1014, 1022 (Md. 1977).

[22]*Sard v. Hardy*, 379 A.2d 1014 (Md. 1977).

[23]The case involved a sterilization operation – bilateral tubal ligation. The Court envisaged *five options* for the purpose of sterilization: (1) female sterilization; (2) oral contraception; (3) the use of an intrauterine device; (4) male vasectomy; and (5) the option of undergoing sterilization *at a later date* with a correspondingly greater likelihood of success rather than at the time of Caesarean section delivery, because the fail-rates of tubal ligation diminished dramatically when performed at some time other than Caesarean birth. As regards the female sterilization by tubal ligation, the Court also identified *six methods* employed in the United States: Madlener technique; Pomeroy technique; Irving method; Uchida method; Aldridge method; and Erlich method. These methods have varying fail-rates. The problem was that the defendant did not make the patient aware of the possibility of vasectomy, the option of undergoing sterilization at a later time and the six methods of performing a tubal ligation. According to the formulations of the Court, "the proper test for measuring the physician's duty to disclose risk information is whether such *data* will be *material* to the patient's decision" (emphasis added). Applying the test, the Court did not encounter difficulty in holding that a reasonable person in the patient's position would have attached "considerable" or "material" significance to the risk of fertility (the operation not being 100 % successful) and the option of undergoing sterilization at a later time. Because it was customary for physicians to discuss the possibility of vasectomy with patients consulting for sterilization, the omission to do that, in the opinion of the Court, was an obvious breach of the duty of disclosure. *See*, *Sard v. Hardy*, 379 A.2d 1014, 1019–1023 (Md. 1977).

[24]For example, General Medical Council (UK) expects their doctors to give their patients the *information* they want or need. The information includes: (1) "options for treating or managing the condition, including the option not to treat"; (2) "the purpose of any proposed investigation or treatment and what it will involve"; (3) "the potential benefits, risks and burdens, and the likelihood of success, for each option". *See*, General Medical Council (UK) *Consent: Patients and Doctors Making Decisions Together* (2008), paragraph 9 (c) (d) (e) at <www.gmc-uk.org> (Last accessed 24 April 2010). *See also*,

about alternatives can creatively and proactively incorporate "alternatives" into "information" that falls within the duty to disclose. As witnessed by England, Canada, and New Zealand law, that can be done either by requiring disclosure of "risks" and "comparative risks" of different treatments, or by courts actively borrowing academic wisdom, or by enacting legislation.[25]

Although there are many open possibilities for the duty of disclosure to encompass alternatives, the law's move from risks disclosure to alternatives disclosure was very cautious. The biggest problem seems to be that doctors are ordinarily not happy with disclosing alternatives that they *do not favour or do not offer*. They prefer to mention only treatment options with which they are technically familiar and emotionally comfortable. Courts also share a concern that overextending the scope of disclosure would overburden the medical profession.[26] In one Canadian case, the appellants audaciously raised the following difficult questions:

> would it be necessary to inform of every possible alternative available, whether or not generally considered reliable by the profession? Would each professional need to become knowledgeable on, and inform patients of, alternative medicine practices such as chiropractic treatment or holistic medicine treatments? [27]

Apparently those questions are framed in a very general fashion, without paying attention to particular circumstances in a particular case. Although difficult to answer, these questions deserved to be entertained. However, the Alberta Court of Appeal in that case did not grasp this opportunity to make the law clearer and left these questions unanswered.[28]

A Canadian case has helpfully highlighted the controversial nature of the issue of a doctor's obligation to inform a patient of alternative treatments.[29] There are two lines of authorities in this area, differing in both emphasis and direction. One line of authorities is conservative, giving weighty deference to professional (medical) judgment.

The Royal Australasian College of Physicians (RACP) *Code of Professional Behaviour* (2006) 1.2.1 (I) (i) <http://www.racp.edu.au/page/policy and advocacy/ethics> (Last accessed 27 April 2010) ("The physician must discuss with patients/relatives/carers/legal guardians the available treatment options, including no treatment; outline the relevant risks of treatment"); New Zealand Medical Association *Code of Ethics* (Revised 2008), p. 7 at <http://www.nzma.org.nz> (Last accessed 22 April 2010) ("Doctors should ensure that patients are involved, within the limits of their capacities, in understanding the nature of their problems, the range of possible solutions, as well as the likely benefits, risks, and costs, and should assist them in making informed choices.").

[25] *See*, Chap. 9.

[26] *Seney v. Crooks* (1998), 166 D.L.R. (4th) 337, 352, at [57] (arguing that to overextend the duty to inform of alternative treatments will place an "unpredictable and monumental", "much too onerous" responsibility upon the medical profession).

[27] *Seney v. Crooks* (1998), 166 D.L.R. (4th) 337, 352, at [57].

[28] The Court's omission to demarcate the boundaries of the duty to inform was justified by the factual circumstances in that case. The alternative medical procedure involved in that case was one treatment that the profession had been familiar with for many years and that some of specialists in that profession preferred. It is not a fringe alternative, not an alternative offered outside the relevant specialty or by some other form of health care. *See*, *Seney v. Crooks* (1998), 166 D.L.R. (4th) 337, 352–353, at [58].

[29] *Van Dyke v. Grey Bruce Regional Health Center* (2005), 255 D.L.R. (4th) 397, at [65].

In the eyes of these authorities, "the treating physician is only obliged to disclose options that *in his or her reasonable medical judgment* are appropriate for the patient".[30] The appropriateness of one option will be determined by the prospect of the option's being capable of bringing some advantage to the patient over the proposed treatment and the potential of achieving a beneficial result for the patient.[31] This line of authorities creates the effect of narrowing the scope of the duty of disclosure of alternatives, keeping it within a realistic boundary.

Another line of authorities is mostly motivated by the patients' rights arguments. These authorities take the position that imposing too many restrictions on the necessity of disclosure of alternatives will "unnecessarily diminish a patient's right to choose from among reasonable medical alternatives".[32] In their view, honouring the patient's right to make an informed decision dictates that the doctor should advise the patient of all medically reasonable alternatives and give the patient the benefit of the doctor's advice as to the merits and demerits of various alternatives, even if the treating physician considers the alternative inappropriate in the particular circumstances.[33]

I do not want to see both lines of arguments to develop into two extremes. They are not irreconcilable. Those two lines of authorities differ on the issue of how much weight should be attached to medical judgment in determining what kinds of alternatives fall within a doctor's duty to inform. As observed before, this book prefers to draw a distinction between appreciation of information and judgement of the materiality of information. That dictates that although the information prong of the materiality test, such as the "menu" or the availability of treatment options, is subject to medical judgment, the question of whether a patient would be likely to attach significance to a treatment option involves a human judgment. In the realm of information disclosure, the law needs to be well-prepared to answer the situation that a doctor's preferences may be expressed in guise of medical judgment, although this situation is not the norm.

3.3 Disclosure of Alternatives: Conventional Wisdom

In this part I will highlight a conservative line of authorities where it was held that disclosure of alternative treatments only targets *recommended* ones. One of the typical examples of jurisdictions which endorse a restrictive approach to alternatives disclosure is California, USA. The basic position in that jurisdiction is that the duty of disclosure is predicated upon a recommended procedure,[34] and, thus, a physician's

[30] *Van Dyke v. Grey Bruce Regional Health Center* (2005), 255 D.L.R. (4th) 397, at [65] (emphasis added).

[31] *Van Dyke v. Grey Bruce Regional Health Center* (2005), 255 D.L.R. (4th) 397, at [65].

[32] *Van Dyke v. Grey Bruce Regional Health Center* (2005), 255 D.L.R. (4th) 397, at [66].

[33] *Van Dyke v. Grey Bruce Regional Health Center* (2005), 255 D.L.R. (4th) 397, at [66].

duty to disclose only attaches to the recommended or proposed procedures, not to the nonrecommended procedures.[35] A corollary of this position is that a physician has no duty to inform his patient of another or contrary school of medical treatment.[36]

Responding to the argument that the duty to disclose should extend to nonrecommended procedures, this line of authorities raised several concerns. First, "a new duty-to-disclose-line", proposing disclosure of nonrecommended procedures, "like one drawn with a finger in the air, is *without precision and predictability*. It would impose significant new burdens on already harried doctors without awarding demonstrable benefits to their patients."[37] Second, "[o]ne difficulty with [such kind of proposal] is that it is inherently and irrevocably wedded to medical hindsight".[38] Third, such a proposal "tends to suggest that a physician should defer his or her medical judgment to the patient's wishes."[39]

The judicial denial to extend the duty of disclosure to nonrecommended procedures was buttressed by a big excuse, namely, the failure to recommend a procedure has already been, and must be, addressed under *ordinary medical negligence* standards. By *reframing a nondisclosure case as a selection/recommendation case*, the courts frequently cited this line of argument as a strong reason for denying extending the duty to disclose to nonrecommended procedures:

> In addressing [the plaintiff's] contention it is necessary to keep in mind that we are considering *a medical procedure which, in the exercise of professional judgment, a doctor does not recommend*. If the procedure is one which *should have been proposed*, then *the failure to recommend* it would be negligence under *ordinary medical negligence principles* and there is *no need to consider an additional duty of disclosure*. (emphasis added)[40]

---

[34] *Scalere v. Stenson*, 260 Cal. Rptr. 152, 153–155 (Cal. App. 2 Dist. 1989) (after having visited four California cases, the court concluded that the predicate for the duty to disclose is the existence of "some proposed therapy" or "a recommended medical procedure"), *but compare*, the dissenting opinion in *Scalere v. Stenson*, 260 Cal. Rptr. 152, 158 (Cal. App. 2 Dist. 1989)(per Johnson J. dissenting) ("It is clear from *Cobbs* and *Truman* the patient's right of choice is not limited to a veto power over treatment recommended by her doctor.").

[35] *Vandi v. Permanente Medical Group, Inc.*, 9 Cal.Rptr.2d 463 (Cal. App. 3 Dist. 1992); *Jamison v. Lindsay*, 166 Cal.Rptr.443, 446–447 (Cal. App. 1 Dist. 1980) (courts finding that the respondents did not propose any therapy/treatment or tests).

[36] *Parris v. Sands*, 25 Cal.Rptr.2d 800 (Cal.App. 2 Dist., 1993).

[37] *Scalere v. Stenson*, 260 Cal.Rptr.152, 156 (Cal. App. 2 Dist. 1989) (emphasis added).

[38] *Vandi v. Permanente Medical Group, Inc.*, 9 Cal.Rptr.2d 463, 467 (Cal. App. 3 Dist. 1992).

[39] *Vandi v. Permanente Medical Group, Inc.*, 9 Cal.Rptr.2d 463, 467 (Cal. App. 3 Dist. 1992) ("It would be anomalous to create a legally imposed duty which would require a physician to disclose and offer to a patient a medical procedure which, in the exercise of his or her medical judgment, the physician does not believe to be medically indicated.").

[40] *Vandi v. Permanente Medical Group, Inc.*, 9 Cal.Rptr.2d 463, 467 (Cal. App. 3 Dist. 1992). *Also see*, *Parris v. Sands*, 25 Cal.Rptr.2d 800, 803 (Cal.App. 2 Dist., 1993) ("[The patient], however, was not without an appropriate legal theory to recover damages. *Negligent failure to advise a patient to pursue a necessary course of treatment* is an action under *ordinary medical negligence*,

As far as the possibility of extending the duty of disclosure to nonrecommended procedures or contrary schools of thought is concerned, some more liberal voices surfaced in California, but were suppressed. For example, following *Jamison v. Lindsay*,[41] the *Jamison*-type special instruction targeting disclosure of *divergent schools of thought* emerged. One version of the instruction was as follows:

> A physician rendering a diagnosis or providing treatment has a duty to inform the patient that *other members of the medical profession* might render a different diagnosis or provide a different treatment based on *a contrary recognized school of thought* within the medical community. A failure to fulfill such a duty is negligence. (emphasis added)[42]

However, this "*Jamison*-type jury instruction" was put to one side or distinguished either by pointing out that it only applied to "surgery, cancer diagnosis or cancer treatment or other serious, life-threatening procedures",[43] or by noting that the factual predicate to giving such an instruction must be that the defendant was aware of conflicting "schools of thought" with respect to diagnosis or treatment,[44] or

upon which the jury here received proper instructions.") (internal citations omitted, emphasis added); *Jamison v. Lindsay*, 166 Cal.Rptr.443, 447 (Cal. App. 1 Dist. 1980) ("Appellant was not without an appropriate legal theory under which she might recover damages. Negligent failure to advise a patient to pursue a potentially necessary course of treatment is actionable under ordinary medical negligence standards, on which the jury was instructed."). Although, according to these authorities, there is no general duty of disclosure with respect to nonrecommended procedures, the courts did not close the door absolutely. *See, Vandi v. Permanente Medical Group, Inc.*, 9 Cal. Rptr.2d 463, 468 (Cal. App. 3 Dist. 1992) ("In an appropriate case there may be evidence that would support the conclusion that a doctor should have disclosed information concerning a nonrecommended procedure .... It follows that even though a physician has no general duty of disclosure with respect to nonrecommended procedures, he nevertheless must make such disclosures as are required for competent practice within the medical community.").

[41] *Jamison v. Lindsay*, 166 Cal.Rptr.443 (Cal. App. 1 Dist. 1980) (The surgeon performed a surgery, removed the patient's right ovary and a large cystic mass, and sent the cystic mass to a pathologist for analysis. The pathologist had observed that the teratoma contained both mature and *immature* tissue. Having been aware that "for many years there had been divergent opinions among pathologists as to whether immature tissue in a teratoma is potentially malignant", the pathologist adhered to his stance that such immature tissue was not malignant, and thus released a report identifying the mass as a benign teratoma, without informing the surgeon of either the presence of immature tissue or that some pathologists would consider the mass to be potentially malignant. The bad thing was that, after being told that the mass was benign, the patient did not seek further treatment, and subsequently developed a malignancy.).

[42] *Parris v. Sands*, 25 Cal.Rptr.2d 800, 803 (Cal. App. 2 Dist.,1993). *See also Traxler v. Varady*, 16 Cal.Rptr.2d 297, 303 (Cal. App. 1 Dist. 1993) (involving almost identical instruction: "A physician rendering a diagnosis has a duty to inform the patient that other members of the medical profession might render a different diagnosis based on a contrary recognized school of thought."); *Mathis v. Morrissey*, 13 Cal.Rptr.2d 819 (Cal. App. 3 Dist. 1992) (the plaintiff proposed a *special instruction* which reads: "When surgery or other dangerous therapeutic procedures are being considered, the physician must inform the patient of the available alternatives or schools of thought and the hazards involved so that the patient is able to give effective consent to the proposed treatment.").

[43] *See, Parris v. Sands*, 25 Cal.Rptr.2d 800, 803 (Cal. App. 2 Dist., 1993).

[44] *Traxler v. Varady*, 16 Cal.Rptr.2d 297, 303 (Cal. App. 1 Dist. 1993) (the proposed special instruction was refused because the appellant cited no evidence that there were divergent "schools of thought" regarding any of the decisions made by her treating physicians).

by warning that the standard instructions on informed consent (such as standard BAJI duty-of-disclosure instructions[45]) have been already adequate.[46]

Another liberal voice surfaced in *Mathis v. Morrissey*.[47] The *Mathis* Court described a hypothetical scenario and illustrated a physician's need to disclose different schools of thought on the correct treatment.[48] The scenario was based on two assumptions. The first assumption was that

> *there are two schools of thought concerning the optimum treatment* for breast cancer. One school posits that a mastectomy is the appropriate procedure, while the other asserts that a lumpectomy followed by radiation is the preferred treatment. (emphasis added)[49]

The second assumption was that "an explanation of these two differing methods of treatment constitutes *material information* for the purposes of informed consent".[50] Under these hypostatized circumstances, the court correctly distinguished the context of selection of a procedure from that of information disclosure, and observed that:

> Once a doctor has made a treatment decision then *the fact* that other doctors would disagree or that *there are other schools of thought* on the correct treatment may be *material information* which should be disclosed to the patient in obtaining consent to the procedure. (emphasis added)[51]

Sadly, these positive thoughts have not received the judicial reinforcement and promotion. In a newly-emerged but not officially-reported Californian case,[52] the plaintiff-patient proposed a special jury instruction which was a verbatim copy of the above-quoted *Mathis* statement.[53] The plaintiff-patient argued that the jury needed to be alerted that "different schools of thought might be material information

---

[45] It reads: "When a doctor recommends a particular procedure then he or she must disclose to the patient *all material information* necessary to the decision to undergo the procedure, including a reasonable explanation of the procedure, its likelihood of success, the risks involved in accepting or reject the proposed procedure, and any other information a skilled practitioner in good standing would disclose to the patient under the same or similar circumstances."(emphasis added)

[46] *Mathis v. Morrissey*, 13 Cal.Rptr.2d 819, 826–827 (Cal. App. 3 Dist. 1992) ("By adding the requirement of informing the patient of 'school of thought', plaintiffs' suggested instruction would go further and impose liability upon a physician as *a matter of law* for the failure to inform a patient of the possible *views of other health care providers merely because* at trial and *in hindsight* an expert *disagreed* with the defendant's treatment decision. Such a result is not supported by any authority and would impose *an excessively onerous burden* upon treating physicians. What the duty of disclosure requires for purposes of informed consent is the divulgence of *material information*, not necessarily the revelation of the existence of various schools of thought." (emphasis added)).

[47] *Mathis v. Morrissey*, 13 Cal.Rptr.2d 819 (Cal. App. 3 Dist. 1992).

[48] *Mathis v. Morrissey*, 13 Cal.Rptr.2d 819, 826 (Cal. App. 3 Dist. 1992).

[49] *Mathis v. Morrissey*, 13 Cal.Rptr.2d 819, 826 (Cal. App. 3 Dist. 1992).

[50] *Mathis v. Morrissey*, 13 Cal.Rptr.2d 819, 826 (Cal. App. 3 Dist. 1992) (emphasis added).

[51] *Mathis v. Morrissey*, 13 Cal.Rptr.2d 819, 826 (Cal. App. 3 Dist. 1992).

[52] *Peukert v. Roncone*, Not Reported in Cal.Rptr.3d, 2004 WL 2915476 (Cal. App. 4 Dist., 2004).

[53] *Peukert v. Roncone*, Not Reported in Cal.Rptr.3d, 2004 WL 2915476 (Cal. App. 4 Dist., 2004), 2 ("Once a doctor has made a treatment decision then the fact that other doctors would disagree or that there are other schools of thought on the correct treatment may be material information which must be disclosed to the patient in obtaining consent to treatment.").

that should be disclosed to the patient".[54] However, the Court of Appeal (Fourth District, California) was not persuaded by such arguments, finding that the standard BAJI instructions given by the court adequately instructed the jury with respect to the duty of disclosure.[55]

I have two observations about the Californian case law regarding alternatives disclosure. First, the judicial unwillingness to impose on a physician a duty to inform his patient of nonrecommended procedures, or existence of an opposing school of thought, is based on confusing the context of information disclosure with the context of diagnosis and treatment. By allowing medical judgment (representing one body of opinion), which deserves higher respect in the field of diagnosis and treatment, to continue to play an influential, even decisive, role in the realm of alternatives disclosure, these authorities in effect blurred the distinction drawn between a physician's clinical freedom or discretion to select, recommend and perform one treatment option, on the one hand, and a physician's obligation to inform his patient of treatment options, on the other. Moreover, the judicial attitudes were heavily influenced by its fear of hindsight bias, and buttressed by the rationale underlying the law's respect for divergence among medical opinions in selecting and recommending one particular procedure. Those factors deserve to be weighed heavily in the context of selection/recommendation of treatment options, but not in the context of information disclosure.

Second, the judicial refusal to give a special or supplementary[56] instruction regarding disclosure of different schools of thought was due to its confidence in the adequacy of the general informed consent instruction, especially the "material information" component. The court not only drew attention to the comprehensive nature of the phrase "material information" but also rightly highlighted the threshold inherent in the "materiality" test. It appears that what the courts really objected to is not the inclusion of information disclosure about various schools of thought under

---

[54] *Peukert v. Roncone*, Not Reported in Cal.Rptr.3d, 2004 WL 2915476 (Cal. App. 4 Dist., 2004), 3.

[55] *Peukert v. Roncone*, Not Reported in Cal.Rptr.3d, 2004 WL 2915476 (Cal. App. 4 Dist., 2004), 4. As regards the special instruction, the court expressed several concerns. First, the *Mathis* court's statement, along which the plaintiff's proposed special instruction was formulated, was deemed as "dicta". Second, the *Mathis* court's statement regarding disclosure of schools of thought was narrowly and restrictively interpreted as applying only to "an entirely different context" involving "a serious surgery or other 'dangerous therapeutic procedure[]' such as mastectomy". The court did not want to read that statement, "which was a prelude to a hypothetical situation dealing with the treatment of breast cancer", "as designed to set out a principle applicable to all cases". Third, in the words of the court, "[the plaintiff-patient's] use of verbatim language from *Mathis* illustrates the hazard posed by directly relying on language from a case, as opposed to offering a clear, concise and neutral statement of the legal principle embodied in the holding of the case."

[56] *Traxler v. Varady*, 16 Cal.Rptr.2d 297 (Cal. App. 1 Dist. 1993) (The appellant proposed an instruction, which highlighted disclosure of the "available choices" with respect to recommended therapy, to *supplement* the standard informed consent (material information) instruction. The plaintiff's request was declined because the proposed instruction, which was formulated in specific words and "simply a slightly more specific restatement" of the general principle, was already covered by a complete, a more encompassing, and a more general instruction.).

the duty to inform, but giving it *a special mention* in the context of jury instructions. This is in sharp contrast to the judicial attitudes in the context of selection of treatment options where special instructions and special protection are offered to pay respect for diversity in medical judgment.

The conservative line of authorities is also present in Canadian and Australian case law. The Canadian case of *Bucknam v. Kostuik*[57] is a good example of the court's paying more respect for physicians' discretion in the context of disclosure of alternative options. In this case, the court noted,

> It seems to me that it may well be imposing an unreasonable standard on an orthopaedic surgeon, who *reasonably believes* that to treat the patient's scoliosis is a necessity and that a simple fusion at the area of the proven ruptured disc is not the answer to the plaintiff's problem, to require him to inform the patient of that option, an option that, by definition, *in his or her mind* is entirely unreasonable. (emphasis added)[58]

The above quotation has been re-formulated by followers as meaning that "[t]he duty to advise of alternative treatments may not apply where the surgeon reasonably believes the alternative is not a reasonable option".[59] By conferring much more weight to the physicians' medical perspectives in the realm of information disclosure, the court actually blurred the legal distinction between information disclosure and treatment, and between selection/recommendation and disclosure.

Similarly, in another Canadian case of *Van Mol v. Ashmore*[60], Justice Goldie also showed reluctance to broaden the scope of alternatives disclosure.[61] In his opinion, Canadian law does not "require[] a surgeon to volunteer a comparative assessment of alternative surgical techniques".[62] In delivering a dissenting opinion, this Justice said, "[w]here a number of techniques exist, *the surgeon's experience and skill* will be a rational factor".[63] Justice Goldie's view was influenced by courts' traditional respect for medical judgement and preference in the context of diagnosis and treatment.[64] As noted below, whether this approach is still comfortably applicable to the different context of information disclosure is doubtful.

The Australian case of *Richards v. Rahilly*[65] also voiced the same concerns as its Canadian counterparts. Envisaging that selection of treatment options was a part of diagnosis and treatment, the court in this case noted that if the submission that the provision of advice should take place before a decision as to treatment is made and

---

[57] *Bucknam v. Kostuik* (1984) 3 D.L.R. (4th) 99 (An orthopaedic surgeon performed surgery on a woman with scoliosis. One alternative operation (a single fusion) is less serious than the proposed one.).

[58] *Bucknam v. Kostuik* (1984) 3 D.L.R. (4th) 99, 111.

[59] *Nattrass v. Weber*, 2008 ABQB 259, at [393].

[60] *Van Mol v. Ashmore* (1999), 168 D.L.R. (4th) 637.

[61] *Van Mol v. Ashmore* (1999), 168 D.L.R. (4th) 637, 711, at [238].

[62] *Van Mol v. Ashmore* (1999), 168 D.L.R. (4th) 637, 714, at [251].

[63] *Van Mol v. Ashmore* (1999), 168 D.L.R. (4th) 637, 714–715, at [253] (emphasis added).

[64] *Van Mol v. Ashmore* (1999), 168 D.L.R. (4th) 637, 714, at [252].

[65] *Richards v. Rahilly* [2005] NSWSC 352.

the patient should make the decision as to what treatment should be provided is correct, "its implications are far-reaching." It explained,

> No longer would a doctor be required before embarking on treatment to warn a patient of its risks, but *at an earlier point in time* the doctor would be required to discuss with the patient the various treatment options, raising in relation to each its advantages and disadvantages and then allowing the patient to choose his or her particular treatment option. That, it seems to me, would involve *a substantial abrogation* by the doctor concerned of *his expertise as a doctor* and to blur the clear distinction identified by the High Court in *Rogers v Whitaker* between diagnosis and treatment on the one hand and the provision of information. (emphasis added)[66]

As to the distinction between diagnosis/treatment and the provision of information, which was highlighted in *Rogers v. Whitaker*, it is obvious that the court in this case only reads that distinction as meaning that the doctor, exercising his expertise, selects and administers one particular treatment option and, before embarking on that particular treatment option, discloses to his patient the risks of that option. It does not contemplate that the information that needs to be provided includes not only the risks of one particular treatment option, but also the availability and comparative risks of other treatment options.

The court tried to differentiate the disclosure of alternatives from the disclosure of risks:

> It is quite different to the situation *where a certain form of treatment has been recommended*, but before undergoing the treatment the patient has the advantages and disadvantages of the treatment fully explained. … An obligation to warn of a "material" risk *inherent in a proposed treatment* is a *significantly different obligation* to one requiring the provision of full information concerning *a number of treatment options* preparatory to the patient choosing his or her treatment.[67]

As to the issue of disclosure of alternatives, the court took the view that the approach that required doctors to discuss all "legitimate treatment options which could have worked" and then request the patients to choose the treatment option which they preferred "is unrealistic, involves enormous practical difficulties and unfairly imposes on patients/parents a decision which they are *unqualified* to make".[68] The court added that such a broadly framed approach is "unworkable as a matter of practicality":

> It would impose an impossible burden on the medical profession if a doctor was bound to offer a patient every "legitimate" treatment option that "could work" and discuss the advantages and disadvantages of each option with the patient and then allow the patient to choose his or her option.[69]

---

[66] *Richards v. Rahilly* [2005] NSWSC 352, at [225].

[67] *Richards v. Rahilly* [2005] NSWSC 352, at [236] (emphasis added).

[68] *Richards v. Rahilly* [2005] NSWSC 352, at [236] (emphasis added).

[69] *Richards v. Rahilly* [2005] NSWSC 352, at [235].

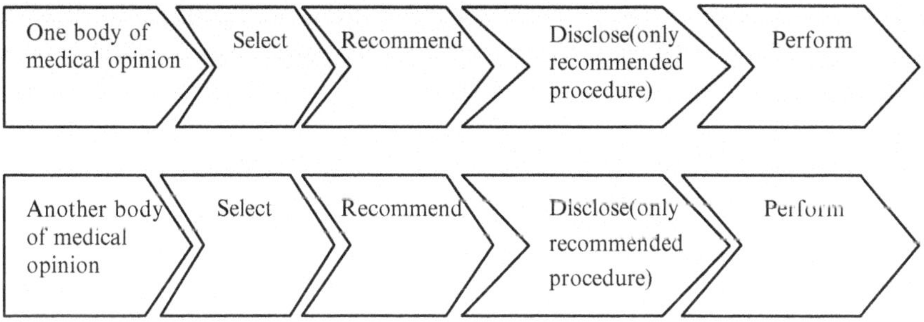

Fig. 3.1 Disclosure of alternatives: a parallel, linear model

Obviously, in the *Richards v. Rahilly* case, the court did not distinguish recommendation from information disclosure. What the court envisaged is such a scenario: a doctor selects and recommends a particular treatment option and, before performing that option, reveals the positive and negative aspects of his option to his patient. Under this scenario, the sequence is that choosing a treatment option (by a doctor) runs first and disclosing information (only of the selected treatment option) comes second. A doctor's selection and recommendation of treatment runs ahead of disclosure of information (only about the treatment option favoured by a doctor). Under this scenario, ultimately a patient only has two choices: to follow a doctor's recommendation and undergo the recommended procedure, or to reject a doctor's recommendation and forgo the recommended procedure. The scenario does not require a doctor to disclose all available treatment options first and allow a patient, with the aid or benefit of a doctor's recommendation, to make an informed choice among divergent treatment options (Fig. 3.1).

The approach of confining the duty to disclose alternatives only to recommended procedures fails to reflect the patient-oriented standard's important distinction between *recommended* treatments and *reasonable* treatments (Bulen 2003, 346). It reinforces both technical fragmentation and informational fragmentation. It builds an informational wall between the divergent bodies of medical opinion. It acknowledges the existence of divergent bodies of medical opinion. However, it allows medical judgment to sweepingly govern all aspects of health care, including information disclosure. It only gives patients two options: accept the recommended procedure or refuse it. It does not expect the patients to be informed of all available treatment options. It leaves the patients with no choice but to do their own research about available treatment options. It comforts and brings convenience to the doctors who may hold a narrow, biased medical opinion. It does not defer and give priority to the patients' informational needs. It still follows the paternalistic notion that the doctors always know the best for their patients and the patients are always ill-equipped to make their choices. It fails to respond sensitively to the different focuses that different aspects of health care have. Due to these reasons, I do not favour a parallel and linear model of health care delivery where the selection and recommendation of treatment option, which is based on a body of medical opinion, precedes the disclosure of treatment options. I will propose a new model in the following part of this chapter. The new model is constructed on several delicate and fine distinctions, rather than allowing one body of professional opinion to sweepingly govern every aspect of health care.

3.4 General Distinction: Selection, Recommendation, Performance v. Disclosure

As far as alternative treatment options are concerned, generally the law needs to draw a distinction between selection/recommendation/performance of one treatment option and disclosure of treatment options. That is an honest reflection of a more general distinction drawn between diagnosis/treatment and information disclosure.

The Canadian law indicates that the question of whether a doctor has acted in accordance with the applicable standard of care in his selection or performance of a particular procedure is distinct from the question of whether the doctor obtained an informed consent from the patient to the proposed procedure.[70] While adoption of one treatment rather than the other may be a matter of judgment for the physician and may be shielded from liability by the "error of judgment" rule, the possibility of liability under the informed consent theory is still alive.[71] One logical consequence of the selection/recommendation – disclosure distinction is that while the doctor is at liberty to recommend to the patient only the procedure he believes superior or more appropriate, the doctor is still obliged to advise the patient of other acceptable and appropriate procedures.[72] Conversely, while it may have been open for the doctor not to recommend some treatment options, his patient is entitled to be advised that these alternatives are open to him.[73]

There is also a line of cases in the USA where the selection/recommendation/performance – disclosure distinction is clearly drawn and honoured.[74] For example,

---

[70] *Patterson v. Hryciuk*, 2004 ABQB 934, (2004) 45 Alta. L.R. (4th) 219, at [45]. *See also Seney v. Crooks* (1998), 166 D.L.R. (4th) 337, 351, at [54] ("Lack of negligence in the choice of treatment or the manner in which that treatment is performed does not negate a physician's additional duty to inform his patient of the risks of proceeding in one way as opposed to another.").

[71] *Haughian v. Paine* (1987), 37 D.L.R. (4th) 624, 635.

[72] *Patterson v. Hryciuk*, 2004 ABQB 934, (2004) 45 Alta. L.R. (4th) 219, at [48] (citing *Seney v. Crooks* (1998), 166 D.L.R. (4th) 337 at 353–354 (Alta.C.A.)).

[73] *Haughian v. Paine* (1987), 37 D.L.R. (4th) 624, 643; *Thibault v. Fewer*, [2002] 1 W.W.R. 204, 217, at [59].

[74] *Stover v. Surgeons*, 635 A.2d 1047, 1050 (Pa. Super. 1993) ("the choice of prosthesis, by medical common sense, must be left with the physician. ... However, where other potential implants are recognized as medically sound alternatives, the attending physician must inform the patient as to the risks and benefits of those alternatives."); *Harrison v. U.S.*, 233 F.Supp.2d 128, 133 (D. Mass., 2002) ("because there are only two methods of childbirth, once there is a material risk to vaginal birth, the doctor's duty to disclose that risk also encompasses the duty to present information about C-sections."); *Dewes v. Indian Health Service, Public Health Service*, 504 F.Supp. 203, 208 (D.C.S.D. 1980) (acknowledging that the method employed by the defendant was a "recognized" method in dealing with the plaintiff's situation, but holding that the defendant "had a duty to inform plaintiff's parent of at least two alternative forms of treatment" for the plaintiff's condition); *Harwell v. Pittman*, 428 So.2d 1053–1054 (La. App. 1 Cir., 1983) (acknowledging that "[w] hether or not to operate is a matter of clinical judgment for the treating surgeon after weighing all

in the *Salis v. U.S.* case,[75] the court accorded a considerable degree of latitude towards the defendant's "personal" decision to employ a diagnostic "angiogram" (then surgery),[76] holding that "a doctor cannot be held liable for following a course of treatment accepted by *a substantial segment of the medical community*".[77] However, when the context shifts to information disclosure, the court found that there is no justification for withholding information regarding the conservative treatment in the context of informed consent, even though a physician's personal choice in favour of the surgical treatment can be justified.[78]

3.5 Further Distinction: Selection – Recommendation – Performance – Disclosure

3.5.1 Performance

3.5.1.1 Performance Versus Selection/Recommendation

A physician's performance of a particular procedure is distinct from his selection and recommendation of the same procedure, and disclosure of options.[79] Even if a

---

the facts before him", but rejecting the defendant's contention that his failure to discuss non-surgical alternative treatments was arguably based on his opinion that plaintiff's condition justified surgery); *Backlund v. University of Washington*, 975 P.2d 950, 954–955 (Wash., 1999)(involving a more conservative form of treatment (phototherapy) and a riskier treatment (blood transfusion) for an infant's jaundice; holding that the jury's exoneration of a physician from liability for negligence did not forestall a plaintiff's claim for failure to obtain informed consent).

[75] *Salis v. U.S.*, 522 F.Supp. 989 (D.C.Pa. 1981).

[76] *Salis v. U.S.*, 522 F.Supp. 989, 996 (D.C.Pa. 1981). Intermittent claudication was the condition the patient suffered from and the physician dealt with. As to the treatments for this condition, two important facts were established by the expert testimony. First, there is a general approach. Surgery is not the ordinary course of treatment for claudicants. In a large majority of cases, the condition will stabilize or improve with a program of "conservative" treatment, e.g. drugs, physical therapy. Second, there are exceptions to the general approach. There exists "a highly personal" decision to undergo an operation to relieve the claudication. The appropriateness of surgery depends on the relative weight of these considerations: "(1) the patient's lifestyle, (2) the extent to which the disease had developed, (3) the inherent risks, and (4) the likelihood that the problems can be remedied through conservative methods".

[77] *Salis v. U.S.*, 522 F.Supp. 989, 996–997 (D.C.Pa. 1981) (emphasis added).

[78] *Salis v. U.S.*, 522 F.Supp. 989, 1000 (D.C.Pa. 1981). The court noted that the patient had three options open: (1) to risk the surgery and its incidental procedures, (2) to adjust his life style in light of the intermittent claudication, and (3) to continue pursuing conservative therapy. Each alternative had a separate set of dangers and potential benefits. In the court's opinion, the conservative treatment needs to be accorded a higher priority than the surgical intervention. The court made it clear that not all options are at the same level of priority. Angiography is a diagnostic test which is only appropriate when surgery is under consideration. Thus, the primary alternative would have been a course of "conservative" therapy to handle the problem without surgery. *See*, *Salis v. U.S.*, 522 F.Supp. 989, 1004 (D.C.Pa. 1981).

[79] *Sim v. Weeks*, 7 Cal.App.2d 28, 45 P.2d 350, 354 ("A charge of negligence in *a choice of treatment* is refuted, *as a matter of law*, by showing that a respectable minority of expert physicians

physician's *performance* of one particular procedure is held not to be negligent, he may be proven to be negligent in *recommending* one particular procedure and in failing to *disclose* viable alternatives.[80] "The factual inquiry concerning the *technical* performance of [one surgery] involves somewhat different considerations, and *does not call for any balancing of competing risks, or of expert opinions as to the appropriate clinical judgment*."[81] The inquiry, in this regard, is "somewhat more stark, namely, whether any technical error was shown to have occurred during surgery."[82]

3.5.1.2 Performance Versus Disclosure

The law needs also to keep disclosure a distance from performance. While it would not be reasonable to expect a doctor to offer or to perform a procedure that he does not believe is a viable option, he needs to raise that option, and, if he knows it is a viable option, explain why he thinks the risks outweigh any potential benefit.[83] In *Harrison v. U.S.*, one of the defendant's argument was that, even if the plaintiff opted for a C-section, the defendant "would not have been willing to perform" it.[84] Although acknowledging that the defendant "was under no legal duty" to perform C-section, the court lent an unconditional support to the First Circuit's view that "the duty to inform a patient of the existence of an alternate procedure, and the duty to perform that procedure, are *entirely distinct*".[85] The court further clarified that,

> a doctor cannot "save" himself from liability for breach of informed consent merely by arguing that, although he failed to inform his patient about an alternate procedure, causation is lacking because he himself would have been unwilling to perform that

---

approved the method selected. *But* where a physician is charged with negligence in the actual performance of a treatment, after its method was chosen over others, evidence tending to show such negligence presents a case for the *jury*.") (emphasis added).

[80] *Kenny v. Wepman*, 753 A. 2d 924, 926 (R. I. 2000). In this case, a patient lost all vision in her eye following cataract surgery. The surgery was suggested by defendant-ophthalmologist to remove a cataract in her left eye. Expert witnesses established that the mere presence of a cataract does not justify surgery. The cataract surgery is justified only when the cataract causes visual problems or interferes with a patient's lifestyle. Although there was no negligent performance of surgery, the Supreme Court of Rhode Island agreed with the trail justice that the defendant failed to apprise plaintiff of viable alternatives.

[81] *Crisp v. Keng* NSW (Common Law Division), Wood J, 2 December 1992, unreported, BC9201449, at [109], [110] (emphasis added).

[82] *Crisp v. Keng* NSW (Common Law Division), Wood J, 2 December 1992, unreported, BC9201449, at [109], [110].

[83] *Opinion 02HDC18414* (Health and Disability Commissioner, 6/4/04) (failure to provide contextualised information).

[84] *Harrison v. U.S.*, 233 F.Supp.2d 128, 134 (D. Mass., 2002).

[85] *Harrison v. U.S.*, 233F.Supp.2d 128, 134 (D. Mass., 2002) (emphasis added).

> procedure upon the patient's request. Such a rule would remove all force from the doctor's duty of informed consent. Rather, by disaggregating the duty to inform about alternate procedures from the duty to perform those procedures, the First Circuit highlighted the very purpose of informed consent: empowerment of the patient. Once a doctor has informed a patient about alternatives, the patient can then make her own assessment and seek out medical care that is in accordance with her decision. (internal citations omitted)[86]

Some commentators advocate "a clear bifurcation between the duty to provide information and the duty to provide care",[87] so that the "mere inability to provide requested care does not absolve the physician of the duty to provide information – an approach that can conserve resources while maximizing patient autonomy" (Krause 1999, 368).

It needs to be noted here that the fear of full information disclosure and the patients' choices, especially in the context of limited resources, is partly attributable to the misconception that providing patients with choices means giving them the right to *require* treatments. The patients do not have the right to require that they be treated in a particular way (Skene 2004, 87). Informing patients of all available treatment options, including those not readily available due to resource reasons, aims to provide them opportunities to explore avenues to pursue their values. That does not mean the patients have a right to require non-resource-sensitive treatments. The disclosure – treatment distinction is still available in the cost-containment environment. This will be fully explored in Chap. 7.

3.5.2 Selection

In selecting procedures, the medical profession is accorded considerable latitude.[88] In the context of proposing a particular procedure rather than others, the difference of opinions does not necessarily mean negligence. A number of theories or doctrines are offered to afford a special protection to the defendant doctors and their exercise of medical judgment.

---

[86] *Harrison v. U.S.*, 233 F.Supp.2d 128, 134 (D. Mass., 2002).

[87] Ben Sones (2006). *See also*, Joan H. Krause (1999), 368.

[88] For example, Aaron D. Twerski and Neil B. Cohen (1992), 9 (noting that "Where the plaintiff alleges that the doctor was negligent for *choosing a given surgical procedure in light of the patient's risk profile*, it is likely that a physician will have considered many of the factors in her own *impressionistic judgment to recommend* the procedure. If the doctor's *rationale* was sufficient to overcome her own ex ante internal evaluation of the risk factors, it is likely to be equally convincing in the context of ex post external review at trial in which the statistical information is considered. … [U]nless the doctor's impressionistic evaluation is *substantially off the mark*, it is unlikely that the statistical data, even though more precise, will convince a jury that the doctor's risk valuation was negligent."(emphasis added)).

3.5.2.1 Non-negligent Error in Judgment

The law does not blame an honest and intelligent exercise of judgment.[89] A defendant-doctor should not be liable for non-negligent errors in judgment.[90] The rule of "error in judgment" reinforces the ideas "that liability should not automatically follow from the mere fact of an adverse outcome nor from the fact that a choice among professionally acceptable courses of action turned out, in retrospect, to have been more harmful or less beneficial than an alternate course might have been" (King 1999, 59–60).

3.5.2.2 No Perfection, No Result Guarantee and Avoiding Hindsight Bias

Highly related to the theory of "error of judgment" is the notion that doctors cannot guarantee success or ensure a cure. Special caution is needed to guard against giving undue weight to the results of medical treatment in considering the conduct of the doctor.[91] Negligence cannot be assumed on the basis of the consequences of the medical treatment to the patient.[92] The rationale behind the "adverse outcome admonition" is that the liability for medical malpractice is fault-based, not based on strict liability principles (King 1999, 57). As with the error of judgment defence, the no guarantee argument also underlies the legal principle that the law only requires exercise of reasonable care, not perfection and infallibility.

---

[89] *Wilson v. Swanson* (1956), 5 D.L.R. (2d) 113, 120.

[90] There is a long-standing honoured distinction between error of judgment and negligence. Although these two concepts may overlap, they are different. The relationship between error of judgment and negligence has been described as: (1) an error of judgment may be negligent, depending on the circumstances; (2) an error of judgment is not necessarily negligence; (3) an error of judgment is a valid defence, only if it is an error made by a doctor exercising reasonable care. *See*, *Pelletier v. Stewart*, 2005 ABQB 484, at [11]. *See also*, *McHugh v. Audet*, 72 F. Supp. 394, 399 (D.C.PA. 1947) ("Where a physician or surgeon exercises such ordinary care and skill keeping within recognized and approved methods he is not liable for the result of a mere mistake or error of enlightened judgment. There is no responsibility for an error of judgment unless it be so gross as to be inconsistent with the degree of skill which it is the duty of every physician to possess.").

[91] *Pelletier v. Stewart*, 2005 ABQB 484, at [28].

[92] *Pelletier v. Stewart*, 2005 ABQB 484, at [11]. *See also*, USA: *McHugh v. Audet*, 72 F. Supp. 394, 400 (D.C.PA. 1947) ("A physician is not an insurer of the health of his patient. The fact that an unfortunate result follows the use of a recognized method does not make out a prima facie case of malpractice against the physician or surgeon who makes the choice."); Australia: *Dunning v. Scheibner*, NSW (Common Law Division), Wood J, 15 February 1994, unreported, BC9402391, at [76], [77] ("For an express warranty to that effect to be found, there would need, in my view, to be a very clear and specific promise on the part of the medical practitioner, which was understood by the patient as such."); *Crisp v. Keng* NSW (Common Law Division), Wood J, 2 December 1992, unreported, BC9201449, at [111] ("There is no expectation that surgery, whether it be spinal surgery or otherwise, will be invariably successful. It would be a serious mistake to approach this field of professional negligence upon the basis that upon proof of a particular surgical procedure being unsuccessful, negligence is automatically established.").

It has long been recognised that medical judgment should not be scrutinised using the "perfect vision afforded by hindsight".[93] A physician should not be held to a standard of perfection.[94] The purpose of "adverse outcome admonition" is not only to emphasise the fault-based nature of medical malpractice liability, but also to underscore the appropriate perspective for the fact-finders in evaluating a defendant's performance in a malpractice claim, and, more specifically, to remind the fact-finders that the defendant's conduct must be evaluated in light of the facts known or reasonably available to the defendant at the time, rather than focusing on "hindsight" (King 1999, 57).

3.5.2.3 The Doctrine of "Two Schools of Thought"

A physician should be allowed to choose among a number of professionally acceptable alternatives. The doctrine of "two schools of thought" was created "as a defense in medical malpractice cases in order to allow each legitimate medical approach to be judged on its own merits and not solely by the rules and principles of a different, albeit authoritative, way of thinking."[95] Pennsylvania is a home of many cases dealing with the "two schools of thought" doctrine.[96] An authoritative formulation of the doctrine is as follows:

---

[93] *Lapointe v. Hôpital LeGardeur* (1992), 90 D.L.R. (4th) 7, 14.

[94] *Turkington v. Lai*, 52 C.C.L.T. (3d) 254, 273, at [71] (Ont. S. C. J.).

[95] *Gala v. Hamilton*, 715 A.2d 1108, 1115 (Pa., 1998) (Nigro Justice, dissenting).

[96] Other jurisdictions have similar doctrines. For example, Tennessee: *O'Neill v. Kiledjian*, 511 F.2d 511, 513 (C.A.Tenn. 1975) ("a doctor will not be held responsible for the exercise of his professional judgment in the selection of one method of treatment over another when both alternatives have the support of a considerable body of competent medical opinion in the community"); Arizona: *Borja v. Phoenix General Hosp., Inc.*, 727 P.2d 355, 357–358 (Ariz. App., 1986) ("a doctor does not commit malpractice simply because he employs a method of diagnosis or a course of treatment some doctors do not find efficacious. So long as a respectable minority of physicians approve the disputed technique and so long as the defending doctor properly employed that technique, he has not fallen below the standard of care."); Missouri: *Haase v. Garfinkel*, 418 S.W.2d 108 (Mo.1967) ("as long as there is room for an honest difference of opinion among competent physicians, a physician who uses his own best judgment cannot be convicted of negligence, even though it may afterward develop that he was mistaken."); Arkansas: *Rickett v. Hayes*, 511 S.W.2d 187, 195 (Ark. 1974) ("Where a physician or surgeon, in the exercise of his best judgment, follows an alternative course of treatment sanctioned and approved by competent medical authority, he cannot be held liable because he failed to pursue another and different course."); Connecticut: *Wasfi v. Chaddha*, 588 A.2d 204, 209 (Conn., 1991) (noting that physicians may choose between alternative acceptable methods without incurring liability solely because that choice may have led to an unfortunate result); Washington: *Gruginski v. Lane*, 30 P.2d 970, 971 (Wash. 1934) ("the mere fact that a bad result followed was not of itself evidence of negligence on the part of the appellant. We also recognize the rule that, if the treatment actually employed had the approval of at least a respectable minority of the medical profession and was recognized by such as a proper method, there would not be negligence.").

> Where competent medical authority is divided, a physician will not be held responsible if in the exercise of his judgment he followed a course of treatment advocated by *a considerable number of recognized and respected* professionals in his given area of expertise. (emphasis added)[97]

It provides a medical practitioner *an absolute defence* to a claim of negligence "when it is determined that the prescribed treatment or procedure has been approved by one group of medical experts *even though an alternate school of thought recommends another approach*, or it is agreed among experts that alternative treatments and practices are acceptable." [98] Once the expert states the factual reasons to support his claim that there is a considerable number of professionals who agree with the treatment employed by the defendant, an instruction on the two "schools of thought" is warranted.[99] If it is found that there are two legitimate schools of thought, the defendant should be insulated from liability.[100] The doctrine is applicable only where there is more than one method of accepted treatment or procedure.[101]

The doctrine recognises that laymen, such as jury members and judges, have limited competency in face of complicated, disputed medical questions.[102] The justification for the doctrine is that "a jury should not be required to judge which school of thought is the best when medical practitioners themselves differ on the point."[103] The intended purpose of the "two schools of thought" doctrine is to make sure that the "practitioners of a reputable school of medicine are not to be harassed by litigation and mulcted in damages because the course of treatment prescribed by that school differs from that adopted by another school".[104] The doctrine "reflects important realities in the practice of medicine."[105]

---

[97] *Jones v. Chidester*, 610 A.2d 964, 969 (Pa., 1992).

[98] *Jones v. Chidester*, 610 A.2d 964, 965 (Pa., 1992) (emphasis added).

[99] *Jones v. Chidester*, 610 A.2d 964, 969 (Pa., 1992).

[100] *Jones v. Chidester*, 610 A.2d 964, 969 (Pa., 1992).

[101] *Jones v. Chidester*, 610 A.2d 964, 965 (Pa., 1992).

[102] *Remley v. Plummer*, 79 Pa.Super. 117, 121–123; 1922 WL 2863, 3 (Pa.Super. 1922).

[103] *Colangeli v. Pallone*, 63 Pa. D. & C.4th 386, 390 (Pa.Com.Pl. 2003). *See also, Gala v. Hamilton*, 715 A.2d 1108,1115 (Pa.,1998) (Nigro, Justice, dissenting) ("The doctrine is rooted in the principle that juries, with their limited medical knowledge, should not be forced to decide which of two acceptable treatments a defendant physician should have performed."); *D'Angelis v. Zakuto*, 556 A.2d 431, 433 (Pa.Super.,1989) (the purpose underlying the doctrine is "to remove from the jury's discretion those matters requiring medical expertise, and on which medical experts disagree among themselves").

[104] *Remley v. Plummer*, 79 Pa.Super. 117, 121–123; 1922 WL 2863, 3–4 (Pa.Super. 1922) ("[A] reputable physician should not be subjected to the risk of loss of his professional standing and the payment of damages" because in the exercise of his best judgment he followed one school of thought rather than another.).

[105] Joseph H. King, Jr. (1999), 58 ("The science of healing is dynamic, subject to continuing change and scientific advances. Going hand in hand with this dynamism is an inherent pluralism in medicine – a scientific world characterized by multiple therapeutic approaches to a medical problem all of which may command respect within at least some significant segment of the medical profession.").

3.5.2.4 Alternative Methods Instruction

California has an equivalent to the Pennsylvania's "two schools of thought" doctrine, namely the Alternative Methods of Diagnosis or Treatment Instruction. It reads,

> Where there is more than one recognized method of diagnosis or treatment, and no one of them is used exclusively and uniformly by all practitioners of good standing, a physician and surgeon is not negligent if, in exercising his best judgment, he selects one of the approved methods, which later turns out to be a wrong selection, or one not favored by certain other practitioners.[106]

This instruction, which serves as a defence for the defendant, embodies the notion that

> different doctors may disagree in good faith upon what would encompass the proper treatment or diagnosis of a medical problem in a given situation. Medicine is not a field of absolutes. There is not ordinarily only one correct route to be followed at any given time. There is always the need for professional judgment as to what course of conduct would be most appropriate with regard to the patient's condition.[107]

Like the "two schools of thought" doctrine, this kind of instruction accords potential benefits to health practitioners when they exercise independent judgment and choice of treatments.[108]

3.5.2.5 The *Bolam* Test and Its Modified Forms

In a situation where there was *conflicting* expert testimony or difference in expert opinions on what was acceptable medical practice, in England and other Commonwealth countries, the *Bolam* test provides a good starting point. The *Bolam* test asks courts to give weighty deference to a responsible body of medical opinion, even though there exists a contrary medical opinion.[109] Underlying the *Bolam* test is the notion that "[i]n

---

[106] California Civil Jury Instruction (BAJI) 6.03. *See also*, BAJI instruction 214-A, California Jury Instructions, Civil, 4th Revised Edition.

[107] *Barton v. Owen*, 71 Cal.App.3d 484, 501–502 (Cal.App.2.Dist. 1977).

[108] *Fraijo v. Hartland Hospital*, 99 Cal.App.3d 331, 342–344 (Cal. App. 2.Dist. 1979) (agreeing that the trial court properly tailored the two instructions (BAJI 6.02 and 6.03), ordinarily applicable only to physicians and surgeons, to apply also to *nurses*; reasoning that: "If standard medical practice permits physicians to confer upon nurses in certain medical situations the exercise of independent judgment, nurses in those situations must be accorded the potential benefits to be derived from BAJI Nos. 6.02 and 6.03. To hold otherwise would impose upon nurses a standard of care exceeding that applicable to the medical profession, hardly a fair result.") (BAJI 6.02 is the "error in judgment" instruction, which "tells the jury that an error in medical judgment is not considered in a vacuum but must be weighed in terms of the professional standard of care".).

[109] *Bolam v. Friern Hospital Committee* [1957] 2 All E.R. 118,122 ("A doctor is not guilty of negligence if he has acted in accordance with a practice accepted as proper by a responsible body of medical men skilled in that particular art. … Putting it the other way round, a doctor is not negligent, if he is acting in accordance with such a practice, merely because there is a body of opinion that takes a contrary view.").

the realm of diagnosis and treatment [involving medical expertise] there is ample scope for genuine difference of opinion and one man is clearly not negligent merely because his conclusion differs from that of other professional men",[110] and the law should give doctors sufficient discretion to practice an inexact science.

In England, the *Bolam* test was confirmed and reinforced in the House of Lords by *Maynard v. West Midland Regional Health Authority*,[111] and *Sidaway v. Governors of Bethlem Royal Hospital*.[112] Although the *Bolam* test was qualified by the *Bolitho* case,[113] in "the vast majority of cases", the law still acknowledges that courts should accord weighty deference to medical experts and medical opinions.[114] Similar lines of formulation having the same effect as the *Bolam* test are also present in the Irish law,[115] Scottish law,[116] Canadian law[117] and Australian law.[118] The *Bolam* test

---

[110] *Bolam v. Friern Hospital Management Committee* [1957] 2 All ER 118, 121 (quoting Scottish case *Hunter v. Hanley* [1955] S.L.T. 213, 217). *See also*, *Maynard v. West Midlands Regional Health Authority* [1985] 1 W.L.R. 685, 638, per Lord Scarman ("Differences of opinion and practice exist, and will always exist, in the medical as in other professions. There is seldom any one answer exclusive of all others to problems of professional judgment. A court may prefer one body of opinion to the other: but that is no basis for a conclusion of negligence."); *Rogers v. Whitaker* (1992) 175 C.L.R. 479, 484 (HCA).

[111] *Maynard v. West Midlands Regional Health Authority* [1985] 1 W.L.R. 685, 638, per Lord Scarman ("It is not enough to show that there is a body of competent professional opinion which considers that theirs was a wrong decision, if there also exists a body of professional opinion, equally competent, which supports the decision as reasonable in the circumstances.").

[112] *Sidaway v. Bethlem Royal Hospital Governors* [1985] AC 871, 892–893 (Lord Diplock) and 897 C (Lord Bridge).

[113] *Bolitho v. City and Hackney HA* [1997] 4 All ER 771, 778.

[114] *Bolitho v. City and Hackney HA* [1997] 4 All ER 771, 779 ("In the vast majority of cases the fact that distinguished experts in the field are of a particular opinion will demonstrate the reasonableness of that opinion.... The assessment of medical risks and benefits is a matter of clinical judgment which a judge would not normally be able to make without expert evidence.").

[115] *Dunne (an infant) v. National Maternity Hospital* [1989] IR 91, 109, per Finlay C.J. ("An honest difference of opinion between doctors as to which is the better of two ways of treating a patient does not provide any ground for leaving a question to the jury as to whether a person who has followed one course rather than the other has been negligent"; "It is not for a jury (or for a judge) to decide which of two alternative courses of treatment is in their (or his) opinion preferable, but their (or his) function is merely to decide whether the course of treatment followed, on the evidence, complied with the careful conduct of a medical practitioner of like specialisation and skill to that professed by the defendant.").

[116] *Honisz v. Lothian Health Board & Ors* [2006] ScotCS CSOH_24, at [39].

[117] *Bauer v. Seager et al.*, [2000] 11 W.W.R. 621, 676–680 (Man. Q. B.) ("There is a 'respectable minority' principle which says that if a doctor acts in accordance with a respectable body of opinion (that is, a respectable minority of the profession), even though it is not the opinion of the majority, he or she will normally be absolved from liability."; "The courts do not have jurisdiction to settle scientific disputes or to choose among divergent opinions of physicians on certain subjects; courts should not involve themselves in resolving scientific disputes which require the expertise of the profession."); *Sharp v. Hurlbert*, 2007 CarswellAlta 464, 2007 ABQB 221, 76 Alta. L.R. (4th) 142, [2007] 9 W.W.R. 657, at [30] ("Where expert evidence establishes that there is more than one recognized and accepted body of medical opinion, a physician is not negligent if he or she adhered to one accepted school of thought.").

[118] *Civil Liability Act 2003* (Qld), s 22(1) (2) (3) (4); *Civil Liability Act 2002* (Tas), s 22; *Civil Liability Act 2002* (WA), s 5 PB; *Civil Liability Act 1936* (SA), s 41; *Civil Liability Act 2002* (NSW), s 5O.

dictates that "as a general rule, where there are two opposing schools of thought among the relevant group of responsible medical practitioners as to the appropriateness of a particular practice, it is not the function of the court to prefer one school over the other".[119]

In summary, all of these principles serve to reinforce the need for caution against passing too cavalierly upon the conduct and decision of experts. Applying those principles in the context of selecting and recommending treatment options, the result seems that, if there are two opposing schools of thought within the defendant's specialty, it is not negligent for the defendant physician to subscribe to one of them by recommending one option rather than another.[120] Having recognised that different doctors of different schools of thought will have different attitudes to particular treatment options, it is not negligent to adopt or propound or offer one to the exclusion of the other so long as those attitudes are not inconsistent with a reasonable standard of care.[121] "[T]he decision as to treatment is that of the doctor provided that there is a legitimate and recognised school of thought in medical circles which supported that treatment."[122] When confronted with two generally recognized schools of thought, the court will not interfere with the reasonable choice of one or the other.[123]

3.5.3 *Recommendation*

3.5.3.1 Recommendation Versus Disclosure

Disclosure of treatment options is different from recommendation of a particular treatment option.[124] A patient's informed decision needs not only a doctor's *unbiased*

---

[119] *Honisz v. Lothian Health Board & Ors* [2006] ScotCS CSOH_24, at [39], per Lord Hodge. This opinion has been frequently quoted by other cases, for example, *Lowe v. Yorkhill NHS Trust* [2007] ScotCS CSOH_111, at [107]; *Dineley V. Lothian Health Board* [2007] ScotCS CSOH_151, at [37]; *Scott v. Lothian University Hospitals NHS Trust* [2006] ScotCS CSOH_92, at [35]; *McEwan v. Ayrshire & Arran Acute Hospitals NHS Trust* [2009] ScotCS CSOH_22, at [232]; *McColm v. Borders General Hospital NHS Trust* [2006] ScotSC 59, at [313].

[120] *Finch v. Carpenter*, 1993 CanLII 1240 (BC S.C.).

[121] *Richards v. Rahilly* [2005] NSWSC 352, at [230] (citing *Eagle v. Prosser* [1999] NSWCA 166).

[122] *Richards v. Rahilly* [2005] NSWSC 352, at [230] (citing *Eagle v. Prosser* [1999] NSWCA 166).

[123] *Groves v. Morton*, 44 C.C.L.T. (3d) 108 (Ont. S. C. J.).

[124] *SEM v. The Mid Yorkshire Hospitals NHS Trust* [2005] EWHC B3 (QB) (The High Court rightly distinguished the context of information disclosure and that of a doctor's personalised recommendation. On the one hand, the defendant admitted, and the court acknowledged, that the defendant should let the patient know *a menu of* treatment options, not just the treatment option actually proposed and performed by the defendant. On the other hand, after admitting that the defendant was negligent in not advising other treatment options, the court's focus shifted to appropriateness of the defendant's recommendation and reasonableness of the patient's response to that recommendation.); *Tan v. Benkovic* [2000] NSWCA 295 (Mason P, 26 October 2000, unreported, BC200006724) (distinguished the context of recommendation or even persuasion from the context of information disclosure).

presentation or disclosure of merits and demerits of treatment options, but also a doctor's personal exercise of medical judgment and *personalised recommendation.* A doctor is entitled to judge that his patient is a good or poor candidate for one treatment option. But he also has an obligation to appreciate that one condition may have a wide spectrum of treatment options. Recommendation/persuasion should be subject to the general requirement that a practitioner should present his patient with balanced and contextualised information. A full picture is needed before a practitioner lets his patients know his preferences and his own judgement. Recommendation/persuasion is sometimes part of the treatment process. It is basically motivated by medical judgment.

In ethical terms, a physician's honest and accurate presentation of medical information should be accompanied by sincere recommendation as to management options.[125] In a legal sense, a doctor has a duty not only to present the alternatives, but also to provide a recommendation.[126] There is an obligation for doctors not only to explain the alternative procedures and the risks but also to make a recommendation.[127]

3.5.3.2 The Laissez-Faire Approach

Just setting out a menu of alternatives and leaving the patient to choose treatments but unaided by any recommendation is not a good approach. Medical matters are often complex. Recommendations of treatment frequently require the application of considerable medical knowledge gained through extensive training and experience.[128] As mentioned before, recommendation is part of exercise of expertise and medical judgment, therefore a part of treatment process. The treatment/disclosure distinction determines that *unbiased presentation* of alternatives information should not be confused with *personalised recommendation.*

It is not enough to just present treatment options on an equal footing and adopt the position of letting the patient decide himself when the treatments actually fall within a progressive scale.[129] The patient is entitled to his doctor's assessment

[125]American Medical Association, Code of Medical Ethics Opinion 8.08 (Issued March 1981; Updated November 2006) at <http://www.ama-assn.org/ama1/pub/upload/mm/Code_of_Med_Eth/opinion/opinion808.html> (Last accessed 24 July 2009) ("The physician's obligation is to present the medical facts accurately to the patient or to the individual responsible for the patient's care *and to make recommendations for management* in accordance with good medical practice. The physician has an ethical obligation to *help the patient make choices from among the therapeutic alternatives* consistent with good medical practice." (emphasis added)).

[126]*Sicard v. Sendziak*, 2008 ABQB 690, at [111] (Court of Queen's Bench of Alberta).

[127]*Bauer v. Seager et al.*, [2000] 11 W.W.R. 621, 672, at [39] (Man. Q. B.).

[128]*Harnish v. Children's Hosp. Med. Center*, 439 N.E.2d 240, 243 (Mass. 1982).

[129]*Zaiffdeen v. Chua*, 2004 ABQB 331, [2005] 358 A.R. 274 (Court of Queen's Bench of Alberta), at [37]–[38]; *Zaiffdeen v. Chua*, 2005 ABCA 290; [2006] 380 A.R. 200 (Court of Appeal of Alberta), at [21] (In these cases, there were two treatment options for the patient's condition: drug treatment or surgery. These options fell within a progressive scale, with surgery being the most

and recommendation in order to place the treatment options in a proper perspective.[130]

In a situation "when the patient's judgment appears to be impaired", the defendant-doctor's "self-confessed approach" – the "laissez-faire attitude", i.e. "present[ing] patients with the options and let them decide whether to undergo a procedure, but not to advise them whether one procedure is better than another or better than nothing at all", "may not be sufficient".[131] Particularly in the area of cosmetic surgery, when there is no medical need for an operation and only a patient's subjective aesthetic opinion determines her view of whether surgery is to be undertaken, a physician should have some responsibility to provide *objective guidance* to the patient whose capacity for self-assessment is clearly disordered.[132]

In a situation where (1) the condition from which the patient was suffering was not well understood, (2) there were at least three, and perhaps five, well-recognised treatments for it, (3) the treatments were not necessarily alternatives but could be used in combination, (4) it was not understood why patients responded to some treatments and not to others, (5) even the mechanism by which these treatments brought about an improvement in symptoms was not known, and (6) there were no

---

severe, and drug treatment being the conservative option. However, the defendant doctor presented drug treatment on an equal footing to surgical treatment. Both the trial court and the Court of Appeal found the doctor breached the standard of care by failing to disclose the various treatment options in the proper perspective.).

[130] *Zaiffdeen v. Chua*, 2004 ABQB 331, [2005] 358 A.R. 274 (Court of Queen's Bench of Alberta), at [37]–[38]; *Zaiffdeen v. Chua*, 2005 ABCA 290; [2006] 380 A.R. 200 (Court of Appeal of Alberta), at [21].

[131] *Lynn G. v. Hugo*, 710 N.Y.S.2d 334, 338 (A.D. 1 Dept. 2000). It involves cosmetic surgeries and a patient suffering from Body Dysmorphic Disorder (a disproportionate preoccupation with minor or imaginary physical flaws). The patient's identification of the problem and dissatisfaction with her body may be a matter of personal taste, motivated by subjective vanity rather than objective physical impairment. The patient's mental state affected her ability to assess the risks and benefits of elective cosmetic surgery because persons with this disorder have irrationally exaggerated perceptions of their bodily imperfections.

[132] *Lynn G. v. Hugo*, 710 N.Y.S.2d 334, 338 (A.D. 1 Dept. 2000). *But compare*, an Australian case *Tan v. Benkovic* [2000] NSWCA 295 (Mason P, 26 October 2000, unreported, BC200006724). The Australian case also involved a patient who "was anxious to improve her appearance through cosmetic surgery and was, to that extent, in a dependant and vulnerable position." Faced with such an eager patient, the appellant-doctor did not choose to cool her down by highlighting the dark side of cosmetic surgery, but encouraged her to undergo the cosmetic surgery with pleasant promises and persuasive "blandishments". Although the appellant-surgeon was found negligent in not informing his patient of full range of risks inherent in the cosmetic surgery, the court did not find it improper for the appellant to encourage his patient to proceed with the facelift that she was anxious to obtain. The court's reasoning was basically patient-autonomy-controlled, noting that it was improper to treat a patient as lacking autonomy. It needs to be noted that, in this case, the appellant-surgeon was alleged to have paid inadequate attention to the *threshold* matter of whether the patient was *a psychologically appropriate candidate* for a cosmetic plastic surgery procedure. This invites discussing a wider topic about women and cosmetic surgery. Feminist scholars argue that "the regulation of cosmetic surgery, instead of simply applying professional and clinical standards of excellence, ought to look beyond such 'technical' considerations and heed the cultural and societal pressures that drive women to seek these interventions". *See*, Melanie Latham 2008, 440.

clear-cut alternative treatments to choose between, a doctor is "not only entitled but bound" to recommend to patients the treatment which the doctor considers most appropriate in the circumstances.[133] "It is not a question of that choice involving the personal preference of the doctor but rather the doctor performing the fundamental duty for which he or she has been retained, i.e. to diagnose and treat."[134] There may arise a situation where a doctor's personal preference and recommendation serves not only as an inevitable part of treatment or as an *duty/obligation*, but also *as an entitlement*.

3.5.3.3 Personalised Recommendation

The law should give a physician's recommendation even persuasion more allowance than a physician's selection of treatment. The courts should accord considerable latitude to a doctor's personalised, subjective professional judgments in recommending a particular procedure. "[C]ourts should not rush into areas in which subjective professional judgments predominate".[135]

In deciding whether a patient has been properly advised by a particular defendant, "one cannot eliminate from consideration the *particular views and experience of [a particular doctor]*, provided of course that expression of those views and reliance on that experience would fall within the scope of what a doctor *exercising proper skill and care* would have said and done."[136] "[I]f [a particular doctor] held *a*

[133] *Richards v. Rahilly* [2005] NSWSC 352, at [233]–[234].

[134] *Richards v. Rahilly* [2005] NSWSC 352, at [234].

[135] *Tan v. Benkovic* [2000] NSWCA 295 (Mason P, 26 October 2000, unreported, BC200006724), at [19]–[20] (making a distinction between "the realm of professional practice and conduct and the realm of morality", on the one hand, and "the realm of the tort of negligence", on the other). This Australian case explores the appropriateness of a surgeon's persuasion for an elective cosmetic surgery in the context of aggravated damages and exemplary damages. Although the appellant-surgeon was found negligent in not informing his patient of full range of risks surrounding the cosmetic surgery, the court concluded that the appellant did not act improperly in *encouraging* his eager patient to undergo cosmetic surgery. The court acknowledged the subjective and individualized nature of giving recommendation and gave a medical professional a substantial allowance to express his or her personal views.

[136] *SEM v. The Mid Yorkshire Hospitals NHS Trust* [2005] EWHC B3 (QB), at [39] (emphasis added). In this case, the patient suffered from a somatoform disorder. A consultant urogynaecologist and obstetrician proposed and performed a surgical procedure which comprised a vaginal hysterectomy, McCall's culdoplasty, and anterior and posterior repair of the vaginal walls. McCall's procedure involves tying the utero-sacral ligaments into the vault of the vagina using non-absorbable sutures: the object is to prevent future prolapse. Sadly the hysterectomy did nothing to solve her problems. It had been established that, in addition to the vaginal hysterectomy with McCall's procedure, there were five options, two non-surgical alternatives and three surgical alternatives, that should have been disclosed by the defendant to the plaintiff. The two non-surgical alternatives are: (1) *doing nothing*, apart from reassurance and physiotherapy; (2) the use of medical devices, such as

firm view as to the best way of proceeding, she would have been *duty bound to express that view*, so long as she did not do so in such a way as to pre-empt her patient's freedom of choice."[137] However, the personalised recommendation should be made "within the parameters of the range of options" which a doctor is obliged to lay before his patient.[138] Personalised recommendation needs to be balanced by contextualised information disclosure.

Some case law has imposed on a practitioner a duty to point out the *risks involved in the failure to follow a recommendation*, such as a patient's decision of non-treatment.[139] That will be expected to produce the effect of encouraging a patient's following a physician's treatment recommendation or discouraging a patient's not accepting necessary treatments.

---

ring or Hodge *pessaries*. The three viable surgical alternatives are: (1) merely repairing the anterior wall of the vagina (*anterior repair*); (2) the so-called *Manchester-Fothergill operation* (its availability "is dependant on the surgical expertise of the surgeon"); (3) *vaginal hysterectomy* and anterior repair, i.e. *without McCall's procedure*. This High Court (Queen's Bench) case highlighted how a practitioner, by expressing qualifications, can and has to recommend the only *one* treatment option s/he preferred from *"a menu"* of treatment options offered, giving due weight to his or her own personal and particular views and experiences (see Appendix 1).

[137] *SEM v. The Mid Yorkshire Hospitals NHS Trust* [2005] EWHC B3 (QB), at [39] (emphasis added) ("The question 'what would you do, doctor?' is frequently asked and has to be answered.").

[138] *SEM v. The Mid Yorkshire Hospitals NHS Trust* [2005] EWHC B3 (QB), at [50].

[139] *Truman v. Thomas* 611 P.2d 902, 906–907 (Cal. 1980) (A physician failed to inform a patient of the material risks of *not submitting to a recommended pap smear*, i.e. the potentially fatal consequences of allowing cervical cancer to develop undetected by a pap smear; the Supreme Court of California supported the opinion that a patient must be apprised not only of the risks inherent in the proposed procedure, *but also the risks of a decision not to undergo the treatment or a diagnostic test*; to reinforce the need of disclosure in the instant case, the Court highlighted the following facts: (1) the pap smear test is "an accurate detector" of cervical cancer; (2) the potential harm of failing to detect the disease at an early stage is death; (3) there was no evidence that the plaintiff was aware of the serious danger entailed in not undergoing the test; (4) the defendant knew that the plaintiff would not undergo the test.); *Elbourne v. Gibbs* [2006] NSWCA 127 (Beazley, Ipp and Basten JJA, 24 May 2006, unreported, BC200603589), at [57] ("it is nevertheless important to see the identification of material risks *in context*. Thus, a medical practitioner is required not only to identify the risks involved in a particular treatment or procedure, but also *the need for the procedure and the possible risks attendant on a failure to undergo that which the practitioner is recommending*. It is only with that knowledge, that the patient can sensibly address the relevance and magnitude of the particular risks."(emphasis added)); per Basten JA (noting that in the present case "the doctor gave evidence that a 'wait and see policy' was not an appropriate option, and would have been rejected by him as 'irresponsible in the extreme'" (at [58])). *But compare*, *Landon v. Zorn*, 884 A.2d 142, 156 (Md., 2005) (the doctor recommended a diagnostic test, but the patient *refused to submit* to that test; the patient argued that he was never advised of any potential risks associated with not having a CAT scan, specifically the fact that failure to submit to the CAT scan could have life-threatening consequences for him; the court held that the informed consent rule exists only where the injury suffered arises from an *affirmative* act on the patient, or affirmative violation of the patient's physical integrity).

3.5.3.4 Persuasion

Persuasion may be revealed in the form of exposing the patient to some information (emphasising the positive profile of one option or emphasising the negative profile of its competitors), or directly expressing a preference for one option over another. Persuasion/recommendation may also take the forms of adding *qualifications or reservations* to treatment options that a physician does not prefer. However, the message of favouring one option over another, sent by a practitioner to his patients, should not be too persuasive so as to undermine the rationale of the doctrine of informed consent. The law needs to be alert to the overly persuasive, explicitly one-sided, or inappropriately manipulative message.[140] The patients need protection against manipulative messages.

Some courts approached the issue of persuasion with great caution. One English judge warned that "[c]ounselling should be non-directive".[141] There is hesitancy for courts to hold that "a doctor is under a legal duty, not just to advise and warn fairly and appropriately but to *persuade* or … to express his wishes in such a way as to *secure compliance*".[142] There is no scope for a duty to "push".[143]

The non-interventional approach was criticised by some scholars as treating patients as "objects" and failing to recognise that patient autonomy is enhanced by the dialogical involvement of a "well-informed physician" (Maclean 2006, 322). Alasdair Maclean argued that healthcare professionals should be under a legal duty to persuade their patients to change their minds when they have made an apparently irrational decision (Maclean 2006, 322).

I agree that there is a long gulf between a genuine persuasion and "bullying". The law should give persuasion some room. The duty of information disclosure should not be simply satisfied by disclosing the relevant information and leaving the patient to make the decision whether to undergo the treatment offered. Letting patients make decisions without assistance reduces the physician's role from professional adviser to technical information provider (Maclean 2006, 325).

The "nondirective" disclosure of "neutral" information is almost impossible. "Given the complexity of the beliefs, attitudes, anxieties, and expectations that will lie in the background of any listener, it may be virtually impossible to transmit infor-

---

[140] Jocelyn Downie, Timothy Caulfield and Colleen Flood (2002), 130 (warning that doctors may use information to purposely manipulate a patient's decision, or simply for the purpose of persuading patients to agree to treatments or to medical goals the doctors have determined to be in the patient's best interests).

[141] *Al Hamwi v. Johnston, The North West London Hospitals NHS Trust* [2005] EWHC 206; [2005] Lloyd's Rep Med 309, para. [44], per Simon J.

[142] *Attwell v. McPartlin* [2004] EWHC 829, para. [60] (emphasis added) (adding that "[s]ome doctors may wish to make an effort to persuade a reluctant patient to act in what the doctor sees as the patient's best interests; some doctors may even feel the need to adopt an overbearing or bullying attitude in order to secure compliance. But, in the end, in the ordinary case it is for the professional to advise and for the patient … to decide.").

[143] *Attwell v. McPartlin* [2004] EWHC 829, para. [60].

mation in a form that carries no potentially misleading reverberations" (Tomlinson 1986, 116). The order in which information is disclosed may influence the patient's appreciation of that information. Bias may be added by the use and selection of words. The information disclosed by the expert will necessarily be biased by the selection of what is believed to be relevant to the decision. Both the concepts of risk and benefit rely on subjective value judgments (Maclean 2006, 326). "[P]art of the professional's role is to advise and to recommend treatment, which, by definition, cannot be a neutral endeavour. … [I]nsistence on neutrality sterilises the dialogue and, while it formally respects consent as permission, it undermines consent as agreement" (Maclean 2009, 205).

Information disclosure involves dialogue, communication and mutual persuasion. On the one hand, clinicians need to respect the patient's autonomy. On the other hand, patients need to listen receptively to the professional and be open to persuasion (Maclean 2006, 330). By challenging the patient's decision, the professional may facilitate patients to do necessary reflection about their decisions (Maclean 2006, 331). Overly focusing on the outcome of the process that culminates in the patient's consent rather than the process necessary to facilitate an autonomous consent prejudices the vulnerable and less well-educated patients without providing any significant additional protection for the more capable (Maclean 2006, 336). Courts need to take more interest in the dialogical process that precedes the patient's decision about whether or not to consent and permit the treatment offered by the professional.

Having said that, persuasion should be confined to medical views and clinical perspectives. Professionals cannot impose their personal moral views on patients. Persuasion cannot frustrate the basic rule that patients are the ultimate decision-makers. Obviously, persuasion involves many subtle areas. Fine lines need to be drawn. The bottom line is that persuasion should not cross the line of *not inducing or coercing* the patients.[144] There is a duty not to present the information in such a way that the patient's right to make his or her own decisions is usurped.[145] More importantly, to avoid patient's autonomy being unduly compromised, balanced and contextualised information, coupled with personalised recommendation and persuasion, is necessary.

3.5.3.5 Tainted Recommendation

Recommendation can be unavoidably influenced by medical judgment and preferences, but the law does not tolerate the fact that it was tainted by factors *beyond medical considerations*, such as conflict of loyalties or interests. On the one hand,

---

[144] *See*, General Medical Council (UK) *Consent: Patients and Doctors Making Decisions Together* (2008), para. 19 at <www.gmc-uk.org> (Last accessed 24 April 2010) ("You should give information to patients in a balanced way. If you recommend a particular treatment or course of action, you should explain your reasons for doing so. But you must not put pressure on a patient to accept your advice.").

[145] Alasdair Maclean (2009), 180–181 (citing *Thompson v. Bradford* [2004] EWHC 2424).

the law should honour and respect a doctor's choice and recommendation regarding plausible course of action if that is "motivated only by the patient's best therapeutic interests".[146] On the other hand, the law should guard against tainted recommendations.

A doctor has a loyalty to his patient's medical interests. That loyalty is expected to be "undivided". However, a physician who treats a patient in whom he also has a research interest has potentially conflicting loyalties.[147] A physician who adds his own research interests to the risk-benefit balance may be tempted to order a scientifically useful procedure or test "that offers marginal, or no, benefits to the patient."[148] A physician who does have a pre-existing research interest might, "consciously or unconsciously", take that into consideration in recommending the procedure.[149] Moreover, in a cost-containment environment, a doctor's recommendation may be tainted by financial incentives.[150]

"[A] physician's advice about treatment options should be free from self-serving financial considerations".[151] If not, there is a duty on physicians to disclose conflicting loyalties because management may be tainted by such conflicts. "[A] physician must disclose personal interests unrelated to the patient's health, whether research or economic, that may affect the physician's professional judgment".[152] A physician who orders a procedure partly to further a research interest unrelated to the patient's health should not be able to avoid disclosure with the argument that the patient might object to participation in research.[153]

[146] *Niblack v. U.S.*, 438F. Supp. 383, 388 (D.C.Colo. 1977).

[147] *Moore v. The Regents of the Univ. of California*, 793 P.2d 479, 484 (Cal. 1990) (defendants using a patient's cells in potentially lucrative medical research without the patient's permission; the Supreme Court of California (majority) supporting causes of action based on lack of *informed consent* and breach of *fiduciary duty*, but not on *conversion*). However, there was dissenting opinion which observed that the nondisclosure cause of action was *not an adequate substitute* for a conversion cause of action. *See*, *Moore v. The Regents of the Univ. of California*, 793 P.2d 479, 519–521 (Cal. 1990) (Mosk Justice, dissenting).

[148] *Moore v. The Regents of the Univ. of California*, 793 P.2d 479, 484 (Cal. 1990).

[149] *Moore v. The Regents of the Univ. of California*, 793 P.2d 479, 484 (Cal. 1990).

[150] *Pegram v. Herdrich*, 530 U.S. 211, 219 (U.S., 2000) (noting that the physician incentives under HMOs model reward physicians for *decreasing* utilization of health-care services, and penalize them for excessive treatment); American Medical Association, The Council on Ethical and Judicial Affairs Report 13 – A-94 *Ethical Issues in Managed Care* (1994–1995), p. 6 (opining that incentives to limit care are more problematic than incentives to provide care).

[151] *D.A.B. v. Brown*, 570 N.W.2d 168, 172 (Minn. App., 1997).

[152] *Moore v. The Regents of the Univ. of California*, 793 P.2d 479, 483 (Cal. 1990) (further adding that "a physician's failure to disclose such interests may give rise to a cause of action for performing medical procedures without *informed consent* or breach of *fiduciary duty*"(emphasis added)). However, the Court acknowledged that "[i]n some cases, … a physician's research interest might *play such an insignificant role in the decision to recommend a medically indicated procedure* that disclosure should not be required because the interest is not material"(emphasis added). This concession was made in the context of avoiding excessive disclosure to harm the patient (therapeutic privileges). *See*, *Moore v. The Regents of the Univ. of California*, 793 P.2d 479, 485 (Cal. 1990), footnote 9.

[153] *Moore v. The Regents of the Univ. of California*, 793 P.2d 479, 485 (Cal. 1990), footnote 9.

A physician's duty to disclose financial incentives may be recognised under the legal theories of negligent misrepresentation,[154] or ordinary medical negligence (including breach of informed consent).[155] The concept of informed consent is "broad enough to encompass" the situation where a physician failed to disclose such personal interests.[156] "The possibility that an interest extraneous to the patient's health has affected the physician's judgment" is something that a reasonable patient would want to know in deciding whether to consent to a proposed course of treatment.[157] A physician's "extraneous motivation may affect his judgment and is, thus material to the patient's consent".[158]

3.5.3.6 Recommendation and Negligence

In addition to disclosure of extraneous motivations, a doctor needs also to realise that a poor recommendation or non-recommendation may end up being regarded as negligent. That may be involved in the failure-to-recommend cases, or the wrong recommendation cases, or the unnecessary procedure cases. Ordinary medical negligence principles will govern the context of recommendation.[159]

It would be safer for a physician if, compared to alternative procedures, the procedure he proposed is less invasive and carried less risks.[160] However, a physician will not be negligent in recommending the contemplated procedure so long as his recommendation is a reasonable and competent exercise of his judgment,[161] and is

---

[154] *Shea v. Esensten (Shea II)*, 208 F.3d 712 (8th Cir. 2000) (the plaintiff claimed that the defendants' failure to disclose a financial incentive caused the patient *the independent injury of having been prevented from making an informed choice of whether to seek what might have been a life-saving referral at his own expense*).

[155] *D.A.B. v. Brown*, 570 N.W.2d 168 (Minn. App., 1997) (patients arguing that physician, manufacturer, and distributor failed to disclose the kickback scheme; the court holding that the doctor's duty to disclose the kickback scheme "presents a classic informed consent issue")

[156] *Moore v. The Regents of the Univ. of California*, 793 P.2d 479, 483 (Cal. 1990). The Supreme Court of California was not persuaded by the argument that "[t]o require disclosure of research and economic interests may corrupt the patient's own judgment by distracting him from the requirements of his health". *See*, *Moore v. The Regents of the Univ. of California*, 793 P.2d 479, 484–485 (Cal. 1990).

[157] *Moore v. The Regents of the Univ. of California*, 793 P.2d 479, 484 (Cal. 1990).

[158] *Moore v. The Regents of the Univ. of California*, 793 P.2d 479, 484 (Cal. 1990).

[159] Even if a plaintiff claimed that the medical practitioner fraudulently induced her into consenting to elective surgery by misrepresenting his experience and training and misrepresenting the merits and demerits of the proposed procedure, it seems that some courts still favoured the doctor-friendly informed consent claim (malpractice claim) rather than the fraud claim, because, in the eye of the court, those representations are relevant to the question of "whether [the defendant's] *selection* of the surgical procedure and *performance* of it met the standard of care for doctors in such circumstances and whether he *adequately disclosed* the risks of the surgical procedure to her". *See*, *Theroux v. Vick*, 163 S.W.3d 111, 114 (Tex. App.-San Antonio, 2005).

[160] *Thibault v. Fewer*, [2002] 1 W.W.R. 204, 217–218.

[161] *Turkington v. Lai*, 52 C.C.L.T. (3d) 254, 272–274 (Ont. S. C. J.).

not premature or otherwise unfounded. If the recommendation is in keeping with current medical standards, the fact that other well-qualified physicians may have recommended other options is a legitimate difference of professional opinions, but not evidence sufficient to establish negligence.[162]

3.5.4 *Disclosure and Doctors' Preferences*

Health practitioners have a tendency to mention and recommend only treatment options with which they are technically familiar and emotionally comfortable. As one expert testimony indicated, "[s]urgeons are cutter-uppers and they operate, and they recommend, usually, the operative procedure".[163] While this phenomenon may be understandable, a side-effect of it is that *a doctor's personal preferences* may constitute an impediment to sufficient disclosure.

A doctor's preferences about options may colour his presentation of treatment options. For example, what is, in reality, the real and substantial matter of election may be presented as a matter of no real choice at all.[164] A doctor is more often inclined to present information in such a manner that the patient will choose the alternative the doctor favours. A doctor may be so convinced himself that the optimum procedure for his patient's condition is the procedure he proposed that he "glossed over the disadvantages of that procedure and any benefits associated with [its alternatives]".[165] A doctor may give undue weight to his preference for a procedure, may exaggerate the benefits of the proposed procedure by raising and overstating the negative aspects of other alternatives.[166] In overall, a doctor may allow his own very strong preference for one option to "stand in the way of his giving a fair assessment of" the options available to his patient.[167]

As reflective of the treatment-disclosure distinction, there is a distinction drawn between *the duty to select/recommend/perform* a treatment procedure and the *duty to disclose/advise* treatment options. The traditional respect for medical opinions in exercising purely medical judgment dictates that legal authorities will be more deferential to a doctor's preference in selecting and recommending treatment. However, a patient's autonomy rather than a doctor's preference will prevail when the context is shifted to advising and disclosing treatment options.

---

[162] *Bauer v. Seager et al.*, [2000] 11 W.W.R. 621, 672–673, at [39]–[41] (Man. Q. B.).

[163] *Archer v. Galbraith*, 567 P.2d 1155, 1158 (Wash.App. 1977) (emphasis added).

[164] *KL v. Farnsworth* [2002] NSWSC 382, at [137] (In this case, the differences between two alternative methods were presented by the doctor to be no more than "cosmetic".).

[165] *KL v. Farnsworth* [2002] NSWSC 382, at [133].

[166] *Opinion 01/05619* (Health and Disability Commissioner, 31/7/2002) (failure to provide balanced information about alternatives).

[167] *KL v. Farnsworth* [2002] NSWSC 382, at [136].

Whatever the doctor's preference as to treatment options, the patient is entitled to be advised of other available options for treatment.[168] The doctor might decide against the alternate treatments or care, he might try to persuade the patient against utilising them, but he must disclose them when a reasonable person would want to know.[169] "Although a physician *may*, and indeed *should*, *express his opinion* regarding *preferable methods of treatment*, he may not neglect to *set out in a fair manner* the alternatives to the procedure he advocates."[170] A patient needs to be advised of a known treatment which others in the same specialty consider superior, even if the doctor does not agree.[171] If one physician does not prefer one alternative, he could have explained that to his patient, together with his reasons for preferring the proposed treatment.[172] The spirit of informed consent means that the patient should be given a chance to choose among "medically[173] acceptable options, not simply to accept or reject the medically preferable option" (Prillaman 1990, 47). A physician has a duty to mention not only alternatives that he recommends, but also "medically reasonable alternatives that the physician does not recommend".[174] Otherwise, the physician, by not discussing those alternatives that he does not favour, effectively makes the choice for the patient.[175] A doctor should guard against substituting his preferences for those of his patients. Different individuals have different lifestyles and value systems; have different risk-benefit balances and levels of risk aversion. What the law offers to the patients is not just a veto power to a physician's proposed and recommended procedure, but "a choice of undergoing the proposed treatment, or selecting an alternative process, or preferring refusal of all medical relief".

In this respect, New Zealand's law has a good performance. The Health and Disability Commissioner (HDC) Opinions have consistently emphasised that a health care provider's stance that one option is not a realistic option for his patient's condition – although consistent with mainstream opinion – does not absolve him of

[168] *Nattrass v. Weber*, 2007 ABQB 577; 53 C.C.L.T. 105, 118, at [39] (Alta. Q. B.); *Nattrass v. Weber*, 2008 ABQB 259, at [391] (citing *Seney v. Crooks*, 1998 ABCA 316 at para. 55; 223 A.R. 145); *Seney v. Crooks* (1998), 166 D.L.R. (4th) 337, 354, at [64] ("[T]he mere fact that a doctor prefers one treatment over another does not relieve him of the obligation to advise of other acceptable and known procedures.").

[169] *Martin by Scoptur v. Richards*, 531 N.W.2d 70, 81 (Wis. 1995) ("It may well be *a "medical decision"* under these circumstances to decide not to do a CT scan, or to decide not to hospitalize the patient in a hospital that can treat an intracranial bleed if it should occur. The statute on its face says, however, that the patient has the *right to know*, with some exceptions, that there are alternatives available."(emphasis added)).

[170] *Marino v. Ballestas*, 749 F. 2d 162, 168 (3d Cir 1984) (emphasis added).

[171] *Seney v. Crooks* (1998), 166 D.L.R. (4th) 337, 353, at [60].

[172] *Seney v. Crooks* (1998), 166 D.L.R. (4th) 337, 353, at [60].

[173] *Matthies v. Mastromonaco*, 733 A. 2d 456, 462 (N. J. 1999) (concerning alternatives that the physician does not recommend, the plaintiff alleging that the doctor did not inform her of the riskier, but potentially more successful, alternative of surgery).

[174] *Matthies v. Mastromonaco*, 733 A. 2d 456, 462 (N. J. 1999).

[175] *Downer v. Veilleux*, 322 A.2d 82, 90–91 (Me. 1974).

his obligation to provide his patient with full information that a reasonable patient in his patient's circumstances would expect to receive.[176] A health practitioner has an obligation to inform his patient of one available treatment option and facilitate discussion regarding this option even if he disagree with the viability of this option.[177] The fact that the patient self-referred for a specific operation did not excuse a surgeon from his obligation to provide information about alternative treatments.[178] Health care providers have a duty to provide balanced and fair information about the options available to a patient and to subordinate any private interests to the interests of the patient in making informed decisions about treatment. [179] Providers must take care not to present patients with unbalanced explanations of their condition and treatment options to support their treatment preferences. [180] Doctors have a responsibility "to locate their own opinions within the spectrum of professional views about possible procedures, and to contextualise their views, rather than simply preferring their own, which in effect deprives the patient of informed choice".[181]

3.6 Conclusion: A New Model

A health practitioner has considerable liberty in selecting and recommending a particular treatment option that he prefers, but in the context of disclosure of treatment options, he needs to keep an open mind towards treatment options that he does not personally favour. Confining the duty of disclosure only to recommended treatment options confuses the context of selection/recommendation with the context of disclosure, and does not pay enough respect to the distinctive aspects of the informed consent rule.

The law should adopt and promote an integrated approach (Fig. 3.2), which features *unbiased and contextualised presentation (disclosure), genuine and honest selection*, and *personalised and individualised recommendation* of treatment options, rather than follow a linear approach, under which disclosure only targets the selected/recommended procedure. The former approach not only shows respect

[176] *Opinion 02HDC18414* (Health and Disability Commissioner, 6/4/04) (failure to provide contextualised information); *Opinion 04HDC00031* (Health and Disability Commissioner, 24/2/2005) (Orthopaedic surgeon's failure to inform his patient of the option he did not favor).

[177] *Opinion 04HDC00031* (Health and Disability Commissioner, 24/2/2005) (Orthopaedic surgeon's failure to inform his patient of the option he did not favor).

[178] *Opinion 01HDC00755* (Health and Disability Commissioner, 9/5/2003) (failure to inform surgical weight loss options).

[179] *Opinion 03HDC19128* (Health and Disability Commissioner, 14/9/04) (failure to reveal that the provider's practice was subject to restrictions).

[180] *Opinion 03HDC19128* (Health and Disability Commissioner, 14/9/04) (failure to reveal that the provider's practice was subject to restrictions).

[181] *Opinion 02HDC18414* (Health and Disability Commissioner, 6/4/04) (failure to provide contextualised information).

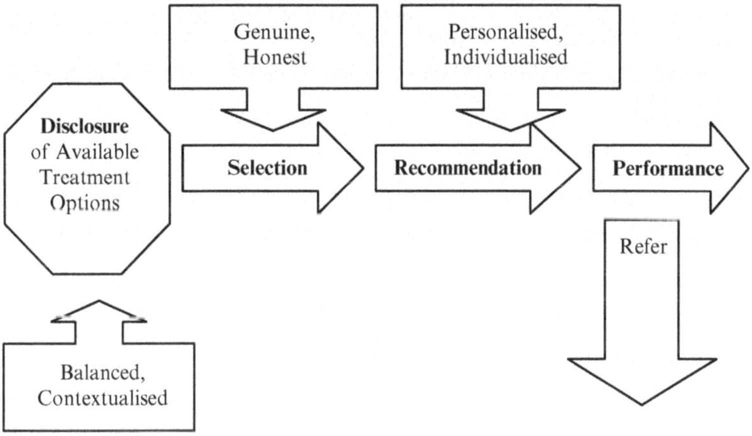

Fig. 3.2 Disclosure of alternatives: an integrated and sensitive model

for medical judgment, but also pays loyalty to the rationale of the doctrine of informed consent. It provides a clear context to the issue of information disclosure about alternatives. It indicates that the unbiased and contextualised disclosure of available treatment options is distinct from, and precedes, the selection, recommendation and performance of treatment.

References

Addison, Thomas. 2003. Negligent failure to inform: Developments in the law since *Rogers v. Whitaker*. *Torts Law Journal* 11: 165–195.

Brophy, Elizabeth. 2003. Does a doctor have a duty to provide information and advice about complementary and alternative medicine? *JLM* 10: 271–284.

Bulen, James A. 2003. Complementary and alternative medicine: Ethical and legal aspects of informed consent to treatment. *The Journal of Legal Medicine* 24: 331–358.

Downie, Jocelyn, Timothy Caulfield, and Colleen Flood. 2002. *Canadian health law and policy*, 2nd ed. Ontario: LexisNexis Butterworths.

Heywood, Rob, Ann Macaskill, and Kevin Williams. 2010. Informed consent in hospital practice: Health professionals' perspectives and legal reflections. *Medical Law Review* 18: 152–184.

King Jr., Joseph H. 1999. Reconciling the exercise of judgment and the objective standard of care in medical malpractice. *Oklahoma Law Review* 52: 49–84.

Krause, Joan H. 1999. Reconceptualizing informed consent in an era of health care cost containment. *Iowa Law Review* 85: 261–386.

Latham, Melanie. 2008. The shape of things to come: Feminism, regulation and cosmetic surgery. *Medical Law Review* 16: 437–457.

Maclean, Alasdair. 2006. Autonomy, consent and persuasion. *European Journal of Health Law* 13: 321–338.

Maclean, Alasdair. 2009. *Autonomy, informed consent and medical law: A relational challenge*. Cambridge: Cambridge University Press.

Manning, Joanna. 2004. Informed consent to medical treatment: The common law and New Zealand's code of patients' rights. *Medical Law Review* 12: 181–216.

Prillaman, Hunter L. 1990. A physician's duty to inform of newly developed therapy. *Journal of Contemporary Health Law and Policy* 6: 43–58.

Skene, Loane. 2004. *Law and medical practice: Rights, duties, claims and defences*, 2nd ed. Chatswood: LexisNexis Butterworths.

Skene, Loane. 2008. *Law and medical practice: Rights, duties, claims and defences*, 3rd ed. Chatswood: LexisNexis Butterworths.

Sones, Ben. 2006. A tale of two countries: Parallel visions for informed consent in the United States and the United Kingdom. *Vanderbilt Journal of Transnational Law* 39: 253–290.

Tomlinson, T. 1986. The physician's influence on patients' choices. *Theoretical Medicine and Bioethics* 7: 105–121.

Twerski, Aaron D., and Neil B. Cohen. 1992. Comparing medical providers: A first look at the new era of medical statistics. *Brooklyn Law Review* 58: 5.

Weir, Michael. 2003. Obligation to advise of options for treatment – Medical doctors and complementary and alternative medicine practitioners. *JLM* 10: 296–307.

Chapter 4
Filters and Circumstances

Abstract This chapter examines four elements that have the effect of narrowing a doctor's duty to inform. They are "medical knowledge", "the patient's condition", "materiality" and "causation". First, the existence and availability of treatment options is subject to medical knowledge and medical judgment. Second, in a real-life scenario, the menu of treatment options is subject to consideration of a particular patient's conditions and stage of illness. Third, a doctor only needs to disclose information about alternatives to which a reasonable person in the patient's position would have attached importance or significance. Fourth, if the duty to inform about alternatives is explored in the tort context, the issue of "causation" always forms a formidable barrier to success. Conversely, this chapter also examines the circumstances which create the potential for broadening a doctor's duty to inform about alternatives. These three circumstances are where procedures have an "elective" or "experimental" nature, or where the patient delivers an inquiry.

4.1 Introduction

In Chap. 2, I highlighted the distinct profile of information disclosure in health care delivery. In Chap. 3, I put the issue of disclosure of alternatives in a wide context of health care, highlighting the distinctive need in the area of information disclosure for a doctor to present a patient with balanced, unbiased and contextualised information about alternatives.

To require a doctor to disclose contextualised information could be burdensome. The patient's right to know must be harmonised with the recognition that an undue burden should not be placed on the physician.[1] In the area of information disclosure

[1] *Harnish v. Children's Hosp. Med. Center*, 439 N.E.2d 240, 243 (Mass. 1982). *See also*, *Stover v. Surgeons*, 635 A.2d 1047, 1051 (Pa. Super. 1993) (noting that the informed consent law "has always recognized the delicate balance which must be maintained between competing interests: the competent patient's right to medical self-determination and the need to alleviate the requirement that the physician disclose every risk to the patient for fear of liability").

X. Zhao, *The Duty of Medical Practitioners and CAM/TCM Practitioners to Inform Competent Adult Patients about Alternatives*,
DOI 10.1007/978-3-642-31647-0_4,

by doctors, there are limits to what society or an individual can reasonably expect of a physician.[2]

From the patient's perspective, the scope of disclosure includes any information that a patient would consider material to a treatment decision. No bright-line rules can be formulated to divide information that needs to be disclosed from which that does not. There is always an argument that it would be onerous to require a doctor to disclose information about the advantages and disadvantages of every available alternative. However, in the words of a court, such an argument "rings hollow".[3] The doctor is not required to give his patient "a short medical education",[4] or a "mini-course in medical science".[5]

First, the doctor's duty to inform has exceptions,[6] such as emergency,[7] "therapeutic privilege",[8] waiver,[9] and the information having already fallen within the

---

[2] *Harnish v. Children's Hosp. Med. Center*, 439 N.E.2d 240, 243 (Mass. 1982).

[3] *Stover v. Surgeons*, 635 A.2d 1047, 1051 (Pa. Super. 1993).

[4] *Canterbury v. Spence*, 464 F.2d 772, 782, n 27 (1972).

[5] *Cobbs v. Grant*, 502 P.2d 1, 11 (1972).

[6] *Holt v. Nelson*, 523 P.2d 211, 218–219 (Wash. App. 1974) (giving a list of nine exceptions, including exceptions based on "causation" and "materiality"); Michael A. Jones (2003), 525 (noting two exceptions to the patient-oriented standard of information disclosure: emergency and "therapeutic priviledge"); The National Health and Medical Research Council (NHMRC) *General Guidelines for Medical Practitioners on Providing Information to Patients* (2004) <http://www.nhmrc.gov.au/publications/synopses/e57syn.htm> (Last accessed 22 August 2010), pages 12 (contemplating three exceptions: (1) the doctor judges on reasonable grounds that the patient's physical or mental health might be seriously harmed by the information; (2) the patient expressly directs the doctor to make the decisions, and does not want the offered information; (3) in an emergency, when immediate intervention is necessary to preserve life or prevent serious harm, it may not be possible to provide information); Loane Skene (2008), 192–196 (exploring Australian law, envisaging two circumstances in which doctors are justified withholding information: (1) therapeutic privilege; (2) the patient has waived the right to be given information).

[7] *Holt v. Nelson*, 523 P.2d 211, 218–219 (Wash. App. 1974) ("A physician need not disclose the various alternatives and risks when an emergency situation exists requiring prompt treatment in the face of the immediate possibility of permanent injury or death and the patient is in no condition to determine for himself."); *Crouch v. Most*, 432 P.2d 250, 254 (N.M. 1967) ("It would indeed by most unusual for a doctor, with his patient who had just been bitten by a venomous snake, to calmly sit down and first fully discuss the various available methods of treating snakebite and the possible consequences, while the venom was being pumped through the patient's body.").

[8] *Holt v. Nelson*, 523 P.2d 211, 218–219 (Wash. App. 1974) ("A physician may not be responsible for failing to disclose a risk to a patient where full disclosure would be detrimental to the patient's best interests."); *Rogers v. Whitaker* (1992) 175 C.L.R. 479, 490 (HCA) (proposing the materiality test which ends with the qualification that "[t]his duty [to inform] is subject to the therapeutic privilege").

[9] *Holt v. Nelson*, 523 P.2d 211, 218–219 (Wash. App. 1974) ("A physician need not disclose the hazards of treatment when the patient has requested she not be told about the dangers, has insisted on remaining ignorant of the perils involved and had the patient been told, the explanation might increase the risks of treatment because of the psychological results of the apprehension that might be produced."). The "right not to know" is implicit in the right to know, since information is offered to a patient as an entitlement or opportunity rather than a duty to receive. It is arguable that there

patient's knowledge.[10] Those exceptions can be the defendant-doctor's defences.

Second, even under the patient-oriented standard of information disclosure, the duty to inform of alternative treatments does not require that the doctor describe every conceivable alternative to every detail of the proposed treatment. To avoid overburdening the medical profession, the law has attached many restrictive adjectives to the word "alternatives/options", such as "available",[11] "reasonable",[12] "possible",[13] "practical",[14] "medically acceptable or significant",[15] "reasonably available",[16] "viable",[17] "feasible",[18] "medically appropriate or acceptable",[19] "medically reasonable",[20] "medically recognized",[21] even "generally recognized and accepted".[22]

---

may be *a duty to know*. Manipulative impositions of information may occur when women should receive information about the stages of fetal development growth before they consent to abortion, as a strategy to discourage consent. *See*, Jocelyn Downie, Timothy Caulfield and Colleen Flood (2002), 155–156.

[10] *Holt v. Nelson*, 523 P.2d 211, 218–219 (Wash. App. 1974) ("A physician has no duty to disclose dangers which are commonly known and it can be assumed that the patient will know of them."; "A physician need not disclose to a patient risks of which he is already aware."); *Spencer By and Through Spencer v. Seikel*, 742 P.2d 1126, 1129 (Okl. 1987) (the patient knew abortion was an alternative to full term pregnancy).

[11] Health and Disability Commissioner (Code of Health and Disability Services Consumers' Rights) Regulation 1996, Schedule, right 6 (1)(b).

[12] Joan H. Krause (1999), 323, footnote 199.

[13] Joan H. Krause (1999), 324, footnote 200.

[14] Joan H. Krause (1999), 324, footnote 201.

[15] *Wachter v. United States*, 689 F. Supp. 1420, 1423–1424 (D. Md. 1988) (If one procedure "was not in general use, was not then known among surgeons to produce better results, and was not the subject of any definitive study showing it would be better than [the proposed treatment]", it will not be viewed as a "medically significant alternative".).

[16] *Doe v. Johnson*, 476 N.W.2d 28, 31–32 (Iowa 1991) ("any kind of truly informed consent must be based on knowledge of reasonably available treatment alternatives").

[17] *Valles v. Albert Einstein Medical Center*, 758 A.2d 1238, 1246–1247 (Pa. Super., 2000) ("[A] physician is only required to inform the patient of those medically recognized or *medically viable* alternate methods of implanting a device."(emphasis added)).

[18] *Thornton v. Annest*, 574 P.2d 1199, 1203 (Wash. App. 1978) ("Only feasible and available treatment must be disclosed.").

[19] Joan H. Krause (1999), 331, footnote 228.

[20] Joan H. Krause (1999), 331, footnote 229.

[21] *Stover v. Surgeons*, 635 A.2d 1047, 1051 (Pa. Super. 1993) ("Under our view of the doctrine of informed consent, a physician would need to discuss alternate prostheses and their relative merits only when the other prostheses represent *medically recognized alternatives*. In such happenstance, the patient is entitled to weigh the risks of the alternative treatments. When, however, there are no other *medically recognized* alternate prostheses, or, for that matter, any other *medically recognized* alternate treatments, the doctor need only discuss with the patient any risks relative to the sole, viable prosthesis [or treatment.]" (emphasis added)).

[22] *Moore v. Baker*, 989 F.2d 1129 (11th Cir. 1993) (finding that ethylene diamine tetra acetic acide chelation (EDTA) therapy was not a generally recognized and accepted alternative to carotid endarterectomy surgery).

In addition to that, in the first part of this chapter, I will highlight four primary factors that may narrow the seemingly broad scope of information disclosure. Those four factors can help to filter information about alternatives that needs to be disclosed. They apply to jurisdictions where a patient-oriented standard of information disclosure and the "materiality" test has been adopted. Some observations about "materiality" and "causation", made in the context of "risks" disclosure, are equally applicable to the context of disclosure of alternatives.

On the other side, although it has the patient-oriented standard of information disclosure and the materiality test, the rule of informed consent cannot be stated with marked precision. The nature and extent of the disclosure required by it depends in each case upon "the peculiar circumstances" giving rise to the duty.[23] There is complexity involved in exploring the varied circumstances of diverse cases. In the second part of this chapter, I take the liberty to explore three well-established circumstances where the duty to disclose information, including information about alternative treatment options, may be potentially enhanced. They are where the proposed procedure has an "elective" and "experimental" nature, or where the patient delivers an inquiry.

4.2 Filters

4.2.1 Medical Knowledge

As I observed in Chap. 2, the "materiality" test has two prongs: the "information" prong and the "materiality" prong. The information prong is profession-oriented and involves medical judgment. The information a physician should reasonably possess is the information possessed by the average qualified physician or, in the case of a specialty, by the average qualified physician *practicing that specialty*.[24] When approaching the issue of medical knowledge, there is a need to distinguish between different categories of doctors. GPs would be expected to know a wider range of medical information than specialists.

Medical knowledge includes actual knowledge (what a doctor has already known) and constructive knowledge (what a doctor should have known). Knowledge is constructive when it is shown that, by the exercise of reasonable or ordinary care or diligence, a person should have known a fact. If one ought to have known of a fact they are deemed to have knowledge of that fact. What a physician knows or should know involves professional expertise and can ordinarily be proved only through the testimony of experts.[25]

[23] *ZeBarth v. Swedish Hospital Medical Center*, 499 P.2d 1, 11 (Wash. 1972).
[24] *Harnish v. Children's Hosp. Med. Center*, 439 N.E.2d 240, 243 (Mass. 1982).
[25] *Harnish v. Children's Hosp. Med. Center*, 439 N.E.2d 240, 243 (Mass. 1982).

Proof of the *existence of alternatives* needs expert medical testimony because the existence of alternatives for a particular physical condition is beyond the knowledge of the layman and falls within the province of the medical profession.[26] The existence of expert medical testimony bolstering ordinary negligence claims cannot negate the need of expert testimony which presents insights on the viable alternatives.[27]

However, there are divergent opinions about who, medical experts or laypersons, decides the "feasibility" or "medical availability" of alternatives. Some USA case law indicates that establishment of the feasibility of alternative courses of treatment needs the help of expert testimony.[28] However, some observes that, where there is evidence of the existence of an available alternative course of treatment, it is for the jury to decide whether the alternative was feasible.[29] The "reasonable availability" of treatment alternatives is decided by the jury (laypersons).[30] These opinions differ on who is the final decision-maker of the "feasibility" or the "availability" of treatment options. They do not undermine the notion that medical knowledge or medical judgement plays an essential role in framing the "menu" or "availability" of treatment options. In my view, the final decision about the "availability" of a treatment option should be reserved to a *third party*, such as judges, rather than the defendant-doctors or the plaintiff-patients. In making that decision, judges need to attach substantial weight to medical expert evidence regarding the "feasibility" or "medical availability" of a treatment option.

---

[26] *Neal by Neal v. Lu*, 464, 530 A.2d 103, 111 (Pa. Super. 1987) (finding that "the weakest aspect of appellants' case, ..., is the lack of expert medical testimony on *three crucial issues*: the nature and magnitude of the undisclosed risks at issue, *the existence of any undisclosed alternative methods of treatment* and the nature and magnitude of the risks presented by the undisclosed alternatives" (emphasis added)); *Archer v. Galbraith*, 567 P.2d 1155, 1161 (Wash. App. 1977) ("Those elements which are the province of the medical profession must be established by the testimony of medical experts in the field of inquiry. Thus, *the existence of the risks and alternatives* which were present in the particular physical condition would be beyond the knowledge of the layman and would have to be established by medical testimony." (emphasis added)); *Sard v. Hardy*, 379 A. 2d 1014, 1025 (1977) (noting that expert testimony was necessary to prove risks and alternatives).

[27] *Neal by Neal v. Lu*, 464, 530 A.2d 103, 112 (Pa. Super. 1987) (finding that although there was expert testimony which explained how the surgery deviated from acceptable procedure, the testimony offered none of the necessary expert insight on risks and viable alternatives).

[28] *Downer v. Veilleux*, 322 A.2d 82, 92 (Me. 1974) ("Expert testimony is necessary to show, not only what the inherent risks of a particular treatment were, but also, that the alternative courses of treatment were feasible. (citations omitted)"); *Stelle v. St. Paul Fire & Marine Insurance Co.* 371 So 2d 843, 849 ("expert medical testimony was necessary ... to establish the feasibility of the procedure.").

[29] *Archer v. Galbraith*, 567 P.2d 1155, 1161 (Wash. App. 1977) ("The concept of choice presupposes that alternatives exist, and where there is evidence of the existence of an available alternative course of treatment, it is for the jury to decide whether the alternative was feasible, whether the physician told the patient about the possible benefits and dangers of pursuing the alternative course, whether a reasonably prudent patient would have chosen the different course of treatment had the alternative been disclosed, and whether the failure to disclose caused injury.").

[30] *Doe v. Johnson*, 476 N.W.2d 28, 31–32 (Iowa 1991) ("Just as with determining whether a risk is 'material', the decision about 'reasonable availability' is best left for the jury except in the rare case where overwhelming evidence compels a verdict as a matter of law.").

4.2.2 The Particular Patient's Condition

Disclosure of alternative treatments means disclosure of alternatives for the *particular patient* and not a recital of medical casebook theory. The extent of disclosure will depend in part on the symptoms and general physical condition actually presented by the patient.[31] A doctor is not obliged to discuss with the patient, *in the abstract*, courses of treatment precluded by his condition.[32] The severity of the patient's condition may ward off any possible alternative treatments.[33] A doctor may argue that the alternative that the doctor omitted to disclose may be not a realistic or real alternative procedure, or the patient has no effective choice, having regard to the patient's conditions and the purpose of treatment. For a particular patient who has particular conditions and is at a particular stage of illness, the number of available treatment options may not be prohibitively large (*see*, Appendix 2).

In the Pennsylvania case of *Valles v. Albert Einstein Medical Center*,[34] although there were six routinely medically recognized sites utilized for the placement of the catheter,[35] the focus of the Superior Court of Pennsylvania was on whether any sites, other than the right subclavian vein which the defendant adopted, was viable in light of the patient's "particular condition" and "particular health considerations".[36] The court rejected the viability of other alternative sites other than the right subclavian vein in light of the patient's particular health concerns, holding that there was no genuine issue of disputed fact that alternate viable sites existed for placement of the catheter.[37] In the Washington case of *Thornton v. Annest*,[38] the patient, complaining that the surgeon unnecessarily removed her fallopian tubes, claimed that the defendant failed to inform her of "four possible alternative courses of action: antibiotic treatment, surgical aspiration of pus, hysterosalpingogram x-ray test, and consultation with a gynecologist".[39] Considering "the physical condition of [the] particular patient", the Court of Appeals of Washington denied the availability and feasibility of all these four alternatives.[40]

---

[31] *Keogan v. Holy Family Hospital*, 622 P. 2d 1246, 1254–1255 (Wash. 1980) (footnote 3).

[32] *Downer v. Veilleux*, 322 A.2d 82, 93 (Me. 1974) (agreeing that the defendant was not negligent for "failing to disclose nonexistent alternatives" to the plaintiff).

[33] *Ziegert v. South Chicago Community Hospital*, 425 N.E.2d 450, 459 (Ill. App. 1981) (the plaintiff's assertion that the defendant failed to inform her of possible alternatives to surgery did not win support from the court because medical witness testified that the severity of plaintiff's varicose veins obviated any possible alternative treatment).

[34] *Valles v. Albert Einstein Medical Center*, 758 A.2d 1238 (Pa. Super., 2000).

[35] *Valles v. Albert Einstein Medical Center*, 758 A.2d 1238, 1247 (Pa. Super., 2000) ("the left and right femoral veins; the right and left internal jugular veins; and the right and left subclavian veins").

[36] *Valles v. Albert Einstein Medical Center*, 758 A.2d 1238, 1247 (Pa. Super., 2000).

[37] *Valles v. Albert Einstein Medical Center*, 758 A.2d 1238, 1247 (Pa. Super., 2000).

[38] *Thornton v. Annest*, 574 P.2d 1199 (Wash. App. 1978).

[39] *Thornton v. Annest*, 574 P.2d 1199, 1203 (Wash. App. 1978).

[40] *Thornton v. Annest*, 574 P.2d 1199, 1203 (Wash. App. 1978).

4.2.3 *"Material" Information*

The "materiality" test is another way of tipping the balance between protecting the patients' right to know and avoiding overburdening the doctors. Patients' interests are accommodated by the rule that a physician owes to his patient the duty to disclose in a reasonable manner all significant medical information that the physician possesses or reasonably should possess that is *material* to an intelligent decision by the patient whether to undergo a proposed procedure.[41]

As I mentioned before, the "materiality" test has two prongs: the information prong, which is profession-oriented, and the materiality prong, which is patient-oriented. The determination of "materiality" is one that lay persons are qualified to make without the aid of an expert. The issue here is whether a reasonable person in the plaintiff-patient's position, not the defendant-doctor, would have attached significance to the undisclosed information. The word "materiality" means that the information that falls within a doctor's duty to disclose should be information to which the patient would have attached "significance". Materiality, therefore, is the cornerstone upon which the doctor's duty to disclose is based.[42] That standard obligates the doctor to disclose only that information material to a reasonable patient's informed decision. Physicians need not disclose information which has "no apparent materiality or relationship to the patient's decision".[43] Nor they need to disclose "all foreseeable risks and possible alternatives, of whatever significance or magnitude".[44] The "materiality" test under the patient-oriented standard of disclosure may play some roles in tightening the scope of alternatives disclosure.[45]

Under the materiality test, "materiality" is usually said to be "the *significance* a reasonable person, in what the physician knows or should know is his patient's position, would attach to the disclosed [information] in deciding whether to submit or not to submit to surgery or treatment."[46] The notion of "significance" is far from favourable to claimants.

As I will show below, although the issues of materiality and causation are interrelated, the materiality test does not have to reach the higher threshold applicable to the causation. That means "[i]t is not necessary when determining materiality

[41] *Harnish v. Children's Hosp. Med. Center*, 439 N.E.2d 240, 243 (Mass. 1982).

[42] *Wheeldon v. Madision*, 374 N. W. 2d 367, 375 (S.D. 1985).

[43] *Holt v. Nelson*, 523 P.2d 211, 218–219 (Wash. App. 1974).

[44] *Kinser v. Elkadi*, 674 S.W.2d 226, 232 (Mo. App. S.D. 1984).

[45] *Matthies v. Mastromonaco*, 733 A. 2d 456, 461 (N. J. 1999).

[46] *Wilkinson v. Vessey*, 295 A.2d 676, 689 (R.I. 1972) (emphasis added). For similar formulation, *see also, Rogers v. Whitaker* (1992) 175 C.L.R. 479, 490 (HCA); *Fitzpatrick v. White* [2008] 3 IR 551, 564 at [35] per Kearns J. I replace "risk or risks" with "information" because of my belief that the materiality test should be applied to all kinds of information disclosure.

to establish that the patient, reasonable or otherwise, *would not have had the treatment* had he or she been warned of the risk in question."[47] A lower threshold may be sufficient in the context of materiality of a risk. The Australian authorities have demonstrated a willingness to lower the threshold. It was said that the doctor needed to disclose "information that is *relevant* to a decision or course of action";[48] the duty to disclose extends "only to matters which might *influence* the decisions of a reasonable person in the situation of the patient",[49] not to risks "which are not *sufficiently substantial* to be a factor in the decision-making of a reasonable person".[50]

However, it was recently clarified that, although the test of materiality is "somewhat lower" than that of causation, "it is necessary that the reasonable patient or particular patient respectively would have been *likely seriously to consider and weigh up the risk* before reaching a decision on whether to proceed with the treatment."[51] The information "may be classified as 'immaterial' in the sense of being unimportant or so rare that they can be safely ignored."[52] The recent formulation of the significance of information in Australia is still a stringent one, raising the threshold from just being "relevant" to being of serious relevance, although lower than the 'but for' causation threshold.

4.2.4 Information "Making a Difference"

There is no need for a doctor to disclose risks which are not material to a patient's decision. In medical negligence law, a doctor can also establish that the patient would have proceeded whether he had been informed of the risks or not.[53] This context involves the issue of causation. I prefer to maintain a distinction between the stage of the *duty* to inform, including the consideration of information "materiality", and the stage of *causation*. However, the fact is that many plaintiff-patients suffer from not being able to prove the causation between the undisclosed information and damages. Causation has an effect on the issue of what kinds of information, if undisclosed, would expose a doctor to a potential tort liability.

---

[47] *Rosenberg v. Percival* [2001] 205 CLR 434, 459, per Gummow J. (emphasis added).

[48] *Rogers v. Whitaker* (1992) 175 C.L.R. 479, 494 (HCA), per Gaudron J. (emphasis added).

[49] *F. v. R.* (1983) 33 S.A.S.R 189, 192, per King C.J. (emphasis added). *See also, Williams v. Golden*, 699 So.2d 102, 107 (La. App. 4 Cir. 1997) ("A physician is required to advise a patient of any material consequences which would *influence* the decision of a reasonable person in the patient's condition." "The second prong … is … to decide whether the probability of that type harm is a risk which a reasonable patient would *consider* in deciding on treatment." (emphasis added))

[50] *F. v. R.* (1983) 33 S.A.S.R 189, 192, per King C.J. (emphasis added).

[51] *Rosenberg v. Percival* [2001] 205 CLR 434, 459, per Gummow J. (emphasis added).

[52] *Rosenberg v. Percival* [2001] 205 CLR 434, 482, per Kirby J.

[53] *Holt v. Nelson*, 523 P.2d 211, 218–219 (Wash. App. 1974).

In most jurisdictions, the battery/assault approach[54] does not win favour in the context of informed consent.[55] Causation is still a filter additional to the "materiality". What the court gave to the plaintiff-patients with a broad duty of disclosure, they often take back with their very narrow rule of causation.[56] The causation requirement is one of the major factors that lead to low success rate in informed consent litigation, even in jurisdictions where the patient-oriented standard of disclosure is adopted (Chalmers and Schwartz 1993, 154). Although running the risk of blurring the distinction between the duty to inform and causation, many cases had sent the message that there was no duty to inform where the patient, even if informed of the alternative, would not have opted for that treatment.[57] Causation is still a big obstacle to the recovery.[58]

Because this is a law book, when I mention causation, I mean causation in law, not causation in science. Moreover, my discussion about causation mainly focuses on *factual* causation. In practice, while proof of factual causation can be a very real problem, questions of remoteness of damage (legal causation) are comparatively rare in medical negligence actions (Jones 2003, 376).

Materiality and causation are interrelated. They share some factors that are of relevance to both issues, such as the likelihood and gravity of the risk, the patient's need for the treatment and the availability of alternatives.[59] The same considerations

---

[54] In jurisdictions, such as Pennsylvania, where the concept of "technical assault" or "technical battery" was adopted and lack of informed consent was a legal equivalent of no consent, the plaintiff needs only to pass the materiality test, without a need to prove the existence of causation. Once the patient who underwent surgery demonstrated, and jury found, that patient was not advised of *material* facts, risks, complications, and alternatives to surgery which reasonable men would have considered *significant* in deciding whether to have operation, the causation inquiry ended, and the sole issue remaining was determination of damages. *See*, *MacDonald v. U.S.*, 767 F.Supp. 1295, 1312 (M.D.Pa. 1991); *Gouse v. Cassel*, 615 A.2d 331 (Pa. 1992); *MacDonald v. U.S.*, 767 F.Supp. 1295 (M.D.Pa. 1991); *Sagala v. Tavares*, 533 A.2d 165, 168 (Pa. Super. 1987).

[55] In *SEM v. The Mid Yorkshire Hospitals NHS Trust* [2005] EWHC B3 (QB), the plaintiff raised an alternative approach of "trespass to the person" in the informed consent context. The High Court's attitude towards this alternative route was: It "[has] a radical impact on the law and practice which currently underlie clinical litigation. …, if this alternative approach were right, there would have been no need for *Chester v. Afshar* to have proceeded to the House of Lords. Ms Chester, who will have been represented by specialist counsel, would have recovered damages without persuading the court to stretch conventional notions of causation to the limit, as she had to do in order to succeed." *See*, *SEM v. The Mid Yorkshire Hospitals NHS Trust* [2005] EWHC B3 (QB), at [59], [60].

[56] *Rosenberg v. Percival* [2001] 205 CLR 434, 484, per Kirby J.; Don Chalmers and Robert Schwartz (1993), 155.

[57] *Seney v. Crooks* (1998), 166 D.L.R. (4th) 337, 355, at [69] (noting that "[i]n many of the cases, it is not the duty that is the problem, but causation").

[58] *SEM v. The Mid Yorkshire Hospitals NHS Trust* [2005] EWHC B3 (QB) (admitting the defendant's negligence in failing to advise the patient about alternative treatments, but rejecting the existence of causation).

[59] Thomas Addison (2003). *See also*, *Rosenberg v. Percival* [2001] 205 CLR 434, 452, per Gummow J. His Honour reasoned that considerations of degree and severity of risk are central to both the question of whether the risk was material and whether the failure to warn of a risk was causative. His Honour continued that "[i]f the Court comes to one view of those considerations when dealing with the materiality issue, the same view will direct the resolution of the causation issue."

which support an inference of materiality with respect to the scope of disclosure may also support an inference of proximate causation.[60] In the context of a patient's revealing particular concerns by inquiring, thus invoking the subjective limb of the *Rogers* test, the standards of both materiality and causation are more likely to be simultaneously satisfied.

However, materiality and causation are different. Even in those jurisdictions where both information materiality and causation are considered in the informed consent cases, causation is seen as a separate issue, distinct from the issue of negligence. There is a "substantial difference" between a finding that the risks of which a medical practitioner has not warned a patient are *material*, and a finding that, had the patient been given the necessary warning, he *would have elected not to undergo the surgery*.[61] The phrase "likely to attach significance to", as it appears in both limbs of the *Rogers* test, does not present a threshold issue of the same nature as to that presented by the issue of causation.[62] It is not necessary when determining materiality of risk to establish that the patient, reasonable or otherwise, would not have had the treatment had he been warned of the risk in question. [63] The threshold for materiality is somewhat lower than that for causation.

Materiality should not be confused with causation. The law should not give the doctors the misleading information that only the risks which would cause the patient to forego the treatment must be divulged.[64] An undisclosed fact could be significant in that a reasonable patient would seriously weigh it in determining whether to undergo the treatment, yet still ultimately choose to consent to the treatment.[65] Depending on the circumstances in a particular case, a patient may well decide to have an operation even when he is advised of significant risks involved in that operation.[66] There is a possibility that while a combination of two or more risks might cause the patient to forgo the proposed treatment, a single risk might not have that effect.[67] There is also a possibility that, while a risk or risks may be material to a patient's decision, the unavailability of alternative treatments may make the proposed treatment ultimately inevitable and may

[60] *Sard v. Hardy*, 379 A.2d 1014, 1025 (Md. 1977).

[61] *Elbourne v. Gibbs* [2006] NSWCA 127 (Beazley, Ipp and Basten JJA, 24 May 2006, unreported, BC200603589), at [6], per Ipp JA (not agreeing the practice of equating a finding that the plaintiff would have *attached significance to* the risks of which he was not warned in making up his mind whether to have surgery with a finding that, had he been warned of those risks, he *would not have had the surgery*).

[62] *Rosenberg v. Percival* [2001] 205 CLR 434, 458 (Gummow J).

[63] *Rosenberg v. Percival* [2001] 205 CLR 434, 458 (Gummow J).

[64] *Canterbury v. Spence*, 464 F.2d 772, 788, n. 89 (1972).

[65] *Arena v. Gingrich*, 733 P. 2d 75, 80 (Or. Ct. App. 1987), Deits J., dissenting. *See also*, *Rosenberg v. Percival* [2001] 205 CLR 434, 463, per Gummow J. (finding that, even if the risk was material, the failure to warn was not causative).

[66] *Elbourne v. Gibbs* [2006] NSWCA 127 (Beazley, Ipp and Basten JJA, 24 May 2006, unreported, BC200603589), at [8], per Ipp JA.

[67] *Canterbury v. Spence*, 464 F.2d 772, 788, n. 89 (1972).

leave the patient no other choice but to proceed with the proposed one (Addison 2003, 190–193).

The patient's condition, the need for treatment and the availability of alternatives have greater relevance in relation to causation than to materiality.[68] On the one hand, a properly advised patient has the right to reject treatment despite the prognosis. The law should hesitate to pre-empt a value judgment which should be properly be made by the patient. Lack of alternatives could be presented as a consideration which diminishes, rather than overwhelms, the significance of the risks and the possibility of establishing causation. On the other hand, the more life-threatening the patient's condition, the more necessary the proposed procedure, the less likely causation will be established.[69] If there are no feasible alternative treatments, the possibility of establishing causation is slim.[70] A reasonable patient would not have foregone the only available treatment in favour of no treatment whatsoever.[71] Furthermore, the nature of the proposed treatment and its alternatives may also be presented as a consideration relevant to causation. The courts would be less prepared to accept that a patient would forgo a relatively safe procedure and opt for a much more immediately hazardous radical procedure.[72] The claimants would be

---

[68] *Elbourne v. Gibbs* [2006] NSWCA 127 (Beazley, Ipp and Basten JJA, 24 May 2006, unreported, BC200603589), per Basten JA, para. [84]; *Chappel v. Hart* (1998) 195 CLR 232, 247–248, per McHugh J. (noting that some evidence may suggest that no causal connection between breach of the duty to warn and the harm exists, such as evidence which indicates that the plaintiff would not have acted on the warning because of *lack of choice* or personal inclination, or, evidence that *no alternative course of action* would have eliminated or reduced the risk of injury; quoted by *Rosenberg v. Percival* [2001] 205 CLR 434, 462, per Gummow J.).

[69] *Brandon v. Karp*, 490 N.Y.S.2d 904, 906 (N.Y.A.D. 3 Dept. 1985) (finding that "plaintiff [] was afflicted with a recurrence of meningitis, which X rays indicated may have been caused by an infected sinus. It was unquestionably necessary for [the plaintiff] to locate the source of the *illness endangering plaintiff's life*, and the sinus wash, according to expert testimony, was *the logical way* to determine if the sinus was infected and was *the means least challenging to plaintiff's health.* The jury could, therefore, rationally have found from this circumstance that a reasonably prudent person in plaintiff's position would have undergone the procedure even if fully informed." (emphasis added)).

[70] *Contreras v. St Luke's Hospital*, 144 Cal.Rptr. 647, 653 (Cal. App. 1978) (the patient raising a choice between an operation and a cast; court noting that use of a cast without an operation was not a feasible alternative treatment).

[71] *Plumber v. State, Dept. of Health & Human Resources*, 634 So.2d 1347, 1351 (La. App. 3 Cir.,1994) (patient undergoing chemotherapy to prevent the cancer from returning or spreading; court finding that the patient was not a candidate for radiation therapy, another widely used cancer treatment, and noting that "[i]n conventional medical wisdom, the alternative to chemotherapy in this situation would simply be to not undergo chemotherapy"; court finding that "a reasonable patient in plaintiff's position, *one who had recently undergone serious cancer removal surgery for which the question of whether the cancer had spread was pathologically inconclusive*, would not have declined chemotherapy had the material information concerning the prospects of success and the lack of known alternative treatment been disclosed to her").

[72] *Niblack v. U.S.*, 438 F. Supp. 383, 388–389 (D.C.Colo. 1977) (plaintiff alleging that the risk of aseptic necrosis inherent in the proposed Decadron therapy (steroid therapy) was not revealed; court noting that other treatments, i.e. radical surgical procedures, entailed greater risks to the plaintiff; court observing that "[w]hen faced with a choice of probable blindness due to scarring,

more likely to succeed in establishing causation where the procedures involved could be more readily described as "elective", such as sterilisation or cosmetic surgery, and the balance of risks between the recommended treatment and the alternative treatments (or the alternative of forgoing any treatment) are more finely balanced, and the medical justification for proceeding is less overwhelming (Jones 2003, 557–558).

In a context involving disclosure of *alternatives*, the situation becomes even more complex. Canadian case law has indicated that where the defendant's breach of duty consists of a failure to advise the patient of an alternative procedure, the claimant will have to prove both that he would have opted for the alternative procedure ("decision causation") and that the alternative procedure would probably have produced a better outcome than the treatment he has actually undergone ("injury causation").[73] The injury may be a fully expected outcome of the recommended treatment. The crucial question is whether it would have been avoided if the plaintiff has been informed of and had chosen the undisclosed alternative treatment. Following the ordinary threshold for causation, the patient is required to establish that the proposed treatment would not have been performed if the alternatives had been disclosed. And, at least, the patient needs to establish the undisclosed alternative might have caused less injury to the patient than the recommended treatment, or the alternative course of action would have eliminated or reduced the risk of injury.[74] This would invite considering the controversial theory of "loss of chance"[75] in medical negligence cases.

---

and possible renewal of brain swelling, the remote risk of aseptic necrosis would not have caused a reasonable patient to reject corticosteroid treatment. Nor would the slight risk of aseptic necrosis cause a reasonable patient to opt for much more immediately hazardous radical surgical procedures.").

[73] *Seney v. Crooks* (1998) 166 D.L.R. (4th) 337, 355; *Sicard v. Sendziak*, 2008 ABQB 690, at [116] (Court of Queen's Bench of Alberta) ("Causation for non-disclosure of alternative treatments involves two steps. First, the Plaintiff establish that a reasonable patient in similar circumstances would have chosen the alternative treatment if properly informed. If a failure to disclose would not have affected the decision to proceed, causation will not be established. Secondly, if the patient would not have chosen to proceed, the Court must consider whether the damage would have been avoided if the alternative had been chosen."). The "decision causation" answers the question of whether a hypothetical reasonable patient, equipped with the undisclosed information, would have opted against the procedure proposed, recommended and performed by the physician. The "injury causation" concerns the question of whether the patient's decision to undergo the procedure caused any harm or whether the patient's decision to forgo the procedure, or to undergo an alternative treatment, could avoid the harm.

[74] *Chappel v. Hart* (1998) 195 CLR 232, 247–248, per McHugh J.; *Rosenberg v. Percival* [2001] 205 CLR 434, 462, per Gummow J. (indicating that evidence that no alternative course of action would have *eliminated or reduced the risk* of injury may suggest that no causal connection between breach of the duty to warn of a risk and the harm existed).

[75] The approach allows evaluation of the plaintiff's loss in terms of comparing the chances of suffering harm (given the breach has occurred) against those that would have existed (if the breach is hypothesised away), even if the chance falls short of 51 %. The approach was applauded as inviting "a more empirical calculation of loss" and offering "outcomes that are more accurate and fair to all concerned". However, the approach has not found favour in medical negligence cases, partly because, in such cases, destiny has taken its course, making an analysis by reference to chance inappropriate or unnecessary. *See, Chappel v. Hart* (1998) 195 CLR 232, 274–275, per Kirby J.

It may be easier for a claimant to succeed on causation where there were other treatment options, especially conservative treatment options, which carried a lower, or no, risk (Jones 2003, 558). Where the proposed treatment and alternatives had *comparable* respective advantages and disadvantages, disclosure of alternative treatments would not have affected a reasonable person's choice of treatments.[76] Where the alternative treatment is more risky than the proposed treatment, or has more disadvantages than the proposed one, the chance of fulfilling the task of proving causation becomes slimmer.

In some jurisdictions, the evidence that, if the undisclosed information had been disclosed, a patient would have had taken a "*second look*" at the necessity of the contemplated procedure is not enough to establish causation, and establishing causation needs a higher threshold, i.e. a reasonable patient in plaintiff's position would "*forego*" the procedure.[77] The plaintiff may testify that, had he been informed of the undisclosed information, he would have *chosen a different doctor*, although he would *not* have *foregone* treatment.[78] As in a situation where the plaintiff claims that, if informed, he would have *declined* treatment, this kind of allegation may be rejected by invoking the necessity of avoiding the 20/20 hindsight bias.[79]

---

[76] *Guebard v. Jabaay*, 452 N.E. 2d 751, 758 (Ill. App. 2 Dist. 1983) (plaintiff alleging that, for her knee injury, she was never informed that an alternative treatment (to the Hauser procedure) involving removal of the patella (knee cap), known as a patellectomy, would yield the desired improvement in function; court finding that the Hauser procedure was also a good treatment, and "although a patellectomy would usually allow the leg good functioning, plaintiff would not have been able to lead as active a sports life as she might have been able to lead with successful Hauser surgery").

[77] *Dessi v. U.S.*, 489 F. Supp. 722, 730 (D.C.Va., 1980).

[78] In the United States case of *Mitchell v. Kayem*, the patient claimed that, had the inherent risks of the procedure been disclosed to her, she would have sought a *second opinion* and had the procedure performed at *a different facility by a more experienced surgeon*, and argued that the phrase "different course of treatment" includes not only having a different medical procedure, but also having a different surgeon performing the same medical procedure. However, the Court of Appeals of Tennessee, by applying an objective standard of causation ("a reasonably prudent person in the patient's position"), encountered no difficulty to deny the patient's argument. In the eyes of the court, "treatment or procedure" refers only to the *type* of procedure and the *manner* of performing it, not to the *person* performing the procedure. The court concluded that,

> [The risk involved] was unavoidable; the only alternative to [the patient] was the same surgical procedure performed by another surgeon; and the generally accepted occurrence rate for these unknown risks and complications of the procedure applies *uniformly* to all qualified surgeons, regardless of their skill level. Therefore, the possibility of the risks and/or complications occurring to [the patient] would not have been different in the hands of another surgeon. The possibility of [the patient's] outcome was *the same in the hands of any and all qualified surgeons*. (emphasis added)

See Mitchell v. Kayem, 54 S.W.3d 775, 781–782 (Tenn. Ct. App. 2001).

[79] *Revord v. Russell*, 401 N. E. 2d 763, 767 (Ind App. 1980) (noting that "[i]n either situation 'we doubt that justice would be served by placing the physician in jeopardy of one patient's bitterness and disillusionment'"). *See also, Geoghegan v. Harris* [2000] 3 IR 536, 551, per Kearns J (noting that patients "may be prejudiced by bitterness and the wisdom of hindsight"); *ZeBarth v. Swedish Hospital Medical Center*, 499 P.2d 1, 13 (Wash. 1972) ("The law does not encourage formulaic or catechistic responses, but looks instead to substance. For the plaintiff to say, after the fact of injury, that he would have refused the initial massive dose, adds little to the credible proof. Although admissible, a statement of that nature is little more than a transparently self-serving response,

More fundamentally, it does not dovetail nicely with the orthodox legal principles of causation. If the patient would have had to undergo the same operation at some stage in any event, if the risk that occurred was inherent in an operation of that sort and could occur irrespective of the experience or skill of the surgeon performing the operation, establishing causation under the conventional logic of causation is almost impossible.[80] Such facts would be translated into arguments that the acts or omissions of the defendant would have "made no difference" to the plaintiff's course of action, and the risk occurring is just a mere "coincidence" rather than an event causally connected to the defendant's negligence.[81]

However, in the context involving the "second opinion" argument, the English law and Australian law seem to have loosened the conventional approach to causation in order to accommodate and reinforce the purpose of the duty to inform.[82]

---

inviting the recital of a formulated catechism to put form above substance."). In *SEM v. The Mid Yorkshire Hospitals NHS Trust* [2005] EWHC B3 (QB), the patient asserted that, if she had been offered a menu of treatments, she would have chosen the least invasive form of intervention. The High Court treated this kind of self-serving evidence with great caution. The court held that the patient acting as a reasonable patient and even if one leaves out of the equation her particular psychiatric condition, would have been likely to follow the surgeon's advice. The failure to warn cases inevitably involve a hypothetical question because they need to construct what the patient would have done if the physician had not been negligent or if a warning had been given. The patient's evidence as to what he would have done is hypothetical in nature and "is very likely to be affected, no matter how honest he is, by his own particular experience" (*Rosenberg v. Percival* [2001] 205 CLR 434, 462, per Gummow J. (quoting *Gover v. South Australia and Perriam* (1985) 39 SASR 543, 566)). To address the hindsight problem inherent in the subject test of causation, the Australian Law of Negligence Review Report recommended that "in determining causation, any statement by the plaintiff about what they would have done if the negligence had not occurred should be inadmissible" (Commonwealth of Australia *Review of the Law of Negligence: Final Report (2002) (Ipp Review)* page 114, para. 7.40). The civil liability legislation followed this recommendation (for example, Section 11 of *Civil Liability Act 2003* (Qld)).

[80] Such as, *Chappel v. Hart* [1998] HCA 55; (1998) 195 CLR 232;156 ALR 517; (1998) 72 ALJR 1344 (HC of A).

[81] *Chappel v. Hart* (1998) 195 CLR 232, 246–247, per McHugh J.

[82] *See, McAllister v. Lewisham and North Southwark Health Authority* [1994] 5 Med L R 343; *Chappel v. Hart* [1998] HCA 55; (1998) 195 CLR 232;156 ALR 517; (1998) 72 ALJR 1344 (HC of A); *Chester v. Afshar* [2004] 4 All ER 587, [2004] UKHL 41; [2005] 1 AC 32. The Australian case of *Chappel v. Hart* presented such a scenario: A doctor performed a surgery on a patient with due skill and care but without having warned of a risk of the surgery. The risk eventuated. The patient had asked the doctor questions about possible risks of the operation. The patient would have required surgery of the kind performed at some time in any event. If she had been properly warned of the risk in question, *she would have delayed the surgery and had it performed by the most experienced surgeon in the field.* The court decided by a majority of three (Gaudron, Gummow and Kirby JJ) to two (McHugh and Hayne JJ) that the patient was entitled to recover substantial damage from the surgeon for the physical injuries suffered as a result of the operation performed on her. The majority opinion holders (Gaudron and Kirby JJ) stressed that the hands of a more experienced surgeon would have reduced the risk of the kind of injury that occurred. There were two main factual differences between *Chappel v. Hart* and *Chester v. Afshar.*

In a context involving alternative treatment options, the arguments based on "second opinion", the timing of the procedure and the identity of the practitioner may have more persuasive power. Had a patient been properly warned and given adequate information, he would have sought a further opinion. It is probable that a second opinion would have revealed the availability of alternative courses.[83] In establishing causation, the plaintiff can satisfy the court that, if he had received proper advice, he would have elected for something other than the proposed surgery which was performed on the chosen date; or, alternatively, that he would have *deferred* having that surgery until such time as *other methods of treatment* had been tried and had failed.[84] In a situation where surgery is not the only option in a plaintiff's case and more conservative treatments are also available, if a warning relating to surgery had been appropriately given, it may be more probable than not that the plaintiff would have at least *deferred/delayed* surgery to enable him to consider alternatives to surgery until *other possibilities* had been tried.[85]

There is one final point to be made about causation. It concerns the informational context in which the patients' reactions or attitudes ought to be explored in establishing the "decision" causation. In *SEM v. The Mid Yorkshire Hospitals NHS Trust*,[86] the patient asserted that, if she had been offered a menu of treatments, she would have chosen the least invasive form of intervention.[87] However, in considering causation, the court noted that, although the doctor would have provided *a menu of approaches*, she would have *recommended* the proposed procedure. [88] Based on the belief that patients do normally follow their doctors' recommendation, the

In the former case, the patient would inevitably have had to undergo the same or almost identical surgical procedure, whereas, in the latter case, *alternative treatments or different form of surgical procedure* would have been open to the patient. Secondly, in the former case, the plaintiff insisted that she would have gone to *the most experienced surgeon* who could be found and a more experienced surgeon would have performed any future procedure, whereas, in the later case, there was no such an assertion. In *Chester v. Afshar*, the House of Lords decided by a majority of three (Lord Steyn, Lord Hope and Lord Walker) to two (Lord Bingham and Lord Hoffmann) that, on policy grounds, the test of causation was satisfied. Under the *Chester* rule, the claimant only needs to demonstrate that she would have postponed the procedure and thereby avoided the risk on that particular occasion. There is no need to further demonstrate that she would never have undergone the procedure carrying the risk that has materialised. Therefore, the judge's further reconstruction of what the claimant would have further responded after the initial postponement is rendered unnecessary.

[83] *Elbourne v. Gibbs* [2006] NSWCA 127 (Beazley, Ipp and Basten JJA, 24 May 2006, unreported, BC200603589), per Basten JA.

[84] *SEM v. The Mid Yorkshire Hospitals NHS Trust* [2005] EWHC B3 (QB), at [36].

[85] *Henderson v. Low* [2001] QSC 496 (Dutney J, 21 December 2001, unreported, BC200108193), at [37] (involving elective surgery; there being more conservative treatment such as ceasing jogging and perhaps physiotherapy or medication; noting that none of other options had been tried except medication).

[86] *SEM v. The Mid Yorkshire Hospitals NHS Trust* [2005] EWHC B3 (QB).

[87] *SEM v. The Mid Yorkshire Hospitals NHS Trust* [2005] EWHC B3 (QB), at [52].

[88] *SEM v. The Mid Yorkshire Hospitals NHS Trust* [2005] EWHC B3 (QB), at [53].

court held that the patient would have been likely to follow the surgeon's advice.[89] This line of thinking confuses the context of information disclosure and context of recommendation at the stage of causation.

A better approach was evident in another English case – *Birch v. University College Hospitals NHS Trust*,[90] which involved the disclosure of alternative procedures. In this case, the court's analysis of causation surrounded the claimant's two seemingly conflicting pieces of evidence. First, the claimant did take the attitude that "doctor knows best", and if the two procedures had been explained, she would not know the difference between them, and if the defendant had *recommended* the catheter angiogram by saying that it was necessary and best to exclude an aneurysm, *she would have followed it*.[91] Another piece of evidence had the effect that if the claimant had been given *the choice between an MRI (without a risk of stroke) and an angiogram (with a risk of stroke)*, she would have chosen an MRI.[92] The court accepted the latter evidence.[93] What needs to be highlighted is that, in establishing the causation element, the court distinguished the context of doctors' recommendation from that of balanced information disclosure. As the judge observed,

> The issue is *not* whether she would have understood the nature of the procedures or what she would have *in the face of a recommendation* as to catheter angiography. The crucial issue is what she would have decided when given *a dispassionate account* along the lines indicated, in other words of the two procedures for imaging, and the advantages and disadvantages of each for someone with her background. … It is clear to me that had she been given *a fair and balanced account* in the way I have held was necessary she would have rejected catheter angiography in favour of MRI. In other words, properly informed she would have declined the procedure leading to her stroke. (emphasis added)[94]

Therefore, causation was established. Obviously, the *Birch* approach of looking at causation within a wider context of all available treatment options makes more sense than the *SEM* approach of exploring causation only within the recommended treatments. It further manifests the need to draw a distinction between recommendation and information disclosure both at the stage of the duty to inform and at the stage of causation.

---

[89] *SEM v. The Mid Yorkshire Hospitals NHS Trust* [2005] EWHC B3 (QB), at [53]. *Compare, Reibl v. Hughes* (1980) 114 D.L.R. (3d) 1, 16 (S.C.C.) ("Merely because medical evidence establishes the reasonableness of a recommended operation does not mean that a reasonable person in the patient's position would necessarily agree to it, if proper disclosure had been made of the risks attendant upon it, balanced by those against it. The patient's particular situation and the degree to which the risks of surgery or no surgery are balanced would reduce the force, on an objective appraisal, of the surgeon's recommendation.").

[90] *Birch v. University College Hospitals NHS Trust* [2008] EWHC 2237 (QB).

[91] *Birch v. University College Hospitals NHS Trust* [2008] EWHC 2237 (QB), at [23], [80].

[92] *Birch v. University College Hospitals NHS Trust* [2008] EWHC 2237 (QB), at [23], [80].

[93] *Birch v. University College Hospitals NHS Trust* [2008] EWHC 2237 (QB), at [81].

[94] *Birch v. University College Hospitals NHS Trust* [2008] EWHC 2237 (QB), at [81].

4.3 Circumstances

4.3.1 "Elective" Procedures

All surgery, in a sense, is elective.[95] Non-elective surgery may arise when (1) the gravely wounded, the gravely ill may be unconscious but in urgent need of surgery; (2) a patient's condition may be such as to demand surgical intervention as the only hope for survival.[96]

It is safe to say that the elective procedures, as opposed to the essential procedures, should not be subjected to "a less stringent" standard of disclosure.[97] However, there are disputes over whether elective procedures should be subjected to a more stringent standard of disclosure. Basically, there are two lines of authorities. One line of authorities espouses the proposition that there is no higher standard of disclosure in the case of elective surgery than with non-elective procedures, although the fact that there is no emergency making the surgery imperative is a relevant consideration.[98] Some courts believed that the significance of the "elective" nature lies in the stage of causation, rather than the duty to inform.[99]

However, it seems that most courts stand in another camp. This line of authorities stands for the proposition that the elective nature of one procedure has an impact on the level of information disclosure. If the procedure is optional, discretional, or cosmetic rather than therapeutic, and may be deferred with relatively minor risk to the patient, then the level of informed consent increases.[100] "[W]here the decision

---

[95] Michael A. Jones (2003), 546 (noting that the courts in England have been reluctant to accept a distinction drawn between the elective and the non-elective procedures, citing *Sidaway v. Bethlem Royal Hospital Governors* [1985] 1 All ER 643, [1985] AC 871 where all operations are deemed as elective because the patient always has a choice).

[96] *Walsh v. Family Planning Services Ltd. & Ors.* [1992] 1IR 496, 518, per McCarthy J. An extreme of elective surgery would be what is purely cosmetic – simply to improve the natural appearance rather than to remedy the physical results of injury or disease. A like argument may be advanced in respect of contraceptive surgery, male or female. Such surgery does not have a direct effect on the health or well being of the patient nor in prolongation of life.

[97] *Lynn G. v. Hugo*, 710 N.Y.S.2d 334, 337 (A.D. 1 Dept. 2000) (involving elective cosmetic surgery; defendant failing to suggest a less invasive alternative; the court holding that the doctor who performs the elective cosmetic surgery has no less of a duty than other doctors to disclose risks of, and alternatives to, the treatment offered).

[98] *Groves v. Morton*, 44 C.C.L.T. (3d) 108, at [89]–[90] (Ont. S. C. J.) (supporting the stance that there is no higher degree of disclosure required in cases of purely selective surgery).

[99] The "elective" nature of the therapy involved can be of little significance in determining what is the duty of care with regard to disclosure of adverse risks. Where the "elective" nature of the procedure becomes of major significance is in the context of establishing *causal connection* between an established negligent failure to disclose and the plaintiff's decision to undergo the therapy. *See*, *Geoghegan v. Harris* [2000] 3 IR 536, 558 (quoting Mr. John White's "Medical Negligence Actions" at p. 190).

[100] *Skeels (Estate of) v. Iwashkiw*, [2006] 11 W.W.R. 632, 659 at [156] (Court of Queen's Bench of Alberta).

was really an elective one, … the informational component must be very high, as the patient had other viable and easily exercisable options."[101] Onerous obligation is necessary in an industry where there is considerable opportunity for financial gain and a reluctance to dwell on risks for fear that the consumer will not proceed with the contemplated procedure.[102]

The fact that the proposed treatment is elective may heighten the need and level of information disclosure, including *disclosure of the "elective" nature, disclosure of risks and disclosure of alternatives*. First, if a procedure is "elective", a doctor should inform his patient of *the "elective" nature* of the procedure.[103] Second, the extent of the obligation to warn about material risks will vary with the elective nature of the surgery concerned. The level of *disclosure of risks* is heightened in the context of elective procedures.[104]

Third, the duty to explain and explore *alternative treatments* is enhanced when the surgery is elective.[105] When an elective surgery is proposed, alternative methods and techniques must be explained and their comparative risks should be disclosed.[106] If surgery is merely one therapeutic option, or of elective nature, there is a need to disclose *conservative, nonsurgical* treatment.[107] The fact that surgery is elective could make the fact-finder to conclude that nonsurgical option is "a more prudent

---

[101] *Skeels (Estate of) v. Iwashkiw*, [2006] 11 W.W.R. 632, 659 at [161] (Court of Queen's Bench of Alberta).

[102] Kelly Scott 2009, 649. *See also, Opinion 07HDC05410* (Health and Disability Commissioner, 28/04/2008) (general surgeon, cosmetic surgery), p. 16 (noting that there is an inherent conflict of interests because the surgeon stands to benefit financially if the consumer agrees to proceed it).

[103] *Delzell v. Moore*, 587 N.E.2d 1131, 1135–1136 (Ill. App. 5 Dist., 1992) (noting that if surgery was not mandatory, or merely one optional course of treatment, a doctor should let his or her patient know *the "elective" nature* of the surgery); *Poole v. Morgan*, [1987] 3 W.W.R. 217, 262 (Alta. Q.B.) (observing that whether the proposed procedure is essential or elective, like whether it involves any innovative techniques or experimental drugs, must voluntarily be disclosed by the physician, as such information would be material to the reasonable patient).

[104] *See, Walsh v. Family Planning Services Ltd. & Ors.* [1992] 1 IR 496, 510, per Finlay C.J. (noting that the obligation to give warning of the possible harmful consequences of a surgical procedure which could be said to be at the other end of the scale to the extent to which it is elective, may be more stringent and more onerous); *White v. Turner* (1981), 31 O.R. (2d) 773, 792–793 (where an operation is elective, even *minimal* risks must be disclosed to the prospective patients, since the frequency of the risk becomes much less material when the operation is unnecessary for his medical welfare); *Groves v. Morton*, 44 C.C.L.T. (3d) 108, 130–131 (where the surgery is purely aesthetic and elective rather than urgent or just necessary for medical reasons, the duty to inform of *rare* complications is heightened); Loane Skene (2008), 184–186 (exploring the Australian case law; observing that if a procedure is regarded as not clinically "necessary", more information should be given because an ordinary person would consider even relatively uncommon risks significant if there is no "need" to have the procedure).

[105] *Ross v. Welsh*, 2003 CanLII 27587 (ON S.C.), at [134].

[106] *Poole v. Morgan*, [1987] 3 W.W.R. 217, 262 (Alta. Q.B.).

[107] *Delzell v. Moore*, 587 N.E.2d 1131, 1135 (Ill. App. 5 Dist., 1992) (in addition to surgery, there involved the option of conservative treatment through diet, exercise, quitting smoking and medication to stop leg claudication).

course" than surgery, or conclude that "a reasonable person might reject surgery in favor of the conservative treatment".[108]

4.3.2 "Experimental" Procedures

There is no bright line that can be drawn between "conventional" or standard procedures and "experimental" or "innovative" procedures. Experimental and conventional treatments represent the ends of a spectrum rather than clearly dichotomous categories. In deciding whether a procedure is experimental or conventional, one may adopt a higher threshold, such as a "general acceptance" standard. However, to avoid unnecessarily hindering advances in science, some courts guard against too readily classifying some innovative procedures as experimental ones.[109] To hold that every new development in medical methodology was "experimental" would be to discourage advances in the field of medicine.

When the procedure favoured by a doctor diverges from or falls outside the ambit of professionally acceptable practices, and it poses a significant risk, or its level of therapeutic effectiveness is different from those associated with acceptable practices, this may present a dangerous situation for the patient. An improvident therapeutic

[108] *Delzell v. Moore*, 587 N.E.2d 1131, 1135 (Ill. App. 5 Dist.,1992) ("After all, if surgery were the only reasonable alternative, if the nonsurgical approach were something that no reasonable person would select if advised of all the significant perils and alternatives, then the surgery would not really have been "elective" at all."). This involves the consideration of the issue of causation. As to the causation and damages in the context of optional/elective surgery, in this case, the Appellate Court of Illinois observed that

> We acknowledge that following a conservative, nonsurgical course of treatment would not necessarily have saved plaintiff's leg in the long run. She may ultimately have had to suffer amputation whether she underwent surgery or not. Nevertheless, there was ample evidence from which the jury could reasonably have concluded that having the surgery when she did not only failed to alleviate any of her pain, but *actually hastened the time when amputation became unavoidable*. Once the surgery was performed, there was no turning back. *The possibility of any less drastic remedial measures was eliminated.* At the very least, the medical evidence established that what should have been optional surgery was directly responsible for causing her to lose her leg *earlier than she would otherwise have had to*. The *premature loss of a limb* is unquestionably a cognizable basis for recovering damages in a medical malpractice action … (emphasis added)

See Delzell v. Moore, 587 N.E.2d 1131, 1135–1136 (Ill. App. 5 Dist., 1992).

[109] For example, in the Canadian case of *Zimmer v. Ringrose*, the court drew a distinction between "a truly 'experimental' procedure" on the one hand, where "no therapeutic benefit is intended to accrue to the participant" and "[t]he subject is simply part of a scientific investigation designed to enhance human knowledge", and a procedure which is "directed towards achieving a therapeutic end" and which is "experimental only in the sense that it represented an innovation … which were relatively untried", on the other hand. The court also drew a distinction between the technique that is "medically unsound" and the technique that merely requires further clinical study. *See, Zimmer v. Ringrose* (1981) 124 D.L.R. (3d) 215, 222–225.

preference expressed by the doctor that lies outside the ambit of more time-honoured modes of therapy may needlessly endanger a patient (King 1999, 79). Therefore, a more guarded approach is needed.

It is a well-established principle that, when advising experimental or non-conventional treatments, the physicians should inform their patients of *conventional treatment options* (if they are available), and *separately* let their patients know *the novel or experimental or non-conventional nature* of the suggested procedure.

First, when mentioning that the experimental procedure is necessary, the physician should not hide the dark side of that kind of procedure. A patient must always be fully informed of the *experimental nature* of the treatment.[110] A doctor should apprise his patient of the fact that one technique had not been approved by the medical profession,[111] or the proposed operation was not in the mainstream of treatment.[112] The absence of established data regarding risks of an experimental procedure cannot constitute an excuse for being silent on the negative side of story.[113] There is no reason to accord more leniency to experimental procedures than to established procedures.[114] Second, the experimental or innovative nature of one procedure reinforces the need of physicians disclosing its *alternatives*, especially *conventional, conservative and well-established alternatives*. The patient should be informed of the full range of professionally acceptable alternatives.

This heightened duty is a reflection of the law's concerns about the *uncertainty* surrounding the benefit-risk profiles of non-conventional options, about the *conflicts*

---

[110] *Ahern v. Veterans Administration*, 537 F.2d 1098, 1102 (C.A.N.M. 1976) (the Court of Appeals observing that "in order for a physician to avoid liability by engaging in drastic or experimental treatment, which exceeds the bounds of established medical standards, his patient must always be fully informed of the experimental nature of the treatment and of the foreseeable consequences of that treatment."(emphasis added)); *See also, Estrada v. Jaques*, 321 S.E.2d 240, 255 (N.C. App. 1984) (holding that "reasonable standards of informed consent to an experimental procedure require disclosure to the patient that the procedure is experimental"); *Heinrich v. Sweet*, 308 F.3d 48, 69 (C.A.1 (Mass.), 2002) (observing that "a doctor who proposes an experimental course of treatment must not only tell the patient about the treatment and its consequences, but must also inform the patient that he is conducting an experimental treatment and that the patient is part of a study").

[111] *Zimmer v. Ringrose* (1981) 124 D.L.R. (3d) 215, 223.

[112] Michael A. Jones (2003), 546 (citing *Newbury v. Bath District Health Authority* (1998) 47 B.M.L.R. 138, QBD which observed that a patient was entitled to be told that a proposed operation was not in the mainstream of treatment "if it involved a method which was entirely new or even relatively untried", or "if the method had fallen out of use because it had been shown to be defective and was not accepted by a responsible body of opinion").

[113] *Heinrich v. Sweet*, 308 F.3d 48, 69 (C.A.1 (Mass.), 2002) ("The doctor must not only tell the patient the *known risks* of the treatment, as he would in *a conventional setting*, but must also inform the patient that there may be *unknown risks*."(emphasis added)).

[114] *Estrada v. Jaques*, 321 S.E.2d 240 (N.C. App. 1984) ("If the health care provider has a duty to inform of known risks for established procedures, common sense and the purposes of the statute *equally require* that the health care provider inform the patient of any *uncertainty regarding the risks* associated with experimental procedures. This includes *the experimental nature of the procedure* and *the known or projected most likely risks*." (emphasis added)).

of interest a practitioner may have in deciding whether a patient is a good candidate for one new option, and about the potential alienation from conventional options that may ensue. Doctors' financial and career benefits from adopting experimental treatments were often cited as a reason for subjecting the patient's consent to undergo such a treatment to heightened scrutiny. Furthermore, because conventional technologies have been tested by and received confirmation from experience, society would do well to deem the time-honoured conventional knowledge less hazardous than the new ones (Parchomovsky and Stein 2008, 311). That justifies the legal rules that induce individuals to use conventional knowledge and exercise caution with innovations.

By requiring mention of the availability of conventional treatments and the non-conventional nature of experimental procedures, the law tries to save the vulnerable patients from forgoing conventional interventions and unknowingly participating in experimental procedures. Disclosure of the experimental nature of a procedure and its conventional alternatives may alert patients about the possibility of a doctor having conflicts of interest on treatment.

The legal requirements that doctors proposing experimental or innovative procedures should inform patients of the "experimental" nature of those procedures and the conventional alternatives to them have raised some concerns. First, they have chilling effects on innovations. Labelling the new treatment or the innovative procedure as "experimental" is likely to frighten away some patients by undermining their confidence in the treatment (Parchomovsky and Stein 2008, 302–303). Second, they do not place innovative treatments on an informational par with conventional ones (Parchomovsky and Stein 2008, 309–310). Some case law shows hesitancy in imposing on providers of conventional medicine a parallel obligation to inform patients about available experimental treatments.[115] Moreover, the lines separating the novel from the conventional are frequently drawn by owners and producers of conventional technologies, who are motivated to obstruct innovations in order to maintain their superiority on the market (Parchomovsky and Stein 2008, 311–312).

The orthodoxy-reinforcing rule has two drawbacks. First, by giving conventional options overwhelming weight and priority, it may hinder innovation and disadvantage medical advances. Second, it is based on the assumption that a treatment option can be easily and clearly defined as conventional or experimental. It ignores the reality that treatment options may present a spectrum rather than a bright-line distinction between standard and experimental interventions. There is a need to treat both conventional and innovative treatments according to their *merits* and adopt a pure risk-benefit approach that gives no deference to convention, rather than simply attach a *label* "conventional" or "experimental" to treatments.

---

[115] *Moore v. Baker*, 989 F.2d 1129 (11th Cir. 1993) (Georgia's informed consent law required disclosure only of alternatives that are "generally recognized and accepted by reasonably prudent physicians").

4.3.3 Patients' Inquiry

In approaching the scope of information disclosure, a question is always raised: Should a distinction be drawn between the *silent* patient and the *inquisitive* one, or "should the scope of the doctor's duty vary according to whether he is giving the information in response to a question raised by the patient or is merely giving unsolicited advice?" (Robertson 1981, 118) And, if yes, what a kind of distinction?

The emergence of the "inquisitive patient" doctrine is due to the restrictive nature of the duty of disclosure imposed on medical practitioners by the *Bolam* test.[116] The New Zealand's case of *Smith v. Auckland Hospital Board*[117] drew a clear distinction between volunteering a warning and responding to questions, indicating that its rule was only confined to the latter context which involved "particular",[118] or "special and somewhat exceptional",[119] or "somewhat uncommon"[120] circumstances. The two contexts had different rules. On the one hand, the patient's "prerogative to decide for himself whether he would submit to the proposed procedures" "placed the doctor under a duty to give a careful and reasonably accurate reply to" the patient's *direct inquiry* as to the risk involved.[121] On the other hand, "*if not asked a specific question*, a doctor would have *no duty to volunteer a warning* as to any risk involved in [a] particular procedure. …"[122] The doctor's duty of care in "the realm of diagnosis or technique" and in "the area of advice" should be measured by the same standards and upon the same principles.[123] The patient's "inquiry" was even interpreted in a restrictive fashion. The patient's inquiry, which only expected a general answer, did not "enlarge" the duty of care, or "alter the scope of the duty".[124]

---

[116] *Geoghegan v. Harris* [2000] 3 IR 536, 563, per Kearns J. (noting that, under the patient-oriented standard of disclosure or the materiality test, there is no room for the operation of the "inquisitive patient" test, because it is subsumed within the new rule).

[117] *Smith v. Auckland Hospital Board* [1964] NZLR 241; revd [1965] NZLR 191.

[118] *Smith v. Auckland Hospital Board* [1964] NZLR 241; revd [1965] NZLR 191, 213, per McGregor J.

[119] *Smith v. Auckland Hospital Board* [1965] NZLR 191, 216, per T.A. Gresson J.

[120] *Smith v. Auckland Hospital Board* [1965] NZLR 191, 219, per T.A. Gresson J.

[121] *Smith v. Auckland Hospital Board* [1965] NZLR 191, 227–228, per T.A. Gresson J.

[122] *Smith v. Auckland Hospital Board* [1964] NZLR 241; revd [1965] NZLR 191, 205–206, per Turner J. (emphasis added).

[123] *Smith v. Auckland Hospital Board* [1964] NZLR 241, 247–248 ("Clearly the evaluation of the risks inherent in the treatment and their significance in relation to the malady to be treated is essential for the provision of balanced information and warnings. This must involve the doctor in the same exercise of judgment founded upon the same *medical experience and knowledge* as he exercises in the field of technique. In this area of his responsibility, therefore, his duty of care should logically be measured by the same standards and upon the same principles."(emphasis added)). In hindsight, this paragraph rightly observed that the appreciation and evaluation of information ("risks inherent in the treatment and their significance in relation to the malady to be treated") is subject to "medical knowledge" or "medical judgment", but failed to appreciate that whether those information are *significant to the patient's decision* does not involve medical judgment.

[124] *Smith v. Auckland Hospital Board* [1964] NZLR 241, 252–254.

The old distinction drawn between "volunteering information" and "responding to patients' questions" was also echoed in the Australian case of *F. v. R.*[125] It reflects a misconceived thinking that "the extent of the duty to disclosure must depend greatly upon the patient's expressed or apparent desire for information".[126] In the *Sidaway* case, several of their Lordships expressed an awareness of the distinction drawn between volunteering information and responding to questions, and they qualified their pro-doctor views in the context involving an "inquisitive patient".[127] Those qualifications can be read to mean that the *Bolam* test has no application where the patient has asked for the information.[128]

The context of patients' delivering inquiries has made great contribution to the development of informed consent principles. It is interesting to note that many breakthroughs of informed consent law occurred in the context of physicians facing with *an inquisitive patient.*[129] With the introduction of the patient-oriented standard of information disclosure or the "materiality" test, any real consideration of the "inquisitive patient" doctrine will be subsumed by heavy and onerous obligations of disclosure imposed by those tests.[130]

The consideration of a patient's right to decide has persuaded the court to make a "presumption in favour of disclosure" even in the context of volunteering information.[131] The *Rogers*-like formulations of the "materiality" of information contemplate two contexts: volunteering information to ordinary or *reasonable* patients and responding to concerns revealed by *particular* patients. In the materiality test jurisdictions, the law requires that the patient be informed of any material risk, whether he inquires or not.[132] The doctor's proactive duty to inform is not "dependant upon

[125] *F. v. R.* (1983) 33 S.A.S.R 189, 192–193, per King C.J. (When facing with patient's questions or other signals of desire for information, the doctor will "ordinarily" "give a truthful and careful answer". But in the context of volunteering information, the issue of disclosure becomes an "exercise of a careful professional judgment", and the law does not require a doctor to "inflict on his patients information which they do not seek and do not want".).

[126] *F. v. R.* (1983) 33 S.A.S.R 189, 192, per King C.J. (citing the New Zealand case of *Smith*).

[127] Lord Templeman acknowledged that asking questions will make a difference. Lord Diplock confined his view to the context of "volunteering unsought information" by indicating that "if the patient in fact manifested this attitude by means of questioning, the doctor would tell him whatever it was the patient wanted to know". Lord Bridge also added a caveat to his argument by saying that "when questioned specifically by a patient of apparently sound mind about risks involved in a particular treatment proposed, the doctor's duty must, in my opinion, be to answer both truthfully and as fully as the questioner requires". *See, Sidaway v. Bethlem Royal Hospital Governors* [1985] 1 All ER 643, 659, [1985] AC 871, 895–902.

[128] *Compare*, Shaun D. Pattinson (2006), 113 (revealing a view which opined that a "general" enquiry, even a "specific" enquiry, cannot be divorced from the *Bolam* test).

[129] Such as: *Rogers v. Whitaker* (1992) 175 C.L.R. 479 (HCA); *Chappel v. Hart* [1998] HCA 55; (1998) 195 CLR 232;156 ALR 517; (1998) 72 ALJR 1344 (HC of A); *Chester v. Afshar* [2004] 4 All ER 587, [2004] UKHL 41; [2005] 1 AC 32.

[130] *Geoghegan v. Harris* [2000] 3 IR 536, 563.

[131] *F. v. R.* (1983) 33 S.A.S.R 189, 192–193, per King C.J.

[132] *Geoghegan v. Harris* [2000] 3 IR 536, 563.

questions asked by the patient who might be completely unaware of the issues to which his or her mind should be addressed".[133]

The "presumption in favour of disclosure" can be rebutted by a patient's waiver of information, although the question of whether a patient has a "right" to ignorance involves controversy.[134] The law has no reason to ask medical practitioners to overload a patient who expresses his wish of waiver with too much information. It seems that there is another "defensive medicine" tendency[135] in the context of information disclosure, in addition to that in the context of diagnosis and treatment, both of which may be attributable to the law and could be detrimental to the doctor-patient relationship. If the underlying purpose of informed consent law is to respect and protect patient autonomy, there is no reason why the law should not recognise a patient's right of waiver, although the law still needs to define what constitutes a valid waiver.

There was a line of case law which suggested that doctors have a discretion as to the terms and manner in which they deal with patient's questions (Jones 2003, 551–554). Some judges subjected the question of whether or not to answer truthfully the patient's inquiry to medical judgment.[136] It was claimed that the question of what a plaintiff should be told in answer to a general enquiry "cannot be divorced from" the *Bolam* test.[137] The *Bolam* test was regarded as relevant even in relation to the question of what answers are properly to be given to specific enquiries.[138]

---

[133] *Rosenberg v. Percival* [2001] 205 CLR 434, 477, para. 141, per Kirby J. Medical practitioners need to realise that patients may sometimes feel intimidated and vulnerable in the face of medical expertise and show reluctance to ask questions for fear of embarrassment caused by poor understanding, anxiety over difficulties articulating questions appropriately, or a reluctance to engage deriving from the notion that the "doctor knows best". *See*, Rob Heywood, Ann Macaskill, Kevin Williams (2010), 165.

[134] Shaun D. Pattinson (2006), 119–120 (exploring moral points of view about whether force-feeding the basic or minimal information to competent patients is desirable).

[135] The "defensive medicine" in the context of information disclosure was defined to mean that medical practitioners expose the patient to *excessive* information about risks and alternatives that may be unnecessary in the circumstances, and refuse to acknowledge the patient is entitled to waive their right to certain information, and their practices are justified on the ground of the need to avoid legal liability. *See*, Rob Heywood, Ann Macaskill, Kevin Williams (2010), 168.

[136] In the Australian case of *F v. R*, the South Australian Supreme Court explicitly identified the patient's desire for information as a factor in determining what a careful and responsible doctor would disclose. King CJ sent a little mixed message on how to respond to a patient's inquiry. First, "[a]n express and apparently seriously intended request for information necessary to make an informed decision will *ordinarily* place the doctor under an obligation to give a truthful and careful answer." Second, King CJ envisaged that "there may be circumstances" "in which reasonable care for the patient may justify or even require an evasive or less than fully candid answer even to a direct request; and a doctor may in the exercise of his skill and judgment reasonably judge that a request is made, not out of a desire for a frank answer, but out of a desire for reassurance". Third, King CJ hastened to add that a doctor should "hesitate long" before withholding the full truth as to real risks of harm or failure when asked to explain them. *See*, *F. v. R.* (1983) 33 S.A.S.R 189, 192.

[137] *Blyth v. Bloomsbury Health Authority* [1993] 4 Med. L.R. 151, 157.

[138] *Blyth v. Bloomsbury Health Authority* [1993] 4 Med. L.R. 151, 157.

However, according to the subjective limb of the *Rogers* test, the doctor needs to be very sensitive and responsive to a particular patient's individual concerns. In a situation which approximated to *Roger*'s, where the plaintiff "expressly and unequivocally brought to the defendant's notice" his concerns, there was "the clearest need" for him to be fully informed as to the procedure and its risk.[139] The patient asking questions will make the doctor "aware" of matters the patient considers significant, and the questions should be answered as fully as possible (Skene 2008, 186). If a patient asks specifically about risks, that will "almost always" place the doctor under an obligation to give a truthful and careful answer (Skene 2008, 196). The only exception is the little-used "therapeutic privilege".[140]

The inquisitive nature of a patient would impact on the extent or the scope of information disclosure. In a situation where a patient asks specific questions, the extent of disclosure required will "obviously be greater".[141] The courts would consider it more culpable to deliberately evade a request for information than to fail to volunteer that information (Pattinson 2006, 114). The judges might be expected to be more likely to intervene to override professional standards or practice in the context of the patient seeking information than in relation to the doctor volunteering information (Montgomery 2003, 249).

The notion that a patient's making inquiries would broaden the scope of information disclosure undoubtedly will apply to disclosure of alternatives. It seems that, even in a jurisdiction where common law regarding the duty to inform overwhelmingly focuses on risks rather than alternatives, if a patient expressed his wish to have more information about comparative failure rates of different treatment options by request or enquiry, the court is likely to broaden the doctor's duty to inform to encompass disclosure of information about alternative treatment options.[142]

---

[139] *Dunning v. Scheibner*, NSW (Common Law Division), Wood J, 15 February 1994, unreported, BC9402391, at [85].

[140] *Rogers v. Whitaker* (1992) 175 C.L.R. 479, 487 (HCA) ("Subject to the therapeutic privilege, the question would require a truthful answer.").

[141] *Zimmer v. Ringrose* (1981) 124 D.L.R. (3d) 215, 221. For Canadian law, *see*, *Reibl v. Hughes* (1980) 114 D.L.R. (3d) 1, 12 (S.C.C.) (what the doctor knows or should know that the *particular* patient deems relevant to a decision whether to undergo prescribed treatment *goes equally to* his duty of disclosure as do the material risks recognized as a matter of required medical knowledge); *Patterson v. Hryciuk*, 2004 ABQB 934, (2004) 45 Alta. L.R. (4th) 219, at [46] (citing *Hopp v. Lepp*, [1980] 2 S.C.R. 192 at 209–210; *Videto v. Kennedy*, (1981), 125 D.L.R. (3d) 127 at 133–134 (Ont.C.A.)) ("[A] patient's expressed interest in the procedure, questions asked and concerns expressed may elevate the duty of the doctor to discuss special or unusual risks though they may be extremely rare or remote."). Canadian scholars even argued that doctors may have to ask patients relevant questions to make them reasonably informed, and failure to ask these questions may constitute negligence in law. *See*, Jocelyn Downie, Timothy Caulfield and Colleen Flood (2002), 136–137.

[142] The Australian case of *Burke v. Humphrey* involved disclosure of the risks (failure) of tubal ligation and its alternative (vasectomy). The court observed that, "especially *in the absence of any request for further information or detail*", "a general statement" that there was a small risk of failure "adequately fulfilled [the] duty of care", and there was no obligation for the defendant "to specify the precise failure rate". The court also noted that there was no obligation for the defendant to compare the relative merits and/or failure rates between a vasectomy and tubal ligation.

4.4 Conclusion

The purpose of the first half of this chapter is to relieve doctors that they are not exposed to an unlimited, unpredictable and unrealistic duty to disclose. First, their medical knowledge, including actual knowledge and constructive knowledge, would determine the parameters of available treatment options. Second, they are entitled to tailor the availability of treatment options to a particular patient's conditions. Third, only the undisclosed information that is material to a patient's decision and has a causal link to the patient's injury has the possibility of exposing a doctor to the negligence liability.

I devote some time to highlight the differences between "materiality" and "causation". First, they are at the different stages of determining a defendant-doctor's tort liability. The issue of information "materiality" is still at the stage of determining whether there is a breach of the *duty* to inform. Second, they have different focuses. The "materiality" is determined by gauging the influence of the undisclosed information on a patient's *decision* to undergo the proposed procedure. However, causation is explored in the sense of the probability of the undisclosed information changing a patient's *decision* and avoiding or reducing a patient's *injury*. Third, they have different thresholds. The threshold for the information being "material" to a patient's decision is basically lower than that for the undisclosed information being a "causative" factor to a patient's injury. Therefore, the scope of information that falls within a doctor's *duty* to disclose would be *broader* than the scope of information that succeeds in satisfying the *causation* test and finally exposes a doctor to a tort liability. Or, putting it in another way, there will be some amount and kinds of information that are *material* to a patient's decision, and therefore have fallen within a doctor's *duty* to disclose, but, cannot satisfy a more stringent *causation* test, and therefore do not matter anyway in the sense of subjecting a doctor to a tort liability. This gap demonstrates the difference between the tort approach, which involves consideration of both materiality and causation, and other approaches, which do not involve causation, such as the New Zealand's Code approach. (For the comparison of the Tort approach with the New Zealand's Code approach, *see*, Chap. 9).

In this part, I also observe some courts' moves to loosen the traditional causation test and other courts' insistence on the conventional approach to causation. This is an evolving area. In my view, the steps of loosening the conventional test of causation in the context of informed consent would not go very far. Once incorporated into a tort framework, the doctrine of informed consent, even if promising to protect a patient's right to choice, cannot easily evade the constraints of traditional negligence principles.

The court reasoned that *"[i]n the absence of any request for advice on alternative procedures*, including a vasectomy, it is asking too much,... to expect a gynaecologist in the defendant's position to lay the foundations of some kind of feasibility study upon which the patient may or may not wish to embark." These observations invite a converse thinking. In addition, at the causation stage, the court thought it "highly unlikely in ... that [the plaintiff] or her husband would have contemplated his undergoing a vasectomy *in lieu of or in addition to* her undergoing [the proposed] form of tubal ligation". (emphasis added). *See*, *Burke v. Humphrey* [2001] TASSC 133 (Cox CJ, 21 November, unreported, BC200107222), at [20]–[28].

When determining the "decision" causation, including, I think, determining the "materiality" of information, I am of the view that a patient's mind and the possibility of change of that mind should be judged against the background that the patient has been informed of all available treatment options, rather than against the notion that a doctor normally recommend a procedure and a patient usually follow the recommendation. This is consistent with my view that disclosure of available treatment options should not be confused with recommendation of treatment. The notion that contextualised information disclosure is distinct from personalised recommendation needs to be implemented at the stages of both breach of the *duty* to inform, including measuring the "materiality" of information, and *causation*.

The scope of information disclosure, including disclosure of alternatives, does not have a bright line. It needs the judiciary weighing varied circumstances in diverse case scenarios. In the second part of this chapter, I take the liberty, from a wide range of circumstances, to single out and explore whether the "elective" and "experimental" nature of a procedure and a patient's making an inquiry have the potential of enlarging the scope of a doctor's duty to inform. The answer is yes.

The portion regarding the "elective" and "experimental" procedures would produce another effect. It gives readers an impression that, when faced with a choice between conservative treatments and invasive (and elective) treatments (such as surgery), or between conventional treatments and experimental treatments, the law has a tendency to favour the former category of treatment rather than the latter. That impression would be gained when readers read Chap. 5.8 about whether doing nothing is an option. The orthodoxy-reinforcing nature of current law is further demonstrated in Chap. 6 (emerging treatment options). Although both Chap. 6 and this chapter cover "experimental" procedures, they have different focuses. This chapter explores a doctor's duty to disclose when *proposing*, recommending and administering experimental procedures. Chapter 6 focuses on the possibility of a doctor *disclosing* emerging treatment options.

This chapter concludes my *general* observations about information disclosure, especially disclosure of alternatives. In the next chapter, I will categorise "alternatives". Then, from Chaps. 6, 7, and 8, I will focus on three specific categories of alternative, and examine the potential of the duty to inform encompassing disclosure of emerging treatment options, financially unavailable treatment options and CAM alternatives.

References

Addison, Thomas. 2003. Negligent failure to inform: Developments in the law since *Rogers v. Whitaker*. *Torts Law Journal* 11: 165–195.

Chalmers, Don, and Robert Schwartz. 1993. *Rogers v.* Whitaker and informed consent in Australia: A fair dinkum duty of disclosure. *Medical Law Review* 1: 139–159.

Downie, Jocelyn, Timothy Caulfield, and Colleen Flood. 2002. *Canadian health law and policy*, 2nd ed. Ontario: LexisNexis Butterworths.

Heywood, Rob, Ann Macaskill, and Kevin Williams. 2010. Informed consent in hospital practice: Health professionals' perspectives and legal reflections. *Medical Law Review* 18: 152–184.

Jones, Michael A. 2003. *Medical negligence*. London: Sweet & Maxwell.

King Jr., Joseph H. 1999. Reconciling the exercise of judgment and the objective standard of care in medical malpractice. *Oklahoma Law Review* 52: 49–84.

Krause, Joan H. 1999. Reconceptualizing informed consent in an era of health care cost containment. *Iowa Law Review* 85: 261–386.
Montgomery, Jonathan. 2003. *Health care law*, 2nd ed. New York: Oxford University Press.
Parchomovsky, Gideon, and Alex Stein. 2008. Torts and innovation. *Michigan Law Review* 107: 285–315.
Pattinson, Shaun D. 2006. *Medical law and ethics*. London: Sweet & Maxwell.
Robertson, Gerald. 1981. Informed consent to medical treatment. *The Law Quarterly Review* 97: 102–126.
Scott, Kelly. 2009. Under the knife: An analysis of the medical council of New Zealand's statement on cosmetic procedures. *JLM* 16: 625–652.
Skene, Loane. 2008. *Law and medical practice: Rights, duties, claims and defences*, 3rd ed. Chatswood: LexisNexis Butterworths.

Chapter 5
Categorisation of Alternatives

Abstract This book formulates the term "alternatives" in a wide fashion. It is categorised into four groups: (1) available treatment options; (2) legally, financially or geographically unavailable treatment options; (3) alternative providers; (4) choices between conventional medicine and CAM. First, the majority of "alternatives" are "treatment options". Second, treatment options, which are medically available, may in fact be unavailable because of non-medical (legal, financial and geographical) factors. That raises the issue of whether to disclose legally, financially or geographically unavailable treatment options. Third, a doctor's inexperience in performing a complex procedure might expose the patient to additional risks, leading to the notion that a patient has a right to be informed of the option of having the procedure performed by alternative (more experienced) practitioners or in a better-equipped and better-staffed institution. Fourth, with the increasing prevalence of CAM, there is a pressing issue of whether a practitioner has a duty to inform about alternative therapies that are beyond the scope of their variety of "medicine".

5.1 Introduction

This chapter will illustrate some categories of alternatives. Alternatives are mainly expressed as *diagnostic or treatment* options. The informed consent rule mainly targets and surrounds "treatment"[1] or "procedure"[2] (including diagnostic

[1] *Gallant v. U.S.*, 392 F.Supp.2d 1077, 1081 (D. Alaska, 2005) (defining "treatment" as "the action or manner of treating a patient medically or surgically").

[2] *Gallant v. U.S.*, 392 F.Supp.2d 1077, 1081 (D. Alaska, 2005) (defining "procedure" as "a particular course of action"). Assignment of a hospital patient to a room with another patient does not qualify as a "treatment or procedure," requiring informed consent. *See*, *Gallant v. U.S.*, 392 F.Supp.2d 1077 (D. Alaska, 2005) (patient alleging that hospital assigned her to hospital room with another patient who was HIV-positive, exposing her to HIV/AIDS).

X. Zhao, *The Duty of Medical Practitioners and CAM/TCM Practitioners to Inform Competent Adult Patients about Alternatives*,
DOI 10.1007/978-3-642-31647-0_5,

procedure[3]). Compared to conventional treatment options, disclosure of emerging treatment options involves more controversy and complexity.

Sometimes alternatives express themselves not directly in term of treatments, but in terms of providers (practitioners and institutions with which practitioners are affiliated), location, legality and financial feasibility.[4] For example, a health care provider may need to admit his inexperience and limitations, and, as the next logical step, reveal to his patient the availability of *alternative (more experienced) provider*. Similarly, a provider may need to make his patient aware of the availability of an *alternative (better-staffed, better-equipped) facility/institution*. Although these kinds of information are extrinsic to treatments, they are intimately related to and finally go to the choice of treatment options.

Alternatives may be "unavailable" to a patient for a variety of reasons, such as: (1) *geographical* constraints on the availability of the treatment; (2) *legal* constraints prohibiting performance of the treatment in a particular jurisdiction; (3) *institutional* constraints precluding the performance of the treatment at a particular institution or by a particular doctor; (4) *financial* constraints that place treatment beyond the means of the patient in question.[5] That presents the possibility of *geographically unavailable alternatives* (including out-of-institution, out-of-state, and out-of-country alternatives), *financially unavailable alternatives and legally unavailable alternatives*.[6] These treatment options are already there, but unavailable for geographical, financial and legal reasons.

---

[3] *Gates v. Jensen*, 595 P.2d 919, 922–923 (Wash. 1979) ("The patient's right to know is not confined to the choice of treatment once a disease is present and has been conclusively diagnosed. Important decisions must frequently be made in many non-treatment situations in which medical care is given, including procedures leading to a diagnosis…").

[4] I am still struggling to find a good term to comfortably embrace all of the above-mentioned alternatives. The Health and Disability Commissioner of New Zealand adopted the term "alternative management options" to include "the option of having the surgery performed by *another surgeon* (whether in private or public)" (emphasis added). *See*, *Opinion 03HDC19128* (Health and Disability Commissioner, 14/9/04) (failure to reveal that the provider's practice was subject to restrictions). Obviously the term "management options" is more encompassing than the term "treatment options", but it still needs to see if it is broad enough to cover all those alternatives formed on the basis of providers, location, legality and financial feasibility.

[5] Joan H. Krause (1999), 334. *See also*, Note, Halle Fine Terrion (1993), 493.

[6] One commentator invented the term "unreadily available alternatives" to encompass four categories of alternatives: geographical, institutional, experimental, and financial. *See*, Note, Halle Fine Terrion (1993), 493.

There are different ways of categorising alternatives, such as "distinct" v. "additional" alternatives[7] and lifestyle-involved alternatives.[8] In this and the following chapters, I will focus on the following alternatives: (1) conventional v. emerging treatment options; (2) legally unavailable alternatives; (3) financially unavailable alternatives; (4) geographically unavailable alternatives; (5) alternative providers; (6) Complementary and Alternative Medicine (CAM) alternatives; (7) the option of doing nothing.

5.2 Conventional and Emerging Treatment Options

In the area of diagnosis and treatment, many legal mechanisms, such as the *Bolam* test and the "two schools of thought" doctrine, are promoting adoption of more wide-accepted, more well-established, and more conventional procedures, although they do accord leeway to the use of minority treatment options. In this area, the law can give more room to a doctor choosing more innovative, emerging and experimental procedures by applying the more innovation-friendly test of "a reasonable doctor" and the analysis of risks-benefits. When administering experimental procedures, a doctor needs to follow the informed consent rule.

When the context is shifted to information disclosure, there are still disputes over whether the law should be orthodoxy-reinforcing. The law needs to approach a doctor's suggesting experimental treatments with caution, especially when conventional treatments are readily available. The contexts that all treatments are conventional or there is no conventional treatment involve less controversy. If both conventional and non-conventional treatments are available and they compete with each other, one issue arises: does a doctor need to disclose non-conventional or emerging treatments? Will conventional treatments always prevail over non-conventional treatments?

I will examine this topic in more detail in a separate chapter (Chap. 6).

---

[7] *Kalsbeck v. Westview Clinic, P. A.*, 375 N. W. 2d 861, 869 (Minn. App. 1985) (the doctrine of informed consent applies "only to situations where the choice is between two or more *distinct*, alternative methods of treatment" and does not apply to "situations where the patient's decision is whether to submit to treatment *in addition to* the basic treatment given" (emphasis added)); *Madsen v. Park Nicollet Medical Center*, 431 N.W. 2d 855, 861 (Minn. 1988) (the court denied the application of informed consent rule to the case by highlighting the "identical", rather than distinct, nature of the two options); *Masquat v. Maguire*, 638 P. 2d 1105, 1106–1107 (Okla. 1981) (the difference between treatments should be "significant" or "go to the nature" of a procedure); *Matthies v. Mastromonaco*, 733 A. 2d 456, 463–464 (N. J. 1999) (noting that the physician's duty to inform the patient of alternatives is especially important when the alternatives are *mutually exclusive*; and, if, as a practical matter, the choice of one alternative *precludes* the choice of others, or even if it *increases appreciably the risks* attendant on the other alternatives, the patient's need for relevant information is critical).

[8] *See*, *Matthies v. Mastromonaco*, 733 A. 2d 456, 463–464 (N. J. 1999) (observing that the patient's need for relevant information intensifies when the choice turns not so much on purely medical considerations as on the choice of one lifestyle or set of values over another).

5.3 Legally Unavailable Alternatives

Gauged by the degree of judicial readiness to embrace under the umbrella of informed consent, alternatives that are not readily available can be categorised into three groups: (1) legally unavailable alternatives; (2) provider/institution-based alternatives, geographically unavailable alternatives; and (3) financially unavailable alternatives.

If a treatment option is characterised as *"legally unavailable"*, it has the least prospect of being encompassed by the physician's duty of disclosure. As the Supreme Court of Oklahoma observed, "[h]olding that physicians must inform patients of treatment alternatives not [legally] available in [the jurisdiction in question] but available in other states is beyond what the law expects from physicians" and "[s] earching for legal alternatives is a job more suitable for lawyers."[9]

The vulnerability of the argument that unconventional therapies should be disclosed when those therapies are labelled as "legally unavailable" was vividly demonstrated in the American case of *Schiff v. Prados*.[10] The case involved a cancer child and choices between conventional chemotherapy and radiation, on the one hand, and unconventional antineoplaston treatment, on the other.[11] The plaintiffs alleged that the defendant did not obtain their informed consent for their child's treatment because he failed to advise them of the antineoplaston treatment.[12] The

[9] *Spencer By and Through Spencer v. Seikel*, 742 P.2d 1126, 1129 (Okl. 1987). This case involved a child born with virtually no brain. The plaintiff's argument that the defendant failed to inform her of the *option of abortion* when the 23 or 24-week-old fetus was discovered to be suffering from hydrocephalus was rejected by the Supreme Court of Oklahoma on the basis that, when the defendant first discovered hydrocephalus, the fetus had reached the *viability* stage, and therefore abortion was *not a legally available option* for the mother, under the Oklahoma statute, unless the mother's life or health was in danger. The patient also argued that, even if abortion was forbidden by Oklahoma statute once the fetus was viable, because physicians in Oklahoma must conform to national, not local, standards of care in treatment of patients, the physician should inform her that an abortion might be available and performed *in other states (outside Oklahoma)*. The court held that "[n]ational standards are applicable in measuring the standard of medical care physicians owe their patients in *rendering treatment* to them" (emphasis added).

[10] *Schiff v. Prados*, 92 Cal.App. 4th 692, 112 Cal.Rptr.2d 171(Cal.App. 1 Dist. 2001).

[11] The child patient suffered from a malignant rhabdoid tumor, a rare and aggressive form of cancer, in her brain and around her spinal cord. There was a surgery on the tumor, most of the tumor was removed, but residual tumor remained in the brain and around the spinal cord. After the surgery, only two options were presented to the plaintiffs: having the child undergo intensive chemotherapy and radiation, or "taking her home and letting her die". The defendants proposed and recommended aggressive chemotherapy and radiation for the child. Although the plaintiffs made it clear that they were interested in knowing of "any alternative treatment or options that might possibly be advantageous to [their] daughter" in addition to radiation and chemotherapy which, they think, would be very difficult to the child, the defendants responded that none of them knew of any appropriate alternative treatments.

[12] *Schiff v. Prados*, 112 Cal.Rptr.2d 171, 177 (Cal.App. 1 Dist. 2001).

plaintiffs called two experts (one is a California-licensed physician, another is a physician licensed in Texas) who testified that the defendant breached the professional standard of care applicable in the circumstances by failing to inform the plaintiffs of antineoplaston treatment as an alternative to the chemotherapy and radiation proposed for the patient.[13]

It was established that the defendant was *aware of* the existence of antineoplaston treatment.[14] The defendant raised the concern that "there were many alternative treatments for cancer known to exist, including laetrile, vitamin C, immuno-augmentative therapy, coffee enemas, Chinese herbal medicines, and others".[15] In his view, although "[a]ny patient is free to explore these potentialities," "[t]he standard of care does not require *controversial and/or alternative methods which have not been subjected to scientific scrutiny*, such as antineoplastons, to mandatorily fall within the range of options discussed during tumor board meetings."[16]

Although the defendant's argument did not raise the issue of legal unavailability of the antineoplaston treatment, the Court of Appeal's reasoning centred on the issue of "whether a treatment that is *illegal* in (California) is nonetheless an *'available'* alternative that a physician could be required to disclose in order to obtain a patient's informed consent".[17]

The court did notice that there was an opposing expert testimony which advocated disclosure of the antineoplaston treatment as an alternative to the recommended chemotherapy and radiation.[18] However, after observing that there was no duty of disclosure with respect to *unrecommended* procedures, the court quickly shifted the focus to the question of whether antineoplastons were an "available" treatment alternative.[20] Although the alternative procedure in question – injection of antineoplastons into children with brain tumors – did exist, the court highlighted "the unusual situation" of the instant case, i.e. the alternative treatment in question was *outlawed* by statute in California.[21] The court found that it would have been illegal to *administer* antineoplastons to the patient in California when the defendant allegedly should have disclosed the existence of that treatment.[22] Without distinguishing the duty to administer and the duty to inform, the court held that "as a matter of law, a

[13] *Schiff v. Prados*, 112 Cal.Rptr.2d 171, 178 (Cal.App. 1 Dist. 2001). One expert even indicated that the defendant's failure to disclose the availability of antineoplastons at tumor board discussions of the patient's case "would be regarded by the average physician as morally offensive and unethical."

[14] *Schiff v. Prados*, 112 Cal.Rptr.2d 171, 178 (Cal.App. 1 Dist. 2001).

[15] *Schiff v. Prados*, 112 Cal.Rptr.2d 171, 178 (Cal.App. 1 Dist. 2001).

[16] *Schiff v. Prados*, 112 Cal.Rptr.2d 171, 178 (Cal.App. 1 Dist. 2001) (emphasis added).

[17] *Schiff v. Prados*, 112 Cal.Rptr.2d 171, 180 (Cal.App. 1 Dist. 2001) (emphasis added).

[18] *Schiff v. Prados*, 112 Cal.Rptr.2d 171, 179 (Cal.App. 1 Dist. 2001).

[19] *Schiff v. Prados*, 112 Cal.Rptr.2d 171, 179 (Cal.App. 1 Dist. 2001).

[20] *Schiff v. Prados*, 112 Cal.Rptr.2d 171, 180 (Cal.App. 1 Dist. 2001).

[21] *Schiff v. Prados*, 112 Cal.Rptr.2d 171, 182 (Cal.App. 1 Dist. 2001).

[22] *Schiff v. Prados*, 112 Cal.Rptr.2d 171, 173 (Cal.App. 1 Dist. 2001) (emphasis added).

treatment that *cannot legally be administered* in this state is *not 'available'* within the meaning of (the informed consent) rule, and thus that a physician cannot be held liable for *failing to disclose* the existence of such a treatment".

5.4 Financially Unavailable Alternatives

In clinical care, doctors cannot avoid questions, such as "should practitioners be required to disclose information about alternatives that the patient has no possibility of accessing?" or "does a practitioner have a duty to disclose alternative that is beyond a patient's reach?"

If a treatment option is viewed as a *"financially unavailable alternative"*, there is the most potential for it to be embraced by a physician's duty to disclose. Financial unfeasibility is the weakest excuse for withholding information about alternative treatment options. The recommendation-disclosure distinction indicates that, while the law can tolerate a physician's recommendation being contaminated by economic considerations, the physician's information disclosure should be free from financial incentives. That requires that a physician inform his patient of all available treatment options/management options, whether or not the option is covered by insurance or is available in publicly-funded health care.

I will examine this topic in a separate chapter (Chap. 7), which has a focus on the English context, although it also takes account of academic discussion in other jurisdictions. There I argue that the resource-blind disclosure of treatment options is more desirable and cost-effective.

5.5 Geographically Unavailable Alternatives

Sometimes doctors are inevitably faced with the question of whether or not a practitioner has a duty to disclose treatments available only overseas (out-of-country alternatives)? That raises the issue of disclosure of "*geographically unavailable*" alternatives. If a treatment option is categorised as "*geographically unavailable*", that option may fall within the ambit of disclosure.[23] In situations where the location of treatment, rather than the choice of treatment, is the informational focus, the location of treatment becomes a material risk factor that needs to be disclosed.[24]

Locations have different scales. Depending on the scales of locations, alternatives may come as *out-of-institution, out-of-state or even out-of-country alternatives.*

[23] *Thibault v. Fewer*, [2002] 1 W.W.R. 204, 217, at [61] ("[T]he decision with respect to the financial consequences of choosing to undergo a procedure outside of the patient's province of residence should be left with the patient. The physician should provide the relevant information. The final decision remains that of the patient, after consideration of all factors, including cost.").

[24] *Skeels (Estate of) v. Iwashkiw*, [2006] 11 W.W.R. 632, 659, at [157] (Court of Queen's Bench of Alberta).

A doctor may need to make his patient aware of a better-equipped, better-staffed facility.[25] Disclosing one facility's deficiency and mentioning the availability of other better-served facilities are two sides of the coin.[26] They are linked together. Out-of-institution alternatives or institutionally unavailable alternatives have more resemblance to the provider-based alternatives, although they involve geographical elements.

However, in the area of a doctor's duty to inform about *alternative facilities/institutions*, to curtail the potential of expansion, the law will incorporate the "causation" thinking into the issue of a doctor's duty to inform. To deserve disclosure, the two institutions/facilities should entail real difference in treatment (i.e. simple difference in place is not enough), [27] and that difference should be significant enough to satisfy both the "materiality" and "causation" thresholds.[28]

In some cases, the reason why a treatment option is not available in the *jurisdiction* (state or country) in question but available in other jurisdictions is that the doctors in the home jurisdiction lack expertise on the treatment. That treatment can be safely categorised as a "geographically unavailable alternative", and may fall within a doctor's duty to disclose. However, in some cases, the procedures, such as abortion, may be illegal in the jurisdiction in question but available in a neighbouring jurisdiction. Those procedures will become "legally unavailable" options. "States" become a valuable demarcation line when they entail different legal landscapes. Therefore, out-of-state alternatives could be vulnerably couched as "legally unavailable alternatives" and be excluded from items that need to be disclosed.[29]

---

[25] *Johnson By Adler v. Kokemoor*, 545 N.W. 2d 495, 508–510 (Wis. 1996) ("Given the *difficulties involved in performing the surgery* at issue in this case, coupled with evidence that the defendant *exaggerated his own prior experience while downplaying the risks* confronting the plaintiff, the circuit court properly exercised its discretion in admitting evidence that a physician of good standing would have made the plaintiff aware of the alternative of lower risk surgery with *a different, more experienced surgeon in a better-equipped facility*." (emphasis added)).

[26] *Barriocanal v. Gibbs*, 697 A.2d 1169, 1172 (Del. Supr., 1997) (involving a doctor's failure to inform his patient of his *lack of recent aneurysm surgery*, of the *difference in hospital staffing on a holiday*, and of the *option of transfer to a teaching institution*).

[27] *Madsen v. Park Nicollet Med. Ctr.*, 431 N.W.2d 855, 861 (Minn. 1988) (finding that "the option of hospitalization was *not an alternative* but was rather an *additional* available treatment"; "Whether [the patient] was or was not hospitalized, her *treatment would have been the same in either place* and with the same risks. Any choice would affect only the *situs* of the patient's care, not the *care* itself. … [T]he home treatment was *identical* to that available in the hospital." (emphasis added)).

[28] *Estate of Lapping v. Group Health Co-op. of Puget Sound*, 892 P.2d 1116, 1123 (Wash. App. Div. 2, 1995) (asking "whether a rational trier of fact could have found, by a preponderance of evidence, that a reasonably prudent person in [the patient's] position *would have attached significance to* the fact that the endometrial biopsy could have been done in *a hospital with more equipment and greater precautions* than were available in the clinic."(emphasis added)); *Martin by Scoptur v. Richards*, 531 N.W.2d 70, 80–81 (Wis. 1995) (agreeing that the plaintiff *would attach significance to* the undisclosed information, and, had he been informed of those information, would have agreed to seek *the alternative forms of care and treatment, i.e. to have a CT scan done, and to take the patient to another hospital with a neurosurgeon*).

[29] For example, *Schiff v. Prados*, 112 Cal.Rptr.2d 171, 173 (Cal.App. 1 Dist. 2001) (holding that an unconventional treatment that cannot legally be administered in a state is *not 'available'* within the meaning of the informed consent rule).

In some jurisdictions, public health care system does leave open the possibility of patients applying for payment for the costs of out-of-country treatments, but subjects it to legal conditions and approval process, and the courts show deference to funding decisions.[30] With the increasing popularity of medical/health tourism, there is urgency to explore what role the informed consent rule (including a doctor's duty to inform about *overseas* alternatives) should play in this emerging industry. [31]

Through international medical travel, patients may pursue: (1) elective procedures that are expensive in their home country, and which are available at a fraction of the cost in destination countries; (2) medically necessary procedures for which there are long domestic waiting lists; (3) medical interventions unavailable in their home country because they have not yet been shown to be safe and effective; and (4) medical interventions that are illegal in their home country because they harmfully exploit vulnerable third-parties (Crozier and Baylis 2010, 299). With the "gap" between procedures or interventions in home country and those overseas, it is possible, although difficult, for the plaintiff-patients to establish the elements of "materiality" and "causation", when a doctor's duty to inform about overseas alternatives is acknowledged and discussed in the context of medical negligence.

5.6 Alternative Provider

Compared to legally unavailable alternatives and financially unavailable alternatives, disclosure of *a provider's experience or limitation*, and disclosure of *alternative provider*, presents a more complex issue because it involves more personal information. When answering the question of whether the doctrine of informed consent can encompass disclosure of provider-specific information, neither an unqualified "yes" or an unqualified "no" is desirable.

5.6.1 The USA Approach

In the USA, the expansive approach of suggesting disclosure of the experience-related information started with the revolutionary (Twerski and Cohen 1999, 3) case *Johnson By Adler v. Kokemoor*,[32] where the Supreme Court of Wisconsin audaciously embraced the need of disclosure to the patient of the provider-specific risk

---

[30] *See*, Canada: *C.C.W. v. Ontario Health Insurance Plan*, 2009 CanLII 712 (ON S.C.D.C.); 305 D.L.R. (4th) 538; *Flora v. Ontario Health Insurance Plan*, 2008 ONCA 538; 295 D.L.R. (4th) 309; *Cameron v. Nova Scotia (Attorney General)*, 1999 CanLII 7243 (NS C.A.); 177 D.L.R. (4th) 611.

[31] G K D Crozier, Françoise Baylis (2010) (raising and exploring the question of "What role should physicians in more-developed home countries play in promoting or constraining international medical travel towards less-developed destination countries?").

[32] *Johnson By Adler v. Kokemoor*, 545 N.W. 2d 495 (Wis. 1996).

information (such as inexperience) and the availability of a better-equipped facility in certain circumstances.[33] However, there is also an opposing camp of those who prefer to adopt a limited approach to informed consent, confining a provider's duty to disclose to information *intrinsic to treatments/procedures*, and oppose to an expansive approach in interpreting "material information".[34]

The post-*Kokemoor* case law reveals that a flexible approach, driven by *facts and circumstances* and answered on a case-by-case basis, rather than a blanket approach or a bright-line approach, to the issue of a doctor's duty to acknowledge inexperience and disclose the availability of more experienced doctors, is favoured by some courts. Under the fact-driven approach, the facts and circumstances that are considered may include: (1) the high complexity of the procedure;[35] (2) the substantially different success rates between the more experienced providers and the less experienced providers;[36] (3) the

---

[33] *Johnson By Adler v. Kokemoor*, 545 N.W. 2d 495, 498 (Wis. 1996) ("[I]nformation regarding a physician's experience in performing a particular procedure, a physician's risk statistics as compared with those of other physicians who perform that procedure, and the availability of other centers and physicians better able to perform that procedure would have facilitated the plaintiff's awareness of 'all of the viable alternatives' available to her and thereby aided her exercise of informed consent."). *See also*, *Goldberg v. Boone*, 912 A.2d 698, 717 (Md. 2006) (holding that it was the combination of the patient's special condition, which *elevated the complexity* of the procedure, with the fact the defendant had *a very limited experience* in performing the procedure, that "gave rise to [the defendant's] duty to inform [his patient] that there were *other more experienced surgeons* in the region that could perform the procedure" (emphasis added)).

[34] Some examples are: *Foard v. Jarman*, 326 N.C. 24, 31, 387 S.E.2d 162 (1990) (no affirmative duty for health care provider to discuss his or her experience where provider perforated patient's stomach wall while performing gastroplasty, resulting in severe complications, including renal failure); *Duttry v. Patterson*, 565 Pa. 130, 136, 771 A.2d 1255 (2001) (the fact that defendant indicated to patient that he had performed procedure approximately once a month when defendant in fact had performed procedure nine times previously is "evidence of a physician's personal characteristics and experience [that] is irrelevant to an informed consent claim"). *See also*, *DeGennaro v. Tandon*, 873 A.2d 191, 197 (Conn. App. 2005), footnote 4; *Abram by Abram v. Children's Hosp. of Buffalo*, 542 N.Y.S.2d 418 (N.Y.A.D. 4 Dept., 1989); *Ditto v. McCurdy*, 947 P.2d 952, 958 (Hawai'i, 1997); *Whiteside v. Lukson*, 947 P.2d 1263, 1265 (Wash. App. Div. 3, 1997); *Duttry v. Patterson*, 771 A.2d 1255, 1258 (Pa., 2001).

[35] The *Kokemoor* case involved a complex surgery – basilar bifurcation aneurysm surgery. The complexity of the surgery dictates that a surgeon's experience or success rate genuinely matters. Less complicated procedures or "routine uncomplicated surgery" could not invite the *Kokemoor* rule. *See*, *Jalowitz v. Physicians Insurance Company of Wisconsin, Inc.*, 691 N.W.2d 926 (Table) (Wis. App. 2004), at [41] (involving "a relatively simple surgery for a trained cardiac surgeon").

[36] The *Kokemoor* case involved a scenario that, due to the complex nature of the surgery, different physicians have *substantially different success rates* in performing the surgery. Under such a scenario, whether surgery is performed by one rather than another represents a choice between "alternate, viable medical modes of treatment". Under such circumstances, the accurate physician-specific information was shown to be material because it was evidence of greater risk of the proposed treatment. *See also*, *Jalowitz v. Physicians Insurance Company of Wisconsin, Inc.*, 691 N.W.2d 926 (Table) (Wis. App. 2004), at [42] (holding that there was no evidence that the "morbidity and mortality rate expected when a surgeon with the defendant's experience [or background] performed the surgery would be significantly higher than the rate expected" when any other trained cardiac physician performed the same surgery); *Prissel v. Physicians Insurance Company of Wisconsin, Inc.*, 674 N.W.2d 680 (Table) (Wis. App. 2003), at [36].

undisclosed but *material* information;[37] (4) the availability of an alternative provider and facility;[38] (5) satisfaction of the *causation* (decision causation and injury causation) threshold;[39] (6) a dishonest provider or misrepresentation;[40] (7) an inquisitive patient.[41] The success/failure rates of complex procedures are more experience-dependant than routine procedures. Substantial difference between the more experienced providers and the less experienced providers, coupled with a patient's inquiry, make it more revealing

[37] *DeGennaro v. Tandon*, 873 A.2d 191, 200 (Conn. App. 2005). *See also*, *Wlosinski v. Cohn*, 713 N.W.2d 16, 25 (Mich. App., 2005) (Borrello, J. dissenting) ("It is axiomatic that a reasonable patient would find information regarding a kidney transplant surgeon's statistical success and failure rates for kidney transplants to be *material* in making the decision whether to proceed with a surgical procedure as *serious* as a kidney transplant. Moreover, [the doctor] had a duty to supply such information *regardless of whether the decedent sought to elicit such information*."(emphasis added)).

[38] Evidence adduced at trial in the *Kokemoor* case established that surgeons with much more experience and higher success rate, and a "tertiary care facility", which contain the proper neurological intensive care unit and microsurgical facilities staffed by neurosurgeons with the requisite training and experience to perform basilar bifurcation aneurysm surgeries, were available and in relatively close proximity (such as Mayo Clinic, only 90 miles away) to the hospital in which the defendant intended to perform the surgery. The unavailability of an alternative provider/more experienced, more competent provider has been used as a distinguishing factor in citing *Kokemoor*, and may constitute an excuse for a court's denial to encompass disclosure of a provider's experience in the context of informed consent. *See*, *Jalowitz v. Physicians Insurance Company of Wisconsin, Inc.*, 691 N.W.2d 926 (Table) (Wis. App. 2004), at [43] (no evidence that a more qualified surgeon or facility was available); *Prissel v. Physicians Insurance Company of Wisconsin, Inc.*, 674 N.W.2d 680 (Table) (Wis. App. 2003), at [37] (no evidence that another experienced cardiovascular surgeon was available to perform the surgery or that another cardiovascular surgeon was available to assist).

[39] *Johnson By Adler v. Kokemoor*, 545 N.W. 2d 495, 506–507 (Wis. 1996) (establishing that a reasonable patient in the plaintiff's position, if accurately apprised of all the risks, would have declined surgery from the defendant-doctor and the undisclosed risk actually materialized and was caused by the treatment); *Howard v. University of Medicine*, 800 A.2d 73, 85 (N.J. 2002) (offering a two-prong test for establishing causation when doctors misrepresent their experience: (1) whether the more limited experience or credentials possessed by the doctor could have substantially increased the patient's risk; and (2) whether that substantially increased risk would cause a reasonably prudent person not to consent to undergo the procedure). Because a provider-specific information disclosure case normally already involves a *gap* or *difference* in risk factors between a more risky provider and a less risky provider, compared to the ordinary risk information disclosure case where the risk-benefit balance between two options is relatively unclear, it is relatively easier for the plaintiff-patient to succeed in establishing both decision causation and injury causation in the context of provider-specific information disclosure. *See*, Aaron D. Twerski and Neil B. Cohen (1999), 12–17.

[40] The *Kokemoor* case involved the defendant-surgeon's *overstatement* about his rather limited experience with the particular type of aneurysm surgery and *understatement* about the morbidity and mortality rate associated with the contemplated surgery. In medical context, because misrepresentation normally invites battery argument, the courts showed caution in characterizing a physician's words or conduct as misrepresentation. The law should do something to blame dishonest physicians. Compared to other avenues for addressing liability, informed consent is more lenient and friendly for defendant-physicians.

[41] The *Kokemoor* case involved an inquisitive patient. Some courts did draw a distinction between the proactive aspect and the reactive aspect of the duty to inform in the context of provider-specific information disclosure, making it clear that, although a physician did not have to volunteer personal information to patients, he should give truthful and accurate answers when a patient

that, if equipped with undisclosed provider-specific information, a reasonable person in the patient's position would have attached significance to such information and would have foregone treatment in the hands of the defendant-provider.

5.6.2 The Canadian Approach

In some Canadian cases, a physician was not required to advise a patient that he was performing a procedure *for the first time*.[42] However, it is too early to conclude that Canadian case law had answered an unqualified "no" to the question of whether a physician has a duty to present his patient with physician-specific information. What Canadian case law has offered is either a routine surgery which can be performed well by any qualified surgeon and in any well-equipped facility,[43] or pieces of provider-specific information which do not have any relevance to a physician's competence or do not affect a physician's capacity to perform his job.[44]

The courts have not yet faced a very complex surgery whose success rate depends heavily on a surgeon's skill/experience and the ready availability of alternative staff and facilities. It still needs to be seen whether Canadian judicial attitudes towards disclosure of provider-specific information would change if the facts and circumstances in a case point clearly to the conclusion that a physician's personal information creates an independent risk, is material to a patient's decision to undergo a procedure in the hands of one physician rather than another, and has a satisfying link to the patient's injury. The *Halkyard v. Mathew* holding[45] was, to a great extent, based on policy considerations and worry about the negative consequences that an expansive approach to informed consent would exert, rather than a genuine appreciation of and loyalty to the informed consent rule. The *Turner v. Bederman* case

affirmatively questioned the physician about his competence, experience and expertise. The materiality of information is more obviously demonstrated when a patient makes an affirmative inquiry about a physician's personal information. *See*, Brad M. Rostolsky (2002), 556–557. Also *see*, *Kaskie v. Wright*, 589 A. 2d 213 (Pa. Super. 1991) (The patient did not ask the physician about his prior surgical experience. The superior court held that a physician did not have to voluntarily reveal his level of experience.).

[42] *Hopp v. Lepp* (1980), 112 D.L.R. (3d) 67 (S.C.C.); [1980] 2 S.C.R. 192; *Turner v. Bederman*, 1996 CarswellOnt 1766, 2 O.T.C. 215, at [12].

[43] *Hopp v. Lepp* (1980), 112 D.L.R. (3d) 67 (S.C.C.); [1980] 2 S.C.R. 192, at [22]. The routine nature of operation dictates that there is no need for the patient to be referred and transferred to a better-staffed facility.

[44] *Turner v. Bederman*, 1996 CarswellOnt 1766, 2 O.T.C. 215; *Halkyard v. Mathew*, 2001 CarswellAlta 273, 2001 ABCA 67, 4 C.C.L.T. (3d) 271, [2001] 7 W.W.R. 26, 277 A.R. 373, 242 W.A.C. 373, 91 Alta. L.R. (3d) 201. In *Stefanyshyn v. Rubin* (1996), 34 C.C.L.R. (2d) 88 (Man. C.A.), a doctor's failure to wear prescribed eyeglasses during surgery was considered not in the context of information disclosure, but in the context of negligent treatment.

[45] The case involved an allegation that the defendant-surgeon failed to disclose his personal medical condition (epilepsy) to a patient, which "might have a bearing on the patient's decision to have or not have the surgery by the attending surgeon". Apparently deeply moved by the arguments

attempted to generalise the Canadian case law and keep a dichotomy between the "*procedure*"-related risks and the "*physician*"-created risks.[46] Such a bright-line approach does not show much regard to the rationale underlying the duty to inform and the informed consent rule itself. When the provider-specific information reflects a choice between available modes of treatment and is incorporated into a patient's weighing in favour of or against a particular mode of treatment, the dichotomy maintained between "procedure" and "physician" will collapse.

A Canadian case has indicated that a general practitioner must make clear to the patient the limitations in his care and the limitations of the facility.[47] The Canadian case law concerning provider-specific information disclosure also illustrates the point that a fact-driven and context-specific approach is preferable when considering risk factors beyond the risks related directly to treatments. It further shows the distinguishing powers that those *Kokemoor*-created factors (such as the complexity of a procedure, an inexperienced provider, the substantial gap between the experienced providers and the inexperienced providers, causation, an inquisitive patient, a dishonest provider (misrepresentation)) have when dealing with the plaintiff's argument that the defendant has a duty to disclose information external to treatments.[48]

The Canadian case law has indicated several qualifications to its seemingly clear rule that "Canadian courts have distinguished between the risks attending the

---

revealed in an academic article (B. R. Furrow "Must Physicians Reveal Their Wounds?" (1996) 5 *Cambridge Quarterly of Healthcare Ethics* 204, 211), the Alberta Court of Queen's Bench concluded that

> [the defendant-surgeon] was not obligated to disclose to [the patient] his personal medical history. … It is the duty of [the defendant's] *personal physician* to determine whether [the defendant] can continue doing surgery. It is also the duty of *the hospital* to determine whether [the defendant] or any other doctor performing surgery in its hospital can continue his or her practice in that hospital if the doctor, for whatever reason, is not capable of performing surgery. It is also the duty of *any doctor* to determine if he or she can continue their medical responsibilities when a physical or mental incapacity exists. (emphasis added)

See Halkyard v. Mathew, 1998 CarswellAlta 822, 43 C.C.L.T. (2d) 171, 67 Alta. L.R. (3d) 174, [1999] 5 W.W.R. 643, 231 A.R. 281, [1998] A.J. No. 986, at [18].

[46] *Turner v. Bederman*, 1996 CarswellOnt 1766, 2 O.T.C. 215, at [11] ("Canadian courts have distinguished between the risks attending the *procedure* and the risks attending the *physician*" (emphasis in the original)).

[47] *Skeels (Estate of) v. Iwashkiw*, [2006] 11 W.W.R. 632, 658 at [149] (Court of Queen's Bench of Alberta).

[48] In *Hopp v. Lepp* (1980), 112 D.L.R. (3d) 67 (S.C.C.); [1980] 2 S.C.R. 192 (at [36], [38]), the Supreme Court indicated a lack of "decision causation" by noting that "the record does not support a conclusion that the plaintiff had made the question of the *place* of performance of the operation *central to his consent*" (emphasis added). The Court also touched "injury causation" by holding that a suggestion that the patient might possibly have suffered less damage if he had gone to Calgary in the first place was "highly conjectural and cannot form the basis of a judgment for the patient". *See also*, *Halkyard v. Mathew*, 2001 CarswellAlta 273, 2001 ABCA 67, 4 C.C.L.T. (3d) 271, [2001] 7 W.W.R. 26, 277 A.R. 373, 242 W.A.C. 373, 91 Alta. L.R. (3d) 201, at [9] (holding that at least where the provider-specific information has *no nexus* to the injuries

procedure and the risks attending the *physician*".[49] For example, it keeps open the question of whether an *inexperienced* physician has a duty to reveal his inexperience and refer his patient to a better-staffed and better-equipped facility when an *inquisitive* patient makes a specific inquiry about his experience and *attaches much importance to the place and expertise*.[50]

5.6.3 The Australian Law

In the Australian case of *Chappel v. Hart*,[51] Mrs. Hart underwent surgery at the hands of Dr. Chappel without warning as to the possible consequences should her oesophagus be perforated and infection set in. The condition for which Dr. Chappel operated on Mrs. Hart is one which is relentlessly progressive. Thus, Mrs. Hart would inevitably have required surgery of the kind performed. Mrs. Hart's major argument was that

---

suffered by the patient, the courts did not think that a physician has a duty to disclose his personal information); *Hopp v. Lepp* (1980), 112 D.L.R. (3d) 67 (S.C.C.); [1980] 2 S.C.R. 192, at [7] (noting that it would be ridiculous to require a licensed specialist to tell a patient (*at least without being asked*) how many operations of the kind in question he had performed *when it was clear that he was not inexperienced*); *Halkyard v. Mathew*, 1998 CarswellAlta 822, 43 C.C.L.T. (2d) 171, 67 Alta. L.R. (3d) 174, [1999] 5 W.W.R. 643, 231 A.R. 281, [1998] A.J. No. 986, at [9], [12] and [13] (finding that there was no *misrepresentation or fraud* in the part of the defendant because there is no evidence to indicate he was covering up his personal medical condition to obtain her consent to the surgery).

[49] *Turner v. Bederman*, 1996 CarswellOnt 1766, 2 O.T.C. 215, at [11](emphasis in the original) (citing *Reibl v. Hughes*, [1980] 2 S.C.R. 880, 884–886: "The relationship between surgeon and patient gives rise to a duty of the surgeon to make disclosure to the patient of what I would call material *risks attending the surgery* which is recommended." The duty of the doctor "relates to the specific *risks* within the surgeon's knowledge *peculiar* to the contemplated *treatment*." (emphasis added by the *Turner* court)).

[50] *Hopp v. Lepp* (1980), 112 D.L.R. (3d) 67 (S.C.C.); [1980] 2 S.C.R. 192, at [7].

[51] *Chappel v. Hart* [1998] HCA 55; (1998) 195 CLR 232;156 ALR 517; (1998) 72 ALJR 1344 (HC of A). In this case, the patient alleged that if she had been properly warned of the risk in question, she would have delayed the surgery and had it performed by the most experienced surgeon in the field. The court decided by a majority of three to two that the patient was entitled to recover substantial damage from the surgeon for the physical injuries suffered as a result of the operation performed on her. The majority opinion stressed that the skills of a more experienced surgeon would have reduced the risk of the kind of injury that occurred. The Ipp report and some Civil Liability Acts, which have implemented the recommendations of the Ipp report in various states and territories, have clarified the law on causation in Australia. For example, in New South Wales, s 5D of *Civil Liability Act 2002* (NSW) stipulates the general principles on causation:

(1) A determination that negligence caused particular harm comprises the following elements: (a) that the negligence was a necessary condition of the occurrence of the harm ("factual causation"), and (b) that it is appropriate for the scope of the negligent person's liability to extend to the harm so caused ("scope of liability").
(2) In determining in an exceptional case, in accordance with established principles, whether negligence that cannot be established as a necessary condition of the occurrence of harm should be

had she been aware of that risk, she would have taken steps to have it performed by *the most experienced surgeon* with a record and a reputation in the field. *Chappel v. Hart* is a case of "risks" disclosure. However, in the eyes of Gaudron J., "[t]he matter can be put another way." She reformulated as follows: "[i]f the foreseeable risk to Mrs. Hart was the loss of an opportunity to undergo surgery at the hands of a more experienced surgeon, the duty would have been a duty to inform her that there were more experienced surgeons practising in the field." She explicitly extends a doctor's duty to provide information beyond the giving of information about the "risks" appertaining to the actual procedure, and includes within the categories of information that need to be disclosed by a practitioner the information related to *the competence or levels of experience and skills of the person* undertaking the procedure for the patient. A medical practitioner may be negligent in failing to advise patients of *the option of having other medical practitioners of greater skill and experience conduct the proposed procedure*, because that knowledge could make a difference to the patient's medical decision. However, other judges who formed part of the majority in *Chappel v. Hart* did not join with Justice Gaudron in this formulation. A scholar observed that the obligation to provide information by professionals about levels of proficiency and experience "will be difficult to translate into practice and may have adverse ramifications for the conduct of medicine" (Freckelton and Petersen 1999, 115).

5.7 CAM Alternatives

The term "alternatives" in this book includes not only "alternative treatment options" and "alternative management options", such as unreadily available alternatives, both of which are in the domain of conventional/orthodox/western medicine, but

---

accepted as establishing factual causation, the court is to consider (amongst other relevant things) whether or not and why responsibility for the harm should be imposed on the negligent party.

(3) If it is relevant to the determination of factual causation to determine what the person who suffered harm would have done if the negligent person had not been negligent:

(a) the matter is to be determined subjectively in the light of all relevant circumstances, subject to paragraph (b), and
(b) any statement made by the person after suffering the harm about what he or she would have done is inadmissible except to the extent (if any) that the statement is against his or her interest.

(4) For the purpose of determining the scope of liability, the court is to consider (amongst other relevant things) whether or not and why responsibility for the harm should be imposed on the negligent party.

S 5E of *Civil Liability Act 2002* (NSW) lays down the rule about the onus of proof of causation: "In determining liability for negligence, the plaintiff always bears the onus of proving, on the balance of probabilities, any fact relevant to the issue of causation." Similar formulations concerning the determination of causation and the onus of proof of it are also evident in *Wrongs Act 1958* (Vic) (s 51, s 52); *Civil Law (Wrongs) Act 2002* (ACT) (s 45, s 46); *Civil Liability Act 2002* (Tas) (s 13, s 14); *Civil Liability Act 2002* (WA) (s 5C, s 5D); *Civil Liability Act 2003* (QLD) (s 11, s 12); *Civil Liability Act 1936* (SA) (s 34, s 35).

also "alternatives formed between orthodox medicine and Complementary & Alternative Medicine (CAM)." That raises the issues of the duty of medical practitioners to disclose CAM (including Traditional Chinese Medicine (TCM)) options, the duty of CAM (including TCM) practitioners to disclose conventional/orthodox medicine options, and the duty of dual (orthodox medicine + CAM) practitioners to disclose alternatives.

Does a doctor's duty to disclose alternatives encompass CAM therapies? There is very little by way of precedent to provide an answer. The main excuse for the absence of a duty to disclose is that CAM therapies lack evidence of effectiveness. With the evidence base of some CAM therapies being increasingly established, with the patient being more aware of the existence and availability of CAM therapies, the current practice of closing the door to CAM information disclosure will become more questionable.

Health practitioners should honour divergence of both value systems and cultural connections of different groups of patients. Where conventional treatments have been exhausted and proved to be ineffective, and one CAM therapy provides some promise, a physician has no reason to deny his patient an opportunity to try. Where the risks of the proposed conventional treatment are high and/or the magnitude of potential harm is great, and a CAM therapy has a lower risk/harm profile, a physician has no excuse for not letting his patient know of an alternative possibility, especially when the patient has raised the inquiry, or when, even if alternatives fail, the conventional treatment is still available. Alternative medicine therapies also involve two contexts: adoption and disclosure. These two contexts are both interrelated and distinct. I will devote one separate chapter (Chap. 8) to this topic.

5.8 Doing Nothing: An Option?

There are some disputes over whether doing nothing constitutes a treatment option. Somebody may argue that doing nothing is only *an alternative to treatment*, not *an alternative treatment*.[52] There are three contexts that involve "doing nothing" and informed consent: (1) the context of *doctors electing* nontreatment or "doing nothing"; (2) the context of *patients electing* to "do nothing"; and (3) the context of *doctors not raising* "doing nothing". The first context involves the question of whether nontreatment can trigger the application of the informed consent rule.[53]

[52] *Wheeldon v. Madison*, 374 N.W.2d 372, 376 (S.D. 1985).

[53] There are two lines of views about this. One line of view argues that a cause of action for lack of informed consent can only be allowed in the context of "some *affirmative* violation of plaintiff's physical integrity" *See*, *Smith v. Fields*, 702 N.Y.S.2d 364, 366 (N.Y.A.D. 2 Dept. 2000). Another line of opinion leaves open the possibility that a negligent nondisclosure action can be brought where injuries result from *nontreatment* rather than affirmative treatment. *See*, *Gates v. Jensen*, 595 P.2d 919, 922–923 (Wash. 1979) ("[t]he existence of an abnormal condition in one's body, the presence of a high risk of disease, and *the existence of alternative diagnostic procedures to conclusively determine the presence or absence of that disease* are *all facts* which a patient must know in order to make an informed decision on the course which future medical care will take" (emphasis added)).

A patient needs to be informed of "material facts" in medical decision-making. These facts include "the *risks* of a course of treatment and the feasible alternatives to the proposed treatment", and "the 'treatment' encompasses all aspects of patient care, including the doctor's *resolve to do nothing* about medical abnormalities in the patient's condition."[54]

As to the second context, it has been widely accepted that information that falls within the duty of disclosure under the informed consent rule includes not only the material risks inherent in a proposed procedure, and the availability of any reasonable alternative procedures, but also the "material risks incident to *abstention from treatment*".[55] The informed consent law or professional guidelines of many jurisdictions has happily embraced the rule that a doctor should inform patients of the consequences of *refusing* treatments proposed or recommended by the doctor.

In the context of a doctor withholding or not raising the option of "doing nothing", a reasonable person would choose not to undergo unnecessary surgery if properly advised that there was *a viable alternative to surgery: the option of doing nothing*.[56] Where a doctor undertakes high risk surgery on a patient and it is likely that the injury would resolve on its own, without surgery, the patient will not have given informed consent unless he has been made aware that non-treatment is a viable medical option.[57]

5.9 Conclusion

The term "alternatives" can be formulated in a wide and liberal fashion. The common law has demonstrated that it is not wise to confine the alternatives that fall within a doctor's duty to inform only to "available treatment options". "Alternatives" may include: (1) legally, financially or geographically unavailable treatment options; (2) alternative providers; (3) CAM alternatives; and (4) the option of "doing nothing". The key thing here is not whether it is nice to create those issues, but how we approach those issues nicely. To acknowledge that there may be a *duty* for a doctor to inform the patient of financially or geographically unavailable treatment options,

[54] *Keogan v. Holy Family Hospital*, 622 P. 2d 1246, 1254–1255 (Wash. 1980) (emphasis added).

[55] *Wheeldon v. Madision*, 374 N. W. 2d 367, 375 (S.D. 1985) (emphasis added). *See also*, *Truman v. Thomas* 611 P.2d 902 (Cal. 1980). In this case, the respondent physician had recommended to the appellant's mother that she submit to a pap smear test, but there was evidence that the patient refused to undergo the test and that respondent did not inform her of its purpose or of the risks involved in her refusal to submit to it. The patient subsequently died of cervical cancer. As the Supreme Court of California clarified in the final part of its opinion, this case did not involve a physician's *failure to recommend an appropriate test*, but involved a physician's failure to "inform a patient of the *risks entailed in refusing to follow his advice*". The Court held that the physician must inform the patient of the risks involved in *refusal* to undergo the proposed diagnostic tests.

[56] *Jacobs v. Painter*, 530 A.2d 231, 236–237 (Me. 1987) (emphasis added).

[57] *Lotocky et al v. Markle et al*, 2006 BCSC 1295, at [188].

alternative providers, and CAM alternatives is one thing. Wisely defining the *circumstances* under which those alternatives fall within the duty to inform is another thing. Even if the door is open, it has many thresholds. A cautious, fact-driven and circumstance-based approach is better than a blanket approach. Some "filters", such as the "materiality" of information and causation, will play their roles in this area.

Among those "alternatives", the issues of whether there is a duty for a doctor to inform about emerging treatment options, financially unavailable alternatives, and CAM alternatives are much more frequently raised. Examining these issues also has a practical value. My journey of examining some specific categories of "alternatives" will start with "emerging treatment options" (Chap. 6), followed by "financially unavailable alternatives" (Chap. 7), ending with "CAM alternatives" (Chap. 8).

References

Crozier, G.K.D., and Françoise Baylis. 2010. The ethical physician encounters international medical travel. *Journal of Medical Ethics* 36: 297–301.

Freckelton, Ian, and Kerry Petersen (eds.). 1999. *Controversies in health law*. Sydney: The Federation Press.

Krause, Joan H. 1999. Reconceptualizing informed consent in an era of health care cost containment. *Iowa Law Review* 85: 261–386.

Rostolsky, Brad M. 2002. Practice makes perfect: Experience-related information should fall within the purview of Pennsylvania's doctrine of informed consent. *Duquesne Law Review* 40: 543.

Terrion, Halle Fine. 1993. Informed choice: Physician's duty to disclose non readily available alternatives. *Case Western Reserve Law Review* 43: 491–523.

Twerski, Aaron D., and Neil B. Cohen. 1999. The second revolution in informed consent: Comparing physicians to each other. *Northwestern University Law Review* 94: 1–54.

Chapter 6
Emerging Treatment Options

Abstract This chapter raises the concern that the law is convention-reinforcing in that it gives overwhelming weight and priority to conventional treatment options in formulating legal rules and chills efforts to adopt and disclose emerging treatment options. It raises the issue of whether it is appropriate to apply the "two schools of thought" theory or the *Bolam* test, which is popular in the context of diagnosis and treatment, in the context of disclosure of treatment options. It is argued that the range of treatment options that fall within the duty to inform may be wider than the range of treatments that satisfy the threshold for the "two schools of thought" doctrine or the *Bolam* test. A doctor's duty to inform should not be confined only to conventional, standard and well-established treatment options. In the context of adopting emerging treatment options, the law gives doctors some leeway in trying innovative or new therapies. Doctors have latitude in deciding whether to adopt emerging treatment options. For those who opt against adopting an emerging treatment option, information about that may still fall within the scope of the duty to disclose.

6.1 Introduction

Medical science and medical advances may present a wide spectrum of treatment options for one condition, which can range from very well-established options to very newly-developed options. To avoid overburdening the physicians, the law's main task is to define the ambit or scope of alternatives disclosure, that is, what alternatives should be disclosed in a specific context.

The *two extreme ends* of the spectrum of options involve less controversy and have more clear-cut answers. At the one end, the law does not expect the duty to inform about alternative treatments to be over-extended to include even fringe alternatives

X. Zhao, *The Duty of Medical Practitioners and CAM/TCM Practitioners to Inform Competent Adult Patients about Alternatives*,
DOI 10.1007/978-3-642-31647-0_6, © Springer-Verlag Berlin Heidelberg 2013

or "quackery",[1] while at the other end, the law does not allow the physicians to ignore treatment options that are well-established, time-honoured or offering brighter prospects.[2]

The real difficulty that the law encounters in the process of defining what alternatives should be subject to disclosure lies in *the middle of the spectrum*. Between the two ends of the spectrum, there emerges a variety of "grey" treatment options, something that lie between that of general acceptance and that of universal denial, something that may not be so promising but have some positive prospects, and something that do not have clear-cut advantages or disadvantages.

A question is open: should the law require physicians to disclose alternatives that are only a minority, or even a small minority, within a specialty favour, that are non-conventional or even experimental in nature, that are not so mature, or do not have a clear risk/benefit picture, and if so, under what circumstances? Can the "school of thought" theory, which is so popular in the context of diagnosis and treatment, be used to establish the availability of alternatives in the context of information disclosure?

In this chapter, the concept "emerging treatment options" refers to treatment options that are not well-established or generally-accepted, but offer promising therapeutic possibilities. While the question of whether or not to disclose well-established, conventional, or standard treatment options involves more clear-cut answers, disclosure of emerging, non-conventional treatment options involve more controversy. This chapter also shows loyalty to the distinction between selection/adoption of treatment options and information disclosure about treatment options. They are distinct, but interrelated.

6.2 "A School of Thought" in the Context of Selection of Treatment Options

The doctrine of "two schools of thought" and its equivalents, such as the *Bolam* test and the alternative methods instruction, are designed to protect a *respectable minority*.[3] A physician will not be held liable for exercising clinical judgment when he follows a recognised course of treatment, even if it is recognised by only a minority

[1] *Nattrass v. Weber*, 2008 ABQB 259, at [392] (warning "against over-extending the duty to inform of alternative treatments to the point of including fringe alternatives").

[2] *Seney v. Crooks* (1998), 166 D.L.R. (4th) 337, at [60] (involving an alternative treatment that was not unreasonable, was more reliable to achieve some effects, and was well-known and preferred by some doctors within his community; the court holding that a patient should be advised of a known treatment which others in the same speciality consider superior, even if the doctor does not agree); *see also, Pozdzik (next friend of) v. Wilson*, 2002 ABQB 351, [2003] 311 A.R. 258, at [65]–[66].

[3] It has been repeatedly observed that "[a] charge of negligence in a choice of treatment is refuted, as a matter of law, by showing that a respectable minority of expert physicians approved the method selected." *See, Church v. Bloch*, 182 P.2d 241, 245 (Cal.App. 2 Dist. 1947); *Sim v. Weeks*, 7 Cal. App.2d 28, 37; 45 P.2d 350, 354.

of experts (Kowalski 1998, 518). These doctrines are innovation-friendly because they "give[] physicians some leeway in deviations from customary medical practice" (Kowalski 1998, 506).

However, to qualify as a school of thought under this doctrine, a line of thought should pass both the qualitative and quantitative thresholds. Provided here are a few examples from a variety of jurisdictions. In *Jones v. Chidester*,[4] the Supreme Court of Pennsylvania prescribed an integrated formula for "a school of thought", embracing both qualitative and quantitative hurdles:

> A school of thought should be adopted not only by "reputable and respected physicians" in order to insure *quality* but also by a "considerable number" of medical practitioners for the purpose of meeting *general acceptance* even if it does *not* rise to the level of a *majority* (emphasis added).[5]

In the view of the court, "[i]t is … insufficient to show that there exists *a "small minority*" of physicians who agree with the defendant's questioned practice.… Rather, there must be a *considerable number* of physicians, *recognized and respected* in their field, sufficient to create another 'school of thought' ".[6] The court seems to attempt to form a hierarchy among "small minority", "considerable number" (maybe in minority, but having general acceptance) and "majority". The court's willingness to elevate the quantitative criterion from "small minority" to "considerable number" came from its appreciation of the nature of the "two schools of thought" doctrine, i.e. it provides "a complete defense" to malpractice.[7]

Similarly, the alternative methods instruction only embraces "recognized" and "approved" methods of diagnosis or treatment.[8] As far as the *Bolam* test is concerned, the *qualitative* limitations on medical practices was highlighted in *Bolitho v. City and Hackney HA*:

> The use of these adjectives – *responsible, reasonable and respectable* – all show that the court has to be satisfied that the exponents of the body of opinion relied on can demonstrate that such opinion has *a logical basis*. In particular, in cases involving, as they so often do, the weighing of risks against benefits, the judge before accepting a body of opinion as being

---

[4]*Jones v. Chidester*, 610 A.2d 964 (Pa., 1992).

[5]*Jones v. Chidester*, 610 A.2d 964, 969 (Pa., 1992) (Justice McDermott concurring, noting that "[w]hen each group has its advocates, and each has its arguable reasons, a doctor of either, cannot be faulted if he properly administers the one to his knowledge and experience seems the better, so long as that group is comprised of *a sufficient number of reputable and respected members*." (emphasis added)).

[6]*Jones v. Chidester*, 610 A.2d 964, 969 (Pa., 1992) (emphasis added). Although favouring to keep a quantitative limitation, the Court did not place a numerical certainty on what constitutes a 'considerable number'. Under the doctrine, three experts are sufficient to create another school of thought, but one expert, no matter how accomplished, is not a "school". *See*, *Choma v. Iyer*, 871 A.2d 238, 246 (Pa.Super., 2005) (Lally-Green J. (concurring)).

[7]*Jones v. Chidester*, 610 A.2d 964, 969 (Pa., 1992).

[8]*Barton v. Owen*, 71 Cal.App.3d 484, 502 (Cal.App.2.Dist. 1977).

responsible, reasonable or respectable, will need to be satisfied that, in forming their views, the experts have directed their minds to the question of *comparative risks and benefits* and have reached a *defensible* conclusion on the matter (emphasis added).[9]

Some forms of qualification on medical opinions that deserve judicial special honour and high deference were recommended by Australian review report on law of negligence, intending to "filter out idiosyncratic opinions" (Commonwealth of Australia 2002, 40):

> A medical practitioner is not negligent if the treatment provided was in accordance with an opinion *widely held* by *a significant number* of *respected* practitioners in the field, unless the court considers that the opinion was irrational (emphasis added).[10]

This line of recommendation, with some variation, was followed by the later civil liability legislation of some jurisdictions in Australia.[11] It was intended to introduce a modified *Bolam* test. Such a provision provides "a defence" because it has the effect that, "if the defendant's conduct accorded with professional practice regarded as acceptable by some …, then subject to rationality that professional practice sets the standard of care."[12]

Similarly, under Irish law, although there is no need for a medical practice to be universal, the "general and approved practice" must be "approved of and adhered to

[9]*Bolitho v. City and Hackney HA* [1997] 4 All ER 771, 778. Only in "a rare case", where "it can be demonstrated that the professional opinion is not capable of withstanding a logical analysis", that "the judge is entitled to hold that the body of opinion is not reasonable or responsible". Thus, the court's focus is, first, to see whether the defendant's conduct was consistent with a body of competent professional opinion then prevailing, and, if there was such a body of opinion, then the subsidiary question arises of whether the practices thereby sanctioned can be held to be incapable of withstanding logical analysis and, correspondingly, to be unreasonable or irresponsible. *See*, *Bolitho v. City and Hackney HA* [1997] 4 All ER 771, 779; *Mirza v. Birmingham Health Authority* [2001] EWHC QB 1, at [48].

[10]Commonwealth of Australia (2002), recommendation 3, page 42. In this formulation, "widely held" is designed to prevent reliance being placed on localised, isolated practices; "respected practitioners" is designed to ensure that the opinion deserves to be treated as soundly based.

[11]*Civil Liability Act 2003* (Qld), s 22(1) (2) (3) (4). It needs to be noted that the "significant number" qualification is absent from the clause on the standard of care for professionals in many other jurisdictions' civil liability legislation. *See, Civil Liability Act 2002* (Tas), s 22; *Civil Liability Act 2002* (WA), s 5 PB; *Civil Liability Act 1936* (SA), s 41; *Civil Liability Act 2002* (NSW), s 5O.

[12]*Dobler v. Halverson* (2007) 70 NSWLR 151, 167, at [59], [60] (talking about 5O of the Civil Liability Act 2002 (NSW) (Standard of care for professionals), which reads: (1) A person practising a profession (a professional) does not incur a liability in negligence arising from the provision of a professional service if it is established that the professional acted in a manner that (at the time the service was provided) was widely accepted in Australia by peer professional opinion as competent professional practice. (2) However, peer professional opinion cannot be relied on for the purposes of this section if the court considers that the opinion is irrational. (3) The fact that there are differing peer professional opinions widely accepted in Australia concerning a matter does not prevent any one or more (or all) of those opinions being relied on for the purposes of this section. (4) Peer professional opinion does not have to be universally accepted to be considered widely accepted.).

by *a substantial number* of *reputable* practitioners holding the relevant specialist or general qualifications".[13]

It appears that, to avoid a finding of negligence, a body of medical opinion should satisfy a few qualifications, such as the qualitative "respected" qualification and the quantitative "significant number" limitation. Although intended to protect a minority, the quantitative "number" qualification was alleged to suffer from its weakness that it will prejudice a very small minority opinion at its infancy stage, and, thus, it will weaken physicians' innovative incentive and hinder medical progress (Dailey 1994, 724). The "respectable minority" standard or the "considerable number" test was criticised as conveying "the incorrect notion that the standard for malpractice is to be determined by a poll of the medical profession".[14] By quantifying medical acceptance, the "considerable number" and "respectable minority" standards unfairly bias the fact-finders against medical situations that demand experimentation (Brown 1993, 233–234).

It is good to see that, in order to honour diversity and to protect a respectable minority, in the context of selection/recommendation of treatment options, a course of treatment qualified as one school of thought under the "two schools of thought" theory does not need to find acceptance with the majority. However, due to the absolute defence nature of the doctrine of "two schools of thought" and other equivalent formulations, and the weighty deference the judiciary accords to "a school of thought" or "a responsible body of opinion", it is understandable that these doctrines set *a high threshold* for a school of thought or a body of medical opinion to benefit from such legal mechanisms. They provide *special* protection for doctors adopting more *established, mature and conventional* treatments.

The "two schools of thought" theory and the *Bolam* test are well-established legal principles developed *in the arena of diagnosis and treatment,* especially in the context of *selecting* treatment. A question posed is: are these principles applicable to the new context of *information disclosure*? If yes, how does the law define "a school of thought" in the context of disclosure of treatment options?

It needs to be noted that the scope of information disclosure is basically patient-oriented. The ambit of the duty to disclose would not only be preliminarily defined by medical knowledge but also substantially shaped by the patients' needs and expectations. That dictates that a medical practitioner needs to be sensitive to his patient's needs, including more individual and more subjective needs revealed by the particular patient. That requires a medical practitioner to *keep open* a wider range of treatment options, including ones he would not recommend or contrary views another segment of practitioners prefer. The scope of medical interventions that fall within a doctor's duty to inform may be *wider* than that safely falling within "a school of thought". It may include emerging or burgeoning treatment options.

[13]*Dunne (an infant) v. National Maternity Hospital* [1989] IR 91, 109, per Finlay C.J. (emphasis added).

[14]*Hood v. Phillips*, 554 S.W.2d 160, 165 (Tex. 1977).

In the context of information disclosure where the ambit of disclosure was mainly driven by the patient's needs, expectations and inquires, rather than by medical practice, a more relaxed or generous qualitative and quantitative criteria may be justified. In this new area, the law may feel the need to lower the thresholds. I will further clarify this in the following part of this chapter.

6.3 Adoption of Emerging Treatment Options

6.3.1 According Priority to Conventional Treatments

As mentioned above, in the context of selection of treatment options, the courts accord great deference to a body of medical opinion which satisfies the thresholds set by the *Bolam* test and the "two schools of thought" doctrine. To secure deference embodied in the *Bolam* test or the "two schools of thought" doctrine, a doctor needs to choose or adopt a course of treatment which is acceptable to a "responsible body of opinion" or a "respectable minority" of the medical profession, or attracts a sufficiently wide following.

When faced with a choice between conventional treatments and emerging treatments, due to the uncertainty and potential conflicts of interests surrounding innovations, the law will understandably give priority to conventional ones. In a publicly-funded health care system, emerging or controversial interventions are unlikely to be allowed to be adopted if the patient has not previously received standard or conventional interventions.[15] The judges would like to see a patient has exhausted conventional treatments before he opts for experimental ones.

Another context which illustrates the law's giving priority to convention is that, while the law accords latitude to doctors in selecting or recommending innovative or experimental treatment options, in doing that, as I mentioned in Chap. 4, the doctors should inform the patients of the experimental nature of the proposed

[15]The National Advisory Committee on Health and Disability (New Zealand) *New Health Interventions: A Report to the New Zealand Minister of Health* (2005) <http://www.nhc.health.govt.nz/moh.nsf/indexcm/nhc-new-health-interventions?Open> (last accessed 25 May 2010), page 22. *See also*, *Smith v. Shalala*, 954 F. Supp. 1 (D.D.C., 1996). In this case, the patient challenged FDA's decision to exclude him from its experimental treatment program (Antineoplastons, an experimental anti-cancer agent). The FDA's decision to exclude the patient from experimental Antineoplastons treatment was based on the great concern that he had not received and tried potentially curative chemotherapy, an available, proven treatment for his illness. The court expressed great concern about the efficacy of Antineoplastons treatment because the efficacy of Antineoplastons in the treatment of Hodgkin's disease has not been scientifically established. The court found that, even if the patient had a fundamental right to "choose among available medical treatments," Antineoplastons treatment was not regarded as "available" treatment as a matter of law because it had not been approved for general use by FDA.

treatment[16] and the full range of treatment options, especially conventional or standard options. The patients should be made fully aware of the ready availability of time-honoured or well-established treatments. Doctors should not prevent patients from choosing conventional treatment options. However, practitioners who favour conventional therapies have no parallel obligation to inform patients about available non-conventional/experimental treatments.[17]

Although the law is basically convention-reinforcing, it does give room for doctors and patients to opt out of standard treatments and choose innovative treatments. That can be done by the way of a doctor and his patient entering into a special agreement, such as invoking the "assumption of risk" mechanism.[18] The court "see[s] no

[16]*Ahern v. Veterans Administration*, 537 F.2d 1098, 1102 (C.A.N.M. 1976) (the defendants administering excessive amounts of radiation (2,999 rads over a 5-day period) which was deemed as experimental because it was not within the bounds of recognized medical standards within the medical community; the Court of Appeals observing that "[w]e recognize that there are many considerations that may influence a doctor's decision on the amount of radiation to be administered in any given case. However, our legal system requires that the treatment to be administered must be *within the bounds of recognized medical standards* in order to overcome legal challenges such as that presented in this case. Accordingly, in order for a physician to avoid liability by engaging in *drastic or experimental treatment, which exceeds the bounds of established medical standards*, his patient must always be fully informed of the experimental nature of the treatment and of the foreseeable consequences of that treatment." (emphasis added)); *See also*, *Estrada v. Jaques*, 321 S.E.2d 240, 255 (N.C.App. 1984) (holding that "reasonable standards of informed consent to an experimental procedure require disclosure to the patient that the procedure is experimental"); *Heinrich v. Sweet*, 308 F.3d 48, 69 (C.A.1 (Mass.), 2002) (observing that "a doctor who proposes an experimental course of treatment must not only tell the patient about the treatment and its consequences, but must also inform the patient that he is conducting an experimental treatment and that the patient is part of a study").

[17]*Moore v. Baker*, 989 F.2d 1129 (11th Cir. 1993) (Georgia's informed consent law required disclosure only of alternatives that are "generally recognized and accepted by reasonably prudent physicians").

[18]The doctor and the patient may, by reaching a special agreement, opt for non-conventional therapy. *See*, *Schneider v. Revici*, 817 F.2d 987 (2nd Cir. 1987) (The plaintiff-patient, suffered from breast cancer, refused a biopsy and possibly a partial mastectomy recommended by conventional circle of physicians, and decided to seek the *"non-toxic", non-invasive, nonconventional* treatment methods (selenium and dietary restrictions) that have not been adopted by the medical community. The defendant did not alienate the patient from pursuing conventional therapies. The defendants actually recommended the plaintiff to have the tumor surgically removed on several occasions. The plaintiff brought a diversity action against the defendant, alleging, among other claims, medical malpractice. The defendant raised *express assumption of risk* as an affirmative defense. The Court of Appeals concluded that a jury instruction on express assumption of risk is proper in medical malpractice cases where a patient knowingly forwent conventional medical treatment and instead accepted the risks that caused the injuries.); *Boyle v. Revici*, 961 F.2d 1060 (2nd Cir. 1992) (It involved the same non-conventional physicians as in *Schneider v. Revici*, 817 F.2d 987 (2nd Cir. 1987). A cancer patient did not heed the advice of conventional cancer specialists (undergoing surgery to resect her tumor), instead, chose first to explore a non-invasive alternative consisting of urine monitoring, urinalyses and the ingestion of various mineral compounds; the court held, a charge on *express assumption of risk* was appropriate.); *Charell* v. *Gonzales*, 660 N.Y.S.2d 665 (Sup. 1997) (A patient, being diagnosed with uterine cancer, forwent the recommended chemotherapy and radiation after undergoing hysterectomy, instead decided to undergo alternative treatment which included special diet and six coffee enemas a day.

reason why a patient should not be allowed to make an informed decision to go outside currently approved medical methods in search of an unconventional treatment."[19] The law does not preclude a patient from giving informed consent to experimental procedures even if they are untested and involve uncertainty regarding risks.[20] That is a recognition of the reality that "medical innovation must go forward, and there will also be some cases in which no recognized procedure will offer any prospect of success".[21]

That agreement would override or trump the custom default and enable the doctor to offer innovative treatments to the patient. The signing of an "experimental treatment" agreement bars the patient from complaining about the treatment's unconventional nature (Parchomovsky and Stein 2008, 302). A patient's agreeing to undergo experimental treatments should be accompanied by full information disclosure. The informed consent rule applies not only in the conventional context of *established procedures*, but also has special value in the context of *experimental procedures*.[22] Before making such an agreement, the doctor should inform the patient of the *experimental or innovative* nature of the new treatment and its *conventional alternatives*. The functions of informed consent in the context of research or experimental/innovative treatments are not only to promote individual autonomy, but also to avoid fraud and duress and to encourage rational decision-making.[23]

The alternative treatment practitioner *never inform* his patient that his protocol was *experimental* and not generally accepted in the medical community. The alternative treatment practitioner *dissuaded* the patient from having conventional chemotherapy and radiation, advising his patient not to "mess" with chemotherapy. Even though a practitioner persuaded a patient to opt for a non-conventional therapy and there was no express assumption of risk which would have exonerated defendant, the court found the presence of *implied assumption of risk* which would trigger the comparative fault analysis.). In the English context, *see*, *Shakoor (Deceased) v. Situ* [2000] 4 All ER 181, 188 ("it seems to me that the fact that the patient has chosen to reject the orthodox and prefer the alternative practitioner is something important which must be taken into account. Why should he later be able to complain that the alternative practitioner has not provided him with skill and care in accordance with the standards of those orthodox practitioners whom he has rejected?").

[19] *Schneider* v. *Revici*, 817 F.2d 987, 995 (2nd Cir. 1987) (adding that "[w]hile a patient should be encouraged to exercise care for his own safety, … an informed decision to avoid surgery and conventional chemotherapy is within the patient's right 'to determine what shall be done with his own body' "). *See also*, *Boyle v. Revici*, 961 F.2d 1060, 1063 (2nd Cir. 1992) ("[A] patient may expressly assume the risk of malpractice and dissolve the physician's duty to treat a patient according to the medical community's accepted standards."). *Compare*, *Smith v. Shalala*, 954 F. Supp. 1 (D.D.C., 1996) (court upholding the FDA's decision to exclude a patient from an experimental treatment program (Antineoplastons) because the patient has not tried conventional therapies).

[20] *Estrada v. Jaques*, 321 S.E.2d 240, 254 (N.C.App. 1984).

[21] *Estrada v. Jaques*, 321 S.E.2d 240, 254 (N.C.App. 1984).

[22] *Estrada v. Jaques*, 321 S.E.2d 240, 254 (N.C.App. 1984).

[23] The context of innovative and experimental treatments involves more complicated things. Experimentation is always done with a mixture of motives. Though doctors want the best for their patient, they will also have an eye to the scientific value of their work. The development of new interventions is driven both by commercial imperatives and the individual clinician's desire to improve patient outcomes. A combination of eager researchers and desperate relatives may obscure the fact that the patient's condition is best addressed with conservative, rather than aggressive, therapy.

Both the "informed consent" rule in the context of experimental treatments, which reinforces the orthodox nature of conventional treatments and the uncertain nature of innovative treatments, and the "assumption of risk" mechanism, which serves as a defence for defendants, have an alarming effect, even chilling effect, on a patient's choosing non-conventional therapies. It gives freedom to patients to opt for non-conventional procedure. But it alerts patients to rethink the negative consequences before entering into an agreement with the defendant-doctor about opting for non-conventional therapies.

6.3.2 Leeway in Adopting Emerging Treatment Options

If the patient's informed consent requirements have been satisfied, the law will accord substantial latitude to the medical profession in adopting innovative treatments. Too readily holding a doctor's departure from conventional practice to be negligent could have an inhibiting effect on doctors who seek and adopt novel treatments in their patients' interests. The law has to reach a delicate balance between these competing considerations. Courts have to balance the dangers of too readily condemning novel procedures which went wrong as negligent, against the potential progress that innovation could produce.

Obviously, adopting emerging treatments does not necessarily equate with medical negligence. Courts do not make a finding of negligence simply because a doctor had adopted an innovative therapy and the patient has sustained injury.[24] Courts recognise the public interest in promoting medical progress and allowing the medical profession to develop innovative and more effective treatments without fear of liability.[25]

Because innovative treatments are regarded as inherently "risky" until it has become tried and tested, the law ordinarily imposes on doctors a high degree of care in adopting unconventional treatments. A defendant-doctor employing experimental procedures has to demonstrate that he exercised a high degree of care both in assessing

[24] *Wilsher v. Essex Area Health Authority* [1987] QB 730, 749 ("[I]f the decision to embark on the treatment at all was justifiable and was taken *with the informed consent of the patient*, the court should … be particularly careful not to impute negligence simply because something has gone wrong." (emphasis added)); *Zimmer v. Ringrose* (1981) 124 D.L.R. (3d) 215, 223–224 (noting that the mere adoption of an innovative treatment was not negligence per se); *Cryderman v. Ringrose* [1977] 3 W.W.R. 109; affirmed [1978] 3 W.W.R. 481 (Alta. S. C. Appellate Division) (holding that the defendant-doctor was not negligent just because he had not followed the usual and normal practice).

[25] For example, *Sidaway v. Bethlem Royal Hospital Governors* (1985) AC 871, 893 ("Those members of the public who seek medical or surgical aid would be badly served by the adoption of any legal principles that would confine the doctor to some long-established, well-tried method of treatment only, although its past record of success might be small, if he wanted to be confident that he would not run the risk of being held liable in negligence simply because he tried some more modern treatment, and by some unavoidable mischance it failed to heal but did some harm to the patient. This would encourage 'defensive medicine' with a vengeance.").

the risks of the proposed treatment and the possible alternatives (Jones 2003, 220). If a doctor's decision to adopt a less-conventional treatment had been carefully arrived at, having weighed up all the possibilities, and can be rationally and responsibly supported, the courts would show unwillingness to intervene.

If the defendant-doctor's practice of adopting non-conventional treatments constitutes a responsible body of medical opinion, he can benefit from the ready protection of the *Bolam* test. Even if adopting the new treatment has not yet accepted as proper by a responsible body of medical opinion, thus not eligible for the deference embodied in the *Bolam* test, the doctor still can justify his decision by reference to the "reasonable doctor" standard and the ordinary risks-benefits analysis.[26]

The *Bolam* test is different from the "reasonable doctor" standard. Compared to the *Bolam* test, which is more convention-oriented and orthodoxy-reinforcing, the ordinary "reasonable doctor" standard is more friendly towards innovative or emerging treatments. When utilising the "reasonable doctor" standard and the risks-benefits analysis, the seriousness of the patient's condition, the availability and effectiveness of the conventional treatments, and the relative risk-benefit of the proposed treatment in comparison to the alternative treatments would be taken into account.

In deciding whether or not the adoption of an innovative treatment option amounts to negligence, the courts may consider a few factors, such as any dangers the innovative therapy entails, previous response of the patient to more conventional treatment, the seriousness of the patient's condition, and the attitude of the patient himself towards the novelty and risk (Mason and Laurie 2006, 317).

The English case of *Simms*[27] provided some hints about how the courts should respond to emerging treatment options in the context of there being no available alternatives and the emerging treatment being the *only option* or the last resort for a

[26]Michael A. Jones (2003), 218. In the USA context, *see*, the Texas case of *Hood v. Phillips*, 554 S.W.2d 160 (Tex. 1977). It involved an assertion that "the mode or form of treatment was not a remedy for the diagnosed condition". The Supreme Court of Texas compared four standards that may be applied to such a medical malpractice suit: (1) the "respectable minority" or "considerable number" standard; (2) the "any variance" standard; (3) the "reasonable surgeons would disagree" standard; (4) the "reasonable and prudent doctor" standard. The court expressed its preference for the "reasonable and prudent doctor" standard ("Did the physician undertake a mode or form of treatment which a reasonable and prudent member of the medical profession would not undertake under the same or similar circumstances?"). This standard should be applied whether the mode or form of treatment is *"experimental," "outmoded," or "rejected." See also*, Douglas Rader Brown 1993, 233–234 ("The 'reasonable and prudent doctor' standard is preferable because it allows for the use of 'experimental' methods of treatment. By quantifying medical acceptance, the 'considerable number' and 'respectable minority' standards unfairly bias the jury against medical situations that demand experimentation."); *Leech v. Bralliar*, 275 F. Supp. 897, 902–903 (D.C.Ariz. 1967) ("Prolotherapy as practiced by the defendant in his treatment of the plaintiff was not proper medical practice anywhere as *no physician* would have practiced prolotherapy as the defendant did in treating the plaintiff." (emphasis added)).

[27]*Simms v. An NHS Trust* [2003] 1 All ER 669; [2002] 2 WLR 1465; [2002] EWHC 2734 (Fam).

patient.[28] It recognises that doctors have a certain leeway to adopt therapies that have not yet been well-established as to safety or efficacy. Emerging treatments would be in the patients' best interests having regard to their dire prognosis without therapy and the lack of available alternatives.

After noting that "[t]he '*Bolam* test' ought not to be allowed to inhibit medical progress",[29] Dame Elizabeth Butler-Sloss, P, in this case, held that, consistent with the philosophy that underpins the *Bolam* test, there was *a responsible body of relevant professional opinion* which supports the innovative treatment.[30] Justified by the notion that to search for affirmative support for every type of novel therapy would run counter to the public interest in medical progress, she adopted a fairly weak version of the *Bolam* test: one which allows innovative treatments to fall within a responsible body of medical opinion *in the absence of negative opinion*, rather than on foot of positive endorsements. She had evidence from "responsible medical opinion which does *not reject the research*".[31]

In determining that giving the innovative treatment to the patients is in their best interests, Dame Elizabeth Butler-Sloss, P gave weight to several factors: the nature of the treatment,[32] the wishes of the patients' families,[33] the unavailability of

---

[28]The case involved two young patients, the variant Creutzfeldt-Jakob disease (vCJD) and a treatment that was new and untested on human beings at that time. The variant CJD, widely known as the human form of "mad cow disease", was recognised as a new and rare disease. The disease is characterized by a multiplication of abnormal proteins in the brain, leading at the clinical stage to progressively impaired neurological functioning. Symptoms include an inability to walk or stand, loss of memory, and failure of speech. There were gaps in the knowledge of the mechanism of the disease and in the precise relationship between the abnormal proteins, the loss of nerve cells and neurological dysfunction. The proposed Pentosan Polysulphate treatment (PPS) was not licensed in the United Kingdom. It had no firm scientific basis and no evidence of efficacy and safety. It was not possible at that stage to have any scientific proof of the efficacy of the proposed treatment. The patients' prognosis was dire. There was no cure and there were no recognised effective drugs which have been able to prolong life or arrest the continuing neurological deterioration. *See*, *Simms v. An NHS Trust* [2002] EWHC 2734 (Fam), paras. [3], [9], [31], [59].

[29]*Simms v. An NHS Trust* [2002] EWHC 2734 (Fam), para. [48] ("The '*Bolam* test' ought not to be allowed to inhibit medical progress. And it is clear that if one waited for the '*Bolam* test' to be complied with to its fullest extent, no innovative work such as the use of penicillin or performing heart transplant surgery would ever be attempted.") (citing Lord Diplock in *Sidaway v. Bethlem Royal Hospital Governors* [1985] AC 871 at page 893).

[30]*Simms v. An NHS Trust* [2002] EWHC 2734 (Fam), para. [51].

[31]*Simms v. An NHS Trust* [2002] EWHC 2734 (Fam), para. [48] (emphasis added). The evidence the court relied on were from three English medical witnesses and a distinguished Japanese neuropathologist whose PPS-related paper was in the process of being peer-reviewed by a prestigious medical journal. The evidence revealed that "it would not in itself be irresponsible or unethical" to give the treatment to the patients, although the requirement for surgery raises issues as to the assessment of the risks of that surgery.

[32]In the eyes of the court, the proposed PPS treatment complies with the *Bolam* test. It was not futile. The pioneering treatment could offer possible benefits to the patients. There was, from the medical evidence, a possibility of arresting the disease temporarily, and the possibility of prolonging the life of these two patients to some extent, although whether that be in weeks, months or years is impossible to tell. Although the chance of improvement is slight, it was not non-existent. *See*, *Simms v. An NHS Trust* [2002] EWHC 2734 (Fam), paras. [58] and [61].

[33]*Simms v. An NHS Trust* [2002] EWHC 2734 (Fam), para. [64] ("the views of both families should carry considerable weight in the circumstances of these two young people").

alternatives,[34] and the patients' prognosis.[35] The *Simms* case provides a very special context where the court showed willingness to loosen the requirement of "a responsible body of medical opinion" inherent in the *Bolam* test in considering whether offering a highly experimental therapy was allowable. It reveals that when a patient's prognosis is very poor and resorting to an innovative treatment option is the only or last option, trying the innovative treatment does not run counter with the *Bolam* test. In my view, there is no need to loosen and liberalise the *Bolam* test under these circumstances. The case involved a treatment which had no evidence of efficacy and safety. The *Bolam* test is a special scheme, prepared for the more established body of medical opinion. The *Bolam* test should not be available. When the *Bolam* test is not available, the court can resort to the ordinary "reasonable doctor" test and the risk-benefit analysis to acknowledge a doctor's selecting an experimental treatment.

As I mentioned before, the substantial leeway that the law accords to medical opinions in selecting or adopting emerging treatments is accompanied by the doctor's duty of information disclosure. Adopting innovative treatments and disclosing the bad side of the innovative treatments are two different issues involving different contexts. Even if the defendant-doctor was not held to be negligent in adopting experimental or innovative treatments, he could be held to be negligent in failing to inform the patient of the fact that the treatment was new and risky, or experimental, or had not been approved or not generally accepted by the medical profession.[36] A doctor's decision to expose a patient to uncertainty should be based on the patient's appreciation of the risks and benefits of the proposed treatment and its alternatives, and the patient's informed consent.

For patients with serious illness who have exhausted the existing well-established treatment options but do not have satisfactory results, and who are invited to enrol in an experimental option, the scenario of "medical vulnerability" may ensue (*See* Menikoff 2009, 51). Part of the cause of the patients' vulnerability is the non-availability or under-desirability of conventional treatments and the desperate nature of the patient's pursuit of alternative treatments. For the "medically vulnerable" patients, the "therapeutic misconception" may arise. Therapeutic misconception points to a situation where patients misunderstand the nature of an experimental intervention because of overly optimistic influences promulgated by a variety of formal and informal elements within the clinical and research environment

[34]*Simms v. An NHS Trust* [2002] EWHC 2734 (Fam), para. [61] ("There is no alternative treatment available.").

[35]There was agreement about the inevitable outcome in the absence of any new treatment. The patients were bound to die. There was no cure and there were no recognised effective drugs which had been able to prolong life or arrest the continuing neurological deterioration. The two young people had "very little to lose" in the treatment going ahead. It was a reasonable risk to take on their behalf. *See*, *Simms v. An NHS Trust* [2002] EWHC 2734 (Fam), paras. [9], [62].

[36]*See*, *Zimmer v. Ringrose* (1981) 124 D.L.R. (3d) 215, 223 (but the claimant failed to establish causation because the claimant would have undergone the procedure in any event).

(Ford 2009, 80). Therefore, for "medically vulnerable" patients, there is an additional need to offset the potentially favourable image created by therapeutic misconception. That may be done by the way of over-emphasizing the negative aspects of experimental options or mentioning alternatives to experimental intervention.

6.4 Disclosure of Emerging Treatment Options

The leeway that doctors have in selecting or adopting emerging treatment options means not only that doctors have latitude in opting *for* innovative treatment options, but also that doctors have freedom in *not* offering innovative treatment options. A doctor has no duty to *offer* treatment options that are still at the experimental stage or are still developing.[37] But that is distinct from the question of whether the doctor has the duty to *inform* about the existence of experimental or emerging treatments.

On the one hand, as I mentioned earlier, adoption of emerging treatment options and disclosure of emerging treatment options are two different contexts involving different rules. In the context of adopting emerging treatment options, the law accords great leeway to medical judgment. Doctors have latitude to decide whether or not to offer innovative treatments, subject to the patient's informed consent requirement in the case of opting for experimental or innovative treatments. Both the *Bolam* test and the reasonable doctor standard can provide protection for doctors' discretion and genuine medical judgment. However, the fact that a doctor did not commit malpractice by offering or failing to apply an experimental treatment does not necessarily answer the different question of whether a doctor has a duty to *inform* his patients of the existence of the experimental treatment (Prillaman 1990, 53). Answering the question of whether a doctor should inform his patient of emerging treatment options is mainly driven by particular circumstances, such as medical knowledge of those options, the condition of the patient, the patient's needs, the availability of conventional treatments, and the eagerness of the patient to seek alternatives.

On the other hand, the latitude that the law gives doctors in selecting or adopting emerging treatment options has some bearing on the availability of emerging treatment options and the duty to disclose them. More and more doctors opting for an emerging treatment would increase the presence of the treatment in the relevant medical specialty, helping to elevate it to "a school of thought" or "a responsible body of medical opinion". That would increase the awareness of and medical knowledge about the emerging treatment among practitioners in the relevant medical field. A duty to present patients with *contextualised* information about alternatives

---

[37] *Del Valle Rivera v. United States*, 630 F. Supp. 750 (D.P.R. 1986) (the court found no duty to offer sclerotherapy, a treatment that was not "an available developed therapy" and was utilized on "an experimental basis" in some medical centers).

dictates that the scope of disclosure for a doctor should not be confined to his own "school of thought". An emerging treatment option may fall within a doctor's duty to inform, even if he does not favour, adopt and administer it.

As I said, the requirement that a doctor has a duty to disclose conventional, well-established treatment options, or the "majority" view, involves less controversy. The issue of whether a doctor has a duty to disclose non-conventional, experimental treatment options, or the "minority" view, invites more disputes. How sizable or respectable should the minority be before it falls within the duty to disclose? There is no easy answer to that question. There is difficulty in defining the exact thresholds for a "minority" treatment falling within a doctor's duty to disclose. However, in this part, I will argue that a doctor's duty to inform should not be confined to conventional alternatives only. We should leave open the possibility that emerging and "minority" treatment options may fall well within the scope of a doctor's duty to inform. The adoption-disclosure distinction dictates that the threshold for a treatment option falling within a doctor's duty to inform may be *lower* than the threshold for a treatment option falling within "a school of thought" or "a responsible body of opinion". Or the potential scope of disclosure of alternative treatment options is *wider* than the range of treatment options that satisfy the "two schools of thought" doctrine or the *Bolam* test in the context of a doctor adopting treatment options.

6.4.1 Only More Promising Alternatives?

In the USA landmark informed consent case – *Canterbury v. Spence* – the court expected physicians to disclose only alternative treatments "promising greater benefit than that being pursued"[38] This cautionary approach was followed by some courts in other jurisdictions. Under the Canadian case law, the duty to inform about alternatives and their material risks is based on the assumption that the alternative offers some prospect of therapeutic benefit.[39] Some courts have limited the obligation to inform patients of alternative treatment options only to those options that the doctor believes would offer some advantage and are reasonably likely to achieve a beneficial result.[40] Australian case law also indicates that, if "no other method had any advantage over that employed by the defendant", the plaintiff's allegation of the defendant's failure to advise other methods should fail.[41]

---

[38] *Canterbury v. Spence*, 464 F.2d 772, 781 (D.C.Cir. 1972).

[39] *Sicard v. Sendziak*, 2008 ABQB 690, at [111] (Court of Queen's Bench of Alberta).

[40] *Bucknam v. Kostuik* (1986), 55 OR (2d) 187, upholding (1983), 44 O.R.(2nd) 102 (Ont. S.C.); *Turkington v. Lai*, 52 C.C.L.T. (3d) 254, 281, at 101 (Ont. S. C. J.).

[41] *Burke v. Humphrey* [2001] TASSC 133 (Cox CJ, 21 November, unreported, BC200107222), at [21] (involving methods of tubal ligation). Under the causation analysis, the court also noted that it was "highly unlikely that [the plaintiff] would have put off to a future occasion some other procedure, especially invasive surgery, when *a potentially reversible but equally, if not more effective, method of tubal ligation* was offered to her during a laparoscopy she was due to undergo the next day in any event" (emphasis added) (at [28]).

The courts will be more ready to consider conservative treatment as an alternative to operative treatment if the conservative option is less risky, less invasive, likely to be less painful than the operative one. The duty to obtain informed consent incorporates the duty to advise of material, special or unusual risks and of available alternatives, especially where these are *more conservative* and involve *fewer risks* than the treatment proposed.[42] Conversely, if the suggested alternatives are much more radical and invasive than the proposed treatment, or they present greater risks to the patient, they will not be regarded as reasonable alternatives.[43]

The legal requirement that an alternative should have some advantage over the proposed treatment in one respect or in some respects (risks or benefits) is facing challenge. Some courts have held that alternatives need to be disclosed even if they would be more hazardous than the proposed therapy.[44] The reason for that is,

> The instruction [that an alternative that is more hazardous is not a viable alternative] ... has the effect of limiting the physician's duty to disclosure of *only the least hazardous procedure available, presumably the one contemplated.* The issue then becomes, not whether the patient has been informed of viable alternatives, but *whether the doctor has recommended the least dangerous of them*, because those which are more hazardous need not be discussed. This instruction, therefore, wholly relieves physicians of any obligation to discuss alternatives with their patients and *substitutes merely a duty to recommend the safest procedure*. It is incompatible, therefore, with the view ... that the patient must be provided with sufficient information to allow him to make an intelligent choice (emphasis added).[45]

---

[42]*Sicard v. Sendziak*, 2008 ABQB 690, at [111], [149] (Court of Queen's Bench of Alberta). In the United States case of *Smith v. Karen S. Reisig, M.D., Inc.*, 686 P.2d 285 (Okl. 1984), the patient underwent a surgical procedure (hysterectomy), not being aware of non-surgical alternative (hormonal therapy). The physician's testimony and records established that the non-surgical hormonal therapy as viable and possibly preferable to the surgery. The Supreme Court of Oklahoma held that the patient established a prima facie case under the theory of a physician's failure to disclose alternative treatment, giving rise to liability under "informed consent". It held that the surgery was "unnecessary" or "not an 'absolute' necessity". *See*, *Smith v. Karen S. Reisig, M.D., Inc.*, 686 P.2d 285, 287–288 (Okl. 1984).

[43]*Stockford v. Johnston Estate*, 57 C.C.L.T. (3d) 135, 148–149 (N.B.Q.B.).

[44]*Logan v. Greenwich Hosp. Ass'n*, 191 Conn. 282; 465 A. 2d 294 (Conn. 1983). In order to determine the extent of lupus involvement in kidneys, there was a need for the patient, who had systemic lupus erythematosus (lupus), to undergo a kidney biopsy. The defendant proposed and performed *a closed needle kidney biopsy*, which involved a local anesthetic and insertion of a surgical needle into her back in order to obtain a specimen of kidney tissue, without discussing the alternative of *an open biopsy*, which would require an incision and a general anesthesia, because he did not consider the latter procedure advisable. The *Logan* case centred on the propriety of the court instruction which directed that the duty of a physician to advise a patient of possible alternatives in obtaining an informed consent to a contemplated operative procedure does not require the disclosure of *a more hazardous alternative*. The Supreme Court of Connecticut rejected the instruction. *See also*, *Gemme v. Goldberg*, 626 A.2d 318, 327 (Conn. App. 1993) ("We cannot say as a matter of law that a doctor is any more justified in withholding information from a patient on the ground that the *result* would have been *less perfect* than our Supreme Court could conclude as a matter of law that a more hazardous procedure need not be disclosed." (emphasis added)); *Parkins v. U.S.*, 834 F. Supp. 569 (D. Conn. 1993) (The undisclosed option did *not* carry with it the *risk of paralysis* since the aorta would be clamped in the abdominal region, but it was *more dangerous*.).

[45]*Logan v. Greenwich Hosp. Ass'n*, 465 A.2d 294, 301 (Conn. 1983).

The perception that an alternative that is "more hazardous", or "more dangerous", or "having less perfect result" is not a viable alternative exclusively focuses on the dark side (risks) of undisclosed treatment options and ignores the bright side of them. As quoted above, it translates a physician's duty to disclose alternative treatment options into "a duty to recommend [only] the safest procedure". It fails to recognise the fact that patients may have a different risk-benefit assessment from that of physicians. Furthermore, a simple rule that "more hazardous" alternatives need not be disclosed ignores the reality that there is often controversy within the medical profession about the respective risks and benefits of competing treatments that have different risk-benefit balances (Prillaman 1990, 49). It is not conclusive that the alternative that the physician recommends is more or less invasive than other alternatives.[46]

6.4.2 Only More Mature Alternatives?

If one alternative is well-established, time-honoured, evidence-based, and has already attracted a sufficiently wide following within one specialty of health profession, a physician will find it difficult to excuse his practice of not mentioning it to his patient.[47] The answer to the issue of a doctor's duty to inform about conventional and well-established treatment options is more clear-cut.

Courts are more inclined to endorse mainstream (generally used and generally accepted) treatments as treatment alternatives. However, courts are less inclined to deem minority therapies as alternatives that should be disclosed.[48] In a jurisdiction where the informed consent law requires disclosure only of treatment options that are "generally recognized and accepted" by reasonably prudent physicians, there is difficulty for a minority therapy being seen as an alternative to a mainstream

[46] *Matthies v. Mastromonaco*, 733 A. 2d 456, 464 (N. J. 1999) (involving alternatives that the physician does not recommend, the plaintiff alleging that the doctor did not inform her of the riskier, but potentially more successful, alternative of surgery).

[47] For example, the Canadian case of *Seney v. Crooks* (1998), 166 D.L.R. (4th) 337 is concerned with well- known alternative. In that case, the alternative treatment not discussed by the doctor was not unreasonable, it was a more reliable method of achieving some effects, and was well-known and preferred by some doctors within his community. The court did not hesitate to hold that a patient should be advised of a known treatment which others in the same speciality consider superior, even if the doctor does not agree.

[48] *Wachter v. United States*, 689 F. Supp. 1420, 1423–1424 (D. Md. 1988) (If one procedure "was not in general use, was not then known among surgeons to produce better results, and was not the subject of any definitive study showing it would be better than [the proposed treatment]", it will not be viewed as a "medically significant alternative".).

treatment.[49] A single expert should not be permitted to "second-guess an entire profession" when it comes to establishing a professional standard of care.[50]

However, there is still room for emerging and "minority" treatments being characterised as alternative treatment options that need to be disclosed. It is arguable that a doctor is obliged to make the patient aware of all alternative treatments, including those he does not favour, so long as they are supported by respectable medical opinion. Another possible criterion would be that "the treatment in question must be 'accepted' (as opposed to 'acceptable') as an appropriate treatment by some substantial percentage of practitioners in the relevant specialty" (Prillaman 1990, 55). Expert medical testimony may be necessary to establish the existence and feasibility of one procedure, to explore the number and respectability of those accepting the procedure. An individual expert may represent a respectable segment of profession.[51]

My view is that, in the context of information disclosure about alternative treatment options, it is not wise to simply cite the *Bolam* test or the "two schools of thought" doctrine to determine the thresholds that an alternative treatment option must cross before it can fall within the scope of information disclosure. More conventional, time-honoured, well-established and popular treatment options can easily pass the thresholds set by the *Bolam* test or the "two schools of thought" doctrine, and therefore can easily be regarded as alternatives to the proposed treatment. Less conventional, less time-honoured, less well-established and less popular treatment options are still have a chance of being regarded as "a responsible body of medical

[49]*See*, *Moore v. Baker*, 989 F.2d 1129 (11th Cir. 1993). In this case, the split among professional opinions surrounded a choice between invasive neurosurgical procedure (carotid endarterectomy) and a non-surgical procedure (ethylene diamine tetra acetic acide chelation (EDTA) therapy) for treatment of a blockage of carotid artery. The minority view, asserted by two experts testimony produced by the plaintiff-patient, supported treating EDTA therapy as an alternative to surgery. The plaintiff-patient even alleged that EDTA therapy was a more promising alternative because "[it] is as effective as carotid endarterectomy in treating coronary blockages, but it does not entail those risks that accompany invasive surgery". However, the minority view was overwhelmed by majority view. The overwhelming evidence produced by the defendants suggested that EDTA was not recognized in the "mainstream medical community" as an alternative to a carotid endarterectomy in treating coronary blockages because it was not only ineffective but also dangerous.

[50]*Spann v. Irwin Memorial Blood Centers*, 34 Cal.App.4th 644, 655 (Cal.App.1.Dist. 1995) (citing *Osborn v. Irwin Memorial Blood Bank*, 5 Cal.App.4th at p. 276).

[51]*Archer v. Galbraith*, 567 P.2d 1155, 1161 (Wash.App. 1977) ("The doctor testifying about possible alternatives set forth a means of therapy pursued by *a respectable segment* of the medical profession. The patient was entitled to be told about that alternative. The testimony was not a recitation on a course of treatment followed only by the medical witness himself." (emphasis added)). In this Washington case, the defendant doctor recommended and performed a surgery because, in his opinion, surgery was absolutely necessary and was the only acceptable and successful treatment for the patient's condition. The defendant's opinion was shared by some other physicians who testified that surgery was the preferred method of treatment for the patient. However, one physician's testimony revealed that, although surgery may be recommended, the patient actually had three choices: (1) a choice of removing a nodule (surgery); (2) a choice of keeping a nodule under observation for a period of time to see whether it would increase in size or regress under medication; (3) a choice of leaving it alone. *See also*, *Wenger v. Oregon Urology Clinic*, 796 P. 2d 376 (Or. App. 1990).

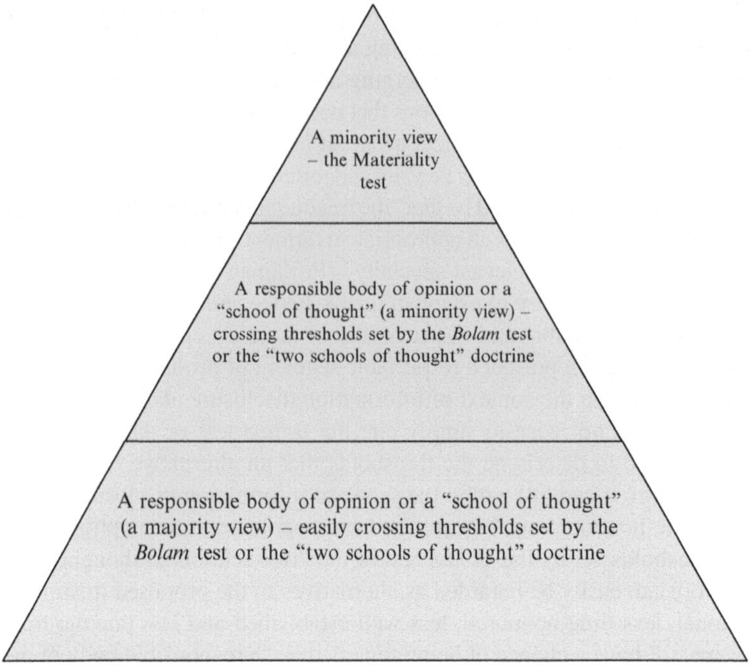

Fig. 6.1 "A minority view"

opinion" or a "school of thought", thus have ample opportunity to be deemed as alternatives to the contemplated treatment (Fig. 6.1).

However, in the context of information disclosure, it is not wise to arbitrarily hold that only conventional and well-established treatments fall within a doctor's duty to inform. The scope of alternatives that should be disclosed is wider than that contemplated by the *Bolam* test or the "two schools of thought" doctrine. The scope of information disclosure is driven by the patient-oriented materiality test. For controversial treatment options, there is always dichotomy in opinions among doctors. There may be a majority of doctors who do not favour the controversial treatment option. There also may be a minority of doctors who believe in the efficacy of the treatment and has a commitment to the controversial treatment. In most cases, the reason why a defendant-doctor did not disclose a "minority" treatment is not that the treatment was not available, but that he did not prefer or recommend it, even if he knew it and acknowledged it as an option.[52] While the legal principles can accord

[52]For example, *Logan v. Greenwich Hosp. Ass'n*, 191 Conn. 282; 465 A. 2d 294 (Conn. 1983) (The reason why the defendant did not consider open biopsy to be a viable alternative for the plaintiff was that there is a greater risk of complications, especially those involving general anaesthesia. The defendant personally did not recommend and mention an open biopsy procedure, although he had performed such operation previously and conceded that "it was a more controlled procedure in terms of visualizing the kidney").

substantial latitude to doctors in selecting treatment options, which is tolerant of technical fragmentation, I doubt the soundness of legal rules that confine the doctor's duty to inform only to treatment options they favour and, thus, reinforce the "informational" dichotomy.

Both the "majority" view holders and the "minority" view holders should give patients a more balanced and contextualised picture of treatment options. Their personal views and preferences can be revealed and voiced in the context of recommendation. But that does not excuse doctors from presenting a full picture to patients. It is always safe to say that a doctor's duty to inform only encompasses the mature or "majority" treatment options or treatments favoured by a significant number of reputable practitioners in the field. But it is not wise for the law to completely close the door to the novel, innovative, experimental or "minority" treatment options. The scope of information disclosure should be patient-oriented and circumstance-tailored.

6.5 Conclusion and Suggestion

In a situation involving selection and disclosure of conventional therapies and non-conventional therapies, in order to protect patients from being subjected to uncertain risks and conflicts of interests, the law accords priority to more conventional therapies rather than experimental, or innovative, therapies. The law is basically orthodoxy-reinforcing.

The latitude and deference the law accords to medical practitioners in selecting a course of action under the "two schools of thought" doctrine or the *Bolam* test is given only to a school of thought that has passed the required qualitative and quantitative thresholds. The mature, time-honoured, and well-established treatment options can easily cross those thresholds and fall within the territory of the *Bolam* test or the "two schools of thought" doctrine. For those innovative treatment options which do not readily fall within the scope of the *Bolam* test or the "two schools of thought" doctrine, the doctor can justify his adopting novel options by utilising the "reasonable doctor" standard and the ordinary risks-benefits analysis. The law normally gives doctors leeway in exercising medical judgment and selecting treatments. But it also subjects a doctor's choosing non-conventional treatments to heightened scrutiny.

To avoid potential liability, the medical practitioners who intend to adopt the non-conventional therapies, especially the controversial and highly experimental therapies, may pursue a special arrangement with the patients, such as a patient's consent, or a patient's "assumption of risk". Such a mechanism, through offering defendants a defence, would frighten a patient away from opting for non-conventional treatment options.

There are concerns that non-conventional therapies may entail unclear risks and a practitioner's opting for a non-conventional alternative may involve conflict of interests. To alert patients of the uncertainty and to avoid potential abuse, the law requires that, before undergoing non-conventional treatment or reaching agreement, the practitioner must satisfy the informed consent requirements. That means the doctor must fully inform the patient of the "dark side" (the uncertainty of risks/benefits or the non-conventional/experimental nature) of the proposed therapy and the availability of conventional treatments. The practitioner should not hide the dark side of the non-conventional therapies and should not alienate the patient from pursuing conventional therapies.

Greater uncertainty about risks and benefits and fears of conflicts of interests account for demanding more thorough consent in the experimental context. Before subjecting the patient to non-conventional treatments, the patient is entitled to information about the merits and demerits of the proposed treatment and its alternatives, including conventional alternatives. However, the experiment-convention dichotomy actually honours an all-or-nothing approach. It ignores the reality that treatment options may present a spectrum rather than a bright-line distinction between standard and experimental interventions. In medical practice, the distinctions between research, innovation, and treatment sometimes are almost indistinguishable. A treatment option may not be easily and clearly defined as conventional or experimental.

In many relationships between professionals and their clients, custom serves as a modifiable contractual default. A doctor's compliance with the relevant custom, practice, or "school of thought" "*is* adequate care as a matter of substantive law".[53] Provision of non-customary care exposes physicians to a heightened prospect of liability (Parchomovsky and Stein 2008, 291). Relying on customs and conventional technologies as the benchmark for assigning tort liability chills innovation and distorts its path.[54] It "subsidizes producers and users of conventional technologies while taxing innovators" (Parchomovsky and Stein 2008, 288).

In a similar fashion, labelling innovative procedures as "experimental" is likely to frighten away some patients. It entails more than the extra cost of securing the patient's informed consent. Too readily labelling a treatment as experimental could stultify medical progress. Giving conventional options overwhelming weight and priority may hinder innovation and disadvantage medical advances. A solution may be that the law can lower the thresholds for convention so as to embrace more non-conventional wisdom or elevate some types of experimentation to the camp of custom so as to let them to benefit from the convention-reinforcing rules.

---

[53]Gideon Parchomovsky and Alex Stein 2008, 301 (emphasis in the original).

[54]Gideon Parchomovsky and Alex Stein 2008, 286 (highlighting the distortionary effect of the torts system on innovation; proposing two possible reforms: (1) "policymakers can make tort law more welcoming to innovation by eliminating the privileged status of custom and moving to a pure cost-benefit system" ("equalizing down."), (2) "[i]nstead of abolishing the custom rules, it is possible to keep them and grant certain innovations, approved by special boards of industry experts, the same privileged status as enjoyed by custom" ("equalizing up")).

To enable fair competition between conventional and non-conventional practices, the legal system needs to shift the focus from *the conventional or experimental "nature"* of the procedure to a pure *merits-demerits* or risks-benefits analysis of procedures. It needs to place innovative treatments on an informational par with conventional ones. If a potential recipient of an innovative treatment needs to be aware of the conventional alternatives to the proposed innovative treatment, conventional doctors also need to make patients receiving conventional treatments aware of the available innovative alternatives to the proposed conventional treatments, if the innovative alternatives have merits, promises and advantages in some respects.

In the context of selection of treatment options, judicial deference only attaches to genuine medical judgment, and medical opinions or schools of thought that cross the qualitative or/and quantitative thresholds. Some legal theories, such as the *Bolam* test and the "two schools of thought" doctrine, are intended to protect diversity and the minority. However, due to the absolute defence nature of the doctrines and the heavy weight that the courts accord to the "school of thought", setting a high threshold for a "school of thought" is both warranted and understandable. A medical opinion attracting only a small minority of followers will not be regarded as being generally accepted, and will therefore not benefit from such a special protection.

However, uncritically copying the "school of thought" thresholds, which are developed in the arena of diagnosis and treatment, to the context of information disclosure may not be appropriate. The two contexts have different focuses and rationales. In the context of disclosure of treatment options, lower thresholds may be needed. The threshold for a treatment option falling within a duty to inform should be lower than the threshold required by the "two schools of thought" doctrine or the *Bolam* test. If warranted, a medical practitioner may need to mention less mature, or less time-honoured, or less popular treatment options. Disclosure and adoption of innovative treatments is sincerely needed in a context where the patient suffers from serious illness and conventional treatment options have been exhausted or are not available.

Again, I would like to emphasise that a more contextualised disclosure of conventional and non-conventional treatment options could be complemented by doctors' recommendation and persuasion. Doctors still have a place to voice their personal views and preferences. For standard/mature/conventional treatment options, the law can allow a high level of persuasion. For non-conventional or innovative treatments, whether they are minor deviations from standards in clinical setting or purely experimental interventions, the law can keep them open as alternative treatment options but only give a low allowance of persuasion. For medically vulnerable patients for whom conventional treatment options have been exhausted or are not available, although innovative or experimental options should be made open as alternatives, the law should give doctors a low allowance of recommendation. A weak "suggestion", rather than strong recommendation or persuasion, may be enough.

To overcome or alleviate the problems that the convention-experiment dichotomy produces, I propose a more gradual approach of categorising conventional and experimental treatments (Fig. 6.2). The approach encompasses both the adoption and disclosure of conventional and experimental treatment options. It honours the

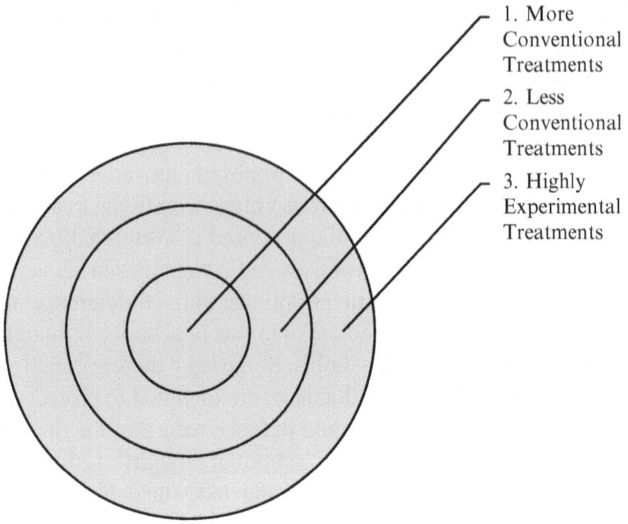

Fig. 6.2 A more gradual approach

adoption-disclosure distinction. It also encourages a more contextualised and balanced information disclosure. It is more merit-based rather than orthodoxy-reinforcing.

1. **More conventional treatments**: *easily satisfying* the *Bolam* test or the "two schools of thought" doctrine; having *more opportunities* of being adopted and disclosed; applying *the Bolam test* (in the context of adoption), and the *ordinary informed consent* requirements regarding disclosure of the risks-benefits of the proposed treatment and its alternatives (including *conventional and,* if warranted, *emerging* treatment options) (in the context of information disclosure); allowing *a higher level of recommendation and persuasion.*
2. **Less conventional treatments**: having *the possibility of satisfying* the *Bolam* test or the "two schools of thought" doctrine; if not forming "a responsible body of medical opinion" or "a school of thought", still can be justified by the reasonableness test and the risks-benefits analysis; having *opportunities* of being adopted and disclosed; applying *the Bolam test or the "reasonable doctor" test* (in the context of adoption) and the *ordinary informed consent* requirements regarding disclosure of the risks-benefits of the proposed treatment and its alternatives (including *conventional and,* if warranted, *emerging* treatment options) (in the context of information disclosure); *allowing recommendation and persuasion.*
3. **Highly experimental treatments**: having *little possibility of satisfying* the *Bolam* test or the "two schools of thought" doctrine; can be justified by the reasonableness test and the risks-benefits analysis; having *less opportunities* of being adopted and disclosed; applying *the "reasonable doctor" test* (in the context of adoption) and the *strengthened or heightened informed consent* requirements (in the context of infor-

mation disclosure) under which, in addition to the disclosure of the risks-benefits of the proposed treatment and its *conventional alternatives*, the *"experimental" nature* of the proposed treatment needs to be disclosed; inviting *the "assumption of risk" mechanism* for adoption; allowing *a low level of recommendation.*

References

Brown, Douglas Rader. 1993. Panacea or Pandora's Box: The "two schools of medical thought" doctrine after *Jones v. Chidester*, 610 A.2D 961 (PA. 1992). *Washington University, Journal of Urban and Contemporary Law* 44: 223.

Commonwealth of Australia. 2002. Review of the law of negligence: Final report. http://revofneg.treasury.gov.au/content/review2.asp. Accessed 22 July 2008.

Dailey, Joan P. 1994. The two schools of thought and informed consent doctrines in Pennsylvania: A model for integration. *Dickinson Law Review* 98: 713–737.

Ford, Paul J. 2009. Vulnerable brains: Research ethics and neurosurgical patients. *Journal of Law, Medicine & Ethics* 37: 73–82.

Jones, Michael A. 2003. *Medical negligence*. London: Sweet & Maxwell.

Kowalski, Michael. 1998. Applying the "two schools of thought" doctrine to the repressed memory controversy. *Journal of Legal Medicine* 19: 503–547.

Mason, J.K., and G.T. Laurie. 2006. *Law and medical ethics*, 7th ed. New York: Oxford University Press.

Menikoff, Jerry. 2009. The vulnerability of the very sick. *Journal of Law, Medicine & Ethics* 37: 51–58.

Parchomovsky, Gideon, and Alex Stein. 2008. Torts and innovation. *Michigan Law Review* 107: 285–315.

Prillaman, Hunter L. 1990. A physician's duty to inform of newly developed therapy. *Journal of Contemporary Health Law and Policy* 6: 43–58.

Chapter 7
Financially Unavailable Treatment Options

Abstract This chapter addresses the issue of whether or not a doctor should inform patients of treatment options not available in the publicly-funded health care system due to limited resources in that system. It answers many concerns raised about disclosing treatment options not available in publicly-funded health care, such as it may cause distress and discomfort to patients and doctors, it may disrupt rationing, and it is time-consuming. It critically examines an approach of tailoring the extent of disclosure based on whether the patient is "inquisitive", "well-informed", "well-educated" and has the ability to afford the treatments. This chapter follows and reinforces a distinction between the "provision" of care and information disclosure. It is argued that, in an effort to reconcile the conflict between resource limitations and patients' freedom of choice, the profession-oriented, community-regarding, and resource-conscious rule concerning the "provision" of health care should be complemented by a patient-oriented, autonomy-regarding and resource-blind rule concerning information disclosure.

7.1 Introduction

Publicly-funded health care systems are not immune from cost-containment pressures (Jones 2003, 351). Finite resources and potentially infinite demands dictate that, in a public health care system, resources allocation or prioritisation is an inevitable fact of life. In this chapter, I pose three questions: (1) Should the provision of services be subject to the "resource constraints" qualification? (2) If the first question is answered affirmatively, should the adequacy of information disclosure, especially the disclosure of treatment options not readily available in publicly-funded health care, be equally qualified by resource constraints? (3) If we differentiate the context of information disclosure from that of diagnosis/treatment and make the former context less resource-sensitive, what consequences (including resources implications) that would entail? Is resource-blind disclosure of treatment options "cost-effective"?

X. Zhao, *The Duty of Medical Practitioners and CAM/TCM Practitioners to Inform Competent Adult Patients about Alternatives*,
DOI 10.1007/978-3-642-31647-0_7, © Springer-Verlag Berlin Heidelberg 2013

I will try to use the wisdom and evidence demonstrated by some jurisdictions, especially the UK, to inform the answers. Because there is dearth of case of law to inform the answer, I rely a little heavily on academic debates and health care statistics, which are more universally applicable than the case law, to clarify the issue. The arguments this chapter makes have some universal value. They can be applicable to every jurisdiction where cost-containment is a component of health care delivery, no matter whether it provides mainly publicly-funded heath care, such as in the UK, Canada, Australia and New Zealand, or it is dominated by private health care, such as the USA.

This chapter continues to adhere to the general distinction between the context of diagnosis/treatment and that of information disclosure. It is evidenced by the division between Part 7.2 and Part 7.3 of this chapter. Following this distinction, I will argue that, in a public heath care system where resource-consciousness is essential, the law needs to encourage and turn a green light to the medical profession's cost-sensitive provision of treatment, but the law should honour and promote the doctor's resource-blind disclosure of information to patients, including information regarding treatment options unavailable in publicly-funded health care. The resource-blind information disclosure is more desirable and "cost-effective" than the resource-conscious information disclosure.

7.2 Provision of Treatments: Resource-Conscious?

The legal principles surrounding medical negligence, including the standard of care, developed in an ideal environment where doctors had little concern for resource limitation and when the best interests of patients could be the all-encompassing motivational force (Caulfield 1994, 689). Medical malpractice law is built upon a culture in which doctors have sole authority to define the quality of health care and the standard of care is set without reference to the patient and public resources. In an era where there is resource constraint on access to health care and where resource considerations are an integral part of professional judgment, some have reason to question the wisdom of utilizing the legal doctrines from an earlier era.

Cost containment does not necessarily mean a decrease in quality of health care (Caulfield 1994, 694). Cost containment measures do not necessarily result in insufficiency of care or even substandard of care. One can even argue that adopting cost containment strategies would actually increase the quality of health care by precluding doctors from prescribing unnecessary procedures. However, there is a possibility that cost containment measures may lead to less than optimal medical services, even adverse outcomes.[1] Therefore, under certain circumstances, cost containment does complicate the existing health law principles.

[1]Laura Athens Mellas 1991, 301 (pointing out that, feeling pressured to contain costs, physicians may react by (1) failing to admit a patient to hospital, (2) foregoing costly diagnostic or treatment services, (3) prematurely discharging a patient, (4) failing to obtain informed consent with respect to decisions based upon cost considerations). *See also*, Samia A. Hurst, Reidun Forde, Stella Reiter-Theil, Anne-Marie Slowther, Arnaud Perrier, Renzo Pegoraro and Marion Danis 2007, 140–142 (a survey revealing that most respondents/physicians (68%) reported adverse outcomes from scarcity); Michael V. Williams 2007, 915 (revealing the negative consequences of "unacceptable" radiotherapy waiting times).

In a medical culture one of whose pursuits is the cost-effectiveness of medical interventions, an inevitable issue is whether the cost-conscious physicians should be assessed by the cost-effective standard of care. That entails an interrelated question of whether economic considerations can be incorporated into standard-setting for doctors. How can one reconcile doctors' standard of care and medical liability with the culture of cost containment? How can one resolve doctors' dilemma of providing patients with quality of care while containing costs and avoiding malpractice liability? In this regard, commentators have proposed three approaches (*See*, Giordani 1989, 1026–1027; Mellas 1991, 306–307; Caulfield 1994, 709–710): (1) adjusting standard of care to reflect cost-containment sentiments[2]; (2) invoking resource constraint as a defence or excuse[3]; (3) extending potential liability to all resource allocation decision-makers.[4]

The problem and the reality is that, compared to the governmental/institutional (administrative) or "macro" rationing makers, the "micro" or individual resource allocation decision-makers (doctors) have more tort liability exposure.[5] It is still

[2]The first approach wants to see customary medical practice to gradually adjust to reflect health care rationing, or to see the professional standard of care to mirror more cost-effective practices, therefore protecting cost-conscious doctors from malpractice liability. The medical profession could incorporate cost containment concerns into their medical protocols and guidelines. Cost conscious guidelines and cost conscious practices could serve as evidence of custom.

[3]The second approach entails creating an immunity based upon cost containment as an excuse for substandard care. It means that a doctor would admit that the care was substandard, but invoke economic circumstances to excuse him, rather than adjust the standard of care.

[4]The third approach – the idea of extending potential liability to third-party decision-makers – is built on the rationale that those parties who are responsible for cost containment decisions and benefit from cost containment should also suffer the adverse consequences of cost containment and bear the costs of any negligent decision making. The biggest advantage that the approach of extending the potential liability to all levels of decision-makers has is that it does not compromise standard of care and does not deny patients compensation of harms caused by cost containment. Therefore, egalitarian and humanitarian values would be served. However, under current legal principles, holding "macro" or "meso" decision-makers to be responsible for the outcome of their resource allocation decisions is not easy. To invoke extended liability, third party payors should have compromised the doctor's sole exercise of medical authority. *See*, *Wickline v. State of California*, 192 Cal. App.3d 1630, 1645–1646 (the California Court of Appeals observing that third party payor liability may arise when cost limitation programs "corrupt" or "override" medical judgment, or treating physicians are "paralyzed" or "rendered powerless to act appropriately" by third party payor).

[5]In the England, the judicial deference to resource-allocation decisions is more likely to be showed in the "menu of care"/judicial review cases rather than in the "inadequacy of care"/negligence cases. The English case law seems to have created a distinction between *no* care being offered because of there being no resources to perform the care at all, on the one hand, and *inadequate* care being provided because of inadequate resources. *See*, Michael A. Jones 2003, 348; Christopher Newdick 1997, 301–305; Frances H. Miller 1992, 54–60 (examining three English cases regarding judicial review of administrative action). Canadian case law seems to present similarly confusing legal landscapes. *See*, Louise R. Sweatman, Diane Woollard 2002, 280; *McLean v. Carr Estate* (1994) 363 A.P.R. 271, 289 (Newfoundland SC); *Law Estate v. Simice* (1994) 21 C.C.L.T. (2d) 228, 240 (B.C.S.C.) (the court being less receptive to the resource restriction arguments at the individual, clinical, or patient-physician level, and observing that

unclear why the judiciary has adopted divergent attitudes towards the resource restraint argument in cases where health care delivery involves the same resource implications.

My view is that the doctors' provision of treatments should be allowed to be resource-sensitive. In a cost-consciousness-promoting environment, the courts should not ignore the impact of resource restriction on the clinical practice.[6] Resource-blind dealing with traditional legal principles exposes doctors to huge potential for liability. If the patient harm were caused by resource-conscious medical practice, blame should be allocated to all responsible parties who joined the chain of resource allocation, not just the end of that chain – "micro" decision makers (doctors). If extending liability to third parties is not feasible, adjusting existing legal principles to accommodate the cost-containment culture is the second best option. Refusing to adjust the standard of care to accommodate resource considerations ignores the fact that, in publicly-funded health systems, doctors are encouraged by professional bodies to make, and are actively involved in making, resources allocation decisions.[7] "[I]t is obvious that many clinical decisions made by doctors in

---

> No doubt such sophisticated equipment [CT scans] is limited and costly to use. No doubt there are budgetary restraints on them. But this is a case where, in my opinion, *those constraints worked against the patient's interest by inhibiting the doctors in their judgment of what should be done for him.* That is to be deplored. I understand that there are budgetary problems confronting the health care system. I raise it in passing only to point out that there were a number of references to the effect of financial restraint on the treatment of this patient. I respectfully say it is something to be carefully considered by those who are responsible for the provision of medical care and those who are responsible for financing it. I also say that *if it comes to a choice between a physician's responsibility to his or her individual patient and his or her responsibility to the medicare system overall, the former must take precedence* in a case such as this. The severity of the harm that may occur to the patient who is permitted to go undiagnosed is far greater than the financial harm that will occur to the medicare system if one more CT scan procedure only shows the patient is not suffering from a serious medical condition (emphasis added).

[6]*See*, *Mathura v. Scarborough General Hospital* (1999) O.J. No. 47 (Ontario Crt of Justice (Gen Div) (1999) 85 O.T.C. 328 (unreported) (commenting that "the court must take into account the availability and cost of procedures, medication and equipment to the attending physician at the time when the cause of action arose. This consideration will affect the standard of care in that a doctor cannot reasonably be expected to provide care, which is unavailable or impracticable due to the scarcity of resources.").

[7]*See*, Medical Council of New Zealand *Statement on Safe Practice in an Environment of Resource Limitation* (August 2008) <www.mcnz.org.nz> (last accessed 22 April 2010), Ethical principles 1 and 4 (Although acknowledging that the care of the patient is a doctor's first concern, Medical Council of New Zealand makes it clear that doctors have a responsibility to *the community at large* to foster the proper use of resources and must balance their duty of care to each patient with their duty of care to the population), Ethical principle 2 (Doctors have a responsibility to try to provide the *best* standards of service possible *with the resources available*); Ethical principle 3 (resource limitation should be recognised as an important part of the environment of medical professional practice); Canadian Medical Association *Code of Ethics* (Update 2004), [43]–[44] at <http://www.cma.ca> (last accessed 24 April 2010) (requiring physicians to recognize their responsibility to promote equitable access to health care resources, and asking them to use health care resources prudently);

public hospitals must of necessity, *have a resource related component*."[8] A standard of care analysis has both *medical or scientific* component and *allocation* component.[9]

Technically, it is not very difficult to incorporate resource-sensitivity into traditional legal principles. For example, the *Bolam* test could be applied to have the effect that, provided a responsible body of professional opinion would endorse a doctor's more "cost-effective" or resource-sensitive practice, the law should not attach negligence to the doctor's provision of care, even though another responsible body of professional opinion would disagree. The *Bolam* test means that the patient is only entitled to the lowest common denominator.[10] "If pressure on resources pushes standards down *in fact*, the minimum acceptable standard *in law* will also decline."[11] The defendant's behaviour is compared to that of similarly placed colleagues. That comparison can be done with respect not only to experience, skill and knowledge, but also to the "circumstances", such as the economic context, in which the doctor is rendering the service (Sweatman and Woollard 2002, 277). Arguably, in a resource-sensitive health care, a doctor's legal standard of care incorporates a duty to take account of resource restrictions reasonably.

To achieve that effect, the law needs to be honest with the resource allocation component of clinical decisions. It is unwise to give a mixed medical and rationing decision a "veil" of pure medical judgment.[12] The judicial deference to ration-

---

General Medical Council (UK) *Management for Doctors* (2006), [10], [20] at <www.gmc-uk.org> (last accessed 24 April 2010) (announcing that all practicing doctors play a role in setting priorities and have a duty to the health of the wider community). The Royal Australasian College of Physicians and Royal Australasian College of Surgeons share very similar formulations, saying that the physician/surgeon should (1) be aware of the importance of wise stewardship of resources, and (2) avoid unnecessary procedures and wasteful practices, and work with colleagues, institutions, government and the community to promote *cost-effective care*, and to develop policy regarding priorities of care. As far as standard of clinical practice is concerned, the surgeon must provide a *good* standard of clinical care, consistent with the prevailing standards of the specialty, *within the constraints of systems and resources*. *See*, The Royal Australasian College of Physicians (RACP) *Code of Professional Behaviour* (2006) 1.4 (II) <http://www.racp.edu.au/page/policy-and-advocacy/ethics> (last accessed 27 April 2010); Royal Australasian College of Surgeons *Code of Conduct* (2006) 1.4 <http://www.surgeons.org/Content/ContentFolders/Policies/FES_PST_2021_P_Code_of_Conduct.pdf> (last accessed 27 April 2010).

[8]*Shortland v. Northland Health Ltd (No. 2)* (unrep, HC Whangarei, M No. 75/97, 6 November 1997, Salmon J.), at p. 13 (emphasis added).

[9]Timothy Caulfield 1995, 989 (but arguing to distinguish these two components; while the medical component involves technical matters that are beyond the expertise of the judge or jury, the allocation component involves the social policy which may be open to a broader examination by the judge or jury).

[10]Michael A. Jones 2003, 353. *See also*, Frances H. Miller 1992, 57–58.

[11]Michael A. Jones 2003, 353 (emphasis in the original).

[12]*See*, *R. v. Cambridge Health Authority* [1995] 2 All ER 129, [1995] 1 WLR 898, [1995] Fam Law 480, [1995] EWCA Civ 49, [1995] 6 Med LR 250 (a father challenging a health authority's decision not to fund further treatment of his child by way of chemotherapy and a second bone marrow transplant; involving *remedial* (as opposed to *palliative*) treatment that might have prolonged the child's life; the health authority categorising the *remedial* treatment as "experimental and unproven" treatment rather than standard therapy; Sir Thomas Bingham MR feeling lack of expertise in judging

ing decisions involving the availability of particular treatments to individual patients is better justified by citing resource restriction rather than disguising them in the name of medical judgment. By admitting the need to allocate resources even at the individualised level, the courts can find a more persuasive basis to establish their opinion that in a cost-containment culture an individual patient's preference should be subordinate to the community's needs, and a more cost-conscious body of medical opinion should prevail over a less cost-sensitive one. In a cost containment environment, the cost-conscious bodies of opinion deserve to be respected and promoted. The judicial deference to divergent medical opinions inherent in the *Bolam* test is not applicable in a cost-containment context.[13]

In a resource-conscious context, how to deal with the relationship between legal authority, medical practice and the patient's wishes or "choice" involves many difficult questions.[14] It raises the issue of whether public health care can afford the patient's choice or "consumerism". Drawing a distinction between the provision of health care and information disclosure would help to reconcile the conflict between resource restrictions on health care delivery and the patients' liberty and choices. On the one hand, the judiciary should stop favouring implicit rationing and acknowledge that the clinical decisions made by medical professionals working in public health care system have a component of resource allocation. The courts should require and show deference to the resource-conscious medical opinions and practices. On the other hand, honouring the patient's autonomy and choices are not furthered by insisting that resource-conscious doctors administer resource-blind procedures, but by informing patients of all treatment options, both resource-driven and resource-free, the rationale for the resource-conscious body of opinion, and helping patients to choose the best available options according to particular circumstances.

---

the "effectiveness" or "merits" of "medical judgment" and adopting a non-interventionist approach towards the more cost-conscious body of medical opinion); *Shortland v. Northland Health Ltd* [1998] 1 NZLR 433, 443 (CA) (noting that "there was no resource dimension" in a decision favouring palliative care rather than curative care). Both the English case of *Cambridge* and the NZ case of *Shortland* presented a scenario of there being divergence on the merits and demerits of the disputed treatment among doctors. If that scenario is involved, how should courts respond? Paying equal respect to different responsible bodies of opinion, or allowing one body of opinion to take precedence over another and favouring a more cost-conscious body of opinion?

[13]*See*, R.J. Paterson 1998, 576–577 (distinguishing two categories of guidelines: if the guidelines are intended to set a benchmark for good practice, judicial scrutiny is likely to be confined to whether that standard accorded with the practice of a responsible body of medical opinion; however, if the guidelines are used to prioritise access to health services, and move from issues of effectiveness to cost effectiveness, judicial review is possibly involved).

[14]Jonathan Montgomery 2006, 185–210 (thinking about the relationship between the law and medical practice; favouring an "integrated" (more deferential) model).

7.3 Disclosure of Treatment Options: Resource-Blind?

7.3.1 Disutility?

There are two ways of rationing of resources: *implicit* rationing and *explicit* rationing.[15] Scholars who favour implicit rationing and hiding information about financially unavailable treatment options from patients allege that explicitness in rationing may cause various members of society to experience disutility. It was claimed that "[g] reater total utility may ... result from the equivocation associated with implicit rationing than from the openness and honesty of explicitness."[16] Firstly, citizens becoming involved in the process of denying care to particular groups of individuals or particular individuals (through either colluding with some form of technical rationing scheme or being directly involved in rationing through some form of public consultation process) may experience disutility (denial disutility) (Coast 1997, 1120). The citizenry who are aware that they have some responsibility for denying treatment to some individuals may experience anguish, especially when the victims are visible (Coast 1997, 1120). Secondly, disutility may result when particular individuals are informed explicitly that their care is being rationed (deprivation disutility). The patients and their relatives, who know that they are being denied services that other patients had received explicitly because of cost, might feel anguish, resentfulness and hopelessness (Coast 1997, 1121).

However, the utilitarian approach of traditional health economics – the disutility theory – presents only part of the story. First, any benefit derived from deception and lack of visibility will be sustained only while patients are kept in ignorance (Doyal 1997, 1117). In a modern well-informed society, any deception is likely to be exposed. Patients who discover that they have been deceived could have a sense of betrayal; their unhappiness would probably far outweigh any distress flowing

[15]The key difference between the two is that, while explicit prioritisation involves the establishment of clear, publicly available criteria and processes specifically designed to set priorities, implicit prioritisation decisions are made without reference to a clear, publicly defined set of criteria. Implicit rationing took place beneath the cover or "veil" of clinical judgment. It was camouflaged under clinical judgment. *See*, The National Advisory Committee on Health and Disability (the National Health Committee or the NHC) (New Zealand) *Prioritising Health Services: A back ground Paper for the National Health Committee* (2004) <http://www.nhc.health.govt.nz/moh.nsf/indexcm/nhc-prioritising-health-services?Open> (last accessed 25 May 2010), page 5; Keith Syrett 2004, 296.

[16]Joanna Coast 1997, 1121. *See also*, J. Thomson et al. 2006, 704–705 (revealing Australian survey results). According to the Australian survey, the most common reasons for not informing the patient of High Cost Drugs (HCDs) were: (1) "the knowledge that they could not obtain this new drug would be too distressing for the patient and their family"; (2) "I would feel bad mentioning a drug that the patient probably cannot afford"; and (3) "the knowledge that some patients can afford to pay for the HCD will only cause distress in those who cannot".

from being told the truth.[17] When a patient, through his own research or discovery, appreciates that his doctor failed to inform him of medically available (although *financially* unavailable) treatments, his trust in his doctor and the profession in general will be undermined (Perry 2007, 915). On the clinician side, sustaining deception over time can itself be distressing, especially in circumstances where the patients ask more direct questions and professional bodies emphasise that the patients' best interests and autonomy should be doctors' primary concern (Doyal 1997, 1117).

Second, the pro-implicit-rationing arguments do not dovetail comfortably with the expectations from patients. A qualitative study[18] done in the UK context revealed that most patients were pleased that they had been provided with all information, regardless of whether or not they had been able to contest successfully the rationing decision or obtain treatment in the private sector. Patients generally favour more explicit rationing, regarding implicit rationing as paternalistic and disempowering (Owen-Smith et al. 2010b, 19). All patient informants had an awareness of health care rationing (Owen-Smith et al. 2010b, 16–17). Of the 31 patients, 21 said that they would *always* want to know about rationing of their own health care, and a further four said they would want to know about rationing in some situations, such as if their life were under threat (Owen-Smith et al. 2010b, 16–17). Only two patients were opposed to explicit rationing, and only one of these completely opposed it in relation to her own treatment (Owen-Smith et al. 2010b, 16–17).

Although it would be cruel and inhumane to tell patients that a therapy might help them, but they have no access to it, silence under such circumstances is equally cruel and inhumane (Miller 1992, 70). Where the patient lacks the money or political influence to secure the preferred care, telling him that his care is inferior, or informing him that a medical beneficial treatment is to be withheld, or is not immediately available, may leave the patient angry and disillusioned with the physician and the health care system as a whole.[19] Despite that, as revealed by the survey I mentioned above, most people would rather have that information than be kept in ignorance. Moreover, despite the fears expressed by clinicians, explicit rationing did not habitually damage relationships with patients, although these were threatened if clinicians did not respond honestly to direct questioning about treatment options, or tried to control patients' reactions to rationing (e.g., through discouraging protests against decision-making) (Owen-Smith et al. 2010a, 91).

---

[17]Len Doyal 1997, 1117. *See* also Amanda Owen-Smith et al. 2010b, 18 (a study revealed that most of the patient informants were understanding of the decision not to disclose and defended their clinicians by arguing they had been forced into a difficult situation by funding bodies, but there are some cases where finding out about implicit rationing had led to complete trust-destroying or a breakdown of the doctor-patient relationship).

[18]Amanda Owen-Smith et al. 2010b, 14–20 (research consisting of in-depth interviews with 31 patients and 21 health care professionals). *See also*, Amanda Owen-Smith et al. 2010a, 88–92.

[19]Timothy A. Caulfield and Diana E. Ginn 1994, 342 ("The suggestion that it would be better for patients not to know would seem to be based either on the paternalistic assumption that patients must not be exposed to unpleasant realities or on an attempt to shield the medical profession from patients' anger regarding rationing.").

However, it should be noted that explicit rationing and openness about treatment options is *not always* the right and best approach for all patients at the consultation level, although it is a preferred option. For example, concerns about the disadvantages of explicitness were raised by the above-mentioned survey. Twenty-four of 31 patient informants acknowledged the distressful nature of openness for patients when they learned that potentially helpful treatments cannot be provided (Owen-Smith et al. 2010b, 17). Six also commented that being explicit about rationing could be distressing for clinical professionals (Owen-Smith et al. 2010b, 17). Searching for the patients' wishes and preferences, and adopting a patient-centred approach are needed.

7.3.2 A Sensitive and Reactive Approach?

For the persons who prefer not to inform a patient of treatments that are available and appropriate but cannot be offered purely for financial reasons, there is another argument which is correlated with the "disutility" argument. That is: when the "availability" of a treatment is effectively a chimera, informing the patient of the treatment serves no useful purpose.[20] If a medical resource is truly beyond the patient's means, disclosure is deemed unnecessary since mere "theoretical availability" does not enhance patient choice.

With those notions in mind, some doctors might take a sensitive, but discriminatory, approach, tailoring the extent of disclosure to the circumstances of whether the patient "is unfamiliar with the internet and has not heard of NICE" or whether he "would … want to cause any trouble" (Firth 2007, 827). Some might adopt a reactive rather than a proactive approach to information disclosure, waiting for patients asking questions about financially unavailable treatments (Firth 2007, 827). A qualitative study revealed that, for some clinical professionals, the question of whether a patient deserves more explicit or cost-blind disclosure would depend on (1) the possibility that patents could pay for private care; (2) the likelihood that patients could successfully contest or overturn decisions; (3) whether patients seemed particularly well-informed or whether patients had raised questions about the availability of particular treatments (Owen-Smith et al. 2010b, 18). Another study also showed that some GPs did not want to embarrass their patients or make them feel that they were getting a second rate care by being open with financially unavailable treatment options (Jones et al. 2004, 97). GPs spoke of making assumptions about their patients' resources and opting not to inform them of certain treatment possibilities on the grounds that they *assumed* the patient could not afford to pay for such treatments (Jones et al. 2004, 97). Their openness about rationing and treatments would

[20]Response to "John Firth: Should you tell patients about beneficial treatments that they cannot have? No" ((2007) 334 *BMJ* 827), "Ethics 101" by Andrew Montgomery, at <http://www.bmj.com/cgi/eletters/334/7598/827#164184> (last accessed 12 June 2010).

to some extent be conditional on whether the patient was "well-educated", "assertive" and "knowledgeable" about current treatments (Jones et al. 2004, 97).

Echoing the "disutility" concerns, these approaches handle the patients' circumstances sensitively. However, these sensitive but discriminatory approaches to disclosure seem to be built on many *paternalistic assumptions*. As I mentioned before, they contradict the preference of the majority of patients, who simply feel that they had a right to be told all relevant information (Owen-Smith et al. 2010b, 20). In answering why patients prefer explicit rationing, a recent qualitative study revealed that the most common justification for explicitness is that openness gives patients the opportunity to overturn decisions, either by paying for private care or by contesting decision-making (Owen-Smith et al. 2010b, 17). Nearly half of the patient informants observed that to be upfront about rationing was a moral obligation for doctors *regardless of* whether the patient was likely to be *able to overturn the decision* (Owen-Smith et al. 2010b, 17). That is said against the background information that the majority (25 of 31) of the patient informants wish to be honestly told about the rationing in their health care (Owen-Smith et al. 2010b, 16–17).

Furthermore, an approach of making full disclosure conditional on the clinicians' perception of patients' abilities to overturn decisions and their prior knowledge of treatment options available may serve to reinforce rather than redress social inequalities in access to information and health care (Owen-Smith et al. 2010b, 20). The sensitive, reactive and discriminatory approach of information disclosure favours the more "inquisitive", "well-informed", "well-educated", or "wealthy" patients. Although deciding to devote their own resource to treatment may be available only to the wealthy or those who take out additional health insurance, it is not right for information disclosure to draw distinctions between the wealthy and the poor and to give information only to those who can afford it and keep the poor in ignorance (Marcus 2007, 826).

In addition to accepting the menu of treatments offered by the cost-containment health care system, there is a wide range of alternative courses of action.[21] Doctors cannot know what resources their patients may have or be able to rally. Just because his patient would appear unable to pay for a treatment that the physician believes could markedly improve his quality of life is not a reason to deny him the knowledge about it.[22] Doctors cannot make "a sweeping judgment" about the patients'

[21]Timothy A. Caulfield and Diana E. Ginn 1994, 336–337 (contemplating that the possibilities that patients may pursue include: (1) purchasing uncovered medical services from personal funds; (2) attempting to obtain the rationed treatment in another jurisdiction using personal economic resources; (3) obtaining access to treatment through supplementary medical benefits provided by an employer; (4) a community raising money for a person to travel to wherever the needed treatment is available; (5) an individual or an advocacy group attempting to convince the health care provider that the individual does not fall within the parameters of the rationing scheme; (6) convincing or pressuring the government or hospital to change the policy).

[22]Response to "John Firth: Should you tell patients about beneficial treatments that they cannot have? No" ((2007) 334 *BMJ* 827), "The inverse care law working again" by Peter B. Hadfield, at <http://www.bmj.com/cgi/eletters/334/7598/827#164184> (last accessed 12 June 2010).

social and economic status.[23] Again, a patient-centred and patient-preference-based approach, rather than a patient-status-dependant approach, is needed.

7.3.3 Undermining Rationing?

The third argument that is frequently raised against explicit rationing and disclosing financially unavailable treatments is that explicitness may disrupt rationing.[24] It has been claimed that bureaucratic and political difficulties would accompany explicit rationing.[25] It is not easy to strike the right balance between competing claims for funding. Consumer and producer lobbying would ensue. Explicit rationing may undermine clinical discretion in rationing.

Although the concern raised above is, on the face of it, reasonable, and needs to be tackled,[26] making rationing more explicit and disclosing financially unavailable treatment options does not mean that it will necessarily compromise the cost-containment efforts. There is a distinction between the provision of care and the disclosure of information. Disclosing alternatives and giving patients information to consider alternative courses of action does not mean that the doctors have a duty to "bend the rules" for individual patients and provide care that the hospital or government has made unavailable (Caulfield and Ginn 1994, 339). Furthermore, contrary to the argument of undermining rationing, full disclosure may be beneficial to the cost-containment initiatives. It can educate the public and raise the awareness of resource restrictions. It can promote the democracy and transparency of rationing process. By disclosing the benefits and risks of all available alternatives, many patients may choose less aggressive, and less costly treatments, therefore helping to control costs in health care (Caulfield and Ginn 1994, 339).

---

[23] Response to "John Firth: Should you tell patients about beneficial treatments that they cannot have? No" ((2007) 334 *BMJ* 827), "The inverse care law working again" by Peter B. Hadfield, at <http://www.bmj.com/cgi/eletters/334/7598/827#164184> (last accessed 12 June 2010).

[24] This line of concern was also echoed by some surveyed patients in a qualitative study. Some patient informants argued that explicit rationing might lead to more protests and lobbying for increased NHS funding. Several patient informants raised the concern that explicit rationing may have negative implications for the long-term viability of the NHS because it might increase demands for expensive treatments, particularly when those who had been denied treatments publicized their plight through the media. *See*, Amanda Owen-Smith et al. 2010b, 17.

[25] Len Doyal 1997, 1115 ("Letting the cat out of the bag would then advantage articulate patients who will know how to play the now transparent system.").

[26] For example, although involving the community or the public in the medicine assessment and prioritisation process is valuable for transparency, experts did not recommend that the patients and their representatives and advocates should be involved in making funding decisions. *See*, Paul McCormack, Joy Quigley & Paul Hansen *Review of access to high-cost, highly-specialised medicines in New Zealand*: Report to Minister of Health (March 2010) <www.beehive.govt.nz/release/access+high+cost+medicines+report+received> (last accessed 4 June 2010), page 65.

Even if the more explicit rationing would lead to more legal challenges and thus expose decision-makers to judicial review, the case law reveals that the judiciary's focus is only on the procedural fairness rather than the substance of the decisions. The judiciary pays high deference to decision-making of the rationing bodies.[27] The judicial deference to resource-driven decisions makes it very hard for patients to shake rationing decisions. On the other hand, legal challenges against rationing decisions would help to enhance the integrity of rationing decision-making. Moreover, legal challenges targeting rationing decisions would compel funding decisions to move closer to responsible medical opinions.[28] Furthermore, legal challenges also may make the rationing process more sensitive to the individualised circumstances.

7.3.4 Time Resource

In answering the question of whether doctors should inform their patients of treatments that they cannot have for financial reasons, some doctors may also adopt a pragmatic approach, raising the "time" constraint, a busy waiting room and "an overbooked clinic" as justification for withholding information or diluting quality of consultation (Firth 2007, 827).

Time appears to be one of the scarcest resources in primary care. There is intimate relationship between time resources and quality and quantity of information disclosure. On the one side, funding constraints would influence quality of consultation. A study shows that, although most GPs tended to identify strongly with the role of patient advocate, they experienced role tensions particularly with respect to wider responsibilities for budgets, populations, and society in general (Jones et al. 2004, 100). Scare resource could affect the extent to which GPs were willing to be open with patients. The availability of GP time was found to play an important role in the gap between professed allegiance to principles and the interpretation and implementation of those principles in practice (Jones et al. 2004, 100). A survey

---

[27]The English case law has shown that the courts are reluctant to intervene into funding decisions on health interventions, if they are resources-driven, no matter at what level they are (macro-, meso-, or micro-layer). *See*, *Pfizer Ltd., R. (on the application of) v. Secretary of State for Health* [2002] EWCA Civ 1566, 70 BMLR 219; *Servier Laboratories Ltd, R. (on the application of) v. National Institute for Health & Clinical Excellence & Ors* [2009] EWHC 281 (Admin), (2009) 108 BMLR 1, [2009] LS Law Medical 163; *R. v. Cambridge Health Authority* [1995] 1 WLR 898, 906; *R. v. North West Lancashire Health Authority* [2000] 1 WLR 977, 991; *Murphy, R. (on the application of) v. Salford Primary Care Trust* [2008] EWHC 1908 (Admin), para [6]; *Otley, R. (on the application of) v. Barking & Dagenham NHS Primary Care Trust* [2007] EWHC 1927 (Admin), para [25]; *Ross, R. (on the application of) v. West Sussex Primary Care Trust* [2008] EWHC 2252 (Admin), para [33].

[28]*North West Lancashire Health Authority v. A & Ors* [1999] EWCA Civ 2022, [2000] 1 WLR 977 (requiring priorities-setting or funding decisions to closely mirror prevailing medical opinions).

revealed that the personal time spent with patients is one of the interventions reported as being rationed the most frequently (Hurst et al. 2006, 1141).

Conversely, maintaining high qualify information disclosure has resource implications. Good ethics and good professional practice cost money (Jones et al. 2004, 101). Patient involvement will have significant implications for funding primary care, particularly in terms of addressing the demands made on consultation time (Jones et al. 2004, 100). Making disclosure resource-blind involves discussion with patients about the cost-containment rationales behind the decisions and the cost-contained or rationed treatment options or management options. That inevitably consumes time and human resources.

However, it needs to be noted that any kind of information disclosure consumes time, not just disclosure of the rationale of rationing decisions and financially unavailable treatment options. The values of empowering patients, promoting good doctor-patient relationship, and improving quality of care outweigh any resources concern.[29] Moreover, the conflict between the time pressure and high quality of disclosure is not irreconcilable. Although consultation involves resources consuming, its resource implications can be alleviated by adopting better strategies of imparting information and making more efficient use of limited human resources.

Finally, I would like to note that, according to an Australian survey, among the reasons for not informing patients of High Cost Drugs (HCDs), the reason that "it is too time consuming to discuss all the potential treatment options" is the *least* favoured explanation for not discussing HCDs in each of the three scenarios[30] (8%, 9% and 4%).[31]

---

[29]*See*, NICE (UK) *Prostate Cancer: Diagnosis and Treatment* – Full Guideline (February 2008), page 9 (The Guideline Development Group did not rate the topic of "communicating with men with prostate cancer, their partners and carers" as a health economic priority; therefore the cost-effectiveness literature on the topic has not been reviewed).

[30]The 3 scenarios are: **Scenario A**: A High Cost Drug (HCD) shown in a phase III study involving people with metastatic cancer to result in an improvement of median overall survival of 5 months (median overall survival extended from around 24 to 29 months). This was based on a study of trastuzumab in combination with chemotherapy for women with metastatic breast cancer. **Scenario B**: A HCD shown in a phase II study (no phase III data available) involving patients with a malignancy resistant to all other forms of treatment, to result in a high objective tumour response. **Scenario C**: A HCD shown in a phase III study to result in similar response and survival benefit as standard chemotherapy, but with significantly improved patient tolerability – based on a study of gemcitabine with cisplatin versus 'MVAC' (methotrexate, vinblastine, doxorubicin, and cisplatin) combination chemotherapy for patients with metastatic bladder cancer.

[31]J. Thomson et al. 2006, 704–705 (most common reasons for not informing the patient of HCDs reflects the "disutility" argument rather than the "time" argument). *See also*, Response to "John Firth: Should you tell patients about beneficial treatments that they cannot have? No" ((2007) 334 *BMJ* 827), "The inverse care law working again" by Peter B. Hadfield ("To use the excuse of a busy waiting room was [] poor"); "Not the doctor's choice any more?" by Steve Choong ("The argument about time spent on explanations and workload is irrelevant and should be addressed through doctors' line management.") at <http://www.bmj.com/cgi/eletters/334/7598/827#164184> (last accessed 12 June 2010).

7.4 Conclusion

In the context of resource constraints and information disclosure, this book follows the same thinking it formed in the context of ordinary therapeutic context. That is, a distinction needs to be drawn between the scenario of diagnosis/treatment and that of information disclosure (Fig. 7.1). As far as the issue of diagnosis/treatment is concerned, the difference between the context of resource constraints and the ordinary therapeutic context is that, in the former context, the law would not honour the diversity of professional opinions, as required by the *Bolam* test. Practising in a cost-containment environment, doctors have to make their provision of service cost-conscious or cost-effective. The standard of care applicable to this context should be profession-oriented or physician-dominated. The law should incorporate cost-effectiveness or cost-consciousness consideration into the task of setting standard of care. In a resource-conscious medical culture, the law needs to favour a resource-sensitive or "cost-effective" body of opinion in delivering health care.

Information disclosure is different from other aspects of health care, such as diagnosis and treatment. Resource/cost constraints should not restrict the adequacy of information disclosure. The scope of a doctor's duty to inform about treatment options includes the duty to disclose treatment options that are not available in publicly funded health care. First, the concern that being open with patients about financially unavailable treatment options may cause unhappiness and stress seems to be too generalised and to be based on paternalistic assumptions. Most patients like, expect and will not be upset by, honest information about financially unavailable treatments. Second, a sensitive and reactive approach in offering information about financially unavailable treatments is discriminatory in nature, and it reinforces social inequalities. Whether or not to inform patients of financially unavailable treatment options should depend on the patients' preferences, rather than their economic, educational and other social status. Third, the worry that raising awareness of rationing and financially unavailable treatments would undermine rationing is over-emphasised. Fourth, the attention drawn

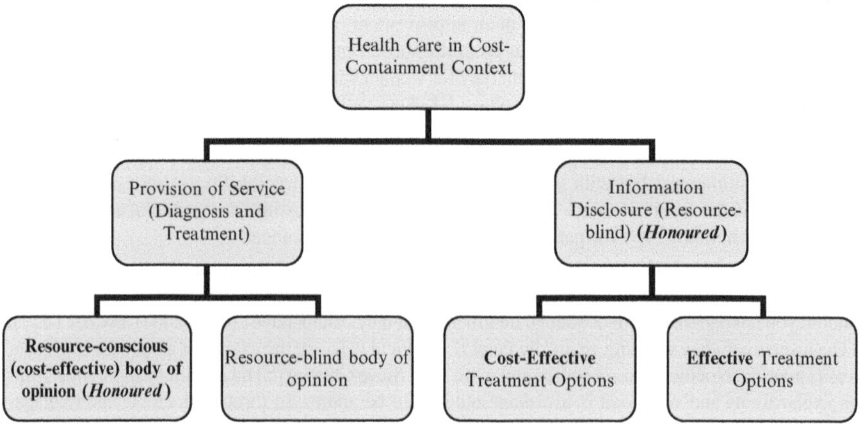

Fig. 7.1 Divisible health care in cost-containment context

to the time resource implications of sufficient information disclosure does not seem to reflect the health care reality. Time is not, should not be, the main consideration when doctors decide to withhold information about financially unavailable treatments. The law needs to allow and promote resource-blind information disclosure.

Technically, the requirement of making rationing more explicit and disclosing information about treatment options not readily available to patients can be easily achieved by interpreting a doctor's duty to inform about *risks and alternatives*. Appreciation of risks and awareness of alternatives are interrelated. One may demand disclosure of a cost containment policy by arguing that, by using less expensive medicines with more side effects or having to be placed on a waiting list for a surgical procedure, it might add to the "material risks" of a given treatment program.[32] The requirement of disclosing cost-contained treatment options can also be argued by utilising the "alternatives" component of information disclosure. A patient needs to be informed of alternative treatments, including those that are made unavailable because of cost-containment measures. A more patient-oriented standard of information disclosure embraces two limbs or two kinds of duty to inform: (1) the objective (a reasonable person in the patient's position) limb or a proactive duty to inform; (2) the subjective (a particular patient) limb or a reactive duty to inform. A doctor's proactive duty to inform about financially unavailable treatment options may arise if a reasonable person in the patient's position would be likely to attach significance to such information in making decisions. Moreover, a doctor's reactive duty to inform would be triggered if a particular patient delivered enquires about resource limitations and their effect on the availability of treatment options.

The argument that the "alternatives" that fall within a doctor's duty to inform may encompass financially unavailable treatment options does not mean that *all* patients *should* be exposed to such a disclosure. A blanket approach of exposing every patient to information about rationing and financially unavailable treatment options, like the approach of denying all patients the right of being told of such information, is paternalistic in nature. There will be some patients, although in a small minority, who do not favour explicit rationing and full information disclosure. Therefore, a search for a patient's wishes is preferred.

Disclosure should be patient-preference-dependant. First, a doctor should honestly answer a patient's *inquiry* about financially unavailable treatment options. Second, in a context where *no specific inquiry* involves, the law needs to make a "presumption in favour of disclosure" about financially unavailable treatment options. That is based on the preferences of the majority of patients who would want to know the rationing of their care and the availability of treatment options that is made unavailable because of cost. Third, the "presumption in favour of disclosure" needs to leave room, such as by acknowledging the possibility of a patient *"waiving" information* about financially unavailable treatment options, to the patient's wishes that he does not want to be upset by such information.

[32]Timothy A. Caulfield and Diana E. Ginn 1994, 330–331 (trying to answer the question of whether the law of informed consent requires a physician to disclose cost containment policies or programs that might affect the treatment available to a patient).

Finally, there is a need to note that, even if there is a duty, and a breach of it, for a doctor to inform about financially unavailable treatment options, and even if the patient has already established the "materiality" of the undisclosed information to his decision to follow the proposed treatment, the patient still needs to establish "causation" in a medical negligence case (*see,* Chap. 9, for comparing the New Zealand's Code approach with the Tort approach). That may entail demonstration that (1) the patient, if being informed of financially unavailable treatment options, probably would not have followed the proposed treatment, and would have taken alternative actions ("decision causation"); and (2) pursuing alternative actions would have avoided the injury the patient suffered ("injury causation"). That poses a difficult, if not insurmountable, task for patients.

References

Caulfield, Timothy A. 1994. Health care reform: Can tort law meet the challenge? *Alberta Law Review* 32: 685.

Caulfield, Timothy A. 1995. Case comment: *ter Neuzen v. Korn* and the standard of care: A call for caution. *Alberta Law Review* 34: 986.

Caulfield, Timothy A., and Diana E. Ginn. 1994. The high price of full disclosure: Informed consent and cost containment in health care. *Manitoba Law Journal* 22: 328–344.

Coast, Joanna. 1997. The rationing debate: Rationing within the NHS should be explicit – The case against. *British Medical Journal* 314: 1118–1122.

Doyal, Len. 1997. The rationing debate: Rationing within the NHS should be explicit – The case for. *British Medical Journal* 314: 1114–1118.

Firth, John. 2007. Head to head: Should you tell patients about beneficial treatments that they cannot have? No. *British Medical Journal* 334: 827.

Giordani, Leslie C. 1989. A cost containment malpractice defense: Implications for the standard of care and for indigent patients. *Houston Law Review* 26: 1007.

Hurst, Samia A., Anne-Marie Slowther, Reidun Forde, Renzo Pegoraro, Stella Reiter-Theil, Arnaud Perrier, Elizabeth Garrett-Mayer, and Marion Danis. 2006. Prevalence and determinants of physician bedside rationing: Data from Europe. *Journal of General Internal Medicine* 21: 1138–1143.

Hurst, Samia A., Reidun Forde, Stella Reiter-Theil, Anne-Marie Slowther, Arnaud Perrier, Renzo Pegoraro, and Marion Danis. 2007. Physicians' views on resource availability and equity in four European health care systems. *BMC Health Services Research* 7: 137.

Jones, Michael A. 2003. *Medical negligence*. London: Sweet & Maxwell.

Jones, Ian Rees, Lee Berney, Moira Kelly, Len Doyal, Chris Griffiths, Gene Feder, Sheila Hillier, Gillian Rowlands, and Sarah Curtis. 2004. Is patient involvement possible when decisions involve scarce resources? A qualitative study of decision-making in primary care. *Social Science & Medicine* 59: 93–102.

Marcus, Robert. 2007. Head to head: Should you tell patients about beneficial treatments that they cannot have? Yes. *British Medical Journal* 334: 826.

Mellas, Laura Athens. 1991. Adapting the judicial approach to medical malpractice claims against physicians to reflect Medicare cost containment measures. *University of Colorado Law Review* 62: 287.

Miller, Frances H. 1992. Denial of health care and informed consent in English and American Law. *American Journal of Law & Medicine* 18: 37–71.

Montgomery, Jonathan. 2006. Law and the demoralisation of medicine. *Legal Studies* 26: 185–210.

Newdick, Christopher. 1997. Resource allocation in the National Health Service. *American Journal of Law & Medicine* 23: 291–318.
Owen-Smith, Amanda, Joanna Coast, and Jenny Donovan. 2010a. Are patients receiving enough information about healthcare rationing? A qualitative study. *Journal of Medical Ethics* 36: 88–92.
Owen-Smith, Amanda, Joanna Coast, and Jenny Donovan. 2010b. The desirability of being open about health care rationing decisions: Findings from a qualitative study of patients and clinical professionals. *Journal of Health Services Research & Policy* 15: 14–20.
Paterson, R.J. 1998. Rationing health care and human rights: The *Northland Health* case. *New Zealand Law Review* 1998: 571–584.
Perry, John. 2007. Candour on unfunded treatments: Patients do not live in an information vacuum. *British Medical Journal* 334: 915.
Sweatman, Louise R., and Diane Woollard. 2002. Resource allocation decisions in Canada's health care system: Can these decisions be challenged in a court of law. *Health Policy* 62: 275–290.
Syrett, Keith. 2004. Impotence or importance? Judicial review in an era of explicit NHS rationing. *The Modern Law Review* 67: 289–304.
Thomson, J., et al. 2006. Do oncologists discuss expensive anti-cancer drugs with their patients? *Annals of Oncology* 17: 702–708.
Williams, Michael V. 2007. Candour on unfunded treatments: Ignorance is a public health issue. *British Medical Journal* 334: 915.

Chapter 8
CAM and Alternatives

Abstract This chapter explores the issue of informing patients of choices between conventional medicine and Complementary and Alternative Medicine (CAM). "Practitioners" are categorized into three types: orthodox (conventional) medicine practitioners, dual practitioners and CAM practitioners. It is noted that the current law involving CAM and conventional medicine disclosure seems to be conventional-medicine-reinforcing. The chapter concludes with a call for both conventional medicine practitioners and CAM practitioners to provide their patients with unbiased and contextualised information that overcomes the boundaries of their "schools" of medicine. An "integrated" model, where all practitioners provide patients with contextualised information about divergent schools of thought, is better than a "fragmented" model, where every practitioner presents patients with information only about his "school" of thought, leaving patients to search for information about other "schools" of thought themselves.

8.1 Introduction

Unlike China where Traditional Chinese Medicine (TCM) is an important part of mainstream medicine, in the developed countries where orthodox medicine dominates, TCM is categorized into Complementary and Alternative Medicine (CAM). In this chapter, I will examine issues relating to CAM in "Western" and developed countries. The Chinese context will be explored in Chap. 10.

For the purpose of this chapter, the term *orthodox medicine* or *conventional medicine* is used when referring to what most readers would consider contemporary, allopathic, Western medicine. Several definitions have been used to differentiate CAM from conventional medicine,[1] although their boundaries blurred. The general

[1]Lois Snyder (ed.) 2007, 9–10 (revealing some definitions of CAM, including: (1) "a broad domain of healing resources that encompass all health systems, modalities and practices and their accompanying theories and beliefs, other than those intrinsic to the politically dominant health care system of a particular society or culture in a given historical period. CAM

X. Zhao, *The Duty of Medical Practitioners and CAM/TCM Practitioners to Inform Competent Adult Patients about Alternatives*,
DOI 10.1007/978-3-642-31647-0_8, © Springer-Verlag Berlin Heidelberg 2013

theme that those definitions have is that CAMs are practices, techniques, and therapies not considered by most as part of mainstream health care.[2]

Available data regarding the prevalence of use of CAM reveals that the public interest in CAM is remarkable.[3] The rationales for CAM use are yet to be fully understood. Patients use CAMs most frequently for chronic conditions (Snyder 2007, 11). Patients use CAMs for a myriad of reasons, including (1) conventional therapies have been exhausted; (2) conventional therapies are of indeterminate effectiveness or are commonly associated with side effects or significant risks; (3) no conventional therapy is known to relieve the patient's condition; (4) the conventional approach is perceived to be emotionally or spiritually without benefit; (5) a perception that CAM is more patient-focused and less disease-specific than conventional medicine; (6) the belief that CAM systems have stood the test of time.[4] Many CAM users are individuals seeking more autonomy and personal control over

---

includes all such practices and ideas self-defined by their users as preventing or treating illness or promoting health and well-being. Boundaries within CAM and between the CAM domain and the domain of the dominant system are not always sharp or fixed." (The National Institute of Health (NIH) Office of Alternative Medicine); (2) a group of diverse medical and health care systems, practices, and products that are not presently considered to be part of conventional medicine (The National Center for Complementary and Alternative Medicine (NCCAM)); Federation of State Medical Boards *Model Guidelines for the Use of Complementary and Alternative Therapies in Medical Practice* (2002) <http://www.fsmb.org/pdf/2002_grpol_complementary_alternative_therapies.pdf> (last accessed 20 November 2010), Sections II Definitions ("CAM refers to a broad range of healing philosophies (schools of thought), approaches and therapies that mainstream Western (conventional) medicine does not commonly use, accept, study, understand, or make available." "Conventional medical practices refer to those medical interventions that are taught extensively at U.S. medical schools, generally provided at U.S. hospitals, or meet the requirements of the generally accepted standard of care.").

[2] Lois Snyder (ed.) 2007, 10. *Complementary* refers to the practice of using a nonconventional approach or therapy *along with* a conventional treatment; *Alternative* refers to the use of a therapy *in place of* conventional medicine; and *integrative* medicine combines mainstream medical therapies and CAM therapies for which there is some degree of high-quality scientific evidence of safety and effectiveness.

[3] Timothy Caulfield and Colin Feasby 2001, 186–187. *See also*, Tat-Leang Lee 2006, 749 (Studies showed that 42% of Americans, 52% of Australians, 76% of Singaporeans and between 20 and 65% of Europeans use some form of CAM); Lois Snyder (ed.) 2007, 10–14 (statistics concerning United States).

[4] Other reasons include: (1) health promotion and disease prevention; (2) curiosity and preference to self-treat; (3) cultural traditions; (4) a suggestion or testimonial from a friend, medical claims. *See*, Lois Snyder (ed.) 2007, 14–15. *See also,* Timothy Caulfield and Colin Feasby 2001, 188 (outlining the following elements of CAM use: (1) individual empowerment; (2) belief in the efficacy of the CAM, (3) concurrence with a particular philosophical or holistic orientation; (4) failure of standard care; (5) the existence of chronic health problems; (6) cultural differences; (7) increasing market pressure); Charlie C.L. Xue et al. 2010, 303 (confining to TCM rather than CAM; proposing that at least three reasons might have contributed to the increasing popularity of TCM over the last decade: (1) the holistic approach of TCM treatments for both health management and general health enhancement; (2) individuals proactively seeking alternative therapies where conventional medicine fails to adequately address their health problems; and (3) the increasing body of scientific evidence concerning the safety and effectiveness of TCM interventions);

health care decisions (Caulfield and Feasby 2001, 187). There may be some social reasons that can explain the popularity of CAMs.[5]

CAM has certainly become a permanent part of the health care landscape as the borders between conventional medicine and CAM begin to blur. Somebody even refers CAM as the "invisible mainstream" (Brophy 2003, 274). However, compared to the medical landscape, the legal landscape regarding CAM is relatively new. Most CAM practices are only subjected to voluntary self-regulation. Few judicial opinions address malpractice and CAM therapies. The legal landscape is subject to rapid change as CAM therapies increasingly penetrate mainstream healthcare.

This chapter attempts to answer a two-way question about disclosure of alternatives: (1) whether an *orthodox medicine practitioner* has a duty to disclose CAM therapies, and if so, under what circumstances? (2) whether a *CAM practitioner* has a duty to inform about orthodox medicine treatments, and if yes, under what context? There is also the question of how *dual practitioners* present information about alternative treatment options.

I will continue drawing a distinction between adoption and information disclosure, and examine the issue of "disclosure" of alternatives alongside the context of "adopting" treatment. The purpose of this book is not to advocate for or against CAM, but to expose the CAM-involving medical landscape to the prevailing legal framework and see how to interpret the duty of alternatives disclosure in contexts involving CAM.

8.2 Orthodox Medicine Practitioners and CAM

8.2.1 Adoption of CAM

In dealing with CAM, the difficult job for medical profession is straddling the fence so as not to marginalise and eliminate CAM approaches that have benefits

Andrew M. Knoll 2004, 360 (offering two explanations for resurgence of CAM: (1) CAM filled a void in biomedicine, namely providing a more fulfilling and caring experience within the practitioner-patient relationship as well as offering an alternative form of therapy for certain conditions where biomedicine has not been very efficacious; (2) patients, while becoming increasingly educated and sophisticated about the limitations of biomedicine in treating certain chronic conditions, are frustrated with biomedicine methods and are turning to alternatives).

[5] A scholar has identified a number of social influences that account for increased use of CAM by the public and by doctors. Orthodox medical care continues to be perceived as generally deficient in terms of attention to the individual, to the spiritual dimension, and to the healing potential of the harmonies between the patient and the therapist and between the patient and nature. Social changes including egalitarianism, the emphasis on personal autonomy, and the rejection of post-war monoculture in favour of diversity and choice, have led to a plural landscape which has been fertile ground for the development of a consumerist approach to life generally and to health in particular. Among doctors there is also a degree of dissatisfaction with traditional biomedicine and its therapeutics, perceived as limited to symptom treatment, limited in efficacy in many chronic conditions, overly bureaucratic and institutionalised, too dependant on drugs, and not conductive to satisfying and effective healthcare. *See*, Malcolm Parker 2007, 10–12.

to offer patients while not throwing open the doors of medicine to practices that compromise the quality of health care, encouraging reliance on CAM that is inappropriate and discouraging the appropriate use of conventional care (Brophy 2003, 280). A difficult issue to decide is whether, when and how a CAM therapy should be introduced into the clinical setting and be made available to patients. Or, in an era of evidence-based medicine, how much and what kind of evidence about the safety and efficacy of CAM treatments is sufficient for them to be made available in the clinical setting?

Most CAMs do not have strong evidence base or have not been subjected to high quality research.[6] The reasons for sparse evidence of CAM effectiveness may include: (1) lack of funds; (2) no training in research methods; (3) no motivation to do research; (4) non-acceptance or indifference towards the validity of the scientific method[7]; (5) a belief that CAM is not worth studying, especially with public funds, because it is fundamentally unscientific and quackery[8]; and (6) bias and prejudice.[9] It seems that TCM is no exception.[10]

[6] There is a measure of the quality of the evidence regarding treatment effectiveness. That is called "Levels of Evidence Ratings": Level IV – Opinion evidence of experts; Level III – Non-randomised controlled studies; Level II – Randomised controlled trials (RCT) and Level I – Meta-analysis of all randomised controlled trials. Apart from acupuncture for a limited number of conditions (Level III evidence), and a few herbal medicines (Level II evidence), CAM treatments have only Level IV evidence for their effectiveness, or at least Level III evidence with only historical controls. *See*, Randall Kune and Gabriel Kune 2007. *See also*, Zhang, C.S. et al. 2010, 6–12 (the benefit of ear-acupressure for symptomatic relief of allergic rhinitis is unknown due to the poor quality of included studies).

[7] Randall Kune and Gabriel Kune 2007. *See also,* David J. Hufford 2003 (arguing that there are important limits in science that constrain its ability to evaluate CAM effectively). Some commentators even attributed the "poor" evidence base for TCM to the facts that "many of [TCM] trials have taken place in China and are not only inaccessible but fail to meet Western standards". *See*, Anne Tran 2006, 366.

[8] For example, a clinical trial testing moxibustion's efficacy in correcting breech position in pregnancy suggested that it has statistically significant positive effects on fetal positioning at the time of birth. That result attracted controversy. Conventional sceptics argued against moxibustion as a legitimate, ethical topic for a research study because there was "clearly" no "biologic plausibility" to the study's hypothesis. Moxibustion is a traditional Chinese method that uses the heat generated by burning herbal preparations containing Artemisia vulgaris (mugwort) to stimulate acupuncture points. That is a mechanism that makes no sense in a Western biomedical paradigm. *See*, Lois Snyder (ed.) 2007, 212–214 (the author is of the view that the prevalent use of CAM by the public is strong reason to suggest that further investigation of CAM may be necessary to meet beneficence and nonmaleficence obligations).

[9] Arnold S. Relman and Andrew Weil 1999, 2126 (claiming that "[t]here is very strong prejudice against accepting ideas that run counter to preconceptions such as Chinese medicine being superstitious and on the face of it absurd; such attitudes lead journal editors and heads of medical institutions to ignore or at worst to suppress evidence that comes in contrary to expectations.").

[10] *See*, Charlie C.L. Xue et al. 2010, 310–312 (pointing out some reasons for lack of evidence of safety and effectiveness of TCM: (1) limited resources from governmental and industry support available for quality studies; (2) lack of quality and quantity of trials; (3) difficulty to align traditional medicine philosophies with modern scientific methods).

Prospective, randomized controlled trials (RCTs) were considered the level of evidence required for most doctors to consider incorporating a CAM therapy into their practice (Wahner-Roedler et al. 2006, 498). However, there are concerns regarding the feasibility of RCTs in the CAM context. Many CAM treatments are holistic and individualised in nature and are not readily responsive to a randomised controlled trial.[11] As a scholar observed,

> This 'softness' of alternative medicine, which many regard as its main strength, is from the standpoint of conventional regulation, its chief weakness. It cannot stand up to standard modes of scientific inquiry – randomized clinical trials, double-blind studies, and the like – because, in important dimensions, it is more a philosophy than a protocol.[12]

There is a strong and frequently-cited argument that RCTs simply does not fit with most of what alternative medicine, a holistic approach to health, is about.[13] For CAMs, there is a methodological obstacle to research.[14] Many CAM practitioners are convinced about the correctness of their approach and their ideologies, particularly for treatments with a long tradition. Many CAM advocates claim that the scientific method is simply not applicable to their remedies.[15]

---

[11] *See*, Timothy Caulfield and Colin Feasby 2001, 189; Barbara L. Atwell 2004, 608; Richard L. Nahin and Stephen E. Straus 2001 (noting that clinical investigations of complementary and alternative medicine are made difficult by factors such as use of complex, individualised treatments, lack of standardisation of herbal medicines, difficulties in accruing, randomising, and retaining patients and in identifying appropriate placebo interventions); Charlie C.L. Xue et al. 2010, 301–312 (warning that data from limited RCTs and systematic reviews need to be interpreted with great caution); The National Advisory Committee on Health and Disability (New Zealand) *New Health Interventions: A Report to the New Zealand Minister of Health* (2005) <http://www.nhc.health.govt.nz/moh.nsf/indexcm/nhc-new-health-interventions?Open> (last accessed 25 May 2010), page 24 (admitting that the "gold standard" of randomised clinical trials (RCTs) are not appropriate for some types of interventions including areas of surgery, complementary and alternative medicines, community health approaches and disability technologies).

[12] Kathleen M. Boozang 1998, 207–208 (citing David G. Warren, *Book Review*, 18 *Journal of Legal Medicine* 257 (1997) (reviewing Julie Stone & Joan Matthews, *Complementary Medicine and the Law* (1996))). The author did not agree with the view that because randomised clinical trials are inappropriate for unconventional treatments, no testing at all need to occur before a new therapy becomes the standard of care.

[13] Kathleen M. Boozang 1998, 207. *See also,* Tat-Leang Lee 2006, 750 (noting that RCTs, the gold standard of evidence-based medicine, lend themselves less comfortably to CAM practices, particularly as the practice involves individualised and prolonged treatments). However, numerous commentators have concluded that most CAMs *can be studied* using already established methodologies. *See*, Timothy Caulfield and Colin Feasby 2001, 190–191; E. Ernst et al. 2007, 24 (disproving the view that EBM is not applicable to areas of "alternative medicine"; noting that application of evidence-based medicine (EBM) to acupuncture is both possible and constructive, and it is conceivable that EBM will eventually generate a list of indications for which acupuncture is demonstrably effective).

[14] Su Mason et al. 2002 (acknowledging that complementary medicine has a different philosophy from conventional medicine, presenting challenges to research methodology, but insisting that rigorous evaluation of complementary medicine could provide much needed evidence of its effectiveness).

[15] Barbara L. Atwell 2004, 607–608 (arguing that one reason for continued uncertainty surrounding the efficacy of many CAM treatments is that modern technology is not always capable of effectively measuring their efficacy).

There are also practical difficulties to embrace RCTs in the CAM context. Some CAMs, such as acupuncture, cannot do placebo control because of the specific physical nature of the treatment. Controlled experiments for acupuncture are difficult to administer – blinding the patient to the use or non-use of acupuncture needles has its obvious limitations (Lois Snyder (ed.) 2007, 22). Sham acupuncture procedures have been employed, but in a limited fashion.

The requirement that a CAM should be subjected to RCTs before it is considered in conventional setting raises the suspicion that a double standard is applied. Like most CAMs, many conventional procedures that are a part of current medical practice also have not been scientifically proven.[16] Even if conventional medicine can rightly take credit for remarkable successes in healing what ails humankind, much of actual clinical practice does not and never can measure up to the scientific standard to which critics of CAM would like to hold alternative modalities.[17]

On the one hand, we should admit that, until new and specific methodology is developed that can adequately address the methodology challenges for RCTs in CAM, evidence from quality RCTs and systematic reviews still holds the credibility of CAM in the scientific community (Xue et al. 2010, 301–312). Therefore, we should encourage to expose CAM to more rigorous research. On the other hand, we should also admit that RCTs does not represent the whole picture in the CAM context.

If RCTs or even systematic reviews of such trials are not the only way, or arguably the appropriate or necessary way, of testing CAMs, what level of scientific validation, or what amount and kind of evidence is sufficient for a CAM to be positively acknowledged in a clinical setting? Are observational studies, case studies and qualitative research all acceptable evidence? Is there any place for a history of traditional use when evaluating the potential safety and efficacy of a CAM modality?

The safety and efficacy of many CAM therapies are evidenced by their prolonged existence, traditional use, anecdotal and empirical evidence of patient successes, rather than by scientific testing. Traditional use has been considered to be a sufficient basis for making defined claims under therapeutic goods regulation.[18] The concept of evidence-based medicine is not restricted to RCTs and meta-analyses but involves the use of the best external evidence available (Brophy 2003, 281). In order for a CAM to be made available in clinical setting, I would argue that the law needs to loosen the evidence base requirements for CAMs. That means, even if a CAM does not have a very strong, but some, evidence base, the law needs

[16] *See*, Arnold S. Relman and Andrew Weil 1999), 2125 (revealing that fewer than 30% of procedures currently used in conventional medicine has been rigorously tested).

[17] E. Haavi Morreim 2003, 222 (claiming that any attempt to throw out or discredit CAM on grounds of scientific inadequacy is sure to toss out large portions of conventional medicine alongside and appears to bode far worse for conventional medicine than for CAM).

[18] Elizabeth Brophy 2003, 281 (Australian context); Vincent Kurata 2007 (Canadian context). The European Union has created a new regulatory framework for traditional herbal medicinal products, embracing the notion of "traditional use". *See*, Directive 2004/24/EC of the European Parliament and of the Council of 31 March 2004 amending, as regards traditional herbal medicinal products, Directive 2001/83/EC on the Community code relating to medicinal products for human use.

to give doctors latitude to adopt it.[19] RCTs should not be the sole arbiter for determining the appropriateness of CAM being embraced in conventional setting. In the absence of definitive evidence, there is a need to honour doctors' genuine medical judgments. As a debater said,

> There is a great difference between being a researcher and being a practitioner. As a researcher, [he has] the luxury of insisting on rigorous scientific testing and … have the leisure to wait for results to come in. As a practitioner, [he is] in the trenches working with patients who have medical needs and … often have to guess to use [his] best medical judgment in the absence of definitive evidence (Relman and Weil 1999, 2125).

That latitude the law accords to doctors in selecting therapies means that the law needs to leave room for doctors who favour a CAM even if its RCT result is not available. It also means that doctors cannot be compelled to adopt CAM therapies that they are reluctant to adopt because of their worry about lack of sufficient evidence, although a duty to refer may arise (Knoll 2004, 361). Doctors have liberty to adopt or not to adopt CAMs.

However, in addition to the patient preference and demand, arguably there are other circumstances where doctors may feel external pressures to integrate CAM into practice: (1) CAM>no treatment; (2) CAM>conventional treatment; (3) CAM+conventional treatment>conventional treatment alone. Some alternative treatments may be superior to conventional medicine, because they offer relief, have fewer side-effects, or are less expensive (Boozang 1998, 212). Alternative providers can provide effective care for chronic conditions and routine illnesses.[20] Once an alternative therapy is shown to be curative, such as acupuncture to relieve back pain, or important to the patient wellness, doctors become obligated to include such options among those they offer to their patients.[21]

One scholar divided CAM therapies into three categories: invalidated (pure quackery); nonvalidated (plausible but not yet proven); and validated (proven to be efficacious).[22] I agree with the scholar that doctors should not *offer*, agree to manage

---

[19] *Compare*, Australian Medical Association *AMA Position Statement. Complementary Medicine* (2002) <http://www.ama.com.au/node/2214> (last accessed 20 November 2008) 2.2 (emphasising that the principle of evidence based assessment should be the basis of evaluating complementary medicines and therapies and their use by the medical profession, and should be the basis of any collaborative relationships between medical practitioners and complementary therapists).

[20] B.H. May et al. 2009, 447–459 (Systematic review reveals that: (1) All studies reported Chinese herbal medicine (HM) had significant effects in improving dementia symptoms; (2) In studies that employed active controls, HM was at least as effective as the pharmaceutical intervention; (3) Meta-analyses found HM more effective than no treatment or placebo and at least equivalent to control interventions, although the overall effect was small; (4) No severe adverse events were reported. These trials provide overall positive evidence for the effectiveness and safety of certain HMs for dementia management.).

[21] Kathleen M. Boozang 1998, 208. However, even if there is necessity for a CAM to be incorporated into conventional care, I still have concerns about conventionally trained doctors' competency to administer CAM therapies because orthodox medicine and CAM are different medical cultures.

[22] Kathleen M. Boozang 1998, 187. The scholar noted that doctors are gradually succumbing to external pressures to integrate alternative therapies and conventional medicine (at p. 191).

jointly, or accede to patient demands for *invalidated* treatments (Boozang 1998, 187), even if offering such treatments will, in a psychological or emotional sense, make the patient "feel better" (Boozang 1998, 205). This is especially so when conventional treatment is available and the delay in obtaining conventional treatment could cause irreparable harm.[23] Doctors have reasons to wait for safety and efficacy data to become available before they offer or accede to patient demands for unproven treatments.[24]

The wide latitude in selecting/adopting CAMs should be supplemented by appropriate informational disclosure, especially for those therapies whose evidence base is emerging. Basically, there are two opposing theories regarding informed consent and CAM. First, it has been commonly suggested that all unproven CAM therapies be treated as *experimental* treatments[25] and thereby deserve a *heightened informed consent* standard. That means the doctor who provides the patient's receipt of an innovative alternative therapy should advise the patient, in addition to that information generally given as part of the informed consent process, that he should consider the treatment to be experimental.

However, characterising a treatment as experimental has many legal ramifica tions. Treating *nonvalidated* CAMs as experimental actually exposes CAMs to a higher informed consent standard than modern scientific medicine interventions since a good proportion of these interventions are also nonvalidated (Sugarman 2003). Moreover, doctors offering nonvalidated "alternative" treatments is different from their offering nonvalidated *experimental* treatment. The source of pressure to offer the treatment may differ.[26] Consistent with my suggestions regarding emerging treatment options in Chap. 6, I am of the view that it is more appropriate to mention the merits-demerits of a CAM and emphasise the fact of nonvalidation of it rather

[23] Kathleen M. Boozang 1998, 205–210. The scholar also proposed that doctors should only agree to patients' requests for *nonvalidated* treatments under narrow conditions: if the research is very promising; if the doctor believes that the patient may benefit; if the risk of harm is very low; and if the doctor adheres to the conventions that govern the doctrine of informed consent for experimental treatment. In the case of nonvalidated treatment, doctors should start with a strong presumption against acceding to the patient's demands.

[24] Kathleen M. Boozang 1998, 209–210 (claiming that traditional ethical principles are not outweighed by the competing principle of patient autonomy).

[25] Eric Ritigstein 2005, 938–939 (revealing an argument that there are only three permissible categories of medical practice: (1) experimental and investigational; (2) accepted by a reputable minority of the profession; and (3) standard community practice; and, if a medical practice is not one of the latter two categories, it should be governed by laws regulating experimental treatments).

[26] Kathleen M. Boozang 1998, 200 ("The traditional paradigm for an unproven treatment involves a clinician-researcher who recommends an innovative therapy. In such cases, the analysis is on the potential for patient coercion due to the possibility that the clinician-researcher may have an ulterior research motive. With alternative medicine, the pressure to integrate an unproven treatment into conventional treatment is more likely to come from patients. In these cases, the concern is not the physician having an ulterior research motive, but rather his offering an intervention that has neither a proven *nor any scientific expectation* of any health benefit." (emphasis in the original)).

than simply label it as "experimental", while at the same time highlight the need for evidence of safety and efficacy in carefully designed controlled clinical trials.

The second, and contrasting, argument concerning CAM and informed consent is that the informed consent doctrine is *not feasible* in the CAM context. Adopting informed consent requirements is seen as a hegemonic imposition of the Western values. I am not convinced by this line of argument. It seems both difficult and unfair to subject conventional medicine and CAM to different informed consent rules. The fact that many CAMs are relatively benign, and the belief that the benefits that a patient could receive, via the placebo effect, may outweigh the possible harms associated with not disclosing information about the lack of scientific evidence, are insufficient to allow the creation of a different disclosure standard for CAM (Caulfield and Feasby 2001, 196–198). It will be difficult for a doctor to argue that he opted not to disclose information about the lack of known efficacy purely for the purpose of inducing a placebo effect or for fear of upsetting the patient. Moreover, the questionable efficacy of many CAM treatments reinforces the need for a thorough disclosure process (Caulfield and Feasby 2001, 196).

Therefore, a doctor adopting a CAM should inform his patient of risks, including known risks and unknown risks, adverse side effects, efficacy associated with the CAM, and alternatives to the CAM. I will leave the issue of the doctor's duty to inform about *alternatives* to the section concerning "dual practitioners" of this chapter.[27] First, doctors who are involved in the provision of CAM therapies must provide patients with information about the *known risks*. Though there is a perception that many CAM therapies are relatively harmless, there are, in fact, many identified risks and adverse side effects. Given the liberal approach that the courts have taken in the assessment of materiality, there are undoubtedly many risks associated with CAM therapies which could be considered worthy of disclosure. Many patients equate what has been promoted to them as "natural" care – especially regarding herbal products – with "safe" care. As part of informed consent and shared decision making, the doctor should actively strive to deconstruct this notion. Patients should be reminded that just because a product is marketed as "natural" does not necessarily mean it is safe. In addition to disclosing known risks, doctors should candidly discuss available information about the *efficacy* of the proposed or requested CAM therapy, because this is information that has a potential to influence treatment decisions and is something that a reasonable person in the patient's position would want to know. Thirdly, doctors may need to tell patients about the lack of evidence concerning CAM efficacy and that there may be *unknown risks*. Doctors should seek to provide information in a manner that is respectful to a patient's beliefs and values. The goal should not be to dissuade a patient from using a CAM but to provide objective information that will allow a well-informed decision about the use of CAMs (Caulfield and Feasby 2001, 198).

[27] *See*, Chap. 8.3.2.

8.2.2 *Disclosure of CAM*

8.2.2.1 Knowledge and Attitudes

There is a large and growing gulf between what patients expect of doctors and what medical schools are training them to do. A survey revealed that more than half of the doctors stated that the patient rather than the doctor initiated the discussion about the benefits and risks of CAM therapy (Wahner-Roedler et al. 2006, 497). Many mainstream doctors find themselves asked about alternative treatments and asked for referrals (Doyle 2001, 534). One reason doctors are hesitant to embrace CAM is the lack of understanding or believability of the proposed mechanisms of action (Snyder 2007, 38).

There are practical difficulties in requiring conventional medical practitioners to consult with patients about CAM therapies as they may lack the requisite knowledge and training, and CAMs do not readily fall within the conventional profession's realm of understanding.[28] But, as one scholar said, "[i]n essence, we could ask ourselves whether a reasonable doctor, practising medicine in the 21st century, in light of increasing knowledge regarding patient behaviour and alternative medicines, should be aware of, and advise patients of, the presence of alternative approaches."[29] It seems to me that the answer should be "yes".

As the public's use of various healing practices outside conventional medicine increases, ignorance about CAMs poses a communication gap between the public and the healthcare profession. Hopefully, this situation will definitely change.[30] A survey of medical undergraduates from the National University of Singapore showed that 86% of students welcomed the inclusion of CAM in the medical curriculum (Lee 2006, 750). Mainstream medical publications, such as *The New England Journal of Medicine*, *JAMA*, and *The Archives of Internal Medicine*, have developed an interest in CAMs and have published articles about CAMs.

---

[28] Australian Medical Association *AMA Position Statement: Complementary Medicine* (2002) <http://www.ama.com.au/node/2214> (last accessed 20 November 2008) 5.2–5.4 (highlighting the need for medical practitioners to have a basic understanding of Complementary Medicine and to receive sufficient training in their undergraduate, vocational and further education to enable them to discuss such issues with their patients on an informed basis; calling on educational institutions and professional colleges to ensure that medical education provides basic information about Complementary Medicine).

[29] Richard A. Haigh 2000, 203. *See also,* D.K. Owen et al. 2001 (observing that, to advise about complementary and alternative medicine, doctors need to understand its potential benefits and limitations).

[30] For example, Australian Medical Association *AMA Position Statement: Complementary Medicine* (2002) <http://www.ama.com.au/node/2214> (last accessed 20 November 2008) 4.4 (requiring medical practitioners to specifically ask patients about their use of Complementary Medicine and to be sufficiently well informed about Complementary Medicine to be able to provide advice to patients when appropriate).

In recent years there have emerged reports of potential herb–drug interactions. However, patients are reluctant to reveal their use of CAMs to their doctors. The rate of non-disclosure of those using CAMs is as high as 77% in some studies (Robinson and McGrail 2004, 90–95). The main reasons that patients provided for not disclosing their use of CAMs to their medical practitioners were concerned about a negative response by the practitioners, the belief that the practitioner work within a biomedical framework and did not need to know about their CAM use, and the fact that the practitioner did not ask, or appeared disinterested (Robinson and McGrail 2004, 90–95).

Patients expect non-judgemental, respectful and compassionate care from their practitioners (Robinson and McGrail 2004, 96). Orthodox medicine profession needs to exercise some degree of caution in making judgments about healing paradigms outside the biomedical model of health and disease – a kind of professional humility (Snyder 2007, 209). Conventional medicine doctors need to appreciate that many CAM healing practices have their own logic and way of interpreting information that may differ significantly from those of conventional medicine (Snyder 2007, 203). Many CAM approaches are based on different philosophical assumptions. Orthodox medicine doctors need to keep open-minded towards the patients' CAM use and to be actively involved with discussing CAMs with patients.

8.2.2.2 Disclosure of CAM Therapies

In the "Adoption of CAM" part of this chapter,[31] I have examined that doctors who adopt CAM therapies need to show the same loyalty to the informed consent doctrine and reveal the risk-benefit profiles of CAM therapies they select. I have also formed the view that doctors are entitled to have latitude in selecting and adopting therapies, no matter conventional or CAM's. The law needs to show generosity in setting and lowering the evidence base threshold for a doctor adopting CAM therapies, rather than citing RCTs as the sole source for evidence base. Doctors who favour conventional medicine also should enjoy the same freedom in choosing therapies. The question still left open here is whether or not the doctor who does *not adopt* CAM therapies has the duty to *disclose* available CAM therapies.

No court has yet found an obligation for doctors to inform of CAM therapies.[32] A Canadian court hinted that the scope of a medical practitioner's duty to inform about alternatives might not include a "fringe alternative" or "alternative medicine

[31] Chap. 8.2.1.

[32] Michael H. Cohen 2001, 2288–2289 (noting that (1) in deciding that providers must offer patients "feasible and available options," US courts typically have not included a requirement that such options involve CAM therapies, which are outside consensus and conventional standards; (2) US courts have not yet had occasion to address whether combination of conventional and CAM therapies must be included in the range of feasible and available options that must be disclosed to the patient).

practices".[33] There is significant scholarly disagreement about whether conventional doctors have a duty to inform about CAM therapies. There are two main arguments *against* CAM disclosure. The primary one is conventional practitioners' lack of *knowledge* about CAMs. Patients cannot expect doctors, who are trained in a conventional setting, to evaluate CAM treatments that they do not understand. Because CAMs are grounded in bodies of knowledge outside doctors' professional and educational experience, it is arguably not practicable for doctors to assume detailed knowledge of these treatment modalities (Bulen 2003, 350). The second argument that critics of expanded disclosure have proposed is the perceived lack of RCTs supporting CAM efficacy (Bulen 2003, 350).

Those arguments have strengths. However, recent changes in doctor education and a significant increase in published clinical trials have begun to undermine the validity of these arguments. First, some CAMs have increasingly been embraced in conventional medical curriculum. Instead of offering a sole CAM elective, some medical schools weave relevant CAM modalities into each course in the 4-year program (Bulen 2003, 353). Second, CAM therapies range from those that are totally unproven, to those reliant upon anecdotal and traditional use, such as herbal medicine, to those based upon scientific proof of variable quality, such as acupuncture (Weir 2003, 300). The evidence profiles of CAMs are diverse. It seems that more published CAM research exists than is typically acknowledged (Bulen 2003, 354).

For example, in his publication,[34] the Australian scholar Charlie Xue helpfully summarised the research and evidence profile of TCM. The paper revealed that a significantly increased number of RCTs and systematic reviews on these trials have advanced understanding of the therapeutic potential of TCM modalities for the treatment of a broad range of conditions. Other systematic reviews of the trial data revealed that, within the observation period (2000–2005), the evidence base of acupuncture has become more solid (Ernst et al. 2007, 24).

With the increased exposure to CAMs in conventional medical education and the increased availability of evidence data for CAMs in clinical setting, *medical* hurdles against CAM disclosure would disappear. The issue left would be a *legal* one: whether or not, if yes, under what circumstances, a conventional doctor has a legal duty to disclose a CAM, even if he does not favor, select and administer the CAM? The ordinary informed consent rules, such as the patient-oriented standard of information disclosure and the materiality test, should apply in the CAM context.

---

[33] *Dickson v. Pinder*, 2010 ABQB 269, at [79] (citing *Seney v. Crooks*, 1998 ABCA 316, 223 A.R. 145 at paras. 57–58 (the Alberta Court of Appeal)).

[34] Charlie C.L. Xue et al. 2010. *See also*, Charlie C.L. Xue et al. 2003, 80–87 (Chinese herbal medicine extract capsule (formulation containing 18 herbs) offers symptomatic relief and improvement of quality of life for some patients with seasonal allergic rhinitis); Zhen Zheng et al. 2008, 671–676 (Real Electroacupuncture demonstrates promising short-term reduction of OLM (Opioid-like medications) for participants with chronic non-malignant pain, but such effect needs to be confirmed by trials with adequate sample sizes).

As I mentioned at the beginning of this book, the availability and feasibility of treatment options is subject to medical knowledge and medical judgment. The first thing is to ascertain what options, including CAMs, are reasonably available for a particular condition. On the one hand, the task of establishing the cluster of reasonably available treatment options involves consideration of the state of medical knowledge at the time.[35] On the other hand, a doctor needs to keep abreast of developments in medical practice and not lag behind medical progress and current medical knowledge.

As CAMs become more legitimate through their recognition by the government and the medical community, and as more insurance companies provide coverage for CAM therapies, CAM options may be considered more "feasible" and "available" (Doyle 2001, 540). Some objective criteria may indicate that a new treatment has become sufficiently "accepted" to create a duty of disclosure. That may include acceptance by a professional medical organisation or medical specialty associations, acceptance by leading textbooks of the relevant specialty, acceptance by articles in medical journals.[36] One could argue that certain CAM therapies are acceptable under the theory of "two schools of thought", and that conventional doctors have a duty to disclose CAM treatment options (Doyle 2001, 542). If the patient had been able to show there was a sufficient level of professional recognition of a CAM as an appropriate treatment for the patient's condition, the court may find that there is a duty for doctors to disclose the existence of the CAM as an alternative. Once a CAM crosses the "general acceptance" or "sufficient acceptance" threshold, it may fall within the ambit of both a doctor's duty to disclose and the duty to offer and recommend.[37] CAM therapies that are well-supported by evidence of safety and efficacy are potentially material treatment options.[38]

Competent adult patients should be entitled to decide (and refuse) not simply between competing orthodox treatments, or between treatment and no treatment, but also between the specific form of medical procedure, including orthodox or

[35] Elizabeth Brophy 2003, 277 (opining that the *Rogers* materiality test is probably subject to the doctor first ascertaining just what alternative options are reasonably available for a particular condition).

[36] Hunter L. Prillaman 1990, 53–55. Some CAMs, such as chiropractic, acupuncture and naturopathy, have their own professional organisations, their own textbooks, their own professional journals and insurance coverage.

[37] Michael H. Cohen 2001, 2291 (noting that to the extent that a CAM is generally accepted within the medical community as safe and effective, the doctor may be liable for malpractice not only for failure to inform, but also for failure to provide the CAM); Lois Snyder (ed.) *Biomedical Ethics Reviews: Complementary and Alternative Medicine: Ethics, the Patient, and the Physician* (Humana Press, Totowa, NJ, 2007) 178 (noting that, as medical evidence begins to show safety and effectiveness for CAM therapies, and these therapies become more generally accepted within the medical community, there may be liability for clinicians who fail to make appropriate adjunctive recommendations involving CAM therapies).

[38] Michael H. Cohen and Mary C. Ruggie 2003, 714. A salient example of a therapy that arguably should be disclosed, together with any evidence-based risks and benefits, is use of acupuncture to reduce nausea following chemotherapy.

alternative (Haigh 2000, 203). There are quite a few circumstances where a doctor's potential duty to inform of CAM is called for. First, CAM therapies may fall within the scope of information disclosure if there is scientific evidence of efficacy and safety for them. *Safe and effective* CAM treatments constitute material information that must be disclosed to patients under the patient-oriented standard of information disclosure.[39] For example, the efficacy of acupuncture is supported by a substantial degree of scientific evidence, particularly in the areas of pain management, nausea and vomiting. The risks associated with acupuncture are considered to be less than the risks associated with conventional/Western medicine. One could argue that a doctor should discuss acupuncture as an option for treatment in those cases where it has proven to be effective (Weir 2003, 300). If the doctor is unable to perform acupuncture, but the patient indicates a preference for it, he should make a referral to an acupuncturist.

Second, CAM therapies that compare *favourably* with those of conventional medicine would more easily and readily fall within the ambit of disclosure. The doctor might be required to disclose CAM therapies if they are safer or less invasive than conventional treatments. A reasonable person is more likely to attach significance to an alternative treatment option, including a CAM alternative, if the risks of the proposed treatment are high or where the risks are low but the magnitude of the harm would be great (Brophy 2003, 277). Where a CAM option offers an outcome similar to the proposed treatment with no risks or fewer risks, this information would be significant to a hypothetical patient.[40] The good candidates for CAM disclosure are ones that "have a favorable risk/benefit ratio compared to other treatments for the same condition; be based upon a reasonable expectation that it will result in a favorable patient outcome, including preventive practices; and be based upon the expectation that a greater benefit will be achieved than that which can be expected with no treatment."[41] It is in a context where conventional therapies have been exhausted or do not relieve the patient's condition or are of indeterminate effectiveness that patients are interested in exploring CAMs (Brophy 2003, 278).

Third, the patient-oriented disclosure standard requires doctors to disclose legally available treatments that a reasonable patient or a particular patient considers *material*

[39] James A. Bulen 2003, 350. *See also*, Michael H. Cohen 2001, 2292 (noting that the doctor can meet informed consent obligations, and thus reduce the risk of malpractice liability, by disclosing the availability of CAM therapies that have sufficient evidence of safety and efficacy to make their availability material to a particular treatment decision).

[40] Elizabeth Brophy 2003, 277. *See also*, Malcolm Parker 2007, 14 (observing that doctors should be aware of CAM treatments which may have similar efficacy to, but are safer than, orthodox medications, particularly where the CAM option is reasonably available and material to the patient); James A. Bulen 2003, 351 (noting that if a CAM treatment has a reasonable likelihood of success, and the treatment's risks and benefits are comparable to other conventional treatments, then it is permissible for the doctor to prescribe and disclose the CAM treatment).

[41] Federation of State Medical Boards *Model Guidelines for the Use of Complementary and Alternative Therapies in Medical Practice* (2002) <http://www.fsmb.org/pdf/2002_grpol_complementary_alternative_therapies.pdf> (last accessed 20 November 2010), Section III. Guidelines.

to a treatment decision (Bulen 2003, 354). Under the patient-oriented standard of information disclosure, a "reasonable patient" might very well want to be informed of CAM options. Although the patient-oriented standard of disclosure is an objective test, more and more subjective elements have been injected into it, either by liberally construing the objective limb – "a reasonable person in the patient's position", or by adding a subjective limb targeting a particular patient. The amount of information to be disclosed also depends greatly on the patient's desire for information. A patient's inquiry is the main means of triggering the physician's reactive duty to warn, although it is not an exclusive one. The doctor is obligated to respond to a patient's questions by disclosing more individualised information.

The patient's need for information about reasonable treatment options supersedes the doctor's decision to offer treatments. A patient's direct questions about CAM treatments should make the doctor aware that the patient attaches significance to this information.[42] Even if a patient does not ask direct questions, some evidence of a patient's use of or preference for CAM treatments, would create an environment where a doctor should reasonably be aware that the patient would attach significance to such information (Brophy 2003, 278).

As I demonstrated in Chap. 3, there is a distinction between *disclosing* CAMs and *recommending/offering* CAMs. Doctors would not necessarily have to recommend CAM therapies, but might be required to inform patients of the availability of some CAM therapies as treatment options. A doctor may prioritise recommendations depending on assessment of the quality of the evidence supporting different options (Parker 2007, 12). However, a doctor's information disclosure needs to be more contextualised.

Information about available CAMs is especially important when conventional medicine treatments have been exhausted or are not available. However, doctors should exercise caution in encouraging patients to use CAM therapies at the expense of the proven and conventional modalities. When a doctor suggests and offers, or a patient asks, a CAM therapy over a well-established conventional therapy, the doctor should fully engage the patient in a conversation about the risks and options, continue to monitor conventionally and make the conventional therapy readily available (Cohen 2001, 2292).

As I highlighted in the contexts of disclosing other alternatives, if a conventional doctor's failure to inform about CAMs is explored in the context of torts, the patient must be able to show not only the "materiality" of the undisclosed CAM information, but also the "causative injury" (Cohen 2001, 2289). Like other kinds of information disclosure, that involves the task of establishing both "decision causation" and "injury causation". The patient needs to demonstrate that he would have declined the conventional treatment had he received full information about CAM options. Another part of causation is that he would have avoided, or at least reduced, the injury had he opted for CAM options. Fulfilling the task is difficult.

[42] Elizabeth Brophy (2003), 278. *See also*, Michael Weir (2003), 301.

8.3 Dual Practitioners

There are disputes over the question of whether CAMs can and should be combined with conventional medicine to create a new entity called integrative medicine. Opponents of integrative medicine argue that integrating alternative medicine with mainstream medicine would not be an advance but a return to the past, an interruption of the remarkable progress achieved by science-based medicine over the past century (Relman and Weil 1999, 2122). Their assertions are based on allegations that the rationales for CAMs are irreconcilable with those of conventional medicine.[43] However, proponents feel optimistic about the future of integrative medicine,[44] regarding CAMs' lack of evidence base not as a fatal factor in embracing CAMs.[45] Integrative medicine has won some popularity. A survey revealed that 57% of physicians thought that incorporating CAM therapies would have a positive effect on patient satisfaction, and 48% believed that offering CAM would attract more patients (Wahner-Roedler et al. 2006, 497). "Integrative" medicine is, and will become, a phenomenon.

Even if integration is feasible, there are still disputes over the forms of integration. The convergence of CAM and evidence-based medicine (EBM) has two models: the totally integrated evidence-based model (TI) and the multicultural-pluralistic model (MP) (Parker 2007, 7). In the case of TI-convergence, EBM dominates by including only CAM treatments whose efficacy has been demonstrated according to the EBM principles (Parker 2007, 8). MP-convergence is deemed as epistemologically, clinically and ethically unjustified (Parker 2007, 12). Combining the diagnostic and treatment processes derived from science-based and non-science-based theoretical backgrounds is potentially confusing and dangerous (Parker 2007, 12). The TI model of convergence actually embraces CAMs at the sacrifice of their unique identities.

---

[43] Arnold S. Relman and Andrew Weil 1999, 2123 ("Most alternative systems of treatment are based on irrational or fanciful thinking and false or unproven factual claims. Their theories often violate basic scientific principles and are at odds not only with each other, but with current knowledge of the structure and function of the human body as now taught in our medical schools. They could not be woven into the fabric of the medical curriculum without confusion, contradiction, and an undermining of the scientific foundation upon which modern medicine rests."). *See also*, Michael H. Cohen and Mary C. Ruggie 2003, 690 (noting that the attempt to create an "integrative" health care did present challenges, such as lack of a shared knowledge base between conventional providers and CAM providers and ideological barriers existed between the two medical cultures).

[44] Arnold S. Relman and Andrew Weil 1999, 2126 ("I feel strongly that integrative medicine is the future, not only because people want it, but because very powerful forces operating both within science and outside of science are moving us in this direction."); Andrew M. Knoll 2004, 360 (advocating integration of the two paradigms in the health care while acknowledging the problems of it).

[45] Arnold S. Relman and Andrew Weil 1999, 2124 ("If a patient has tried a method and found that it works, that patient needs no further proof, does not need to read the reports of a randomised double-blind controlled trial in a medical journal to be convinced of the efficacy of treatment.").

8.3.1 Delivering CAMs

Conventional medicine doctors are being allowed increasing professional latitude in embracing CAMs, although there are variations in the degree of latitude.[46] While the medical profession has, in the past, used its privileged position to fight aggressively against CAM by setting narrow parameters for licensing and revoking licenses of non-conforming practitioners,[47] it is giving an increasing amount of latitude to a doctor providing CAM (Caulfield and Feasby 2001, 191). A registered practitioner shall not be found guilty of unbecoming conduct or be found to be incapable or unfit to practice medicine solely on the basis that the registered practitioner employs a therapy that is non-traditional or departs from the prevailing medical practices, unless it can be demonstrated that the therapy has a safety risk for that patient unreasonably greater than the prevailing treatment.[48] That would be likely to allow more and more doctors to get involved in the provision of CAM therapies. That would facilitate the formation and development of "a school of thought" favouring, recommending and administering a CAM therapy.

---

[46] Eric Ritigstein 2005 (revealing an attempt to excuse conventional doctors from disciplinary punishment by providing that a licensed physician or surgeon is not subject to discipline for certain unprofessional conduct solely on the basis that the treatment or advice rendered is "alternative or complementary medicine"; the term of "alternative or complementary medicine" being defined as "those health care methods of diagnosis, treatment or healing that are not generally used but that provide a reasonable potential for therapeutic gain in a patient's medical condition that is not outweighed by the risk of the health care method"); Andrew M. Knoll 2004, 365 (revealing that some states have enacted State Medical Freedom Acts (MFAs), which provide that doctors who utilize CAMs are not per se engaged in professional misconduct); Joseph A. Barrette 2003, 107(noting that the enactment of the Alternative Medical Practice Act (AMPA) gives doctors the right to use effective nonconventional medical care and gives patients the right to choose innovative medical care).

[47] Joseph A. Barrette 2003, 80 (highlighting that doctors integrating CAM into conventional care risked having their licenses suspended or revoked, even though their patients were neither harmed nor complained to the medical board); Michael H. Cohen (1996), 86 (noting that "[b]y separating medical from nonmedical practitioners, and granting state medical boards broad authority to punish deviation from medical orthodoxy, irrespective of patient injury, the existing regulatory environment favors a health care system dominated by orthodox medicine, based on technological approaches to disease and healing, and modelled on the assumption that patients lack the requisite sophistication to choose who may minister to the diseased body.").

[48] Timothy Caulfield and Colin Feasby 2001, 191–192 (in Canadian context). In the USA context, *Model Guidelines for the Use of Complementary and Alternative Therapies in Medical Practice*, approved by the Federation of State Medical Boards, recognizes "that a licensed physician shall not found guilty of unprofessional conduct for failure to practice medicine in an acceptable manner solely on the basis of utilizing CAM." It recommends that conventional professional guidelines need to allow a wide degree of latitude in physicians' exercise of their professional judgment and not preclude the use of any methods that are reasonably likely to benefit patients without undue risk. *See*, Federation of State Medical Boards *Model Guidelines for the Use of Complementary and Alternative Therapies in Medical Practice* (2002) <http://www.fsmb.org/pdf/2002_grpol_complementary_alternative_therapies.pdf> (last accessed 20 November 2010), Section I. Preamble.

Before embracing a CAM, a doctor should assess the risk-benefit profiles of both the CAM treatment and conventional medicine treatments (or no treatment).[49] When recommending and offering CAM therapies, conventional medicine doctors need to take full advantage of their knowledge of both conventional medicine and CAMs, and realise the importance of conventional diagnosis and monitoring. Continuing to monitor conventionally, and intervene conventionally when medically necessary, helps ensure that the standard of care will have been met, and the possibility of patient injury minimised.

A doctor who favours a CAM can choose to refer his patient to a CAM specialist or deliver the CAM himself. The potential liability exposure for physician referrals to a CAM practitioner is not large.[50] The general rule that there is no liability merely for referring to a specialist should apply to both conventional care and the CAM context.[51] However, there are real risks for conventional medicine doctors who actually *deliver* CAM therapies. The risks may include the risk of their licenses being suspended or revoked and the risk for malpractice. Mainstream doctors who practice the more widely-accepted CAMs might not run the same risk of losing their licenses as doctors who practice CAM therapies considered more "on the fringe" (Doyle 2001, 546).

The convergence of CAM and orthodox medicine complicates the determination of negligence in both the diagnosis/treatment and information disclosure areas (Parker 2007, 14). One difficulty is to determine the standard of care applicable to doctors who deliver alternative therapies. Academically, there are three different standards applicable to dual practitioners: the alternative medicine standard, the mixed practice standard, and the medical standard (Studdert 1999, 175–176). Obviously, subjecting dual practitioners to *alternative medicine standard* would

---

[49] *See*, Federation of State Medical Boards *Model Guidelines for the Use of Complementary and Alternative Therapies in Medical Practice* (2002) <http://www.fsmb.org/pdf/2002_grpol_complementary_alternative_therapies.pdf> (last accessed 20 November 2010), Section I. Preamble (In evaluating appropriateness of a doctor's integrative or CAM care practice, the following question needs to be considered: Is the physician using a treatment that is: (1) effective and safe? (having adequate scientific evidence of efficacy and/or safety or greater safety than other established treatment models for the same condition); (2) effective, but with some real or potential danger? (having evidence of efficacy, but also of adverse side effects); (3) inadequately studied, but safe? (having insufficient evidence of clinical efficacy, but reasonable evidence to suggest relative safety); (4) ineffective and dangerous? (proven to be ineffective or unsafe through controlled trials or documented evidence or as measured by a risk/benefit assessment).); Section III. Guidelines (The treatment offered should: (1) have a favorable risk/benefit ratio compared to other treatments for the same condition; (2) be based upon a reasonable expectation that it will result in a favorable patient outcome, including preventive practices; (3) be based upon the expectation that a greater benefit will be achieved than that which can be expected with no treatment.).

[50] Federation of State Medical Boards *Model Guidelines for the Use of Complementary and Alternative Therapies in Medical Practice* (2002) <http://www.fsmb.org/pdf/2002_grpol_complementary_alternative_therapies.pdf> (last accessed 20 November 2010) Section III. Guidelines ("The physician may refer the patient as necessary for additional evaluation and treatment in order to achieve treatment objectives and may include referral to a licensed or otherwise state-regulated health care practitioner with the requisite training and skills to utilize the CAM therapy being recommended. However, the physician is responsible for monitoring the results and should schedule periodic reviews to ensure progress is being achieved.").

[51] Lois Snyder (ed.) 2007, 178–179 (subject to some exceptions, such as "joint treatment" and the "known incompetent").

allow the standard for dual practitioners to deteriorate into a lower standard.[52] Among the three, applying the medical standard to the CAM context is the most conservative and the harshest. It raises the prospect of negligence per se when a dual practitioner chooses a CAM treatment.[53]

Although the mixed practice standard is criticised as illogical and potentially unjust,[54] applying a double standard seems to be fairer to a dual practitioner. A double standard shows a genuine loyalty to the "same school" rule. On the one hand, in judging whether a doctor who administered a CAM therapy to his patient did so with the requisite degree of skill and care, the alternative medicine standard may have some logical appeal (Studdert 1999, 175). It would make little sense to allow the standards to be set by doctors with no experience or knowledge of the CAM therapies. On the other hand, setting standards for dual practitioners should reflect the fact that they possess both the conventional knowledge and alternative knowledge.

8.3.2 Disclosure of Alternatives

For doctors who practise both conventionally and alternatively, what kinds of treatment options should fall within their duty to disclose? Many of those conventional medicine doctors who deliver CAMs seem to have an undivided loyalty to *CAMs* and forget their capacity as conventional medicine practitioners. However, that should not negate the need that dual practitioners make their knowledge about both conventional medicine and CAMs available in the context of information disclosure.

There is a slight distinction in setting standards for dual practitioners between in the context of administering CAMs and in the context of disclosing information about alternatives. In the technical realm that requires specific expertise, the law allows fragmentation, and alternative medicine practitioners who are trained and skilled in this realm are better positioned to give an evaluation and get involved in

---

[52] It is based on the assumption that the alternative medicine standard is lower than the medical standard. As far as delivering CAM therapies is concerned, this is not always the case. Arguably the skills of orthodox medicine practitioner in offering CAMs may be lower than that of CAM practitioners.

[53] David M. Studdert 1999, 175. *Compare*, Robert T. Vlasis 2006, 505–506 (opining that when a doctor incorporates CAM therapies with allopathic treatments, the CAM treatments do not become grounds for a malpractice action per se; interpreting case law as meaning that the standard of care in allopathic treatment looks not to the conventionality or unconventionality of the method but rather to the appropriateness and effectiveness of the treatment in light of the patient's condition). *See*, *Charell v. Gonzales*, 660 N.Y.S.2d 665, 668 (Sup. 1997) ("it would seem that no practitioners of alternative medicine could prevail on such a question as the reference to the term 'non-conventional' may well necessitate a finding that the doctor who practices such medicine deviates from 'accepted' medical standards").

[54] Timothy Caulfield and Colin Feasby 2001, 202 (noting that patients should be able to rely on doctors to employ the same stringent standards regardless of the nature of the treatment).

producing expert evidence (Studdert 1999, 175). However, where the claim against dual practitioners is failure to *disclose* a full range of treatment options, the law will not allow dual practitioners to ignore the medical knowledge they possess or are reasonably expected to possess. In such situations, the medical standard rather than the alternative medicine standard may be applied.[55]

The dual practitioner needs not only to inform patients of the availability, the nature, and the risks of the proposed CAM therapies, but also to disclose any *conventional* treatments. The ambit of information disclosure for dual practitioners should not be confined to CAM therapies. A dual practitioner's duty to inform needs to encompass both available conventional and available CAM treatment options.

My view is that, for both medical practitioners and CAM practitioners, providing an "integrative" or "dual" health care is not possible, but possessing an "integrative" knowledge is necessary in the area of information disclosure. There is a wide philosophical gulf between conventional medicine and alternative medicine. A true integration or assimilation of one into another is almost impossible unless it occurs at the expense of losing identity or the unique value of one that is assimilated. Most of CAMs are not comfortable with and not readily amendable to modern scientific thinking. There is a conflict of loyalties for dual practitioners. However, wide knowledge about different medicines helps to present patients with full, unbiased information about treatment options.

8.4 CAM Practitioners

Most CAMs are at the stage of voluntary self-regulation.[56] A high proportion of health services is provided by CAM practitioners, but they are not subject to formal statutory regulation.[57] It is interesting to explore why CAMs are insufficiently regulated in an orthodox-medicine-dominated society. It seems that the idea of statutory

[55] David M. Studdert 1999, 175 ("while arguments for application of alternative medicine standards may have some force in cases where physicians are alleged to have been negligent in administering techniques that are foreign to medicine, a medical standard of care probably better reflects the dual practitioner's duty in clinical situations that implicate knowledge of both alternative and conventional medicine.").

[56] John Lunstroth 2006 (regarding voluntary self-regulation as the most viable model for CAM practitioners).

[57] For example, although there is an open clause (section 3(2)) that makes it possible for "additional health profession" to be subjected to the Act, the *Health Practitioners Competence Assurance Act* 2003 (NZ) (2003 No. 48) only embraced Chiropractic in its 2003 version. New Zealand is still at the discussion and consultation stage of implementing regulation of some CAM practitioners. Victoria is the only jurisdiction in Australia that has adopted a statutory approach to the regulation of Chinese medicine practitioners (including acupuncturists). It has taken international lead by introducing the *Chinese Medicine Registration Act* 2000 (Vic).

regulation is unpopular to both parties arguing for or against CAMs. Some jurisdictions showed hesitancy in regulating CAMs because statutory regulation of CAMs was seen as legitimatising a form of health care that is yet to establish a compelling scientific evidence base for the safety and efficacy of treatments, and falsely giving consumers an impression that CAM is as effective and safe as orthodox medicine.[58] They approach statutory regulation of CAMs very cautiously because of the fear that regulation may mislead public perception and confer an unwarranted status on CAM practitioners.

Statutory regulation may not even be favoured by CAM practitioners themselves because regulating CAMs, especially along the model of medical professional regulation, would undermine their distinct identity. Applying a statutory regulation that is modelled on existing medical legislation to CAM contexts is not free from problems (Tran 2006, 352–369). Standardisation of practices may cause CAM practitioners to lose their claim to offer treatment that is a true alternative to orthodox medicine, and "medicalisation" of CAM may cause the philosophies that underpin CAM methods to be watered down (Tran 2006, 367). The question whether CAMs should be subjected to statutory regulation may be translated into the issue of whether alternative medicines require an *alternative legal framework*, including an alternative regulatory model.

Leaving CAMs unregulated is not advisable. A risk the under-regulation creates is that CAM practitioners are not subject to effective forms of professional accountability in relation to CAM services which have the potential to be seriously counter-therapeutic for their clients if they breach norms of propriety generally accepted within their professions and expected by their clients.[59]

Under-regulation of CAM has effects both on the provision of service and on information disclosure. Several questions arise. In the context of provision of service, the question is whether or not CAM practitioners deserve the protection of the "same school" rule. In the context of information disclosure, the question is whether or not CAM practitioners have ability to present information about the risk-benefit profiles of CAM treatments and alternative conventional medicine treatments.

8.4.1 The Context of Diagnosis and Treatment: The "Same School" Rule?

8.4.1.1 The *Shakoor v. Situ* Case: Standard of Care for CAM Practitioners

There is criticism about the approach of allowing peer review or peer judgment to decide the competency and disciplinary issues. It was argued that peer review or

[58] Anne Tran 2006, 365–367 (mentioning UK and New Zealand).

[59] Ian Freckelton 2008, 413–418 (talking in the Australian and New Zealand context).

self-regulation per se does not amount to adequate regulation.[60] This view reflects the argument that clinical practice should be evidence-based and, in setting standards of care for health practitioners, courts should be more ready to intervene and be informed by evidence-based medicine rather than peer judgments. It raises the issue of how to deal with the relationship between professional judgment, professional guidelines which are more evidence-based, and the courts' roles. While making judgments more evidence-based is applaudable, considering that, even in the context of conventional medicine, only a small part of it have been subjected to the "gold" clinical trials and applying the evidence-based thinking to the task of setting standard of care is not free from concerns and doubts, exposing CAM practitioners to the evidence-based requirements, no matter in the context of regulation and clinical care, is not realistic.

The concerns surrounding the question whether it is wise to leave CAM practitioners to define their standard of care were also echoed in the English case of *Shakoor v. Situ*.[61] The case raised the question of whether or not CAM professions should be accorded the same judicial deference as conventional medicine profession. It answers "yes", but a qualified one. It imposes on CAM practitioners an additional duty to actively appreciate the risk information released from conventional medicine sources. The court shows some unease with the thought of leaving CAM professions themselves to define their standard of care.

The case concerned a practitioner of traditional Chinese herbal medicine (TCHM).[62] Because there is a discrepancy between the standards applicable to orthodox medical practitioners and TCHM practitioners, and the choice between these two standards has great implications, the main task of the High Court was to address the following issue: "[i]s [the defendant] to be judged by the standards of the reasonably careful practitioner of CHM [Chinese Herbal Medicine] or according to the standards applicable to orthodox medical practitioners in [the United Kingdom]?"[63] Therefore the main issue of the case is to define *the standard of care for CAM practitioners*.

---

[60] Malcolm Parker 2007, 13 ("[I]t is no longer acceptable for peer review to be informed simply by the clinical experiences, accumulated wisdom and consequent opinions of one's peers. Within medicine, the status of tradition, hierarchy and personality has yielded to that of sound scientific evidence, so that it is the rule of evidence (like the rule of law in social life), not the rule of men and their status and charisma, which increasingly has final say. The validation of the particular practice must now come from beyond the professional 'black box' of consensus or opinion.").

[61] *Shakoor (administratrix of the estate of Shakoor (deceased) v. Situ (t/a Eternal Health Co)* [2000] 4 All ER 181.

[62] Chinese herbal medicine, together with acupuncture and Chinese message, is a part of Traditional Chinese Medicine (TCM). The defendant had been trained in China for 5 years in the theoretical and practical application of both traditional Chinese (including herbal) medicine and western medicine. He was not qualified as a "doctor" in the United Kingdom and, thus, was not subject to regulation either by licensing or registration. However, he is a voluntary member of an association called the 'Register of Chinese Herbal Medicine'. Members of the Register are required to have achieved minimum standards of competence by examination and are subject to a 'Code of Ethics', the rules of which are formulated similarly to those governing the medical profession in the United Kingdom.

[63] *Shakoor (Deceased) v. Situ* [2000] 4 All ER 181, 186.

The *Shakoor v. Situ* case does not concern a TCM practitioner's *disclosure of conventional medicine alternatives* because the patient had *already been aware of* orthodox treatment option (surgery), but opted against it and chose in favour of alternative medicine treatments.[64]

In the case, the patient's window alleged that the defendant had been negligent in (1) *prescribing* the decoction, or alternatively, (2) failing to *warn* the deceased of the *risk* of injury posed by the remedy.[65] The first allegation concerns the context of diagnosis and treatment. The second allegation relates to information (risks) disclosure. The defendant responded that (1) according to the Chinese medical textbooks and periodicals which were available to him, the *prescription* of the decoction had been established, over centuries, to be completely safe with no adverse effects; (2) he was unaware of the matters reported in Western/conventional medical journals.

Although the claimant's allegations covered the contexts of both diagnosis/treatment and information disclosure, the court focused mainly on the first of these issues. As to the issue of *failure to warn of risks*, the court's conclusion is that (1) even if the risk had already fallen within a doctor's knowledge, an adverse reaction of the type which occurred is such a *rare* event that a doctor would not be obliged to give a warning; and (2) even if a warning were to be given, the risk could legitimately have been presented as being so small that an appropriate warning would not have had the effect of dissuading anyone, let alone the deceased, from taking the treatment.[66] It seems that the claimant's nondisclosure allegation failed at the stage of both breach of duty and causation.

---

[64] The deceased suffered from multiple benign lipomata. A benign lipoma does not constitute any risk to health. In the eyes of orthodox medicine, there is not any known treatment other than removal by surgery. It might reasonably be inferred that the deceased had been told by his general practitioner that *surgery was the only orthodox medical treatment*. The deceased consulted the defendant. The defendant prescribed a course of a Chinese herbal remedy prepared with reference to a traditional recipe or classic formula, consisting of a mixture of 12 different herbs. After taking nine doses of the remedy, the patient suffered acute liver failure. After liver transplant surgery he died. Histological analysis of the removed liver showed acute sub-total hepatic necrosis. The coroner's examination established the identity of ten of the ingredients, including *Bai Xian Pi*, which might be hepatotoxic but the evidence was unclear. There was not any basis for doubting that the herbs conformed to acceptable standards of quality. The expert evidence adduced on each side agreed that (1) the injury to and failure of the deceased's liver (and therefore his death) were, on a balance of probabilities, caused by the decoction; (2) the ingredients are biologically active but not toxic or hepatotoxic either individually or collectively; (3) in the deceased they induced an *"idiosyncratic" reaction*; that such *a reaction is extremely rare and cannot be predicted in any person. See, Shakoor (Deceased) v. Situ* [2000] 4 All ER 181, 184.

[65] In support of her allegation, the claimant adduced evidence from the *field of orthodox medicine* rather than Chinese medicine, including western medicine experts and western medicine publications. Those evidences suggested that (1) there were certain known risks of liver damage from the ingestion of a similar Chinese herbal medicine; (2) the decoction did not, according to the judgment of western medicine, have any prospect of ameliorating or curing the deceased's lipomata; (3) the risk/benefit analysis pointed against allowing the use of the decoction at all; (4) if it were to be prescribed, it could only be properly prescribed after an appropriate warning to the patient of the risks of injury.

[66] *Shakoor (Deceased) v. Situ* [2000] 4 All ER 181, 191–192.

Although the *Shakoor* case is not primarily a failure to warn case, it assists in answering the following question: in a jurisdiction where orthodox medicine dominates medically, culturally and even politically, such as the United Kingdom, should an alternative medicine practitioner take active steps to appreciate the risks that are revealed by orthodox medicine but are not available in the field of alternative medicine to which the alternative medicine practitioner showed commitment?

The *Shakoor* court answered the question in the affirmative. The court placed great but undue weight on the fact that "the practitioner is practising his art alongside orthodox medicine",[67] unnecessarily highlighting that "the alternative practitioner has chosen to practice in [the United Kingdom] alongside a system of orthodox medicine and must abide by the laws and standards prevailing in [that] country",[68] and blindly assuming that the standard of care prevailing in Beijing may fall below that in London.[69] In modern societies, it should be very difficult, if not impossible, to find a corner where an alternative medicine practitioner does not practise his art "alongside orthodox medicine".[70] The situation is almost the same at every corner of the world. There is no need to highlight a geographical or jurisdictional difference on this issue. Contrary to the court's assumption, more rigorous legislative interventions into the practice of traditional Chinese medicine, higher level of integration of Western medicine and Chinese medicine, and more involvement of Western medicine in TCM education in China has made it probable that the standard of care applicable to TCM practitioners in Beijing would be higher, not lower, than that prevailing in London.

Based on this over-emphasised fact, the court drew three observations: (1) because the practitioner is holding himself out as competent to practise "within a system of law and medicine", this "system of law and medicine", such as the UK's, would review the standard of care provided to the patient[71]; (2) it is not enough to say that the remedy the alternative practitioner has prescribed is "traditional and believed not be harmful", he has "a duty to *ensure* that the remedy is *not actually or potentially harmful*"[72]; (3) an alternative medicine practitioner must recognise that an adverse reaction to a traditional remedy is quite likely to have come to the attention of orthodox medicine providers and have revealed in orthodox medical journals, and he "must take steps to satisfy himself that there has not been any adverse report in such [orthodox medicine] journals on the remedy which ought to affect the use he makes of it".[73]

---

[67] *Shakoor (Deceased) v. Situ* [2000] 4 All ER 181, 188.

[68] *Shakoor (Deceased) v. Situ* [2000] 4 All ER 181, 188.

[69] *Shakoor (Deceased) v. Situ* [2000] 4 All ER 181, 188. The court actually admitted that it "know not what is the standard of skill and care which prevails in China or how it compares with the standard which is practised [in the Britain]". *See*, *Shakoor (Deceased) v. Situ* [2000] 4 All ER 181, 187.

[70] The *Shakoor* court actually admitted that Traditional Chinese Medicine is "practised alongside modern medicine in China". *See*, *Shakoor (Deceased) v. Situ* [2000] 4 All ER 181, 187.

[71] *Shakoor (Deceased) v. Situ* [2000] 4 All ER 181, 189.

[72] *Shakoor (Deceased) v. Situ* [2000] 4 All ER 181, 189 (emphasis added).

[73] *Shakoor (Deceased) v. Situ* [2000] 4 All ER 181, 189.

Reading those observations, one can conclude that the court imposed upon alternative medicine practitioners an additional duty to keep informed of relevant discoveries in orthodox medicine, a duty to cross-reference with orthodox literature. One method that the court suggested to discharge this duty is to subscribe to an association which arranges to search the relevant literature and promptly report any material publication to its members.[74] But the "relevant literature" must be that "which would be taken by an orthodox practitioner practising at the level of specialty at which the alternative practitioner holds himself out".[75] The workability of this suggestion is open to doubt (Fordham 2001, 11). The doubt may be justified when the law becomes aware that orthodox medicine and most of alternative medicines cannot be easily translated into each other because they employ different languages and terminologies.

Imposing on alternative practitioners a duty to ensure that their remedies are not harmful is a very high requirement. The duty of alternative practitioners to keep their eyes on reports released in the Western medicine world is burdensome. By imposing such a duty, the acting judge actually lent a hand in reinforcing the orthodox medicine dominant culture. As one scholar noted, the standard established in *Shakoor* was "heavily influenced by the 'apparent facticity' of orthodox medicine" (de Prez 2001, 86). It requires non-conventional practitioners to "aspire to the values" of orthodox medicine and to "demonstrate an affinity with the principles of orthodox medicine" (de Prez 2001, 86). It imports "a degree of empiricism/'evidence-based' practice" and "values from the scientific rationale of orthodox medicine" into the practices of alternative medicine (de Prez 2001, 87).

As far as the standard of care for CAM practitioners is concerned, rather than consistently showing respect and even taking a non-intervention attitude to professionals that underlies the *Bolam* test, the English court showed more readiness to modify the test and rigorously scrutinise the practitioner's conduct in the case of practitioners of alternative medicine. When applying the *Bolam* test, the court distinguished orthodox medicine from alternative medicine:

> Had this been a case involving a practitioner of an accepted branch of 'orthodox' medicine I would have been disposed to agree with the defendant's submission [that the court should defer to a medical opinion supported by a reputable body of experts skilled in that particular art]. But the question is whether the same principles necessarily apply in the case of alternative practitioners.[76]

The court raised a deep concern about the risk of an unmodified application of the *Bolam* test in the context of alternative medicine by asking that

> Does the application of the *Bolam* principle mean that, whatever the alternative therapy, those who practice 'in the same art' as the practitioner are able to dictate to the court the standards in accordance with which he is to be judged?[77]

[74] *Shakoor (Deceased) v. Situ* [2000] 4 All ER 181, 189.

[75] *Shakoor (Deceased) v. Situ* [2000] 4 All ER 181, 189.

[76] *Shakoor (Deceased) v. Situ* [2000] 4 All ER 181, 187.

[77] *Shakoor (Deceased) v. Situ* [2000] 4 All ER 181, 187.

Although acknowledging that TCHM has "a long and distinguished history", the court still cast doubt on "the extent of current teaching, research, monitoring and verification of its practices in China or elsewhere".[78] The court wanted to see that the approaches adopted by orthodox medicine ought to be followed by alternative medicine:

> in hospitals, teaching schools and medical research establishments throughout the world attention is paid to questioning the validity of treatments, measuring their efficacy and observing and reporting upon side effects, with the results of such observation and research being published to the medical profession in peer reviewed articles and papers.[79]

The court suspected that the same practices may not prevail in China.[80] By adding a bracket, the court cautiously admitted that this suspicion was perhaps quite wrong.[81] It did have a wrong suspicion. China is not only a Western-medicine-dominated society, but also shares a medical culture which honours evidence of efficacy and safety. As I will reveal in Chap. 10, China's efforts to "modernise" and "scientificise" Traditional Chinese Medicine (TCM) have resulted in TCM losing much of its identity.[82]

The court presented an *extreme* example to justify its approach of differentiating between western medicine and alternative medicine:

> Would the court be bound to accept the evidence of fellow practitioners of [a cult whose practitioners believed that the administration of arsenic was an appropriate remedy for various ill] that prescription of arsenic was in accordance with their accepted practice and therefore non-negligent? The short and obvious answer is 'no'...[83]

In such extreme situations, as the court rightly pointed out, other tactics rather than that of imposing on an alternative medicine practitioner an additional duty to appreciate the orthodox medicine information are sufficient to avoid unfair outcome. Those tactics may include refusing to regard such a 'cult' as a body engaged in the practice of 'medicine' or defining the expert evidence of a particular practice as not being responsible, reasonable or reputable.[84] The law of torts and the *Bolam* test can play their roles by requiring a "responsible" opinion and a more substantial "body" of professional opinion to defend non-orthodox practices (de Prez 2001, 84). There is no need to be driven by such extreme examples and to overburden alternative medicine practitioners by requiring them to keep familiar with relevant risk information expressed in another medical language with which they may absolutely not be familiar, especially in a medical culture which has a low level of integration of conventional and CAM medicines.

---

[78] *Shakoor (Deceased) v. Situ* [2000] 4 All ER 181, 187.

[79] *Shakoor (Deceased) v. Situ* [2000] 4 All ER 181, 187.

[80] *Shakoor (Deceased) v. Situ* [2000] 4 All ER 181, 187.

[81] *Shakoor (Deceased) v. Situ* [2000] 4 All ER 181, 187.

[82] *See*, Chap. 10.3.2.

[83] *Shakoor (Deceased) v. Situ* [2000] 4 All ER 181, 187.

[84] *Shakoor (Deceased) v. Situ* [2000] 4 All ER 181, 187–188.

Although the court did not want to uncritically apply the profession-honoured *Bolam* test "without alteration or qualification"[85] in a CAM context, it is good to see that the court did not go further and follow the claimant's argument that the conduct of alternative medicine practitioners should be measured by the standard of care applicable to *orthodox medicine practitioners*.[86] The court offered two explanations to its position. First, the defendant did not "hold himself out as a practitioner of orthodox medicine".[87] It is well-established that the standard required depends on what a professional holds himself out as able to do.[88]Second, the fact that the claimant rejected orthodox medicine treatments and chose in favour of alternative medicine should have a say in deciding the relevant standard of care:

> More particularly, the patient has usually had the choice of going to an orthodox practitioner but has rejected him in favour of the alternative practitioner for *reasons personable* and best known to himself and almost certainly at some personal financial cost. Those reasons may include a passionate belief in the superiority of the alternative therapy or a fear of surgery or of reliance (perhaps dependence) on orthodox chemical medications which may have known undesirable side effects either short or long-term or both. (In the instant case, where the deceased was not known to have been predisposed to favour alternative medicine, his motivation may, for all we know, have been a fear of surgery or merely a desire to avoid the delays attendant nowadays on non-surgical cases.) The decision of the patient may be enlightened and informed or based on ignorance and superstition. Whatever basis of his decision, it seems to me that *the fact that the patient has chosen to reject the orthodox and prefer the alternative practitioner is something important which must be taken into account.* Why should he later be able to complain that the alternative practitioner has not provided him with skill and care in accordance with the standards of those orthodox practitioners *whom he has rejected*? (emphasis added).[89]

It needs to be noted that this line of reasoning embodies the notion of "assumption of risk".[90] It needs to be seen if this line of reasoning would produce a chilling effect on the patient's choosing a CAM as an alternative to orthodox medicine. It makes it clear that a patient, who rejected orthodox medicine in favour of alternative medicine, could not legitimately expect the alternative medicine practitioner to reach the high standard of care that is applicable to orthodox practitioners.

Therefore, as to the standard of care in the field of alternative medicine, the *Shakoor* court actually adopted a middle way. On the one hand, it showed reluctance to allow the unqualified *Bolam* test as a blind shield for alternative medicine practitioners and urged such practitioners to keep an open and active mind to what orthodox medicine practitioners have formulated about their therapies. It would be dangerous

---

[85] *Shakoor (Deceased) v. Situ* [2000] 4 All ER 181, 186.

[86] *Shakoor (Deceased) v. Situ* [2000] 4 All ER 181, 188.

[87] *Shakoor (Deceased) v. Situ* [2000] 4 All ER 181, 188.

[88] *Philips v. William Whiteley Ltd* [1938] 1 All ER 566.

[89] *Shakoor (Deceased) v. Situ* [2000] 4 All ER 181, 188.

[90] *See,* Robert T. Vlasis 2006, 514–515 (holding that the policy underlying the assumption of risk doctrine justifies its application to CAM providers because patients electing experimental CAM treatments likely have full knowledge of the danger and intelligently acquiesce in the treatment).

and irresponsible to give an unregulated alternative medicine group "effective *carte blanche*" with respect to their practices (Fordham 2001, 9). On the other hand, the court accepted the traditional negligence rule that a professional's conduct is best judged by his peers. To judge an alternative practitioner by exactly the same standards as those of an orthodox one would be to ignore the sensible and fair rule that a professional should be judged by his "own art" rather than by someone else's (Fordham 2001, 9). It would be perverse to assess the practice of alternative medicines by the standards developed by orthodox medicine, "given that many non-orthodox practices are founded on an outright rejection of orthodox thinking and that their patients often seek non-conventional therapies due to their disillusionment and/or rejection of orthodox therapies" (de Prez 2001, 84).

Under this modified *Bolam* rule, a claimant has two options to win an action against an alternative practitioner. One is to make the *Bolam* test workable in the area of alternative medicine, that means, by calling an expert in the specialty in question, to prove that the defendant has failed to exercise the skill and care appropriate to that art.[91] Another alternative is, if the experts under the first option are not available, to prove that the prevailing standard of skill and care in that art is deficient having regard to the risks which were not and should have been taken into account.[92] The claimant's allegation in this case centred on the second optional argument.[93]

The court found that the defendant-practitioner was not negligent in prescribing the decoction.[94] The *Shakoor* findings are applaudable for their compromise and common sense (Fordham 2001, 8). They are also applaudable in the sense that they did not absolutely deny the safety and efficacy of TCM and allowed their peers to judge the conduct of TCM practitioners. But the court showed less deference to

[91] *Shakoor (Deceased) v. Situ* [2000] 4 All ER 181, 189.

[92] *Shakoor (Deceased) v. Situ* [2000] 4 All ER 181, 189.

[93] The claimant argued that (1) the warnings revealed by orthodox medicine world were enough to put any practitioner on notice of the serious potential risk from the herbs; (2) it becomes negligent for any practitioner to prescribe the decoction because orthodox doctors confirm that herbal medicine cannot alleviate or cure the lipomata; (3) the risk/benefit analysis points unequivocally against the prescription where there is no conceivable benefit and only the risk of serious harm, however rare the incidence of it might be. *See*, *Shakoor (Deceased) v. Situ* [2000] 4 All ER 181, 190–191.

[94] The court had four main reasons for its finding. Firstly, having read the relevant evidence, the court was not prepared to conclude that TCHM cannot alleviate or cure lipomata. Secondly, the court was not prepared to find that an ordinary careful general practitioner – the appropriate equivalent orthodox specialty – would have been negligent if he had failed to read and take notice of the warnings contained in orthodox medical journals. Thirdly, even if a reasonably competent general practitioner had seen the letters in question, due to the letter's equivocality, lack of peer review and non-resemblance to the patient's clinical situation, he would not have been realised that the preparation was too hazardous to prescribe. Finally, the court accepted that "the risk of unpredictable responses leading to liver disease with Chinese herbal medicines is very substantially lower than that seen with modern chemical medicines". Experts on both sides had acknowledged that adverse drug reactions leading to liver injury could arise with a range of commonly prescribed western medications, including some antibiotics, anti-epileptics and anti-psychotic drugs. *See*, *Shakoor (Deceased) v. Situ* [2000] 4 All ER 181, 190–191.

these peer opinions. The court seemed to be accustomed to view the conduct of CAM practitioners through the spectacles of orthodox medicine because they practise within an orthodox medicine context. The requirement of 'evidence-based' medicine in CAM context may be criticised for applying a double standard to alternative medicine and lending judicial support to the medical efforts of orthodox medicine to retain dominance in the therapeutic division of labour (de Prez 2001, 87). The court's approach, if generally adopted, would confirm the superior status of orthodox medicine over alternative forms of healing (Weir 2003, 304).

In the context of information disclosure, the *Shakoor* case has the effect of encouraging CAM practitioners to step out of their traditional knowledge and try to appreciate the orthodox medicine thinking. The CAM practitioners should keep continued "awareness of orthodox reflections, findings and reports" on their non-orthodox remedies (de Prez 2001, 87). CAM practitioners should have an understanding of evidence-based medicine.[95] A CAM practitioner should be appropriately trained to reflect high standards for his modality. Where appropriate, this training should incorporate sufficient biomedical education to assist in identifying conditions that should be attended to by a medical practitioner with a clear understanding that in no case should a patient be dissuaded from attending a medical practitioner (Weir 2003, 306). The problem is that there is no corresponding duty on orthodox medicine practitioners to appreciate CAMs.

The *Shakoor* case and judgment arose in a context where Chinese medicine practitioners were not formally regulated. It is still to be seen whether the judgment would be different if the TCM practitioners have been subject to rigorous and formal professional regulation. For example, Singapore has the *Traditional Chinese Medicine Practitioners Act 2000*.[96] In my view, that would make a difference when courts decide whether or not to accord deference to peer opinions. However, inspired by a judgment in a criminal case, a Singaporean scholar predicted that Singaporean courts might adopt an even stricter approach than that in *Shakoor*, and hold that all practitioners of all forms of medicine must be governed by the standards applicable to *practitioners of conventional medicine* (Fordham 2001, 10–11). That means subjecting CAM practitioners to orthodox medicine standard of care. I do not share with this view. The judiciary should show more confidence to professional practices and adopt a more non-interventionist approach if a profession has more formal regulation, higher quality education and higher professional integrity.

The *Shakoor* judgment seems to send a message that CAM practitioners should have in mind that the society within which their art is practised has certain legitimate expectations based on its mainstream medical culture (Fordham 2001, 11). But I still doubt the necessity of attaching importance to the nature of medical culture in *one society or jurisdiction*. Does China, which pays respect to Traditional

[95] House of Lords Select Committee on Science and Technology, 6th Report Complementary and Alternative Medicine (1999–2000) HL 123, chapter 6, para. 20.

[96] No. 34 of 2000.

Chinese Medicine, have a weak mainstream medical culture? Absolutely not. As I will explain in Chap. 10, China has a very strong Western medical culture. The "integrative" approach that China adopts is actually Western-medicine-reinforcing, which is at the expense of diluting the uniqueness of Traditional Chinese Medicine. The real issue is whether or not a society is open-minded towards the diversity of medical cultures.

8.4.1.2 The "Same School" Rule and CAM Practitioners

As far as the standard of care for health care practitioners is concerned, the "same school" rule is generally accepted. That means that health care practitioners are entitled to have their treatment of patients tested by the rules and principles that conform to their training and the standards set by their immediate professional peers, not by those of some other school.[97] The *Shakoor* judgment still showed fidelity to the "same school" rule in the CAM context, meaning that the standard of care applicable to CAM practitioners should be a CAM standard rather than an orthodox medicine standard. However, it also expressed concerns about the appropriateness of uncritically applying the "same school" rule to the CAM context. There is a further argument that health care practitioners, including CAM practitioners, should be judged by the "rule of evidence" rather than by the "rule of men" or peer review (Parker 2007, 13).

I would argue that the law continues to apply the "same school" rule to CAM practitioners, at the same time making it sure that the CAM "schools" *deserve* peer judgment and judicial deference. The latter task needs rigorous professional regulation for CAMs. Formal education and regulation for CAM practitioners would give courts more confidence to accord deference to CAM professions.

It is unfair to judge a defendant-practitioner by the standards that do not conform to his education, training, and peer expectations (Studdert 1999, 174). In general, a court will hold a CAM practitioner to the skill he claims to possess (Vlasis 2006, 516–517). Another rationale for applying "school-specific" standards is that, when a patient knowingly chooses or consents to treatment from a given practitioner, he may expect the skills, but must assume the risks that are common to that practitioner's healing method (Studdert 1999, 174).

Applying the "same school" rule to the CAM context means that a court would accord deference to "a responsible body of professional opinion" or "a school of thought" in the CAM field, as witnessed by the *Bolam* test. That means that, in a jurisdiction which reformulated the *Bolam* test, such as Australia, the defence to

[97] David M. Studdert 1999, 174. There are several exceptions to the "same school" rule: (1) where principles or standards at issue are common to both schools; (2) where a practitioner strays outside his scope of permissible practice; (3) where a court cannot identify a coherent school of practice. Evidence that an approach to healing is licensed is an important marker of its status as a discrete "school" of practice. *See*, David M. Studdert 1999, 174.

liability, i.e. the treatment concerned has been widely accepted as proper professional practice by peer professional opinion, is also available to CAM practitioners.[98] That also means that CAM expert testimony is required to establish the customary CAM practice.[99] All of these assertions are subject to the qualification that CAM professions are well regulated.[100] The judicial deference is accorded only to a CAM approach, which is qualified as "a responsible body of professional opinion", not all CAM approaches.

8.4.2 The Context of Information Disclosure: A Duty to Inform About Conventional Medicine Alternatives?

As with orthodox medicine, practising of CAM should be subject to the informed consent rule.[101] The purpose of the doctrine of informed consent is to safeguard a patient's right of autonomy and self-determination. Because of its patient-oriented nature, the informed consent rule should not make distinctions between different medicines. If a jurisdiction decides to adopt the doctor-oriented standard of disclosure, the same standard should also apply to CAM practitioners, rather than setting a harsher standard for CAM practitioners.[102] I prefer the patient-oriented standard of information disclosure. Actually the CAM context, which contains diverse, or even no, practice of information disclosure, vividly demonstrates the inappropriateness of applying the profession-oriented standard of disclosure in the CAM context.

---

[98] *Kocev v. Toh* [2009] NSWDC 169 (applying s 50 (defence of treatment given being widely accepted in Australia by peer professional opinion as competent professional practice) of the *Civil Liability Act* to chiropractors, holding that defendant's treatment of the plaintiff was in accordance with *acceptable professional standards of competent chiropractic practice*).

[99] *Bronneke v. Rutherford* 120 Nev. 230, 89 P.3d 40 (Nev. 2004).

[100] *Bronneke v. Rutherford* 120 Nev. 230, 89 P.3d 40 (Nev. 2004) (plaintiff arguing that chiropractors are not entitled to the deference given to medical doctors because medicine is based upon the scientific method, whereas the practice of chiropractic is not scientific; court disagreeing with that and noting the rigorous educational requirements for chiropractic practitioners).

[101] For example, *Doreika v. Blotner* 666%S.E.2d 21 (Ga. App.) (holding that the doctrine of informed consent, i.e. a medical professional must inform a patient of the material risks of a proposed treatment or procedure which are or should be known and must inform the patient of available alternatives to the proposed treatment or procedure, applies to chiropractors). *Compare*, *Blotner v. Doreika*, 285%Ga. 481, 678%S.E.2d 80 (Ga.) (Because Georgia does not recognize a common law duty to inform patients of the material risks of a proposed treatment or procedure, because chiropractic treatment is not included among the matters for which informed consent is required by OCGA § 31-9-6.1, and because the Legislature has not otherwise required informed consent for chiropractic treatment, Supreme Court of Georgia refused to expand the informed consent rule to chiropractors).

[102] *Bronneke v. Rutherford* 120 Nev. 230, 89 P.3d 40 (Nev. 2004) (in a jurisdiction which adopted professional medical standard for informed consent, the patient argued for adopting a patient-oriented standard for chiropractors).

Requiring CAM practitioners to conform to standard informed consent rules would be harsh and onerous because most CAMs do not have clear and established risk-benefit profiles. However, even if the risks of a CAM therapy are unclear, patients opting for the CAM need to know the fact that the risks are unknown.

In addition to the question of informing about the CAM risk-benefit profiles, there are disputes about whether CAM practitioners have an obligation to advise of alternative treatment options, including orthodox medicine treatments.[103] Basically there are two kinds of voices. Some scholars think it unreasonable for CAM practitioners, when fulfilling their obligation to advise of options for treatment, to advise on orthodox medicine treatments.[104] Maybe due to their narrow scope of practice and weak knowledge base of orthodox medicine, the law does not expect CAM practitioners to inform their patients of orthodox medicine alternatives. There are some differences between orthodox medicine practitioners and CAM practitioners. The obligation of medical practitioners to advise of potential options for treatment, including arguably some CAM options, derives from the role of medical practitioners and the assumption that they are entitled to perform any medical procedure (Weir 2003, 302). As one scholar observed,

> [The] hegemony [enjoyed by medical doctors] supports a broad ethical and legal obligation upon medical doctors to outline the various options for treatment. If a medical practitioner is assumed to be entitled to provide virtually any form of therapy, it is not unreasonable to expect a broad discussion of treatment options (Weir 2003, 302–303).

Compared to orthodox medicine practitioners, CAM practitioners may not be entitled by law to perform the broad range of *conventional medicine* treatments that may be available for a particular malady (Weir 2003, 303). To require CAM practitioners to undertake the onerous task of advising on conventional medicine treatment options would be unrealistic and potentially dangerous (Weir 2003, 307).

However, other scholars expect CAM practitioners to disclose conventional medicine options, reasoning that

> If complementary practitioners are what their name suggests, they "complement" orthodox medicine. A key part in their *training* is, and should be, awareness not just of their own limitations but *of what orthodox medicine can offer to the provision of co-ordinated or variegated treatment.* Few patients are in a position to evaluate their treatment modality options scientifically. They rely upon health care practitioners for the provision of sufficient reliable, dispassionate information for them to be able to exercise their decision-making in an informed manner. If this information is not made available to patients, their ability to discern amongst their options is compromised and their autonomy diminished (emphasis added).[105]

---

[103] This issue may be less important than expected because conventional medicine treatments are more likely to have already fallen within the patients' knowledge before they opt for CAMs. A survey revealed that, out of 56 patients who elected CAMs, only three patients have bypassed conventional medicine and 54 patients stated that failure of conventional medicine was their reason for attending CAMs. *See,* Judith Moore et al. 1985, 28.

[104] *See*, Michael Weir 2003 (highlighting disputes on this issue).

[105] Freckelton 2000, 225. *See also*, Richard A. Haigh 2000, 205.

A scholar cites homeopathy as an example, arguing that homeopaths have a duty not only to disclose the risks inherent in homeopathic treatment, but also to inform about available *conventional* medical treatments (Richardson 2008, 595). Alternatives that fall within a CAM practitioner's duty to inform include alternative treatments offered by the competing conventional schools of medicine, and alternatives which may even pose more risks than the treatment proposed (Richardson 2008, 607–608). The rationale underlying the scholar's argument is that, in order to protect the public and individual patient autonomy, homeopathic practitioners should be held to the same informed consent standard, such as the patient-oriented standard of information disclosure and the materiality test, as conventional medical doctors (Richardson 2008, 607–608). The patient should be well informed before making the decision to forego conventional treatments. It is unclear whether or not the scholar's argument could be generalised from the better-established schools or professions, such as homeopath, to all CAMs that may encompass many poorly established and under-regulated schools of profession.

Both views make good sense. The view arguing against expanded disclosure highlights the reality that most CAMs are marginalised and CAM practitioners are allowed a narrow scope of practice in conventional-medicine-dominated societies. The view arguing for expanded disclosure draws our attention to the fact that the law cannot expect patients to identify treatment options themselves. Patients are not in a good position to do that. However, honouring the latter view needs some prerequisites. First, as I highlighted in the paragraph cited, CAM practitioners need to be exposed to, or required to have integrated education and conventional medicine training, so they are well-qualified to present conventional medicine information. Second, the whole health care system needs to honour the presence of CAM practitioners and embrace them in providing high quality health care. Third, to increase confidence invested on CAM practitioners, CAM practitioners, together with conventional medicine practitioners, should be subjected to similarly rigorous professional regulation.

Consistent with my view that, in the context of information disclosure, health care professionals should overcome their preferences and views of their "schools of thought" and present patients with full, balanced and contextualised information, I prefer the view that the scope of alternatives disclosure for CAM practitioners should not be confined to CAM therapies they prefer. Distinctions drawn between treatment and information disclosure indicates that a narrowly defined scope of practice is not a good justification for narrow information disclosure. In the area of diagnosis and treatment, I would like to see health care practitioners, including orthodox medicine practitioners, to show fidelity to their specialty rather than to practise in two different medical "worlds". I do not think that the emergence of dual practitioners is attractive. That is due to the fact that conventional medicine and CAMs have absolutely different cultures, adopting different languages and different diagnostic and treatment paradigms. Hopefully technical fragmentation created by health professionals' specialty and commitment could be remedied by informational integration witnessed by health professionals' balanced disclosure of treatment options.

Having said that CAM practitioners also have a duty to disclose orthodox medicine treatment options, I have deep concerns about CAM practitioners' competency to present conventional medicine information, especially when CAM practitioners are insufficiently regulated and insufficiently embraced in health care delivery. Like the rationale underlying my call for orthodox medicine practitioners to disclose effective CAM therapies, the basic thinking behind my argument for contextualised information disclosure is that health care practitioners should not be allowed to only present information they technically prefer and leave patients themselves to explore the full options available. Patients are not well positioned to survey treatment options available themselves.[106]

Even if there is no general duty for CAM practitioners to inform about orthodox medicine treatments, a strong appreciation of their limitations, the obligation to encourage continuing contact with orthodox medicine practitioners, and the need to refer when appropriate is important.[107] CAM providers have a duty to refer if the patient needs medical attention from a conventional doctor. They need to understand their legal and ethical obligations to refer to a medical practitioner when the patient does not respond to treatment or the condition is outside their scope of practice.

Again, in the context of negligence law, we cannot ignore the element of "causation". Both allegations claiming that a conventional medicine practitioner has a duty to inform of a CAM and a CAM practitioner has a duty to inform about orthodox medicine options will meet with the hurdle of "causation". For example, even if a CAM practitioner is under a duty to inform about conventional medicine treatments, the patient must show that he would have chosen another treatment and the harm suffered could have been avoided had he been presented with all material risks and alternative conventional treatments.[108] The injury suffered is a loss incurred from

---

[106] *Compare,* Australian Medical Association *AMA Position Statement: Complementary Medicine* (2002) <http://www.ama.com.au/node/2214> (last accessed 20 November 2008) 1.2 (relying too heavily on *patients* to access and present information: "It is essential that consumers have improved access to well researched information about Complementary Medicine so that they are empowered to question and to raise relevant issues with any complementary therapist they consult and to make well informed choices. The AMA considers it important that education campaigns are provided to assist the public to take an informed role in relation to Complementary Medicine and to be aware of the importance of continuing to consult medical practitioners in relation to medical conditions and health concerns. It is important that patients inform their medical practitioner of complementary medicines and/or therapies they are using.").

[107] Michael Weir 2003, 307. *See also,* Anna M. Richardson 2008, 611 ("Proponents of homeopathy may argue that homeopaths are unable to inform their patients of the risks inherent in refusing the conventional treatment because homeopaths are not trained in the conventional medical field. However, requiring the unlicensed homeopath to recommend the patient to a licensed physician if there is a reasonable likelihood the patient needs to be seen by a licensed conventional physician eliminates any concern that the homeopath be required to diagnose an ailment which he is unqualified to detect. There is not a need for specific diagnosis, but only the reasonable determination that the patient should seek conventional treatment from a licensed physician.").

[108] Anna M. Richardson 2008, 609.

not pursuing any other treatment as a result of the failure to disclose the availability of the conventional treatment.

As to the burden of proof, it is for *the claimant* to prove, on the balance of probabilities, that the defendant's breach of duty caused the damage. The "shift of burden of proof" approach did not win much popularity in the Commonwealth jurisdictions.[109] In comparison, the approach of drawing an inference of causation has met with greater acceptance.[110] The approach allows the court to draw robust inferences of causation in some cases of uncertainty. A court may draw an inference of causation even if there is no positive scientific evidence, or expert evidence is not conclusive or even conflicting. However, a court may only draw a valid inference based on facts supported by the evidence and not on the basis of supposition or conjecture.[111]

An issue remaining is whether, as far as alternatives disclosure is concerned, there is a need to draw a distinction between dual practitioners and pure CAM practitioners. Understandably, dual practitioners are likely to be expected to canvas a fuller range of treatment options than their non-physician counterparts before allowing a patient to commit to a care plan involving alternative medicine (Studdert 1999, 175), because dual practitioners are formally regulated as mainstream conventional practitioners and have more ready and more accurate knowledge about conventional medicine than pure CAM practitioners. Dual practitioners do have more competency than pure CAM practitioners in presenting conventional medicine information. However, the difference should lie in the degree of information disclosure rather than in the nature of the duty to inform. The knowledge base of practitioners is not fatal to the presence or absence of the duty to inform. While dual practitioners' duty to inform about conventional medicine treatment options centres on more detailed and accurate presentation, the emphasis of CAM practitioners' duty to disclose conventional treatments is more on acknowledging limitations, raising awareness of conventional options and fulfilling the duty to refer.

8.4.3 A Canadian Case: A CAM Practitioner and the Duty of Care

Finally I would like to examine a Canadian case[112] to support my view that CAM practitioners should be exposed to "peer review" in setting the standard of care, and they have a duty to disclose alternative treatments, including CAM options and conventional medicine options. The case also illustrates the complexity of the issues involved.

[109] *Wilsher v. Essex AHA* [1988] 1 All ER 871, [1988] AC 1074 (HL).

[110] *Snell v. Farrell* (1990) 72 DLR (4th) 289; *Accident Compensation Corp v. Ambros* [2008] 1 NZLR 340 (CA).

[111] *Accident Compensation Corp v. Ambros* [2008] 1 NZLR 340, 358 (CA), para. [67].

[112] *Dickson v. Pinder*, 2010 ABQB 269 (Court of Queen's Bench of Alberta).

The case involved a patient who suffered from neck pain and a headache, and a chiropractor who had practised chiropractic for about 27%years. The chiropractor manipulated the patient's neck using spinal manipulative therapy ("SMT"). Later the patient suffered a stroke. She alleged that the SMT caused her stroke, and the chiropractor failed to obtain her informed consent to the SMT and that he negligently performed the SMT on her. The patient testified that had she been aware of risks of the SMT and other available alternative treatments, such as massage therapy, she would not have allowed the chiropractor to perform the SMT.[113] The patient's allegations were concerned with the contexts of both treatment and information disclosure, although both contexts are subject to the same medical negligence law. The Court of Queen's Bench of Alberta subjected chiropractors to ordinary medical negligence law.[114]

In setting the standard of care for chiropractors, the court opined that "[s]ince courts have held that chiropractors are *treated like other 'medical practitioners,'* the principles that relate to *non-chiropractic medical professionals* apply with equal force to chiropractors".[115] However, the court seemed to endorse the view that the standard of care that the defendant-chiropractor had to meet was "the degree of care, diligence, judgment and skill which is exercised by a normal, prudent or reasonable *chiropractor* under like or similar circumstances and with the same experience and training".[116] Therefore the court did not offer a clear view on the standard of care for CAM practitioners. The medical standard and the CAM standard may be divergent.

The court found that the defendant-chiropractor did not address *non-chiropractic alternatives*.[117] The defendant-chiropractor did not usually provide patients with the option of alternative therapies to resolve their neck pain and headaches, other than SMT.[118] In the case of neck pain, the alternative therapies might include mobilization, massage therapy, trigger point therapy or physiotherapy.[119]

There were two "chiropractors" who gave an expert opinion concerning the standard of care expected of a chiropractor in 2002. But they had divergent opinions on a chiropractor's duty to inform about alternatives. Although they agreed that the patient could have received other alternative treatments, chiropractic and

[113] *Dickson v. Pinder*, 2010 ABQB 269, at [26].

[114] *Dickson v. Pinder*, 2010 ABQB 269, at [3]. Under the Canadian medical negligence law, the patient has the onus of proving on a balance of probabilities that: (1) the defendant owed her a legal duty of care; (2) the defendant breached the standard of care that he owed to her; (3) the patient suffered an injury or loss; and (4) the defendant's conduct was the actual and legal cause of her injury or loss (citing Ellen I. Picard and Gerald B. Robertson, *Legal liability of doctors and hospitals in canada*, 4th ed. (Toronto: Thomson, 2007) at 212).

[115] *Dickson v. Pinder*, 2010 ABQB 269, at [16] (citing *Heughan v. Sheppard*, [2000] O.T.C. 413 at para. 160 (Sup. Ct. J.)) (emphasis added).

[116] *Dickson v. Pinder*, 2010 ABQB 269, at [15] (emphasis added).

[117] *Dickson v. Pinder*, 2010 ABQB 269, at [39].

[118] *Dickson v. Pinder*, 2010 ABQB 269, at [34].

[119] *Dickson v. Pinder*, 2010 ABQB 269, at [34].

non-chiropractic, the two experts diverged on the approach to alternatives disclosure. One expert was a chiropractor, but with *a strong conventional medicine education background.*[120] In his opinion, the defendant-chiropractor should have informed the patient of reasonable treatment alternatives, such as activator treatment, mobilization, stretching, physiotherapy, *medication, as prescribed by a physician*, or doing nothing.[121] However, another chiropractor expert, who co-edited *Clinical Guidelines for Chiropractic Practice in Canada* (1994), was more conservative in formulating the approach to alternatives disclosure for chiropractors. In his view, the chiropractor need not actively pursue alternative treatments. In this view, a chiropractor need discuss alternative treatments only if the patient showed apprehension concerning the proposed treatment.[122] He defined the approach of waiting for patients to raise the issue of alternative treatments before the chiropractor discussed them as a "patient-centred" approach, although he acknowledged that this approach was not realistic or practical for all patients, because patients may not have any knowledge of what alternative treatments are available.[123] The court did not favour this approach.[124]

I should emphasise that Canada is a jurisdiction where the patient-oriented standard of information disclosure has been adopted and a medical practitioner's *common law duty* to inform about alternative treatments has been accepted.[125] In Canada, a medical practitioner must inform a patient about the risks associated with the proposed medical treatment; and the alternatives to the proposed medical treatment, and the advantages and risks of those alternatives.[126] Canadian jurisprudence has established that, as part of the informed consent process, a medical practitioner must canvas alternative treatments with the patient.[127] In the court's view, "[a] patient cannot meaningfully choose a therapy unless the medical practitioner places that therapy in *context*, with alternatives and the consequence of inaction."[128]

Although highlighting that the two experts had divergent opinions on the scope of a chiropractor's duty to disclose alternatives, or *what alternatives* fall within the chiropractor's duty to inform, the court noted that they shared the view that the chiropractor must present the patient with *alternatives to the proposed treatment.*[129] SMT

[120] *Dickson v. Pinder*, 2010 ABQB 269, at [52]. He attended medical school from 2004 to 2008 and received his doctor of medicine degree in 2008.

[121] *Dickson v. Pinder*, 2010 ABQB 269, at [56].

[122] *Dickson v. Pinder*, 2010 ABQB 269, at [65].

[123] *Dickson v. Pinder*, 2010 ABQB 269, at [66].

[124] *Dickson v. Pinder*, 2010 ABQB 269, at [105] (asking "How can a patient pose questions or appear apprehensive when the patient has no idea what alternatives are available to the patient?").

[125] *Dickson v. Pinder*, 2010 ABQB 269, at [67]. *See*, Chapter 9.4.1.

[126] *Dickson v. Pinder*, 2010 ABQB 269, at [68].

[127] *Dickson v. Pinder*, 2010 ABQB 269, at [75] (citing *Zimmer v. Ringrose*, 124 D.L.R. (3d) 215 at para. 16 (C.A.) (the Alberta Court of Appeal), *Haughian v. Paine*, [1987] S.J. No. 240, 37 D.L.R. (4th) 624 (C.A.) (the Saskatchewan Court of Appeal)).

[128] *Dickson v. Pinder*, 2010 ABQB 269, at [75] (emphasis added).

[129] *Dickson v. Pinder*, 2010 ABQB 269, at [104], [106].

was not the only possible treatment for the plaintiff-patient's condition, and her pain may have resolved over time without any steps beyond rest. Therefore, the court's task was narrowed to answer the question whether the chiropractor should present the option of *conservative or no treatment* to the patient. The court acknowledged that when conservative or no treatment had already been tried, and the patient was already aware of them, those options are not, strictly speaking, alternative treatments.[130] However, if inaction had never been tried by the patient, it should fall with a practitioner's duty to inform. Therefore, the court found that the defendant-chiropractor failed to discharge his duty properly to inform his patient of the reasonable alternative therapies.[131]

Even though the chiropractor was found to have failed to disclose alternative therapies, the patient lost the informed consent lawsuit because the causation element was not proven. The court found that the patient would have consented to the SMT even if the chiropractor had explained in more detail the risk of stroke, the nature and effects of a stroke, and the alternative treatments for her condition.[132] The patient had previously seen her (non-chiropractic) physician for her headaches and neck pain. These problems continued, so it was reasonable that she would investigate an alternative source for her relief. [133] The chiropractor's breach of his duty to inform was of no consequence and was not the cause of the patient's injuries.

This Canadian case raised the issue of a CAM practitioner's duty to disclose alternatives. In the case, an expert even raised the issue of a chiropractor's duty to disclose *orthodox medicine treatment options*, although the court's response and reasoning did not go so far. The court treated chiropractors "like other 'medical practitioners'" and adopted uncritically the informed consent legal principles that have been developed in the context of conventional medicine to the context of CAM.

In many conventional-medicine-dominated societies, chiropractic professionals have been statutorily regulated, formally educated and somewhat mainstreamed. They also enjoy relatively wide latitude in choosing diagnostic and treatment options.[134] Chiropractic care often overlaps with conventional medical care (Morrison 2009). One has reason to be hesitant before concluding that the rules for chiropractors would apply universally to other CAM professionals. Even for chiropractors, the court did not voice a final answer to the question of whether or not the "reasonable alternative therapies" that fall within a chiropractor's duty to inform include *orthodox medicine treatment options*. Furthermore, as the case revealed, although a doctor's *duty* to inform and "causation" are distinct issues, consideration of "causation" in the context of negligence law diminishes the possibility of

[130] *Dickson v. Pinder*, 2010 ABQB 269, at [80] (citing *Guay v. Wong*, 2008 ABQB 638, 463 A.R. 289 at para. 114).

[131] *Dickson v. Pinder*, 2010 ABQB 269, at [107].

[132] *Dickson v. Pinder*, 2010 ABQB 269, at [120].

[133] *Dickson v. Pinder*, 2010 ABQB 269, at [120].

[134] Peter Morrison 2009 (arguing to narrow the chiropractors' scope of practice).

exposing a practitioner to a tort liability, and therefore dilutes the significance of a practitioner's duty to disclose alternatives.

Talking about "causation", the basic and conventional test for *factual* causation is the "but for" test and "balance of probabilities". Where the claimant brings an action in negligence for breach of the doctor's duty to inform, he does have to establish causation by proving that had he been properly warned he would not have accepted the treatment.[135] However, it needs to be noted that the "but for" test is not the sole, comprehensive, and exclusive standard for testing causation.[136] There are many forms of departure from the general rules of causation, such as the "material contribution" test,[137] the "material increase of risk" approach,[138] and the "loss of chance" theory.[139] In the arena of information disclosure, some jurisdictions have witnessed the effort to loosen the conventional approach to causation in order to reinforce a doctor's duty to inform and a patient's right to be informed.[140] That suggests recognition of a more rights-based approach to damage. Driven by considerations of policy and justice, loss of right seems to be regarded as a new form of damage.

8.5 Conclusion

A health practitioner is often inclined to present information in such a manner that a patient will choose the alternative the practitioner thinks preferable. That will happen more frequently and rigorously in the context of CAM and conventional medicine where conventional medicine practitioners and CAM practitioners are more likely to be hostile to each other. That reinforces the need for both practitioners to overcome personal preferences and biases, to place treatment in context, and to present patients with balanced information about alternative treatment options. While the law accords wide latitude to practitioners' *selecting* medicines, conventional or alternative, the *information disclosure* by orthodox, dual and CAM practitioners should be contextualised and balanced (Table 8.1).

Most CAMs have weak evidence base and most orthodox practitioners have weak knowledge base about CAMs. Because of that, the current law on the standard of care

[135] *Bolam v. Friern Hospital Management Committee* [1957] 2 All ER 118, 124.

[136] *Chappel v. Hart* (1998) 195 CLR 232, 243, per McHugh J.; 255 per Gummow J.; 269 per Kirby J.; 282 per Hayne J.

[137] *Bonnington Castings Ltd v. Wardlaw* [1956] AC 613.

[138] *McGhee v. National Coal Board* [1973] 1 WLR 1; *Fairchild v. Glenhaven Funeral Services Ltd* [2002] 3 WLR 89 (industrial disease cases).

[139] *Chaplin v. Hicks* [1911] 2%KB 786, [1911–1913] All ER Rep 224; *Allied Maples v. Simmons & Simmons* [1995] 1 WLR 1602; *Sellars v. Adelaide Petroleum NL* (1994) 179 CLR 332 (economic cases).

[140] Australia: *Chappel v. Hart* [1998] HCA 55; (1998) 195 CLR 232;156 ALR 517; (1998) 72 ALJR 1344 (HC of A); The UK: *Chester v. Afshar* [2004] 4 All ER 587, [2004] UKHL 41; [2005] 1%AC 32.

Table 8.1 Orthodox/Dual/CAM practitioners and alternatives disclosure

	Adoption (wide latitude)	Alternatives disclosure (more contextualised)
Orthodox practitioners	Conventional medicine	Conventional medicine (+CAM (with clear evidence base))
Dual practitioners	Conventional medicine + CAM	Conventional medicine + CAM
CAM practitioners	CAM	CAM (+conventional medicine?)

and information disclosure in the contexts involving CAM is orthodoxy-reinforcing and convention-medicine-dominating. Both the evidence base for CAMs and CAM knowledge base for conventional practitioners are being increasingly established.[141] The law will respond correspondingly.

Orthodox practitioners have latitude in choosing to adopt CAMs. They have a potentially wide scope of practice. The latitude that conventional medicine practitioners have in adopting CAMs would make it possible that, eventually, a significant number of respected conventional medicine practitioners would favour a CAM therapy. That would facilitate the formation and development of "a responsible body of professional opinion" or "a school of thought", which may fall within a practitioner's duty to present contextualised information, even if he does not favour that "school". Furthermore, more and more rigorous research about CAMs and "integrative" education would expose orthodox practitioners to information about CAM treatments. Those factors lend weight to the argument that the orthodox practitioners' duty to inform should not be confined only to orthodox medicine treatments. Not all CAM therapies would fall within a conventional medicine practitioner's duty to inform. The duty may encompass disclosure of CAM alternatives which have some clear evidence base, or which can compare favourably with conventional medicine options, or which are material to patients' decision-making.

CAM practitioners have a narrow scope of practice in the sense that they are not allowed to practise conventional medicine. They also have weak knowledge base about conventional medicine. That reduces weight of the argument that CAM practitioners have a duty to inform about conventional medicine alternatives. However, practising a treatment and disclosing treatment options are two distinct issues. Moreover, CAM practitioners' knowledge base about conventional medicine can be enhanced by integrated education and rigorous regulation. There is no strong reason to explain why patients cannot obtain full and unbiased information from CAM practitioners.

Conventional medicine treatment options would more readily fall within a *dual practitioner*'s duty to inform even if he favours a CAM therapy. That is because the

141 Australian Medical Association *AMA Position Statement: Complementary Medicine* (2002) <http://www.ama.com.au/node/2214> (last accessed 20 November 2008) (noting that increasingly it will be possible for judgements to be based on evidence of safety, quality and efficacy of CAMs).

information about conventional medicine treatments would more readily fall within the scope of a dual practitioner's knowledge. Moreover, the practitioner's "dual" capacity as both a conventional medicine practitioner and a CAM practitioner justifies a patient's expectation that the dual practitioner would present him with more balanced information. A dual practitioner's fidelity to a CAM can only explain the fragmentation of the provision of services, but cannot excuse him from the duty to disclose unbiased information.

Information disclosure is patient-oriented. It does not depend on practitioners' preference of one "school" of medicine over another "school" of medicine. The requirement of contextualised information disclosure applies to both the context of conventional medicine and the context involving conventional medicine *and* CAM. The "integrated" model of both orthodox practitioners and CAM practitioners providing patients with contextualised information is better than the "fragmented" model of both orthodox practitioners and CAM practitioners presenting patients with information only about their "schools" of medicine and leaving patients themselves to search information about other "schools" of medicine.

References

Atwell, Barbara L. 2004. Mainstreaming complementary and alternative medicine in the face of uncertainty. *UMKC Law Review* 72: 593–630.

Barrette, Joseph A. 2003. The Alternative Medical Practice Act: Does it adequately protect the right of physicians to use complementary and alternative medicine? *St. John's Law Review* 77: 75–122.

Boozang, Kathleen M. 1998. Western medicine opens the door to alternative medicine. *American Journal of Law & Medicine* 24: 185–212.

Brophy, Elizabeth. 2003. Does a doctor have a duty to provide information and advice about complementary and alternative medicine? *Journal of Law and Medicine* 10: 271–284.

Bulen, James A. 2003. Complementary and alternative medicine: Ethical and legal aspects of informed consent to treatment. *The Journal of Legal Medicine* 24: 331–358.

Caulfield, Timothy, and Colin Feasby. 2001. Potions, promises and paradoxes: Complementary and alternative medicine and malpractice law in Canada. *Health Law Journal* 9: 183–203.

Cohen, Michael H. 1996. Holistic health care: Including alternative and complementary medicine in insurance and regulatory schemes. *Arizona Law Review* 38: 83–164.

Cohen, Michael H. 2001. Informed consent in complementary and alternative medicine. *Archives of Internal Medicine* 161: 2288–2292.

Cohen, Michael H., and Mary C. Ruggie. 2003. Integrating complementary and alternative medical therapies in conventional medical settings: Legal quandaries and potential policy models. *University of Cincinnati Law Review* 72: 671–729.

de Prez, Paula. 2001. Something "old", something "new", something "borrowed" … The continued evolution of *Bolam*. *Professional Negligence* 17: 75–87.

Doyle, Aimee. 2001. Alternative medicine and medical malpractice: Emerging issues. *The Journal of Legal Medicine* 22: 533–552.

Ernst, E., M.H. Pittler, B. Wider, and K. Boddy. 2007. Acupuncture: Its evidence-base is changing. *The American Journal of Chinese Medicine* 35: 21–25.

Fordham, Margaret. 2001. The standard of care applicable to practitioners of alternative medicine. *Singapore Journal of Legal Studies* 2001: 1–11.

Freckelton, I. 2000. Review of the book entitled complementary medicine: Ethics and law. *Journal of Law and Medicine* 8: 224.

Freckelton, Ian. 2008. Regulating the unregistered. *Journal of Law and Medicine* 16: 413–418.
Haavi Morreim, E. 2003. A dose of our own medicine: Alternative medicine, conventional medicine, and the standards of science. *Journal of Law, Medicine & Ethics* 31: 222–235.
Haigh, Richard A. 2000. Alternative Medicine and the doctrine of patient disclosure. *Journal of Law and Medicine* 8: 197–206.
Hufford, David J. 2003. Evaluating complementary and alternative medicine: The limits of science and of scientists. *Journal of Law, Medicine & Ethics* 31: 198–212.
Knoll, Andrew M. 2004. The reawakening of complementary and alternative medicine at the turn of the twenty-first century: Filling the void in conventional biomedicine. *Journal of Contemporary Health Law & Policy* 20: 329–366.
Kune, Randall, and Gabriel Kune. 2007. Mainstream medicine versus complementary and alternative medicine in the witness box: Resolving the clash of ideologies. *Journal of Law and Medicine* 14: 425–432.
Kurata, Vincent. 2007. "Traditional use" and regulatory change in the arena of natural health products. *Health Law Review* 15: 14.
Lee, Tat-Leang. 2006. Complementary and Alternative Medicine, and Traditional Chinese Medicine: Time for critical engagement. *Annals Academy of Medicine Singapore* 35: 749–752.
Lunstroth, John. 2006. Voluntary self-regulation of complementary and alternative medicine practitioners. *Albany Law Review* 70: 209–286.
Mason, Su, Philip Tovey, and Andrew F. Long. 2002. Evaluating complementary medicine: Methodological challenges of randomised controlled trials. *British Medical Journal* 325: 832–834.
May, B.H., et al. 2009. Herbal medicine for dementia: A systematic review. *Phytotherapy Research* 23: 447–459.
Moore, Judith, Kathy Phipps, Donald Marcer, and George Lewith. 1985. Why do people seek treatment by alternative medicine? *British Medical Journal* 29: 28–29.
Morrison, Peter. 2009. Adjusting the role of chiropractors in the United States: Why narrowing chiropractor scope of practice statutes will protect patients. *Health Matrix* 19: 493–537.
Nahin, Richard L., and Stephen E. Straus. 2001. Research into complementary and alternative medicine: Problems and potential. *British Medical Journal* 322: 161–164.
Owen, D.K., G. Lewith, and C.R. Stephens. 2001. Can doctors respond to patients' increasing interest in complementary and alternative medicine? *British Medical Journal* 322: 154–158.
Parker, Malcolm. 2007. Two into one won't go: Conceptual, clinical, ethical and legal impedimenta to the convergence of CAM and Orthodox Medicine. *Bioethical Inquiry* 4: 7–19.
Prillaman, Hunter L. 1990. A physician's duty to inform of newly developed therapy. *Journal of Contemporary Health Law and Policy* 6: 43–58.
Relman, Arnold S., and Andrew Weil. 1999. Is integrative medicine the medicine of the future? *Archives of Internal Medicine* 159: 2122–2126.
Richardson, Anna M. 2008. Informed patients go *Homeo* happy: Applying the doctrine of informed consent to homeopathic practitioners. *Ohio Northern University Law Review* 34: 593–612.
Ritigstein, Eric. 2005. Chapter 742: Paving the way for "Alternative and Complementary Medicine" in California? *McGeorge Law Review* 36: 933.
Robinson, A., and M.R. McGrail. 2004. Disclosure of CAM use to medical practitioners: A review of qualitative and quantitative studies. *Complementary Therapies in Medicine* 12: 90–98.
Snyder, Lois (ed.). 2007. *Biomedical ethics reviews: Complementary and alternative medicine – Ethics, the patient, and the physician*. Totowa: Humana Press.
Studdert, David M. 1999. Legal issues in the delivery of alternative medicine. *JAMWA* 54: 173–176.
Sugarman, Jeremy. 2003. Informed consent, shared decision-making, and complementary and alternative medicine. *Journal of Law, Medicine & Ethics* 31: 247–250.
Tran, Anne. 2006. The regulation of Traditional Chinese Medicine practitioners in Australia. *Journal of Law and Medicine* 13: 352–369.
Vlasis, Robert T. 2006. The doctor is out, or unconventional methods for healing: Resolving the standard of care for an Alternative Medicine practitioner. *Houston Law Review* 43: 495–525.

Wahner-Roedler, Dietlind L., Ann Vincent, Peter L. Elkin, Laura L. Loehrer, Stephen S. Cha, and Brent A. Bauer. 2006. Physicians' attitudes toward complementary and alternative medicine and their knowledge of specific therapies: A Survey at an academic medical center. *eCam* 3: 495–501.

Weir, Michael. 2003. Obligation to advise of options for treatment – Medical doctors and complementary and alternative medicine practitioners. *Journal of Law and Medicine* 10: 296–307.

Xue, Charlie C.L., et al. 2003. Treatment for seasonal allergic rhinitis by Chinese Herbal Medicine: A randomized placebo controlled trial. *Alternative Therapies in Health and Medicine* 9: 80–87.

Xue, Charlie C.L., et al. 2010. Traditional Chinese Medicine: An update on clinical evidence. *The Journal of Alternative and Complementary Medicine* 16: 301–312.

Zhang, C.S., et al. 2010. Ear-acupressure for allergic rhinitis: A systematic review. *Clinical Otolaryngology* 35: 6–12.

Zheng, Zhen, et al. 2008. The effect of electroacupuncture on opioid-like medication consumption by chronic pain patients: A pilot randomized controlled clinical trial. *European Journal of Pain* 12: 671–676.

Chapter 9
New Zealand Context and Beyond

Abstract This chapter concentrates on the New Zealand context, especially New Zealand's Code of Patients' Rights, but draws distinctions between jurisdictions, mainly England, Australia and Canada. It is highlighted that, although they share similarly rigorous professional and ethical principles regarding information disclosure, England, Australia, Canada and New Zealand differ from each other on the legal principles regarding a doctor's duty to inform about alternatives. New Zealand offers the most encompassing range of alternatives that may fall within the duty to disclose. This chapter also compares the New Zealand's Code approach with the tort law approach. It concludes that, compared to the approaches of either heavily relying on tort law or relying exclusively on professional regulation, the New Zealand's Code approach has the merit of combining the authority, stability, and proactive character of legislation, with the flexible and embracing nature of professional regulation, at the same time avoiding the inconveniences of medical negligence lawsuits.

9.1 Introduction

The preceding chapters were constructed around topics and sub-topics, rather than jurisdictions. Chapter 2 acknowledged the divisibility of health care. It drew a dichotomy between diagnosis/treatment and information disclosure and highlighted the distinctive dimension of information disclosure, one of the elements of the rule of informed consent. It set a basic tone for the following chapters. Following the distinction drawn by Chap. 2 between diagnosis/treatment and information disclosure, Chap. 3 put the issue of disclosure of alternatives in a context and intended to build a comprehensive model covering the disclosure, selection, recommendation and performance/provision of treatment options. The model drew fine distinctions between the four aspects of health care, and embraced the notion that the unbiased/balanced/contextualised disclosure of treatment options should be distinct from

X. Zhao, *The Duty of Medical Practitioners and CAM/TCM Practitioners to Inform Competent Adult Patients about Alternatives*,
DOI 10.1007/978-3-642-31647-0_9, © Springer-Verlag Berlin Heidelberg 2013

the genuine selection and personalised recommendation of treatment options. This approach serves as a core principle in the whole book. Chapter 4 highlighted three circumstances where the duty to disclose information, including information about alternative treatment options, may be enhanced, and four "filters" that may narrow the seemingly broad scope of information disclosure. Chapter 5 attempted to categorise the alternatives that may fall within the scope of disclosure. Among them, whether a doctor's duty to inform encompasses disclosure of emerging treatment options, financially unavailable alternatives, and CAM therapies involves much more controversy. The book devoted three separate chapters (Chaps. 6, 7 and 8) to these alternatives.

In Chaps. 9 and 10, I will focus on two jurisdictions: New Zealand and China. New Zealand has a unique legal context, where the no-fault compensation scheme/ACC scheme, the Code of Patient's Rights/Health and Disability Commissioner (HDC) jurisdiction, and other jurisdictions (such as Health Practitioners Disciplinary Tribunal (HPDT) and Human Rights Review Tribunal (HRRT) jurisdictions) complement each other. China offers a unique medical and legal context, where both the integrative health care system and legislation embrace Western medicine and Traditional Chinese Medicine (TCM) with warm arms.

In this chapter, I will devote substantial time to the New Zealand law, especially the Code of Patients' Rights and the HDC jurisdiction. Before doing that, I would like to take this opportunity to draw distinctions between some major Commonwealth jurisdictions about information disclosure and disclosure of alternatives, which I did not provide in earlier chapters, partly because those chapters are basically content-dominated rather than jurisdiction-oriented. The distinctions I draw here will illustrate the point that England, Australia, Canada and New Zealand have different *legal* landscapes in the context of disclosure of alternatives. More importantly, drawing distinctions helps highlight the distinctive dimension of the New Zealand law.

9.2 The English Model

9.2.1 The Less Demanding Common Law

9.2.1.1 From *Bolam* to *Birch*

Building on the notion that, due to lack of expertise, laypersons are not well-equipped to second-guess the medical issues, the orthodox *Bolam* test accords weighty deference to genuine difference of medical opinions in the realm of diagnosis and treatment involving medical expertise.[1] When faced with two or more schools of thought, the court was deprived of a substantial degree of liberty to adjudicate

[1] *Bolam v Friern Hospital Management Committee* [1957] 2 All ER 118, 121–122.

over the *substance* of medical opinions.[2] The *Bolam* test mainly targeted the context of diagnosis and treatment. There is doubt about whether it could dovetail nicely with the context of information disclosure.[3]

The subject of a doctor's duty of disclosure was exhaustively discussed by the House of Lords in *Sidaway v Bethlehem Royal Hospital Governors*.[4] In the *Sidaway* case, the majority privileged beneficence over autonomy. The medical profession was conferred significant discretion in determining the scope of information disclosure. Only Lord Scarman honoured the treatment-disclosure distinction and warmly embraced the patient-oriented standard of information disclosure and the notion of "materiality" of risks.[5]

Given the divergence in opinions between their Lordships and inherent ambiguity of the *Bolam* test, it is not surprising that commentators disagreed on the implications of the *Sidaway* case (Maclean 2009, 167). Basically, the *Sidaway* case confirmed the applicability of the *Bolam* test in the context of information disclosure. The post-*Sidaway* era witnessed the judiciary's continued deference to the bodies of professional opinion (Maclean 2009, 170–172). But inconsistency and ambiguity remained (Maclean 2009, 171–172).

The *Bolitho* case[6] is a diagnosis and treatment case, not an information disclosure case. Although a number of qualitative limitations on medical practices were highlighted, their Lords envisage that only in "a rare case", where it can be demonstrated that the professional opinion is not capable of withstanding a logical analysis, that the judge is entitled to hold that the body of opinion is not reasonable or responsible.[7] The judicial evaluation of medical opinions is still not normative in nature. It only goes to the credibility of the experts rather than the substance of the opinion. Like *Sidaway*, the academic reaction to *Bolitho* was mixed (Maclean 2009, 173). The *Bolitho*'s implications were limited.[8]

The *Pearce* case[9] was regarded as a natural development of the trilogy of *Bolam-Sidaway-Bolitho*, because, in the *Pearce* case, Lord Woolf MR quoted at length and with approval the majority opinion of *Sidaway* and *Bolitho*. Although the appellant's case was dismissed, Lord Woolf MR's words about "a significant risk"[10]

---

[2] *Maynard v West Midlands RHA* [1985] 1 All ER 635, 639, per Lord Scarman ("in the realm of diagnosis and treatment the negligence is not established by preferring one respectable body of professional opinion to another").

[3] *See*, Chap. 2.

[4] *Sidaway v Bethlem Royal Hospital Governors* [1985] 1 All ER 643, (1985) AC 871.

[5] *Sidaway v Bethlem Royal Hospital Governors* [1985] 1 All ER 643, 645–654.

[6] *Bolitho v City and Hackney HA* [1998] AC 232 (HL); [1997] 4 All ER 771.

[7] *Bolitho v City and Hackney HA* [1997] 4 All ER 771, 779.

[8] Alasdair Maclean 2009, p. 174. *Compare* Catherine Tay Swee Kian 2003, p. 384 (regarding the *Bolitho* case as representing a significant nail in *Bolam*'s coffin).

[9] *Pearce v United Bristol Healthcare NHS Trust* (1999) 48 BMLR 118, [1999] PIQR 53.

[10] *Pearce v United Bristol Healthcare NHS Trust* [1999] PIQR 53, 59; (1998) 48 BMLR 118, 124 ("if there is a *significant risk* which would *affect the judgment* of *the reasonable patient*, then in the normal course it is the responsibility of a doctor to inform the patient of that significant risk, if the information is needed so that the patient can determine for him or herself as to what course he or she should adopt" (emphasis added)).

caught both the judiciary's and commentators' attention. Similar to the responses following *Sidaway* and *Bolitho*, academic reactions to the *Pearce* case was varied, with some commentators seeing it as a closer move to the prudent *patient* standard,[11] while some deeming it as a further preservation of the *professional* standard by relying on the *experts* for a determination of the significance of the risk (Maclean 2004, 408–409. *See* also Maclean 2009, 174–176), and some regarding it as "conflation" of the reasonable doctor test and the reasonable patient test (Miola 2009, 97).

Here I doubt the value of complicating the issue by introducing a "mixed" model into the issue of the standard for information disclosure. The standard of information disclosure answers the question of, in whose eyes or perspectives, the patients' or the doctors', the scope of information disclosure should be determined. There is no practical value and significance to draw a distinction between "whether *a reasonable patient* would attach importance to a piece of information" and "whether *a reasonable doctor* believes *a reasonable patient* ought to attach importance to a piece of information" (Pattinson 2006, 112). The issue of whether a reasonable patient would attach significance to information does not involve medical judgment.

In the arena of information disclosure, the English approach is basically doctor-oriented. Although Lord Woolf's remark in the *Pearce* case signified a potential of the English law shifting from the doctor-dominated standard of information disclosure to the patient-oriented standard and the "materiality" (or significance) test, as the *Birch* case[12] witnessed, it was overwhelmed by the line of *Bolam-Sidaway-Bolitho* authorities.

Allowing the doctor-oriented *Bolam* test as the measure of a doctor's duty to disclose information means that what must be disclosed depends upon the practice of a responsible body of professional opinion. Judicial deference to divergent bodies of medical opinion embodied in the *Bolam* test dictates that non-disclosure of a particular piece of information is not necessarily negligent merely because some doctors would have disclosed it, if other responsible practitioners would not have

[11] Kenyon Mason and Douglas Brodie 2005, 301; Sara Fovargue and José Miola 2010b (reading Lord Woolf MR's words as formulating a "reasonable patient" standard), Shaun D. Pattinson 2006, 111 (it "brings the English legal position very close to Lord Scarman's 'prudent patient' test"). The perceived trend towards the patient-oriented standard of information disclosure is confirmed by *Wyatt v Curtis*, where Sedley LJ highlighted the importance of having regard to the patient's perception when judging the "significance" of risks. *See, Wyatt v Curtis* [2003] EWCA. Civ 1779, [16] ("Lord Woolf's formulation refines Lord Bridge's test by recognising that what is substantial and what is grave are questions on which the doctor's and the patient's perception may differ, and in relation to which the doctor must therefore have regard to what may be the patient's perception."). *See* also, Alasdair Maclean 2009, 176–177 (arguing that the courts would still rely on the *medical experts* to determine the significance of a particular risk; commentating that Sedley LJ's generous interpretation of Lord Woolf's test was "conspicuously absent" from Lord Woolf's judgment).

[12] *Birch v University College Hospitals NHS Trust* (2008) 104 BMLR 168, (2008) 105 L.S.G. 19, [2008] All ER (D) 113 (Sep), [2008] EWHC 2237 (QB).

disclosed it.[13] The latitude permitted by the *Bolam* test was designed to recognise the legitimacy of differences of opinion (Montgomery 2003, 248). Where there is no independent expert evidence as to the professional practice, the court may treat the defendant's own usual practice as evidence of the appropriate standard.[14] Applying the *Bolam* test in the field of information disclosure cannot provide much predictability because the amount of information to which patients are entitled would be dependant on the professional attitudes and change of those attitudes to the question of information disclosure (Jones 2003, 544–545).

9.2.1.2 The *Birch* Case

Before the advent of the *Birch* case, there were no English cases which focused on the issue of disclosure of *alternative* treatments.[15] Although the duty to disclose probably encompasses the disclosure of alternative treatments, the English cases have been universally concerned with the disclosure of *risks*, emphasising the link between consent and outcome responsibility (Maclean 2009, 203). If a treatment is not the one that the professional would recommend, and if it is reasonable under the *Bolam* test to take this stance, there may be no duty to disclose the treatment even if another doctor would have recommended it (Maclean 2009, 203). Benefiting from the notion of "significant risks" formulated by Lord Woof MR in *Pearce*, the *Birch* case contemplates that there will be circumstances where a doctor's duty to inform may encompass disclosure of the "comparative risks" of *different* procedures. However, the *Birch* court formulated its ruling with great caution.

The *Birch* case was concerned with a choice between two imaging methods, catheter angiography (angiogram) and magnetic resonance imaging (MRI) (Tables 9.1 and 9.2). The patient was allegedly exposed to an "unnecessary" procedure. While the defendant was not found negligent in *deciding to undertake an angiogram*, the High Court (Queen's Bench Division) (per Mr Justice Cranston) found the defendant liable to the claimant because it failed to *discuss with the claimant the different imaging methods – catheter angiography and MRI – and the comparative risks.*

The *Birch* case lends some support to the arguments I made in Chap. 3. First, the case involved the situation of failing to disclose a procedure *not recommended* by the defendant-doctor. The traditional practice of "recommending first, disclosing only the recommended procedure" was challenged. Second, the *Birch* court drew a clear distinction between *selection* of a procedure from a range of available procedures and *information disclosure* regarding available procedures. That was witnessed

[13] Michael A. Jones 2003, 545 (citing *Gold v Haringey Health Authority* [1988] 1 QB 481).

[14] Michael A. Jones 2003, 545, footnote 57 (citing *Thake v Maurice* [1986] QB 644).

[15] Rob Heywood 2009, 31 (commentating that the *Birch* case, although only a decision of the High Court, is the first English case where the court's focus was invested on disclosure of alternative treatments and their comparative risks, and the duty to disclose alternative treatments became central to the finding of liability).

Table 9.1 Three possible diagnoses

Possible diagnosis	Characteristics
An ischaemic lesion of the third cranial nerve	It could be expected to heal itself spontaneously with time
An aneurysm	It is life-threating, needs to be ruled out *urgently*
Cavernous sinus pathology	It is not so potentially life-threatening, but needs to be ruled out

Table 9.2 Two different imaging methods entailing different advantages and disadvantages

	Catheter angiography (angiogram)	Magnetic Resonance Imaging (MRI)
Advantages	(1) Ruling out an aneurysm *with 100% certainty*	(1) Non-invasive, without a risk of stroke; (2) *excluding both* a posterior communicating artery aneurysm and cavernous sinus pathology
Disadvantages	(1) Invasive, more risky, with a risk of stroke; (2) *only excluding* a posterior communicating artery aneurysm but *not cavernous sinus pathology*	*But* there is a disagreement on whether MRI would have detected *an aneurysm* or whether unenhanced MRI would have sufficient *sensitivity* to exclude an aneurysm

by the court's effort to separate the issue of the defendant's decision to *choose* the catheter angiogram over MRI from the issue of the defendant's failure to *inform* of comparative risks associated with the alternative procedure (MRI). The High Court found that the defendant's decision to *choose* angiography over MRI represents "a responsible body of medical opinion"[16] and can withstand "logical analysis" and "logical attack".[17] Although there was a *bias* among *neurosurgeons* in favour of excluding an aneurysm because of the dramatic consequences of missing such a diagnosis,[18] the defendant's choice in favour of catheter angiography, albeit focusing on the aneurysm, involved a risk benefit balancing.[19] However, when it comes to information disclosure, the court found that the defendant had a duty to discuss

[16] *Birch v University College Hospitals NHS Trust* [2008] EWHC 2237 (QB), at [68] (despite the facts that there was no consensus within the profession in 2003 as to the better imaging method for diagnosing aneurysms of the type the claimant-patient might have had, and there has been a trend since 2003 in favour of MRI and other non-invasive techniques as the diagnostic tool of choice).

[17] *Birch v University College Hospitals NHS Trust* [2008] EWHC 2237 (QB), at [69]–[70].

[18] *Birch v University College Hospitals NHS Trust* [2008] EWHC 2237 (QB), at [69] ("In that culture the risks of carrying out a catheter angiogram were not a deterring factor and even in recent years catheter angiography has been regarded as the best first-time method of urgently excluding aneurysms large enough to cause third nerve palsy.").

[19] *Birch v University College Hospitals NHS Trust* [2008] EWHC 2237 (QB), at [69].

comparative risks of catheter angiography *alongside MRI*,[20] envisaging that "there will be *circumstances* where … the duty to inform a patient of the *significant risks* will not be discharged unless she is made aware that *fewer, or no risks*, are associated with *another procedure*".[21] Third, the court distinguished "information disclosure" from "recommendation". Doctors are free to offer patients recommendations and preferences on the issue of which course of action would provide the optimum outcome for the patients and should be pursued instead of others. However, that should not inhibit them from presenting patients with "dispassionate", "fair" and "balanced" information.[22]

Despite those positive moves, we should approach the *Birch* case with great caution. The move in *Birch* is to be applauded, but it is very fact-driven and easily distinguished. It has narrow parameters. First, the court's expansive approach to information disclosure is confined only to "unusual" or "special" circumstances in that case.[23] The court felt difficulty "in delineating, *in general terms*, the circumstances in which the duty arises to inform of comparative risks".[24]

Second, the court only envisages that the patient needs to be made aware that "fewer, or no risks" are associated with the alternative procedure.[25] In the case, the undisclosed alternative procedure is non-invasive, conservative, and less risky than the proposed procedure. The case involves a specific context where the undisclosed

---

[20] *Birch v University College Hospitals NHS Trust* [2008] EWHC 2237 (QB), at [77].

[21] *Birch v University College Hospitals NHS Trust* [2008] EWHC 2237 (QB), at [74] (emphasis added).

[22] But in the context of establishing causation in the informed consent cases. *See*, *Birch v University College Hospitals NHS Trust* [2008] EWHC 2237 (QB), at [81] ("The issue is *not* whether she would have understood the nature of the procedures or what she would have *in the face of a recommendation* as to catheter angiography. The crucial issue is what she would have decided when given *a dispassionate account* along the lines indicated, in other words of the two procedures for imaging, and the advantages and disadvantages of each for someone with her background. … It is clear to me that had she been given *a fair and balanced account* in the way I have held was necessary she would have rejected catheter angiography in favour of MRI. In other words, properly informed she would have declined the procedure leading to her stroke" (emphasis added)).

[23] Those "unusual" or "special" circumstances include: (1) the claimant was correctly diagnosed by a *neurologist*, and the initial plan was sensible; (2) things started to go wrong when, for reasons which were unclear, the specifically recommended MRI for the claimant was blocked; (3) the claimant was then transferred to the defendant-hospital (centre) to exclude two life-threatening possible diagnoses; (4) due to the unavailability of bed in the neurology wards, the claimant fell into the hands of the *neurosurgeons*; (5) initially both an MRI and catheter angiography were identified as possibilities; (6) however, later on, maybe due to the *ascertainment bias among neurosurgeons* at the defendant-hospital, the focus was shifted to the possibility of an aneurysm, the priority was given to eliminate the possibility of an aneurysm by catheter angiography, and, thus, the possibility of MRI was discarded; (7) it turned out that, with hindsight, the claimant was subject to an unnecessary procedure which caused a stroke. *See*, *Birch v University College Hospitals NHS Trust* [2008] EWHC 2237 (QB), at [78], [82].

[24] *Birch v University College Hospitals NHS Trust* [2008] EWHC 2237 (QB), at [74] (emphasis added).

[25] *Birch v University College Hospitals NHS Trust* [2008] EWHC 2237 (QB), at [74].

alternative procedure offered brighter prospects than the proposed procedure.[26] This factual context warrants a reservation about the *Birch* court's seemingly expansive approach.[27]

Third, although the *Birch* case raised the possibility of a doctor disclosing an "alternative" procedure, its focus is still on the "risks" aspect of information disclosure. The task of the court was to explore what the duty to inform of "significant risks", as formulated by Lord Woof MR in *Pearce*, would encompass.[28] The question the court posed was, in addition to informing the patient of *significant risks associated with the procedure which was performed*, the catheter angiogram, "[w]as it necessary for the defendant to go further and to inform [the claimant] of *comparative risk, how this risk compared with that associated with other imaging procedures*, in particular MRI?".[29]

Fourth, in formulating the rule regarding a doctor's duty to inform about comparative risks of an alternative procedure, the court still followed the *Bolam-Bolitho* line of words, looking at whether there is a responsible body of medical opinion that withstands logical scrutiny. The court felt "troubled on reading" the *Sidaway* case, mainly because of the divided nature of the opinions.[30] With the paucity of authorities, the court turned to the *Bolam-Bolitho* line of two-step analysis to justify its conclusion that the defendant's failure to provide the claimant with the information constituted a breach of duty.[31] That creates confusion. As the court noted, there was

---

[26] The un-revealed diagnostic procedure was non-invasive and conservative. It entailed less or no risk. It was capable of ruling out two possible diagnoses, albeit with disputed certainty for one possible diagnosis. On the contrary, the proposed procedure was invasive. It carried an inherent risk of stroke. Although having a high degree of certainty, it can only eliminate one life-threatening condition. It cannot rule out another potentially life-threatening possible diagnosis.

[27] *See*, Rob Heywood 2009, 31 ("[T]he case only succeeded because there were two options available and, even though one was thought to be slightly more effective than the other at ruling out a potentially serious condition, they both broadly could have reached a similar diagnosis. *This, of course, will not always be the case*. There may be circumstances *where alternative medical procedures differ significantly in terms of what they are intended to achieve and the frequency of their success*. In this situation it may well be that the alternative medical procedure is simply *not a feasible option* and thus it would be inappropriate for the law to hold medical practitioners accountable for failure to disclose"(emphasis added)).

[28] *Birch v University College Hospitals NHS Trust* [2008] EWHC 2237 (QB), at [74].

[29] *Birch v University College Hospitals NHS Trust* [2008] EWHC 2237 (QB), at [74] (emphasis added).

[30] *Birch v University College Hospitals NHS Trust* [2008] EWHC 2237 (QB), at [73] ("That decision appears to contain differences as to how a court is to assess whether risks are to be conveyed to the patient, even putting to one side the dissent of Lord Scarman. Lord Diplock's approach, based firmly on *Bolam* [1957] 1 WLR 582, asks what a reasonable body of medical opinion would regard as proper to be disclosed (at 893). At least three of their Lordships added the gloss that in some circumstances the proposed treatment may involve a substantial risk of serious consequences which, notwithstanding reasonable medical opinion, must be disclosed to the patient.").

[31] *Birch v University College Hospitals NHS Trust* [2008] EWHC 2237 (QB), at [79]. Firstly, in the opinion of the Court, in the claimant's case "no reasonable prudent medical practitioner" would have failed to discuss the respective modalities and risks with the claimant, and "[i]n their absence [the claimant] was denied the opportunity to make an informed choice". Secondly, in the view of the Court, even if the first observation was wrong, the defendant's failure "could not be described in law as reasonable, responsible or logical".

disagreement among medical practitioners as to whether the claimant should have been informed of comparative risks of alternative procedures,[32] and the defendant had many *followers*. The *Bolam* test, if applied, should save him. To justify its reasoning under the *Bolam-Bolitho* line of analysis, the court had no other choice but to favour and rely heavily on what *one* expert said.[33] It seemed that a piece of non-self-serving expert evidence changed the direction of the case. One has good reason to wonder how the court's *Bolam-Bolitho* reasoning would go in the absence of such a kind of expert evidence.

A recent empirical study investigating informed consent in hospital practice revealed that, in the UK, medical practitioners decide what treatment to offer patients based on *their personal preferences* for evidence-based practice (Heywood et al. 2010, 162). Where alternatives are available, the decision to opt for one course of action over another was left to the *professional judgement of the doctors* (Heywood et al. 2010, 162). From a legal perspective, this is dubious practice, which may be open to future challenge. Denying patients a choice by reference to "evidence-based practice" may be viewed by some as little more than medical paternalism in the sense that medical practitioners are not painting a complete picture for patients and are actually preventing them from having the final say on their treatment (Heywood et al. 2010, 178–179). The study also revealed that, to make the patient to feel that the treatment is desirable, medical practitioners tend to frame things in a positive light (Heywood et al. 2010, 161–162). If doctors frame things in a positive way, this has the potential to overshadow the seriousness of the risks. If many options are available, medical practitioners would be likely to guide the patient towards their preferred course of action (Heywood et al. 2010, 162). All of those phenomena point to the need for English law to clarify the relationship between *disclosure* of alternatives and *selection/recommendation* of treatment options. The difficulty in gauging the exact amount of information disclosure has been exacerbated by the uncertain nature of the English law in respect of the required standard for information disclosure (Heywood et al. 2010, 172–174).

9.2.2 The More Demanding Professional Regulation

In contrast to the profession-protective tenor and the conservative approach adopted by common law, the UK professional regulation has opted for a more demanding and encompassing standard of information disclosure. As far as the scope of information disclosure is concerned, in the UK, there is a big discrepancy between the

[32] *Birch v University College Hospitals NHS Trust* [2008] EWHC 2237 (QB), at [79].

[33] *Birch v University College Hospitals NHS Trust* [2008] EWHC 2237 (QB), at [79] ("In the light of Mr Kitchen's important evidence, I am convinced that …"). The Court had favourable impression of that piece of expert evidence because, as the defendant's own neurosurgeon, the expert conceded mistakes occurred at the defendant-hospital, admitted to neurosurgical bias, and clearly testified that someone should have discussed with the claimant the different imaging methods and their associated risks. *See*, *Birch v University College Hospitals NHS Trust* [2008] EWHC 2237 (QB), at [76] ("Given the heavy reliance I have already placed on Mr Kitchen's evidence in the resolution of this case it is difficult to gloss over so clear a view.").

case law requirements and professional ethical guidance. The General Medical Council (GMC) guidance (General Medical Council (UK) 2008, paras. 5, 7, 8 and 9) on information disclosure is more stringent than the legal standards. If doctors followed the GMC's *guidance* on providing information prior to obtaining a patient's consent to treatment, they would be going beyond what was technically required by the *law*.

The GMC (2008) Guidance is basically patient-needs-oriented. It recommends that doctors give patients the information about (1) options for treating or managing the condition, including the option not to treat; (2) the purpose of the proposed treatment; (3) the potential benefits, risks and burdens, and the likelihood of success, for each option; (4) if available, whether the benefits or risks are affected by which organisation or doctor is chosen to provide care; (5) the experimental or innovative nature of treatments; (6) any treatments that the doctor believe have greater potential benefit for the patient than those the doctor or his or her organisation can offer (General Medical Council (UK) 2008, para. 9). In terms of this book, the alternatives that the Guidance contemplates include not only alternative treatment options and emerging treatment options, but also alternative health care providers and alternatives not readily available in the doctor's organisation. It confirms the notions, as I argued in Chap. 3, that contextualised information disclosure should proceed before recommendation, it should not be confined to recommended options, and it should be distinguished from other activities of health care delivery.

To further illustrate the point, I would like to cite a more specific example – the National Institute for Health and Clinical Excellence (NICE) clinical guideline on diagnosis and treatment of prostate cancer.[34] Like the GMC Guidance, the NICE guideline on prostate cancer is patient-centred.[35] The Guideline realises that being diagnosed with cancer and the specific nature and side effects of many of the treatments used in prostate cancer can have an effect on a man's sense of masculinity.[36] Some men will not trade quality for quantity and may wish to forgo the "best" treatment from the healthcare professional's perspective and would prefer to keep their potency for example.[37] Radical treatment of prostate cancer carries the threat of significant disturbance to quality of life and functioning. For some men the prospect of side effects of radical treatments may be less acceptable than the disease itself – especially when there is uncertainty about whether prostate cancer is a threat to their

[34] NICE (UK) *Prostate Cancer: Diagnosis and Treatment* – Full Guideline (February 2008). The purpose of National Institute for Health and Clinical Excellence (NICE) is to encourage not only the most efficient use of the NHS's finite resources, but also the best clinical practice and consistency of treatment throughout the NHS. Its recommendations take the forms of Guidance and Guidelines. *See*, *Eisai Ltd. v The National Institute for Health and Clinical Excellence (Nice)* [2007] EWHC 1941 (Admin), para [4].

[35] NICE (UK) *Prostate Cancer: Diagnosis and Treatment* – Full Guideline (February 2008), page 7 ("Information and care should be centred on the needs of individual men as they arise from prostate cancer or its treatment, as well as the needs of their partners and carers.").

[36] NICE (UK) *Prostate Cancer: Diagnosis and Treatment* – Full Guideline (February 2008), page 11.

[37] NICE (UK) *Prostate Cancer: Diagnosis and Treatment* – Full Guideline (February 2008), page 11.

longer term survival.[38] Therefore, decisions about treatment options rely on men being sufficiently well informed at each stage of their illness to understand the choices they face and with sufficient time to consider the options carefully.[39] The Guideline recommends that the information needs of men with prostate cancer include[40]:

- Basic anatomy and pathology to enable men and their carers to understand how prostate cancer might affect them;
- Aims, risks and likely effects of *proposed diagnostic procedures*;
- The likely range of impact and rate of progression of prostate cancer;
- *Potential treatment options*, including known benefits, uncertainties about benefits, known risks, potential short and long-term adverse effects, and the probability of improved survival or symptom reduction;
- *Reasons why a man might decide to opt for or not opt for radical treatment*, whether provisionally or for the long term;
- The effect which treatment for prostate cancer may have on a man's quality of life, including his relationship with his partner;
- *Reasons for not offering interventions which men might expect*;
- Urological, oncological, radiological, palliative care and other relevant services;
- Other sources of information, possible self help action and sources of support.

The Guideline also realises that, since both the nature of the disease and the benefits of treatment may be uncertain, decision-making in prostate cancer treatment is complex.[41] Decision support or decision aids is recommended, although such aids are not a substitute for a comprehensive communication process.[42]

9.2.3 Law or Professional Regulation?

When talking about informed consent and information disclosure, many UK scholars mentioned the GMC's professional guidance and invested great hope in it (e.g., Jones 2003, 549–550; Montgomery 2003, 250–251; Pattinson 2006, 114; Brazier and Cave 2007, 114). Michael A. Jones argued that GMC guidance is a strong evidence of what amounts to good medical practice and hence responsible medical practice within the context of the *Bolam* test (Jones 2003, 550). A failure to conform to professional guidance constitutes negligence, at least in the absence of very good, and logical, reasons for not complying with them (Jones 2003, 550). Noting that *Sidaway* offers insufficient safeguards for patients' rights to information and there is little indication that the courts wish to take advantage of the scope left by *Sidaway*

[38] NICE (UK) *Prostate Cancer: Diagnosis and Treatment* – Full Guideline (February 2008), page 10.

[39] NICE (UK) *Prostate Cancer: Diagnosis and Treatment* – Full Guideline (February 2008), page 10.

[40] NICE (UK) *Prostate Cancer: Diagnosis and Treatment* – Full Guideline (February 2008), page 7.

[41] NICE (UK) *Prostate Cancer: Diagnosis and Treatment* – Full Guideline (February 2008), page 7.

[42] NICE (UK) *Prostate Cancer: Diagnosis and Treatment* – Full Guideline (February 2008), page 9.

for judicial activism in establishing higher standards, Jonathan Montgomery shifted confidence from legal doctrine to professional standards (Montgomery 2003, 251). Moves towards greater involvement of patients in decision-making and less paternalistic care should be led by the medical profession rather than the legal doctrines (Montgomery 2003, 251).

Deficiencies in the legal standards to informed consent can be, to some extent, diminished by the higher standards required in professional guidance with which doctors have to comply. The medical profession (such as GMC) standard can be at least as rigorous as the Australian patient-oriented *Rogers* test (Fovargue and Miola 2010a, 15). The demanding nature of the professional ethical guidance mitigates the courts' lack of coherence with regard to the scope of information disclosure and how patient autonomy might be protected. Furthermore, the medical profession's own standards can feed the legal standards. Guidelines might serve to inform the legal standard of care more proactively by providing an added dimension to the evaluation of the legal standard of care and representing a shift from the traditional *Bolam* standard (Samanta et al. 2006, 323).

However, even the *Bolam* test arguably has the potential of achieving the effect of the *Rogers* test by the help of a *Rogers*-like professional guidance, its realisation will depend on at least two conditions. Whether or not professional guidelines can be used to define a new legal standard of care in respect of information disclosure is uncertain (Heywood et al. 2010, 183). The first condition is that medical profession promises to make, and to *keep*, its guidance as patient-oriented, or as stringent as the *Rogers* test. Relying exclusively on professional regulation to achieve a high quality information disclosure is vulnerable because professional guidance could be subject to future change by the medical profession.[43] Second, the *judiciary* should show willingness to use the GMC's ethical guidance as the legal standard.[44] The reality is that the judiciary has some degree of scepticism about the weight of guidelines in determining the legal standard (Samanta et al. 2006, 351–354). Moreover, for doctors, the NICE's Guidance and Guidelines is not compulsory.[45] They do not override

[43] Sara Fovargue and José Miola 2010a (arguing that, while the previous UK 1998 professional guidance asked more of doctors than was strictly legally required, the 2008 version brings the professional ethical imperative down and closer to the legal standard); Shaun D. Pattinson 2006, 114.

[44] José Miola 2009, 106–108 (arguing that "[b]y using *Bolam* to acknowledge the guidance as a 'gold standard' that the reasonable doctor should follow, the law could do far more to protect patient autonomy than by drifting into the rather cosmetic changes that the Australian model would bring"; but admitting that "this would leave the law as a hostage to fortune with regard to the continued excellence of the guidance").

[45] For example, at page xxvi, NICE (UK) *Prostate Cancer: Diagnosis and Treatment* – Full Guideline (February 2008) has a disclaimer: "The GDG assumes that health care professionals will use clinical judgment, knowledge and expertise when deciding whether it is appropriate to apply these guidelines. The recommendations cited here are a guide and may not be appropriate for use in all situations. The decision to adopt any of the recommendations cited here must be made by the practitioner in light of individual patient circumstances, the wishes of the patient and clinical expertise."

clinical judgment of healthcare professionals.[46] Furthermore, an empirical study of hospital practice in UK revealed that, although they are aware of the existence of professional guidelines, medical practitioners paid minimal attention to them and were unaware of their substantive content (Heywood et al. 2010, 170). Detailed and elaborate guidelines are largely ignored by those who should be relying on them most (Heywood et al. 2010, 170). If compliance with professional guidelines is unachievable in practice and cannot realistically be met by clinicians, there is difficulty in allowing them to mould the legal standard of care (Heywood et al. 2010, 183). Overall, although high quality professional guidance can inform the legal standard of care, there is still a need for the law to catch up with the professional ethical guidance.

9.3 The Australian Model

9.3.1 The Modestly Demanding Common Law and Legislation

Adopting a patient-oriented standard of disclosure and a test of "materiality" does not necessarily mean that the law would require the doctor to disclose alternative treatments.[47] This was evidenced by Australian law. The Australian law explicitly rejected the *Bolam* test as the standard of information disclosure and embraced the patient-oriented standard. It offered the *Rogers* test.[48] The *Rogers* test presented two very encompassing limbs (objective and subjective) of the "materiality" test. The *Rogers* test not only survived the High Court's reconsideration in *Rosenberg v Percival*,[49] but also survived the Australian civil liability legislation.[50] However, the *Rogers* test only concerned disclosure of material "risks" and was silent about disclosure of alternatives.

[46] *Eisai Ltd, R (on the application of) v National Institute for Health and Clinical Excellence (NICE)* [2008] EWCA Civ 438, para [6].

[47] *Compare* Michael A. Jones 2003, 525 (equating the patient-oriented standard of disclosure and the materiality test with the requirement that the doctor should communicate the inherent and potential hazards of the proposed treatment, *the alternatives to that treatment,* if any, and the likely results if the patient remains *untreated*).

[48] *Rogers v Whitaker* (1992) 175 C.L.R. 479, 490 (HCA) ("The law should recognize that a doctor has a duty to warn a patient of a material risk inherent in the proposed treatment; a risk is material if, in the circumstances of the particular case, *a reasonable person in the patient's position*, if warned of the risk, would be likely to attach significance to it or if the medical practitioner is or should reasonably be aware that *the particular patient*, if warned of the risk, would be likely to attach significance to it" (emphasis added)).

[49] *Rosenberg v Percival* [2001] 205 C.L.R. 434, 476–481 (Kirby J.), 501 (Callinan J.).

[50] Commonwealth of Australia 2002, page 48 (confirming a medical practitioner's two kinds of duty to inform: "the proactive duty to inform" and "the reactive duty to inform"); *Civil Liability Act 2003* (Qld), s 21(1); *Civil Liability Act 2002* (Tas), s 21.

In the area of information giving, the Australian tort law reform and civil liability legislation showed loyalty to the common law. The reinstatement in the civil liability legislation of the modified *Bolam* test as the standard of care for doctors[51] does not apply to the context of doctors providing information to patients.[52] In relation to information giving, the common law principles continue to apply. It needs to be noted that, although the Australian Review of the Law of Negligence Report recommended that both the proactive limb and the reactive limb of the duty to inform should be retained (Commonwealth of Australia 2002, 48, para. 3.49), only two jurisdictions (Queensland and Tasmania) crystallised the two-pronged *Rogers* approach in their civil liability legislation.[53] Similarly to the *Rogers* test, their focus is still only on the disclosure of information about the "risk".

The Australian landmark cases regarding a doctor's duty to inform all concerned the disclosure of *risks* of an operation.[54] Much of the Australian informed consent case law concerned non-disclosure of *risks* of treatment where the risk had, in fact, eventuated to the detriment of the patient. So was the *Rogers* test framed by Australian common law.

There are *academic comments* arguing for including disclosure of *treatment options* in the *Rogers* test. An Australian scholar argued that the parameters of the *Rogers* materiality test should not be so narrowly defined. In order for the patients to make an informed choice, the information that patients should be given extends not only to information about material risks but also to *other types of information* that the doctor know, or should know, the patient would be likely to consider significant (Skene 2008, 190). Another Australian scholar expects the *Rogers* rule to be applied more broadly and wants to see the duty to inform encompass a duty to disclose *treatment options*, especially where the contemplated procedure has substantial attendant risks and there is evidence that no treatment, or a less risky or non-interventionist treatment, may prove successful even if it produces a lower rate of success.[55] The necessity to disclose the less dramatic intervention is further

[51] *Civil Liability Act 2003* (Qld), s 22(1) (2) (3) (4); *Civil Liability Act 2002* (Tas), s 22; *Civil Liability Act 2002* (WA), s 5PB; *Civil Liability Act 1936* (SA), s 41; *Civil Liability Act 2002* (NSW), s 5O.

[52] *Civil Liability Act 2003* (Qld), s 22(5); *Civil Liability Act 2002* (NSW), s 5P; *Civil Liability Act 1936* (SA), s 41(5); *Civil Liability Act 2002* (Tas), s 22(5).

[53] *Civil Liability Act 2003* (Qld), s 21(1) ("A doctor does not breach a duty owed to a patient to warn of risk, before the patient undergoes any medical treatment (or at the time of being given medical advice) that will involve a risk of personal injury to the patient, unless the doctor at that time fails to give or arrange to be given to the patient the following information about the risk – (a) information that a reasonable person in the patient's position would, in the circumstances, require to enable the person to make a reasonably informed decision about whether to undergo the treatment or follow the advice; (b) information that the doctor knows or ought reasonably to know the patient wants to be given before making the decision about whether to undergo the treatment or follow the advice."); *Civil Liability Act 2002* (Tas), s 21.

[54] *See*, Michael Weir 2003, 297 (noting that there is a surprising paucity of case law in Australia on the specific issue of the duty to disclose treatment options).

[55] Michael Weir 2003, 297 (reading the Canadian case of *Haughian v Paine* (1987), 37 D.L.R. (4th) 624; [1987] 4 WWR 97).

emphasised if the riskier procedure is still possible after the more conservative option has proven unsuccessful (Weir 2003, 297). Another scholar also prefers to read the materiality test broadly, proposing that a doctor should advise a patient about *material alternative treatment options* (Brophy 2003, 276). The content of a doctor's duty involves more than the obligation to provide information about material risks (Brophy 2003, 275). Materiality is likely to be the test for the general duty to provide information and advice and therefore applicable to all types of information, including alternative treatment options (Brophy 2003, 276). To take an alternative view is to contemplate different tests for different types of information and advice (Brophy 2003, 276). The scholar suggested that the types of information encompassed by the duty to provide information and advice include: the benefits and likely outcomes of treatment; the risks involved in the treatment; the possibility and probability of complications; and side-effects and alternative treatment options.[56] An Australian High Court judge seemed also to suggest that the doctor's duty to inform should be more encompassing, observing that, in order for the patients to make meaningful choices, health professionals have a duty to inform patients of not only the material risks of contemplated procedures but also "any available alternatives".[57]

However, as highlighted in Chap. 3, in the Australian case of *Richards v Rahilly*,[58] the court devoted much more attention to a doctor's *selection and recommendation* of a treatment option than to *disclosure* of treatment options. In the minds of the judges, the sequence of the health care activities should be that a doctor proposed and recommended "a certain form of treatment" first, and then warned the patient of the "material risk" inherent in the proposed treatment. In the eyes of the court, a doctor's duty to inform only encompasses disclosure of *material risks inherent in a proposed treatment.* The court did not contemplate a doctor's recommendation of a treatment option being accompanied by and preceded by disclosure of available treatment options. To highlight the "impossible", "unrealistic", and "unworkable" nature of disclosure of available treatment options, the court adopted some extreme words, such as "every 'legitimate' treatment option that 'could work'",[59] ignoring the fact that information disclosure should be tailored to the patient's needs, and its scope could be constrained by the patient's condition, consideration of elements of "materiality" and causation in medical negligence cases.

Lastly, I should note that, in the context of non-disclosure of risks, to succeed in medical negligence actions under Australian law, the plaintiff/patients must clear

[56] Elizabeth Brophy 2003, 275 (citing *The Laws of Australia* (Lawbook Co., subscription service) Medical Practitioners 27.2 "Negligence: Standard of Care" at [31]).

[57] *Rosenberg v Percival* [2001] 205 CLR 434, 465, per Kirby J. (observing that health providers have a duty "to inform patients contemplating invasive procedures (such as surgery) of the material risks involved in the treatment proposed, and any available alternatives. Any 'choice' by the patient, in respect of such procedures, without the provision of such information, is meaningless.").

[58] *Richards v Rahilly* [2005] NSWSC 352.

[59] *Richards v Rahilly* [2005] NSWSC 352, paras. [235]–[236].

many hurdles, such as: (1) the doctor did not provide particular information to the patient; (2) the particular information was "material"; (3) the patient has suffered an injury or loss; and (4) the patient would have acted differently if properly informed (*See*, Skene 2008, 198–215). Moreover, because of the hindsight problem and the self-serving character of the patient evidence, several jurisdictions in Australia have adopted the Ipp Committee's recommendation[60] that the plaintiff's statements about what they would have done if properly informed should be inadmissible, unless against their interests.[61]

It still needs to be seen whether Australian scholars' argument that the *Rogers* test should extend to the disclosure of alternative treatment options will be translated into common law rules. Even if disclosing alternatives to the recommended treatments is held to fall within a practitioner's duty to inform, the plaintiff/patients still must clear the hurdles I mentioned above, especially the "materiality", "causation" and "injury".

9.3.2 The More Demanding Professional Regulation

Compared to the Australian common law's narrow focus on disclosure of risks, Australian professional guidelines' formulation of the scope of information disclosure is broad. Both the Royal Australasian College of Physicians and the Royal Australasian College of Surgeons require that physicians and surgeons discuss with patients *the available treatment options*, including non-operative or no treatment, outline the relevant risks of treatment, and provide the opportunity for questions to be asked within the bounds of confidentiality and privacy (The Royal Australasian College of Physicians (RACP) 2006, 1.2.1(I); Royal Australasian College of Surgeons 2006, 1.2(a)). If the patient is involved with "a new surgical procedure",[62] the patient needs to be advised that (1) the technique is new and/or experimental;

---

[60] Commonwealth of Australia 2002, page 113, paras. 7.38 and 7.40 (continuing to adopt a subjective test of causation, but recommending that "in determining causation, any statement by the plaintiff about what they would have done if the negligence had not occurred should be inadmissible").

[61] *See*, *Civil Liability Act 2003* (Qld) s 11(3) ("If it is relevant to deciding factual causation to decide what the person who suffered harm would have done if the person who was in breach of the duty had not been so in breach:

(a) the matter is to be decided *subjectively* in the light of *all relevant circumstances*, subject to paragraph (b); and

(b) any statement made by the person after suffering the harm about what he or she would have done is *inadmissible* except to the extent (if any) that the statement is against his or her interest.") (emphasis added). *See also*, *Civil Liability Act 2002* (NSW) s 5D (3); *Civil Liability Act 2002* (Tas) s 13(3); *Civil Liability Act 2002* (WA) s 5C(3).

[62] A new surgical procedure is defined as one that has not previously been used in that particular hospital or health service, and represents a significant departure from previous practice. *See*, Royal Australasian College of Surgeons 2008, 1.1.

(2) the potential risks of the new procedure, including any areas of uncertainty; (3) the criteria for selection of patients for the new procedure; and (4) *alternative treatments which are available* (Royal Australasian College of Surgeons 2008, 4.2). Patients should be able to access information about how many of these procedures have been performed at the hospital and by the surgeon who will perform the procedure (Royal Australasian College of Surgeons 2008, 4.2).

Guidelines published by the National Health and Medical Research Council (NHMRC)[63] give doctors an even more encompassing list of information that may be subject to disclosure (The National Health and Medical Research Council (NHMRC) 2004b, 11):

- the possible or likely nature of the illness or disease;
- *the proposed approach to investigation, diagnosis and treatment*: (1) what the proposed approach entails; (2) the expected benefits; (3) common side effects and material risks of any intervention; (4) whether the intervention is conventional or experimental; (5) who will undertake the intervention;
- any significant long term physical, emotional, mental, social, sexual, or other outcome which may be associated with a proposed intervention;
- *other options for investigation, diagnosis and treatment*;
- the degree of uncertainty of any diagnosis arrived at;
- the degree of uncertainty about the therapeutic outcome;
- the likely consequences of *not choosing the proposed diagnostic procedure or treatment, or of not having any procedure or treatment at all*;
- the time involved; and
- the costs involved, including out of pocket costs.

The Guideline has a counterpart focusing on communication, which presents a more detailed check list for information disclosure.[64]

---

[63] The National Health and Medical Research Council (NHMRC) is Australia's peak body for supporting health and medical research; for developing health advice for the Australian community, health professionals and governments; and for providing advice on ethical behaviour in health care and in the conduct of health and medical research. The current legislative basis of the Council is the National Health and Medical Research Council Act 1992 (NHMRC Act). The NHMRC is responsible to the Commonwealth Minister for Health and Ageing. One of the NHMRC's strategic objectives is to maintain high ethical standards. *See*, <http://www.nhmrc.gov.au/about/org/role.htm>.

[64] When discussing *the proposed intervention* with the patient, it envisages that the following information should be conveyed in plain language: (1) a description of the intervention; (2) what will happen to the patient; (3) whether the proposed intervention is critical, essential, elective or discretionary; (4) whether the proposed intervention represents current accepted medical practice; (5) whether the proposed intervention is conventional, experimental or innovative; (6) whether the proposed intervention is part of a clinical trial or other research project; (7) the potential consequences of any proposed intervention: the expected benefits; common side-effects, common complications, contraindications and possible harms, including their likelihood and degree; uncommon side-effects to which the particular patient may be exposed, or which are of concern to that patient; any outcomes that may require further intervention; and any significant long-term adverse outcomes

The emergence of the NHMRC Guidelines was a response to a concern that there was a lack of clarity in the *law* concerning information which should be given by doctors to patients. Empirical studies conducted by the Victorian Law Reform Commission in 1986–1987 revealed that doctors were giving patients less information than they wanted, and on occasion less than was required to fulfil the common law standard of reasonable care (The National Health and Medical Research Council (NHMRC) 2004b, 13). The Commission felt the need to change an attitude prevalent among doctors, that the patient's best interests were served if doctors decided what information to give and what treatment was best. In their June 1989 report, the Law Reform Commissions recommended the approach of the NHMRC's formulating guidelines for the medical profession concerning the provision of information to patients about proposed treatment and procedures, rather than replacing the common law standard of reasonable care concerning the provision of information to patients with a statutory standard (The National Health and Medical Research Council (NHMRC) 2004b, 13). Legislation was deemed an impractical way of dealing with giving information because it was too rigid and incapable of covering the wide range of situations which might arise (The National Health and Medical Research Council (NHMRC) 2004b, 13).

The status of the NHMRC Guidelines is subject to disputes. On the one hand, they claim that they reflect the common law right of legally competent patients to make their own decisions about medical treatment, and their right to grant, withhold or withdraw consent before or during examination or treatment, and the doctor's existing common law responsibility to take reasonable care (The National Health and Medical Research Council (NHMRC) 2004b, 7–8). NHMRC Guidelines have an expectation that they might be consulted in disciplinary or civil proceedings in deciding whether the doctor has behaved reasonably in giving information (The National Health and Medical Research Council (NHMRC) 2004b, 7–8). On the other hand, however, they are not "law" (Skene 2008, 176). Their purpose is to foster better communication between doctor and patient rather than to set mandatory standards of behaviour in giving information (The National Health and Medical Research Council (NHMRC) 2004b, 3). Guidelines have greater flexibility than the

---

(physical· emotional, mental, social, sexual, financial or other); (8) the degree of uncertainty about the benefit(s) of the proposed intervention; (9) how quickly a decision about the proposed intervention needs to be made; (10) who will undertake the proposed intervention, including their status and the extent of their experience, and that of any supervising doctor, where this information is known; (11) how long the proposed intervention will take; (12) how long until the results of any intervention will be available; (13) how long will be needed for recuperation and/or rehabilitation; (14) what the estimated costs are (where known), including out-of-pocket costs; and what, if any, conflicts of interest the doctor may have, including financial ones. In addition, the patient should be advised of *alternative options* including: what those options are; their availability and potential consequences; likely short- and long-term consequences that may arise if they choose not to proceed with the proposed intervention or with any intervention at all. It is noted that *complex interventions* usually require the provision of detailed information, as do *treatments where the patient has no physical illness*, for example cosmetic surgery. *See*, The National Health and Medical Research Council (NHMRC) (2004a), p. 10, 6.6.

law. In appropriate circumstances, divergence from the guidelines would not inevitably be regarded as negligent or unprofessional behaviour (The National Health and Medical Research Council (NHMRC) 2004b, 7–8).

9.4 The Canadian Model

9.4.1 The More Stringent Common Law

9.4.1.1 Information Disclosure

The Canadian law on the doctrine of informed consent is based on the two 1980 Supreme Court of Canada cases – *Hopp v Lepp*[65] and *Reibl v Hughes*.[66] Both judgments rejected the professional or doctor-oriented standard of information disclosure and favoured the "reasonable patient" standard. The questions of whether a risk is material and therefore should be disclosed, and whether there has been a breach of the duty of disclosure are not to be determined solely by the professional standards of the medical profession at the time.[67] The scope of information disclosure relates what is material to the need for information of *a reasonable or prudent person in the patient's circumstances* (Downie et al. 2002, 131). The duty of disclosure also embraces what a doctor knows or should know that *the particular patient* deems relevant to the patient's decision whether or not to undergo the procedure.[68]

The disclosure of risks centres on "material", special or unusual risks. Whether a particular risk is material and whether disclosure made satisfies the test of materiality are a matter for the trier of fact.[69] The scope of the duty of disclosure and whether it has been breached must be decided in relation to the circumstances of each case.[70] The risks must be disclosed when they are common and significant even though not necessarily grave in effect, and when they are rare but particularly serious in effect (Downie et al. 2002, 141). If the patient asks specific questions about

[65] *Hopp v Lepp* (1980), 112 D.L.R. (3d) 67 (S.C.C.); [1980] 2 S.C.R. 192.

[66] *Reibl v Hughes* [1980] 2 S.C.R. 880, (1980) 114 D.L.R. (3d) 1 (S.C.C.).

[67] *Hopp v Lepp* (1980), 112 D.L.R. (3d) 67, 80 (S.C.C.); *Reibl v Hughes* (1980) 114 D.L.R. (3d) 1, 12–13 (S.C.C.).

[68] *Reibl v Hughes* (1980) 114 D.L.R. (3d) 1, 12 (S.C.C.) ("The patient may have expressed certain concerns to the doctor and the latter is obligated to meet them in a reasonable way. What the doctor knows or should know that the particular patient deems relevant to a decision whether to undergo prescribed treatment goes equally to his duty of disclosure as do the material risks recognized as a matter of required medical knowledge."); *Videto v Kennedy* (1981) 125 D.L.R. (3d) 127, 133–134 (Ont. C.A.).

[69] Jocelyn Downie et al. 2002, 131; *Videto v Kennedy* (1981) 125 D.L.R. (3d) 127, 133–134 (Ont. C.A.).

[70] *Videto v Kennedy* (1981) 125 D.L.R. (3d) 127, 133–134 (Ont. C.A.).

the procedure, including even unorthodox questions, this may show materiality, and the patient is entitled to be given accurate, reasonable answers.[71]

9.4.1.2 Disclosure of Alternatives and Causation

As to the content of information that falls within the scope of disclosure, Canadian scholars have contemplated a wide range of information that is beyond the risks. According to their formulations, the doctor's duty to disclose may encompass disclosure of: (1) the prognosis if the patient remains untreated; (2) the doctor's recommendation about whether treatment should be undertaken; (3) alternative goals of treatment, and reasonably accessible alternative treatment means of pursuing such goals; (4) success and failure rates of different methods of treatment; (5) known effects, material risks, discomforts and side-effects of different methods of treatment and the likelihood of occurrence, even when treatment is successfully undertaken (Downie et al. 2002, 141). Such a formula acknowledges that a doctor's duty to inform not only attaches to risks of the prescribed treatment, but also goes to the consequences of leaving the ailment untreated and alternative treatment options.

Canadian common law has offered a line of authorities that favoured disclosure of alternative treatment options. That line of authorities started with *Zimmer v Ringrose*, where the Alberta Court of Appeal held that the doctor should discuss "the benefits to be gained from the recommended treatment or operation, the advantages and disadvantages associated with *alternative procedures* and the consequences of *forgoing treatment*".[72]

Then came the *Haughian v Paine*,[73] where the neurosurgeon performed disc operation on a patient without informing him of the small risk of paralysis or the riskless alternatives to surgery and the patient suffered paralysis. The *non-surgical treatment* did not have risk, but had a significant rate of success, and the same surgical option would still be available if the non-surgical treatment was unsuccessful.[74]

The Saskatchewan Court of Appeal distinguished the context of recommendation and that of information disclosure by framing two different questions and giving them two different answers. The first question was whether the neurosurgeon was negligent in not *recommending* a period of conservative management before undertaking surgery. Noting that the method of treatment, conservative management and surgery, was a matter of judgment for the surgeon, the court answered the question negatively.[75] An error of judgment, as distinguished from an act of unskilfulness, carelessness or lack of knowledge, does not make the surgeon liable.[76] The trial

[71] *Videto v Kennedy* (1981) 125 D.L.R. (3d) 127, 133–134 (Ont. C.A.).

[72] *Zimmer v Ringrose* (1981), 124 D.L.R. (3d) 215, 222 (Alta. C.A.) (emphasis added).

[73] *Haughian v Paine* (1987), 37 D.L.R. (4th) 624; [1987] 4 WWR 97.

[74] *Haughian v Paine* (1987), 37 D.L.R. (4th) 624, 635.

[75] *Haughian v Paine* (1987), 37 D.L.R. (4th) 624, 635.

[76] *Haughian v Paine* (1987), 37 D.L.R. (4th) 624, 635.

judge even found that since the doctor was a *neurosurgeon* it was understandable that the doctor and the patient expected *surgery* rather than conservative management.[77] However, holding that the neurosurgeon was not negligent in recommending surgery rather than conservative management did not deter the court from framing a question concerning *informed consent*, and holding that the neurosurgeon was negligent in failing to inform the patient of the risk of paralysis inherent in the recommended surgery and the available options of *no treatment or conservative management*.[78]

The court emphasised that disclosure of risks and disclosure of alternatives are two elements of informed consent, and they are not independent of and in isolation from each other.[79] On the one hand, one cannot make an informed decision to take a risk without knowing the alternatives to undergoing the risk.[80] On the other hand, although the risk of paralysis attendant on surgery was small, given that alternative non-surgical treatment was available, with lack of risk, a significant chance of success, and the paucity of evidence that the condition disabled the patient significantly, disclosure should have been made.[81]

The court followed the Canadian line of authorities focusing on disclosure of *risks* – *Hopp v Lepp*, *Reibl v Hughes* and *Videto v Kennedy*.[82] However, after quoting these cases and the Lord Scarman's opinion in *Sidaway* with approval, Sherstobitoff J.A., who delivered the judgement of the court, creatively observed that,

> I would *add* to the principles outlined above *a matter which was not under direct consideration* in the forgoing cases: In order to enable a patient to give informed consent, a surgeon must *also*, where the circumstances require it, explain to the patient *the consequences of leaving the ailment untreated, and alternative means of treatment and their risks* (emphasis added).[83]

The court found the support for this observation from *Reibl v Hughes*, where a commentator quoted *Canterbury v Spence* and noted that expert testimony is necessary to establish not only the risks inherent in a given procedure, but also "the consequences of leaving the ailment untreated, and alternative means of treatment and their risks".[84] The court distinguished *Hopp v Lepp* because that case did not involve alternatives.[85] In the view of the court, in the instant case, there was no adequate discussion about the consequence of leaving the ailment untreated or of undergoing

[77] *Haughian v Paine* (1987), 37 D.L.R. (4th) 624, 634.

[78] *Haughian v Paine* (1987), 37 D.L.R. (4th) 624, 643.

[79] *Haughian v Paine* (1987), 37 D.L.R. (4th) 624, 644.

[80] *Haughian v Paine* (1987), 37 D.L.R. (4th) 624, 644.

[81] *Haughian v Paine* (1987), 37 D.L.R. (4th) 624, 643.

[82] *Haughian v Paine* (1987), 37 D.L.R. (4th) 624, 636–638 (citing *Hopp v Lepp* (1980), 112 D.L.R. (3d) 67 (S.C.C.); *Reibl v Hughes* (1980) 114 D.L.R. (3d) 1 (S.C.C.); *Videto v Kennedy* (1981) 125 D.L.R. (3d) 127 (Ont. C.A.)).

[83] *Haughian v Paine* (1987), 37 D.L.R. (4th) 624, 638–639.

[84] *Haughian v Paine* (1987), 37 D.L.R. (4th) 624, 639.

[85] *Haughian v Paine* (1987), 37 D.L.R. (4th) 624, 643.

conservative management. The consequence was, at worst, a continuation of pain and discomfort and possible need for surgery in the future. If the condition deteriorated, surgery was always an option in the future.

Because the duty to inform was explored in the context of negligence, the court in *Haughian v Paine* could not avoid the issue of *causation*. First of all, it needs to be noted that, unlike England and Australia which still favour a *subjective* test of causation,[86] Canada has adopted an *objective* or a modified objective approach to causation in informed consent cases.[87] The focus of the objective standard of causation is what *a prudent or reasonable person in the patient's position* would have decided if suitably informed of the withheld information.

The *Haughian v Paine* dealt with a situation where *conservative management* involved no risk and a significant success rate, and *invasive surgery* carried not only the usual risks associated with major surgery but also the additional risks, albeit minimal, of paralysis or death. The court had no difficulty in holding that, if the risks inherent in the surgery and the alternatives to surgery had been disclosed, a reasonable person in the patient's position would not have agreed to the surgery.[88]

Unlike the *Haughian v Paine*, which involved weighing conservative management and invasive intervention, one other Canadian case, *Seney v Crooks*,[89] involved *two divergent professional opinions* on two different treatment options. The plaintiff-patient broke her wrist and visited an orthopaedic surgeon. On her second visit, the x-rays indicated that the wrist was not healing in alignment. It was obvious at that time that she would require surgery if this was to be corrected. The surgeon recast the wrist. The surgeon did not inform the patient of the alignment problem and of the availability of an alternative treatment to casting. By the third visit, the patient had developed reflex sympathetic dystrophy (RSD). Because of the RSD, the alternative treatment would not have been available. After the fourth visit, the patient discontinued seeing the surgeon. Eventually she attended a Hand Clinic in Calgary and had corrective surgery to her wrist. After the surgery, she had an obvious deformity of her wrist with limited movement in one aspect. The plaintiff brought an action against the surgeon alleging negligent treatment, failure to inform

[86] **England**: *Chatterton v Gerson*, (1981) 1 QB 432; *Hills v Potter*, (1984) 1 WLR. (4). **Australia**: *Rogers v Whitaker* (1992) 175 C.L.R. 479, 490 (HCA); *Chappel v Hart* (1998) 195 C.L.R. 232, 272; *Ellis v Wallsend District Hospital* [1989] 17 NSWLR 553 (C.A.); *Civil Liability Act 2003* (Qld) s 11(3); *Civil Liability Act 2002* (NSW) s 5D (3); *Civil Liability Act 2002* (Tas) s 13(3); *Civil Liability Act 2002* (WA) s 5C(3).

[87] *Reibl v Hughes* (1980) 114 D.L.R. (3d) 1, 17 (S.C.C.); *Arndt v Smith* (1997), 148 D.L.R. (4th) 48, 51 (S.C.C.). The Canadian landmark informed consent case – *Reibl v Hughes* – presented a context where the patient was offered the choice of having the recommended operation or not having it, and disclosure of material information (risk of stroke) could have made the patient to postpone surgery until his disability and pension entitlements were complete. In the eyes of the Court, a reasonable person in the plaintiff's position would have declined surgery *at the particular time* if undisclosed information had been revealed.

[88] *Haughian v Paine* (1987), 37 D.L.R. (4th) 624, 644–647.

[89] *Seney v Crooks* (1998), 166 D.L.R. (4th) 337 (Alta. C.A.).

of the seriousness of the injury and failure to advise of available alternative treatment.

The alternative treatment to mere casting involves placing a fixation device on the wrist to keep the wrist more stable while healing occurs. First, the alternative treatment was *more intrusive* than the treatment the surgeon had employed, but less intrusive than the corrective surgery that the patient eventually had to undergo. Second, the alternative was *preferred by a minority of orthopaedic specialists* practising in Calgary. This minority held the view that a fixation device which holds the bone in place was the preferable treatment because mere casting allows a greater opportunity for slippage. The external device is more invasive than a cast but holds the fracture in a more secure fashion than a plastic cast. Third, the alternative treatment was a *known* procedure. The alternative treatment had been in use for some 50 years and both of the medical experts testified that the alternative treatment was a common method of treatment for a wrist fracture. The profession has been familiar with it for many years. It was *not a fringe alternative, not an alternative offered outside the specialty of orthopaedics or by some other form of health care.*[90] The defendant-surgeon was aware of the alternative method but he was of the view that a satisfactory result could be attained without it.[91]

Like the *Haughian v Paine* Court, in this case, the Alberta Court of Appeal drew a distinction between the context of treatment/recommendation and that of information disclosure. The defendant-surgeon owed "more than one duty of care" to his patients.[92] In addition to the duty to provide treatment, the doctor had a duty to inform the patient of the status of her condition, the treatment being proposed, *an alternative mode of treatment preferred by some specialists*, and the risks associated with proceeding with mere casting rather than the alternative treatment.[93] On the one hand, the court acknowledged the divergence of professional opinions on which treatment, mere casting or a fixation device, should be *recommended*. The defendant-surgeon followed and recommended a treatment that would have been opted for by a *majority* of average, reasonably prudent, orthopaedic surgeons practising in Calgary in 1991.[94] There was no negligence attributed to that treatment. However, lack of negligence in the *choice* of treatment does not negate a doctor's duty of information disclosure. The court observed that,

> From a physician's viewpoint, a particular treatment may be successful in 95% of the cases and therefore they would not recommend putting all patients through a more intrusive treatment. While that may be a practically sound position, and while many of the patients may opt for the less intrusive treatment, the patient is entitled to participate in the decision for his or her treatment.[95]

---

[90] *Seney v Crooks* (1998), 166 D.L.R. (4th) 337, 353 (Alta. C.A.).

[91] *Seney v Crooks* (1998), 166 D.L.R. (4th) 337, 356, at [70] (Alta. C.A.).

[92] *Seney v Crooks* (1998), 166 D.L.R. (4th) 337, 351 (Alta. C.A.).

[93] *Seney v Crooks* (1998), 166 D.L.R. (4th) 337, 351, at [53] (Alta. C.A.).

[94] *Seney v Crooks* (1998), 166 D.L.R. (4th) 337, 347–348 (Alta. C.A.).

[95] *Seney v Crooks* (1998), 166 D.L.R. (4th) 337, 356, at [70] (Alta. C.A.).

The majority of doctors may prefer not to do the more cumbersome and intrusive treatment, but the choice was left to the patient.[96] The court agreed with the trial judge that the defendant was negligent in failing to disclose information about alternative treatments. The court's willingness to embrace disclosure of "alternative treatments as well as the risks of treatments" under the duty to inform was triggered by an *academic* comment, which formed the view that although the language in Canadian landmark informed consent cases was couched in terms of disclosure of *risks*, the duty of disclosure is not confined to risks but extends to *other material information* which a reasonable patient would want to have, particularly available alternatives to the proposed treatment and the material risks associated with those alternatives.[97] The court distinguished several cases[98] cited by the defendant because the real concern of those authorities was *causation* rather than the *duty* to inform.

A finding of negligent conduct would not have led automatically to recovery. In considering *causation*, the court proposed two questions: (1) Would the patient have opted for the alternative treatment had she been properly informed of the availability of the alternative? (2) Would any alternative treatment have made a difference? Or, had the patient undergone the alternative procedure, would her condition have been better? In answering the first question, the court noted that, if properly informed, the patient would not have remained with the defendant-surgeon and followed his advice.[99] In the view of the court, once the patient has proven the first step (involving answering the first question) in causation, there is a good argument that the onus should shift to the party who is medically knowledgeable and has breached his duty to prove that it would not have made any difference.[100] Anyway, the court agreed with the trial judge's finding that, had the patient undergone the alternative procedure, the unfortunate outcome could have been minimised. The surgery that was done later was far more extensive than the alternative treatment. It was more probable than not that the patient's condition could have been avoided.[101] There was a risk that the alternative treatment would not have completely avoided the injury. It may be that damages could have been assessed at less than the full extent.[102]

---

[96] *Seney v Crooks* (1998), 166 D.L.R. (4th) 337, 353, at [59] (Alta. C.A.).

[97] *Seney v Crooks* (1998), 166 D.L.R. (4th) 337, 352, at [55] (Alta. C.A.) (citing Picard J.A. and Robertson, *Legal liability of doctors and hospitals in Canada*, 3rd ed. (Scarborough: Carswell, 1996), pp. 129–130).

[98] *Bucknam v Kostuik* (1984) 3 D.L.R. (4th) 99 (H.C.J.); *Martins v Barsoum*, unreported (15 March 1995) (Ont. H.C.J.); *Ferron v Yadav*, [1990] OJ No. 473 (QL) (H.C.J.).

[99] *Seney v Crooks* (1998), 166 D.L.R. (4th) 337, 361, at [95] (Alta. C.A.).

[100] *Seney v Crooks* (1998), 166 D.L.R. (4th) 337, 362–363, at [99] and [101] (Alta. C.A.).

[101] *Seney v Crooks* (1998), 166 D.L.R. (4th) 337, 364, at [108] (Alta. C.A.). *Compare*, *Seney v Crooks* (1998), 166 D.L.R. (4th) 337, 344, at [26] (Alta. C.A.) (Hetherington J.A. dissenting) (holding that the surgeon's failure to disclose an alternative treatment did not cause the plaintiff's loss: "The question for the trial judge was not whether there was a *possibility* that the damage to [the patient] could have been avoided. Nor was it whether the *risk* of damage could have been reduced. The question for the trial judge was whether he was satisfied on a balance of probabilities that the alternative treatment, [], would have prevented or reduced the damage." (emphasis in the original)).

[102] *Seney v Crooks* (1998), 166 D.L.R. (4th) 337, 364, at [108] (Alta. C.A.).

A further Canadian case summarised that causation for non-disclosure of alternative treatments involves two steps.[103] First, the plaintiff establishes that a reasonable patient in similar circumstances *would have chosen the alternative treatment* if properly informed ("decision causation"). If a failure to disclose would not have affected the decision to proceed, causation will not be established. Secondly, if the patient would not have chosen to proceed, the court must consider *whether the damage would have been avoided* if the alternative had been chosen ("injury causation").

Finally, in the *Van Dyke v Grey Bruce Regional Health Centre*,[104] the Ontario Court of Appeal endorsed the view that a doctor's disclosure obligation includes not only the duty to disclose all material risks of the proposed treatment, but also the duty to advise the patient of "all available reasonable alternative treatments".[105] The court highlighted that there were two lines of authorities on the *scope* of a doctor's obligation to inform a patient of alternative treatments.[106] Believing that it is impossible to delineate the reach of a doctor's disclosure obligation without regard to the facts and circumstances of specific cases, the court noted that the extent to which a doctor must disclose and discuss alternative treatments will depend on a myriad of *factual circumstances*. Despite that, the court proposed a "generalised" approach to the scope of the disclosure obligation:

> The ultimate decision whether to proceed with a particular treatment rests with the patient and not the doctor. The doctor must equip the patient with the information necessary to make an informed choice. *Where there is more than one medically reasonable treatment* and *the risk/benefit analysis engaged by the alternatives involves different considerations*, a reasonable person would want to *know about the alternatives* and would want *the assistance of the doctor's risk/benefit analysis* of the various possible treatments before deciding whether to proceed with a specific treatment. Put differently, a reasonable person could not make an informed decision to proceed with treatment "A" if that patient was unaware of the risks and benefits associated with treatment "B", *a medically appropriate alternative treatment* (emphasis added) [107]

Such an approach provides a good balance between a patient's choice and a doctor's duty to disclose. It leaves open that alternative treatments may fall within a doctor's duty to inform. It contemplates that alternative treatments that fall within the duty of disclosure should be "medically reasonable" or "medically appropriate". It also realises that doctors' information disclosure should be accompanied by recommendation. In making decisions about treatment options, patients need doctors' assistance and guidance.

---

[103] *Sicard v Sendziak*, 2008 ABQB 690, at [116] (Court of Queen's Bench of Alberta).

[104] *Van Dyke v Grey Bruce Regional Health Centre* (2005), 255 D.L.R. (4th) 397.

[105] *Van Dyke v Grey Bruce Regional Health Centre* (2005), 255 D.L.R. (4th) 397, 414, at [63]–[64].

[106] *Van Dyke v Grey Bruce Regional Health Centre* (2005), 255 D.L.R. (4th) 397, 414–415, at [65]–[66] (one line of authorities is: *Bucknam v Kostuik* (1984) 3 D.L.R. (4th) 99 (H.C.J.); *Ferron v Yadav*, [1990] OJ No. 473 (QL) (H.C.J.); another line is *Seney v Crooks* (1998), 166 D.L.R. (4th) 337 (Alta. C.A.)).

[107] *Van Dyke v Grey Bruce Regional Health Center* (2005), 255 D.L.R. (4th) 397, at [67].

9.4.2 *The Similarly Stringent Legislation and Professional Regulation*

The Province of Ontario codified Canadian common law requirements about informed consent in health care. The *Health Care Consent Act* crystallised the two-pronged, patient-oriented approach to the standard of information disclosure by promulgating that

> A consent to treatment is informed if, before giving it, (a) the person received the information about the matters [set out in the Act] that *a reasonable person in the same circumstances would require* in order to make a decision about the treatment; and (b) the person received responses to *his or her requests for additional information* about those matters.[108]

The "matters" referred to in the first prong of the above-quoted test are: "1. The nature of the treatment. 2. The expected benefits of the treatment. 3. The material risks of the treatment. 4. The material side effects of the treatment. 5. *Alternative courses of action*. 6. The likely consequences of *not having the treatment*."[109] The information that may be encompassed by the duty to inform includes not only the merits and demerits of proposed treatment, but also alternative courses of action. The policy released by the College of Physicians and Surgeons of Ontario echoes the *Health Care Consent Act* requirements.[110]

In its Guide on consent, the Canadian Medical Protective Association highlights the "reasonable patient" standard of information disclosure and the test of risk "materiality" favoured by some precedent-setting judgments (The Canadian Medical Protective Association 2006, 7–8). It endorses the position that, for a patient's consent to be "informed", the duty to disclose should not be confined to the risks. It encompasses explanation about *alternatives available*.[111] The patient should be told about the consequences of leaving the ailment untreated, and about available alternative forms of treatment and their risks. Although there should be no coercion by unduly frightening patients who refuse treatment, there is a positive obligation to inform patients about the potential consequences of their refusal (The Canadian Medical Protective Association 2006, 10). There is no obligation to discuss what might be clearly regarded as unconventional therapy, but patients should know there are other accepted alternatives and why the recommended therapy has been chosen (The Canadian Medical Protective Association 2006, 10).

---

[108] *Health Care Consent Act*, 1996 S.O., c. 2, Sched. A, s 11(2).

[109] *Health Care Consent Act*, 1996 S.O., c. 2, Sched. A, s 11(3) (emphasis added).

[110] The College of Physicians and Surgeons of Ontario 2005, 2. Consent must be informed. ("A physician must provide a patient with information about the nature of the treatment, its expected benefits, its material risks and side effects, alternative courses of action and the likely consequences of not having the treatment." "If the patient requests additional information, he or she must receive a response.").

[111] The Canadian Medical Protective Association 2006, page 7 ("the patient must have been given an adequate explanation about the nature of the proposed investigation or treatment and its anticipated outcome as well as the significant risks involved and alternatives available.").

The Canadian Medical Association has prepared the *Code of Ethics* as an ethical guide for Canadian physicians, reminding them that they should be aware of the legal and regulatory requirements that govern medical practice in their jurisdictions (Canadian Medical Association 2004, p. 1). The *Code* is patient-oriented. When formulating the scope of information disclosure, it adopts the more encompassing word "information" rather than the "risks". It recommends physicians should: (1) provide their patients with the *information* they *need* to make informed decisions about their medical care, and answer their questions to the best of their ability; (2) recommend only those diagnostic and therapeutic services that they consider to be beneficial to their patient or to others; (3) respect the right of a competent patient to accept or reject any medical care recommended (Canadian Medical Association 2004, [21], [23], [24]).

9.5 Common Law, Professional Regulation, Legislation?

In the context of disclosure of alternatives, England, Australia and Canada present different models (Table 9.3). All three jurisdictions have very demanding *professional guidelines*, especially the UK and Australia. Happily those guidelines have embraced both disclosure of risks and disclosure of alternatives under the duty to inform. However, leading English and Australian *common law* judgements have said much less about the issue of disclosure of information about alternatives (especially about the alternatives not recommended by the treating doctor) than have leading Canadian judgements. Unlike England, Australia has adopted a very embracing test of information disclosure in the Commonwealth jurisdictions. But that "materiality" test is confined only to the context of giving information about *risks*. The Australian tort law reform and civil liability legislation[112] followed the narrow focus of common law and did not proactively expand the parameters of the two-pronged, patient-oriented standard to include disclosure of alternatives.

Canadian case law embraces a broader scope of information disclosure, encompassing disclosure of alternative treatment options. The approach of Canadian courts overcoming the common law narrow focus on disclosure of "risks" is to proactively interpret the meaning of information disclosure and to follow Canadian writers

[112] *Civil Liability Act 2003* (Qld), s 21(1) ("A doctor does not breach a duty owed to a patient to warn of *risk*, before the patient undergoes any medical treatment (or at the time of being given medical advice) that will involve a *risk* of personal injury to the patient, unless the doctor at that time fails to give or arrange to be given to the patient the following information *about the risk:* (a) information that a reasonable person in the patient's position would, in the circumstances, require to enable the person to make a reasonably informed decision about whether to undergo the treatment or follow the advice; (b) information that the doctor knows or ought reasonably to know the patient wants to be given before making the decision about whether to undergo the treatment or follow the advice" (emphasis added)); *Civil Liability Act 2002* (Tas), s 21.

Table 9.3 Scope of information disclosure and some commonwealth jurisdictions

	England	Australia	Canada	New Zealand
Common law: *Doctor-oriented* standard	√[1]			
Common law: *Patient-oriented* standard		√[5]	√[9]	√[15]
Common law: Disclosure of *risks*	√[2]	√[6]	√[10]	√[16]
Common law: Disclosure of *treatment options*	√ (under "unusual" or "special" circumstances)[3]		√ (a line of authority)[11]	
Legislation: Disclosure of *risks*		√[7]	√[12] (Ontario)	√[17]
Legislation: Disclosure of *treatment options*			√[13] (Ontario)	√[18]
Professional regulation: *Patient*-oriented standard and disclosure of *risks and treatment options*	√[4]	√[8]	√[14]	√[19]

Notes:

[1] *Bolam v Friern Hospital Management Committee* [1957] 2 All ER 118, [1957] 1 WLR 582; *Sidaway v Bethlem Royal Hospital Governors* [1985] 1 All ER 643, (1985) AC 871

[2] *Sidaway v Bethlem Royal Hospital Governors* [1985] 1 All ER 643, (1985) AC 871; *Pearce v United Bristol Healthcare NHS Trust* (1999) 48 BMLR 118; [1999] PIQR 53

[3] *Birch v University College Hospitals NHS Trust* (2008) 104 BMLR 168, (2008) 105 L.S.G. 19, [2008] All ER (D) 113 (Sep), [2008] EWHC 2237 (QB)

[4] General Medical Council (UK) *Consent: Patients and Doctors Making Decisions Together* (2008)

[5] *Rogers v Whitaker* (1992) 175 C.L.R. 479 (HCA); *Rosenberg v Percival* [2001] HCA 18; 205 CLR 434; 75 ALJR 734

[6] *Rogers v Whitaker* (1992) 175 C.L.R. 479 (HCA)

[7] *Civil Liability Act 2003* (Qld), s 21(1); *Civil Liability Act 2002* (Tas), s 21

[8] The Royal Australasian College of Physicians (RACP) *Code of Professional Behaviour* (2006); Royal Australasian College of Surgeons *Code of Conduct* (2006); The National Health and Medical Research Council (NHMRC) *General Guidelines for Medical Practitioners on Providing Information to Patients* (2004); The National Health and Medical Research Council (NHMRC) *Communicating with Patients: Advice for Medical Practitioners* (2004)

[9] *Hopp v Lepp* (1980), 112 D.L.R. (3d) 67 (S.C.C.); *Reibl v Hughes* (1980) 114 D.L.R. (3d) 1 (S.C.C.)

[10] *Hopp v Lepp* (1980), 112 D.L.R. (3d) 67 (S.C.C.); *Reibl v Hughes* (1980) 114 D.L.R. (3d) 1 (S.C.C.)

[11] *Haughian v Paine* (1987), 37 D.L.R. (4th) 624; [1987] 4 WWR 97

[12] *Health Care Consent Act*, 1996 S.O., c. 2, Sched. A

[13] *Health Care Consent Act*, 1996 S.O., c. 2, Sched. A

[14] Canadian Medical Association *Code of Ethics* (Update 2004); The Canadian Medical Protective Association. *Consent: A guide for Canadian physicians*, 4th ed. (2006); The College of Physicians and Surgeons of Ontario *Consent to Medical Treatment* (Reviewed September 2005)

[15–16] *Smith v Auckland Hospital Board* [1965] NZLR 191; *Doyle v Accident Compensation Corporation* [1997] 3 NZLR 160; *B v Medical Council* (Note) [2005] 3 NZLR 810

[17] Health and Disability Commissioner (Code of Health and Disability Services Consumers' Rights) Regulation 1996, Schedule, Right 6

[18] Health and Disability Commissioner (Code of Health and Disability Services Consumers' Rights) Regulation 1996, Schedule, Right 6

[19] Medical Council of New Zealand *Information, Choice of Treatment and Consent* (2011)

who argued for expanding the duty to disclose so as to encompass alternative treatments.[113] In Australia, academics have frequently argued for expansive readings of the *Rogers* test (Skene 2008, 190; Weir 2003, 297; Brophy 2003, 275–276). It is not yet clear whether these academic arguments will be translated into legal principles.[114]

The *common law* is reactive rather than proactive, in that it can only develop in response to actual cases. Most landmark informed consent cases are concerned with seeking compensation for the harm caused by *undisclosed materialized risks*. Thus, the courts have only been asked to decide on whether or not a doctor should have informed the patient of a particular risk (Maclean 2006, 324). Furthermore, cases that reach a court must be decided within the common law institutional constraints of precedent and legal policy. Any development in common law is likely to be piecemeal. All of this can lead to a law that may be out of synch with ethical mores, uncertainty and a lack of predictability (Maclean 2009, 214).

Admittedly, *professional regulation* can play a more proactive role. It will play an important role in encouraging the virtues of professionalism. Professional guidelines not only improve practice, but also indirectly influence legal standards. Professional regulatory bodies can make some remedies, such as an explanation, an apology and assurance, available. But there is still the question of whether professional regulation could be developed sufficiently to avoid the need for a direct legislative response (Maclean 2009, 218). The main problem with the approach of professional regulation is the possible perception that the professional regulatory bodies are insufficiently independent of the practitioners and are biased in their favour (Maclean 2009, 218). At present there may be insufficient public confidence in these bodies to support an expanded role (Maclean 2009, 218).

The law can be more proactive by *legislation* and by translating ethical expectations into legal principles. Legislating "would have the advantage of allowing the development of a conceptually coherent law, with well-defined guidance" (Maclean 2009, 217). However, as illustrated by Australian and Canadian law, the law of torts

[113] *Haughian v Paine* (1987), 37 D.L.R. (4th) 624, 639 (citing a commentary from *Reibl v Hughes* which quoted *Canterbury v Spence* and noted that expert testimony is necessary to establish not only risks inherent in a given procedure, but also "the consequences of leaving the ailment untreated, and alternative means of treatment and their risks"); *Seney v Crooks* (1998), 166 D.L.R. (4th) 337, 352, at [55] (Alta. C.A.) (citing Picard J.A. and Robertson *Legal liability of doctors and hospitals in Canada*, 3rd ed. (Scarborough: Carswell, 1996), pp. 129–130, where scholars argues that although the language in Canadian landmark informed consent cases was couched in terms of disclosure of *risks*, the duty of disclosure is not confined to risks but extends to other material information which a reasonable patient would want to have, particularly available alternatives to the proposed treatment and the material risks associated with those alternatives).

[114] In *Rosenberg v Percival*, an argument that a duty to inform covers "any available alternatives" was hinted, but not pursued. *See*, *Rosenberg v Percival* [2001] 205 CLR 434, 465, per Kirby J. (noting that health providers have a duty "to inform patients contemplating invasive procedures (such as surgery) of the material risks involved in the treatment proposed, and any available alternatives. Any 'choice' by the patient, in respect of such procedures, without the provision of such information, is meaningless.").

or medical negligence suffers from some disadvantages. The liability in negligence will depend on the materiality of risks, materialisation of a risk and the establishment of causation. It has higher thresholds and entails harsh consequences. Moreover, the law of torts is limited in the flexibility of its remedies. It only makes the option of damages available. Disgruntled patients often want an explanation, an apology or an indication that steps will be taken to prevent the problem recurring (Maclean 2009, 214).

All three approaches – the professional regulation, common law and medical negligence legislation – have disadvantages. First, although necessary in promoting a good sense of professionalism and restoring confidence in medical profession, the approach of relying on *professional guidelines* suffers from lack of authority and independence.

Second, *common law* operates retrospectively, by providing redress for wrongs in the past, rather than prospectively and preventatively by clearly setting out permissible standards of conduct and trying to avoid harm in the future. Because common law is precedent-based, with each case being limited to its own facts, it grows in a piecemeal fashion. As shown by the Canadian case law, extending the duty to inform to the context of alternatives disclosure could not be accomplished without the courts' proactive reading of case law (even just *obiter*) and actively seeking support from academic literature.

Third, *medical negligence legislation* could be the most proactive way of reformulating the scope of information disclosure. However, the medical negligence context does not provide an ideal soil to nurture the doctrine of informed consent. It focuses on compensation and has many high thresholds for compensation. It suffers from rigidity. Moreover, civil liability or medical negligence litigation under common law is always slow, cumbersome, not readily accessible, and too financially burdensome.

Therefore, an approach of combining the law's authority, the regulation's flexibility, and the legislation's proactive propensity, but at the same time avoiding the inconveniences of medical negligence lawsuits, needs to be pursued. In this respect, New Zealand's Health and Disability Commissioner Act and its related Code of Patients' Rights offer a good example.

9.6 New Zealand Law and Its Code of Patients' Rights

9.6.1 The Unique "Code"

The Code of Health and Disability Services Consumers' Rights,[115] or New Zealand's Code of Patients' Rights (hereafter "the Code"), resulted from the Cartwright

[115] Health and Disability Commissioner (Code of Health and Disability Services Consumers' Rights) Regulations 1996, Schedule.

Report[116] in which Judge Dame Silvia Cartwright's two of her key recommendations were enactment of a statement of patients' rights and the appointment of a Health Commissioner. The Cartwright Report signalled a fundamental shift in public attitudes toward the medical profession (Paterson 2002, 71–72). The Report highlighted the importance of public scrutiny of the medical profession and awareness of patients' rights.

The Code and its "parent Act" offer an unique jurisdiction. First, as a piece of legislation, it has legal authority and enforceability. Second, as a code of rights and a complaints-resolving regime, its scope and content is rights-oriented and very encompassing. It serves as a tool of professional regulation. Scrutiny of the medical profession is done by an independent, external third party. Third, as a code aiming to promote and protect the patients' rights, it is distinct from the accident compensation regime. It does not involve the hurdles of causation and damage. Therefore, the "Code" approach enjoys the benefits of both the authoritative and proactive character of legislation, and the flexible and embracing nature of regulation, but at the same time, avoids the inconveniences the patients experience when they are involved in medical negligence or accident compensation lawsuits.

9.6.1.1 Legally Enforceable

The Code is set out in the Schedule to the Health and Disability Commissioner (Code of Health and Disability Services Consumers' Rights) Regulations 1996. Its "parent Act" is the Health and Disability Commissioner Act 1994,[117] which established the office of the Commissioner to promote and protect the rights of patients, provide for the promulgation of a Code of Rights, and set up a complaints regime to secure the fair, simple, speedy and efficient resolution of complaints of breaches of rights in the Code. As a piece of delegated (or subordinate) legislation, the Code has full legal effect (Skegg and Paterson 2006, 25). Although formulations of rights in the Code are similar to those in professional guidelines and charters of patients' rights, the Code rights are legally enforceable. They are "not merely aspirational statements or quasi-voluntary guidance of the kind found in codes of ethics or professional statements" (Manning 2009, 316).

Every Code right is matched by a correlative duty.[118] A provider's failure to fulfil duties may result in the provider being subject to a complaint to the Health and Disability Commissioner (HDC). The Commissioner may refer the complaint to

[116] *The Report of the Committee of Inquiry into Allegations Concerning the Treatment of Cervical Cancer at National Women's Hospital and into Other Related Matters*, Auckland, Committee of Inquiry, 1988. The Cartwright Inquiry was triggered by an article published in the *Metro* magazine, alleging unethical experimentation at National Women's Hospital. The Cartwright Report led to major reforms to patient rights in New Zealand. *See*, DB Collins and CA Brown 2009, 601.

[117] 1994 No. 88, Amendment 2003 No. 49.

[118] *See*, cl 1 (2) ("Every provider is subject to the duties in this Code.") and cl 2 ("The rights of consumers and the duties of providers under this Code are as follows: … ") of the Code.

another agency, such as to the relevant health professional registration authority, if it appears that the competence, fitness to practise, or appropriateness of conduct of a health practitioner may be in doubt.[119] The complaint may trigger formal investigation by the Commissioner. The Commissioner has a wide range of recommendatory, reporting, and referral powers at the end of an investigation in which the provider has been found in breach of the code. The Commissioner is required to notify the appropriate registration authority in the case of an investigation of a health practitioner.[120] The Code and Commissioner jurisdiction may end up with the Commissioner referring the provider to the independent Director of Proceedings (DP) for the DP to decide whether to institute a disciplinary charge before the Health Practitioners Disciplinary Tribunal (HPDT), and/or to the civil proceedings before the Human Rights Review Tribunal (HRRT) which has a limited damages jurisdiction.[121]

9.6.1.2 Encompassing

The Code applies to all providers of health and disability services, both registered and unregistered, private or public, including organisations such as District Health Boards (DHBs) and hospitals as well as individual providers.[122] Clause 2 of the Code provides a list of ten rights: (1) the right to be treated with respect; (2) the right to freedom from discrimination, coercion, harassment, and exploitation; (3) the right to dignity and independence; (4) the right to services of an appropriate standard; (5) the right to effective communication; (6) the right to be properly informed; (7) the right to make an informed choice and give informed consent; (8) the right to have support; (9) the right in respect of teaching or research; and (10) the right to

[119] *Health and Disability Commissioner Act 1994* (NZ), s 34(1)(a).

[120] *Health and Disability Commissioner Act 1994* (NZ), s 43(2)(d).

[121] P.D.G. Skegg and Ron Paterson (General Editors) 2006, 608–609. In deciding whether to refer to the DP, the Commissioner must have regard to three considerations: (1) the wishes of the complainant (if any) and the aggrieved person (if not the complainant) in relation to the matter; (2) any comments made by the provider on the proposed referral; and (3) the public interest. The HPDT jurisdiction is only available to *registered health practitioners*, and is not available for non-registered (such as complementary and alternative medicine) providers. The HRRT jurisdiction is available for both registered health practitioners and CAM providers. It has power to award complementary and punitive damages. According to the *Health and Disability Commissioner Act*, an action before the HRRT may result in a declaration (s 54(1)(a)), a restraining order (s 54(1)(b)), an order to perform some acts(s 54(1)(e)), or/and the award of damages(s 54(1)(c)). The damages sought by the Director or the aggrieved person include compensatory damages (s 57(1)(c)) and exemplary/punitive damages(s 57(1)(d)), but do not cover "personal injury" damages (s 52(2)).

[122] Joanna Manning 2009, 315. As far as the definition of "provider" is concerned, section 3 of the *Health and Disability Commissioner Act* lists categories of person who will fall within the meaning of "health care provider". This section also has a very open paragraph (k). By virtue of this paragraph, the term "health care provider" will also cover "any other person who provides, or holds himself or herself or itself out as providing, health services to the public or to any section of the public, whether or not any charge is made for those services".

complain. The Commissioner is contemplating to introduce a right to privacy into the Code (Manning 2009, 319–320).

Notably, Right 4(2) of the Code adopted the very encompassing words – "legal, professional, ethical, and other relevant standards" – to describe the standards that providers should comply with. It elevates professional and ethical duties to legal obligations. Failure to fulfil a guideline that is considered to be aspirational and an expression of best practice rather than setting a minimum standard is unlikely to lead to a breach of Right 4(2) (Skegg and Paterson 2006, 38). However, "legal standards underpinned by statute, professional standard set by colleges, ethical standards set by registration authorities, and other relevant standards are *potentially* legal enforceable via the Code" (Skegg and Paterson 2006, 38 (emphasis added)). Given that in other jurisdictions, such as England and Australia, there is a big discrepancy between the legal standard and the professional standard and both standards are separate and distinct, New Zealand is unique in incorporating or integrating the professional and ethical standards into the legal arena.

9.6.1.3 Distinct from the Context of Accident Compensation

New Zealand has a comprehensive, no-fault accident compensation scheme. Medical accidents used to be governed by "medical misadventure" (including "medical error" and "medical mishap") provisions.[123] The New Zealand's *Injury Prevention, Rehabilitation, and Compensation Amendment Act (No 2) 2005*[124] substituted the concept of "treatment injury" for the notion of "medical misadventure". The new concept of "treatment injury" shifted the focus from an individual health professional's fault and blaming culture to the "system approach" to medical accidents and learning culture.[125] It rejects the fault-based test of medical error. It moved

[123] According to Section 5 of the *Accident Rehabilitation and Compensation Insurance Act 1992*, "medical misadventure" means personal injury resulting from medical error or medical mishap. "Medical error" means the failure of a registered health professional to observe a standard of care and skill reasonably to be expected in the circumstances. It is not medical error solely because desired results are not achieved or because subsequent events show that different decisions might have produced better results. "Medical mishap" means an adverse consequence of treatment by a registered health professional, properly given if: (a) The likelihood of the adverse consequence of the treatment occurring is rare; and (b) The adverse consequence of the treatment is severe. Under the notion of "medical misadventure", there was still a need to establish that the health professional had acted *negligently*. *Fault* still needed to be established, *blame* still needed to be attributed. That formed "an oddity in a scheme essentially based on the principle of no-fault cover" (Petra Butler "A Brief Introduction to Medical Misadventure" (2004) 35 VUWLR 811, 816). *See also*, P.D.G. Skegg and Ron Paterson (General Editors) 2006, 687–694.

[124] By section 5(1)(a) of the Accident Compensation Amendment Act 2010 (2010 No. 1), the name of the principal Act changed. The principal Act is now called the Accident Compensation Act 2001. "Accident Compensation" is substituted for "Injury Prevention, Rehabilitation, and Compensation".

[125] P.D.G. Skegg and Ron Paterson (General Editors) 2006, 696. *See also*, Ken Oliphant 2007, 387 (noting that the 2005 reform – particularly the rejection of the fault-based test of medical error – evidences a paradigm shift in attitudes to injury prevention, the role of ACC and the state's responsibility for personal injury).

closer to the no-fault nature of the rest of accident compensation scheme.[126] However, cover under "treatment injury" still needs existence of "personal injury" suffered by the patient and establishment of causal nexus between personal injury and treatment (Skegg and Paterson 2006, 709). "Treatment injury" is defined as personal injury *caused* by treatment.[127]

The term "treatment" in the concept "treatment injury" is not confined to the context of diagnosis and treatment. It also embraces information disclosure and obtaining or failing to obtain informed consent.[128] The requirements of injury and causation apply to the context of information disclosure.[129] Deficient medical advice (including failure to inform) *per se* did not amount to "medical misadventure". The claimant must prove three elements: (1) deficient medical advice; (2) injury, or physical or mental consequences; (3) a causal link between the two.[130] The question of whether an incapacity has been "caused" by an accident or otherwise remains the key gatekeeper question, and its importance has only been increased by the change from "medical misadventure" to "treatment injury" (McLay 2008, 65).

Furthermore, it seemed that the New Zealand Court of Appeal has showed less preparedness to relax the traditional rules of causation in the context of information disclosure. The *Chester v Afshar* and *Chappel v Hart* approach of relaxing the conventional causation test[131] was mentioned and commented in the New Zealand

[126] Reforms in 2005 removed the final fault element from the compensation criteria for medical injuries, making it a true no-fault system. However, there are still some situations in which fault continues to play some part in the new treatment injury provisions. *See*, Ken Oliphant 2007, 381.

[127] *Injury Prevention, Rehabilitation, and Compensation Act 2001*, s 32(1)(b). *See*, *Edwards v Accident Compensation Corporation* [2009] NZACC 116, [22] (holding that the appellant falls at the first hurdle of establishing that she has suffered personal injury *"caused by treatment"* (s 32(1)(b)), and there is no link between the appellant's development of rheumatoid arthritis, and her treatment with co-trimoxazole despite an apparent temporal connection).

[128] *Injury Prevention, Rehabilitation, and Compensation Act 2001*, s 33(1)(a) (b) (c) (d) (e). Section 36(2)(a) of the Accident Insurance Act 1998 provided that "medical error" includes a negligent failure to obtain informed consent to treatment. In the context of "medical misadventure", "a medical mishap" may flow from "deficient medical advice" – whether through failure to inform or misrepresentation, innocent or fraudulent. *See*, *Green v Matheson* [1989] 3 NZLR 564, 573 (CA). Misrepresentation about the risks inherent in proposed treatment would be treated as "medical misadventure". *See*, Ken Oliphant 1996. A negligent failure to obtain an informed consent where the relevant risk eventuates and results in personal injury is covered by the compensation scheme, and patients suffering physical injury cannot bring a civil claim in negligence for damages for breach of the duty to warn. *See*, Joanna Manning 2004, 184.

[129] *J v Accident Compensation Corporation* [2006] NZACC 33, para. [99] ("The allegation of a lack of informed consent includes an assertion that the appellant would not have proceeded to have the termination had she been properly informed of the risks of the operation.").

[130] *Doyle v Accident Compensation Corporation* [1997] 3 NZLR 160, 166 (HC), per Fisher J. *See also*, *XYZ v Accident Compensation Corporation* [2002] NZACC 53, para. [20] ("the injury suffered must be attributable to the medical error"). Although these observations were given in the old context of "medical misadventure" founded upon deficient medical advice, they are also applicable to the new context of "treatment injury" caused by failure to give appropriate information.

[131] *See*, Sect. 4.2.4.

case of *Accident Compensation Corp v Ambros*,[132] a case extensively examining the traditional test for causation (the "but for" test and the "material contribution" test) and its modified alternatives (such as "material increase in the risk of injury", "loss of chance", "shifting of the evidential onus", and "drawing of an inference") in the context of medical malpractice, and trying to locate the best approach in New Zealand context. Although the Court of Appeal did not close the door for further considering "the applicability (or otherwise) of the informed consent cases under the accident compensation regime",[133] the court noted that "[t]o the extent that the informed consent cases are based on *the policy imperative of upholding patient rights to be informed* by imposing liability to pay damages, then they have *little relevance* to a non-fault accident compensation regime".[134] In the court's view, the *Chester v Afshar* and *Chappel v Hart* approach "would mean that causation in fact ('but for') always equates to causation in law in that context".[135] The court also shared a concern that adopting the *Chester v Afshar* and *Chappel v Hart* approach "is similar to saying that a win at the casino was caused by going there on Tuesday because the chances are slight that there would have been a win had the punter gone to the casino on Wednesday".[136] This lends a support to Joanna Manning's concern that ironically "claimants may be in a better position to prove causation at common law than under New Zealand's statutory compensation scheme, a purpose of which is to avoid the arbitrariness of a negligent action" (Manning 2004, 211).

However, in the context of the Code of Rights, there is no need to consider *causation and damage*.[137] Breach of the Code does not depend upon proof of injury and a causal link between the injury suffered and a breach of a Code right (Manning 2004, 208). Therefore, in the context of information disclosure, breaches of the Code rights can result where the patient's right to be sufficiently informed or given an informed consent has not been observed, even though no injury has resulted, or where the injury suffered is not physical, or where injury suffered is unrelated to the risk that should have been disclosed (Manning 2004, 209). The patient is entitled to appropriate information irrespective of whether it would have been a determinative factor in the decision to proceed (Manning 2004, 209).

The Code is a unique and distinctive legal scheme in New Zealand medical law. The Code, enshrined in the form of Regulation, and along with its parent legislation Health and Disability Commissioner Act 1994, "have the effect of creating a new

---

[132] *Accident Compensation Corp v Ambros* [2008] 1 NZLR 340 (CA).

[133] *Accident Compensation Corp v Ambros* [2008] 1 NZLR 340, 355 (CA), at [52] (waiting until a case arises in the New Zealand context).

[134] *Accident Compensation Corp v Ambros* [2008] 1 NZLR 340, 354 (CA), at [50] (emphasis added).

[135] *Accident Compensation Corp v Ambros* [2008] 1 NZLR 340, 355 (CA), at [51].

[136] *Accident Compensation Corp v Ambros* [2008] 1 NZLR 340, 355 (CA), at [51].

[137] P.D.G. Skegg and Ron Paterson (General Editors) 2006, 40–41 ("Failure to supply the requisite information is a breach of Right 6, irrespective of whether the consumer would have gone ahead with the procedure if the information had been disclosed.").

form of liability, which takes its place alongside the criminal, tortious, professional disciplinary and other forms of liability to which the provider may already be subject" (Skegg 1997).

The New Zealand's Code and HDC jurisdiction provides contrast and complement to the no-fault accident compensation (ACC) scheme. In contrast to ACC, which is compensation-focused, the Code and HDC jurisdiction is basically *fault-based* and *accountability-focused*. The compensation role is performed by the ACC scheme, but other functions of the civil action – corrective justice (vindication and professional accountability) and deterrence – are intended to be fulfilled principally by an independent complaints regime (the Code and HDC), supplemented by professional discipline and residual civil claims for exemplary damages (Manning 2008, 120–155).

The Code and HDC play a *pivotal* role in resolving complaints. The Commissioner's Office has three focuses of work: resolution of complaints; protection of the public; and learning from complaints.[138] The Commissioner is a constant interpreter of the Code of Rights. The Commissioner is readily accessible. The Commissioner is a "watchdog" to public interests and a gatekeeper to other available jurisdictions.

First, HDC jurisdiction has *a low threshold, less hurdles*, and, therefore, promises a *high potential* of the Commissioner's getting involved in the health practitioners' professional practice. Behind the HDC's jurisdiction is a right-advocated legislation. Ordinary negligence on the part of health practitioners is sufficient to invoke the Commissioner's response.

Second, HDC jurisdiction is a *low-level* complaint resolution mechanism.[139] Firstly, it is, at least notionally, a sole-person jurisdiction. Accessibility and efficiency are its prevailing considerations. Secondly, sanctions for breach of the Code are normally non-punitive (Manning 2008, 130). HDC cannot award damages.[140] Once breach of the Code was established, the provider was usually recommended to apologise to the complainant and review his practice. The Commissioner seeks to ensure that lessons are learned and steps taken to prevent similar occurrences. Thirdly, although HDC has the power of formal investigation and further referral to other mechanisms, some very low-level resolution methods (without public exposure), such as advocacy and mediation, are also on the list of options that are available to HDC. Only a small minority of complaints are formally investigated, as opposed to being resolved through low-level means or referred to other agencies.[141] Sometimes, HDC is a *peacekeeper*. The wider application of the Code to provider

[138] R. Paterson "Commissioner's Report" in *Health and Disability Commissioner Annual Report* 2007, p. 1.

[139] Ron Paterson 2002, 74–75 ("the focus of the complaints system is resolution of complaints at the lowest appropriate level, acknowledgement of a patient's concerns, and, where necessary, review and rehabilitation of a substandard practitioner or system").

[140] For example, in the above-mentioned *Opinion 02HDC18414* (Health and Disability Commissioner, 6/4/04), what the Commissioner recommended was that the provider (1) apologise to his patient; and (2) review his explanation of treatment options available to patients, in light of the Opinion. *Also see*, P.D.G. Skegg and Ron Paterson (General Editors) 2006, 56 (noting that there is "no general right to damages" for breach of the Code).

[141] Joanna Manning 2008, 129 (also offering an explanation based on resources).

conduct can be balanced by a relatively low level response to its breach in most cases (Manning 2004, 216).

Third, HDC jurisdiction serves as "gateway" or "gatekeeper" to other jurisdictions. The Commissioner can make Health Practitioners Disciplinary Tribunal (HPDT) and Human Rights Review Tribunal (HRRT) jurisdictions available to the complainant, but for the great majority of investigations, the Commissioner's opinion and recommendations conclude the process. Only very small minority of complaints will go to the other two jurisdictions.[142] For patients whose pursuit is for purposes other than or in addition to compensation, the HDC jurisdiction is an attractive and convenient avenue. Due to its gatekeeper nature, most of complaints would stop there.[143]

Fourth, HDC jurisdiction offers a high potential for quality control and improvement of care. HDC has a wide range of recommendatory, reporting and referral powers. Those powers have the "rehabilitative and constructive" potential (Collins and Brown 2009, 609). The Commissioner encourages health practitioners to reflect positively and/or constructively on their practice. Complaints are used as a "window of opportunity" to improve health services (Bismark and Paterson 2006, 281–282). The investigative reports are not just retrospective analyses of how and why a patient's rights were breached. They are used for educational purposes (Paterson 2002, 75). Educational purposes are served by media statements on matters of public concern, publication of investigation reports (in anonymised form) on the commissioner's Web site, and sending copies of reports (also anonymised) to colleges and professional bodies (Paterson 2002, 75). Most medical practitioners are extremely sensitive to official criticism and tend to take an HDC "breach" finding very seriously (Manning 2008, 130).

9.6.2 Scope or Standard of Information Disclosure

New Zealand has an early landmark informed consent case – *Smith v Auckland Hospital Board.*[144] It used to be frequently cited by judges. It has narrow parameters. In the *Smith* case, the Court of Appeal indicated that its opinion was only confined

[142] Joanna Manning 2008, 130–131 (revealing that commissioners have referred only tens of complaints to the Director of Proceedings out of more than 1,000 complaints concluded annually); DB Collins and CA Brown "The impact of the Cartwright Report upon the regulation, discipline and accountability of medical practitioners in New Zealand" (2009) 16 *JLM* 595, 609 (noting that the lower incidence of disciplinary hearings may be attributed to the Commissioner's discretion to make adverse findings against practitioners).

[143] Although there has been a dramatic increase in the number of complaints since the Commissioner's Office was founded, the number of disciplinary charges before professional bodies and disciplinary bodies has declined. In 2000–2001, of 111 cases where the commissioner found that a doctor had breached the code, only twelve were referred for professional discipline. *See*, Ron Paterson 2002, 77–78.

[144] *Smith v Auckland Hospital Board* [1964] NZLR 241; revd [1965] NZLR 191.

to the "particular",[145] or "special and somewhat exceptional",[146] or "somewhat uncommon"[147] circumstances, rather than laying down a general rule. *Smith* is "a case in which there was an *express inquiry* as to the risks involved", not a case involving a doctor volunteering information.[148]

The *Smith* case created a dichotomy between a doctor's volunteering information and a doctor's responding to the patient's inquiry. On the one hand, a patient asking a specific question will expose the doctor to "a duty to give a reasonably adequate answer",[149] or "responsibility for a careful, although not necessarily a detailed, answer"[150]; or "at least to give an answer substantially more informative than was furnished by the gesture and conversation which were deposed to".[151] On the other hand, "*if not asked a specific question*, a doctor would have no duty to volunteer a warning as to any risk involved in [the] particular procedure (in which the risk admittedly was not great)".[152]

Smith was an informed consent case, but the standard of disclosure that the court preferred was still profession-oriented.[153] It did not distinguish "the area of advice" from "the realm of diagnosis or technique":

> Clearly the evaluation of the risks inherent in the treatment and their significance in relation to the malady to be treated is essential for the provision of balanced information and warnings. This must involve the doctor in the *same exercise of judgment* founded upon the *same medical experience and knowledge* as he exercises in the field of technique. In this area of his responsibility, therefore, his duty of care should logically be measured by the *same standards* and upon the *same principles* (emphasis added).[154]

The *Smith* case distinguished the *Bolam* case because the latter one was not involved with answering a patient's questions.[155] Therefore, the *Smith* case leaves the *Bolam* test[156] intact.

---

[145] *Smith v Auckland Hospital Board* [1964] NZLR 241; revd [1965] NZLR 191, 213, per McGregor J.

[146] *Smith v Auckland Hospital Board* [1965] NZLR 191, 216, per T.A. Gresson J.

[147] *Smith v Auckland Hospital Board* [1965] NZLR 191, 219, per T.A. Gresson J.

[148] *Smith v Auckland Hospital Board* [1964] NZLR 241; revd [1965] NZLR 191, 197 (emphasis added). Hutchison J. also expressly noted that his view "relates only to the present case, in which, as must be accepted, the appellant made the inquiry" (at 212).

[149] *Smith v Auckland Hospital Board* [1964] NZLR 241; revd [1965] NZLR 191, 206, per Turner J.

[150] *Smith v Auckland Hospital Board* [1964] NZLR 241; revd [1965] NZLR 191, 213, per McGregor J.

[151] *Smith v Auckland Hospital Board* [1964] NZLR 241; revd [1965] NZLR 191, 206, per Turner J.

[152] *Smith v Auckland Hospital Board* [1964] NZLR 241; revd [1965] NZLR 191, 205–206, per Turner J. (emphasis added).

[153] *Smith v Auckland Hospital Board* [1964] NZLR 241; revd [1965] NZLR 191, 205–206, per Turner J. ("What is proper in specific circumstances must, … be measured by what other competent and experienced medical men would conceive as their duty in like circumstances").

[154] *Smith v Auckland Hospital Board* [1964] NZLR 241, 247.

[155] *Smith v Auckland Hospital Board* [1965] NZLR 191, 226–227, per T.A. Gresson J.

[156] *Bolam v Friern Hospital Management Committee* [1957] 2 All ER 118, 122, per McNair J. ("A doctor is not guilty of negligence if he has acted in accordance with a practice accepted as proper by a responsible body of medical men skilled in that particular art. … Putting it the other way round, a doctor is not negligent, if he acting in accordance with such a practice, merely because there is a body of opinion that takes a contrary view.").

There was a period when *Smith* was restrictively interpreted to mean that, unless the patient asks the doctor specifically about the risk, the doctor is under no obligation to inform the patient (Oliphant 1996, 9–10). That left open the question of what sort of question would trigger the duty to inform, or how specific the inquiry had to be.

The advent of *Rogers* transformed the New Zealand law. *Rogers* has been cited by New Zealand case law on several occasions.[157] In a 1997 High Court case, the court stated that deficient medical advice can take one of two forms. The first involves breach of a doctor's duty to use due care in *answering a patient's question* where the patient, to the knowledge of the doctor, intends to rely on the answer in making a decision with respect to a potential medical procedure.[158] The other form mirrors the *Rogers* approach, i.e. a doctor has a duty to warn a patient of *a material risk inherent in proposed treatment*.[159] A risk is material: (i) if in the circumstances a reasonable person in the patient's position, if warned of the risk, would be likely to attach significance to it; or (ii) if the medical practitioner is aware, or reasonably should be aware, that if warned of the risk, the particular patient would be likely to attach significance to it.[160]

In the *B v Medical Council*,[161] after providing extensive quotation from *Rogers*, Justice Elias noted that "[i]n the case of diagnosis and treatment, conduct which falls short of the mark will be assessed substantially by reference to *usual practice* of comparable practitioners. In the case of adequacy of communication of information to the patient, however, *wider considerations* are relevant."[162] The survey of courts and other decision-makers' opinions in New Zealand indicates that the evidence of medical practice or common practice is only relevant to, not conclusive of, the standard of care (Manning 2007, 401). The decision-maker, the court, the Health Practitioners Disciplinary Tribunal or the Health and Disability Commissioner, enjoys a more freedom, than under *Bolitho*, to undertake a broader normative assessment of the reasonableness of medical practice, not just the logical consistency of the practice (Manning 2007, 401–407).

Partly because of the introduction of accident compensation scheme, nowadays in New Zealand, the *Smith* case is "all but ignored" (Skegg and Paterson 2006, 209). With the advent of the Code, talk about informed consent at the clinical level has

---

[157] *Doyle v Accident Compensation Corporation* [1997] 3 NZLR 160 (HC), 165, per Fisher J. (in the context of "medical misadventure"); *B v Medical Council of NZ* (Note) [2005] 3 NZLR 810 (involving professional conduct for disciplinary purposes).

[158] *Doyle v Accident Compensation Corporation* [1997] 3 NZLR 160, 165 (HC), per Fisher J. (citing *H v ACC* [1990] NZAR 289 and *Hazel v ACC* [1991] NZAR 362).

[159] *Doyle v Accident Compensation Corporation* [1997] 3 NZLR 160, 165 (HC), per Fisher J. (citing *Rogers v Whitaker* (1992) 109 ALR 625 (HCA)).

[160] *Doyle v Accident Compensation Corporation* [1997] 3 NZLR 160, 165 (HC), per Fisher J. (citing *Rogers v Whitaker* (1992) 109 ALR 625 (HCA)).

[161] *B v Medical Council of NZ* 8/7/96, Elias J, HC Auckland HC 11/96, noted at [2005] 3 NZLR 810.

[162] *B v Medical Council* (Note) [2005] 3 NZLR 810, 812 (emphasis added).

been overwhelmed by the Code's formulation of the patients' rights and the Commissioner's interpretation of those rights. The Commissioners have developed the New Zealand law on informed consent, taking it into areas beyond the common law (Manning 2004, 183).

The Code distinguishes disclosure of information from provision of services and maintains a dichotomy between Right 4 (Right to Services of An Appropriate Standard) and Right 6 (Right to be Fully Informed). Right 4 of the Code, which is profession-oriented, is mostly suitable to be used in a context involving clinical judgment, such as diagnosis and treatment. It makes it clear that every consumer has the right to have services provided with "reasonable care and skill" and the right to have services provided that "comply with legal, professional, ethical, and other relevant standards".[163] It "encompasses the traditional duty of care (reasonable care and skill) with modern concepts of patient safety (minimization of harm) and care coordination" (Paterson 2002, 73). Right 6 of the Code is a statutory acknowledgment of the distinctive aspects of information disclosure. Unlike Right 4, Right 6 is formulated from the consumers' (patients') perspective. It provides a patient-oriented standard of information disclosure.

9.6.3 A "Materiality" Test?

One scholar read Right 6 of the Code as adopting the notion of "materiality" in deciding whether information should be disclosed.[164] It seems that the case of the Code is not so simple. Although the previous New Zealand case law quoted the *Rogers* "materiality" test,[165] the Code omitted the word "material" in formulating the scope of information disclosure.

Although the threshold for information "materiality" is lower than that required to satisfy causation, it is still a high hurdle. Most jurisdictions use the word "attach[ing] significance to" or "significant" to describe the "materiality" of information.[166] Some judge regards the words "significant risk" and "material risk" as

---

[163] *Health and Disability Commissioner (Code of Health and Disability Services Consumers' Rights) Regulation 1996*, Schedule, Right 4(1) and (2).

[164] José Miola 2009, 94 ("As can be seen, Right 6 seems at first glance to consist of the first, objective, part of the *Rogers* test, but with additional, wide-ranging details *being classed as material*, such as information about the doctor's qualifications and alternative treatments" (emphasis added)).

[165] *Doyle v Accident Compensation Corporation* [1997] 3 NZLR 160, 165 (HC), per Fisher J.

[166] *Rogers v Whitaker* (1992) 175 C.L.R. 479, 490 (HCA) ("a risk is material if, in the circumstances of the particular case, a reasonable person in the patient's position, if warned of the risk, would be likely to *attach significance to* it or if the medical practitioner is or should reasonably be aware that the particular patient, if warned of the risk, would be likely to *attach significance to* it" (emphasis added)); *Pearce v United Bristol Healthcare NHS Trust* [1999] PIQR 53, 59;

interchangeable.[167] Some cases witnessed the use of diverse words, such as "relevant",[168] "influence",[169] or "sufficiently substantial" factor,[170] to describe the relationship between the risks and a patient's medical decision. According to the new Australian formula, for a risk to be material, it is necessary that the patient "would have been *likely seriously to consider and weigh up the risk*" before making a decision.[171]

Moreover, the "materiality" of information should be measured against medical *decisions*. Only the risks that are material to "a decision or course of action",[172] or "the decision-making of a reasonable person",[173] or "a decision on whether to proceed with the treatment",[174] or "deciding whether to submit or not to submit to surgery or treatment",[175] can fall within the scope of disclosure.

The Code's formulation of the scope of information disclosure is a little different from those of overseas jurisdictions. Right 6(1) and (2) impose a proactive duty of information disclosure on providers. Right 6(1) provides that every consumer has the right to the information that "a reasonable consumer, in that consumer's circumstances, would *expect to receive*",[176] even if there is *no treatment decision* to be made. Right 6(2) promulgates that "[b]efore making a choice or giving consent, every

---

(1998) 48 BMLR 118, 124 ("if there is a *significant* risk which would affect the judgment of the reasonable patient, then in the normal course it is the responsibility of a doctor to inform the patient of that *significant* risk, if the information is needed so that the patient can determine for him or herself as to what course he or she should adopt" (emphasis added)); *Fitzpatrick v White* [2008] 3 IR 551, 564 at [35] per Kearns J. ("a risk may be seen as material if, in the circumstances of the particular case, a reasonable person in the patient's position, if warned of the risk, would be likely to *attach significance to* it" (emphasis added)); *Wilkinson v Vessey*, 295 A.2d 676, 689 (R.I. 1972) ("materiality may be said to be "the *significance* a reasonable person, in what the physician knows or should know is his patient's position, would *attach to* the disclosed risk or risks in deciding whether to submit or not to submit to surgery or treatment" (emphasis added)).

[167] *Fitzpatrick v White* [2008] 3 IR 551, 564 at [35] per Kearns J.

[168] *Rogers v Whitaker* (1992) 175 C.L.R. 479, 494 (HCA), per Gaudron J. (the doctor needs to disclose "information that is relevant to a decision or course of action").

[169] *F. v R.* (1983) 33 S.A.S.R 189, 192, per King C.J. (the duty to disclose extends "only to matters which might influence the decisions of a reasonable person in the situation of the patient"). *See also*, *Williams v Golden*, 699 So.2d 102, 107 (La.App. 4 Cir. 1997) ("A physician is required to advise a patient of any material consequences which would *influence* the decision of a reasonable person in the patient's condition." "The second prong … is … to decide whether the probability of that type harm is a risk which a reasonable patient would *consider* in deciding on treatment" (emphasis added)).

[170] *F. v R.* (1983) 33 S.A.S.R 189, 192, per King C.J. (a doctor do not need to disclose risks "which are not sufficiently substantial to be a factor in the decision-making of a reasonable person").

[171] *Rosenberg v Percival* [2001] 205 C.L.R. 434, 459, per Gummow J. (emphasis added).

[172] *Rogers v Whitaker* (1992) 175 C.L.R. 479, 494 (HCA), per Gaudron J.

[173] *F. v R.* (1983) 33 S.A.S.R 189, 192, per King C.J.

[174] *Rosenberg v Percival* [2001] 205 C.L.R. 434, 459, per Gummow J.

[175] *Wilkinson v Vessey*, 295 A.2d 676, 689 (R.I. 1972).

[176] *Health and Disability Commissioner (Code of Health and Disability Services Consumers' Rights) Regulation 1996*, Schedule, Right 6(1) (emphasis added).

consumer has the right to the information that a reasonable consumer, in that consumer's circumstances, *needs* to make an informed choice or give informed consent."[177]

Two distinctions could be drawn between the formulations of Right 6(1) and (2).[178] First, they adopt different words ("expect to receive" and "needs to make an informed choice") in describing the potential scope of information disclosure. It is arguable that information that a patient "expects" and "needs" may be broader than information that is "material" to his medical decision. The thresholds of "expectation" or "need" may be lower than that of "materiality" or "significance".[179] Second, under Right 6(1), a provider has the duty of information disclosure *regardless of whether or not there will be decision-making*. However, under Right 6(2), information disclosure is treated as a condition precedent to a treatment decision (Skegg and Paterson 2006, 40). This strengthens the argument that what the Code envisages is more than simply information that is *material to the patient's decision-making*.[180]

9.6.4 A Two-Pronged Test?

As I mentioned above, Right 6(1) and (2) offer the proactive limb or prong of the duty of information disclosure. Right 6(1) and (2), by asking practitioners to volunteer information, actually articulate a practitioner's proactive duty to inform. That duty targets an objective group of patients ("a reasonable consumer, in that consumer's circumstances").

Right 6(3) declares that every consumer has the right to "honest and accurate answers to questions relating to services".[181] Right 6(3), by asking practitioners to

---

[177] *Health and Disability Commissioner (Code of Health and Disability Services Consumers' Rights) Regulation 1996*, Schedule, Right 6(2) (emphasis added). "Choice" means a decision (a) to receive service; (b) to refuse services; and (c) to withdraw consent to services.

[178] However, it seems that these distinctions are not important in practice, as both provisions are variously cited in Commissioner Opinions. *See,* P.D.G. Skegg and Ron Paterson (General Editors) 2006, 40.

[179] *See*, Joanna Manning 2004, 201 (favouring the Australian formulation about "likely to attach significance to", which is "likely to seriously consider and weigh up the risk before reaching a decision"; noting that "[t]he information does not have to be determinative of the patient's choice, so long as it would have been considered as *reasonably relevant* to that choice; a piece of information that a reasonable patient would have *wanted to consider and weigh in the balance*" (emphasis added)).

[180] *See*, the "list" of the information in Right 6(1) of the Code ("(a) An explanation of [consumer's] condition; and (b) An explanation of the options available, …; and (c) Advice of the estimated time within which the services will be provided; and (d) Notification of any proposed participation in teaching or research, including whether the research requires and has received ethical approval; and (e) Any other information required by legal, professional, ethical, and other relevant standards; and (f) The results of tests; (g) The results of procedures.").

[181] *Health and Disability Commissioner (Code of Health and Disability Services Consumers' Rights) Regulation 1996*, Schedule, Right 6(3).

respond honestly to questions a particular patient may raise, creates a practitioner's reactive duty to inform. The duty is triggered by a particular patient's (subjective) individualized concerns. The duty to answer a patient's inquiries is not governed by the *Bolam* test.[182]

The formulation of the Code was probably influenced by case law (such as the *Smith* case). Right 6(3) only contemplates one, although main, method of a patient's raising concerns – asking questions. It does not explicitly embrace other means of the patient's drawing a practitioner's attention to his concerns. Compared to the *Rogers* test, the Code lacks a more embracing, reactive limb of the duty to inform. However, this insufficiency does not seem to be a fatal flaw in relation to its scope of information disclosure. Two ways could compensate the deficiency: by inviting a more subjective reading on the phrase "in that consumer's circumstances" under Right 6(1) and (2),[183] or by giving a more liberal interpretation about Right 6(3).

9.6.5 *Disclosure of Options/Alternatives*

Like many other jurisdictions, before the era of the Code, New Zealand case law confined the duty to disclose to information about "risks". The Code took advantage of the proactive potential of legislation and extended the ambit of the duty to disclose to cover other information. In formulating the subject matter of disclosure, the Code adopted the very encompassing word "information" rather than "risks".[184]

Right 6(1) gives a list of "information"[185] that a reasonable consumer, in that consumer's circumstances, would expect to receive: (a) An explanation of his condition; (b) *An explanation of the options available*, including an assessment of the expected risks, side effects, benefits, and costs of each option; (c) Advice of the estimated time within which the services will be provided; (d) Notification of any proposed participation in teaching or research, including whether the research requires, and has received, ethical approval; (e) *Any other information required by legal, professional, ethical, and other relevant standards*; (f) The results of tests;

[182] Joanna Manning 2004, 204 (also noting that whether it is an accurate answer will be judged by the Commissioner in the light of responsible medical opinion).

[183] Joanna Manning 2004, 193–194 (quoting with approval Professor Peter Skegg's opinion, arguing that "[t]he closer the focus on the individual circumstances of the particular patient, the closer in practice the test in Right 6 approaches a subjective one"); José Miola 2009, 94 ("[D]espite not containing a subjective element, Right 6 lacks little in comprehensiveness in comparison to *Rogers*.").

[184] *Health and Disability Commissioner (Code of Health and Disability Services Consumers' Rights) Regulation 1996*, Schedule, Right 6(1) and (2).

[185] I agree with Professor Peter Skegg that the "list" is best viewed as a checklist of the kinds of information that should be sometimes provided, and the word "including" is better read as synonymous with "such as". In many circumstances, a reasonable consumer, in that consumer's circumstances, would *not* expect to receive *all* of the information listed in paragraphs (a)–(g) of Right 6(1). *See*, P D G Skegg and Ron Paterson (General Editors) 2006, 212.

and (g) The results of procedures.[186] A patient's questions relating to services may expose a provider to a duty to disclose: (a) The *identity and qualification of the provider*; (b) The *recommendation of the provider*; (c) How to obtain an opinion from another provider; and (d) The result of research.[187] The word "including" that appears in both Right 6(1) and (3) indicates that both lists are not exhaustive. The open-ended nature of the over-arching Right 6 enables the standards of disclosure to develop over time (Manning 2004, 203).

The duty to volunteer information about treatment options is not dependant on the patient asking questions.[188] Under the Code, disclosure of treatment options is high on the list of information that a reasonable consumer can expect to receive. The information that the patient would "expect to receive" includes "[a]n explanation of the options available, including an assessment of the expected risks, side effects, benefits, and costs of each option".[189] Even if this piece of information about "options" is absent from the list, it still has a high potential of falling within the scope of disclosure because of the presence of Right 6(1)(e). Right 6(1)(e) is very embracing: "[a]ny other information required by legal, professional, ethical, and other relevant standards"[190] is included in the provider's legal duty to inform. Functioning very similarly to Right 4(2), it has the *potential* effect of elevating "professional, ethical, and other relevant standards" into legal standards.[191]

Right 4(2) and 6(1)(e) focus on the context of diagnosis/treatment and the context of information disclosure respectively. They shorten the distance between professional, ethical standards and legal standards in both contexts. Many professional guidelines are very open-minded towards information disclosure. They embrace the disclosure of alternatives. New Zealand's is no exception.[192] Even without Right 6(1)(b), applying the requirement of Right 6(1)(e) can attain the goal of embracing disclosure of alternatives.

To embrace disclosure of alternatives within the ambit of the duty to inform, New Zealand takes full advantage of the proactive nature of *legislation*. Legislation

[186] *Health and Disability Commissioner (Code of Health and Disability Services Consumers' Rights) Regulation 1996*, Schedule, Right 6(1)(a)–(g).

[187] *Health and Disability Commissioner (Code of Health and Disability Services Consumers' Rights) Regulation 1996*, Schedule, Right 6(3)(a)–(d).

[188] *See, Opinion 02HDC18414* (Health and Disability Commissioner, 6/4/04) (failure to provide contextualised information), page 14.

[189] *Health and Disability Commissioner (Code of Health and Disability Services Consumers' Rights) Regulation 1996*, Schedule, Right6(1)(b).

[190] *Health and Disability Commissioner (Code of Health and Disability Services Consumers' Rights) Regulation 1996*, Schedule, Right 6(1)(e).

[191] There is a need to realise that the professional and ethical standards "will not always have been drafted with a view to their being used in a legal context". *See*, P.D.G. Skegg and Ron Paterson (General Editors) 2006, 213 (opining that Right 6(1)(e) be read with the opening words of Right 6(1) and clause 3 of the Code).

[192] Medical Council of New Zealand 2002 (reiterating the legal (the Code's) requirements, including Right 6).

can move beyond the common law focus on disclosure of "risks". Legislation can overcome the piecemeal fashion of common law development and allow for a comprehensive formulation of information disclosure. Moreover, by elevating professional and ethical standards to legal standards, the New Zealand Code eradicates or shortens the discrepancies that may be formed between the two standards, and harmonises the standard of care for health practitioners. The New Zealand's approach of embracing disclosure of alternatives by proactive legislation is a better alternative to the Canada's approach of embracing disclosure of alternative treatment options by judiciary's proactive interpretation of the informed consent rule.

9.6.6 Options: "Available"?

The only statutory restriction imposed on the ambit of *options* that fall within the duty to inform is to see if they are "available".[193] The availability of treatment options will be constrained by medical knowledge (including constructive knowledge). To determine the availability of treatment options, a health practitioner should also have regard to the patient's conditions. The circumstances (such as the elective, experimental nature of the proposed treatment and the patient's enquiry) and filters (such as medical knowledge and the patient's condition) that I elaborated in Chap. 4 will apply.[194] Those circumstances and filters can enlarge and narrow the scope of alternatives disclosure. Having said that, it should be noted here that the Code does not involve consideration of causation. Arguably, at the stage of the duty to inform, it even has a lower threshold than that of "materiality". That means that the Code's ambit of information (including alternatives) disclosure may be broader than that envisaged by other jurisdictions. In considering the Code's scope of disclosure, one needs to approach the patient's will and concerns with greater sensitivity. One needs to avoid the risk of blurring the duty and causation.

The availability of one option can be explored from different perspectives – medically, financially, geographically, and even legally. The availability of treatment options may be affected by factors external to medical considerations. Consistent with its liberal tenor, the Code and HDC jurisdiction entertained "alternatives" or "options" in a quite loose fashion. The jurisdiction is very open-minded towards disclosure of geographically, financially unavailable treatment options and alternative provider.

---

[193] *Health and Disability Commissioner (Code of Health and Disability Services Consumers' Rights) Regulation 1996*, Schedule, Right 6(1)(b). *Compare*, Medical Council of New Zealand advises doctors to make themselves aware of all the "reasonable" alternatives. *See*, Medical Council of New Zealand *Information, Choice of Treatment and Consent* (2011), para. 8.

[194] For example, where a procedure is elective and cosmetic, a consumer needs to be told of all the treatment options, the risks, benefits, and likely outcome of each. In situations where the provider wishes to offer an innovative treatment s/he believes is effective, the provider should attempt to present the patient with a clear and balanced summary of the information available. *See*, Joanna Manning 2004, 197–198.

Firstly, showing loyalty to Right 6 of the Code, if *the publicly funded service* was not available to people with the patient's level of need at that time, the provider needs to promptly and clearly inform the patient about *management options*, including the *option of seeking private treatment*, and the risks (if any) of no treatment.[195] According to Right 6(1)(c) of the Code, the estimated time within which services will be provided may fall within a provider's duty to disclose. If warranted, the patient should be given clear and specific advice about the option of seeking *private* assessment and treatment.[196] Conversely, a practitioner should give his patient adequate information about the alternative of treatment in the *public* system.[197] When surgery may be performed in both the public and the private sector, patients should be informed that they have a choice between the two sectors. [198] In providing information about these two options, the surgeon should inform the patient of the estimated waiting times for each sector (where possible) and provide the patient with an indication of the differences between the two systems, for example, whether the patient will have access to the surgeon of choice and the freedom to choose the timing of the surgery, in the public sector.[199]

Secondly, although it is an *obiter* in the HDC opinion, the Commissioner has hinted that "[a]t a time when New Zealand patients are not infrequently referred overseas for medical care (even in the publicly funded system), the information that a reasonable patient in [a patient's] circumstances would expect to receive includes information about treatment options available (albeit in private) *overseas*".[200] It opens the possibility of a provider having a duty to disclose treatment options that is not available in New Zealand, but is available in other jurisdictions.

Thirdly, in the Commissioner's view, "[a] reasonable patient, in [a particular patient's] circumstances, would expect to be informed of [his physician's] *restrictions* and of *alternative management options*, including *the option of having the surgery performed by another surgeon* (whether in private or public)".[201] The duty to inform encompasses disclosure of provider-specific information and the availability of an alternative provider. The types of information a reasonable patient

[195] *Opinion 09HDC00891* (Health and Disability Commissioner, 31/3/2010) (prioritization and management of a patient), pp. 17–18.

[196] *Opinion 04HDC13909* (Health and Disability Commissioner, 4/4/06) (failure to provide accurate information about the expected waiting time).

[197] *Opinion 01/05619* (Health and Disability Commissioner, 31/7/2002) (failure to provide balanced information about alternatives).

[198] *Opinion 03HDC19128* (Health and Disability Commissioner, 14/9/04) (failure to reveal that the provider's practice was subject to restrictions).

[199] *Opinion 03HDC19128* (Health and Disability Commissioner, 14/9/04) (failure to reveal that the provider's practice was subject to restrictions).

[200] *Opinion 02HDC18414* (Health and Disability Commissioner, 6/4/04) (failure to provide contextualised information) (emphasis added).

[201] *Opinion 03HDC19128* (Health and Disability Commissioner, 14/9/04) (failure to reveal that the provider's practice was subject to restrictions) (emphasis added).

may expect to receive include the risk of having a procedure performed at a certain *location* (for example, where fewer back-up services are available) or specific relevant information about having a *particular provider* perform the proposed procedure (for example, where the provider has *limited experience* in performing that procedure, or the provider's practice in that area has been restricted).[202] Health care providers should be honest about their limitations. A provider who does not have an access agreement at the local maternity facility should inform her patient of the reasons for this and the management options available, in particular, the option of immediate transfer to specialist care in hospital.[203]

Theoretically, the provider's duty to disclose the provider-specific information can be drawn from Right 6(1)(b) of the Code, where the "expected risks" of "each option" may fall within the duty to disclose. Arguably, a provider's duty to inform of risks inherent in each option applies not only to the risks inherent in *the proposed treatment* and its alternatives, but also to the risks attaching to *the person or organisation* providing the chosen option, because the latter category of risks forms part of the risks of an option (Manning 2004, 203). A provider's insufficiency in qualifications and experience may expose his patient to additional risks. The relative inexperience of the doctor in the chosen technique is a matter that a reasonable patient would want to know before making a choice to proceed.[204]

According to the Commissioner, such a broad scope of information disclosure is "not intended to place an undue burden on the provider but to support a culture where patients' rights and medical professionalism are protected".[205] The Commissioner reminds that a provider should not underestimate the impact that openness and candour can have on the doctor-patient relationship.[206]

9.6.7 A Doctor's Recommendation and Preferences

Although the main focus of Right 6 is on information disclosure, it is not silent about the issue of recommendations. First, the provision of information about treatment options available includes "an assessment" of both the negative and positive

[202] *Opinion 03HDC19128* (Health and Disability Commissioner, 14/9/04) (failure to reveal that the provider's practice was subject to restrictions). *See also*, HDC opinions *00HDC10159* and *00HDC08628*.

[203] *Opinion 00HDC08628* (Health and Disability Commissioner, 30/7/02) (A provider who did not have an access agreement at the local maternity facility).

[204] *Opinion 08HDC20258* (Health and Disability Commissioner, 11/11/09) (a relatively new procedure).

[205] *Opinion 03HDC19128* (Health and Disability Commissioner, 14/9/04) (failure to reveal that the provider's practice was subject to restrictions).

[206] *Opinion 03HDC19128* (Health and Disability Commissioner, 14/9/04) (failure to reveal that the provider's practice was subject to restrictions).

aspects ("the expected risks, side effects, benefits, and costs") of each option.[207] The practice of a practitioner's just setting out options *without assessment* of risks-benefits of different treatments does not fit comfortably with his proactive duty to inform imposed by Right 6(1). Second, "[t]he recommendation of the provider" is also one of the subject matters of the *reactive duty* to inform.[208] Providers should honestly and accurately answer the questions that the patient raised about the "recommendation of the provider". Even without such provisions, the necessity of a provider's recommendation is also obvious. Selecting, recommending and performing one particular procedure is a part of the treatment process. That is the essence of a health practitioner's work. A health practitioner has *a duty or right* to make recommendations.

According to their professional code of ethics, doctors should recommend only those diagnostic or screening procedures which seem necessary to assist in the care of the patient and only that treatment which seems necessary for the well being of the patient.[209] In some areas of medical practice where the concepts involved in treatment are complex and most consumers will be able to grasp only some of the considerations surrounding the recommended treatment or procedure, it is wise for the doctor to make a specific recommendation based on his experience, although the final choice about whether to accept or reject such a recommendation is the patient's.[210] There are rare occasions when a doctor does not wish to discuss a particular treatment with a patient because that treatment conflicts with the values or beliefs of the doctor. In this case the doctor must inform the patient of this conflict and refer the patient to a doctor who can discuss the currently recommended and accepted treatment options.[211]

The HDC opinions demonstrate a good awareness that a health care provider's preferences may colour his presentation of treatment options. Therefore, they consistently advocate more *balanced* and more *contextualised* information disclosure.

---

[207] *Health and Disability Commissioner (Code of Health and Disability Services Consumers' Rights) Regulation 1996*, Schedule, Right 6(1)(b). For example, in the context of cosmetic procedure where the procedure being carried out is elective and has no medical benefit, and where the consumer often has *heightened expectations* about what can be achieved, it is particularly important that the provider give his patient enough information, both positive and *negative*, at the preoperative consultation to make the patient to have a *realistic expectation* about the final outcome. *See*, *Opinion 07HDC05410* (Health and Disability Commissioner, 28/04/2008) (general surgeon, cosmetic surgery), page 16 (finding that the provider did not give the patient adequate information about the size and extent of scarring involved in a cosmetic procedure, noting that there is an inherent conflict of interests because the surgeon stands to benefit financially if the consumer agrees to proceed it).

[208] *Health and Disability Commissioner (Code of Health and Disability Services Consumers' Rights) Regulation 1996*, Schedule, Right 6(3)(b).

[209] New Zealand Medical Association 2008, page 7, [18].

[210] Barnett Bond "Chapter 11: Informed consent" in Cole's medical practice in New Zealand 2008, page 88.

[211] Barnett Bond "Chapter 11: Informed consent" in Cole's medical practice in New Zealand 2008, page 89.

A patient is entitled to information that fully reflects not only an individual surgeon's own opinion but also the majority opinion within the particular field.[212] The provider's stance that a treatment option was not a realistic option for the patient did not absolve him of his obligation to provide his patient with full information (all the information that a reasonable patient in that patient's circumstances, would expect to receive) to enable him to make an informed choice.[213] A doctor has an obligation to inform his patient of one available treatment option and facilitate discussion regarding this option even if he *disagree* with the viability of this option.[214] Providers have a duty to provide balanced and fair information about the options available to a patient and to subordinate any private interests to the interests of the patient in making informed decisions about their treatment.[215] Providers must take care not to present patients with unbalanced explanations of their condition or options to support their treatment preferences.[216] Doctors have a responsibility to locate their own opinions within the spectrum of professional views about possible procedures, and to contextualise their views, rather than simply preferring their own, which in effect deprives the patient of informed choice.[217]

The developing duty to provide balanced and contextualised information about options indicates an awareness that subtle pressures can be exerted by practitioners on patients to opt for the procedure they recommend (Manning 2004, 198). It provides a potentially important counterweight to any tendencies for practitioners to place their own interests ahead of patients' interests in making informed decisions for themselves about their treatment (Manning 2004, 198).

9.6.8 Minority Treatment Options

As far as the question of what categories of treatment options should fall within the scope of disclosure is concerned, HDC *Opinion 02HDC18414* deserves some time to be noted. It shows that the provider's duty to present balanced and contextualised information not only applies to the context of two *divergent* medical opinions, but also applies to the situation involving the *majority* and *minority* treatment options.

---

[212] *Opinion 01/05619* (Health and Disability Commissioner, 31/7/2002) (failure to provide balanced information about alternatives).

[213] *Opinion 04HDC00031* (Health and Disability Commissioner, 24/2/2005), page 9 (Orthopaedic surgeon's failure to inform his patient of the option he did not favor).

[214] *Opinion 04HDC00031* (Health and Disability Commissioner, 24/2/2005), page 9 (Orthopaedic surgeon's failure to inform his patient of the option he did not favor).

[215] *Opinion 03HDC19128* (Health and Disability Commissioner, 14/9/2004) (failure to reveal that the provider's practice was subject to restrictions).

[216] *Opinion 03HDC19128* (Health and Disability Commissioner, 14/9/2004) (failure to reveal that the provider's practice was subject to restrictions).

[217] *Opinion 04HDC00031* (Health and Disability Commissioner, 24/2/2005), page 9 (Orthopaedic surgeon's failure to inform his patient of the option he did not favor).

The Opinion surprised many doctors in New Zealand because it made a *controversial* treatment option, which was *not widely accepted* by mainstream neurological opinions in both Australia and New Zealand but was available in the private health care system in Australia, to fall with the ambit of a neurosurgeon's duty to disclose.[218] In my view, the surprise was partly due to many doctors' misguided perception that the duty to *offer* treatments and the duty to *disclose* treatments were the same thing.[219]

The Opinion involved a patient diagnosed with brain tumour and two treatment options, namely palliative radiotherapy and aggressive surgery. The neurosurgeon told the patient that he had a terminal condition – a malignant primary glioblastoma – and there was no surgical option "that would make any difference".[220] He offered palliative radiotherapy as the only management option. Although the surgeon was *aware* of the availability of the more aggressive surgery for glioblastomas, he did not favour it because, in his view, the aggressive surgery "has never been shown to prolong longevity significantly and has certainly never been shown to be curative".[221] It was acknowledged that the prognosis associated with glioblastomas is very poor – they are resistant to all known forms of treatment (chemotherapy, radiotherapy and surgery) and a wider excision of the tumour carries an increased and significant risk of hemiparesis.[222] The neurosurgeon would *not perform* radical surgery for the patient because of fear of damaging him by causing paralysis. The patient did *not ask* the surgeon about the option of surgery.

The patient and his family searched the internet for information about glioblastomas. It was through the help of their friends and the media that he found out that the aggressive surgery was the best option for his type of tumour.[223] The patient travelled to Australia and underwent a surgical resection of the tumour there.[224] Later on, the patient had undergone operations for several times because of recurrence of glioblastoma. The patient survived nearly 2 years from the date of the first surgery

---

[218] Tim Dare *et al.* 2010, 263–264 (describing the case as "striking").

[219] The National Advisory Committee on Health and Disability (New Zealand) 2006, page 12–13 (some clinicians read this case as patients giving them pressure to "consider" interventions for which they didn't feel there was strong evidence; "Some clinicians expressed concern about the *potential conflict* between making *information* on new interventions available to patients and *providing* quality care in a setting of constrained resources" (emphasis added)).

[220] *Opinion 02HDC18414* (Health and Disability Commissioner, 6/4/04) (failure to provide contextualised information), page 3.

[221] *Opinion 02HDC18414* (Health and Disability Commissioner, 6/4/04) (failure to provide contextualised information), page 4.

[222] *Opinion 02HDC18414* (Health and Disability Commissioner, 6/4/04) (failure to provide contextualised information), page 12.

[223] *Opinion 02HDC18414* (Health and Disability Commissioner, 6/4/04) (failure to provide contextualised information), page 6.

[224] The Australian surgeon informed the patient that surgery was certainly not curative and there is no good scientific evidence to suggest that further resection of the tumour would necessarily increase his life span. *See, Opinion 02HDC18414* (Health and Disability Commissioner, 6/4/04) (failure to provide contextualised information), page 7.

performed by the Australian surgeon. The complainant – the patient's wife – claimed that the surgery improved the patient's quality of life and prolonged his life.[225]

On a television programme, the Australian surgeon hinted that the surgery could be done in New Zealand funded by the public health system. The New Zealand provider/neurosurgeon admitted that radical surgery is performed in neurosurgical units in public hospitals and in private institutions when it is deemed safe and beneficial to the patient.[226]

The HDC found that the extent of tumour resection in glioblastomas and its role in prolonging survival was controversial.[227] There was a *divergence of opinions* whether radical surgery significantly prolongs longevity and whether the risks associated with radical surgery outweigh the potential benefits. The practice of radical excision of glioblastomas was *not widely accepted* in Australia and New Zealand.

What prompted the complainants – the patient and his wife – to submit the complaint is that they felt angry that the providers did not offer them the option of further surgery or raise it as a possibility, and they had to learn about the surgical treatment via a television current affairs programme.[228]

Realising that the controversies surrounded the disputed surgery, in this case, the Commissioner made it clear that his function is not to comment on the merits and benefits of different medical procedures, but to read and interpret the Code.[229] In interpreting Right 6(1)(b) of the Code, the Commissioner embraced the notion that a doctor's recommending and performing a procedure and a doctor's disclosing treatment options are two different contexts. In the view of the Commissioner, while it would not be reasonable to expect the surgeon *to offer or perform* a procedure that he did not believe was a viable option, he needed to *raise the option of further surgery*, which he *knew* to be *a viable option*, and *explain* why he thought the risks outweighed any potential benefit.[230] In the opinion of the Commissioner, the neurosurgeon had an obligation to inform the patient of the option of surgery and to facilitate discussion of the feasibility of that option, *even if he did not recommend it or was unwilling to perform it himself.*[231] By failing to provide full and contextualised

[225] *Opinion 02HDC18414* (Health and Disability Commissioner, 6/4/04) (failure to provide contextualised information), page 9.

[226] *Opinion 02HDC18414* (Health and Disability Commissioner, 6/4/04) (failure to provide contextualised information), page 8.

[227] *Opinion 02HDC18414* (Health and Disability Commissioner, 6/4/04) (failure to provide contextualised information), page 15.

[228] *Opinion 02HDC18414* (Health and Disability Commissioner, 6/4/04) (failure to provide contextualised information), page 9–10. In their view, the provider made a choice for them, and it was up to the patient to make the decision of whether or not to undergo surgery.

[229] *Opinion 02HDC18414* (Health and Disability Commissioner, 6/4/04) (failure to provide contextualised information), page 15.

[230] *Opinion 02HDC18414* (Health and Disability Commissioner, 6/4/04) (failure to provide contextualised information), page 12.

[231] *Opinion 02HDC18414* (Health and Disability Commissioner, 6/4/04) (failure to provide contextualised information), page 14.

information, the health care provider deprived the patient and his family of the opportunity to weigh the very limited options for themselves.[232]

Although acknowledging that the prognosis associated with glioblastomas was very poor, the neurosurgeon may deem that radical surgery was *not a realistic option* for his patient, and this stance may be consistent with *mainstream opinion* in New Zealand, the Commissioner observed that *a surgeon's stance* that one option is *not a realistic option for his patient's condition* does not absolve him of his obligation to provide his patient with full information that a reasonable patient in his patient's circumstances would expect to receive about alternative treatment options.[233] The fact that the patient is a general practitioner does not affect his Code right to the information that an "ordinary" patient would expect.[234] Health care providers have a responsibility to locate their own opinions within the spectrum of professional views about possible procedures and to contextualise their recommendations, rather than simply "announce" their stance.[235]

9.6.9 Innovative Treatment Options

According to Right 6 of the Code, a patient who is subjected to an experimental or innovative treatment is entitled to receive the information that a reasonable patient would expect to receive in the circumstances. That information may include the fact that the procedure is new, and experimental or innovative, and/or it is unorthodox and not generally approved of by medical profession, and/or the effectiveness and attendant risks of the proposed innovative treatment, compared with conventional alternatives.[236] A reasonable patient would expect to receive the information that the majority of practitioners in the field would not perform the procedure that the provider recommends in the circumstances.[237] If a patient is choosing between evidence-based medicine and innovative treatments for which there is no scientific evidence, the doctor should attempt to present to the patient a clear and balanced summary of the *scientific information* available.[238] The requirement of providing

[232] *Opinion 02HDC18414* (Health and Disability Commissioner, 6/4/04) (failure to provide contextualised information), page 13.

[233] *Opinion 02HDC18414* (Health and Disability Commissioner, 6/4/04) (failure to provide contextualised information), page 12.

[234] *Opinion 02HDC18414* (Health and Disability Commissioner, 6/4/04) (failure to provide contextualised information), pages 13–14 (noting that the patient, a general practitioner, saw the neurosurgeon in his specialist capacity; raising the argument that, given the particular circumstance of the patient's being a general practitioner, even greater information disclosure was required).

[235] *Opinion 02HDC18414* (Health and Disability Commissioner, 6/4/04) (failure to provide contextualised information), pages 12–13.

[236] *Opinion 08HDC20258* (Health and Disability Commissioner, 11/11/09) (a relatively new procedure); P.D.G. Skegg and Ron Paterson (eds) 2006, 139.

[237] *Opinion 01HDC05619* (Health and Disability Commissioner, 31/07/02) (Hepatobiliary Surgeon).

[238] Medical Council of New Zealand *Information, Choice of Treatment and Informed Consent* (2011), para. 18.

patients with balanced and contextualised information is especially important in a situation involving innovative or complementary therapies.[239] If we draw a fine distinction between the issue of a practitioner's duty to *inform* when *proposing an innovative treatment* and that of a practitioner's duty to *inform about an innovative treatment*, we find that, like the status of law in other jurisdictions, there is a paucity of Commissioner opinions on the latter issue, although the legal principles about the former issue has been well-established.

9.6.10 The Opening Words of Right 6(1) and Clause 3

Right 6(1) of the Code begins with the words "Every consumer has the right to the information that a reasonable consumer in that consumer's circumstances, would expect to receive, including – ", followed by a list of the information that may fall within a provider's duty to inform. These opening words were absent in the Draft Code (Skegg and Paterson 2006, 211). Their presence at the beginning of Right 6(1) in the Code signifies that it qualifies all that follows (Skegg and Paterson 2006, 212). That means a provider has a duty to disclose only the information that "a reasonable consumer in that consumer's circumstances, would expect to receive", not all of the information listed in paragraphs (a)–(g) of Right 6(1).

Adding these opening words to Right 6(1) has the effect of either restricting or broadening the scope of information disclosure. It leaves the Commissioner the task of exploring, in circumstances of a particular case, what "a reasonable consumer in that consumer's circumstances, would expect to receive", when deciding whether a piece of information falls with a provider's duty to disclose. Some "circumstances", such as a practitioner's lack of both actual and constructive knowledge about a piece of information, may warrant the information not being disclosed (Skegg and Paterson 2006, 212). However, other "circumstances", such as the fact that a consumer has a much-greater-than-average concern about a particular piece of information, may enlarge the duty to disclose (Skegg and Paterson 2006, 213). This line of observation also applies to Right 6(2), where a similar line of words ("a reasonable consumer, in that consumer's circumstances, needs") is embraced.

The phrase "a reasonable consumer/patient, in the consumer/patient's circumstances/position" is popular among common law jurisdictions, when formulating the standard for information disclosure. It is not unique in New Zealand. As I demonstrated in Chap. 2, it has been adopted in many other jurisdictions when formulating the patient-oriented standard of information disclosure, such as the *Rogers* test in Australia. What the New Zealand's Code distinctively offers is its use of the word "information" and its embracing a long and non-exhaustive list of information when adopting the phrase "a reasonable consumer/patient, in the consumer/patient's circumstances/position", rather than restricting the information that falls within a

[239] Joanna Manning 2004, 197–198 (noting that giving balanced information "has obvious significance for providers of complementary or innovative therapies").

duty to disclose only to "risks". That creates the *potential* that a wide range of information, including information about treatment options, *may* fall within what "a reasonable consumer in that consumer's circumstances" would "expect to receive" or "needs". It opens the door or *possibility* for the information about treatment options falling within a provider's *legal* duty to inform, although that information does not always fall within the ambit of a provider's duty of disclosure in every case or under every circumstance. It requires a flexible, fact-driven, circumstance-oriented and context-based explanation of the scope of information disclosure, rather than a blanket, all-or-nothing, and bright-line approach to the scope of information disclosure.

The phrase "a reasonable consumer in the consumer's circumstances" has both an objective limb ("a reasonable consumer") and a subjective limb ("in the consumer circumstances"). It points to the need for, in the context of the Code, the Commissioner to feel the "expectation" and "need" from a consumer/patient's perspective. It is the third-party (the Commissioner) who, with the help of medical expert opinions (but not exclusively relying on them), and looking at information from a (particular) patient's perspective rather than a doctor's, decides whether a piece of information falls within a doctor's duty to disclose. It confers great discretion in the hands of the Commissioner (Skegg and Paterson 2006, 213).

In comparison with Right 6(1) and (2), which invite consideration of *the "reasonableness" of a patient* when defining the potential scope of information disclosure, Clause 3 of the Code, which is entitled "provider compliance", draws the Commissioner's attention to the *"reasonableness" of a provider's actions* before concluding that there is a breach of the Code. It provides that "[a] provider is not in breach of [the] Code if the provider has taken *reasonable actions* in the *circumstances* to give effect to the rights, and comply with the duties, in [the] Code."[240] The "circumstances" means "all the relevant circumstances, including the consumer's clinical circumstances and the provider's resource constraints."[241] The introduction of Clause 3 into the Code was attempted to address the concern that, in the real world, providers do not have unlimited funding, many consumers compete each other for the available time, space and funding, and therefore there should be a limit on a provider's duty to give full effect to all the rights of all consumers (Skegg and Paterson 2006, 46–47).

The New Zealand's practice of attaching a "reasonable actions" defence to the patients' rights, including a patient's right to be fully informed, reminds me of the Australian effort to tame the pro-patient rule, such as the *Rogers* test, by clarifying that the content and scope of the duty to inform should not be looked at solely from the point of view of the patient. It was alerted that the nature of the duty is "a duty to take *reasonable* care to inform", and that considerations should be given to the

[240] Clause 3(1) of the Code (emphasis added).

[241] Clause 3(3) of the Code. Other relevant circumstances might include abusive behaviour that thwarts effective "history taking" during a consultation, or withholding information the consumer knows to be relevant. *See*, P.D.G. Skegg and Ron Paterson (General Editors) 2006, 48.

situations of the practitioner.[242] This qualification may help to reassure doctors that the law does not require of them unrealistic standards of behaviour (Commonwealth of Australia 2002, 47, para. 3.46). Despite that, the Review Panel emphasised that "the information that the doctor must take reasonable care to provide is the information necessary to enable *the patient* to give informed consent, not the information that the reasonable doctor would consider necessary for this purpose" (Commonwealth of Australia 2002, 47–48, para. 3.47 (emphasis added)).

The Australian "reasonable care" qualification was raised and talked about in the context of tort, or in the framework of negligence, where the "reasonableness" test dominates in establishing the standard of care. It addressed the concern that personal injury damages had become financially unsustainable (Parker 2003, 136. *See also*, Commonwealth of Australia 2002, ix.). Compared to that, New Zealand's "reasonable actions" qualification is introduced in a Code, which is rights-oriented, distinct from the context of accident compensation and characterised with low thresholds for Commissioner's intervention and low-level complaint resolution mechanisms. Another difference is that one of main concerns the New Zealand Code addresses is resource constraints rather than controlling injury damages.

How to reconcile the patient-right-advocating nature of the whole Code, especially the patient-oriented standard of information disclosure, with the provider-oriented nature of Clause 3? On the one hand, played as a contrast and complement to the New Zealand's no-fault accident compensation (ACC) scheme, which is compensation-oriented, focuses on community responsibility and cultivates a learning culture rather than a blaming culture, the Code is basically fault-based, individual-accountability-focused and deterrence-aimed. Ordinary negligence on the part of health practitioners should be present to invoke the Commissioner's response. That justifies the consideration of "reasonableness" of a health practitioner's behaviour in the Code context.[243] The Code already removes the need of the Commissioner considering "causation" and "damage" in weighing whether there is a breach of the Code, the hurdle of "negligence" is sincerely needed to prevent the practice of defensive medicine and the effect of overkilling from occurring.

On the other hand, however, remembering that there is a distinction between diagnosis/treatment and information disclosure, as this book argued for consistently, I always wonder whether Clause 3 applies comfortably to the contexts of both provision of diagnosis/treatment and information disclosure. I admit that Clause 3 has great value in the context of provision of services (diagnosis and treatment). For example, as I pointed out in Chap. 7, the reality that health care resources are

---

[242] Commonwealth of Australia 2002, page 47, para. 3.44 (emphasis added). Legislation followed the Panel's recommendations. For example, Section 50 of *Wrongs Act 1958* (Vic) provides that "A person (the defendant) who owes a duty of care to another person (the plaintiff) to give a warning or other information to the plaintiff in respect of a risk or other matter, satisfies that duty of care if the defendant takes *reasonable care* in giving that warning or other information" (emphasis added).

[243] *See*, Right 4(1) of the Code ("Every consumer has the right to have services provided with *reasonable care and skill*" (emphasis added)). It reflects the common law standard of care in negligence.

limited requires that a doctor's provision of services should be resource-conscious. Clause 3 provides a justification for resource-conscious delivery of public health care. I also admit that Clause 3 is a good place to host the *exceptions* to the duty to inform, such as "therapeutic privilege",[244] emergency, the patient's waiver, the undisclosed information already falling within the patient's knowledge, and a provider's lack of actual and constructive knowledge about the undisclosed information. However, I am suspecting the soundness of Clause 3 compromising, undermining and qualifying the *duty to disclose information* about what a reasonable patient, in the patient's circumstances, "would expect to receive" and "needs". We should show hesitancy to allow that.

For example, Clause 3 does not make a distinction between the context of diagnosis/treatment and that of information disclosure in formulating the qualifier of "resource constraints".[245] As I argued in Chap. 7, there is a need to differentiate information disclosure from diagnosis/treatment in the law's responding to the cost-containment feature of health care. In the context of diagnosis and treatment, a doctor's practice should be cost-conscious and cost-effective. However, in the context of information disclosure, resource constraints should not be allowed to excuse doctors from presenting available treatment options, including those that are unavailable because of cost-containment considerations.

In New Zealand, even in the context of diagnosis and treatment, the Commissioner has showed some degree of reluctance to accept the defence of "resource constraints" too readily.[246] In the context of information disclosure, scholars,[247] the

[244] P.D.G. Skegg and Ron Paterson (General Editors) 2006, 48 (noting that the provider's duty to provide information might in practice be reduced if there was a significant risk that the consumer's health would be directly and detrimentally affected if the information was provided).

[245] The situation is very similar in the context of ACC. *See, Injury Prevention, Rehabilitation, and Compensation Act 2001*, s 32(2)(b). The New Zealand *Injury Prevention, Rehabilitation, and Compensation Amendment Act* excludes "personal injury that is solely attributable to a resource allocation decision" from cover. That means injury resulting from lack of access to treatment or timely treatment because of resource decisions will not result in cover. Only if a resource allocation decision is the *sole or only* reason for treatment being unavailable or delayed, which itself results in injury or death, does the exclusion apply. The exclusion would not apply to situations where an injury was caused by a resource allocation decision *in conjunction with* a clinical decision (a "mixed" decision). "Treatment" not only encompasses provision of treatments and failure to provide treatment, or to provide treatment in a timely manner, but also embraces information disclosure and obtaining or failing to obtain informed consent. *See, Injury Prevention, Rehabilitation, and Compensation Act 2001*, s 33(1)(a) (b) (c) (d) (e).

[246] Where scarcity of resources is involved, an organisational provider may need to show it took at least some steps to give effect to the consumer's rights, and made some attempt to bring the shortage of resources to the attention of management or the relevant funding agency. In dealing with the issue of the understaffing of the emergency department, the Commissioner has chosen to find the district health board vicariously liable for the breach, rather than accepting the Clause 3 defence in relation to the register. *See*, P.D.G. Skegg and Ron Paterson (General Editors) 2006, 47–49.

[247] R.J. Paterson 1998, 583 (observing that medical decision-making/recommendation and disclosure are two different contexts).

Commissioner opinion[248] and the professional standard[249] have acknowledged the need for doctors to present patients with full information, including information about treatment options unavailable in publicly-funded health care system. By virtue of Right 4(2) of the Code, a *professional* duty to inform about treatment options unavailable in publicly-funded health care system has the potential of being elevated into a *legal* duty. All of these indicate the need to exercise caution when invoking Clause 3 in the context of disclosure of treatment options.

9.7 CAM, Conventional Medicine and Disclosure of Alternatives

9.7.1 CAM Practitioners

The Code applies to CAM practitioners.[250] A CAM practitioner can be a health care provider since he provides or holds himself out as providing health services to the public. To carry out their duties under the Code, CAM practitioners have the same

[248] *Opinion 09HDC00891* (Health and Disability Commissioner, 31/3/2010) (prioritization and management of a patient). In this Opinion, the Commissioner hinted that Right 4 (right to services of an appropriate standard) and Right 6 (right to be fully informed) of the Code have different remits. In a context where insufficiency of public funding necessitates prioritisation of patients, Right 4 required providers to appropriately assess and prioritise a patient's level of need using relevant standards and/or guidelines. However, under the Right 6 of the Code, if the publicly funded service was not available to people with the patient's level of need at that time, the provider needs to promptly and clearly inform the patient about: (1) the decision and *reasons* for it; (2) the need to monitor her condition and notify the DHB if any deterioration; and (3) *management options*, including the *option of seeking private treatment*, and the risks (if any) of no treatment.

[249] In the opinion of Medical Council of New Zealand, where there are delays in the publicly funded health system and the public system is not the only avenue for treatment, the doctor should also advise the patient where services may be obtained privately. When a decision has been made by the funder not to fund a specific service, what the Council expects doctors to do is: (1) Doctors who are placed in a position where they are unable to provide a preferred treatment are advised to inform the patient what the preferred treatment involves, what the next best option is and what this next best option involves. (2) Where possible, doctors should outline the rationale for treatment being limited or denied. Where the reasons have dimensions that go beyond the technical expertise of the doctor to resolve, the doctor should instead refer the patient to the funding or responsible agency for an explanation. *See*, Medical Council of New Zealand 2008, [25]–[28], [32].

[250] *Health and Disability Commissioner Act 1994* (NZ), s 3. *See also*, *Opinion 97HDC9933* (Health and Disability Commissioner) (a homeopath); *Opinion 97HDC4036* (Health and Disability Commissioner) (a naturopath); *Opinion 98HDC14193* (Health and Disability Commissioner, 7/1/2000) (Massage Therapist); *Opinion 04HDC17805* (Health and Disability Commissioner, 8/11/2005) (Massage Therapist); *Opinion 06HDC09882* (Health and Disability Commissioner, 25/1/2007) (Natural Therapies Practitioner); *Opinion 06HDC12937* (Health and Disability Commissioner, 21/6/2007) (Massage Practitioner); *Opinion 07HDC12714* (Health and Disability Commissioner, 31/1/2008) (Acupuncturist); *Opinion 07HDC20616* (Health and Disability Commi-ssioner, 24/6/2008) (Chiropractor); *Opinion 08HDC00218* (Health and Disability

duty to inform their patient of the risks and side effects of their CAM treatments,[251] and any other information required by legal, professional, ethical, and other relevant standards.[252]

The Code keeps a critical eye on a patient's foregoing conventional medicine treatments in favour of CAM therapies. A CAM practitioner should act very carefully not to alienate patients from seeking help from conventional therapies. Faced with a patient who had an adamant aversion to seeking conventional medical treatment, a CAM practitioner should not inappropriately raise the patient's healing expectations about the CAM treatment, should always have conventional treatments in mind, should frequently and regularly make the patient aware of the risks and benefits of continuing the CAM treatment and the ready availability of the conventional medical treatment options, particularly when it becomes apparent that the patient's condition is not responding to the CAM treatment.

That is what led to *Opinion 08HDC00218*.[253] The Opinion involved a life-threatening condition – cancer. The patient already knew the availability of conventional medical treatments, but did not opt for them. The Opinion allowed some room for a try of alternative therapies when a patient, out of fear or out of her own value or

---

Commissioner, 16/12/2008) (Alternative therapy – Bioptron light therapy). Actions of CAM practitioners also fall within the jurisdiction of Human Rights Review Tribunal. *See*, *Director of Health and Disability Proceedings v A* [2003] NZHRRT 35 (1 December 2003) (an acupuncturist and practitioner of traditional Chinese medicine); *Director of Health and Disability Proceedings v DG* [2005] NZHRRT 2 (25 February 2005) (a practitioner of traditional Chinese medicine); *Director of Health and Disability Proceedings v D G* [2005] NZHRRT 3 (25 February 2005) (a practitioner of traditional Chinese medicine).

[251] *Opinion 07HDC12714* (Health and Disability Commissioner, 31/1/2008) (Acupuncturist's failure to warn the risks of coughing when the patient had needles in her back); *Opinion 97HDC9933* (Health and Disability Commissioner) (a homeopath's lack of recording and failure to provide information about possible side effects of a homeopathic remedy). However, information disclosure about the "risks, side effects, benefits" of treatment options is mainly formulated in the context of orthodox/conventional medicine. It remains questionable whether Right 6 can be applied smoothly and comfortably to the context of CAM. More and more people realise that clinical trials are not suitable to CAM. Should CAM providers give patients a clear risk-benefit analysis when CAMs are poorly researched?

[252] *Opinion 97HDC4036* (Health and Disability Commissioner) (a naturopath, a deviation from the usual instructions on the product label was required due to the child's age and feeding requirements, failure to provide information about how to administer a naturopathic remedy).

[253] *Opinion 08HDC00218* (Health and Disability Commissioner, 16/12/2008) (Alternative therapy – Bioptron light therapy – A patient with breast cancer initially being resistant to pursuing conventional treatment (mastectomy plus chemotherapy)). In that Opinion, the patient (then aged 44) was diagnosed with cancer in her right breast. A breast surgeon advised the need of a mastectomy. The patient wanted to pursue alternative therapies even after being warned that there was no guarantee of a cure. The provider ran a Bioptron light therapy clinic. On her first encounter with the provider, the patient informed the provider of her diagnosis of breast cancer and her decision against having conventional medical treatment. The provider tried persuading her to reconsider her decision and told her of a successful case where a breast cancer patient combined chemotherapy with Bioptron light therapy. Despite this, the patient remained "adamant" against having medical treatment.

lifestyle, adamantly refused to pursue conventional treatments. However, it did not allow the provider to alienate the patient from conventional medical treatments. The Opinion imposes on a CAM practitioner a duty to inform the patient of both the risks-benefits of the proposed therapies and available options.[254]

It needs to be noted that the Opinion was concerned with a cancer patient, and the conventional medical cancer treatments (such as surgery, chemotherapy) were more ready to fall within a person's knowledge, and the provider knew the existence and availability of conventional options. If CAM practitioners have not been subjected to good professional regulation and education, and the information about conventional medical treatments and their risks-benefits is not within their knowledge, do the practitioners still have a duty to disclose those information? Should a CAM provider present patients with balanced and contextualised information, such as information about available conventional medicine options? Are the Code's requirements attainable for CAM providers, especially in a context where CAMs are not well researched, and CAM providers are not well regulated and are not well educated?

The requirement to present balanced and contextualised information mainly targets providers of *innovative/experimental* treatments and *CAM* providers. It is good to require providers to present with patients full and balanced information about treatment options, especially when the proposed therapy does not have good evidence base and the more evidence-based alternatives are readily available. However, contextualised information disclosure needs knowledge. To secure that knowledge, requiring CAM practitioners to have high quality education about conventional medicine and CAM, and subjecting them to a high level of professional regulation are necessary.

Applying the opening words of Right 6(1) to a CAM provider's duty to inform would lead to the conclusion that, in a context where CAM practitioners are not rigorously regulated, are not allowed to practise conventional medicine and are ill-informed about conventional medicine, conventional medicine treatment options may not fall within a CAM provider's duty to inform, because the information is not what "a reasonable patient, in the patient's circumstances" would "expect" him to provide. In addition, a CAM provider can invoke Clause 3 of the Code as a defence to allegation that he does not inform a patient of conventional medicine treatment options, claiming that he has taken "reasonable actions in the circumstances" to comply with the duties. In my opinion, allowing CAM practitioners to confine their duty to inform only to their CAM treatments is not attractive. Subjecting them to rigorous regulation and requiring them to provide information about conventional medicine treatment options is a preferred option.

---

[254] *Opinion 08HDC00218* (Health and Disability Commissioner, 16/12/2008) (Alternative therapy – Bioptron light therapy), pages 14–15 (noting that when suggesting or recommending alternative therapies, such as CAA tablets, liver tonic and plantain leaves, the provider should present the patient with an explanation of the options available and an assessment of the risks, benefits, and costs of those therapies).

9.7.2 Dual Practitioners

New Zealand law gives latitude to medical practitioners to adopt CAM therapies.[255] Sometimes the problem for a dual practitioner is that he may fall too much in love with unorthodox medicine and ignore his status as a conventional medicine practitioner or a registered medical practitioner. It is essential for a dual practitioner to recognise that "there are limits both to conventional and alternative wisdom", and to "intelligently use his or her knowledge of both, not treating either as totally superior to the other."[256] "[I]t will seldom if ever be the case that an alternative belief can be accepted as overriding all conventional medical science."[257] Patients may expect that dual practitioners would have "the best of both worlds".[258]

[255] In the New Zealand's *Health Practitioners Competence Assurance Act*, there is subsection which is called Hippocratic Clause or "homeopathic clause". *See*, *The Health Practitioners Competence Assurance Act 2003* (NZ), s 100(4) ("No person may be found guilty of *a disciplinary offence* under this Part *merely because* that person has adopted and practiced any *theory of medicine* or healing if, in doing so, the person has acted *honestly and in good faith*" (emphasis added)). It allows some measure of freedom for individual practitioners to choose what they believed to be the best thing for their patients. The stance of Medical Council of New Zealand towards CAM has changed a lot in the past few years. *Compare*, Medical Council of New Zealand *Statement on Complementary and Alternative Medicine* (2011), para. [3] ("When complementary and alternative medicines (CAM) have demonstrated benefits for the patient and have minimal risks, and patients have made an informed choice and given their informed consent, Council does not oppose their use."), and para. [4] (acknowledging s 100(4) of *the Health Practitioners Competence Assurance Act 2003* (NZ)); *with* Medical Council of New Zealand *Guidelines on Complementary, Alternative or Unconventional Medicine* (April 1999) ("There can obviously be no similar waiver for doctors whose practices show incompetence as judged by the standards of the Colleges and Societies the Medical Council uses as referral bodies, or as judged by the Medical Council itself, even if the incompetence arises from 'the adoption in good faith of a particular theory of medicine or healing'."). However, New Zealand medical practitioners should be cautious about adopting too liberal an interpretation of the clause. *See*, *Tizard v Medical Council of New Zealand* Unreported, High Court, Auckland, M. NO. 2390/91, 10 December 1992, Barker, Thorp and Smellie J.J. ("[W] hile several have seen 'theory of medicine' exceptions as being intended to provide room for minority views, no decision has recognized the idiosyncratic view of a single practitioner, unsupported by scientific proof or by a significant number of his or her fellow practitioners, as 'a theory of medicine'."); *Re Gorringe* 5/8/03, Medical Practitioners Disciplinary Tribunal (New Zealand) Decision No. 237/02/89D, available at www.mpdt.org.nz, para. [35], [36] (observing that "honest belief in the efficacy of a particular theory is not necessarily a sufficient answer").

[256] *Tizard v Medical Council of New Zealand* Unreported, High Court, Auckland, M. NO. 2390/91, 10 December 1992, Barker, Thorp and Smellie J.J. *See also*, *Re Gorringe* 5/8/03, Medical Practitioners Disciplinary Tribunal (New Zealand) Decision No. 237/02/89D, available at www.mpdt.org.nz, para. [36].

[257] *Tizard v Medical Council of New Zealand* Unreported, High Court, Auckland, M. NO. 2390/91, 10 December 1992, Barker, Thorp and Smellie J.J.

[258] *Re Gorringe* 5/8/03, Medical Practitioners Disciplinary Tribunal (New Zealand) Decision No. 237/02/89D, available at www.mpdt.org.nz, para. [86]. The *Re Gorringe* decision was concerned with a "dual" practitioner, who was educated in both science and conventional medicine, and was a registered medical practitioner, holding a current practising certificate. The patients alleged that

In New Zealand, a dual practitioner will run some legal risks if he confines his practice and the scope of information disclosure only to non-conventional practices. A dual practitioner should inform his patients of (1) treatment options available, *including conventional options*; (2) *the non-conventional nature of alternative treatments*; (3) the risks, benefits and efficacy of the various treatment options; including the purpose of, risks, benefits and efficacy of the non-conventional treatment options.[259] The purpose for imposing such a wide range of disclosure is to equip the patients with balanced information so that they can assess the comparative worth or values of non-conventional diagnosis and treatments as against conventional treatments. A dual practitioner should not hide information about the material risks of alternative medicine treatment and the existence of other options, even if the practitioner has a strong belief in the likely benefits of the treatment and his ability to perform it efficiently and safely.[260] No such strong beliefs can justify the failure to provide the patient with relevant information which he was entitled to, and needed, before he could make an informed choice as to whether to undergo the treatment which was being offered.[261] A doctor who chooses to recommend an unproved treatment ahead of one with proved effectiveness (or one that is regarded as orthodox) must be prepared to argue, with evidence, that the unproved treatment is safe, that the patient is not harmed by withholding the standard therapy, and that the patient is fully informed and consents.[262]

---

the reason they approached the practitioner was because he was "a medical practitioner" practising homeopathy. The Tribunal agreed that the practitioner was practising and held himself out to the public as a dual practitioner in conventional medicine and complementary remedies.

[259] *Re Gorringe* 5/8/03, Medical Practitioners Disciplinary Tribunal (New Zealand) Decision No. 237/02/89D, available at www.mpdt.org.nz, para. [52] ("where a registered medical practitioner practices '*alternative*' or '*complementary*' medicine, there is an onus on that practitioner to inform the patient not only of the nature of the alternative treatment offered but also the extent to which that is consistent with conventional theories of medicine and has, or does not have, the support of the majority of practitioners. "). The *Gorringe* decision involved allegations of breach of the informed consent rules. It was alleged that (1) the practitioner carried out a non-conventional diagnostic technique, without giving an adequate explanation of it, particularly without advising his patient of "its advantages and disadvantages when compared to conventional and generally recognised diagnostic investigatory techniques" and of the degree to which the technique had been "scientifically evaluated for efficacy" as a diagnostic tool; (2) the practitioner provided and/or arranged to be provided various non-conventional treatments and required his patient to forego conventional medical treatment, without advising his patient of the risks, benefits and efficacy of the treatment options, including the purpose of, risks, benefits and efficacy of the non-conventional treatment. It was found that the practitioner did not respond adequately to his patients' questions, offering his patients "very brief and insubstantial answers". *See also*, Medical Council of New Zealand *Statement on Complementary and Alternative Medicine* (2011) paras [12]–[13] (adopting the *Gorringe* rule).

[260] *Re Jackson* 15/12/1999, Medical Practitioners Disciplinary Tribunal (New Zealand) Decision No. 103/99/49D (a general practitioner using manipulative therapy), para. [8], available at www.mpdt.org.nz.

[261] *Re Jackson* 15/12/1999, Medical Practitioners Disciplinary Tribunal (New Zealand) Decision No. 103/99/49D (a general practitioner using manipulative therapy) para. [13], available at www.mpdt.org.nz.

[262] Ian St George "Chapter 19: The doctor who uses complementary and alternative medicine practices" in Cole's Medical Practice in New Zealand 2008, page [138].

The reasons for expanding the dual practitioner's duty of disclosure to cover conventional medicine perspectives are that: (1) the practitioner was practising and held out as a dual practitioner in both conventional and alternative medicine; (2) the practitioner "must be well aware of the possibility that patients consult them to get 'the best of both worlds' and to avoid those aspects of alternative medicine which are extreme or incredible"[263]; (3) where alternative remedies are offered by a registered medical practitioner, "it is difficult to escape the conclusion that the patient derives considerable assurance from the fact that the practitioner is so registered"[264]; (4) the persons who suffer from chronic complaints or conditions for which no simple cure is available are more readily exploited because they are often willing to undergo any treatment which is proffered as a cure. The faith which such persons place in practitioners offering alternative remedies largely depends on the credibility with which such practitioners present themselves.[265]

In the context of the Code, consistent with the legal requirements imposed on pure conventional medicine practitioners, dual practitioners should also overcome their personal preferences in mentioning treatment options. It is essential that a dual practitioner provide balanced and complete information about options. If a medical practitioner wants to include a holistic/spiritual approach into patient management, he should discuss with his patient all appropriate management options, including conventional treatment options, avoiding weighing too heavily in favour of the holistic/spiritual approach.[266] If the orientation of a practice departs significantly from a standard or conventional approach in a way that impacts on patient management, it is a practitioner's duty to make sure that the patient is informed.[267]

9.7.3 Conventional Medicine Practitioners

As far as pure orthodox medicine practitioners are concerned, the *Statement on Complementary and Alternative Medicine* requires that doctors need to acknowledge and to be aware of CAM therapies, even if they do not intend to use or

[263] *Re Gorringe* 5/8/03, Medical Practitioners Disciplinary Tribunal (New Zealand) Decision No. 237/02/89D, available at www.mpdt.org.nz, para. [53].

[264] *Re Gorringe* 5/8/03, Medical Practitioners Disciplinary Tribunal (New Zealand) Decision No. 237/02/89D, available at www.mpdt.org.nz, para. [52].

[265] *Re Gorringe* 5/8/03, Medical Practitioners Disciplinary Tribunal (New Zealand) Decision No. 237/02/89D, available at www.mpdt.org.nz, para. [52].

[266] *Opinion 03HDC19027* (Health and Disability Commissioner, 16/12/04) (A Christian practitioner offering a spiritual approach to treatment).

[267] *Opinion 03HDC19027* (Health and Disability Commissioner, 16/12/04) (A Christian practitioner offering a spiritual approach to treatment).

recommend them.[268] However, the *Statement* does not encourage doctors to actively learn CAM information. In a situation where a patient expresses an interest in CAM, the *Statement* only requires the doctor to indicate the limits of his knowledge and, where appropriate, to give suggestions of other sources for further information.[269]

In the Code and HDC jurisdiction, disciplinary proceedings, and human rights review jurisdiction, there are no cases that can inform the answer to the question of whether conventional medicine practitioners need to disclose information about CAM therapies, and, if so, under what circumstances. In the context of the Code, Right 6(1) and (2) and Clause 3 play an important role in answering that question. Would a reasonable patient, in a particular patient's circumstances, *expect* a conventional medicine practitioner to be able to provide CAM treatment information? Is the information about CAM therapies the one that a reasonable patient, in a particular patient's circumstances, *needs* to make an informed choice or give informed consent? Is there scope for conventional medicine practitioners arguing that, although they did not disclose CAM options, they have "taken reasonable actions in the circumstances" to give effect to the patient's right to be fully informed?

Those questions may be answered "no". A reasonable patient would not expect the impossible (Skegg and Paterson 2006, 212). Lack of evidence base of a CAM, lack of sufficient acceptance of it in the conventional world and a doctor's lack of knowledge about a CAM option would point to negating a duty for a conventional medicine practitioner to inform his patient of the CAM therapy, even though the patient has a strong interest in and commitment to the unconventional therapy.

However, with the increasing presence of CAM in society (including in health care), increasing academic debate and university medical education about CAM, CAM options would be more readily to fall within a patient's "expectation" and a practitioner's "knowledge". If a CAM therapy has advantages over conventional treatments in treating a particular condition, if the CAM therapy has a well-established and clear risk-efficacy profile, if the therapy has won favour from a responsible body of conventional professional opinion, and if a conventional medicine practitioner has already known or should have known the CAM therapy, there is little room for a conventional medicine practitioner to argue that the CAM information is not what a reasonable patient would expect to receive or not what a reasonable patient needs to make an informed choice. The conventional medicine practitioner needs to disclose it even if he personally does not favour or recommend the therapy. A patient delivering a question about the CAM therapy or showing an interest in it would trigger the use of the subjective limb of the "reasonable patient" test. That increases the possibility of a CAM therapy falling within the scope of a particular patient's expectation and need.

[268] Medical Council of New Zealand *Statement on Complementary and Alternative Medicine* (2011) para [6].

[269] Medical Council of New Zealand *Statement on Complementary and Alternative Medicine* (2011) para. [9].

9.7.4 *Impression: Still Orthodoxy-Reinforcing?*

The New Zealand's Code approach has made great contributions to the informed consent rule by honouring the patients' rights and promoting a contextualised and unbiased information disclosure. However, my impression is that, although New Zealand is very active in promoting a culture of giving balanced information disclosure by medical practitioners, that promotion has a boundary. It only requires *conventional medicine practitioners* to disclose balanced information about *conventional medicine* treatments. It does not contemplate a duty for conventional medicine practitioners to inform about CAM treatments. That is in contrast with the legal requirements about information disclosure for *CAM and dual practitioners*.

In the context involving CAM, *CAM and dual practitioners* are required to make their patients aware of *conventional medicine treatment options* when patients pursue CAM, even though they do not favour, recommend or perform them. CAM practitioners are not allowed to alienate patients from pursuing conventional medical treatments. Dual practitioners are required to use the knowledge of both conventional medicine and CAM, and inform patients of the availability of conventional treatments and the extent to which a CAM is consistent with conventional theories of medicine.

Like other common law jurisdictions, New Zealand does not offer much legal information about the question of whether or not, if yes, under what circumstances, the scope of a medical practitioner's duty to inform may be expanded to encompass disclosure of *unconventional*, including *experimental and CAM*, treatment options. Compared to the duty of CAM practitioners and dual practitioners to disclose information of both CAM and *conventional medicine* treatment options, it seems that there is no comparable duty for conventional medicine practitioners to disclose information about CAM therapies. That indicates that New Zealand is still encouraging an orthodoxy-reinforcing culture. In dealing with the dichotomy and interface between conventional medicine and CAM, New Zealand, like other jurisdictions, including China, is adopting an approach of attaching heavy weight to the labels "conventional" and "non-conventional", rather than focusing on the merits-demerits of conventional medicine and CAM and according them equal status.

9.8 Conclusion: The Code Approach and the Tort Approach

New Zealand law leads other jurisdictions in answering the question of how to sensitively deal with the intricate and fine distinctions that are drawn among different components of clinical practice, namely information disclosure, selection, recommendation, and performance of treatment. New Zealand law, especially its HDC jurisdiction, has adopted a liberal approach to the health care providers' general duty to disclose information and their specific duty to inform about treatment options. It endorses and shows consistent loyalty to the patient-oriented standard of disclosure. It recognises the need and importance of a provider's recommendation in the context of information disclosure. A provider's duty to disclose encompasses information about the risks and benefits of the proposed treatment and its alternatives. It honours the distinction drawn between a provider's recommendation/offer/performance of procedures and information disclosure. It acknowledges that a provider's preference may colour his presentation and requires health practitioners to disclose treatment options that they do not recommend or would not provide.

Driven by the patients' needs and expectations, the Code is very open-minded towards disclosure of alternatives. Following the Code, New Zealand endorses a very embracing duty of alternatives disclosure for health practitioners. Controversial or minority treatment options may fall within a practitioner's duty to inform, even though they are not generally accepted and the practitioner does not favour them. A practitioner may need to disclose treatment options that are not readily available in the public health care system, treatment options that are available overseas, or the availability of another health care provider. By virtue of the Code's expansive approach to information disclosure, more provider conduct is potentially caught by the Code than would attract liability at common law (Manning 2004, 216).

In summary, under the New Zealand's Code approach, a medical practitioner may have a duty to inform patients of a wide variety of alternatives: (1) conventional treatment options (alternatives to the new/experimental treatments); (2) non-recommended treatment options (alternatives to the proposed or recommended treatments); (3) minority treatment options (alternatives to the treatments favoured by the majority of practitioners); (4) treatment options not available in publicly-funded health care, or the option of seeking private treatments (financially unavailable treatment options); (5) treatment options not available in New Zealand but available overseas (geographically unavailable treatment options); (6) the option of having the treatment performed by another medical practitioner or provider (alternative providers).

There are several aspects that demonstrate New Zealand's strong commitment to requiring health practitioners to present patients with *balanced and contextualised* information. First, New Zealand prepares a very wide range of alternatives that may fall within a health practitioner's duty to inform. Second, New Zealand's Code requires health practitioners to disclose not only the divergent "schools" of treatments, but also the treatments that treating practitioners do not recommend or favour, even the treatments that are favoured only by a minority of their colleagues. Third, under the Code, practitioners may need to disclose or mention to their patients options that are made unavailable because of financial, geographical, and other reasons.

Most importantly, unlike the context of medical negligence liability, New Zealand's Code approach does not involve considerations of causation and damage. Whether or not the information about the undisclosed alternatives would make a difference to a patient's decision and injury has no bearing on the issue of whether there is a breach of the Code. The Commissioner will only consider the patients' expectation and need[270] with regard to information disclosure. Arguably that is a lower threshold than the "materiality" test.

[270] *See*, Right 6(1) and (2) of the Code.

The alternatives that fall within a Code's duty to inform in New Zealand can be categorised into three contexts: (1) ordinary (conventional medicine) treatment options; (2) treatment options involving conventional medicine and CAM; (3) financially and geographically unavailable treatment options and alternative providers. Under the Tort approach, all three contexts cannot avoid consideration of causation. I will cite English law, Canadian law, and USA law as examples (Table 9.4). They illustrate that even if the informed consent law can embrace disclosure of the varieties of alternative that the New Zealand's Code approach has done, under the Tort approach, additional consideration of causation will inevitably narrow the effective scope of a health practitioner's duty to inform.

England is still constrained in formulating the rules of disclosing alternative treatments. The *Birch* case indicates that the English law still concentrates on the *"risks"* aspects of information disclosure. The requirement of disclosure of alternatives is deduced from the need of disclosing "comparative risks" of divergent procedures.[271] Moreover, the *Birch* only highlights the need to disclose non-invasive, conservative and less risky alternatives to the proposed procedure. Furthermore, in medical negligence cases, the court needs to consider the issue of causation, i.e. the question of whether or not the patient would have declined the proposed procedure when given a fair and balanced information about divergent treatments or procedures.[272]

Canada is like New Zealand in recognising a doctor's duty to disclose "available reasonable", "medically reasonable", "medically appropriate" alternative treatments.[273] Although Canadian case law shows great caution in recognising a doctor's duty to inform about CAM therapies, alternative treatment options that fall within a doctor's duty to disclose may include *non-recommended treatment options, conservative (non-surgical) treatment options, and minority treatment options*. In addition, CAM practitioners may be exposed to a duty to disclose alternative treatments, including *CAM options and conventional medicine options*. That shows a similar commitment of Canadian law to promote a balanced information disclosure.

However, in medical negligence cases, Canadian courts must consider causation. That requires them to consider what a prudent or reasonable person in the patient's position would have decided if suitably informed of the withheld information.[274] That is divided into two questions concerning "decision causation" and "injury causation" respectively. First, whether a reasonable patient in similar circumstances would have chosen the alternative treatment if properly informed. Secondly, whether the damage would have been avoided if the alternative had been chosen.[275] Causation

[271] *Birch v University College Hospitals NHS Trust* [2008] EWHC 2237 (QB), at [74].

[272] *Birch v University College Hospitals NHS Trust* [2008] EWHC 2237 (QB), at [81].

[273] *Van Dyke v Grey Bruce Regional Health Centre* (2005), 255 D.L.R. (4th) 397, 414–415, at [65]–[67].

[274] *Reibl v Hughes* (1980) 114 D.L.R. (3d) 1, 17 (S.C.C.); *Arndt v Smith* (1997), 148 D.L.R. (4th) 48, 51(S.C.C.); *Haughian v Paine* (1987), 37 D.L.R. (4th) 624, 644–647 (finding that if the risks inherent in the surgery and the alternatives to surgery had been disclosed, a reasonable person in the patient's position would not have proceeded to undergo the surgery).

[275] *Seney v Crooks* (1998), 166 D.L.R. (4th) 337, 361, at [95] (Alta. C.A.).

Table 9.4 Disclosure of alternatives and causation

Jurisdictions	Disclosure of alternatives	Causation?
UK	Non-invasive, conservative and less risky alternatives[1]	√
Canada	"Available reasonable", "medically reasonable", "medically appropriate" alternative treatments[2]	√
	Non-recommended treatment options[3]	√
	Conservative (non-surgical) treatment options[4]	√
	Minority treatment options[5]	√
	CAM options and conventional medicine options (for CAM practitioners)[6]	√
	BUT, NOT "alternative medicine practices" (for conventional medicine practitioners)[7]	–
USA[8]	Geographically unavailable treatment options	√
	Alternative providers	√
	Financially unavailable alternatives	√
NZ	Conventional treatment options (←→ experimental treatment)[9]	–
	Non-recommended treatment options[10]	–
	Minority treatment options[11]	–
	Financially unavailable treatment options[12]	–
	Geographically unavailable treatment options[13]	–
	Alternative providers[14]	–
	Conventional medicine treatment options (for CAM and dual practitioners)[15]	–
	Non-conventional (CAM) treatment options (for conventional medicine practitioners)?	–

Notes:

[1]*Birch v University College Hospitals NHS Trust* [2008] EWHC 2237 (QB)

[2]*Van Dyke v Grey Bruce Regional Health Centre* (2005), 255 D.L.R. (4th) 397, 414–415, at [65]–[67]

[3]*Zimmer v Ringrose* (1981), 124 D.L.R. (3d) 215, 222 (Alta. C.A.)

[4]*Haughian v Paine* (1987), 37 D.L.R. (4th) 624, 643 (the proposed surgery has a small risk of paralysis; the non-surgical treatment has a significant chance of success, and is riskless; surgery is still available if non-surgical treatment is unsuccessful)

[5]*Seney v Crooks* (1998), 166 D.L.R. (4th) 337, 351 (Alta. C.A.) (alternative mode of treatment preferred by *some specialists*)

[6]*Dickson v Pinder*, 2010 ABQB 269 (Court of Queen's Bench of Alberta) (involving a CAM practitioner-chiropractor; an expert opined that the defendant-chiropractor should have informed the patient of reasonable treatment alternatives, such as activator treatment, mobilization, stretching, physiotherapy, medication, *as prescribed by a physician*, or doing nothing; the court held that the chiropractor should present the option of *conservative or no treatment* to the patient)

[7]*Dickson v Pinder*, 2010 ABQB 269, at [79] (citing *Seney v Crooks*, 1998 ABCA 316, 223 A.R. 145 at paras. 57–58 (the Alberta Court of Appeal)) (noting that the scope of the duty might not include a "fringe alternative" or "alternative medicine practices")

[8]*See*, Chap. 5 (5.5 Geographically Unavailable Alternatives; 5.6 Alternative Provider)

[9]*Opinion 08HDC20258* (Health and Disability Commissioner, 11/11/2009) (a relatively new procedure)

[10]*Opinion 04HDC00031* (Health and Disability Commissioner, 24/2/2005) (Orthopaedic surgeon's failure to inform his patient of the option he did not favor)

[11]*Opinion 02HDC18414* (Health and Disability Commissioner, 6/4/2004) (failure to provide contextualised information)

(continued)

Table 9.4 (continued)

[12]*Opinion 09HDC00891* (Health and Disability Commissioner, 31/3/2010) (prioritization and management of a patient); *Opinion 04HDC13909* (Health and Disability Commissioner, 4/4/2006) (failure to provide accurate information about the expected waiting time)
[13]*Opinion 02HDC18414* (Health and Disability Commissioner, 6/4/2004) (failure to provide contextualised information)
[14]*Opinion 03HDC19128* (Health and Disability Commissioner, 14/9/2004) (failure to reveal that the provider's practice was subject to restrictions)
[15]*Opinion 08HDC00218* (Health and Disability Commissioner, 16/12/2008) (Alternative therapy – Bioptron light therapy); *Opinion 03HDC19027* (Health and Disability Commissioner, 16/12/2004) (A Christian practitioner offering a spiritual approach to treatment).

is not always easily established. For example, in a case requiring a CAM practitioner to present the option of conservative treatment to the patient, a court found that causation was not established because even if the chiropractor had explained the risk of the proposed treatment and the alternative treatments for her condition, the patient would have consented to the proposed treatment.[276]

Some cases in the USA showed willingness to expand information disclosure to cover information about limitations/restrictions of providers (institutions or practitioners) and the physician-related information (such as inexperience), promising existence of a doctor's duty to inform about *alternative providers and geographically unavailable treatment options*.[277] However, in these areas, in addition to "materiality", the courts concerned actually incorporated consideration of "causation" at the stage of a doctor's *duty* to inform. Before acknowledging a doctor's duty to disclose the information, the courts want to make sure that a doctor's revealing undisclosed information should make a real difference to a patient's decision in choosing among alternatives.[278]

Similar to Canadian law, the USA courts would consider both "decision causation" and "injury causation", i.e. the question of whether a hypothetical reasonable patient, equipped with the undisclosed information, would have opted against the procedure proposed, recommended and performed by the physician; and the question of whether the patient's decision to forgo the proposed procedure, or to undergo an alternative one, could avoid the harm. Incorporating the "causation" thinking into the issue of whether a doctor has a duty to disclose information confuses the two elements of negligence law. But it indicates the judiciary's caution and hesitancy in adopting a blanket and expansive rule.

Furthermore, the negligence cases regarding non-disclosure of *financially unavailable alternatives* also face difficult hurdles when the question of causation

---

[276] *Dickson v Pinder*, 2010 ABQB 269, at [120].

[277] *See*, Chap. 5 (Sect. 5.5 "Geographically Unavailable Alternatives"; Sect. 5.6 "Alternative Provider").

[278] *See*, *Estate of Lapping v Group Health Co-op. of Puget Sound*, 892 P.2d 1116 (Wash. App. Div. 2, 1995); *Martin by Scoptur v Richards*, 531 N.W.2d 70 (Wis. 1995); *Madsen v Park Nicollet Med. Ctr.*, 431 N.W.2d 855, 861 (Minn.1988); *Johnson By Adler v Kokemoor*, 545 N.W. 2d 495, 506–507 (Wis. 1996); *Howard v University of Medicine*, 800 A.2d 73, 85 (N.J. 2002).

arises. The prospect for success is slim for these cases, especially when the undisclosed treatment options would probably not have been *practically* available to the claimant/pursuer anyway.

Finally, I would cite two survey results to illustrate the encompassing nature of the New Zealand's Code approach and its impact on health care. Two surveys were conducted in both Australia and New Zealand, researching the views and practices of medical practitioners regarding discussion of expensive treatment options that are not available in publicly-funded health care. The Australian survey reveals that if the patient would have to pay for the High Cost Drug (HCD) themselves, or if the HCD were not subsidised, a significant number of oncologists (between 28 and 41% depending on the scenario) would not inform the patient about the HCD (Thomson et al. 2006, 702–708). That is in striking contrast with New Zealand practice. A very similar New Zealand survey reveals that the percentage who would not discuss expensive unfunded drugs was substantially lower in New Zealand (6.4–11.1%) than it was in Australia (28–41%) (Dare et al. 2010, 260–264).

Australia and New Zealand have many similarities. They are culturally and demographically similar. There are extensive interactions between medical professions in the two countries. Given these similarities, one might expect broadly similar professional attitudes towards informing patients about treatment options. The divergence of professional attitudes towards the issue of informing patients of financially unavailable treatment options, as revealed by surveys, should be partly explained by the different legal rules regarding disclosure of alternatives in the two jurisdictions. While New Zealand's Code of Patients' Rights has already recognized a legal duty for doctors to inform about a wide range of alternatives, including alternative treatments not readily available in publicly-funded health care, Australia is still waiting for courts to translate scholars' arguments for disclosure of alternative treatments into legal principles.

In next chapter, I will examine Chinese law. With the advent of Chinese *Tort Liability Law*, people invest much hope in Chinese tort law and medical negligence law to protect the patients' *rights*, including those based on the informed consent rule. As I will illustrate, motivated by an ambition of protecting the patients' "right of informed consent", some Chinese scholars suggest diluting or ignoring the requirements of "causation" and "personal injury" in informed consent cases. Patients' loss of right of autonomy is compensated by awarding a small amount of "mental distress" compensation. This line of suggestion seems to attempt to combine the ready availability of remedial responses, as witnessed by the New Zealand's Code approach, with a high level compensation scheme, as featured by the Tort law.

However, I doubt the wisdom of protecting the patients' rights within the framework of tort law because the avenue of tort is burdensome, costly and time-consuming. I would recommend the New Zealand's Code approach of protecting the patients' rights. In the nondisclosure cases, especially the cases of nondisclosure of alternatives, "causation" provides a huge hurdle. The merit of the New Zealand's Code approach is that it wisely avoids the tort context and provides a legally enforceable, patient-friendly and distinct arena to realise the dream of protecting patients' rights.

References

Bismark, Marie, and Ron Paterson. 2006. No-fault compensation in New Zealand: Harmonizing injury compensation, provider accountability, and patient safety. *Health Affairs* 25: 278–283.

Brazier, M., and E. Cave. 2007. *Medicine, patients and the law*, 4th ed. Edinburgh: LexisNexis Butterworths.

Brophy, Elizabeth. 2003. Does a doctor have a duty to provide information and advice about complementary and alternative medicine? *Journal of Law and Medicine* 10: 271–284.

Canadian Medical Association. 2004. Code of ethics. http://www.cma.ca. Accessed 24 April 2010.

Collins, D.B., and C.A. Brown. 2009. The impact of the Cartwright Report upon the regulation, discipline and accountability of medical practitioners in New Zealand. *Journal of Law and Medicine* 16: 595–613.

Commonwealth of Australia. 2002. Review of the law of negligence: Final report. http://revofneg.treasury.gov.au/content/review2.asp. Accessed 22 July 2008.

Dare, Tim, Mike Findlay, Peter Browett, et al. 2010. Paternalism in practice: Informing patients about expensive unsubsidised drugs. *Journal of Medical Ethics* 36: 260–264.

Downie, Jocelyn, Timothy Caulfield, and Colleen Flood. 2002. *Canadian health law and policy*, 2nd ed. Markham: LexisNexis Butterworths.

Fovargue, Sara, and José Miola. 2010a. How much information is "enough"? *Clinical Ethics* 5: 13–15.

Fovargue, Sara, and José Miola. 2010b. One step forward, two steps back? The GMC, The Common law and "informed" consent. *Journal of Medical Ethics* 36: 494–497.

General Medical Council (UK). 2008. Consent: Patients and doctors making decisions together. www.gmc-uk.org. Accessed 24 April 2010.

Heywood, Rob. 2009. Medical disclosure of alternative treatments. *The Cambridge Law Journal* 68: 30–32.

Heywood, Rob, Ann Macaskill, and Kevin Williams. 2010. Informed consent in hospital practice: Health professionals' perspectives and legal reflections. *Medical Law Review* 18: 152–184.

Jones, Michael A. 2003. *Medical negligence*. London: Sweet & Maxwell.

Kian, Catherine Tay Swee. 2003. Interpretation of the *Bolam* test in the standard of medical care: Impact of the *Gunapathy* case and beyond. *Professional Negligence* 19: 384–394.

Maclean, Alasdair R. 2004. The doctrine of informed consent: Does it exist and has it crossed the Atlantic? *Legal Studies* 24: 386–413.

Maclean, Alasdair. 2006. Autonomy, consent and persuasion. *European Journal of Health Law* 13: 321–338.

Maclean, Alasdair. 2009. *Autonomy, informed consent and medical law: A relational challenge*. Boston, MA: Cambridge University Press.

Manning, Joanna. 2004. Informed consent to medical treatment: The common law and New Zealand's Code of Patients' Rights. *Medical Law Review* 12: 181–216.

Manning, Joanna. 2007. The standard of care and expert evidence of accepted practice in medical negligence. *Journal of Law and Medicine* 15: 394–407.

Manning, Joanna. 2008. New Zealand's remedial responses to adverse events in healthcare. *Torts Law Journal* 16: 120–155.

Manning, Joanna. 2009. Review of New Zealand's Health and Disability Commissioner Act and Code of Rights. *Journal of Law and Medicine* 17: 314–326.

Mason, Kenyon, and Douglas Brodie. 2005. *Bolam, Bolam* – Wherefore art thou *Bolam*? *Edinburgh Law Review* 9: 298–306.

McLay, Geoff. 2008. Accident compensation – What's the Common law got to do with it?. *New Zealand Law Review* 2008: 55–79.

Medical Council of New Zealand. 2002. Information and consent. http://www.mcnz.org.nz/portals/0/Guidance/Information%20and%20Consent.pdf. Accessed 8 September 2010.

Medical Council of New Zealand. 2008. Statement on safe practice in an environment of resource limitation. www.mcnz.org.nz. Accessed 22 April 2010.

Miola, José. 2009. On the materiality of risk: Paper tigers and panaceas. *Medical Law Review* 17: 76–108.

Montgomery, Jonathan. 2003. *Health care law*, 2nd ed. New York: Oxford University Press.

New Zealand Medical Association. 2008. Code of ethics. http://www.nzma.org.nz. Accessed 22 April 2010.

Oliphant, Ken. 1996. Defining "medical misadventure": Lessons from New Zealand. *Medical Law Review* 4: 1–31.

Oliphant, Ken. 2007. Beyond misadventure: Compensation for medical injuries in New Zealand. *Medical Law Review* 15: 357–391.

Parker, Malcolm. 2003. Reforming the law of medical negligence: Solutions in search of a problem. *Torts Law Journal* 11: 136–164.

Paterson, R.J. 1998. Rationing health care and human rights: The *Northland Health* case. *New Zealand Law Review* 1998: 571–584.

Paterson, Ron. 2002. The patients' complaints system in New Zealand. *Health Affairs* 21: 70–79.

Pattinson, Shaun D. 2006. *Medical law and ethics*. London: Sweet & Maxwell.

Royal Australasian College of Surgeons. 2006. Code of conduct. http://www.surgeons.org/Content/ContentFolders/Policies/FES_PST_2021_P_Code_of_Conduct.pdf. Accessed 27 April 2010.

Royal Australasian College of Surgeons. 2008. General guidelines for assessing, approving and introducing new surgical procedures into a hospital or health service. http://www.surgeons.org/AM/Template.cfm?Section=Position_papers&Template=/CM/ContentDisplay.cfm&ContentFileID=41797. Accessed 27 April 2010.

Samanta, Ash, Michelle M. Mello, Charles Foster, John Tingle, and Jo Samanta. 2006. The role of clinical guidelines in medical negligence litigation: A shift from the *Bolam* standard? *Medical Law Review* 14: 321–366.

Skegg, P.D.G. 1997. The New Zealand Code of Health and Disability Services Consumers' Rights. *Journal of Law and Medicine* 5: 124.

Skegg, P.D.G., and Ron Paterson (eds.). 2006. *Medical law in New Zealand*. Wellington: Brookers.

Skene, Loane. 2008. *Law and medical practice: Rights, duties, claims and defences*, 3rd ed. Sydney: LexisNexis Butterworths.

The Canadian Medical Protective Association. 2006. *Consent: A guide for Canadian physicians*, 4th ed. www.cmpa-acpm.ca. Accessed 5 September 2010.

The College of Physicians and Surgeons of Ontario. 2005. Consent to medical treatment. http://www.cpso.on.ca/policies/policies/default.aspx?ID=1544. Accessed 5 September 2010.

The National Advisory Committee on Health and Disability (New Zealand). 2006. District health board decision-making about new health interventions: A background paper. http://www.nhc.health.govt.nz/moh.nsf/indexcm/nhc-new-health-interventions?Open. Accessed 25 May 2010.

The National Health and Medical Research Council (NHMRC). 2004a. Communicating with patients: Advice for medical practitioners. http://www.nhmrc.gov.au/publications/synopses/e58syn.htm. Accessed 22 August 2010.

The National Health and Medical Research Council (NHMRC). 2004b. General guidelines for medical practitioners on providing information to patients. http://www.nhmrc.gov.au/publications/synopses/e57syn.htm. Accessed 22 August 2010.

The Royal Australasian College of Physicians (RACP). 2006. Code of professional behaviour. http://www.racp.edu.au/page/policy-and-advocacy/ethics. Accessed 27 April 2010.

Thomson, J., et al. 2006. Do oncologists discuss expensive anti-cancer drugs with their patients? *Annals of Oncology* 17: 702–708.

Weir, Michael. 2003. Obligation to advise of options for treatment – Medical doctors and complementary and alternative medicine practitioners. *Journal of Law and Medicine* 10: 296–307.

Chapter 10
Chinese Context

Abstract This chapter examines China's legal context, medical context and law relating to TCM. In the legal context, China demonstrates that a jurisdiction can, through statutory intervention or legislation, expand the scope of a doctor's duty to inform to cover the disclosure of alternatives. It also further illustrates that the Tort approach is not always the best way to honour a patient's right to be informed. In the medical context, China presents an "integrative" medical culture. Behind the facade of TCM's flourishing and equal status to Western medicine, TCM's uniqueness has actually been diluted by the Western-medicine-oriented approach of integration. Although it may not be wise to accord practitioners freedom to practise both TCM and Western medicine, because of the irreconcilability of the two medical cultures, the "integrative" approach is consistent with the thesis that health care practitioners would better possess and present patients with contextualised information that transcends the boundaries of the different "schools of thought".

10.1 Introduction

In this chapter, I will introduce the Chinese context, which I divide into "legal context" and "medical context" before I touch the issue of Traditional Chinese Medicine (TCM) and the law. Assuming that readers may not be familiar with Chinese law and Chinese health care, I decide to put analysis of relevant issues, such as the duty of medical practitioners[1] to inform about alternative treatment options, the duty of Western medicine practitioners to inform about TCM therapies and the duty of TCM practitioners to inform about Western medicine treatments, in a wider context. For example, the sequence of examining the Chinese legal context will be: Chinese

[1]In China, that includes Western medicine practitioners and Traditional Chinese Medicine practitioners.

X. Zhao, *The Duty of Medical Practitioners and CAM/TCM Practitioners to Inform Competent Adult Patients about Alternatives*,
DOI 10.1007/978-3-642-31647-0_10,

medical law → Chinese medical negligence law → Chinese informed consent law → Chinese informed consent law about disclosure of alternatives. That starts from a wider context and ends with a narrower context. The ultimate aim is to explore the issue of a practitioner's duty to disclose alternatives, but in a bigger legal context. Talking about an issue in a wide context would give readers a feeling that the book loses focus for some time. However, I hope the approach will give readers a clearer and a more coherent picture about the Chinese context, which, I assume, would be foreign to readers. I have written some background materials, such as the Chinese legal system and the history of Chinese medical negligence law, and have attached them as appendices (Appendices 3 and 4). Readers are free to resort to that information if they like or feel the need to do that.

I also have a note about the citation of Chinese law and literature. Although I offer English translations, I also include the original *Chinese* information about the Chinese legislation and academic literature I cite. I have a concern that, due to the language barrier and the lack of English translation of all legal resources, readers may encounter difficulty in tracing sources back to original Chinese literature, especially academic literature, if they use the English translations *only*. Having the Chinese version of the citations will help in this regard.

10.2 Legal Context

10.2.1 Chinese Medical Law

China has a civil law tradition. Legislation plays a pivotal role in Chinese legal system (for details, *see*, Appendix 3: Chinese Legal System). Although some of them overlap, Chinese medical legislation can be categorised into six main groups: (1) Law that pertains to medical practitioners, medical institutions[2] and clinical care. Because the focus of this book is on *medical practitioners*, I will give more details about this category of legislation in the next paragraph. (2) Law that relates to human health products. It covers legislation concerning pharmaceuticals, medical devices, foods and cosmetic products. In the field of regulating pharmaceuticals and medical devices, there is a "parent" law – *Pharmaceutical Administration Law*,[3] followed by many "child" regulations. (3) Public health law, led by the *Law on Prevention and Treatment of Infectious Diseases*.[4] (4) Mental

[2] Regulation on Medical Institutions (1994, State Council)(医疗机构管理条例, 1994年,国务院).

[3] Law of the People's Republic of China on Pharmaceutical Administration (2001, The Standing Committee of the National People's Congress) (中华人民共和国药品管理法,2001年,全国人大常委会).

[4] Law of the People's Republic of China on Prevention and Treatment of Infectious Diseases (1989, revised 2004, The Standing Committee of the National People's Congress) (中华人民共和国传染病防治法, 1989年,2004年修订,全国人大常委会).

health law.[5] (5) Traditional Chinese Medicine law.[6] (6). Law regulating emerging biotechnology issues.[7]

The basic "law" of regulating medical practitioners in China is *Law on Practising Doctors*.[8] It is applicable to "the professional medical personnel who have legally obtained the qualifications as practising doctors or assistant practising doctors and registered to practice medicine in institutions for medical treatment, disease prevention and health care".[9] The concept of "practising doctors" (执业医师("*Zhi Ye Yi Shi*")) or "medical practitioners" includes "practising doctors" and "assistant practising doctors".

The *Law on Practising Doctors* is enacted to protect public health. It serves two purposes: improving and maintaining the competence of doctors, and promoting professional, ethical and legal standards. The first task is fulfilled by subjecting potential doctors to national examination and registration.[10] Unlike common law countries which follow the State-sanctioned self-regulation model, in China the regulation of medical practitioners, including licensing and disciplinary actions, falls within the functions of governmental bodies – administrative departments of health, although doctors may organise and join their own association.[11] Moreover, the *Law on Practising Doctors* is also full of professional and ethical requirements.[12] It clarifies a doctor's rights and duties.[13] Specifically, it makes it clear

[5] China is still waiting for its *national* Mental Health Law. It has been subjected to more than 25 years' discussion and debate and more than ten revisions since it was drafted in 1985. However, there are some *local regulations* in this area, for example, *Shanghai Mental Health Regulation* (2001, The Standing Committee of Shanghai People's Congress) (上海市精神卫生条例, 2001年, 上海市人民代表大会常务委员会).

[6] I will explore this in the part "Traditional Chinese Medicine and the Law" of this Chapter.

[7] Such as Regulation on Human Organ Transplantation (2007, State Council) (人体器官移植条例, 2007年, 国务院).

[8] Law on Practising Doctors of the People's Republic of China (1998, Standing Committee of the National People's Congress) (中华人民共和国执业医师法, 1998年,全国人大常委会).

[9] Law on Practising Doctors of the People's Republic of China (1998), Article 2 (中华人民共和国执业医师法, 1998年, 第2条)

[10] Law on Practising Doctors of the People's Republic of China (1998), Articles 8–20 (中华人民共和国执业医师法, 1998年, 第8-20条).

[11] Law on Practising Doctors of the People's Republic of China (1998), Articles 4 and 7(中华人民共和国执业医师法, 1998年, 第4, 7条).

[12] For example, according to Article 3, doctors should "have sound professional ethics and high levels of competence for medical practice, demonstrate humanitarianism and fulfill the sacred responsibility for preventing and treating diseases, healing the wounded and rescuing the dying and safeguarding the health of people."

[13] One of the doctors' rights is the right "to conduct medical diagnosis, disease investigation and medical disposal, issue corresponding medical certificate and *choose appropriate plans* for medical treatment, disease prevention and healthcare" (emphasis added). *See*, Article 21 (1) of the Law. Doctors have the following duties in practising medicine: (1) to abide by laws, regulations and the technical and operating rules;(2) to foster the spirit of dedication, follow professional ethics, fulfill the responsibilities as a doctor and serve the patients conscientiously; (3) to care for and respect the patients and guard patients' privacy; (4) to work hard for professional proficiency, update one's knowledge and raise professional and technical competence; (5) to disseminate hygienic and health care knowledge and educate the patients on health issues. *See*, Article 22 of the Law.

that doctors should comply with seven "practising rules", one of which is the "informed consent" rule.[14]

10.2.2 *Chinese Law of Liability for Medical Damage*[15]

Chinese *Law on Practising Doctors* and *Regulation on Medical Institutions* are of the type of professional regulation. They set out professional standards ("practising rules") for medical practitioners and their employers (medical institutions). They incorporate many professional and ethical codes into legal documents. The form of liability they envisaged is of an *administrative* or *disciplinary* nature, although they always leave the *criminal* responsibility open as an avenue of punishment for very serious cases. When the context shifts to *civil* liability for medical practitioners, the *Law on Practising Doctors* and *Regulation on Medical Institutions* are of little relevance. The development of Chinese *medical negligence law* is mainly attributable to the birth, application and interpretation of three other pieces of legislation: the *General Principles of Civil Law* (1986) (GPCL),[16] the *Regulation on the Handling of Medical Accidents* (2002),[17] and the *Tort Liability Law* (2009).[18]

---

[14] In addition to the "informed consent" requirement which I will elaborate later, the six other "practising rules" are: (1) When implementing medical treatment, disease prevention and healthcare measures and signing relevant medical certificates, doctors shall conduct diagnosis and investigations themselves (in person) and timely fill in medical documents according to stipulations, and shall not conceal, forge or destroy medical documents and relevant materials. Doctors shall not issue medical certificates that are not related to their own practising scope or not in line with the practising categories. (2) For emergency and critical cases, doctors shall adopt emergency treatment measures and shall not refuse to give emergency treatment. (3) Doctors shall use medicines, sterilizing drugs and medical equipment approved for use by relevant state departments. Except for proper diagnosis and treatment, doctors shall not use narcotic drugs, toxic drugs for medical use, medicines for mental disease or radioactive medicines. (4) Doctors shall not solicit or illegally accept money or articles from patients or seek other illegitimate gains by taking advantage of one's position. (5) In case of natural disasters, outbreaks of contagious diseases, sudden accidents with heavy casualties and other emergencies that pose a serious threat to people's life and health, doctors shall follow the orders of the health administrative departments of the people's governments at or above the county level. (6) In case of a malpractice or when an epidemic situation is found, doctors shall report in a timely manner to the employer institution or the health administrative departments in accordance with relevant stipulations. When a doctor finds that the patient is suspected of being involved in an injury case or dies of abnormal cause, the doctor shall report to relevant departments in accordance with relevant stipulations. *See*, Articles 23–29 of the Law.

[15] *See also*, Xiju Zhao, *Chinese Medical Negligence Law: How to Distinguish and Accommodate Common Law Principles?* in Chen Lei & C.H. van Rhee (eds). *Towards a Chinese Civil Code: Historical and Comparative Perspectives* Brill 2012. I have done a lot of updating and rewriting about the topic in this part.

[16] General Principles of the Civil Law of the People's Republic of China (1986, NPC) (中华人民共和国民法通则, 1986年,全国人大).

[17] Regulation on the Handling of Medical Accidents (2002, State Council) (医疗事故处理条例, 2002年, 国务院).

[18] Tort Liability Law of People's Republic of China (2009, Standing Committee of NPC) (中华人民共和国侵权责任法, 2009年, 全国人大常委会).

The GPCL provides general guidance on civil liability. It can apply comfortably to the context of medical negligence. A doctor's negligent conduct may cause personal injury and infringe a patient's "rights of life and health",[19] therefore falling within the scope of GPCL. However, the advent of Regulations on Medical Accidents[20] complicated the situation. The *Regulation on the Handling of Medical Accidents* (2002) (hereafter the 2002 *Regulation*) had two components: one being a professional regulation and disputes resolution scheme, and another being a medical accident compensation law. Both the GPCL and the 2002 *Regulation* cover personal injury compensation. The problem is that the two pieces of legislation have different thresholds for compensation and different rules regarding the amount of compensation. That created discrepancies. There have been continuing concerns about the *Regulation*'s inconsistency with the basic tort law principles. The Supreme People's Court (SPC) of China, by releasing several Judicial Interpretations,[21] created a two-layer, parallel approach. It drew a distinction between cases of medical accidents and non-medical-accident cases and subjected them to different legal rules. In addition to these two divergent causes of action, there were two other dichotomies or distinctions, i.e. (1) distinctions between two groups of applicable laws (the 2002 *Regulation* and 2003 Notice[22] *v.* GPCL and the 2003 Interpretation[23]) and (2) two systems of authentication (medical accident *technical* authentication *v. forensic* authentication). The SPC's approach actually solidified the inconsistencies between the two contexts, rather than solved them. Fortunately, the new *Tort*

[19] General Principles of the Civil Law of the People's Republic of China (1986, NPC), Article 98 ("Citizens shall enjoy the rights of life and health.") (中华人民共和国民法通则, 1986年,全国人大, 第98条).

[20] Regulation on Dealing with Medical Accidents (1987, State Council) (医疗事故处理办法, 1987年, 国务院); Regulation on the Handling of Medical Accidents (2002, State Council) (医疗事故处理条例, 2002年, 国务院).

[21] Supreme People's Court's Reply to Tian Jin High People's Court Regarding How to Apply Laws in Adjudicating the Medical Incident Compensation Case of *Li Xin-rong v. The Affiliated Hospital of Tian Jin No. 2 Medical College* (1992, SPC) (最高人民法院关于李荣诉天津市第二医学院附属医院医疗事故赔偿一案如何适用法律问题的复函, 1992年, 最高人民法院); Notice of the Supreme People's Court on Trying Civil Cases on Medical Disputes by Referring to the "Regulation on Handling Medical Accidents" (No. 20 [2003] of the Supreme People's Court) (最高人民法院关于参照《医疗事故处理条例》审理医疗纠纷民事案件的通知, 2003年, 最高人民法院); The Interpretation of the Supreme People's Court Concerning Some Issues on the Application of Law for the Trial of Cases on Compensation for Personal Injury (2003, SPC) (最高人民法院关于审理人身损害赔偿案件适用法律若干问题的解释, 2003年, 最高人民法院); Answers by the Chief Official of the First Civil Court of the SPC to Reporters' Questions on How to Apply Laws in Adjudicating Medical Lawsuits (最高人民法院民一庭负责人就审理医疗纠纷案件的法律适用问题答记者问). The Supreme People's Court has the power to give general *interpretation* on the application of laws in *judicial* proceedings ("judicial interpretation"("司法解释"("*Si Fa Jie Shi*"))).

[22] Notice of the Supreme People's Court on Trying Civil Cases on Medical Disputes by Referring to the "Regulation on Handling Medical Accidents" (No. 20 [2003] of the Supreme People's Court) (最高人民法院关于参照《医疗事故处理条例》审理医疗纠纷民事案件的通知, 2003年, 最高人民法院).

[23] The Interpretation of the Supreme People's Court Concerning Some Issues on the Application of Law for the Trial of Cases on Compensation for Personal Injury (2003, SPC) (最高人民法院关于审理人身损害赔偿案件适用法律若干问题的解释, 2003年, 最高人民法院).

Liability Law (2009) does not echo the concept of "medical accident". However, even after the Tort Law came into being, there are still disagreements about the fate of the 2002 *Regulation*. (For details, *see,* Appendix 4: Chinese Medical Negligence Law: From 1986 to 2009).

The *Tort Liability Law* (2009) (hereafter the Tort Law) has a separate chapter addressing "liability for medical damage" (医疗损害责任("*Yi Liao Sun Hai Ze Ren*")), which defines the liabilities of medical institutions and health care professionals for damages caused by them.[24] In my view, with the advent of the Tort Law, the part of medical accident compensation in the 2002 *Regulation* is destined to fade into history because its incompatibility with the GPCL and the Tort Law. At present, my view is supported by a proposed judicial interpretation regarding how to adjudicate the cases of "liability for medical damage", in which SPC explicitly mentions GPCL, the Tort Law and Chinese Law of Civil Procedure as the legal basis for interpretations, but does not mention the 2002 *Regulation*.[25] The law of "liability for medical damage" in the Tort Law will replace the "medical accident compensation" part of the 2002 *Regulation* and, therefore, will be the main source of Chinese medical negligence law.

The Chapter "liability for medical damage" has 11 articles. In addition to the context of diagnosis, treatment, and information disclosure (Articles 54–58), it also encompasses the contexts of tort liability for medical product defects (Article 59), tort liability caused by invasion of patients' privacy and breach of the duty of confidentiality (Article 62), and tort liability for "unnecessary examination" (Article 63). Some of the provisions of medical negligence in Chinese Tort Law are repetitive and unnecessary. However, in order to present readers with a whole picture of the new law, I will examine them one by one. That will be done in a comparative perspective. The Chinese context will be examined first before we see if common law experience could inform and feed into the development of Chinese law.

10.2.2.1 Article 54: Fault-Based Liability and Vicarious Liability

The Tort Law envisages three approaches to attributing tortious liability: *fault-based liability, liability based on presumption of fault, and no-fault liability or strict liability*. The "default" criterion under which a person may incur tortious liability is the fault-based one. As a general principle, a person will incur liability where he

[24] Academically "medical damage liability" is defined as a tort liability where medical institutions and healthcare professionals in the therapeutic activities, due to negligence or, under the expressly defined circumstances, no matter whether there is negligence or not, caused personal injuries or other injuries to patients, and therefore shall bear damage compensation liability and other liabilities. *See*, Yang Li Xin "Study on the Concept of Medical Damage Liability" (2009) No. 3 Politics and Law 75, 79 (杨立新: "医疗损害责任概念研究", 载《政治与法律》2009 年第3 期, 第79页).

[25] The Supreme People's Court of China *Interpretation on How to Apply Laws in Adjudicating Cases of Liability for Medical Damage (Discussion Paper)* http://www.ahyllaw.com/display.asp?id=1238 (last accessed 20 April, 2012) (最高院关于审理医疗损害责任纠纷案件适用法律若干问题的解释(征求意见稿)). The Interpretation has 38 articles.

infringes upon another person's civil rights and interests and is at *fault*.[26] However, if there are expressly defined circumstances where the law stipulates that the person is *presumed to be at fault*, the person shall assume the tort liability unless he is able to prove that he is *not at fault*.[27] In this context, the defendant concerned has the opportunity to produce evidence to rebut that presumption by proving that he was not at fault. Finally, in some circumstances, the law may specify that the person who infringes on another person's civil rights and interests shall bear tort liability *irrespective of the person's fault*.[28] That is called "no-fault liability".

These general principles of tort law are echoed in Chinese medical negligence law. Article 54 of the Tort Law witnesses the application of the approach of *fault-based liability*. As a general principle, medical institutions are liable and have to pay compensation if the medical institution and/or any of its health care professionals are at *fault* and *damage* is *caused* to a patient during diagnosis and treatment.[29] Here "fault" mainly means "negligence".[30] The plaintiff-patient must prove the existence of the *fault* of the medical institution and/or medical professionals, the *damage* suffered by the patient and the *connection* between the fault and the damage. In addition to Article 54, as I elaborate below, Article 58 and Article 59 of the Tort Law offer the possibilities of imposing on the defendants the *liability based on presumption of fault and no-fault/strict liability*. As I explain below, I have reservation about the soundness of Article 59 which provides the basis for a court to hold that a health care provider is *jointly liable* for damages caused by medical *product defect*. In my view, Article 59 confuses medical negligence law with the law of product liability. The civil liability for medical damage should be fault-based. Moreover, it is questionable whether *presumption of fault*, as witnessed by Article 58, forms a separate approach of attributing tortious liability. Presumption of fault is still fault-based. Therefore, in my view, the health professionals' liability for medical damage should be basically fault-based.

According to Article 54, "[i]f a patient is injured in diagnosis and treatment activities and such injury is caused by the fault of a medical institution and its

---

[26] Tort Liability Law of People's Republic of China (2009, Standing Committee of NPC), Article 6 (1) (中华人民共和国侵权责任法, 2009年, 全国人大常委会, 第6(1)条).

[27] Tort Liability Law of People's Republic of China (2009, Standing Committee of NPC), Article 6 (2) (中华人民共和国侵权责任法, 2009年, 全国人大常委会, 第6(2)条).

[28] Tort Liability Law of People's Republic of China (2009, Standing Committee of NPC), Article 7 (中华人民共和国侵权责任法, 2009年, 全国人大常委会, 第7条). For example, product liability (Chapter 5), liability for environmental pollution (Chapter 8) and inherently hazardous or dangerous activities (Chapter 9).

[29] Tort Liability Law of People's Republic of China (2009, Standing Committee of NPC), Article 54 (中华人民共和国侵权责任法, 2009年, 全国人大常委会, 第54条).

[30] Chinese new law about civil liability for medical damage is deemed as a substitute for Chinese "medical accident" law. According to Article 2 of the Regulation on the Handling of Medical Accidents (2002, State Council), "medical accidents" (医疗事故 ("*Yi Liao Shi Gu*")) is defined as "accidents that have caused personal injury to the patients *negligently* by the medical institutions or the staff members thereof in the activities of medical treatment by violating the laws, regulations, ministerial rules concerning medical treatment and health or the standards or conventions of medical treatment and nursing" (emphasis added).

medical staff members, the medical institution shall be liable for compensation". It is unclear whether Article 54 and its *fault-based* principle are equally applicable to the area of information disclosure. In Chinese law, the concept of "diagnosis and treatment activities" means "any activity that, through different methods, such as examination, applying medicines and medical devices, and operations, aims to diagnose illness, cure illness, alleviate illness, alleviate pain, improve functions, prolong life and help patients to restore health".[31] It seems that it does not include information disclosure. Despite that, I am of the view that the approach of attributing tortious liability in the context of *information disclosure* should also be a *fault-based* one.[32] Admittedly, the doctrine of "informed consent" is committed to respect, honour and protect a patient's right of autonomy or self-determination. That creates a strong motive to argue that the approach of attributing tortious liability should be right-based rather than fault-based. However, as demonstrated by common law, the judiciary shows reluctance to talk about the doctrine of informed consent in the context of battery and assault[33] mainly because battery and assault does not involve the consideration of professional opinions and professional standard of care. "Professional negligence" becomes the common legal framework to explore the issue of a doctor's duty to inform.[34] The move from "battery and assault" to "negligence" is profession-protective in nature. Once imbedded in medical negligence law, the task of protecting a patient's right of being informed cannot be immune from the consideration of the elements of the cause of action "negligence", i.e. the duty of care, the breach of the duty (negligence), injury and causation.

The Tort Law followed the tradition of Chinese negligence law that a *medical institution* is liable to pay damages arising from the negligence of its *health care professionals*.[35] That is an extension and reflection of the general Chinese tort law principle that the employer shall assume tort liability if its employees cause

[31] Rules for Implementing the Regulation on Medical Institutions (1994, Ministry of Health), Article 88 (医疗机构管理条例实施细则, 1994年, 卫生部, 第88条).

[32] *Compare*, Yang Li Xin "On the Principle and System of Imputation for Medical Damage Liability" (2009) 10 Journal of China University of Political Science and Law 62, 62–72 (杨立新: "论医疗损害责任的归责原则及体系", 载《中国政法大学学报》2009 年第2 期, 第62-72页) (suggesting three principles for three different contexts: (1) the principle of *fault* liability for cases of *medical technology liability*; (2) the principle of *presumption of fault* for cases of *medical ethics liability*(including the case of failing to *disclose information*); (3) the principle of *no-fault* liability for cases of *medical products liability*).

[33] For example, *Natanson v. Kline*, 350 P.2d 1093 (Kan. 1960).

[34] That is witnessed by leading informed consent cases in common law, such as *Sidaway v Bethlehem Royal Hospital Governors* [1985] 1 All ER 643, (1985) AC 871 (UK); *Reibl v. Hughes* [1980] 2 SCR 880, (1980) 114 D.L.R . (3d) 1 (S.C .C.) (Canada); *Rogers v Whitaker* (1992) 175 C.L.R. 479 (HCA) (Australia); *Smith v. Auckland Hospital Board*, [1964] NZLR 241; revd [1965] NZLR 191 (New Zealand).

[35] *See*, Tort Liability Law of People's Republic of China (2009, Standing Committee of NPC), Articles 54, 55, 57, 58, 59, 60, 62 (中华人民共和国侵权责任法, 2009年, 全国人大常委会, 第54, 55, 57, 58, 59, 60, 62条).

damages to others in performing their professional tasks.[36] There may be direct liability for a medical institution if it is itself negligent for failing to manage its services properly. Making medical institutions readily available to pay damages caused by its employees brings convenience for plaintiff-patients. Medical institutions cannot avoid vicarious liability by claiming that they have already exercised the duty of supervision over employees or were not negligent in choosing employees. However, there is still a need to explore the mechanisms that could enhance *individual* professionals' sense of accountability. The law would not prohibit medical institutions from having recourse against health care professionals after they have paid the compensation (Lin Wen Xue 2010, 22).

10.2.2.2 Article 57: The Standard of Care and the Tests for Fault

When we talk about the "fault" of medical institutions and health professionals, "fault" mainly means "medical negligence", although it does not exclude intentional fault.[37] The notion of "medical negligence" involves the issue of setting the standard of care for health professionals and clarifying the test for medical negligence. However, unfortunately, Chinese Tort Law does not provide a clear answer to those issues.

According to Article 57 of the Tort Law, when determining "fault" or "medical negligence", the judiciary will ask if a health care professional failed to exercise the "duty of diagnosis and treatment" corresponding to "the then-prevailing medical level" (当时的医疗水平("*Dang Shi de Yi Liao Shui Ping*")).[38] It needs to be noted that the Second Discussion Draft of the Tort Liability Law formulated the first part of Article 57 in the following way: "Medical professionals shall fulfil the *duty of care* corresponding to the then-prevailing medical level."[39] It is not clear why legislators replaced the term "the duty of care" (注意义务("*Zhu Yi Yi Wu*")) with "the duty of diagnosis and treatment" (诊疗义务("*Zhen Liao Yi Wu*")). Maybe they were more familiar with the latter term and merely attempted to adopt the more lay words in formulating legal provisions. However, the absence of the notions of "the duty of care" and "breach of the duty of care" in Article 57 is disappointing. Because of the absence of the basic tort law idea that negligence is the breach of the duty of reasonable care, the significance of the Japanese notion "medical level" has been

[36] *See*, Tort Liability Law of People's Republic of China (2009, Standing Committee of NPC), Article 34(1) (中华人民共和国侵权责任法, 2009年, 全国人大常委会, 第34(1)条).

[37] Project Group of "Study on Judicial Interpretation of Tort Liability Law" 2010, Article 97.

[38] Tort Liability Law of People's Republic of China (2009, Standing Committee of NPC), Article 57 (中华人民共和国侵权责任法, 2009年, 全国人大常委会, 第57条) ("In diagnosis and treatment activities, health professionals fail to exercise the duty of diagnosis and treatment corresponding to the then-prevailing medical level, and cause injuries to the patient, the medical institution concerned shall be liable for compensation.").

[39] Tort Liability Law of People's Republic of China (2d official discussion draft, December. 21, 2008), Article 57 (中华人民共和国侵权责任法(二次审议稿), 第57条) (emphasis added).

undeservedly enlarged. It has been frequently claimed that, in Chinese tort law, the test for fault is the "medical level" standard.

Despite the fact that the term "the duty of care" is replaced by "the duty of diagnosis and treatment", it seems that, when offering explanations about the Tort Law, the Legislative Affairs Commission of the Standing Committee of the National People's Congress (NPC) of China is still loyal to the notions that negligence is a breach of a duty of care and a health professional should fulfil a duty of *reasonable and prudent care* (The Legislative Affairs Commission of the Standing Committee of the National People's Congress 2010, 232). The Commission equates the "duty of diagnosis and treatment corresponding to the then-prevailing medical level" with "the duty of care". The idea of "reasonable care" is also present in Article 60 of the Tort Law. That article creates three defences to medical liability. One of them is that, under the situations of emergency, such as rescuing the life of the patient who is critically ill, if health professionals have exercised *reasonable* duty of diagnosis and treatment, the medical institution does not bear liability for injuries suffered by the patient.[40] All of these indicate that, in addition to the "medical level" test, China's Tort Law also embraces the objective "reasonable doctor" test for medical negligence.

In my view, Chinese provisions regarding the standard of care for health professionals are a little confusing. First, it seems that it confuses the "reasonable" standard and the "medical level" standard. The two standards are actually different. Second, it does not make it clear which one is the fundamental, supreme and ultimate test for the standard of care for health professionals.

The notion of "medical level" is mainly borrowed from the Japanese legal context. Nobody explains why it is introduced into Chinese law. The use of the word "then-prevailing" indicates that Chinese law also rejects "hindsight bias". The theory of "medical level" may incorporate the "locality" rule, meaning that the task of determining the "medical level" includes the considerations of a defendant's location, qualification and rank (The Legislative Affairs Commission of the Standing Committee of the National People's Congress 2010, 232).

In Japanese law, the notion of "medical level" has historical significance. The "medical level" is a legal notion, incorporating in it a few considerations, such as the defendant/doctor's specialty, the nature of medical institution, and the locality of medical institution (Xia Yun 2009, 282). It involves exercising value judgment rather than factual judgment. That makes it different from other notions, such as "medical custom" or "common practice". Therefore, the significance of the notion "medical level" in Japanese medical negligence law is that it helps to keep distance from the term "medical custom" and encourages judges to make their own legal judgments about the standard of care, rather than solely and uncritically relying on "medical custom" to establish the standard of care for health professionals.

The notion "medical level" has made great contribution to Japanese medical negligence law in the sense that it gave judges reasons for not blindly following

[40] Tort Liability Law of People's Republic of China (2009, Standing Committee of NPC), Article 60 (2) (中华人民共和国侵权责任法, 2009年, 全国人大常委会, 第60(2)条).

"medical custom" when establishing medical negligence. However, it has several drawbacks. First, it is misleading. Although it is a legal notion and plays a significant role in helping judges not exclusively rely on medical custom or medical opinions when forming their judgments about the standard of care, the notion "medical level" is still oriented towards medical profession, medical practice and medical opinions. It can be easily misunderstood as a *medical* notion rather than a *legal* one. Therefore, on the one hand, the notion of "medical level" may cause misunderstanding; on the other hand, it adds little value to the legal notion of "breach of the duty of reasonable care". That is the major reason why the notion of "medical level" has lost favour in Japanese law. Recently, when establishing medical negligence, judges in Japan prefer to say that the defendant "breached the duty of reasonable care", rather than invoke the old-fashioned and misleading notion "medical level" (Xia Yun 2011, 39–40).

Second, the "medical level" standard is not competent to serve as a basic and fundamental test for the standard of care. It is not universally applicable. The "medical level" means a clinical level, not a scientific level. It points to the well-established and well-recognised medical practices.[41] As I will indicate in the following Japanese part, the term "medical level" actually only encompasses treatments whose safety and efficacy have already been established, and those treatments that have both technical and human resources and can be readily applicable in clinical care (Xia Yun 2011, 33). A doctor is required to *administer* those treatments. "Medical level" does not embrace innovative, emerging or "experimental" treatments. It does not answer the question of whether a doctor has a duty to *administer* innovative or "experimental" treatments if conventional treatments are not available or have been exhausted, and the question of whether a doctor has a duty to *inform* about emerging or innovative treatments even if well-established treatments are available. The "medical level" standard is somewhat convention-friendly and convention-reinforcing.

Compared with the "medical level" standard, the "reasonable doctor" standard is more friendly towards new and experimental treatments. The basic, fundamental and ultimate test for the standard of care in the area of professional negligence and medical negligence should be the "reasonable professional" or "reasonable doctor" test. The "reasonable" standard is a real legal test, actively engaging judges with the task of undertaking the risk-benefit evaluation rather than simply relying on external standards, such as "common practice". Moreover, the "reasonable" standard is widely applicable. It may allow for the selection, disclosure and administration of emerging and experimental methods of treatment.

Although it cannot serve as a basic test for the standard of care, the theory of "medical level" has some value in Chinese law. As a legal rule, the "medical level" standard offers the convenience of measuring the standard of care by looking at the wide-accepted and well-established nature of medical practices. Therefore, it has the potential of being transformed into a rule, something like the *Bolam* test or the

[41] Yang Li Xin "Proof and Burden of Proof of Medical Negligence" (2009) No. 6 Journal of Law 1, 3 (杨立新: "论医疗过失的证明及举证责任", 载《法学杂志》2009年第6期, 第3页).

doctrine of "two schools of thought". Under this rule, judges honour diversity of professional practices and pay respect to widely-accepted professional opinions, but hold the ultimate power of deciding whether or not such professional practices are reasonable or rational.

Sadly, Chinese Tort Law does not include provisions detailing the pivotal issue of how to establish the standard of care and medical negligence. The term "medical level" is not clearly defined. Maybe National People's Congress (NPC) expected the Supreme People's Court (SPC)'s Judicial Interpretation to fill that void. The official and final version of Judicial Interpretation of Tort Liability Law has not yet surfaced. The discussion paper drafted by SPC (Judicial Interpretation) on how to adjudicate the cases of "liability for medical damage" does not provide enough details about the standard of care for medical professionals. It only restates the old practice that, when deciding "the then-prevailing medical level" or whether or not a health professional is negligent, courts should rely on "external" standards, such as statutory provisions and medical practices (The Supreme People's Court of China 2012, Article 22). In addition to those standards, courts can, if necessary, consider a few other factors, such as the qualification of medical institution, the qualification of medical professionals, and discrepancies between geographical areas (The Supreme People's Court of China 2012, Article 22). Similarly, in interpreting and determining the "then-prevailing medical level", the Discussion Draft proposed by tort scholars only suggests that the law should adopt the controversial "locality rule" and take some factors, such as the location, the level of medical institutions and the qualifications of professionals, into consideration (Project Group of "Study on Judicial Interpretation of Tort Liability Law" 2010, Article 100). Both of them are silent on the detailed test for the standard of care and negligence.

Another possible explanation for the silence is that, as a civil law jurisdiction, Chinese law does not invest hope in judges being actively involved in analysis of negligence. Judges need to resort to external expertise, such as "expert authentication", to obtain judgments about the standard of care and medical negligence. However, legal judgments are different from medical judgments. Even if medical experts are allowed to judge the issue of standard of care, the final decision should be reserved in the hands of the judiciary. SPC has chosen to treat the conclusions of authentication as "evidence" rather than as conclusive judgments.[42] Therefore, giving judges more guidance on the issue of how to establish the standard of care and medical negligence is necessary.

In this respect, the risks-benefits analysis and the *Bolam* test, which have been developed in common law jurisdictions, are advisable. First of all, the general standard of care is the "reasonable doctor" standard accompanied by the risk-benefit

[42] Notice of the Supreme People's Court on Trying Civil Cases on Medical Disputes by Referring to the "Regulation on Handling Medical Accidents" (No. 20 [2003] of the Supreme People's Court), Article 2 (2) (最高人民法院关于参照《医疗事故处理条例》审理医疗纠纷民事案件的通知, 2003年, 最高人民法院, 第2 (2)条). *See also*, The Supreme People's Court of China 2012, Article 20 (affirming that courts shall not admit the conclusions of authentication made by medical experts as evidence if judges have "reasonable doubt" about them).

analysis.[43] However, for professionals, including health care professionals, the legal principles formulated along the line of the *Bolam* test are also available.[44] The *Bolam*-based line of formulations accords medical professionals great deference and considerable latitude in providing professional services. It honours genuine difference of opinions among medical professionals. Other interrelated principles that have a protective effect on the exercise of medical judgment include: (1) an error in judgment is different from negligence; (2) doctors cannot guarantee success or ensure a cure; (3) negligence cannot be assumed on the basis of the consequences of the treatment to the patient; (4) medical judgment shall not be scrutinised using the perfect vision afforded by hindsight.[45] These principles tell people that the law should acknowledge and accept the uncertain and imprecise nature of medicine. The doctors can only be expected to exercise reasonable care. All of these principles and rules could be embraced under Article 57 of the Tort Law. It is not difficult to do that because Article 57 already embraced the notion of avoiding hindsight and the

---

[43] For example, according to the *Queensland (Australia) Civil Liability Act* (2003), the general principles for general standard of care are: (1) A person does not breach a duty to take precautions against a risk of harm unless – (a) the risk was foreseeable (that is, it is a risk of which the person knew or ought reasonably to have known); and (b) the risk was not insignificant; and (c) in the circumstances, *a reasonable person in the position of the person* would have taken the precautions. (2) In deciding whether a reasonable person would have taken precautions against a risk of harm, the court is to consider the following (among other relevant things) – (a) the probability that the harm would occur if care were not taken; (b) the likely seriousness of the harm; (c) the burden of taking precautions to avoid the risk of harm; (d) the social utility of the activity that creates the risk of harm. *See*, *Civil Liability Act 2003* (Qld), s 9 (1) (2). The risk-benefit analysis is applicable in medical negligence law.

[44] For example, in Australia, the standard of care for professionals (including but not limited to medical professionals) are: (1) A professional does not breach a duty arising from the *provision of a professional service* if it is established that the professional acted in a way that (at the time the service was provided) was *widely accepted* by peer professional opinion by a *significant number* of *respected* practitioners *in the field* as *competent* professional practice. This serves as a defense for professionals to a claim of negligence. (2) To benefit from this defense, a professional needs to introduce evidence in support of his or her conduct that satisfies four criteria: (a) The conduct was *widely accepted*. The conduct was not only accepted by one particular regional group, but by various groups. This may mean that the practice may need to be accepted nationally, or internationally, dependent upon the professional concerned. Peer professional opinion does not have to be *universally accepted* to be considered *widely accepted*. (b) The conduct was *accepted by a significant number of practitioners*. Having regard to the number of practitioners in practice, *a large proportion* accepted the behaviour. It does not mean that over half of practitioners need to accept the conduct. It is possible for *a number of "schools of thought"* to exist in relation to the practices within a profession. (c) The practitioners providing evidence in support must be *"in the field'* of practice under review, and *"respected"* in that field. Accordingly, in areas of specialty medicine and research, there will be exist a limited number of professionals who will be able to provide the evidence necessary. (d) The evidence must support that the conduct in question was *"competent"*. (3) The fact that there are *differing* peer professional opinions widely accepted by a significant number of respected practitioners in the field concerning a matter does not prevent any 1 or more (or all) of the opinions being relied on for the purposes of this section. (4) However, peer professional opinion can not be relied on if the court considers that the opinion is *irrational* or contrary to a written law. *See*, *Civil Liability Act 2003* (Qld), s 22 (1) (2) (3) (4); J. A. Devereux 2007, 650–651.

[45] *See*, Sect. 3.5.2.

requirement that doctors follow mature, time-honoured and widely recognised medical practices. What Chinese law needs to do is to announce the supremacy of the "reasonable man (doctor)" standard as the basic test for (medical) negligence, to detail the risk-benefit analysis when formulating the general principle for the general standard of care, and, at the same time, to transform the "medical level" theory into a rule that governs the standard of care for medical professionals and that defines circumstances under which judges accord weighty deference to medical practices. More importantly, in addition to the "medical level" theory or the *Bolam*-like rule, Chinese law needs to acknowledge, and accords supremacy to, the basic tort ideas that medical negligence is the breach of a doctor's duty of reasonable care or the breach of a doctor's duty to take precautions against a risk of harm, and, in establishing medical negligence, courts shall consider the foreseeability of the risk of harm, the probability of the harm occurring, the seriousness of the harm, the burden or cost of taking precautions to avoid the risk of harm, and the social utility of the activity that creates the risk of harm.

However, enshrined in the *Bolam* philosophy is a non-interventionist approach. The *Bolam* test does not encourage scrutinising of the external clinical efficacy and safety of a treatment.[46] Delivering health care is viewed as involving *highly skilled, dedicated and altruistic* staff applying *uncertain but technical knowledge* for *the benefit of patients*. Accordingly deference to medical professional opinions not only reflects the judiciary's admission that they lack sufficient expertise to judge technical issues, but is also underpinned by their confidence on the ethics of medical professionals. Underlining the deferential approach is the notion that the medical profession is well-trained, well-regulated and self-disciplined profession that deserves public trust and respect. A survey of the reasons for judicial non-intervention revealed that the factors behind the reticence of the judiciary include: the characterisation of professionals' work as altruistic, the feeling that they are generally undeserving of liability, the need to provide a comfortable working environment to encourage them to continue to offer their services to society, the importance of permitting them to exercise clinical judgment without constantly worrying about litigation (Montgomery 2003, 177). I am not very confident that this deferential approach is readily transferable to China, especially when I read bad stories[47] about the deteriorating doctor-patient relationship and public dissatisfaction with medical profession.

---

[46] Lachlan McMurtrie 2006, 224 (highlighting that widely accepted medical practice may not concur with what has been scientifically and clinically proven to an appropriate treatment regime; arguing that the law should recognise *clinical practice guidelines* using principles of *evidence-based medicine* as the prima facie standard of care for treatment, rather than allowing customary practice to define standard of care and requiring little or no objective proof of efficacy or safety).

[47] Those stories, reported by Chinese media, are mainly concerned with patients' complaints about doctors' lack of skill and responsibility in providing health care, doctors' over-prescribing expensive medication, doctors' subjecting patients to needless examination and treatment, and doctors' taking bribes and kickbacks from patients and pharmaceutical companies.

The doctor-patient relationship in China suffers from lack of mutual trust and even hostility.[48] That has drawn international attention.[49] In China media exposure of some extreme, high-profile cases reinforced the public's negative perception of the medical profession.[50] Sometimes patients resort to protests, riots and threatened or actual violence to resolve the doctor-patient disputes because they mistrust the existing dispute-resolution schemes.[51] Doctors are also the victims of this bad relationship (*See*, Liu Xue Ying et al. 2008, 87–89). Even the Tort Law devotes a separate provision to show its commitment to protecting doctors' rights and interests.[52]

When people investigate the reasons for the situation, they find that doctors are not the only party to blame, although some wrong doctors may have ruined the reputation of the profession.[53] There are many governmental, economic, legal,

[48] A survey showed that the medical profession is more pessimistic about the doctor-patient relationship than patients. The impression of bad doctor-patient relations may be created by media exposure of extreme cases. *See*, Fu Zi Tang et al. 2006, 11.

[49] *See*, The Lancet 2010; Yi Yang et al. 2010 (responding to the first Editorial); The Lancet 2012.

[50] A survey showed that patients and the medical profession hold divergent opinions towards the media's involvement in medical disputes. While 73.3% of the patients surveyed commented positively towards the media and think that the media contributed to disputes-resolution, almost all hospitals and medical professionals oppose the media being involved in medical disputes and think that the media are destructive to dispute-resolution. *See*, Fu Zi Tang et al. 2006, 38. *See also*, The Lancet 2010, 657; Yi Yang et al. 2010, 1823–1824 (saying the media to "provoke[] tension between doctors and patients", "mislead[]" the public, and "demonise[]" Chinese doctors)).

[51] *See*, Xu Xin and Lu Rong Rong (2008), 82–101. *See also*, Dean M. Harris and Chien-Chang Wu (2005), 456. A survey showed that 56.1% of medical professionals surveyed had experienced the patient's physical threat. *See*, Fu Zi Tang et al. 2006, 14. Violence against doctors, including murder, is commonplace and reportedly increasing. In 2006, the last year for which detailed records on patient-doctor violence was reported publicly (including violence perpetrated by patient family members and friends), the Chinese Ministry of Health stated that 5,519 medical personnel had been "injured" in disputes. And on March 29, the China Daily cited an "official source" who said that in 2010, 17,000 violent incidents took place, affecting roughly 70% of all public hospitals in China. *See*, Adam Minter *Violent Crimes in China's Hospitals Spread Happiness* http://www.bloomberg.com/news/2012-03-29/violent-crimes-in-china-s-hospitals-spread-happiness.html (last accessed April 28, 2012). Two recent examples of violence against health professionals are: (1) In September, 2011, Xu Wen, a 43-year-old otolaryngologist at Beijing Tongren Hospital, had been stabbed 17 times in her arms, head and back by a dissatisfied patient, Wang Baoming. (2) In March, 2012, Wang Hao, a young internist at the First Affiliated Hospital of Harbin Medical University in northeast China, was stabbed to death by a disgruntled patient. Three other doctors were seriously injured in the attack.

[52] Tort Liability Law of People's Republic of China (2009, Standing Committee of NPC), Article 64 ("Lawful interests and rights of medical institutions and its health professionals shall be protected by law. Those who interfere with the order of medical treatment and obstruct the work and life of medical professionals shall assume legal liability according to law.") (中华人民共和国侵权责任法, 2009年, 全国人大常委会, 第64条).

[53] Two phenomena do destroy the reputation of Chinese medical profession. Some Chinese doctors accept or even seek red envelopes ("*Hong Bao*" (红包)) (a monetary gift in exchange for favourable service) from patients against the rules. Second, some doctors receive or even ask for financial kickbacks ("*Hui Kou*" (回扣)) from drug companies. Even doctors acknowledge that "lack of professional ethics" or "deterioration of professional ethics" is one of the main reasons for medical disputes. *See*, Yi Yang et al. 2010.

social, medical, and cultural contributing factors (*See*, Wen Chao Ying et al. 2007, 24–26). The insufficiency in both government supervision, government regulation of the medical profession, and government investment in health care is one of the major reasons.[54] Health professionals are subjected to a system that tolerates and even forces them to over-prescribe expensive or needless medication in order for the hospital to survive. The health care reform, which is market-oriented, has been proved to be a failure. Many doctors are not happy with their job, especially their income (*See*, Yang Hui et al. 2003, 18–20), complaining that they are underpaid, undervalued and mistrusted. The starting salary for a doctor is around $500 per month. In order to supplement their income, doctors legally receive commissions on prescriptions and medical services, and, although illegally, they take red envelopes (filled with cash) from patients and kickbacks from pharmaceutical companies. Most doctors have a very heavy workload.[55] The appointment time that most patients have is between 3 and 10 min (Fu Zi Tang et al. 2006, 17). Doctors always feel the stress that comes from this job and life (*See*, Lei Yi and Wu Ming 2010, 1055–1057).

The remaining issue is whether this Chinese situation should make a difference in formulating legal rules that reflect attitudes towards medical profession. On the one hand, the law may need to send a message to the public that lay people should respect professionals. On the other hand, the public may feel uncomfortable with legal rules that give too much deference to medical practices, especially when they lack confidence in the integrity of the profession. In that case, the courts imposing rigorous scrutiny of the medical profession, or undertaking rigorous risk-benefit analysis, or asking experts to perform the risk-benefit analysis, may be needed, if the *Bolam* test is not readily applicable. In my view, in Chinese clinical care, rebuilding and restoring mutual trust and confidence between doctors and patients is very important.

10.2.2.3 Article 58: Presumption of Fault

Generally, the cause of action "medical negligence" has three elements: the fault of medical institution and/or professionals, the damage suffered by a patient, and the connection between the fault and the damage. That is made clear by Article 54 of the Tort Law. Article 57 of the Tort Law offers a rule, although inadequate, of how to establish fault or medical negligence. However, according to Article 58 of the Tort Law, if a patient suffers from "damage", medical institutions shall be *presumed to be "at fault"* if they: (i) violate Laws, Administrative Regulations, Rules, or other stipulations regarding diagnostic and treatment practices; (ii) conceal or refuse to

[54] A survey done by *Ding Xiang Yuan* (丁香园), a popular biomedical website in China, in 2010, reveals that when asked about the main reasons for the increased tension between doctors and patients, 78% of 14,577 survey participants (including 5,710 residents, 5,132 attending physicians, 2,256 associate chief physicians, and 609 chief physicians) blamed it on a lack of government funding to hospitals and 70% accused the public media for negative reports. *See*, Yi Yang et al. 2010, 1823–1824.

[55] A study showed that almost 90% of doctors surveyed must see 10–40 patients in their 8-h office time. 14.7% of them will see 40 patients in their 8-h office time. *See*, Fu Zi Tang et al. 2006, 16.

provide relevant medical records with respect to the disputes; or (iii) forge, falsify or destroy medical records.[56] Here, two issues need to be addressed: First, is this *presumption of fault rebuttable*? Second, if it is rebuttable, *what* proof may rebut the presumption? All of these questions relate to the basic issue of whether or not the law admits that the "reasonable" doctor standard is the supreme, fundamental and ultimate test for the standard of care and medical negligence.

Following Article 58, violating "Laws, Administrative Regulations, Rules, or other stipulations regarding diagnostic and treatment practices" will result in the defendant-medical institution being presumed to be at fault. My particular concern is that some scholars even suggest that this presumption of fault should *not* be rebuttable.[57] Here the real issue is how much significance we should attach to those statutory and professional standards. The presumption of negligence already accords great authority to the "Laws, Administrative Regulations, Rules, or other stipulations regarding diagnostic and treatment practices" in establishing breach of the standard of care. Making that presumption irrebuttable actually gives those "external standards" absolute authority.

My view is that the law needs to show fidelity to, and accord supremacy to, the basic test for negligence – the objective "reasonable doctor" test, rather than surrendering the judgment of the standard of care to those "external standards". It needs to be noted that Chinese Tort Law's formulations of those "standards" that deserve deference are very encompassing. They not only include "Laws" that have the second highest legal authority in the Chinese legal system, but also embrace "stipulations regarding diagnostic and treatment practices" that may be mere convenient expression of medical custom. Nobody can guarantee that those standards are always of high quality. There is always a risk that poor quality medical practices may function as a shield for medical professionals rather than as a guide for them. Moreover, giving too much authority to "custom" may hinder, chill or even kill medical progress. Statutory standards may lag behind the development of medical science. Chilled by the custom-oriented and orthodoxy-reinforcing rules, medical professionals may show unwillingness to depart from convention and try innovative procedures. Therefore, the wiser way of treating "statutory standards" and "common practice" when establishing the standard of care for doctors, is, as in common law jurisdictions, to deem them to be "important" evidence, rather than "decisive" or "conclusive" evidence.[58]

[56] Tort Liability Law of People's Republic of China (2009, Standing Committee of NPC), Article 58 (中华人民共和国侵权责任法, 2009年, 全国人大常委会, 第58条).

[57] Liang Hui Xing 2010, 38–39; Project Group of "Study on Judicial Interpretation of Tort Liability Law" 2010, Article 101. *See also*, The Supreme People's Court of China 2012, Article 8. *Compare*, Lin Wen Xue 2010, 21 (interpreting "presumption of fault" as giving the defendant an opportunity to rebut the presumption); Wang Yue 2010, 36 (reading "presumption of fault" as meaning that judges can directly presume fault, without the need to organize authentication); Liao Huan Guo 2010, 24 (reading Article 58 as "shifting burden of proof").

[58] For example, in English law, departure from a protocol is not automatically negligent. It raise a prima-facie case of negligence and, unless the circumstances indicate that there were good reasons for departing from the usual practice, the professional will be found liable. *See*, Jonathan Montgomery *Health Care Law* (2 ed, Oxford University Press, New York, 2003) 183–184.

The argument that the presumption of fault is rebuttable should be equally applicable to the circumstances of (ii) and (iii) of Article 58, where medical institutions conceal, refuse to provide, forge, falsify, or destroy medical records. Most medical records are controlled by medical institutions. They provide vital information for an authentication committee or a court to establish whether or not the defendant-medical-institution is negligent and whether or not there is causation between the defendant's negligent conduct and the damage suffered by a patient. The behaviours of medical institutions, which are listed in (ii) and (iii) of Article 58, may hinder an authentication committee or a court from fulfilling, or make it impossible to fulfil, the task of establishing medical negligence and causation. Under those circumstances, it is justifiable for the law to loosen the plaintiff-patient's burden of proof and to presume the defendant-institution to be at fault or negligent. However, the presence of *flawed medical records* does not necessarily mean that the defendant-institution is *negligent in diagnosis, information disclosure and treatment.* The legal effect of a defendant hiding or destroying medical records, or making or presenting defective medical records is to alleviate or revoke the plaintiff-patient's burden of proof rather than to hold the defendant-institution automatically liable for the damage suffered by the patient. The term "fault" in Article 58 should mean the "fault" in *diagnosis, information disclosure and treatment* rather than in making, maintaining and presenting medical records. In the same vein, the term "damage" in Article 58 should mean "damage" *caused by the "fault" in diagnosis, information disclosure and treatment.*[59] There seldom is causation between the *fault in making, maintaining and presenting medical records* and the *damage* suffered by a patient in the process of *diagnosis, information disclosure and treatment.* Therefore, the better approach of explaining (ii) and (iii) of Article 58 is that, even if the defendant's behaviour is defective or flawed in making, maintaining and presenting medical records, and is, therefore, presumed to be at fault, the defendant should be given a chance to rebut this presumption by showing that he had exercised reasonable care in diagnosis, information disclosure and treatment, or had satisfied the reasonable doctor standard, and, therefore, is not at fault or negligent in diagnosis, information disclosure and treatment. That is different from the approach of arguing that the presumption is not rebuttable, which actually equates and confuses the flaw of the defendant in making, maintaining and presenting medical records with his "fault" in diagnosis, information disclosure and treatment.

It is good to see that the Legislative Affairs Commission of the Standing Committee of the National People's Congress seems to support the view that the presumption of fault in Article 58 is rebuttable, admitting that a breach of the duty of care is not equivalent to a violation of statutory provision (The Legislative Affairs Commission of the Standing Committee of the National People's Congress 2010, 232, 235). However, it still needs to wait and see whether or not this view will

[59] *See*, The Legislative Affairs Commission of the Standing Committee of the National People's Congress 2010, 252 (emphasising that the "fault" that is presumed in Article 58 is the "fault" that caused the patient's damage).

become a majority in China because the orthodox view that a violation of statutory provisions and medical norms itself is negligence is still overwhelming. Tracing back to the era of "medical accidents", Chinese law has a tradition of equating "external" standards, such as statutory provisions and medical common practices, with the legal standard of care for health professionals.[60] Chinese law shows excessive deference to the "external" standards rather than focus on the legal test for medical negligence.[61] Because of that, some legal notions, such as the risk-benefit balance, the standard of care for professionals and medical negligence, and "internal" legal rules concerning negligence and medical negligence, are not well developed in Chinese law. Another aspect of Chinese law's excessive deference to "external" standards is that, even if the reasonable doctor standard and "statutes and medical norms" are distinguished, their roles are usually misplaced. There is a view, which is very popular in both academia and the judicial field of China, that the reasonable doctor standard has a role to play only when there is *no* "statutes and medical norms" (Gao Shengping 2010, 617–618; Yu Mingshui 2010, 39). If "statutes and medical norms" are available, they will be regarded as conclusive standards of conduct for health professionals. Whether or not the defendant violates "statutes and medical norms" is given priority and primacy as a test for medical negligence. The basic "reasonable doctor" standard is degraded into a supplementary and secondary test for medical negligence.

Although the Legislative Affairs Commission realises that a violation of statutory provision is different from the breach of the duty of care and, therefore, rebutting the presumption of fault is allowable, it fails to offer persuasive explanations for that. It cites some principles, such as "avoiding hindsight bias" and "no guarantee of result", to explain the difference between a doctor's failure to follow clinical guidelines and a doctor's negligence (The Legislative Affairs Commission of the Standing Committee of the National People's Congress 2010, 232). It fails to explicitly acknowledge the supremacy of the reasonable doctor standard in establishing medical negligence. Moreover, when elaborating the question of what proof can

[60] For example, under the *Regulation on the Handling of Medical Accidents* (2002), the notion of "medical accidents" (医疗事故 ("*Yi Liao Shi Gu*")) means "accidents that have caused personal injury to the patients *negligently* by the medical institutions or the staff members thereof in the activities of medical treatment *by violating the laws, regulations, ministerial rules concerning health care, and norms of diagnosis, treatment and nursing*" (emphasis added). Although "negligence" and "a violation of statutory provisions and medical norms" are two different elements of the notion, when establishing "medical accidents", the authentication committee and the courts seldom consider whether the defendant-doctor is "negligent". The law does not require them to do that. Their focus is simply on whether there is "a violation of statutory provisions and medical norms". "Negligence" is equated and confused with "a violation of statutory provisions and medical norms".

[61] This is also evidenced by Chinese product liability law. According to Article 46 of *Product Quality Law* (2000), there are two tests for the "defect" of a product: (1) "unreasonable risk"; (2) national and industrial standards. It turns out that, in establishing the "defect" of a product, Chinese judges are busy with looking at whether the product conforms to "national and industrial standards", rather than judging whether or not the product has an "unreasonable risk".

rebut the presumption, it mentions a *defence* to medical liability, [62] rather than citing the "reasonable" standard.

The stance of the Legislative Affairs Commission indicates that, even if there is agreement that the presumption of fault in Article 58 is rebuttable, there are divergent views about what proof or evidence that the defendant can present to rebut the presumption. First, some argue that the defendant can present evidence to show that the plaintiff's *claims* that the defendant violates statutory provisions and clinical practices, or the defendant has flaws in making, maintaining and providing medical records, are untrue (Chen Zhihua 2010, 91). Since the presumption of fault is based on the circumstances that have already been established, it seems that, once established, there is no room any more for the claim that they do not exist. Second, as I mentioned in the last paragraph, some scholars allow the defendant to raise *defences* to liability to rebut the presumption of fault (The Legislative Affairs Commission of the Standing Committee of the National People's Congress 2010, 235; Chen Zhihua 2010, 91). Since establishing fault and invoking defences to liability are two different stages of tort liability, the approach of raising defences to liability to rebut the presumption of fault seems to confuse them. Third, there is a suggestion that the presumption may be rebutted by showing that the "diagnostic and treatment practices" have already been superseded by *new or "updated" practices*. This makes sense since professional practices may lag behind medical progress. However, it is not readily and universally applicable to the circumstances relating to medical records. In my view, the presumption of fault in Article 58 may be rebutted by seeking the help of *the basic test for medical negligence – the reasonable doctor standard*. The defendant's conduct mentioned in Article 58 may be justified or excused by proof that he has already exercised reasonable and prudent care in diagnosis, information disclosure and treatment, or he did what might reasonably expected of a person of ordinary prudence, acting under similar circumstances, or he did what a reasonable doctor should have done.

10.2.2.4 Article 59: Medical Product Liability

In a chapter concerning civil liability for "medical" damage, there is a clause that lays down a hospital's liability for defective medical "products" and substandard blood. If a patient suffers damages caused by *defective drugs, disinfectants, medical devices* or transfusion of *substandard blood*, the patient may seek compensation *either* from the manufacturer *or* the blood-supplying institution, *or* from the relevant *medical institution*.[63] Medical institutions, *after paying* compensation to the patient,

---

[62] The Legislative Affairs Commission of the Standing Committee of the National People's Congress 2010, 235 (citing the example of "emergency" to illustrate how to rebut the presumption).

[63] Tort Liability Law of People's Republic of China (2009, Standing Committee of NPC), Article 59 (中华人民共和国侵权责任法, 2009年, 全国人大常委会, 第59条).

are entitled to claim reimbursement from the manufacturer or blood-supplying institution.[64]

The birth and formulation of Article 59 of the Tort Law is heavily influenced by a high-profile case of medical product liability in China – the "*Qi Er Yao*" case, or the case of "Qiqihar No. 2 Pharmaceutical".[65] The facts of the case are as follows. Out of motive for profit because diethyl glycol is much cheaper than propylene glycol, in September 2005 a chemical dealer sold 1 ton of the chemical diglycol, claiming it was propylene glycol, to a pharmaceutical company, Qiqihar No. 2 Pharmaceutical Co. Ltd., in Heilongjiang Province. He forged various documents including his business, drug registration and manufacturing licenses to sell products to pharmaceutical companies. The company failed to test the so-called "propylene glycol" as required under State Drug Administration regulations before purchase nor did it cross-check the licenses provided by the dealer. The company's analysts realised the material was substandard but inexplicably had still put it into production with the consent of company executives. The fake chemical was used as auxiliary material to produce the medication "Armillarisni A". After perfunctory tests the company had released the product. "Armillarisni A" is drug that is administered by injection to treat acute cholecystitis and chronic and atrophic gastritis. The fake Armillarisni A, made by Qiqihar No. 2 Pharmaceutical, was sold in Guangdong Province for 10.5 yuan (US$1.31) per dose while its two competitors sold at 11.68 yuan (1.46 dollars) and 12.9 yuan (1.61 dollars). The Zhongshan (Sun Yat-sen) University No. 3 Hospital is the only one in Guangdong Province that purchased the drug. In April 2006, 65 patients were treated with the drug containing fake ingredients at the hospital. In May, patients receiving the injections at the hospital had developed acute kidney failure and this prompted an immediate investigation. It was found that the drug contained diglycol, which causes pain in the alimentary canal and stomach as well as causing kidney, liver and nerve damage. By the beginning of 2008, 14 patients had died after suffering kidney failure. The scandal ended with arrest, fine, ban and a few trials.[66]

---

[64] Tort Liability Law of People's Republic of China (2009, Standing Committee of NPC), Article 59 (中华人民共和国侵权责任法, 2009年, 全国人大常委会, 第59条).

[65] There were many reports about the case. For example, *see*, Fraudulent dealer forges licenses to sell fatal fake chemical, http://english.peopledaily.com.cn/200605/24/eng20060524_268115.html; Dealer Sells Fake Chemical to Pharmaceutical Company, http://www.china.org.cn/english/2006/May/169289.htm; Fake Medicine Firm Fined, Banned After 11 Deaths, http://www.china.org.cn/english/2006/Jul/173341.htm; Five suspects questioned for fake drug case, http://english.gov.cn/2006-05/21/content_287035.htm; Death toll from contaminated drug rises to 14 in S China, http://english.people.com.cn/90001/90776/90882/6344024.html (last accessed May 1, 2012). Chinese Premier Wen Jiabao chaired a State Council executive meeting, ordering government departments to launch a thorough investigation into the case and intensify supervision and regulation of the pharmaceutical market.

[66] The chemical dealer was arrested by Jiangsu police. The Qiqihar No. 2 Pharmaceutical was fined 19 million yuan (US$2.3 million). The production licence of the company was revoked by the Heilongjiang provincial food and drug administration and the sale of the firm's drugs banned. Five company employees, two deputy factory directors in charge of technology and supply, one material buyer, one general manager, and one testing office director, went on trial in Guangzhou Intermediate People's Court. They were sent to jail for their involvement in the counterfeit drug operation.

The "*Qi Er Yao*" case raised several legal issues, involving Chinese administrative law, criminal law and civil law. In the civil field, 11 patients affected by the fake drug had sued the hospital, the company (the producer) and two sellers for 20 million Chinese yuan (RMB) (2.74 million U.S. dollars) compensation. In July 2008, the Tianhe District Court in Guangzhou held that the four defendants, *including the hospital*, are jointly liable for 3.5 million Chinese yuan compensation.

The case occurred before the inception of the Tort Law. The then-prevailing law is Article 43 of China's *Product Quality Law*, which provides that a victim may claim for compensation either from the *producer* or from the *seller* of the product if the product has *defect* and *causes* damage to others. Accordingly the cause of action "product liability" in China has three elements: the product defect, the damage and the causation between the defect and the damage. In the "*Qi Er Yao*" case, all these elements have been satisfied. The main issue is *who* shall bear the liability for compensation. In the case, there are four parties who had been involved with the chain of selling the product to the patients – the manufacturing company, two selling companies and the hospital, each party making a profit from the selling. The defendant-hospital raised an argument that the *hospital* is the "user" of the drug, not the "*seller*" of it, and, therefore, should be immune from the no-fault product liability. However, the courts found that the hospital bought the drugs from one of the selling companies at 36.005 Chinese yuan per dose, but sold them to patients at 46.10 Chinese yuan per dose, making a 28% profit from the transaction. In the courts' view, that is "sale".[67]

Article 59 of the Tort Law codifies the ruling that a medical institution or a hospital may be liable for damage caused by a defective product, even if it does not have fault in creating the "defect" of the product. Article 59 is cited as an example of imposing no-fault or strict liability on medical institutions.[68] However, this view is not absolutely true. The final and ultimate liability of medical institutions for medical products is still *fault-based* one, but medical institutions are placed in the chain of potential defendants who shall be *jointly liable* for damage caused by defective medical products. First, Article 59 only imposed on *manufacturers* a *no-fault* liability for *defective drugs, disinfectants, medical devices.* Both the liability of *medical institutions* for *defective drugs, disinfectants, medical devices* and *substandard blood*, and the liability of *the blood-supplying institution*, such as blood bank, for *substandard blood* are *fault-based* ones. That is made clearer in Chap. 5

---

[67] *See*, the judgments of the *Qi Er Yao* Armillarisni A case: Guangzhou Tianhe District People's Court (2007) Tian Fa Min Yi Chu Zi NO. 905 (June 26, 2008); Guangzhou Intermediate People's Court (2008) Sui Zhong Fa Min Yi Zhong Zi No. 3082 (December 10, 2008, Appeal) (齐二药亮菌甲素注射液产品质量损害赔偿纠纷案,广州市天河区人民法院(2007)天法民一初字第905号(2008年6月26日,一审);广州市中级人民法院(2008)穗中法民一终字第3082号(2008年12月10日,二审)).

[68] Yang Li Xin "On the Principle and System of Imputation for Medical Damage Liability" (2009) 10 Journal of China University of Political Science and Law 62, 62–72 (杨立新: "论医疗损害责任的归责原则及体系", 载《中国政法大学学报》2009 年第2 期, 第62-72页) (suggesting the principle of *no-fault* liability for cases of *medical product liability*).

(Product Liability) of the Tort Law. If there are defects of products, damages and causation between the defects and damages, the manufacturers of the products shall bear tort liability.[69] That does not involve the consideration of the manufacturers' fault. However, a seller shall be subject to tort liability for damages caused by defective products only if the "defects" of the products result from the "fault" of the seller, although a seller may be subject to tort liability if it cannot identify the producer and the supplier of the defective products.[70] Moreover, Article 59 only stipulates the liability of medical institutions and blood-supplying institutions for "substandard" blood. What Article 59 requires is that those institutions should follow statutes, standards and guidelines in collecting, testing and checking blood. It does not answer the question of who shall be liable for damages caused by contaminated blood that, although not "substandard", still causes infections to patients.[71]

Second, although medical institutions are *not ultimately liable* for damages caused by defective products or substandard blood if they do not have fault, the plaintiff-patients have the freedom to claim for compensation either from the manufacturer/the blood-supplying institution or from the medical institution. This follows the basic principle of Chinese product liability law that the "manufacturer" of a product and the "seller" of the product are jointly liable for damages caused by the defect of the product.[72] Both manufacturers/blood-supplying institutions and medical institutions concerned are potential defendants. In fact, if the plaintiff-patient only sues one party, courts may, on its initiative or by application of the existing defendants, include other parties as defendants (The Supreme People's Court of China 2012, Articles 4–5. *See also*, Beijing High Court 2010, Rules 4–5).

Third, Article 59 accords the medical institution a right to claim reimbursement from the manufacturer or blood-supplying institution after it has paid compensation to patients and the latter body is ultimately liable for the compensation. This right of recourse is subject to a few conditions: (1) the "defect" of the product is not created by the faulty conduct of the medical institution; (2) the product is not made by the medical institution itself; and (3) the medical institution can identify the manufacturer of the product (The Supreme People's Court of China 2012, Articles 27–29). Surely, the story should have the other side. If the medical institution has fault and that results in the defect of the product, the manufacturer of the product, after paying compensation to patients, also has the recourse against the medical institution (*See*, The Supreme People's Court of China 2012, Article 27). That is in accord with the

[69] Tort Liability Law of People's Republic of China (2009, Standing Committee of NPC), Article 41 (中华人民共和国侵权责任法, 2009年, 全国人大常委会, 第41条).

[70] Tort Liability Law of People's Republic of China (2009, Standing Committee of NPC), Article 42 (中华人民共和国侵权责任法, 2009年, 全国人大常委会, 第42条).

[71] If this happens, Chinese practice is to order the medical institution and the blood-supplying institution concerned to give the patients a sum of fee, based on the principle of "fairness". This has been confirmed by Beijing High Court in its interpretation on how to apply Chinese Tort Liability Law. *See*, Beijing High Court 2010, Rule 34.

[72] Tort Liability Law of People's Republic of China (2009, Standing Committee of NPC), Article 43 (中华人民共和国侵权责任法, 2009年, 全国人大常委会, 第43条).

basic product liability law in China.[73] The party who should not bear the ultimate liability for compensation shall have the recourse against the party who has the ultimate liability for compensation (*See*, Beijing High Court 2010, Rules 32–33).

Article 59 has invoked debates, suspicions and criticisms from the start. The second draft of the Tort Law put "medical institutions" as the first option for paying compensation, saying that, for defective medical products, patients may claim for compensation *either from medical institutions* or from manufacturers of the products. However, from the third draft on, the legislature changed the sequence of potential defendants for medical product liability, with "manufacturers and the blood-supplying institutions" being mentioned as the first option of defendants, followed by "medical institutions". The reversal of the sequence of potential defendants for medical product liability indicates the concession the legislature made when faced with disagreements about whether or not it is wise to involve medical institutions in bearing medical product liability.

I have reservation about the soundness of making hospitals jointly liable for damages caused by defective medical products. The purpose of Article 59 is said to provide "convenience" to the patients when they seek compensation after suffering from damages caused by defective medical products and substandard blood (The Legislative Affairs Commission of the Standing Committee of the National People's Congress 2010, 237). The view that medical institutions should be deemed as "sellers" of medical products and be jointly liable for damages caused by defective medical products is still overwhelming in China. However, in a long term, it is not wise to involve health professionals and medical institutions in the task of paying compensation for damages caused by defective medical products. Although the final liability of medical institutions under Article 59 is still fault-based, it actually imposes a strict or no-fault liability for the defects of medical products on health professionals and medical institutions because medical institutions bear the risk of manufacturers getting bankrupt and having no ability to pay back compensation. That is what happened in the "*Qi Er Yao*" case. Medical institutions have little power in preventing the "defect" of a product from occurring. On the one hand, subjecting medical institutions to potential no-fault or strict liability cannot make medical products safer. On the other hand, it may hinder medical progress, increase costs of health care and promote "defensive medicine". Chinese approach of including medical institutions as defendants in cases of medical product liability fails to honour the dichotomy between the sale of goods and the provision of health services. It does not distinguish between services and goods when applying a strict or no-fault liability. It confuses medical negligence law with product liability law.

[73] Tort Liability Law of People's Republic of China (2009, Standing Committee of NPC), Article 43 (中华人民共和国侵权责任法, 2009年, 全国人大常委会, 第43条) ("If damages are caused by defects existing in the products, the infringee may claim for compensation either from the producer or from the seller of the products. If defects in the products are caused by the producer, the seller shall have the recourse against the producer after it has paid the compensation. If defects existing in the products are due to the fault of the seller, the producer shall have the recourse against from the seller after it has paid the compensation.").

It diverts patients' attention from the product to the health care. It decreases manufacturers' incentive to make their products safer. Therefore, the better approach of allocating liability in medical product cases is to classify a doctor's use of medical products as subsidiary to the provision of health care, to apply the fault-based medical negligence law, and to keep health care away from no-fault or strict liability.

The main justification for regarding medical institutions as "sellers" of medical products and exposing them to product liability is that Chinese medical institutions make *a substantial profit from selling* those products to patients. Article 59 reflects China's reality that medical institutions and health professionals play a dual role of prescriber and seller of medical products. That is mainly due to China's health care system which subjects health professionals to the task of "selling" medical products to supplement the insufficient governmental contribution to the health care. However, I have noticed that China has showed a commitment to "separate medicine from health care", promising to gradually abolish the policy of allowing hospitals to make a profit from "selling" medical products (*See*, State Council 2012). If Chinese government keeps that commitment, the now-prevailing practice of medical institutions both prescribing and "selling" medial products will become a history. Article 59 is doomed to be short-lived.

10.2.2.5 Article 60: Defences

Article 60 of the Tort Law envisages three defences to medical institutions' tort liability: (1) the patient or his close family members fail(s) to cooperate with the medical institution in performing diagnosis and treatment that "conforms to diagnostic and treatment practices (norms)"; (2) the health professionals have exercised "the duty of reasonable diagnosis and treatment" under emergency situations such as rescuing the life of the patient who is in critical condition; (3) diagnosis and treatment is constrained by the "then-prevailing medical level". Invoking of the first defence is subject to the prerequisite that health professionals have already exercised the duty of sufficient information disclosure, making the patients aware of their conditions, the proposed treatments and their risks, and the risk of non-treatment (The Legislative Affairs Commission of the Standing Committee of the National People's Congress 2010, 244).

Compared the final version of the Tort Law with the previous versions, some changes deserve attention. First, the third draft of the Tort Law used "necessary" rather than "that conforms to diagnostic and treatment practices (norms)" to describe "diagnosis and treatment" that patients need to cooperate. This change strengthens Chinese law's tendency to treat "medical norms" or "common practice" as an exclusive test for the appropriateness of the proposed diagnosis and treatment. It hinders the effort of developing a flexible, objective and legal test for the standard of care of health professionals. Second, when formulating the second defence, the third draft adopted the tort notion "the duty of reasonable care". Regrettably, that is replaced by "the duty of reasonable diagnosis and treatment". It causes a basic tort notion missing.

Article 60 seems to be only applicable to the context of diagnosis and treatment. It is difficult to apply it to the context of information disclosure and the context of medical product liability. The first defence demonstrates that a patient's negligence or contributory negligence may be cited as a defence to civil liability. The second and third defences actually can be logically drawn from the basic test for medical negligence – the reasonable doctor standard. The second defence itself is the logical application of the reasonable doctor standard to the circumstances of "emergency". Similarly the third defence can be nicely explained by applying the reasonable doctor standard and its related rules, such as the rules that there is no guarantee of result and the law does not allow hindsight bias in medical negligence cases. All of these indicate the significance and the leading role of the reasonable doctor standard in medical negligence law, and the importance of developing such a basic test in medical negligence law. Finally, it should be noted that the notion "the then-prevailing medical level" in the third defence, which is obviously a "medical" notion, is different from the same word in Article 57, which is a "legal" notion. This further demonstrates that the notion "the then-prevailing medical level" has a confusing and misleading effect, which makes it incompetent, as required by Article 57, to serve as a basic test for medical negligence.

10.2.2.6 Article 61: Medical Records

It seems that the "liability for medical damage" part of the Tort Law inherited the all-embracing tenor of Chinese medical law legislation. In addition to tort liability in the traditional context of technical diagnosis/treatment and information disclosure, it also establishes a few professional and ethical duties for medical institutions and medical professionals, the breach of which will lead to tortious liability. They are the duty of a doctor to prepare, preserve and provide medical records (Article 61), the duty of a doctor to respect patients' privacy and maintain confidentiality (Article 62), and the duty of a doctor to avoid "unnecessary examination" (Article 63).

According to Article 61, medical institutions and health professionals are obligated to prepare, keep and preserve hospital admission records, doctors' instruction sheets, laboratory test reports, surgical and anaesthesia records, pathology data, nursing records, medical cost records and *other medical records*.[74] The medical institution has a duty to provide the "above-mentioned" medical records if a patient requests to inspect them and make copies of them.[75]

In Chinese medical law, there is a distinction drawn between "objective" medical records and "subjective" medical records. "Subjective" medical records include the records of discussion of death cases and complicated cases, the records of the

[74] Tort Liability Law of People's Republic of China (2009, Standing Committee of NPC), Article 61 (1) (中华人民共和国侵权责任法, 2009年, 全国人大常委会, 第61(1)条).

[75] Tort Liability Law of People's Republic of China (2009, Standing Committee of NPC), Article 61 (2) (中华人民共和国侵权责任法, 2009年, 全国人大常委会, 第61(2)条).

opinions of superior health professionals, and the records of the opinions of health professionals of other departments or other medical institutions. Before the Tort Law, it seemed to be an established rule, and also an overwhelming view, that medical institutions have a duty to only present to patients "objective" medical records because "subjective" medical records contain the records of divergent personal opinions of different health professionals and may cause patients' misunderstanding about the appropriateness of diagnosis and the treatments proposed by the defendant-doctor. The first section of Article 61 only has an explicit list of those "objective" medical records. It does not overtly mention "subjective" medical records because there is still disagreement on whether patients have a right to view and copy "subjective" medical records (The Legislative Affairs Commission of the Standing Committee of the National People's Congress 2010, 251–252). However, in my view, the duty of medical institutions to provide or present medical records for the purpose of patients' viewing and making a copy points to both "objective" and "subjective" medical records. The word "above-mentioned" in the second section of Article 61 indicates that a doctor's duty to *make and preserve* medical records (Article 61(1)) and a doctor's duty to *provide* medical records (Article 61 (2)) should point to the same objects. The list in Article 61(1) is not exhaustive. A doctor has a duty to make and preserve both "objective" and "subjective" medical records. The same applies to Article 61 (2) (the duty to provide medical records). In fact, courts need both "objective" and "subjective" medical records in the cases of medical negligence. Medical institutions have a duty to present both of them to courts.[76] It is impossible to deny the plaintiff-patients' right to access them. Therefore, it seems that drawing a distinction between "objective" and "subjective" medical records has little or no legal significance.

Another question is whether or not it is necessary to have a clause such as Article 61 *in the Tort Law*, or whether or not a doctor's duty in Article 61 is a *tort* duty. Some scholars suggests that, as far as tort liability and damage compensation is concerned, the liability clause prepared for breach of *the duty to inform* can be applied to the context of breach of *the duty to provide* medical records (Project Group of "Study on Judicial Interpretation of Tort Liability Law" 2010, Article 106 (2)). However, in my view, this is unconvincing. As I said before, a flaw in preparing, maintaining and presenting medical records does not necessarily mean negligence in diagnosis, treatment and information disclosure. A doctor's duty to make, keep and provide medical records is more like a professional and ethical duty than a tort duty. The legal effect of medical institutions refusing to present medical records, according to Article 58 of the Tort Law, is to create a rebuttable presumption of fault, or in procedural law, to alleviate the plaintiff-patients' burden of proof. "Defective" or "flawed" medical records may bring to medical institutions disadvantages in law. However, not all "defective" medical records will put medical institutions in a disadvantaged position. Whether or not "defective" medical records will be admitted by courts as evidence for expert authentication depends on whether or not the "defects"

[76] The Supreme People's Court of China 2012, Article 11; Beijing High Court 2010, Rule 12.

have a "material" impact on the authentication.[77] Medical institutions shall consume negative legal consequence only when their conducts in forging, falsifying, or destroying medical records make it impossible for courts to establish negligence and causation, or when there are apparent inconsistencies or errors in medical records and the producer of the medical records cannot offer reasonable explanations about them (The Supreme People's Court of China 2012, Article 17). If the function of Article 61 is simply to raise awareness that a doctor has a duty to prepare, keep and, when requested, present medical records, and a patient has a right of access to his medical records, there is no need to do that in civil liability legislation.

10.2.2.7 Article 62: Privacy and Confidentiality

According to Article 62, medical institutions and medical professionals are obligated to maintain the *privacy and confidentiality* of patients.[78] If the medical institution infringes a patient's privacy or discloses his medical records without the patient's consent, and that causes damages to the patient, it shall bear tort liability.[79]

Article 62 has a positive aspect. The notion "right of privacy" has not been well developed in Chinese law. China's *General Principles of Civil Law* (GPCL) (1986) is committed to protect a wide range of civil rights, but does not mention the right of privacy. Chinese law used to protect the right of privacy under the name of the right of "reputation", treating invasion of a citizen's privacy as infringement of his right of reputation.[80] The infringee can claim for compensation for mental distress.[81] The new Tort Law explicitly includes the right of privacy in the long list of "civil rights and interests" that it aims to protect.[82] But the Tort Law does not precede further to elaborate how to protect the right of privacy. Article 62 can in some degree

[77] Beijing High Court 2010, Rule 13.

[78] Tort Liability Law of People's Republic of China (2009, Standing Committee of NPC), Article 62 (1) (中华人民共和国侵权责任法, 2009年, 全国人大常委会, 第62(1)条).

[79] Tort Liability Law of People's Republic of China (2009, Standing Committee of NPC), Article 62 (2) (中华人民共和国侵权责任法, 2009年, 全国人大常委会, 第62(2)条).

[80] *See*, Opinions of the Supreme People's Court on Several Issues concerning the Implementation of the General Principles of the Civil Law of the People's Republic of China (For Trial Implementation) (1988, SPC, Fa (Ban) Fa [1988] No. 6), Article 140 (最高人民法院关于贯彻执行《中华人民共和国民法通则》若干问题的意见(试行) (1988年,最高人民法院,法(办)发[1988]6号), 第140条); Interpretation of the Supreme People's Court on Several Issues about the Trial of Cases concerning the Right of Reputation (1998, SPC, Judicial Interpretation No.26 [1998]), Question and Answer 7 (最高人民法院关于审理名誉权案件若干问题的解答(1998年,最高人民法院,回答七)).

[81] Interpretation of the Supreme People's Court on Problems regarding the Ascertainment of Compensation Liability for Emotional Damages in Civil Torts (2001, SPC, Fa Shi [2001] No.7), Article 1 (最高人民法院关于确定民事侵权精神损害赔偿责任若干问题的解释(2001年,最高人民法院,法释[2001] 7号),第1条).

[82] Tort Liability Law of People's Republic of China (2009, Standing Committee of NPC), Article 2 (中华人民共和国侵权责任法, 2009年, 全国人大常委会, 第2条).

make up for that regret. It reinforces the notion that a patient's right of privacy needs to be protected and violation of the right may result in tort liability. However, the task of protecting a *patient*'s right of privacy can be fulfilled by *general* privacy law and tort liability law.[83] I doubt the wisdom of singling out the patient's right of privacy in the Tort Law.

Article 62 also mentions a doctor's duty of "confidentiality". Chinese procedure laws have not yet acknowledged the rule that a doctor has a testimonial privilege in civil or criminal proceedings. Moreover, confidentiality is not absolute. It has limits and exceptions. Public interest, public security, and imminent danger to third parties may justify or tolerate a violation of confidentiality. A doctor's duty of confidentiality may be overwhelmed by a doctor's duty to warn of risks or dangers to third parties.

10.2.2.8 Article 63: "Unnecessary Examination"

Article 63 only has one sentence, that is, medical institutions and health professionals are obligated not to carry out unnecessary examination in violation of diagnosis and treatment norms.[84] There is no definition of the flexible term "unnecessary examination". There is no mention about the liability for "unnecessary examination". The formulation of the same clause in the second and third draft of the Tort Law is as follows, "Health professionals should administer reasonable methods of diagnosis and treatment according to the patient's condition, and shall not adopt unnecessary diagnosis and treatment, such as over-examination. If the aforementioned duty is breached, medical institutions shall refund the costs of the unnecessary diagnosis and treatment. If patients suffer other damages as a result, medical institutions shall bear the liability for compensation." Comparing the two versions, I find that the draft version is better than the final version. First, the final version only targets *over-examination*, without mentioning *over-treatment*. I cannot find persuasive reasons explaining that omission. Second, according to the draft, in determining whether or not a method of diagnosis or treatment is "necessary", judges will see whether or not it is "reasonable". However, following the final version, judges will simply see whether or not it conforms to "diagnosis and treatment norms". It is said that the purpose of the change is to increase the practicability of Article 63 (Gao Shengping 2010, 657). In my view, the change further demonstrates that Chinese law has a predisposition to treat "diagnosis and treatment norms" as final and exclusive standard when examining the appropriateness of diagnosis and treatment. This approach of according excessive deference to professional practices is not

[83] The clauses in the Tort Law that relate to the protection of a patient's right of privacy include Article 15 (the infringee may demand the infringer to stop the infringement, compensate for damage, and make an apology, etc.), and Article 22 ("If the infringement on any personal right and interest results in serious mental injury, the infringee shall have the right to demand compensation for mental distress.").

[84] Tort Liability Law of People's Republic of China (2009, Standing Committee of NPC), Article 63 (中华人民共和国侵权责任法, 2009年, 全国人大常委会, 第63条).

laudable. When the whole professional practice or medical norm is contaminated by financial incentives or external considerations, even if over-examination and over-treatment is widespread and apparent, Article 63 can play little role to change that because it conforms to "common practices". Third, the draft has a liability clause, subjecting over-diagnosis and over-treatment to civil liability. However, in the final version, that part is gone. It is said that the reason for deleting the liability part of Article 63 is that "it is difficult to do the refunding" (The Legislative Affairs Commission of the Standing Committee of the National People's Congress 2010, 262). Only claiming that unnecessary examination is prohibited is not enough. Some scholars propose that compensation liability shall attach to the practice of conducting unnecessary examination if it causes unnecessary medical expenses, or causes personal injury, or causes the loss of best treatment opportunity or best treatment plan (Project Group of "Study on Judicial Interpretation of Tort Liability Law" 2010, Article 108). The Supreme People's Court, through judicial interpretation, decides to restore the missing liability part to make Article 63 whole.[85]

Over-examination and over-treatment is a big problem in Chinese health care delivery. It is a phenomenon. Sometimes it is due to patients' desires to have "unnecessary" intervention. It is also an illustration of "defensive medicine",[86] especially in the old era when Chinese law shifted the burden of proof of both negligence and causation to the defendant-hospital in medical negligence cases. However, the biggest contributing factor of it is Chinese health care system, which motivates doctors to make useless prescriptions, to propose costly diagnostic tests, and to undergo unnecessary but revenue-generating procedures, in order to supplement their income and the revenue of their employers. Combating and removing health professionals' financial incentives is the root approach to responding to over-examination and over-treatment. Another concern of mine is that whether or not Article 63 has a separate value in the Tort Law. In my view, whether or not a procedure is "necessary" can be nicely determined by applying the general "reasonableness" standard or the reasonable doctor standard. Chinese Tort Law has a general provision about the standard of care for health professionals – Article 57. What Article 63 aims to achieve can be achieved by applying Article 57.

Finally, I have some comments about Articles 61, 62 and 63. These provisions reinstate a few of the doctors' professional and ethical duties.[87] They send a strong

---

[85] The Supreme People's Court of China 2012, Article 36. *See also*, Beijing High Court 2010, Rule 6.

[86] According to a survey, 70% of the doctors surveyed think that over-examination helps to produce evidence that can be used in the doctor-patient lawsuits. *See*, Ding Xiang Yuan: *It Is Difficult to Change: What Are the Doctors' Opinions about the Difficulty in Seeing Doctors and Costliness in Having Illness Treated?* http://6d.dxy.cn/article/2012/02/23/19186 (last accessed April 25, 2012) (丁香园: "难言改观:医生眼中的看病难与看病贵", 载 http://6d.dxy.cn/article/2012/02/23/19186,2012年4月25日访问).

[87] *See*, Yang Li Xin "On the Principle and System of Imputation for Medical Damage Liability" (2009) 10 Journal of China University of Political Science and Law 62, 62–72 (杨立新: "论医疗损害责任的归责原则及体系", 载《中国政法大学学报》2009 年第2 期, 第62-72页) (suggesting three categories of medical liability: (1) medical technology liability; (2) *medical ethics liability*; (3) medical products liability).

message to doctors and hospitals that they have a duty to prepare, preserve, and, if requested by patients, provide medical records; a duty to maintain confidentiality; a duty to protect patients' privacy; and a duty not to practise "defensive medicine". They send good messages. However, there is reason to wonder whether tort law provides the best context for exploring those issues. Maybe it is better to leave those issues to professional regulation or professional codes of ethics. Some issues, such as that involving medical records, involve property law, contract law, data protection law, and other branches of law. The issue of privacy and confidentiality is so complicated that one provision is obviously not sufficient to resolve the issue. It also involves exceptions and public law. The parameters of "unnecessary examination" are not easily defined. More importantly, one of the main functions of tort law is compensation. The Tort Law only explicitly points out the potential tort liability for breach of *the duty to protect privacy and maintain confidentiality*. It is silent on the tort liability in the context of *the duty to prepare, preserve, and provide medical records* and *the duty to avoid unnecessary examination*. Even if tort liability is available and those provisions are not mere proclamations, proving *fault, damage and causation* will turn out to be very complex in those situations. Tort law is not a panacea for all medical law problems. Tort law needs to be complemented by professional regulation and ethical guidance in promoting best medical practice.

The *Regulation on Handling Medical Accidents* has already specified administrative or disciplinary punishment for breach of the duty to prepare, preserve and provide medical records.[88] That punishment provision also covers other professional duties, such as the duty to report serious medical negligence and medical accidents. Awarding compensation is not always the best avenue to respond to the breach of professional and ethical duties, especially when personal injury and harm are not directly involved. In the era of Tort Liability Law, the *Regulation on the Handling of Medical Accidents* (2002) would be better transformed into a law of professional regulation. The modified *Regulation* can fulfil the mission of clarifying professional and ethical duties and offering disciplinary and other low-level responses to breach of those duties. That being realised, the Tort Liability Law could devote most of its attention to the conventional context of diagnosis, treatment and information disclosure.

[88] The Regulation on the Handling of Medical Accidents (2002, State Council), Article 56 ("In case any of the medical institutions violates the provisions of the present Regulation by doing any of the following, it shall be ordered by the administrative department of health to make corrections; if the circumstances are serious, the person-in-charge and other people that are held to be responsible shall be given administrative punishments or disciplinary punishments: … (2) Refusing to photocopy or reproduce medical records for the patients without good reasons; (3) Failing to write or properly keep medical records in accordance with the requirements of the administrative department of health under the State Council; (4) Failing to make up medical records of rescue within the prescribed time limit; (5) Failing to seal up, keep and open the medical records or material objects according to the requirements of the present Regulation;…") (医疗事故处理条例, 2002年, 国务院, 第56条).

10.2.2.9 Article 64: Forbidding Disturbing Health Care Delivery

As I mentioned before, violence and disturbance is prevalent in Chinese hospitals.[89] In Chinese, the phenomenon is called "*Yi Nao* (医闹)". The reasons for the phenomenon are complex.[90] One of the reasons is that the patients do not trust the existing avenues of resolving medical disputes. Sometimes *Yi Nao* demonstrates dissatisfaction of patients towards poor health care and unethical professional conducts. Sometimes they are the result of unrealistic expectations by poor families who, having travelled far and exhausted their savings on care, expect medical miracles. In some cases, *Yi Nao* is performed by "professional" men, who obtain authority from the patients and make a profit from compensation by hospitals for the patients' damages, because it seems that the more the extent of *Yi Nao*, the more compensation the patients or their relatives may have. To show response to the phenomenon of *Yi Nao*, Chinese Tort Law include Article 64, which states that, "[l]awful interests and rights of medical institutions and its health professionals shall be protected by law" and "[t]hose who interfere with the order of medical treatment and obstruct the work and life of medical professionals shall assume legal liability according to law." The "interests and rights" of health professionals should have been protected by general clauses that protect *citizens'* rights. The presence of Article 64 in the Tort Law is a shame. It is bizarre that it appears in a chapter handling the civil liability for the patients' damages. It reflects how worse the patient-doctor relationship in China is.[91]

Ironically, violence and disturbance in hospitals did lead to some positive changes. Doctors began to rethink the importance of the process of informed consent and to search the ways of improving communication skills and helping patients to form realistic expectation about the result of treatment.[92] Hospitals began to show

---

[89] According to the statistics of Ministry of Health, in 2010 there are 17,243 cases of violence or disturbance in hospitals. In 5 years, there is an increase of 7,000 cases.

[90] In doctors' eyes, the possible causes of violence against Chinese health professionals are: (1) Because of China's one-child policy, parents and grandparents pay great attention to the health of their child and demand higher-quality health services for their children. (2) Because a high proportion of health care payments is out-of-pocket, and, starved of funds from the government, Chinese hospitals resort to prescribing expensive, and often unnecessary, drugs, diagnostics, and procedures, poor workers and their dependants (children, spouses, and parents) have high expectations of the therapeutic efficacy of such expensive treatments. (3) There is a common lack of reasonable understanding about medicine among the general public. (4) The quality of medical services in some Chinese hospitals is low. *See*, Sheng-Li Huang and Xiao-Yan Ding (2011).

[91] In April, 2012, Ministry of Health and Ministry of Public Security even released to the public a notice, restating their stance against *Yi Nao* and subjecting some kinds of violence and disturbance in hospitals to administrative punishment and criminal responsibility. *See*, Ministry of Health and Ministry of Public Security of People's Republic of China, *Notice to the Public about Maintaining Order in Medical Institutions* (April 30, 2012, Wen Tong [2012] No. 7) (中华人民共和国卫生部 中华人民共和国公安部: "关于维护医疗机构秩序的通告"(2012年4月30日, 卫通〔2012〕7号)).

[92] Ding Xiang Yuan *Chinese Version of Guidelines on How to Prevent Violence in Health Care Workplace* http://www.cmda.gov.cn/xinwen/redianxinwen/2011-11-03/10059.html (last accessed May 1, 2012) (丁香园:《医疗工作场所防止暴力行为中国版指南(2011–2012)》, 载 http://www.cmda.gov.cn/xinwen/redianxinwen/2011-11-03/10059.html, 2012年5月1日访问).

more willingness to seek alternatives to the courts' adjudicating medical lawsuits, such as mediation by impartial third parties, to fairly and efficiently resolve the patient-doctor disputes. The Ministry of Health is hastening health care system reform, aiming to reduce the financial incentive for doctors to prescribe unnecessary examination and treatments.[93] Controversially, in May 2012, the Ministry of Health and the Ministry of Public Security jointly released a notice to big hospitals, requiring them to establish a permanent police base in the workplace and increase police vigilance inside hospitals. Although turning hospitals into high-security institutions may be necessary in a short-term, it is not a long-term root solution. It is essential that Chinese government locate the real root causes of *Yi Nao* and find ways to end it.

10.2.2.10 Causation

Like fault and damage, causation is a major constituent of tort liability theory. Liability for medical damage is not an exception. However, Chinese Tort Law is silent on the basic test for causation and the modified tests in the contexts of some special torts. Sadly, current versions of some judicial interpretations of the Tort Law (The Supreme People's Court of China 2012; Beijing High Court 2010) do not say more words than the Tort Law about the substantive law of causation. This is mostly attributable to the fact, like the case of establishing medical negligence, when establishing causation, Chinese law and the judiciary have an excessive reliance on "external" opinions, such as the authentication made by *medical* experts, thinking that there is no need to elaborate the *legal* rules of causation.

Although the general test of causation is absent from the Tort Law, the Law does envisage some circumstances under which no liability or mitigated liability could be argued. It makes the contributory negligence theory available as a mitigating factor.[94] It recognises that the victim's conduct,[95] the third party's conduct[96] and force majeure[97] may break the causation. In the context of medical liability, the Tort Law also recognises that the patient's failure to follow medical instruction may constitute

[93] State Council 2012 (trying to revoke the link between the income of health professionals and the profits gained through selling drugs and undergoing examinations).

[94] Tort Liability Law of People's Republic of China (2009, Standing Committee of NPC), Article 26 ("Where the infringee is also attributable to the damage, the liability of the infringer may be mitigated.") (中华人民共和国侵权责任法, 2009年, 全国人大常委会, 第26条).

[95] Tort Liability Law of People's Republic of China (2009, Standing Committee of NPC), Article 27 ("If the damage is caused by the victim intentionally, the person who commits the act shall assume no liability") (中华人民共和国侵权责任法, 2009年, 全国人大常委会, 第27条).

[96] Tort Liability Law of People's Republic of China (2009, Standing Committee of NPC), Article 28 ("If the damage is caused by a third party, the third party shall assume the tort liability.") (中华人民共和国侵权责任法, 2009年, 全国人大常委会, 第28条).

[97] Tort Liability Law of People's Republic of China (2009, Standing Committee of NPC), Article 29 ("If any damage is caused to other people for the reason of force majeure, no liability shall be assumed. Where there are otherwise different provisions, such provision shall govern.") (中华人民共和国侵权责任法, 2009年, 全国人大常委会, 第29条).

contributory negligence or even absolute defence to liability.[98] It also acknowledges the limited nature of medical science and medical skills.[99]

It needs to be noted that the *Regulation on Handling Medical Accidents* has already embraced the notion that, in determining the amount of compensation, the law needs to consider the contribution of the negligent medical act to the consequences of the injury, and the relationship between the injury and the patient's existing conditions.[100] There is a need to incorporate that notion into the Judicial Interpretation of the Tort Liability Law.

The Tort Law's silence on the very important issue of causation is not appropriate. In the common law, the general test of causation is the "but for" test and "balance of probability". There may exist intervening acts or causes which break the chain of causation.[101] The common law notion that *legal* causation is different from *scientific* causation[102] is of special value for Chinese law. Given that they lack expertise and knowledge, Chinese judges rely heavily on conclusions of *scientific* experts about negligence and causation.[103] Chinese law should learn that the legal causation is

---

[98] Tort Liability Law of People's Republic of China (2009, Standing Committee of NPC), Article 60 (1) ("A medical institution shall not be liable for compensation if injuries are caused to a patient under any of the following circumstances: (1) the patient or his close family members fail(s) to cooperate with the medical institution in performing diagnosis and medical treatment that conforms to diagnosis and treatment standards; …. The medical institution and its medical staff members who have fault under the circumstance as mentioned in Item (1) of the preceding paragraph shall bear corresponding compensation liability.")(中华人民共和国侵权责任法, 2009年, 全国人大常委会, 第60 (1)条).

[99] Tort Liability Law of People's Republic of China (2009, Standing Committee of NPC), Article 60 (3) (中华人民共和国侵权责任法, 2009年, 全国人大常委会, 第60 (3)条).

[100] The Regulation on the Handling of Medical Accidents (2002, State Council), Article 49 (医疗事故处理条例, 2002年, 国务院, 第49条).

[101] For example, the victims of the negligence may themselves be responsible for breaking the chain of causation. If the patient's conduct contributed to the original injury, the injury would be attributable only *partly* to the professionals. Contributory negligence theory not only can serve as a defence to liability, but also can be raised in the context of causation. Finally, the patient's injury may be the result of natural causes, such as underlying medical problems or an unavoidable accident, rather than the doctor's negligent conduct. According to New Zealand legislation, "Treatment Injury" is personal injury that is caused by treatment. It is "not a necessary part, or ordinary consequence, of the treatment, taking into account all the circumstances of the treatment, including (i) the person's underlying health condition at the time of the treatment; and (ii) the clinical knowledge at the time of the treatment". Treatment injury does not include personal injury that is wholly or substantially caused by a person's underlying health condition. It also excludes personal injury that is a result of a person unreasonably withholding or delaying their consent to undergo treatment. The fact that the treatment did not achieve a desired result does not, of itself, constitute treatment injury. *See*, *Injury Prevention, Rehabilitation, and Compensation Act 2001* (NZ), s 32.

[102] The Commonwealth countries have drawn clear distinctions between law and science and between fact-finders and medical experts. In the realm of proving causation in medical malpractice lawsuits, Australian common law has distinguished legal causation from scientific causation. Unlike the scientific causation, the purpose of legal causation is to ascertain or apportion legal responsibility. It has shown readiness and willingness to embrace common sense, value judgments and policy considerations in determining causation. *See*, *Chappel v Hart* (1998) 195 CLR 232, 242–243.

[103] Liao Tian Ming et al. 2010, 2 (revealing that Chinese judges have high dependence on the conclusions of authentication).

based on "probability" rather than "100% accuracy". Drawing distinctions between scientific and legal causations would give them more courage to exercise discretion in assessing scientific evidence.

Uncritically and blindly applying the general principle of causation to the context of medical negligence is not advisable. In the common law, the "but for" test is not the sole, comprehensive, and exclusive standard for testing causation.[104] There are many forms of departure from the general rules of causation. The "material contribution" test for causation has won wide support. If the defendant's act materially contributed to the plaintiff's injury, the "but for" test is deemed to be satisfied.[105] However, the fate of the "material increase of risk" approach is uncertain. It has been applied in several industrial disease cases.[106] Some judges were prepared to treat the "material increase in the *risk* of injury" as equivalent to a "material contribution" to the injury. But some judges showed reluctance to apply the same approach to the medical malpractice cases.[107] In the same vein, some courts showed the same caution to extend the "loss of chance" theory, which has been applied in economic cases,[108] to the medical negligence sphere.[109] There was a concern about the greater social cost of liability if the loss-of-chance principles are extended to medical negligence cases generally.[110] Elaborating the legal rules of causation, such as the "but for" test and the "material contribution" test, would provide Chinese judges with guidance on how to establish causation.

10.2.2.11 Burden of Proof

The Tort Law does not touch the burden of proof of both *fault and causation*. One explanation for this is that Tort Law is a substantive law rather than a procedural law. To alleviate the difficulty that plaintiff-patients encounter in proving fault and

---

[104] *Chappel v Hart* (1998) 195 CLR 232, 243, per McHugh J.; 255 per Gummow J.; 269 per Kirby J.; 282 per Hayne J..

[105] *Bonnington Castings Ltd v Wardlaw* [1956] AC 613.

[106] *McGhee v National Coal Board* [1973] 1 WLR 1; *Fairchild v Glenhaven Funeral Services Ltd* [2002] 3 WLR 89.

[107] *Accident Compensation Corp v Ambros* [2008] 1 NZLR 340, 351 (CA). The distinction drawn between these two categories of cases is that, in cases involving product liability, industrial pollution and industrial diseases, the creator of the risk is also the beneficiary of the risk which has generally been created for commercial profit, while, in medical cases, there are usually pre-existing conditions of the claimant, and uncertainty is an inherent part of medical practice, and medicine is of high social utility. *See*, *Accident Compensation Corp v Ambros* [2008] 1 NZLR 340, 351 (CA), para. [36].

[108] *Chaplin v. Hicks* [1911] 2 KB 786, [1911–13] All ER Rep 224; *Allied Maples v Simmons & Simmons* [1995] 1 WLR 1602; *Sellars v Adelaide Petroleum NL* (1994) 179 CLR 332.

[109] *Hotson v East Berkshire Area Health Authority* [1987] AC 750; *Gregg v Scott* [2005] UKHL 2; 2 AC 176; *Lawson v Laferrière* (1991) 78 DLR (4th) 609; *Accident Compensation Corp v Ambros* [2008] 1 NZLR 340, 353 (CA), para. [46]. *Compare*, *Rufo v. Hosking*, 2004 NSWCA 391.

[110] *Gregg v Scott* [2005] 2 AC 176, para. [90], per Lord Hoffmann.

causation, Chinese law used to "shift" the burden of proving "lack of negligence" and "lack of causation" to the defendant-medical institution.[111]

The SPC's approach of *shifting* the burden of proof to defendants in medical malpractice cases had aroused concerns and criticism among health care professionals. It seemed that SPC did not want to overestimate the potential impact of shifting the burden of proof on the outcome of litigation. In their opinions, establishing fault and causation will heavily or even solely rely on the conclusions of authentication. The shifting of the burden of proof only produced the effect that the defendant-medical institution shall bear the burden of applying for *authentication* and triggering the procedure of authentication.[112]

The Tort Law's failure to explicitly answer the issue of assigning the burden of proof in medical negligence cases and failure to endorse the exceptional approach of shifting burden of proof can be interpreted as meaning that it re-endorses or restores the *general principle* of burden of proof in medical liability litigation.[113] That means the *plaintiff-patients* shall bear the burden of proving both negligence and causation in medical negligence cases. This is confirmed by some judicial interpretations, where the Supreme People's Court and Beijing High Court make it clear that, *in medical negligence cases*, the *plaintiff-patient* must prove the *fault* of the medical institution and/or professionals, the *causation* between the fault and the damages suffered by the patient.[114] They are of the same opinion that the *defendant-medical institution* has the burden of proving that it has exercised the duty to *disclose information* to the patient.[115] As far as the burden of proof is concerned, Chinese law seems to try to make a distinction between ordinary medical negligence cases and informed consent cases. Although the two courts have the same stance on the issue of burden of proof in the medical negligence cases and the informed consent cases, they are divergent on the allocation of the burden of proof in the cases of liability for defective medical products and substandard blood.[116]

---

[111] Stipulations of the Supreme People's Court on Evidence in Civil Litigation (2001, No. 33, SPC), Article 4 (8) ("In tort litigation caused by medical acts, medical institutions shall bear the burden of proving that there is no causation between medical acts and harms, and there is no medical fault.") (最高人民法院关于民事诉讼证据的若干规定, 法释〔2001〕33号, 最高人民法院, 第4 (8)条).

[112] The Chief Official of the First Civil Court of the SPC 2004.

[113] However, arguably, that also can be interpreted as leaving the *exceptional* approach of shifting burden of proof *intact*. Chinese law needs to clarify this.

[114] The Supreme People's Court of China 2012, Article 6; Beijing High Court 2010, Rule 8.

[115] The Supreme People's Court of China 2012, Article 7; Beijing High Court 2010, Rule 8 (both of them saying nothing about the burden of proof of *causation* in *informed consent cases*).

[116] The Supreme People's Court of China 2012, Article 10 (shifting the burden of proving that there is *no defect* and there is *no causation* between the defect and the damage to *the medical institution and the product manufacturer*; shifting the burden of proving that the blood is *not substandard* and there is *no causation* between the blood transfusion and the damage the patient suffered to *the medical institution and the blood-supplying institution*); Beijing High Court 2010, Rule 10 (the *plaintiff-patient* bearing the burden of proving the *defect* of the product, the *damage* suffered and the *causation* between the defect and the damage; the *plaintiff-patient* bearing the burden of proving the *blood is substandard*, he has suffered *damage* and there is *causation* between the blood transfusion and the damage).

Chinese law should show caution to the approach of shifting the burden of proof to the defendants in medical negligence cases. Determining the ideal balance between helping patients to overcome the difficulties in proving causation, on the one hand, and encouraging medical progress, on the other, is not easy. Among the approaches that are designed to alleviate the burden of proof imposed on the plaintiffs, the approach of "shifting the burden of proof" to the defendants did not win much popularity in the Commonwealth jurisdictions because of its inflexibility, extreme nature and potential negative consequences on medical practices.[117] Compared to the approaches of "shifting burden of proof", "material increase of risk", and "loss of chance", the approach of drawing an *inference* of causation has met with greater acceptance.[118] Drawing a distinction between legal and scientific causation means that a court's assessment of causation can differ from the expert opinion and courts can infer causation in circumstances where the experts cannot.[119] Compared to the approach of "shifting burden of proof", the approach of drawing inference has the advantage of flexibility and leniency. I share some scholars' view that the approach of drawing an inference of causation needs to be available in Chinese medical negligence law under certain circumstances.[120]

10.2.3 Chinese Informed Consent Law and the Duty to Disclose Alternatives[121]

10.2.3.1 The Doctrine of Informed Consent in China: An Alien?

There are academic debates about whether the doctrine of informed consent is compatible with Chinese culture. The difference of opinions originates from the different ways of interpreting Chinese medical culture, rather than the culture itself. Some scholars read the doctrine of informed consent as promoting an individual-centred culture and see it as an "alien" to Chinese family-dominated culture. They argue for the doctrine of informed consent being "localised" or "contextualised" in

---

[117] *Wilsher v Essex AHA* [1988] 1 All ER 871, [1988] AC 1074 (HL).

[118] *Snell v Farrell* (1990) 72 DLR (4th) 289; *Accident Compensation Corp v Ambros* [2008] 1 NZLR 340 (CA). On the one hand, the approach allows the court to draw robust inferences of causation in some cases of uncertainty. A court may draw an inference of causation even if there is no positive scientific evidence, or expert evidences are not conclusive or even conflicting. On the other hand, a court may only draw a valid inference based on facts supported by the evidence and not on the basis of supposition or conjecture. *See*, *Accident Compensation Corp v Ambros* [2008] 1 NZLR 340, 358 (CA), para. [67].

[119] *Accident Compensation Corp v Ambros* [2008] 1 NZLR 340, 358 (CA), para. [67].

[120] Project Group of "Study on Judicial Interpretation of Tort Liability Law" 2010, Article 102. *Compare*, Yang Li Xin 2010, 14–15 (arguing for loosening the burden of proof for *both medical negligence and causation*).

[121] *See also*, Xiju Zhao *The new Tort Liability Law and the journey towards informed consent in China* in *Medical Law International* Vol. 12, No. 2. I have done some updating and rewriting in this part.

Chinese culture rather than copying it uncritically and without adjustment into Chinese context (Zhang Ying Tao and Sun Fu Chuan 2004, 12–15; Chen Hua 2009, 17–19). Some relate Confucianism, "family culture" and traditional Chinese medical culture to the prevalence of paternalism in Chinese health care and the difficulties in translating the informed consent doctrine into clinical care (Dai Qingkang 2003, 54–56; Zhang Ao Hui and Dong Yu Zheng 2010, 30–31).

However, some scholars are reluctant to see Chinese culture and Western culture through a series of dichotomies, such as individualism vs. communitarianism; individual autonomy vs. family decisions; individual liberty vs. social/common good, and argue for recognising the diversity, plurality and complexity of both cultures (Nie Jing Bao 2002, 18–22). "Truth telling on terminal disease" was cited as an example to illustrate that, when concealing or withholding truth in the context of terminal disease, Chinese doctors nowadays actually followed the old *Western* biomedical mode and forgot the standard medical practice of telling the whole truth in traditional China (Nie Jing Bao 2002, 20). Informed consent is deemed to be "not only well compatible with some spirits of Confucian moral traditions and traditional Chinese medical ethics but also can be justified by indigenous ethical terms, such as '*ren*' (humanity or humaneness), '*yi nai renshu*' (medicine as an art of humanity and humaneness), and '*cheng*' (sincerity and truthfulness)" (Nie Jing Bao 2002, 21).

As Professor Nie observed, acknowledging the moral necessity of informed consent in China and its cultural comparability with Chinese moral and medical ethics traditions does not mean claiming that there are no socio-cultural obstacles to realising the moral ideal of informed consent in contemporary Chinese contexts (Nie Jing Bao 2002, 22). A survey taken in 2002 in Taiwan showed that in a Confucian society, the family element often determined the course of decision, and the patient's autonomy was overlooked (Michael Cheng-tek Tai and Tsung-po Tsai 2003, 558–561). A survey done in China revealed that 72.4% of patients surveyed acknowledge the legitimacy of family members being involved in decision-making (Wang Yi Feng and Xu Yi Ping 2009, 53). It seems that both patients, patients' family members and doctors are happy with involving family members, and sometimes giving them priority, when medical decisions need to be made (Wang Yi Feng and Xu Yi Ping 2009, 53). That reflects Chinese social reality that many patients have a close relationship with their family and they trust family members to make medical decisions on their behalf. That is also at least partly because some patients need family contributions when paying the medical bills.

Another phenomenon that can only be understood by deeply appreciating Chinese unique social-cultural context is the high rate of Caesarean Section in China. In the opinion of the World Health Organization, an "ideal rate" of all caesarean deliveries for a population is 15%. However, in most middle and large hospitals in China, the Caesarean Section rate has reached 40–60%, and some hospitals have the 70–80% rate of Caesarean Section (Li Xiao Yun 2010, 103). Globally there are many contributing factors to the rise in Caesarean Section rates. Mother-centric reasons include women's preferences, women's fear and low tolerance of pain. Doctor-centric reasons may include: (1) Caesarean Section is more profitable than the natural delivery; (2) Caesarean Section is more convenient and scheduled than the lengthy vaginal birth that is not easily predetermined; and (3) hospitals are scared of medical malpractice lawsuits. China's health care is not immune from those widely quoted reasons. However, an additional contributing factor that China has is that more and more patients and families believe in and choose the "lucky" month, date, even time for the birth of their children. One survey revealed that, of 380 cases of Caesarean Section that are performed because of "social factors" (factors other than medical necessity), there are 44 cases which are attributable to patients and their families' "unscientific" belief on "lucky" birth dates (Li Xiao Yun 2010, 103–104).

All arguments surrounding the compatibility of the informed consent doctrine with Chinese culture should answer one question: what are the patients' attitudes toward individual autonomy? Do Chinese patients themselves want to be kept informed when receiving health care? A study targeting one specific patient group – cancer patients – reveals that 77.6% of them want to know the true diagnosis and most of them prefer to be fully informed (Su Yin Li and Li Le Zhi 2008, 28). Another study surveying patients with very severe conditions also shows that 92.5% of them want to be informed of the severe nature of their conditions (Su Yin Li and Li Le Zhi 2008, 28).

However, the attitudes of patients' family members towards information disclosure present a different profile. Most of them take the view that disclosure of real conditions and diagnosis will produce a negative effect on cancer patients' feeling and quality of life. One study show that only 27.8% of family members prefer full information disclosure, with 66.8% of them preferring patients being informed of only diagnosis and 42% of them adopting "the less, the better" attitude (Su Yin Li and Li Le Zhi 2008, 29). As to the patients who are terminally ill, only 2.5% of their family members prefer disclosure of true conditions, with 28.4% of them opposing to patients being truly informed and 69.1% of them preferring hiding the information for some time (Su Yin Li and Li Le Zhi 2008, 29). These data show that there are discrepancies between the wishes of patients and those of their family members.

In a legal context, since the 1990s Chinese law has showed commitment to the notion of informed consent. As I explain in the next part, Chinese Tort Liability Law has a continued commitment to accord the right of informed consent to competent patients themselves rather than to their family members. China is moving in the right direction. A psychological study comparing a group of patients who choose to make medical decisions themselves with a group of patients who opt for their family members making medical decisions on their behalf has shown that the former group of patients do not have increased psychological burden even if they know their conditions, the medical risks and complications involved in medical interventions (Zhang Gui Qing and Han Jin Li 2008, 383–386). Although in a Chinese context one cannot avoid, and actually needs, the involvement of family, the law plays a right part in promoting a culture that accords supremacy to the patients' wishes in medical decision-making.

China actually needs the informed consent doctrine very much. As I demonstrated before, both the doctors and patients in China are suffering from a deteriorating doctor-patient relationship. Lack of communication is one of the big contributing factors to that relationship (Fu Zi Tang et al. 2006, 13). A survey reveals that the majority of hospitals and medical professionals surveyed place confidence in the role of information disclosure in avoiding medical lawsuits (Fu Zi Tang et al. 2006, 18). They view the informed consent rule positively. It is beneficial to both patients and medical professionals.

10.2.3.2 The Informed Consent Law

(a) Before the Tort Law

Before the *Tort Liability Law* (2009), there are three pieces of Chinese legislation that have embraced the doctrine of informed consent. They are: the *Law on Practising Doctors* (1998), the *Regulation on Medical Institutions* (1994), and the *Regulation on Medical Accidents* (2002). Among the seven "practising rules" that the *Law on Practising Doctors* sets out for medical practitioners is the requirement that "doctors should truthfully explain the patients' *conditions* to the patients *or* their family members".[122] That is followed by a warning that "care shall be taken to avoid adverse impact on the patients",[123] which embodies the notion of "therapeutic privilege". Doctors shall obtain the approval from the hospital and the consent of the patient or family members before conducting clinical treatments on an *experimental* basis.[124]

Under the *Law on Practising Doctors*, it seems that the ambit of a doctor's duty to disclose is very narrow, encompassing only information about a patient's "condition". Moreover, breach of this duty does not entail any legal liability. According to the *Law*, only breach of the duty to obtain the consent of the patients or their family members in the context of *experimental* clinical treatments results in potential disciplinary and criminal responsibilities.[125]

The insufficiency of information disclosure under the *Law on Practising Doctors* could be supplemented, to some extent, by the *Regulation on Medical Institutions*,[126] under which the duty to disclose is a little more encompassing. Article 33 of the *Regulation on Medical Institutions* stipulates that, when administering "operation, special examination, or special treatment", the medical institution should obtain the

[122] Law on Practising Doctors of the People's Republic of China (1998), Article 26 (中华人民共和国执业医师法, 1998年, 第26条) (emphasis added).

[123] Law on Practising Doctors of the People's Republic of China (1998), Article 26 (中华人民共和国执业医师法, 1998年, 第26条).

[124] Law on Practising Doctors of the People's Republic of China (1998), Article 26 (中华人民共和国执业医师法, 1998年, 第26条).

[125] Law on Practising Doctors of the People's Republic of China (1998), Article 37 (8) (中华人民共和国执业医师法, 1998年, 第37 (8)条). According to the Article 37, a doctor's breach of the "practising rules" may be subjected to the following responsibilities: (1) being warned or having their medical practice suspended for a period between 6 months and 1 year by the administration departments of health; (2) for serious cases, their practising certificates being revoked; (3) for criminal offenses, criminal liabilities being investigated.

[126] Regulation on Medical Institutions (1994, State Council) (医疗机构管理条例, 1994年, 国务院).

consent of the patient *and* his or her family members or relatives. Pursuant to Article 62 of the *Rules for Implementing the Regulation on Medical Institutions*,[127] medical institution should respect the patient's right to be informed of *conditions, diagnosis and treatment,* and, before performing operation, special examination, special treatment, the medical institution should give the patient "necessary explanation". On the one hand, these provisions recognise that a patient has the right to be informed of condition, diagnosis and treatment. The scope of information disclosure is broadened. On the other hand, it seems that the duty to disclose still has a narrow ambit. It only targets "operation, special examination, and special treatment". Moreover, the legislation still lacks clarity in formulating what kinds of information should be disclosed about the "operations, special examination, and special treatment". Furthermore, the "legal liabilities" part of the *Regulation* and *the Rules for Implementing the Regulation*[128] attaches no liability to medical institutions for their employees' failure to disclose, even when "operation, special examination, and special treatment" is involved.

Both the *Law on Practising Doctors* and the *Regulation on Medical Institutions* regulate the main "role-players" – healthcare professionals and medical institutions – in health care delivery. However, the doctrine of informed consent they formulated is almost teethless. Breach of the duty to inform does not even attract disciplinary liability. As mentioned above, the *Regulation on the Handling of Medical Accidents* (2002) (hereafter "*Regulation on Medical Accidents*") not only serves as professional regulation, but also, more importantly, ambitiously claims to be the law dealing with medical accidents compensation. Actually its second, civil law component has been always remembered, mentioned and emphasised by Chinese academia and public. However, even in a piece of legislation whose dominant focus is on compensation for medical accidents, there is still low awareness that breach of the duty to inform may result in *civil* liability. The *Regulation on Medical Accidents* does have a separate provision regarding informed consent, but the provision appears in the Chapter "Prevention and Handling of Medical Accidents".

Of the three pieces of Chinese medical law legislation which touched on the informed consent rule before the advent of Tort Liability Law, the *Regulation on Medical Accidents* offered the best formulation of the rule. It expressly stipulates that "in the activities of medical treatment, medical institutions and medical practitioners should truthfully inform patients of their conditions, treatment measures, medical risks and others". [129] It is more embracing than previous formulations. It does not confine the duty to inform to specified categories of treatments. The range of

[127] Rules for Implementing the Regulation on Medical Institutions (1994, Ministry of Health) (医疗机构管理条例实施细则, 1994年, 卫生部).

[128] Chapter 6 of Regulation on Medical Institutions (1994, State Council); Chapter 7 of Rules for Implementing the Regulation on Medical Institutions (1994, Ministry of Health).

[129] The Regulation on the Handling of Medical Accidents (2002, State Council), Article 11 (医疗事故处理条例, 2002年, 国务院, 第11条).

information that falls within the duty to disclose is wider and not exhaustive. In addition, it asks doctors to respond to a patient's inquires in a timely manner.[130] Like the *Law on Practising Doctors*, it creates a potential exception to the duty to warn: attention should be paid to "avoid an adverse impact on the patients".[131] However, the *Regulation on Medical Accidents* only contemplates making corrections, and, in serious cases, *administrative or disciplinary* punishment for breach of the informed consent provision.[132] There is almost no hope that breach of the duty to inform may fall within the concept of "medical accident", and therefore attract compensation and civil liability. Apparently, when creating the notion of "medical accident", legislators only envisaged the traditional context of diagnosis and treatment, with no awareness of the legal rule that breach of the duty to inform may results in civil liability.

In the context of Chinese *case law*, before 2000, Chinese courts did not recognise a cause of action formulated in terms of breach of the "informed consent" rule (Jiang Chun Ling 2006, 116–117). Since 2000, the "informed consent" cases have gradually and rapidly emerged in the Chinese judicial arena. It seems that Chinese judges are more creative and open-minded than Chinese legislators and the written law. A case survey revealed that, in the opinions of Chinese courts, information that may fall within the duty to disclose include the qualifications and limitations of medical institutions, the purpose, risks and success rate of the proposed treatment, alternative treatment options, and the side effects of medicines (Jiang Chun Ling 2006, 118–119). Some courts allowed compensation for mental distress even when they found that there was no causation between the failure of information disclosure and the patient's injury (Jiang Chun Ling 2006, 120–121).

For Chinese patients who argue for informed choice, a reported case reveals that *contract law* remedies may be available.[133] In that case, two options of human assisted reproduction (IVF and ICSI) were available to the couple. The defendant-hospital changed the option that was initially proposed (ICSI), and actually administered IVF without the consent of the patients. Both the district court and the

---

[130] The Regulation on the Handling of Medical Accidents (2002, State Council), Article 11 (医疗事故处理条例, 2002年, 国务院, 第11条).

[131] The Regulation on the Handling of Medical Accidents (2002, State Council), Article 11 (医疗事故处理条例, 2002年, 国务院, 第11条).

[132] The Regulation on the Handling of Medical Accidents (2002, State Council), Article 56 (1) ("In case any of the medical institutions violates the provisions of the present Regulation by doing any of the following, it shall be ordered by the administrative department of health to make corrections; if the circumstances are serious, the person-in-charge and other people that are held to be responsible shall be given administrative punishments or disciplinary punishments: (1) Failing to truthfully inform the patient of his condition, the measures of medical treatment or medical risks…") (医疗事故处理条例, 2002年, 国务院, 第56 (1)条).

[133] *Zheng Xue-feng, Chen Guo-qing v. Jiang Su Province People's Hospital* (Medical Service Contract) (published in Supreme People's Court Report [2004] No. 8) (郑雪峰、陈国青诉江苏省人民医院医疗服务合同纠纷案(2004年8月10日中华人民共和国最高人民法院公报[2004]第8期出版)).

intermediate court held that, without the presence of emergency, the hospital's unilateral change of treatment options constituted breach of *medical service contract*. The court observed that, under a medical service contract, a hospital has a duty to disclose treatment plans and the patient has the right to choose among treatment plans. According to the court, when two or more treatment plans are available, the hospital should sufficiently inform the patient of the merits and demerits of different treatment options and follow the patient's choices.

(b) The Tort Law: Article 55 and Article 56

The 2009 Tort Law devotes two Articles to the context of information disclosure. Article 55 (1) provides that:

> Medical professional shall, *during diagnosis and treatment*, inform *patients* about their *conditions and treatment measures*. If *surgery, special examination, or special treatment* is required, medical professionals shall, in a timely manner, disclose *medical risks, alternative treatment plans and other information* to *patients*, and obtain their consent in writing. If it is not advisable to disclose information to the patient, information disclosure shall be served to his *close family members* whose written consent shall be obtained. (emphasis added)[134]

Article 55 (1) embraces the idea that under some circumstances, honest information disclosure to the patient may not be desirable. This leaves room for application of the so-called "therapeutic privilege". But the law needs to give more indication of what circumstances warrant applying this exception. Exceptions to the general duty to inform need to be interpreted narrowly and cautiously.

According to Article 55 (2), if a medical professional's failure to inform caused injuries to the patient, the medical institution concerned is liable for compensation.[135] Compared with previous legislation, the big and applaudable step that the Tort Law has taken is to expose a medical professional's breach of the duty of disclosure to the potential *tort liability*.

Article 56 creates another exception to a doctor's duty to inform. If there are emergent situations such as rescuing the life of a patient who is in critical condition, and the opinion of the patient or his *close* family members cannot be obtained, corresponding medical measures may be performed immediately with the approval of the person in charge of the medical institution or the authorised responsible person of the medical institution.[136] It recognises the well-accepted

[134] Tort Liability Law of People's Republic of China (2009, Standing Committee of NPC), Article 55 (1) (中华人民共和国侵权责任法, 2009年, 全国人大常委会, 第55(1)条).

[135] Tort Liability Law of People's Republic of China (2009, Standing Committee of NPC), Article 55 (2) (中华人民共和国侵权责任法, 2009年, 全国人大常委会, 第55(2)条).

[136] Tort Liability Law of People's Republic of China (2009, Standing Committee of NPC), Article 56 (中华人民共和国侵权责任法, 2009年, 全国人大常委会, 第56条). According to Chinese Family Law and Inheritance Law, "close family members" include spouses, parents, children, siblings, grandparents, and grandchildren.

"emergency" exception.[137] However, there are some remaining issues. First, it needs to clarify what circumstances may fall within Article 56. The situation where "the opinion of the patient or his close family members *cannot be obtained*" does not include one where the patient or his close family members explicitly *refuse* the treatment.[138] It is unclear whether Article 56 is applicable to non-emergent situations.[139] If Article 56 is only concerned with "emergent" situations, there is no need to seek the opinions of the patient's close family members. "Emergency" justifies necessary medical intervention that is in the patient's best interests. Second, what is the purpose of having medical measures approved by "the person in charge of the medical institution or the authorised responsible person of the medical institution"? The purposes of it is normally to ensure that due diligence has been performed in checking whether there are indeed any party who can give consent on behalf of the patient, and whether the medical intervention is really necessary. If the situation is emergency, medical intervention may be justified even without the consent of the patient, and, therefore, the first purpose loses some significance. If the purpose of the approval by another person is to double check the necessity of the proposed medical intervention, a person who has expertise in doing that and who is readily available, such as another doctor/consultant, may be a better choice than "the person in charge of the medical institution or the authorised responsible person of the medical institution".

(i) "Who" shall consent?

Before the Tort Law, there existed conflicts and confusion about the issue of who, the patient or his family members, had the right to be informed.[140] Basically there were three different formulations. First, the *Law on Practising Doctors* adopted a "patient *or* family members" approach. Doctors should disclose information to

---

[137] It answers several concerns that raised and highlighted in a high-profile tragedy (the *Xiao Zhijun* (肖志军) episode). In November 2007, a pregnant woman *Li Liyun* (李丽云) and her baby died because a medical institution in Beijing cannot obtain the consent to operation from *Xiao Zhijun*, who was assumed to be *Li*'s husband, but later turned out to be *Li*'s boyfriend. It is not very clear why *Xiao* refused to sign the consent form. *Li*'s parents sued the hospital, claiming that the hospital failed to take measures to rescue the life of *Li* and her baby. In 2009, Beijing High People's Court ruled in favour of the hospital, mainly on the basis that, according to the conclusion of forensic examination, there is no causation between *Li*'s death and the conduct of the hospital.

[138] The Legislative Affairs Commission of the Standing Committee of the National People's Congress 2010, 231. *See also*, Liang Hui Xing 2010, 37 (favouring to protect a patient's right of self-determination).

[139] *See*, The Supreme People's Court of China 2012, Article 23 (clarifying that Article 56 shall apply to the following circumstances: (1) the patient is in critical condition and cannot express opinions, and the explicit opinions of the patient's close family member cannot be obtained; (2) the patient's condition is rapidly deteriorating, if immediate medical intervention is not taken, that will result in irreparable consequences; (3) the patient cannot express opinions, but the opinions of his close family members are not in the patient's interest). The first (1) and (2) circumstances are "emergent", but the third is not.

[140] For detailed discussion, *see*, Ji Tao 2010, 10–13.

patients *or* their family members.[141] It gave "patients" and "family members" equal priority and status. More importantly, it saw the patients' consent as an alternative to the consent of family members. Doctors may obtain the consent of the patient. But alternatively, they are legally allowed to seek and rely only on the consent of the patient's family members.

The second approach, "patient *and* family members", was endorsed in the *Regulation on Medical Institutions*.[142] It treated the "patients' consent" and "consent of family members or next of kin" cumulatively rather than alternatively. Under this approach, the patients' will cannot be contravened or ignored. Compared to the first approach, it strengthened the importance of the patient's autonomy and self-determination. But the patient's exercise of right was constrained by the involvement of family members.

The *Regulation on Handling Medical Accidents* favoured a "patient's consent" approach.[143] This third approach revolutionarily accords the right to know and decide in undergoing treatment to the patients themselves rather than their family members. It moved closer to the spirit and rationale of the informed consent rule. The Tort Law has confirmed the third approach, reinforcing the notion that it is "the patients" rather than "their family members" who should exercise the right of self-determination.

(ii) Distinction between diagnosis/treatment and information disclosure?

As I elaborated above, the Chapter 7 "Liability for Medical Damage" of the Tort Law includes a few *general* provisions, such as the fault-based rule of medical liability (Article 54), the standard of care/negligence provision (Article 57), the presumption of fault provision (Article 58), and the provision regarding defences to medical liability (Article 60). In addition to that, the Tort Law *separately* stipulates the doctors' duty of information disclosure (Articles 55 and 56). At this stage, it is still unclear *how distinctive* these informed consent provisions are. Or what is the relationship between the general medical liability provisions and the informed consent provisions? Should the general provisions govern and universally apply to the contexts of both diagnosis/treatment and information disclosure?

On the one hand, embracing information disclosure in the Tort Law indicates that the doctor's duty to inform is being explored in the framework of tort liability law and medical negligence law. That means some general rules of medical negligence would unavoidably apply to both contexts, including information disclosure. Those rules may include the fault based nature of liability, the general components of medical negligence liability (a duty of care, breach of standard of care, damage and causation),

[141] Law on Practising Doctors of the People's Republic of China (1998), Article 26 (中华人民共和国执业医师法, 1998年, 第26条).

[142] Regulation on Medical Institutions (1994, State Council), Article 33 (医疗机构管理条例, 1994年, 国务院, 第33条).

[143] The Regulation on the Handling of Medical Accidents (2002, State Council), Article 11 (医疗事故处理条例, 2002年, 国务院, 第11条).

and the rules on burden of proof.[144] On the other hand, devoting two separate provisions to the doctrine of informed consent may indicate that the context of information disclosure has some distinctiveness.

The general provisions regarding liability for medical damage cannot be applied uncritically and unthinkingly to the context of information disclosure. For example, the key focus of Article 60 (defences to medical liability) is "diagnosis and treatment" (诊疗("*zhen liao*")),[145] rather than information disclosure. Another example is that Article 58 presumes medical professionals' and medical institutions' violation of laws, administrative regulations, rules and other diagnosis and treatment norms as being "at fault". The laws and professional guidance have significance in the courts' establishing the standard of care and finding negligence. Do those "external standards" provide guidance and criteria on the issue of what kinds of information should be disclosed to patients? Even if the laws and professional guidelines can specify the medical risks and treatment options that a specified illness will have, do they know whether or not a particular patient would attach relevance and importance to those medical risks and treatment options? The third observation is that expert authentications and their conclusions would play a highly influential, if not decisive, role in establishing fault and causation. Does that mean that the persons who decide what information they need and, if the information had been disclosed, whether or not they would have chosen to undergo treatments should be the *experts* rather than the patients? To show loyalty to the rationale of the doctrine of informed consent, I would suggest Chinese law to borrow other jurisdictions' wisdom of drawing distinctions on wide-ranging issues, especially the standard of care, between diagnosis/treatment and information disclosure.[146]

(iii) The standard of information disclosure: doctor-oriented or patient-oriented?

Following the above line of thinking, another issue that arises is whether Article 57 (the standard of care/negligence provision) also controls the situation of

[144] As far as the burden of proof is concerned, I have a concern whether there are convincing reasons for distinguishing the cases of informed consent from the cases of ordinary medical negligence. *See*, The Supreme People's Court of China 2012, Articles 6–7; Beijing High Court 2010, Rule 8 (Both of them opine that, *in medical negligence cases*, the *plaintiff-patient* must prove the *fault* of the medical institution and/or professionals, the *causation* between the fault and the damages suffered by the patient. However, in their view, the *defendant-medical institution* has the burden of proving that it has exercised the duty to *disclose information* to the patient. But they say nothing about the burden of proof of *causation* in *informed consent cases*).

[145] Tort Liability Law of People's Republic of China (2009, Standing Committee of NPC), Article 60(1) (中华人民共和国侵权责任法, 2009年, 全国人大常委会, 第60(1)条) ("A medical institution shall not be liable for compensation if injuries are caused to a patient under any of the following circumstances: (1) the patient or his close family members fail(s) to cooperate with the medical institution in performing *diagnosis and medical treatment* that conforms to *diagnosis and treatment* standards; (2) the medical staff have exercised reasonable duty of *diagnosis and medical treatment* under emergency situations such as rescuing the life of the patient who is in critical condition; (3) effective *diagnosis and medical treatment* is impossible at the current medical treatment level. ..." (emphasis added)).

[146] *See*, Chaps. 2 and 3.

information disclosure. Or, in considering what information should fall within a doctor's duty to inform, or the scope of information disclosure, does the law follow medical practices or patients' informational needs?

As I mentioned before, when drafting and discussing Article 57, regrettably, the legislators substituted the term "the duty of care" with the word "the duty of diagnosis and treatment". It is not clear why they did this. Maybe they simply prefer a lay term over a legal term because not all of them know much about law. Or, maybe in their minds, the duty of information disclosure is a part of the duty of diagnosis and treatment. Whatever the reason, the fact is that the literal meaning of the term "the duty of diagnosis and treatment" is less encompassing than the word "the duty of care".[147] The "duty of care" includes the duty of care in the contexts of both diagnosis/treatment and information disclosure.

Reading the new formulation of the provision regarding the standard of care, it is arguable that Article 57 shall *not* govern the context of information disclosure. That would leave some scope for the effort of reshaping the distinctive dimensions of information disclosure. Article 57 endorses a medical-practice-oriented standard of care. We cannot say that there is no relationship between medical practices and information disclosure. However, keeping some distance from Article 57, when formulating the scope of information disclosure, would give legal rules more allowance to depart from the medical-practice-oriented standard of care and to move forward to a more patient-needs-oriented standard of information disclosure.

The Legislative Affairs Commission of the Standing Committee of the National People's Congress has realised that the duty to inform is different from the duty of "diagnosis and treatment", stating that even if a health professional has exercised the duty of information disclosure under Article 55, there is still possibility that he may bear the liability under Article 57 because he failed to exercise the duty of care in diagnosis and treatment (The Legislative Affairs Commission of the Standing Committee of the National People's Congress 2010, 228). In a frequently-quoted informed consent case, a court in Shanghai also explicitly points out that the duty to inform is distinct from the duty to provide service.[148] Despite that, it seems that

[147] *See*, Liang Hui Xing 2010, 37–38 (interpreting that "the duty of diagnosis and treatment" is a type of "the duty of care").

[148] *Chen Rui Xue v. China People's Armed Police Hospital of Shanghai*, People's Court of Changning District of Shanghai (2000) Chang Min Chu Zi No. 3174; The No. 1 Intermediate People's Court of Shanghai (2000) Hu Yi Zhong Min Zhong Zi No. 900 (Appeal) (陈瑞雪诉中国人民武装警察部队上海总队医院案 一审判决书:上海市长宁区人民法院(2000)长民初字第3174号;二审判决书:上海市第一中级人民法院(2000)沪一中民终字第900号). The case involves a doctor's failure to inform a patient of a complication of an operation. Although the intermediate court acknowledged that the doctor was not negligent in performing the operation, the doctor was found negligent in failing to disclose the risk of the operation. The appellant court changed the trial court's opinion that the doctor is not liable because the harm the patient suffered is an unavoidable complication of the operation and the doctor is not negligent in diagnosing and treating the patient. In the appellant court's opinion, medical activities have two separate stages, i.e. the stage of informing a patient of a risk before operation and that of performing the operation. The appellant court relied significantly on the authentication report (medical expert opinion) in determining whether a doctor is negligent in providing services, but found the doctor in breach of the duty to inform even if the report did not touch on the issue.

Chinese law has a low awareness about the need to adopt *a different standard of care* in the field of information disclosure. For example, although acknowledging that the duty of care in the context of information disclosure is distinct from the duty of care in the context of diagnosis and treatment, the Legislative Affairs Commission still tries to cite a medical-profession-oriented standard of care to explain the duty to inform.[149] It is good to see that some Chinese scholars began to discuss the scope of information disclosure from the perspective of patients' informational needs (Gao Shengping 2010, 608; Yu Mingshui 2010, 231).

In my view, the task of making a choice between the doctor-oriented standard of information disclosure and the patient-oriented one is unavoidable for Chinese law. Although, as I will explain below, Chinese law has already had a list of what kinds of information shall fall within a doctor's duty to inform, that is not enough. There will always be cases where the issue is not whether or not one kind of information, such as *a risk* of a procedure, is the one that falls within Article 55, but whether or not the information, such as *the risk* of the procedure, is the one that needs to be disclosed. For example, Article 55 only stipulates that a doctor needs to disclose medical risks, but fails to clarify what kinds of medical risks shall fall within a doctor's duty to disclose. Chinese law needs a *general* clause in Tort Law that generally defines the scope of information disclosure. The clause shall provide a chance for legislators to choose a doctor-oriented or a patient-oriented standard of information disclosure. That clause may be followed by a section that provides a non-exhaustive *list* of the kinds of information that may fall within a doctor's duty to inform.[150] The information that falls within the "list" may be very extensive, or too remote. The general clause concerning the standard of information disclosure may qualify the "list" section, even if the standard of information disclosure is a patient-oriented one. That means, a doctor has a duty to only disclose the information that a reasonable patient in the patient's position would need, or expect to receive, or deem it as significant in making medical decisions, not any information that falls within the "list".

[149] The Legislative Affairs Commission of the Standing Committee of the National People's Congress 2010, 229 (introducing the Japanese notion of "medical level" as the standard of care in the context of information disclosure).

[150] New Zealand's Code of Patients' Rights offers an example. *See*, Right 6 (1) of the Code ("Every consumer has the right to the information that a reasonable consumer, in that consumer's circumstances, would expect to receive, including –

(a) An explanation of [consumer's] condition; and
(b) An explanation of the options available, including an assessment of the expected risks, side effects, benefits, and costs of each option; and
(c) Advice of the estimated time within which the services will be provided; and
(d) Notification of any proposed participation in teaching or research, including whether the research requires and has received ethical approval; and
(e) Any other information required by legal, professional, ethical, and other relevant standards; and
(f) The results of tests; and
(g) The results of procedures.").

As far as the standard of information disclosure is concerned, there is a dichotomy in Commonwealth jurisdictions. England[151] and Singapore[152] show loyalty to the traditional doctor-oriented *Bolam* test. However, Canada,[153] Australia, [154] New Zealand[155] and Malaysia[156] prefer a patient-oriented standard, such as the *Rogers* test, over the *Bolam* test. I would suggest China to follow the trend and proactively adopt a patient-oriented standard of care in the field of information disclosure. That is because, as I elaborated in Chap. 2, the patient-oriented standard of information disclosure honours the patient's right of self-determination and the distinctions drawn between "medical judgment" and "layperson knowledge", and between knowledge of "information" and "materiality" of information. Although the availability of a piece of information may be subject to medical judgment or medical knowledge, whether or not a patient would attach significance to the information does not involve medical judgment.

(iv) What information?

In expressing what amount of information that the duty of disclosure may encompass, the Second Discussion Draft drew a distinction between "*ordinary* diagnosis and treatment activities" and "surgery, special examination, and special treatment". The two contexts are very different. In "*ordinary* diagnosis and treatment activities", medical professional shall "*concisely* inform patients of conditions and treatment measures".[157] However, when "surgery, special examination, and special treatment" is involved, the requirement of information disclosure is more encompassing. Medical professionals shall "timely inform patients of conditions, treatment measures, medical risks, alternative treatment plans and other information".[158]

Comparing the Second Discussion Draft with the final version of the Tort Liability Law, it is apparent that there are some slight differences between them. The final version keeps unchanged the distinction drawn between "ordinary diagnosis and treatment activities" and "surgery, special examination, and special treatment". But the two contexts form a hierarchy. The first sentence of the provision deleted the adjective "ordinary". That means "diagnosis and treatment activities" will encompass the "surgery, special examination, and special treatment". In "diagnosis and treatment

---

[151] *Sidaway v Bethlehem Royal Hospital Governors* [1985] 1 All ER 643, (1985) AC 871.

[152] *Dr Khoo James and Another v Gunapathy d/o Muniandy and another appeal* [2002] 2 SLR 414; [2002] SGCA 25.

[153] *Reibl v. Hughes* [1980] 2 SCR 880, (1980) 114 D.L.R . (3d) 1 (S.C .C.).

[154] *Rogers v Whitaker* (1992) 175 C.L.R. 479 (HCA).

[155] Health and Disability Commissioner (Code of Health and Disability Services Consumers' Rights) Regulation 1996, Schedule, Right 6 (2).

[156] *Foo Fio Na v Dr Soo Fook Mun and Anor* [2007] 1 MLJ 593.

[157] Tort Liability Law of People's Republic of China (2d official discussion draft, December. 21, 2008), Article 54 (中华人民共和国侵权责任法(二次审议稿), 第54条) (emphasis added).

[158] Tort Liability Law of People's Republic of China (2d official discussion draft, December. 21, 2008), Article 54 (中华人民共和国侵权责任法(二次审议稿), 第54条).

activities", medical professionals shall also inform patients of "conditions and treatment measures".[159] The final version also deleted the word "concisely", indicating that information disclosure should be sufficient and full. If "surgery, special examination, or special treatment" is required, medical professionals shall, in a timely manner, inform patients of "medical risks, alternative treatment plans and other information", and obtain the patient's consent in writing.[160]

The final version of Article 55 envisages a general context and a special context. Generally, the information about "conditions and treatment measures" falls within a doctor's duty to disclose. The general provision targets all diagnosis and treatment activities,[161] including the "surgery, special examination, and special treatment". However, when "surgery, special examination, or special treatment" is involved, medical professionals shall, *additionally*, inform patients of "medical risks, alternative treatment plans and other information".[162] Furthermore, when the *special* context is engaged, the patient's consent should be in writing.

"Special examination" and "special treatment" mean: (1) examination and treatment that entail some risks and possible negative consequences; (2) examination and treatment that may expose the patient to negative consequences and risks because of the patient's idiosyncrasies or critical condition; (3) experimental clinical examination and treatment; (4) examination and treatment that involve charges that may place large financial burden on the patient.[163] It contemplates both the medical and financial

---

[159] Tort Liability Law of People's Republic of China (2009, Standing Committee of NPC), Article 55 (中华人民共和国侵权责任法, 2009年, 全国人大常委会, 第55条).

[160] Tort Liability Law of People's Republic of China (2009, Standing Committee of NPC), Article 55 (中华人民共和国侵权责任法, 2009年, 全国人大常委会, 第55条).

[161] The concept of "diagnosis and treatment activities" is wide-ranging. It means "any activity that, through different methods, such as examination, using medicines and medical devices, and operations, aims to diagnose illness, cure illness, alleviate illness, alleviate pain, improve functions, prolong life and help patients to restore health". *See*, Rules for Implementing the Regulation on Medical Institutions (1994, Ministry of Health), Article 88 (医疗机构管理条例实施细则, 1994年, 卫生部, 第88条). For definitions in other jurisdictions, *See*, *Health Care Consent Act* (Canada), 1996 S.O., c. 2, Sched. A, s. 2 (1) ("'treatment' means anything that is done for a therapeutic, preventive, palliative, diagnostic, cosmetic or other health-related purpose, and includes a course of treatment, plan of treatment or community treatment plan, but does not include, (a) the assessment for the purpose of this Act of a person's capacity with respect to a treatment, admission to a care facility or a personal assistance service, the assessment for the purpose of the *Substitute Decisions Act, 1992* of a person's capacity to manage property or a person's capacity for personal care, or the assessment of a person's capacity for any other purpose, (b) the assessment or examination of a person to determine the general nature of the person's condition, (c) the taking of a person's health history, (d) the communication of an assessment or diagnosis, (e) the admission of a person to a hospital or other facility, (f) a personal assistance service, (g) a treatment that in the circumstances poses little or no risk of harm to the person, (h) anything prescribed by the regulations as not constituting treatment.").

[162] Tort Liability Law of People's Republic of China (2009, Standing Committee of NPC), Article 55 (中华人民共和国侵权责任法, 2009年, 全国人大常委会, 第55条).

[163] Rules for Implementing the Regulation on Medical Institutions (1994, Ministry of Health), Article 88 (医疗机构管理条例实施细则, 1994年, 卫生部, 第88条).

Table 10.1 Disclosure of alternatives: China and some common law countries

	UK	Australia	Canada	New Zealand	China
Common law: *Doctor*-oriented standard	√	–	–	–	–
Common law: *Patient*-oriented standard	–	√	√	√	–
Common law: Disclosure of *risks*	√	√	√	√	–
Common law: Disclosure of *treatment options*	√(under "unusual" or "special" circumstances)	–	√(a line of authority)	–	–
Legislation: Disclosure of *risks*	–	√	–	√	√
Legislation: Disclosure of *treatment options*	–	–	–	√	√
Professional Regulation: *Patient*-oriented standard and disclosure of *risks and treatment options*	√	√	–	√	√

aspects of diagnosis and treatment. According to some courts' interpretation, informed consent may be called for when the diagnosis and treatment is for teaching or research purposes (The Supreme People's Court of China 2012, Article 33), or in circumstances where there is a need to have the cooperation of the patient or his close family members (The Supreme People's Court of China 2012, Article 33), or the use of medical products is involved.[164] There is no evidence that the circumstances necessitating a patient's informed consent in Chinese law is exhaustive.[165]

Following Article 55, for invasive treatments, a doctor may need to disclose to patients their conditions, medical measures, medical risks and alternative treatment plans and other information. The list is wide-ranging and open. The information disclosure in Chinese law includes both disclosure of risks and disclosure of alternatives. As I explored in Chap. 9, not all common law jurisdictions have embraced the disclosure of *alternatives* in the *legal* duty of information disclosure (Table 10.1). China is leading some other jurisdictions in this way: through passing a piece of legislation that has very high legal authority, it has expanded the scope of information disclosure to encompass information about both medical risks *and alternative treatment options*.

(v) What alternatives?

The Tort Law uses two terms – "treatment measures"(医疗措施("*Yi Liao Cuo Shi*")) and "alternative treatment plans" (替代医疗方案("*Ti Dai Yi Liao Fang An*")) – to

[164] Beijing High Court 2010, Rule 38.

[165] The Supreme People's Court of China 2012, Article 33 (anticipating that there are "other" circumstances where informed consent is needed for diagnosis and treatment); Beijing High Court 2010, Rule 38 (envisaging that the rule of informed consent may apply to "other" diagnosis and treatment activities that may cause serious adverse consequences to patients)

describe options. Because they are used together in the same context, it is fair to construe the term "treatment measures" as meaning "treatment options proposed or recommended by treating doctors", and to interpret the term "alternative treatment plans" as covering "alternative treatment options to the proposed or recommended treatments". The literal meaning of "plan" is, arguably, more encompassing than that of "treatment option". Borrowing the Canadian legal thinking, "treatment plan" may deal with more than one health problem, and may combine more than one treatment option.[166]

Reading Article 55 narrowly, the duty to disclose alternatives only applies to the context of administering "surgery, special examination, or special treatment". According to the legal definition of "surgery, special examination, or special treatment", this category of "diagnosis and treatment activities" mainly includes "invasive", "risky", "experimental", and "expensive" ones.[167] Therefore, when a doctor recommends or proposes a *surgical or invasive* treatment, he should also inform patients of non-surgical, non-invasive or less invasive treatment options. [168] Faced with *risky* treatments, a doctor needs to disclose alternatives that have better risk-benefit profiles, or at least, less risky alternative treatments. Where an *experimental* treatment is proposed, conventional or well-established treatment options need to be disclosed. Finally, a doctor needs to mention cheaper alternatives to *expensive* treatments. [169] This is very important in Chinese context. China keeps a fee-for-service health care. Doctors have a strong financial incentive to propose and recommend expensive rather than cost-effective treatments.[170] That is different from jurisdictions where rationing care is adopted and a doctor's duty to inform

[166] *See*, *Health Care Consent Act*, 1996 S.O., c. 2, Sched. A, s. 2 (1) ("'plan of treatment' means a plan that, (a) is developed by one or more health practitioners, (b) deals with one or more of the health problems that a person has and may, in addition, deal with one or more of the health problems that the person is likely to have in the future given the person's current health condition, and (c) provides for the administration to the person of various treatments or courses of treatment and may, in addition, provide for the withholding or withdrawal of treatment in light of the person's current health condition"; "'course of treatment' means a series or sequence of similar treatments administered to a person over a period of time for a particular health problem".).

[167] Rules for Implementing the Regulation on Medical Institutions (1994, Ministry of Health), Article 88 (医疗机构管理条例实施细则, 1994年, 卫生部, 第88条).

[168] *See*, *An Wen Jun v. The People's Hospital of Xinjiang Uygur Autonomous Region, etc.*, The Urumqi Intermediate Court of Xinjiang Uygur Autonomous Region (2010) Wu Zhong Min Yi Zhong Zi No. 840 (安文君诉新疆维吾尔自治区人民医院分院等医疗损害赔偿纠纷上诉案, 新疆维吾尔自治区乌鲁木齐市中级人民法院民事判决书(2010)乌中民一终字840号) (finding that the doctor is negligent in both selecting the proposed surgery and informing the patient of alternatives to the proposed surgery).

[169] *See*, *Xu Gui Shen, etc. v. Guangdong Province People's Hospital*, The Guangzhou Intermediate Court (2004) Sui Zhong Fa Min Yi Zhong Zi No. 1352 (许桂燊等与广东省人民医院医疗损害赔偿纠纷上诉案,广东省广州市中级人民法院民事判决书(2004)穗中法民一终字第1352号) (finding the defendant not negligent in selecting the mode of surgery, but negligent in failing to properly inform the patient of the economic burden of the surgery).

[170] The Lancet 2010 (admitting that Chinese doctors have a financial incentive to over-investigate and over-treat).

about effective (but not cost-effective) treatment options becomes the focus of attention (*see,* Chap. 7).

In the context of diagnosis and treatment, Article 57 ("the then-prevailing medical level") will govern. That means the judiciary will determine negligence by considering "the then-prevailing medical level". The "then-prevailing medical level" will be set by the well-established and wide-recognised medical practices. Therefore, in the context of diagnosis and treatment, it is much safer for doctors to follow more conventional practices or treatments. However, when the context shifts to information disclosure, Article 57 becomes less important and less relevant. Arguably, as I explained above, it does not apply to information disclosure. Therefore, the scope of information disclosure is not confined to conventional and well-established treatment options. Innovative and emerging treatment options may fall within the duty to inform, even if there is not yet good evidence of their efficacy and safety (Liao Huan Guo 2010, 22).

China has an "integrated" health care delivery system. This is because Traditional Chinese Medicine (TCM), a form of "Alternative and Complementary Medicine" in other jurisdictions, is one of the two "mainstream" medicines in China. China's medical education system ensures that Chinese "western medicine" practitioners have some (although limited) knowledge about Traditional Chinese Medicine, and TCM practitioners have substantial knowledge about Western medicine. Many "Western medicine" practitioners prescribe Chinese medicine and almost all TCM practitioners use one form or another of Western medicine diagnostic methods and treatments. That raises the issue of whether disclosure of alternative treatment options needs to cross the dividing line that is drawn between "Western medicine" and Traditional Chinese Medicine. Or, framed in another way, does a Western medicine practitioner have the duty to inform about TCM alternatives? And should a TCM practitioner disclose Western medicine treatment options? If so, under what circumstances? I will follow this in the final part of this chapter.

The medical levels in China have huge discrepancies between the urban areas and the rural areas, between the provincial hospitals and the county hospitals, and between the bigger cities and the smaller towns. That raises another issue of whether a doctor needs to advise patients about "alternative providers". For complicated, highly skill-dependant treatments, I would argue that less experienced practitioners need to honestly acknowledge their limitations and inform their patients of the availability of more experienced or skilled practitioners and medical institutions. It needs to be noted that the information that needs to be disclosed is expressed in very wide-ranging terms in the Chinese Tort Law. The Law adopts a very encompassing word "other information" when formulating the scope of information disclosure. It leaves room for the issue of whether a doctor needs to disclose "doctor-specific information", such as a doctor's inexperience and health, when that information, although extrinsic to treatments, poses additional risks to the patient's health.

(vi) The materiality test?

The information that may fall within the duty to disclose may be very extensive. As I highlighted in Chap. 4, the seemingly expansive scope of information disclosure has several filters, such as medical knowledge, patients' condition, the "materiality" test and causation, which have the potential for restricting the information that needs to be disclosed by medical professionals.

In framing the scope of information disclosure, the Tort Law is silent on the "materiality" test. I strongly recommend that the "materiality" test, together with the patient-oriented standard of information disclosure, be introduced into Chinese informed consent law. The test only requires a doctor to give patient information to which the patient would attach significance. It strikes a good balance between a patient's informational needs and a doctor's disclosure burden. The notion of "materiality" is not absolutely new in a Chinese medical law context. For example, in formulating the doctrine of informed consent, China's Code of Ethics for Human Assisted Reproductive Technologies has already adopted the phrase of "material information".[171]

Some Chinese scholars have an awareness of the materiality test and show an interest to it, but have not yet formed a proper understanding of it. First, some scholars equate "material" with "decisive", and therefore confusing the test for standard of care with the test for causation. In their eyes, a doctor has a duty to disclose information that has a "decisive" influence on a patient's decision-making (Gao Shengping 2010, 608), or information that would prompt a patient to make a "different" medical decision (Yu Mingshui 2010, 231). It needs to be clarified that a doctor has a duty to disclose information to which a patient would attach *significance* in making medical decisions. When determining *materiality*, it is not necessary to establish that a reasonable patient in the patient's position would *not* have had a procedure had he been sufficiently informed. That is the task for courts when they establish *causation*.

Second, when formulating the materiality test, there is inconsistency in Chinese academia about the issue of in "whose" perspective, *a reasonable patient's or a particular patient's*, the "significance" shall be weighed. There is an adamant assertion that, if knowing the information would prompt "a subjective patient" to make a different medical decision, the information shall fall within a doctor's duty to disclose (Yu Mingshui 2010, 231). Some scholars do not maintain consistency when applying rules at the stage of determining materiality and the stage of determining causation. For example, a scholar suggests a subjective test ("a particular patient") at the stage of determining materiality (Yu Mingshui 2010, 231), but adopts an objective test ("a reasonable patient") at the stage of determining causation (Yu Mingshui 2010, 232). China's test for information "materiality" should at least have the objective prong ("a reasonable patient in the patient's circumstances"). Having an additional subjective prong ("a particular patient") of the "materiality" test is also advisable in Chinese law. Whether the test is objective, subjective, or a hybrid, there is a need to keep it same and consistent at the stages of both establishing materiality and establishing causation.

[171] Code of Ethics for Human Assisted Reproductive Technologies (2001, Ministry of Health), Principle 2(2) (人类辅助生殖技术伦理原则, 2001年, 卫生部, 原则(二)(2)).

Finally, uncertainties associated with the concept "materiality" may cause difficulties for courts. It is essential that Chinese law give judges some rules about the factors that need to be considered when determining materiality. As Australian law demonstrates, those factors may include the likelihood and seriousness of the potential harm or risk, the nature of the proposed treatment, the necessity of medical intervention, the desire of the patient for information, and the availability of alternative treatment options.

(vii) Damage?

Pursuant to Article 55 (2) of the Tort Law, if health professionals fail to perform their duty to inform, and the breach *causes damage* to the patient, the medical institution concerned shall bear the liability for compensation.[172] That means that, as a form of tort liability, compensation liability caused by the breach of the duty to inform, has the same hurdles, such as damage and causation, as in the context of diagnosis and treatment. However, the word "damage" or "harm" (损害 ("*Sun Hai*")) is undefined.[173] It is uncertain whether it means personal injury or physical injury, or whether it includes mental injury and property damage.

Beijing High Court holds the view that if the failure of a doctor to exercise the duty to inform leads only to infringement of a patient's *right* of informed consent, with no infringement of a patient's *personal rights* and a patient's right of *property*, tort liability and compensation will not ensue.[174] Under this view, the loss of the right of informed consent does not seem to be damage. In contrast, the Supreme People's Court proposes that if the failure of a medical institution to bear the duty to inform has caused "serious mental injury" to a patient, the patient can sue the medical institution for compensation for mental distress (The Supreme People's Court of China 2012, Article 34). According to Article 22 of the Tort Law, if the infringement on any "personal right and interest" results in "serious" mental injury, the infringee shall have the right to demand compensation for mental distress. "Civil rights and interests" (民事权益 ("*Min Shi Quan Yi*")) include "personal rights and interests" (人身权益 ("*Ren Shen Quan Yi*")) and "property rights and interests" (财产权益 ("*Cai Chan Quan Yi*")).[175] Article 2 of the Tort Law has a long list of "personal" and "property" rights and interests, including the rights to life, health

---

[172] Tort Liability Law of People's Republic of China (2009, Standing Committee of NPC), Article 55 (2) (中华人民共和国侵权责任法, 2009年, 全国人大常委会, 第55 (2)条).

[173] In Australian context, *injury* means personal injury. *Personal injury* includes – (a) fatal injury; and (b) pre-natal injury; and (c) psychological or psychiatric injury; and (d) disease. *Damages* includes any form of monetary compensation. *General damages* means damages for – (a) pain and suffering; or (b) loss of amenities of life; or (c) loss of expectation of life; or (d) disfigurement. *Personal injury damages* means damages that relate to the death of or injury to a person. *Harm* means harm of any kind, including the following – (a) personal injury; (b) damage to property; (c) economic loss. *See*, *Civil Liability Act 2003* (Qld), ss 51, 69, Schedule 2 Dictionary.

[174] Beijing High Court 2010, Rule 39.

[175] Tort Liability Law of People's Republic of China (2009, Standing Committee of NPC), Article 2 (中华人民共和国侵权责任法, 2009年, 全国人大常委会, 第2条).

and privacy, but the "right of informed consent" is not on the list. Because the list is not exhaustive, we need to wait and see whether the "right of informed consent" or the right of autonomy or self-determination will fall within the scope of Article 2. Infringement of the rights and interests of Article 2 shall expose infringer to tort liability, including liability for mental distress (Article 22). Even if Article 22 is applicable, compensation is available only when there is "serious" mental injury.

In the same vein, some scholars suggest that Article 55 (2) can be divided into two contexts: (1) the breach of the duty to inform causes *personal injury* of the patient; (2) the breach of the duty to inform does not cause personal injury of the patient, but causes *damage to the right of informed consent*.[176] If the first context is involved, measuring compensation shall follow the ordinary rules concerning personal injury compensation (Article 16 of the Tort Law).[177] If the context involved is the second one, awarding compensation shall follow the "*mental distress*" provision (Article 22 of the Tort Law).[178] Compared to the approach adopted in the common law jurisdictions, this approach is rather liberal. By embracing the second context in the compensation scheme, it shows respect for the principle that the law needs to protect a patient's *right* of autonomy and self-determination even if there is no personal injury involved. However, this approach actually dilutes the significance of personal injury and causation in medical negligence liability cases. Pursuing tort remedies thorough courts is costly and time-consuming. It does not always provide the best avenue to protect the patient's right to be informed, especially when no personal injury is involved and the patient's motivation for instituting complaints is not for compensation, but for correction and accountability. Lower-level mechanisms, such as disciplinary sanctions, may be more appropriate and convenient options to resolve low-level complaints.

(viii) Causation?

As I repeatedly said, when establishing medical "fault"/medical negligence and causation, Chinese law heavily, and, in most cases, exclusively, rely on the conclusions of expert authentication. That reduces Chinese law's motivation to develop legal substantive rules governing how to establish medical negligence and causation. The case is the same in the arena of information disclosure.

Applying the basic "but for" test to the informed consent cases means that, when establishing the causation between the doctor's failure to inform and the patient's

[176] Project Group of "Study on Judicial Interpretation of Tort Liability Law" 2010, Article 98 (1). *Compare*, Lin Wen Xue 2010, 22 (arguing that the damage in the context of informed consent include physical and mental damage, but does not include the *damage to the right to know*).

[177] Project Group of "Study on Judicial Interpretation of Tort Liability Law" 2010, Article 98 (2).

[178] Project Group of "Study on Judicial Interpretation of Tort Liability Law" 2010, Article 98 (3). For cases, *see*, *Yuan Tian v. Yunnan Province No. 1 People's Hospital*, Kunming Intermediate People's Court (2004) Kun Min Yi Chu Zi No. 80; The High People's Court of Yunnan Province (2005) Yun Gao Min Yi Zhong Zi No. 134 (袁田诉云南省第一人民医院医疗损害赔偿案,昆明市中级人民法院(2004)昆民一初字第80号; 二审:云南省高级人民法院(2005)云高民一终字第134号) (protecting the patient's right of being informed even though the harm the patient suffered is not the cause of the surgery concerned).

Table 10.2 Chinese informed consent law

	The informed consent rules in Chinese Tort Liability Law
Distinction: diagnosis/ treatment – information disclosure	? (Relationship between Article 55 and Article 57)
Doctor-oriented standard	?
Patient-oriented standard	?
The materiality test	?
Disclosure of risks	√
Disclosure of *treatment options*	√
Disclosure of *recommended* treatment options	√
Disclosure of *non-recommended* treatment options	√
Other alternatives	? ("other information")
Exceptions	√ ("therapeutic privilege" and emergency)
Damage hurdle	Including sole "serious" mental injury?
Causation hurdle	?

damage, the patient should prove that, had a reasonable patient in the patient's position been sufficiently informed, he would have elected *not* to undergo the proposed procedure, and therefore the materialised risk would have been avoided. In cases concerning a doctor's failure to inform alternatives, the plaintiff/patient has to prove both the "decision" causation and the "injury" causation, i.e. a reasonable patient in the patient circumstances would have chosen the alternative treatment if properly informed, and the damage would have been avoided or reduced if the alternative had been chosen. There is also a need to make a choice between "objective" causation ("a reasonable patient in the patient's position") and "subjective causation" ("the particular patient"). The choice should be in harmony with the choice made in the context of establishing information "materiality". Furthermore, as in the case of establishing the "materiality" of information, when establishing causation in the informed consent cases, the court needs to weigh several considerations, such as the patient's condition, the likelihood and seriousness of the potential harm or risk, the nature of the proposed treatment, the necessity of medical intervention, the desire of the patient for information, and the availability of alternative treatment options.

10.2.3.3 Information Disclosure: Medical Practices

As illustrated above, China's new *Tort Liability Law* has a new, although unclear in many respects, line of thinking about informed consent law (for summary, *See* Table 10.2). In 2010, after *the Tort Liability Law* became law, the Ministry of Health of People's Republic of China (PRC) sent a letter to provincial departments of health, recommending the standard informed consent forms formulated by People's Hospital of Peking University (Ministry of Health (People's Republic of China) 2010). The Letter adopts a "patient-centred" notion, confirming that patients have "a right to know, a right to choose and a right to consent". It points out that recommending and standardising informed consent formulations is a part of implementing the *Tort Liability Law, Regulation on Medical Institutions* and other sources of laws. The 610-pages long People's Hospital of Peking University version of standard informed consent forms is attached to the letter. It can be expected that the recommended informed consent formulations would play an important role in establishing the standard of care regarding information disclosure in clinical care.

The attachment *Compilation of Medical Informed Consent Forms* adopted by People's Hospital of Peking University (People's Hospital of Peking University 2010) includes 10 general information disclosure forms and hundreds of specialised informed consent forms applicable to different diseases and procedures. When admitting to hospitals, patients will be informed of their rights and obligations. Among those rights, the patient has "the right to know diagnosis of the disease, progress of condition, diagnosis and treatment plans *proposed or suggested* by doctors, fees, risks, efficacy, and prognosis", the right to answer questions and seek clarification.[179] If medicines and medical devices are not covered by some public health and insurance programs, and should be paid by patients themselves, they should sign the informed consent form (People's Hospital of Peking University 2010, 10). By signing the informed consent form, patients can refuse or abandon medical measures suggested by doctors, or ask to be released from a hospital or to be transferred to another hospital (People's Hospital of Peking University 2010, 11–14).

As far as medical information that needs to be disclosed, every specialised informed consent form shares three parts: (1) the introduction of the disease or condition and treatment suggestions (recommendations); (2) the medical risks; (3) the patient's informed choice. In the part of "patient's informed choice", the patient should acknowledge that his doctor has informed him of "the procedure *proposed*, the complications and risks inherent in the procedure, *other available treatment options* and has answered relevant questions concerning the procedure." Reading these parts, one has reason to conclude that the treatments that fall within a doctor's duty to inform include both the proposed or recommended treatments and other available non-recommended treatment options. These parts also inform the patient that a doctor may, according to a patient's condition, adjust procedures, or the procedure needs to be performed by several doctors (a team). They also want patients to acknowledge that doctors did not give them guarantee of 100% success. However, although all procedure-based, specialised informed consent forms have a detailed list of *medical risks*, they fail to specify *what treatment options* are available for those conditions.

I have some suggestions about the harmonisation of informed consent forms. First, China should try to avoid the risk of the informed consent process being so formalised and bureaucratic that it becomes just obtaining a signature on a form.

[179] People's Hospital of Peking University 2010, 1 (emphasis added).

There is a need to tailor the process to the situation of the particular patient. Second, although understandably information disclosure centres mainly on disclosure of *risks*, patients also need to be informed of the *benefits* of the proposed procedure and the consequences of failing to go ahead with the proposed procedure in order to give patients more balanced information. Third, the process of communication and patients' understanding is more important than mere revelation of medical information. Fourth, informed consent should not be viewed as a single event. It is an on-going process.

10.2.3.4 The Japanese Law and the Future of Chinese Informed Consent Law

I am optimistic about the future of Chinese informed consent law, although it is still developing now and is immature in many respects. Chinese legislative process relies heavily on legal scholars' input, and Chinese law scholars are very open-minded towards legal developments of other jurisdictions, including both civil law and common law jurisdictions. Although always claiming to have "Chinese characteristics", Chinese law will inevitably be heavily influenced by the legal wisdom of developed countries, especially their well-established, widely accepted and mature legal rules.

In the medical law area, I have introduced common law principles and rules to Chinese readers, and have also provided observations on Chinese law and reflections on how to distinguish and accommodate common law rules in the Chinese context (For example, Zhao Xiju 2008). I also noticed that another scholar has introduced Japanese medical malpractice law into the Chinese world (Xia Yun 2007). Japan and China not only share the same civil law tradition, but also have some language similarity. That determines that Japanese law, together with the laws of other jurisdictions, may have some influence on the development of Chinese law. Thanks to that author's detailed introduction of Japanese medical malpractice law and translation of Japanese court opinions, I am able to read and know Japanese law. I will summarise Japanese informed consent law here and present some observations. Those observations reflect my hope about the direction in which Chinese law should develop.

In establishing negligence, Japanese law embraced the Learned Hand Formula and the risk-utility analysis (Xia Yun 2007, 64–85). Statutory standards and medical custom or "common practice" are not conclusive in establishing the standard of care (Xia Yun 2007, 86–88). In proving the presence or absence of negligence, Japanese law attaches importance to drawing an inference of negligence, judicial discretion, policy considerations and value judgment (Xia Yun 2007, 88–99). Furthermore, in treating medical authentication conclusions and medical expert opinions on causation, Japanese law also adheres to the idea that legal causation is distinct from scientific causation (Xia Yun 2007, 244–258).

Similar to the common law rules, in establishing medical negligence, Japanese law follows the "reasonable doctor" or "ordinary doctor" test (Xia Yun 2007, 105–108).

For clinical custom to be standard of care, it must meet a standard of reasonableness (Xia Yun 2007, 107). Japanese courts used to simply rely on medical custom, as demonstrated by medical authentication or medical expert opinions, as the standard of care in measuring medical negligence (Xia Yun 2007, 109). Later on, they realised that doctors should follow the "then-prevailing medical knowledge" when practising medicine (Xia Yun 2007, 110). Finally, they embraced the notion of "medical level". The "then-prevailing *medical knowledge*" is divided into two categories: (1) the "academic level" that may encompass *developing* medical knowledge; (2) the "*medical level*" that only covers clinically recognised, widely accepted medical practices whose safety and efficacy have been established (Xia Yun 2007, 111–112). Doctors have a duty to *administer* only medical procedures that have well-established evidence of safety and efficacy, and can be incorporated into clinical care (meaning that they have corresponding equipments, technology and human resources to administer the procedure) (Xia Yun 2007, 114).

Since the creation of the concept of "medical level", it seemed that Japanese judiciary wrongly equated "medical level" with medical "custom", and thus repeated the unwise practice of according medical "custom" a conclusive role in establishing the required standard of care. The Japanese legal academic world also confused the notion of "medical level", clinical "custom" or "common practice", and the "reasonable doctor" test (Xia Yun 2007, 118–139). Some Japanese scholars could not discern the difference between those three standards and questioned the independent value of the newly created notion of "medical level" (Xia Yun 2007, 133–134).

It seems that Chinese Tort Liability Law has already borrowed the notion of "medical level" (医疗水平("*Yi Liao Shui Ping*")) in establishing the standard of care for healthcare professionals. However, China should be very careful in not repeating the Japanese wrong message that the notion of *"medical level"*, *medical "custom"*, and *the "reasonable doctor" test* are the same thing. Benefited from the common law thinking, I would like to emphasise here again that, in determining the standard of care for doctors, Chinese law should accord supremacy and sacredness to the objective "reasonable doctor" standard, and should not be distracted by the notion of "medical level" and medical "custom".

Medical custom does not present conclusive evidence in establishing the standard of care for doctors. The Japanese notion of "medical level" is actually intended to achieve what the modified *Bolam* test, as witnessed by Australian civil liability legislation, has attempted to achieve. It does not cover every treatment. It only warmly embraces the widely accepted and well-established treatments. For those well-established and mature treatments, the judiciary accords weighty deference to doctors when they select and administer them. However, the not-well-established, innovative and experimental treatments would not have the privilege of benefiting from the "medical level" theory. That does not mean doctors' choosing and administering innovative treatments will definitely be labelled "negligence". The "reasonable doctor" test and the risk-utility analysis are still available for them to justify their choice.

The distinct value of the "medical level" theory, or its equivalent – the modified *Bolam* test, rests on the fact that it gives both the judiciary and the medical profession predictability, simplicity and convenience when handling the complicated issue of negligence for medical practitioners. The desirability and attractiveness of the notion of "medical level" is confined to the context of diagnosis and treatment. It has special value in the context of a doctor *selecting* and administering treatments. There is a need to reconsider the desirability of extending the notion of "medical level" into informed consent law.

The legal developments and academic discussion of Japanese *informed consent law* were heavily influenced by the common law (Xia Yun 2007, 321–358). It had been argued that the informed consent rule, which was developed in Western countries, did not fit comfortably with the Japanese native culture. However, it seems that the view that the informed consent doctrine had universal value finally prevailed in Japan (Xia Yun 2007, 354–358).

As far as the standard or the scope for information disclosure is concerned, Japanese courts used to adopt the "reasonable doctor" test, attaching great weight to "the then-prevailing medical level" or "a doctor's reasonable discretion" when measuring whether or not there is a breach of the duty to inform (Xia Yun 2007, 381–384). From the 1990s there had been a move in judicial attitudes towards a *patient-oriented* standard of information disclosure (Xia Yun 2007, 384–390). Courts began to pay attention to the issues of whether or not the patient would attach importance to the undisclosed information and whether or not the doctor had actual or constructive knowledge about that fact and the medical information (Xia Yun 2007, 384–390).

In the views of Japanese scholars, the information that falls within a doctor's duty to disclose includes: (1) the patient's condition; (2) the diagnosis and treatment proposed by the doctor; (3) alternative treatment options; and (4) the consequences of refusing proposed treatments (Xia Yun 2007, 368–369). However, it was only after the 1990s that Japanese courts began to incorporate disclosure of *alternative treatment options* into the duty to inform (Xia Yun 2007, 369–370). The previously prevailing judicial view regarding disclosure of treatment options was that selecting treatment options is a matter of medical *discretion* (Xia Yun 2007, 370–371). Since 1992, many cases concerning disclosure of alternative treatment options emerged. I will categorise this area of Japanese law into three legal situations.

The first situation is where the doctor *proposes* an *experimental* treatment option. Similar to the common law, in this area Japanese law has embraced two basic rules. First, information disclosure should differentiate between experimental treatments and conventional or well-established treatments. A doctor proposing experimental treatment will attract *more rigorous or strengthened* information disclosure (Xia Yun 2007, 435–438). Second, when proposing experimental treatments, the doctor should inform his patient of alternative treatment options, especially *well-established, standard, or mainstream* treatment options (Xia Yun 2007, 371–372). For example, when the new or innovative surgical treatment is proposed, the doctor should inform the patient of the availability of *conservative* treatment options and compare the risks and benefits of both options (Xia Yun 2007, 372).

The second situation involves a doctor *proposing the elective or cosmetic procedures*. Similar to the context of experimental treatment, Japanese law also has two rules in this area. First, the elective or cosmetic nature of the proposed procedure triggers a *heightened* duty of disclosure (Xia Yun 2007, 438–440). If there is no urgency or health necessity to undergo the procedure, or if the procedure does not have any therapeutic purpose, the doctor should fully disclose both sides of the procedure, especially its dark side, in order to counterbalance the patient's unrealistic impression or over-optimistic expectation (Xia Yun 2007, 438–440). Second, a procedure's lack of urgency and necessity demonstrates and reinforces the need to disclose the procedure's alternatives (Xia Yun 2007, 441–442).

The third situation involves a doctor's *proposal of well-established treatments and the availability of less-well-established treatment option*. The controversial issue raised in this context is whether or not a doctor has the duty to disclose *new, minority, or less-well-established* treatment options. It highlights the importance and the need to clarify the relationship between the "medical level" theory and the scope of a doctor's duty to inform.

The issue was raised in a Japanese Supreme Court case.[180] The case involved the choice between the radical surgery (radical mastectomy) and the less disfiguring alternatives (breast-conserving surgery).[181] In this case, patient X, aged 44, was diagnosed with breast cancer in 1991. Doctor Y proposed and performed *radical mastectomy*. He mentioned the *breast-conserving surgery* in an indirect and negative way. Before the surgery, the patient, by writing a letter to Doctor Y, expressed her *desire* for the breast-conserving surgery, but the doctor did not pay much attention to her wishes. The patient claimed damages, alleging that Doctor Y breached his duty to *administer (provide)* and *disclose* the breast-conserving surgery.

At the relevant time, the breast-conserving surgery was *not a well-established or standard* treatment for breast cancer patients in Japan. On the one side, information concerning breast conserving surgery was limited in Japan at the time of operation. Breast conserving measures were utilised in only 12.7% of all breast cancer operations. Most surgeons thought that many problems remained to be resolved before it could become a standard practice for breast cancer treatment. It is safe to say that the breast-conserving surgery was not mature enough to reach the "medical level" at that time in Japan. On the other side, although not widely-accepted and well-established, breast-conserving surgery had *some degree of recognition* in the academic and clinical field. Since 1989, breast-conserving surgery had attracted academic attention and study in Japan. From 1990, more and more medical institutions had tried the treatment. Case study and positive evaluation about the treatment and clinical guidelines for the treatment had

[180] The Supreme Court, 3rd petty bench, 2001.11.27, 55 Minshu 1154, 1769 Hanji 56, 1079 Hanta 198.

[181] In the USA context, the period between the 1950s and the 1970s witnessed the emergence of newer and less disfiguring alternatives to radical mastectomies. Those alternatives (such as lumpectomy and radiation therapy) were equally effective for many patients as the radical mastectomy. However, in the 1970s many surgeons routinely continued to perform radical mastectomy, often without informing their patients of the newer, less disfiguring alternatives. To break this "self-righteous silence", laws guaranteeing breast cancer patients access to *complete* information about treatment alternatives had been enacted in many states of USA. *See*, Joan H. Krause 1999, 379.

emerged. In the USA and Europe, it was then widely recognised that both the recurrence rate and survival rate after treatment with breast-conserving surgery were comparable to radical mastectomy.

Other details that need to be noted are: (1) the doctor *knew* about the breast-conserving surgery and had performed it on two other patients; (2) according to the then-existing breast-conserving surgery guidelines, the patient was an appropriate *candidate* for the surgery.

The Osaka District Court granted the patient's claim, concluding that the doctor had breached his duty of *disclosure*. The District Court reasoned that breast is a symbol of womanhood, and breast cancer surgery has a special nature in the sense that it has both physical and psychological impact on patients (Xia Yun 2007, 691–692). In considering treatment options for breast cancer patients, treating doctors should consider not only the survival rates but also the patients' mental aspects and the quality of life of their families (Xia Yun 2007, 692). In the view of the District Court, the methods of surgery that fall within the duty to inform should not be confined to those that have been widely adopted by general doctors and whose safety and efficacy have been well-established (Xia Yun 2007, 692). The duty to inform should also encompass methods of surgery whose safety and efficacy is being established among specialists and which have already fallen within or should have fallen within the treating doctor's knowledge (Xia Yun 2007, 692).

The Osaka High Court reversed the trial court judgment and dismissed the patient's claim. The Osaka High Court did not differ from the trial court in formulating the legal principles regarding disclosure of treatment options. It shared the view that a doctor should disclose not only the widely adopted methods of surgery whose safety and efficacy have been well-established, but also the methods of surgery about which the treating doctor knew or should have known and whose safety and efficacy is becoming increasingly established among specialists (Xia Yun 2007, 694). What caused the High Court to reach the different conclusions was the different fact-finding, and the High Court's confusing *administration* of treatments with *disclosure* of treatments.

First, in the eyes of the High Court, doctor Y has already disclosed information about the breast-conserving surgery (Xia Yun 2007, 694). Second, in the views of the High Court, *telling* the patient that she is a good candidate for breast-conserving surgery means asking the patient to *receive* the treatment (Xia Yun 2007, 694). That means, to *administer* the breast-conserving surgery, the doctor should obtain the patient's consent to non-standard surgery and explain why he does not *administer* standard or conventional surgery. The High Court also categorised the breast-conserving surgery as treatment that has a low administration rate and whose safety and efficacy had not yet been established. Therefore, even the "assumption of risk" mechanism cannot apply (Xia Yun 2007, 695).

The Japanese Supreme Court quashed the High Court judgment and returned the case to the Osaka High Court. The Supreme Court held that what Doctor Y disclosed to the patient about the breast-conserving surgery was not sufficient. The Supreme Court observed that, when a disease has *multiple* treatment options available and all of the treatments are *well-established*, it is easier to hold that a doctor should disclose the risks-benefits of all of those treatment options (Xia Yun 2007, 696). The court felt it difficult to formulate the legal rules about information disclosure when both well-established treatments and *not-yet-well-established treatments* are involved (Xia Yun 2007, 696). However, in this respect, the court set out some general principles.

First, the treatments that a doctor proposed to *administer* are, generally, ones that are recognised by the "medical level" (Xia Yun 2007, 696). That means doctors generally *propose and administer* treatments which have been widely accepted and whose safety and efficacy have been well-established. Second, for treatments that have not been recognised by the "medical level", a doctor does *not always* have a duty to disclose them (Xia Yun 2007, 696). However, *under some circumstances*, a doctor needs to *inform* his patient of not-widely-accepted treatment options (Xia Yun 2007, 696). The circumstances that the court contemplated to trigger discussion of the not-widely-accepted treatments include:

> *At least*, when one therapy (mode of surgery) has been administered in many medical institutions, has *a significant number of cases of administration*, and is *being positively evaluated* by doctors who had administered it, and if the patient concerned is *a candidate for this therapy* (mode of surgery), and the doctor has already been explicitly informed that the patient has *a strong desire* to know whether or not she is a good candidate for this therapy (mode of surgery) and to know the possibility of administrating it, *even if the doctor adopts negative attitudes towards the therapy (mode of surgery) and refuses to administer it himself*, the doctor has the duty, *within his knowledge*, to inform his patient of content of the therapy (mode of surgery), its possibility of application or its risks-benefits, and the name and address of medical institutions that are administering the therapy (mode of surgery), and other information. (emphasis added) (Xia Yun 2007, 696)

The Supreme Court's approach rightly honoured the distinction between the duty to *administer* treatments and the duty to *disclose* information about treatments. It acknowledges that a doctor's personal attitudes should not hinder him from giving sufficient information disclosure. When formulating the expansive approach, the court also defined *circumstances* under which the approach would be applied. First, the treatment option that needs to be disclosed must have *some degree of acceptance* in medical profession, and *positive evidence* of its safety and efficacy must be *accumulating*. Second, the court attaches importance to the patients' *wishes* and informational needs. By expressing wishes and concerns, a patient may trigger the *reactive* duty to inform. Third, the emerging method of surgery has already fallen within the doctor's actual *knowledge*. Fourth, considering her *conditions*, the doctor would acknowledge that the patient is a *candidate* for the emerging mode of surgery. Finally, the lifestyle-involved nature of breast cancer treatments also played some role in the court's thinking (Xia Yun 2007, 696–697).

In the minds of the Supreme Court, this approach would afford the patient an opportunity to consider whether to undergo the proposed radical mastectomy or to pursue the breast-conserving surgery in other medical institutions which provide it (Xia Yun 2007, 697). Doctor Y's practice actually deprived the patient of the latter possibility. *Disclosing* the option of breast-conserving surgery does not mean that the doctor has a duty to *administer* the option himself (Xia Yun 2007, 697). Nor does it mean that he has a duty to persuade the patient to receive the option in other medical institutions (Xia Yun 2007, 697). The doctor can keep his own judgment that radical mastectomy is the best surgical option for the patient (Xia Yun 2007, 697).

The line of thinking of this 1991 Radical Mastectomy Case has been followed by other Japanese cases (Xia Yun 2007, 698–700). It was seen as a form of honouring patients' right of self-determination (Xia Yun 2007, 698–700). However, the case triggered debates in Japan. Critics held that the Supreme Court's approach ignored the doctor's *personal attitudes* towards treatment and diluted the status of medical experts (Xia Yun 2007, 554). The author who originally provided this account of Japanese law is also of the view that the law should not treat the duty to administer and the duty to inform differently (Xia Yun 2007, 555). She argued that the "medical level" theory should be applied universally to the contexts of both treatment and information disclosure (Xia Yun 2007, 555). I have challenged this view in the Chinese academic world (Zhao Xiju 2009). The significance of the case is that it recognises the inappropriateness of applying the "medical level" theory unthinkingly to the context of information disclosure, and it endorses the view that the scope of treatment options that fall within the *duty to inform* may be *broader* than that of the *duty to administer*. The duty to *recommend* (even persuade) and *administer* is distinct from the duty to *inform*. The case lends some support to my arguments, as I made it clear in the context of common law (*see*, Chap. 3). The medical-profession-oriented and convention-honoured *Bolam* test (or the "medical level" theory in the Japanese and Chinese law) is not appropriate in the context of information disclosure. The law should make sure that a doctor's information disclosure is not adulterated by personal preferences.

The Japanese Radical Mastectomy case involved a lifestyle-involved, not-well-established and not-generally-accepted treatment option. It has special value to discussing the issue of a doctor's duty to disclose the *minority, emerging and developing* treatment options. Confining the duty to inform to the well-established and orthodox treatment options only sometimes does not fit comfortably with the rationale underlying the informed consent rule. It also sends a message that a doctor has a duty to be kept informed of *new* treatment options whose safety and efficacy is becoming more established.

Japanese law acknowledges the legitimacy of a doctor's duty to *persuade* in clinical care, meaning that a doctor has a right or duty to persuade patients to receive the treatments that the doctor deems best for his patient by exercising medical judgment (Xia Yun 2007, 702). Persuading patients to follow a doctor's recommendation and suggestion was legitimised as a part of a professional job (Xia Yun 2007, 702). But that duty and power should not cross the line and become coercion (Xia Yun 2007, 702). Furthermore, recommendation and persuasion is different from information disclosure.

Other aspects of Japanese law, regarding disclosure of alternatives, that support my arguments include: (1) A patient's specific condition may determine the scope and the availability of treatment options. A doctor need only disclose treatment options that fit a patient's condition.[182] A patient's condition may dictate that the

[182] Xia Yun 2007, 376, footnote 2.

treatment proposed by a doctor is the only option for the patient.[183] (2) Where two and more (multiple) treatment options are available to a patient, and one forms the first best option and another constitutes the second best option, the doctor needs to disclose the risks-benefits balance of both options (Xia Yun 2007, 372–373).

Japanese law defines "alternative treatment options" as treatment options that are alternative to the first best treatment proposed by a doctor, and that are beneficial to diagnose a patient's conditions or have some efficacy in curing or alleviating the patient's conditions (Xia Yun 2007, 376). Alternative treatment options generally should have *theoretical feasibility* and *clinical appropriateness* (Xia Yun 2007, 376). That means an alternative treatment option should be deemed by medical theories as one of methods to diagnose and cure diseases, and it can be appropriately applied to a patient's specific conditions (Xia Yun 2007, 376).

However, some aspects of Japanese thinking raise my concerns. For example, when several treatment options have similar risk-benefit profiles, it was held that it is up to a doctor's medical discretion to choose between options and there is no duty to disclose the risks-benefits of treatment options (Xia Yun 2007, 375). It ignores the fact that the patients' values, lifestyles and risk tolerance levels may be different from that of doctors. Another example is that some scholars think that when several treatment options have the same therapeutic significance, if the treatment proposed by the doctor is less risky than alternatives or entails the same risks as alternatives, and has the same benefits or more benefits than alternatives, the doctor does not have a duty to inform about alternative treatment options.[184] This rule suffers from the same weaknesses that existed in the first example of rule. Moreover, both rules fail to recognise that the choice of treatment options is not a mere exercise of balancing medical risks-benefits. It should accommodate patients' personal circumstances. Furthermore, the significance of disclosure of alternatives is described by the author who introduced Japanese law as to convince patients to follow a doctor's judgment and cooperate with treatments (Xia Yun 2007, 374). I cannot agree with this utilitarian and instrumental approach. It does not grasp the real purpose of the informed consent rule.

10.2.4 Conclusion and Suggestion

In conclusion, Chinese Tort Liability Law presents a new line of thinking about Chinese medical negligence law, including informed consent law. It has many merits. It shows loyalty to the basic theory of fault-based liability and the objective test for standard of care. It follows the practice of allowing medical profession to decide the standard of care. It attaches importance to statutory and professional practices in establishing the standard of care and negligence. It, for the first time,

[183] Xia Yun 2007, 376, footnote 2.

[184] Xia Yun 2007, 375, footnote 2.

makes the form of tort liability available for patients when they allege a doctor's breach of the informed consent rule.

However, Chinese Tort Law suffers from lack of detail. For example, in the context of medical negligence, it lacks detailed definitions of some key terms, such as "negligence", "reasonable care", "causation", "damage" and "informed consent". Hopefully, judicial interpretation regarding Tort Liability Law will eventually emerge and could help overcome these uncertainties. In doing this, Chinese law can accommodate common law wisdom in formulating medical negligence principles (Table 10.3).

Correlated to the lack of detail, another weakness that the Tort Law has is that it is somewhat all-embracing and too ambitious. In the context of medical negligence law, it incorporates many of doctors' professional and ethical duties into tort law. We cannot expect tort law to provide a panacea for all medical law issues. Moreover, the tort law is not always the best context in which to discuss medical law issues.[185] If the law wants to lower the threshold for liability for breach of the informed consent rule, and to give a patient's right of self-determination high priority, it can do it in other contexts. In this respect, New Zealand's Code of Patients' Right and a Health and Disability Commissioner (HDC) offers a good example. A Chinese survey revealed that 91% of the patients believe that they need an independent body, something like the existing China's Consumers Protection Association, to protect and advocate their rights (Fu Zi Tang et al. 2006, 48). As I examined in Chap. 9, the New Zealand's Code approach is better than the Tort approach to protect patients' right to be informed. As I argued before, I would like to see Chinese medical negligence law to be supplemented by rigorous medical professional regulation.

10.3 Medical Context

10.3.1 Chinese Health Care

Chinese health care and reform is a very complicated issue. It is beyond the scope of this book. However, to picture a clear but different context, I would like to raise some points. First, choosing China's 1980s reform as a dividing line, the post-1949 Chinese health care can be categorised into two phrases. Prior to 1978, China successfully ran a "barefoot doctor" system under which Government was heavily involved in recruiting, training and sending "barefoot doctors" to deliver public health services and simple medical care in rural areas that otherwise lacked health resources. However, in the post-*Mao* era of modernisation, as a result of the market-oriented economic reforms in the 1980s, the old state-funded health system collapsed.

[185] Medical malpractice legal proceedings are costly and time-consuming. A Chinese survey showed that 73.3% hospitals surveyed attach importance to the hospital *reputation*. 9.5% care a lot about their energy and time involved in dealing with medical accident lawsuits. Only 4.8% of them attach value to economic compensation. *See*, Fu Zi Tang et al. 2006, 12.

Table 10.3 Chinese Tort Law and common law principles

Chinese Tort Law	Common law principles	Suggestions
Article 54: fault-based liability	–	Applying to the contexts of both diagnosis/treatment and information disclosure
Article 57: "the then-prevailing medical level"; standard of care	Objective "reasonable doctor" standard; the risk-utility or risk-benefit analysis; the *Bolam* test; the "two schools of thought" doctrine	(1) Showing loyalty to the basic tort principle that negligence is the breach of the duty of reasonable care; (2) According supremacy to the basic "reasonable doctor" standard; (3) Reinforcing the objective ("reasonable care") nature of standard of care; (4) Subjecting medical practices and medical opinions to judicial scrutiny; (5) Showing deference to wide-accepted and respectable medical practices; (6) Acknowledging genuine difference of medical opinions
Article 58: Presumption of fault	*Rebuttable* presumption; "Statutory standards" and "common practice": not "conclusive"	(1) According supremacy to the "reasonable doctor" standard; (2) Showing caution in giving statutory and professional standards conclusive authority, especially in the context of professional guidelines and medical norms; (3) The presumption is rebuttable; (4) The presumption can be rebutted by applying and seeking the help of the basic "reasonable doctor" standard of care
Article 59: medical product liability	–	Distinguishing between health care and goods in no-fault/strict liability
Article 60: Defences	–	Acknowledging the medical-profession-protective nature of the "reasonable doctor" test

Article 61: the duty to prepare, preserve and provide medical records	–	(1) Not a tort duty; (2) Supplemented by or leaving it to professional regulation
Article 62: the duty to maintain privacy and confidentiality	–	(1) Governed by general law of privacy and data protection; (2) Supplemented by or leaving it to professional regulation
Article 63: "unnecessary examination"	–	(1) Article 57 can govern; (2) Supplemented by or leaving it to professional regulation
–	**Causation and burden of proof**: the "but for" test; intervening causes; contributing factors; legal causation *v.* scientific causation; "material contribution"; "material increase of risk"; "loss of chance"; drawing inference; "shifting burden of proof"	(1) Recognising the "but for" test and the "material contribution" test in medical negligence cases; (2) Drawing a distinction between causation in *law* and causation in *science*; (3) Recognising the intervening and contributing causes in the chain of causation; (4) Loosening the test for causation in the context of medical liability; (5) Adopting the approach of "drawing inference of causation"
Articles 55–56: informed consent law	The "single comprehensive duty" *v.* drawing distinctions and making the duty divisible	Acknowledging the distinctive aspects of informed consent law; Drawing a distinction between diagnosis/treatment and information disclosure
	Doctor-oriented *v.* patient-oriented standard of information disclosure	Adopting the patient-oriented standard and the "materiality" test
	Risks disclosure *v.* risks + alternatives disclosure	Keeping the "risks + alternatives" disclosure
	Disclosure of recommended treatment options *v.* more balanced and contextualised disclosure	(1) Being aware that a doctor's preference may colour disclosure of alternatives; (2) Scope of alternatives disclosure is not confined to recommended procedures
	Damage + causation hurdles?	(1) Keeping damage and causation hurdles; (2) Tort liability + other forms of liability

China evolved from a system based on salaries, public budgets and direct government care provision to a system dominated by fee-for-service health provision that were public in name, but survived mainly on the basis of maximising revenue from private households (Ho 2010, 37–38). People in the rural areas are the biggest victims. While people employed in urban state-owned, governmental and public sectors have the right to enjoy almost free coverage for their health expenses, rural people are struggling with the new burden of healthcare fees.[186] Mirroring the dichotomy formed between rural and urban areas, China's health resources are unevenly distributed, with health professionals and health facilities concentrated in urban areas. All of these raise the issue of equity.[187] Even the Chinese government has acknowledged that the market-oriented health reform has been a failure.

Second, China does not have a mature primary care system, in particular general practice. Despite efforts, since 1999, to introduce general practice in urban areas, acceptance of general practice has been slow against the background of a strong urban tradition of hospitals as primary care providers, the widespread belief that specialists are more skilled than generalists even for minor complaints, and the perceived right of the individual to use the provider of their choice. General practitioners (GPs) failed to perform a gate-keeping role. In China the work load of medical practitioners is heavy, especially for those working in popular hospitals. Some popular doctors in popular hospitals may have 100 patient visits every working day.[188]

Third, due to the fee-for-service nature of health care delivery, health care professionals and hospitals are exposed to strong financial incentives. Public health facilities are permitted to charge for services. Doctors are allowed to make money from prescriptions and investigations. The low costs of routine care are subsidised by charges for more technologically advanced treatments and drugs. The pharmacy is a part of the hospital. Therefore, the system creates incentives for doctors to over-prescribe drugs and expensive procedures. The situation is so serious that even *Chinese Tort Liability Law* was invited to respond to it and, thus, urged medical institutions and medical professionals not to carry out "unnecessary examination" in violation of diagnosis and treatment norms.[189]

---

[186] The New Rural Co-operative Medical Care System (NRCMCS) is a new 2005 initiative to overhaul the healthcare system, particularly intended to make it more affordable for the rural poor.

[187] In 2000, rural residents made up two-thirds of the population, but their health expenditures accounted for only 22.5% of the nation's total. In 2000, the life expectancy for a person living in Shanghai compared to a person living in Guizhou was 13.5 years higher, equivalent to the life expectancy gap between individuals in the developed nations and the most underdeveloped countries in the world. *See*, Ho 2010, 38–39.

[188] In 2007, the average visits per annum that every Western medicine practitioner and TCM practitioner received is 1,508.48 and 1,623.11 respectively.

[189] Tort Liability Law of People's Republic of China (2009, Standing Committee of NPC), Article 63 (中华人民共和国侵权责任法, 2009年, 全国人大常委会, 第63条).

10.3.2 Traditional Chinese Medicine v. "Western" Medicine

Traditional Chinese Medicine (TCM) has a more than 2,000 years' history in China and has roots in Chinese philosophy and culture. In China, Western medicine (conventional or orthodox medicine in the eyes of the Western world) is a newcomer. Over thousands of years TCM has developed a theoretical and practical approach to the treatment and prevention of disease. The earliest records of TCM surfaced as early as the eighth century BC.[190] The first documented source of Chinese medical theory, the *Huangdi Nei Jing* ("Inner Classic of the Yellow Emperor" or "Yellow Emperor's Internal Medicine"), which was written in the *Eastern Han* dynasty between 300 BC and 100 BC, describes the diagnosis and treatment of a huge range of disorders, and gives advice about healthy lifestyles, exercise, and diet which conforms remarkably well with current recommendations for the prevention of chronic disease (Hesketh and Wei Xing Zhu 1997, 115). If taking the compilation of the *Huangdi Nei Jing* as the indication of maturity of TCM, TCM had been well-established and developed for more than 1,000 years before the Jesuit missionaries introduced the modern scientific medicine into China in the sixteenth century.

The philosophical foundation of TCM is different from that of Western medicine.[191] Diagnosis and treatment regimens in TCM are extremely individualised. Various TCM techniques are employed to restore the balance through the unencumbered flow of *qi*. The main modalities of TCM are acupuncture and moxibustion, Chinese herbal medicine, therapeutic massage (*Tuina*), and manipulation (acupressure). These modalities are often used in combination with each other, along with diet and exercise programs. Herbs are used much more commonly than acupuncture. The TCM doctors usually choose from around 500 common classical prescriptions. Nowadays many formulations are available in the more convenient form of tablets, capsules, and ampoules.

TCM is an "alternative" to rather than "complementary" with Western medicine. It is an entirely coherent system, with internal logic and consistency of thought and practice (Hesketh and Wei Xing Zhu 1997, 115). As with most forms of traditional medicine, the theoretical and diagnostic basis of traditional Chinese medicine cannot be explained in terms of Western anatomy and physiology (Hesketh and Wei Xing Zhu 1997, 115). It is rooted in the philosophy, logic, and beliefs of a different civilisation and leads to a perception of health and disease that is alien to Western scientific thinking (Hesketh and Wei Xing Zhu 1997, 115).

---

[190] WHO (2001), Legal Status of Traditional Medicine and Complementary/Alternative Medicine: A Worldwide Review, p 2.

[191] In TCM, there is a fine balance between the two opposing but interrelated and inseparable forces of nature, *Yin* and *Yang*. *Yin* has been described as those aspects of cold, slow, passive, dark, and female, whereas *Yang* is hot, excited, active, light, and male. Health is maintained by achieving and then maintaining the balance between these opposing forces. Disease is the result of imbalance, and imbalance results from a blockage of vital energy (*Qi*) that flows throughout the body along well-defined channels called meridians.

The fate of TCM had fluctuated since the introduction of Western medicine thinking into the Chinese context. The newly introduced modern Western medicine had found a foothold in China only after the Opium War (1840). As the West had asserted economic, political, and military pressure on China, and as modern scientific medicine grew dramatically and established more and more of its hospitals in China, many Chinese intellectuals began to recognise the power of modern scientific medicine and to use modern Western science as the sole standard. They reflected critically on the status of traditional Chinese medicine (Fan Ruiping 2003, 216). As a scholar wrote,

> The ghost of science has since haunted everything Chinese in general and Chinese medicine in particular for the entire twentieth century and into the twenty-first century. The branches of modern Western science have since been introduced to the Chinese not only as valuable tools for their lives, but also as standards for truth. Evaluating whether a traditional Chinese discipline is "scientific" by using modern Western science as the standard has become a substantial value judgment: "Scientific" is true, right, good, advanced, or at least indicating the right direction of future development, while "unscientific" is false, wrong, bad, backward, or indicating the fate of perishing (Ruiping 2003, 216).

The gradually and dramatically established Western medicine posed so a great challenge to traditional medicine in China in the following decades that TCM was once nearly officially abandoned by the Nationalist government in the first half of the twentieth century because TCM was deemed to be "unscientific".[192] In 1929, the First Health Council of the Ministry of Health (with no members from the TCM field) unanimously resolved that traditional Chinese medicine was a kind of witchcraft and formulated concrete methods to abolish TCM within 50 years, including stopping issuing licenses to new TCM practitioners and prohibiting TCM schools from operating (Ruiping 2003, 216). The proposal caused fierce resistance all over the country and generated unprecedented debate regarding the "scientific" status of TCM. The TCM dispute revolved from academic arena to political arena. In 1936, the then Nationalist government promulgated a *Traditional Chinese Medicine Regulation* (中医条例("*Zhong Yi Tiao Li*")). It signalled, for the first time, the official recognition of TCM in China (Wen Xiang 2004, 84–86).

After the People's Republic of China was born, there were still voices against TCM. The first President *Mao Zedong* successfully saved TCM.[193] *Mao* urged the recognition and support of TCM, specifically to treat the millions living in rural areas. Following *Mao*'s instruction that Chinese doctors should inherit the good

---

[192] Yu Yunxiu, a senior officer in the Nationalist government, was a leading advocate for abolishing TCM in China. In his eyes, traditional Chinese medicine is nothing more than accumulation of experiences, without explicit, solid and convincible laboratory evidence. *See*, He Xian Zhong 2004, 72–76.

[193] Soon after the establishment of the People's Republic of China in 1949, *Mao Zedong*, the charismatic leader of the government, called for solidarity between traditional Chinese medical physicians and modern scientific medical physicians. In 1953, noticing that many intellectuals and local officials disregarded traditional Chinese medicine, *Mao* commented that both traditional Chinese medicine and modern scientific medicine included good and bad parts and that what had to be done was to inherit the good parts from each. In 1954, *Mao* emphasized that "it is more

parts of both traditional Chinese medicine and modern Western medicine so as to promote the common cause of pursuing national health, Chinese government and its Ministry of Health began to adopt a positive attitude towards TCM. It endeavored to incorporate TCM into its national health care system. Although protection and use of TCM was initially politically motivated by President *Mao*, the popularity of TCM has not diminished since the end of *Mao*'s era. TCM is still cherished by most of Chinese people as a cultural heritage.

Nowadays it can be said that TCM practitioners do not need to worry about survival although calls for abolishing TCM have not died out entirely. TCM has been incorporated into health care, both politically, legally and clinically. Even the *Constitution of People's Republic of China* voiced its support for TCM, according TCM an equal status to modern Western medicine.[194] As I will demonstrate, all medical laws, statutes and regulations apply to both Western medicine and TCM indiscriminately, uncritically and even unthinkingly.

The *Regulation on Traditional Chinese Medicine* reiterated the well-established policy that China shall protect, support and develop the TCM cause, shall give equal importance to both TCM and Western medicine, shall encourage the two medical systems to learn from each other's merits, to complement and cooperate with each other, and shall promote systematic and coherent unification of the two medical systems.[195]

TCM also enjoys a solid and stable presence at both the executive level and clinical level in China. It has a national administrative agency (the State Administration of Traditional Chinese Medicine), which is distinct from and independent of the Ministry of Health, and local branches at the level of province, autonomous region and municipality. The 2007 statistics from Ministry of Health and the State Administration of Traditional Chinese Medicine show that there were a total of 19,852 hospitals, 7,124 clinics in mainland China, having received 1,637,695,812 visits and 50,768,718 visits in 2007 respectively. Among them, there were 3,066 TCM hospitals, 681 TCM clinics, having 279,089,858 visits and 6,925,147 visits in

important for the modern Western medical physician to learn from the traditional Chinese medical physician than the other way around" because traditional Chinese medicine had accumulated enormous effective experiences in the thousands of years of its practice. In 1955, the Ministry of Health arranged a special delegation of 76 Western medical physicians to learn traditional Chinese medicine from a group of experts in Beijing for two and a half years. Many local cities followed this example and organized similar reeducation programs for the modern Western medical physicians. *See*, Fan Ruiping "Modern Western Science as A Standard for Traditional Chinese Medicine: A Critical Appraisal" (2003) 31 Journal of Law, Medicine & Ethics 213, 217. These people (Western medicine doctors who systematically learned TCM) are called "*Xi Xue Zhong*" ("西学中") and many of them have become leading integrative medicine doctors. This idea has been diluted since *Mao*'s death. Western medicine doctors are no longer pushed to learn and practice traditional Chinese medicine.

194 Art. 21, Constitution of People's Republic of China 1982, as amended (stipulating that "the state develops both modern medicine and traditional Chinese medicine").

195 Regulation on Traditional Chinese Medicine of People's Republic of China (2003, State Council), Article 3 (中华人民共和国中医药条例, 2003年, 第3条).

2007 respectively. In 2007, there were 206,842 licensed TCM practitioners, 35,091 licensed TCM assistant practitioners and 82,494 TCM pharmacists.

In spite of support for the policy of integrating TCM into health care, there are ongoing concerns that TCM has lost much of its unique identity because China's efforts to "modernise" ("*Xian Dai Hua*" (现代化)) and "scientificise" ("*Ke Xue Hua*"(科学化)) TCM. There has been a long-lasting dispute on whether TCM *is* a "science" or *should be* a "science". It has been argued that using modern scientific knowledge as the standard to evaluate and tailor TCM does not really help the development of TCM (*See*, Ruiping 2003).

10.3.3 Dual and Integrative Medicine

The World Health Organization's first global strategy on traditional medicine lists China as one of only four of its member states to have attained an integrative health care system.[196] First, China has a dual and integrative medical *education*. It has both medical (Western medicine) universities or medical (Western medicine) schools and TCM universities or TCM schools. Every Western medicine school contains a department of traditional medicine and every TCM school contains a department of Western medicine. About 10% of the teaching in Western medical schools is allocated to TCM. More percentage (30% or more) of teaching in TCM tertiary institutions is oriented to Western medicine.[197]

Training forms of TCM practitioners and pharmacists has moved from traditional apprentice to modern formal education. TCM used to be taught through apprenticeships. Nowadays tertiary education becomes the leading way of training TCM professionals. Since 1956 China has operated formal tertiary courses of study in TCM, with government accreditation and financial support. Undergraduate university TCM programs in China are generally of 5 years' duration. Like other types of university, admission standards to TCM colleges or universities generally require completion of senior high school. Students need to pass the National University Entrance Examination and have satisfactory marks.

The 2007 statistics tell us that there are 47 higher education institutions of TCM in mainland China, including 12 *universities* of TCM. In 2007 these TCM higher education institutions admitted 112,212 students, including 7,379 Master students and 1,134 PhD students. Moreover, there are 223 non-TCM higher education institutions (including Western medicine universities) which also have TCM programmes and TCM students. Most TCM universities offer both undergraduate

---

[196] World Health Organization *WHO Traditional Medicine Strategy 2002–2005* (Geneva: WHO, 2002): at 8–9, http://www.who.int/medicines/library/trm/trm_strat_eng.pdf (accessed 20 July 2006).

[197] World Health Organization *Legal Status of Traditional Medicine and Complementary/Alternative Medicine: A Worldwide Review 2001.*

and postgraduate programs. TCM bachelor students normally have 5 years of university. TCM master students have additional 3-year learning period. There is further 3 years of study for PhD students. Postgraduate candidates are selected from amongst graduates of tertiary institutions of TCM or Western medicine and on the basis of a National Postgraduate Courses Entrance Examination.

TCM tertiary institutions usually provide Bachelor of Medicine (TCM) and Bachelor of Chinese Pharmacy programs, with specialties in the disciplines of herbal medicine, acupuncture, and herbal pharmacology. The curriculum and textbooks for TCM universities are issued by the National Education Committee in conjunction with the State Administration of TCM. Students undergo systematic training in TCM theories and practice with a focus on TCM diagnostic systems and methods of treatment.

TCM students should study TCM theoretical subjects and TCM clinical subjects. TCM theoretical subjects may include TCM History, Introduction to TCM, *Zang-xiang Xue* (Viscera-state Doctrine of TCM), TCM Etiology and Pathology, TCM Diagnostics, Science of Chinese Materia Medica, Formulary of Chinese Materia Medica, Doctrines of Various Historic Schools and Ancient Chinese Medical Literature. TCM clinical subjects may embrace TCM Internal Medicine, TCM Surgery, TCM Gynaecology, TCM Paediatrics, TCM Traumatology, TCM Ophthalmology, TCM Otorhinolaryngology, and Acupuncture. In addition, TCM students must take quite a few *Western medicine subjects*, both theoretical and clinical, such as Anatomy, Histology and Embryology, Physiology, Biochemistry, Microbiology, Parasitology, Pathology, Pharmacology, Fundamentals of Diagnostics, Western Internal Medicine, Surgery. For TCM undergraduate students, the ratio of TCM courses and Western medicine courses may reach 6:4. For TCM students who have enrolled in programmes that have more strong Western medicine orientation, the ratio can move to 5:5 or even 4:6.

Students spend their fifth year in both TCM teaching hospitals and Western medicine hospitals as interns. During undergraduate and internship training, TCM students obtain clinical experience in hospitals in both *TCM and Western medicine* departments. Graduates from Bachelor of Medicine (TCM) programs are able to diagnose in Western medical terms, prescribe Western pharmaceuticals, and undertake minor surgical procedures.

On the other side, all Western medical schools devote around 10–15% of curriculum time to TCM, so Western medicine students receive an overview of TCM (Hesketh and Wei Xing Zhu 1997, 116). An introductory course in TCM (approximately 100 h) will familiarise them with TCM theory and treatment. However, practitioners trained in Western medicine cannot practise acupuncture or Chinese herbal medicine without undertaking extensive additional training.

Second, at the *clinical* level, there is also some form of integration. There are many Western medicine doctors working hand in hand with TCM practitioners in TCM hospitals. There are also TCM staffs in the Western-medicine-dominated hospitals. The integrated nature of the two systems is well illustrated by the fact that in Western medicine hospitals around 40% of the medicines prescribed are traditional, while, in the TCM hospitals, 40% of all prescribed drugs are Western medicine (Hesketh and Wei Xing Zhu 1997, 116). Traditional herbal therapies represent 30–50% of total national medication consumption in China.

On the one side, TCM practitioners are free to prescribe modern chemical medicines and use modern diagnostic methods (in place of or in additional to TCM diagnostic methods). Many TCM doctors in China administer "double diagnosis" and "double therapy" in their practice. That means that they make both a symptom-complex ("*zheng*"(症)) diagnosis according to the TCM diagnostic theories and methods (looking, smelling, asking, and feeling) and a disease ("*Bing*"(病)) diagnosis according to the modern scientific diagnostic theories and methods (physical, laboratory, and machinery examinations) for every patient.[198] In performing double therapy, they prescribe to the same patient both Chinese herbal medicines based on the TCM diagnosis and modern chemical drugs based on the scientific medical diagnosis.

On the other side, the Western medicine practitioners are not shy of prescribing *Chinese Patent Medicines* (or Prepared or Ready-made Chinese Medicine), which is a *standardisation* of Chinese classic herbal formula, and which can be *uniformly* applicable to the *all* suitable candidates. It seems that such invasion into each other's domain has created a result or an impression that what TCM practitioners are good at is forming and prescribing *individualised* herbal medicine formula that is only applicable to individual circumstances of each patient, while the exclusive expertise of Western medicine practitioners mainly falls within the area of surgery and operations.

Third, in the context of *research*, Chinese government has always emphasised the "scientificisation" of TCM, attempting to find "scientific" explanations and justifications for TCM theories and treatments. For this purpose, tremendous resources have been invested in conducting scientific research on TCM.[199] From a Western medicine standpoint, there is a need to identify the biochemical composition of the active agents in many of the herbal preparations. Some research has produced encouraging results.[200] However, some research ended in vain.[201]

---

[198] Actually they are required by law to administer "double diagnosis", although "double diagnosis" is not easy to be done for every patient. *See*, Stipulations on Many Issues Surrounding Running Traditional Chinese Medicine Hospitals (1980, Ministry of Health), Article 5 (中医医院工作若干问题的规定(试行), 1980年, 卫生部,第5条).

[199] One is to attempt to discover effective chemical ingredients in Chinese medicinal herbs in order to explain their clinical effects. The other is to disclose anatomically observable "lines" behind the channel (*jing-luo*) system of Chinese medicine so as to offer a scientific explanation for the function of acupuncture. *See*, Ruiping 2003, 218.

[200] For example, the herb *qing hao su* (青蒿素) has been used in China for treating fever for over 2,000 years. In 1971 it was found to have specific antimalarial activity and the active compound artemesin was isolated. In clinical trials, parasite clearance times were shorter than with chloroquine, symptoms responded more rapidly, and there was no serious toxicity. *Qing hao su* has now become a first line drug for malaria in many parts of Asia. *See*, Hesketh and Wei Xing Zhu 1997, 117.

[201] Fan Ruiping 2003, 218 (revealing that, although much labor and energy were invested in the hope of finding a physical basis for "jing-luo" (channel) system in Chinese medicine, all was done in vain).

Western medicine and TCM are fundamentally different approaches, having a huge and maybe irreconcilable conceptual and clinical difference. Concerns have been raised about the necessity and appropriateness of the above-mentioned integrative approach. A Hong Kong scholar, Fan Ruiping, argued that TCM and modern scientific medicine are fundamentally incommensurable and cannot be evaluated by the same standards (*See*, Ruiping 2003). He noted that TCM dramatically differs from modern scientific medicine in its basic medical orientation, physiological theories, etiology, diagnostics, therapeutics, and pharmacology (Ruiping 2003, 213). Dramatic differences exist between perspectives for illness (seeing illness as anatomicopathological v. viewing illness as symptom-complex ("*zheng*"(症)) of the whole body); origins of illness (disease entities v. unbalanced climate and/or emotional factors); diagnostic means (advanced laboratory investigations v. ordinary contacts (looking, smelling, asking, and feeling)); clinical focus (pathological anatomy and function v. the patient's complaint and actual experience of being sick); aims of treatment (curing diseases v. balancing functional factors); and means of treatment (chemical drugs or surgeries v. natural herbs or simple needles) (Ruiping 2003, 213).

Fan argued that the scientific standard, and randomised clinical trials, are not appropriate for TCM. The approach of randomised clinical trials, which are appropriate for scientific medicine and studies groups of patients with the same disease diagnosis, is inappropriate for TCM, because symptom-complexes do not describe diseases and a symptom-complex is virtually unique to a particular patient (Ruiping 2003, 219–220). It is impossible for TCM to conduct a stringent randomised clinical trial (Ruiping 2003, 219–220). The method of study that is appropriate for TCM is individual-sensitive observational studies (Ruiping 2003, 219–220). Fan asserted that it is a mere assumption that the standards of modern scientific medicine are more true in accounting for medical reality than the standards of TCM (Ruiping 2003, 218–219). He observed that, beneath the integrative approach, TCM actually has been marginalised by the dominance of scientific medicine. He suggested that successful integration of scientific medicine with TCM can take place only when each is evaluated according to its own standards, rather than subjecting TCM to the same scientific standard as the Western medicine.[202]

Fan's analysis makes sense, although I hasten to add my view that the integrative approach needs to be promoted in the context of information disclosure. Many scholars in China share the sentiment that the survival of TCM is actually put into danger in an integrative culture which is Western-medicine-oriented. Many Chinese scholars express the difficulty of integrating Western medicine with Traditional Chinese medicine, especially in their theoretical rationales (Sun Ze Ting et al. 2006, 77–78; Qian Hua 2008, 1–2). China is trying to follow the NICE (National Institute for Clinical Excellence)'s model and attempting to make evidence-based clinical guidelines for TCM treatments, for example, acupuncture. Many Chinese scholars argue that, in formulating Clinical Practice Guidelines for TCM, China should

[202] Fan Ruiping 2003, 218–219 (proposing a dual standard medical integration).

not simply follow the Western-medicine-based "Levels of Evidence Ratings". Randomised controlled trials results cannot paint the whole picture for TCM. In assessing the evidence base for TCM, importance and value should be accorded to ancient literature, long traditional use, expert opinions, experiences, consensus, and case study (Wu Xi et al. 2010, 2–3; Li Jian Sheng and Yu Xue Qing 2010, 648–649; Chen Ke Ji and Jiang Yue Rong 2009, 302–304).

10.4 Traditional Chinese Medicine and the Law

10.4.1 Integrative or Alternative Legal Framework?

The integrative thinking is also reflected in TCM legislation. Generally speaking, China's health care legislation does not draw a distinction between Western medicine and TCM. Almost all legislation is uniformly applicable to TCM and Western medicine practitioners. The distinctive aspects of TCM are paid respect by the way of creating some minor exceptions to the general provisions or formulating specific provisions. The integrative approach means that almost all health care laws, statutes, and regulations, such as the *Law on Practising Doctors*,[203] *Regulation on Medical Institutions*,[204] *Pharmaceutical Administration Law*,[205] *Regulation on the Handling of Medical Accidents*,[206] and *Tort Liability Law*,[207] govern both Western medicine and TCM.

10.4.1.1 TCM Practitioners

A good example of integration and uniformity is China's *Law on Practising Doctors (1998)*. It opens the door to TCM practitioners. Doctors in China actually include four major categories: Clinical (Western medicine) Practitioners, TCM (including Tibet medicine, Mongolia medicine, Uygur medicine, Dai medicine and other ethnic minority medicines) Practitioners, Dental Practitioners and Public

[203] Law on Practising Doctors of the People's Republic of China (1998, Standing Committee of the National People's Congress) (中华人民共和国执业医师法, 1998年,全国人大常委会).

[204] Regulation on Medical Institutions (1994, State Council)(医疗机构管理条例, 1994年, 国务院).

[205] Law of the People's Republic of China on Pharmaceutical Administration (2001, The Standing Committee of the National People's Congress) (中华人民共和国药品管理法,2001年,全国人大常委会).

[206] The Regulation on the Handling of Medical Accidents (2002, State Council) (医疗事故处理条例, 2002年, 国务院).

[207] Tort Liability Law of People's Republic of China (2009, Standing Committee of NPC) (中华人民共和国侵权责任法, 2009年, 全国人大常委会).

Health Practitioners. They are subject to different examinations but to the same practising rules.

According to the law, "doctors" include medical practitioners (doctors) and assistant medical practitioners (assistant doctors). The law requires uniform examination of qualifications for both doctors and assistant doctors formulated by the health administration department of the State Council.[208] The prerequisites to taking the examination have both academic and clinical components. For example, if a person has a bachelor's degree or a higher degree in medicine from an institution of higher learning and has practised for 1 year under the guidance of licensed doctors at health care institutions, he can take the examination.[209] There are less demanding requirements for assistant doctors.[210] The law shows flexibility by recognising apprenticeship as a form of education for TCM. Those who have learned traditional medicine (TCM and ethnic minority medicine) via apprenticeship or have acquired special and proficient medical skills through many years of practice may take the examination.[211] The examination of qualifications for TCM doctors is administered by the State Administration of Traditional Chinese Medicine.

Similarly, according to *Regulation on Medical Institutions*[212] and its Implementing Measures, "medical institutions" not only include Western medicine hospitals and clinics but also include TCM hospitals and clinics.[213] Western medicine institutions and TCM medical institutions are exposed to the same legal rules.[214]

---

[208] Law on Practising Doctors of the People's Republic of China (1998, Standing Committee of the National People's Congress) Article 8 (中华人民共和国执业医师法, 1998年,全国人大常委会, 第8条).

[209] Law on Practising Doctors of the People's Republic of China (1998, Standing Committee of the National People's Congress) Article 9 (1) (中华人民共和国执业医师法, 1998年,全国人大常委会, 第9 (1)条). Two other circumstances under which a person can take the examination are: (1) after obtaining the certificate for assistant practising doctors and degrees from 3-year colleges, he has worked for 2 years or more at a health care institution; (2) he has a medical degree from a technical secondary school and has worked for 5 or more years at a health care institution.

[210] Law on Practising Doctors of the People's Republic of China (1998, Standing Committee of the National People's Congress) Article 10 (中华人民共和国执业医师法, 1998年,全国人大常委会, 第10条) ("Those who have medical degrees from 3-year medical colleges or technical secondary schools can take examination of assistant practising doctors' qualifications after a probation period of 1 year or more under guidance from practising doctors at institutions for medical treatment, disease prevention or health care.").

[211] Law on Practising Doctors of the People's Republic of China (1998, Standing Committee of the National People's Congress) Article 11 (中华人民共和国执业医师法, 1998年,全国人大常委会, 第11条).

[212] Regulation on Medical Institutions (1994, State Council)(医疗机构管理条例, 1994年, 国务院).

[213] Implementing Measures for Regulation on Medical Institutions (1994, Ministry of Health) Article 3 (医疗机构管理条例实施细则, 1994年, 卫生部, 第3条).

[214] Regulation on Medical Institutions (1994, State Council) Articles 24–39(医疗机构管理条例, 1994年, 国务院, 第24-39条); Implementing Measures for Regulation on Medical Institutions (1994, Ministry of Health) Articles 51–65 (医疗机构管理条例实施细则, 1994年, 卫生部, 第51-65条).

10.4.1.2 TCM Drugs

China subjects both conventional drugs and TCM drugs to the same *Pharmaceutical Administration Law*.[215] According to the Law, the term "pharmaceuticals" means "materials that are used for preventing, treating, or diagnosing diseases of the people, and regulating the physiological functions, with prescribed applicable diseases (indications), main functions, usage, and dosage".[216] It not only covers modern Western medicine pharmaceuticals, such as antibiotics, biochemical pharmaceuticals, radioactive pharmaceuticals, blood serum, vaccine, blood products, and diagnosis pharmaceuticals, but also embraces TCM medical products, including Chinese traditional medicinal materials ("*Zhong Yao Cai*"(中药材)), Chinese medicine crude slices ("*Zhong Yao Yin Pian*"(中药饮片)), and prepared Chinese medicines ("*Zhong Cheng Yao*"(中成药)).[217]

In addition to the "parent" law – the *Pharmaceutical Administration Law*, in most cases, other pharmaceutical legislation also does not distinguish between conventional drugs and TCM drugs. All conventional drugs and TCM drugs (especially prepared Chinese medicines) may fall within the scope of Good Laboratory Practice (GLP),[218] Good Clinical Practice (GCP),[219] Good Manufacture Practice (GMP),[220] and Good Supply Practice (GSP).[221] Chinese traditional medicinal materials have their own Good Manufacture Practice.[222] Regulations regarding prescription drug and OTC drug classification,[223] adverse reactions reporting and

[215] Law of the People's Republic of China on Pharmaceutical Administration (2001, The Standing Committee of the National People's Congress) (中华人民共和国药品管理法,2001年,全国人大常委会).

[216] Law of the People's Republic of China on Pharmaceutical Administration (2001, The Standing Committee of the National People's Congress) Article 102 (中华人民共和国药品管理法,2001年,全国人大常委会, 第102条).

[217] Law of the People's Republic of China on Pharmaceutical Administration (2001, The Standing Committee of the National People's Congress) Article 102 (中华人民共和国药品管理法,2001年,全国人大常委会, 第102条).

[218] Good Laboratory Practice for Pharmaceuticals (2003, State Food and Drug Administration) (药物非临床研究质量管理规范, 2003年, 国家食品药品监督管理局).

[219] Good Clinical Practice for Pharmaceuticals (2003, State Food and Drug Administration) (药物临床试验质量管理规范, 2003年, 国家食品药品监督管理局).

[220] Good Manufacture Practice for Pharmaceuticals (1999, State Food and Drug Administration) (药品生产质量管理规范, 1999年, 国家食品药品监督管理局).

[221] Good Supply Practice for Pharmaceuticals (2000, State Food and Drug Administration) (药品经营质量管理规范, 2000年, 国家食品药品监督管理局).

[222] Good Manufacture Practice for Chinese traditional medicinal materials (2002, State Food and Drug Administration) (中药材生产质量管理规范(试行)(GAP), 2002年, 国家食品药品监督管理局).

[223] Management Measures on Prescription Drug and OTC Drug Classification (1999, State Food and Drug Administration) (处方药与非处方药分类管理办法(试行), 1999年, 国家药品监督管理局).

surveillance,[224] and drug information disclosure[225] also apply to TCM drugs. TCM drug manufacturers can apply for the title of "New Pharmaceuticals" for their TCM drugs.[226] Before that is done, TCM drugs are subjected to rigorous testing.

Within the umbrella of pharmaceutical law, Chinese law devotes some special provisions to TCM drugs. First, apparently responding to the fact that many TCM drugs originate from plants and animals, China makes it clear that the state protects the wild pharmaceutical resources and encourages cultivating Chinese traditional medical materials.[227] Second, Chinese pharmaceutical law creates a few exceptions for Chinese traditional medicinal materials and Chinese medicine crude slices. State Council shall otherwise formulate the administrative measures on cultivation, gathering, and breeding of Chinese traditional medicinal materials.[228] Processing Chinese traditional medicine crude slices is exempt from the ordinary manufacturing requirements.[229] Third, in selling Chinese traditional medicinal materials, the places of origin of them should be indicated clearly.[230] Fourth, China shows special commitment to protect varieties of Chinese medicines by the special way of protecting secrecy.[231] Fifth, according to drug information disclosure law, drug package leaflets should contain information about safety, efficacy of the drug, indications, contra-indications, adverse reactions and other items. However, if there is no reliable testing data to support them, Chinese law allow TCM drug information booklets and leaflets to be silent on pharmacological effects, adverse reactions, contra-indications, or to declare "unclear" on those items.

---

[224] Management Measures on Reporting and Surveillance of Drug Adverse Reactions (2004, State Food and Drug Administration) (药品不良反应报告和监测管理办法, 2004年, 卫生部、国家食品药品监督管理局).

[225] Stipulations on Drug Information Disclosure Booklet and Leaflet (2006, State Food and Drug Administration) (药品说明书和标签管理规定, 2006年, 国家食品药品监督管理局).

[226] Measures on Approving New Pharmaceuticals (1999, State Drug Administration) Article 6 (新药审批办法, 1999年, 国家药品监督管理局, 第6条).

[227] Law of the People's Republic of China on Pharmaceutical Administration (2001, The Standing Committee of the National People's Congress) Article 3 (中华人民共和国药品管理法,2001年, 全国人大常委会, 第3条). *Also see*, Regulations on the Management of Protection of Resources of Wild Medicinal Materials (1987, State Drug Administration) (野生药材资源保护管理条例, 1987年, 国家医药管理局).

[228] Law of the People's Republic of China on Pharmaceutical Administration (2001, The Standing Committee of the National People's Congress) Article 103 (中华人民共和国药品管理法,2001年,全国人大常委会, 第103条).

[229] Law of the People's Republic of China on Pharmaceutical Administration (2001, The Standing Committee of the National People's Congress) Article 10 (中华人民共和国药品管理法,2001年, 全国人大常委会, 第10条).

[230] Law of the People's Republic of China on Pharmaceutical Administration (2001, The Standing Committee of the National People's Congress) Article 19 (中华人民共和国药品管理法,2001年, 全国人大常委会, 第19条).

[231] Law of the People's Republic of China on Pharmaceutical Administration (2001, The Standing Committee of the National People's Congress) Article 36 (中华人民共和国药品管理法,2001年, 全国人大常委会, 第36条); Regulations on the Protection of Varieties of the Traditional Chinese Medicines (1992, State Council) (中药品种保护条例, 1992年, 国务院).

10.4.1.3 Western Medicine Standard or TCM Standard?

TCM practitioners in China and those in other countries may have different feelings about their professional and legal environments. TCM professionals in China are warmly embraced at every level of health care, but they work in a science-promoting or science-advocating world in which all laws, norms and regulations have been formulated according to the modern scientific model. China's integration of TCM with conventional medicine has a strong Western-medicine-oriented culture. That is one of big reasons why some TCM advocates argue that TCM education and health care should keep a distance from Western medicine paradigms. Some universities are experimenting with a decrease in the Western medicine component of TCM education, trying to restore traditional forms of education and to emphasise traditional TCM methods of diagnosis and treatment.

Despite the prevalence of integrative health care in China, I cannot agree with the view that TCM has lost its identity in delivering heath care in China, especially when I read Chinese laws. From *legal* perspectives, China is still committed to preserve and promote TCM's unique features. I have some evidences. First, although TCM doctors in TCM hospitals are encouraged to adopt both Western medicine and TCM diagnostic methods, they are recommended to administer treatments by identifying patients' symptom-complexes rather than diseases and following TCM theories, methods and formulas.[232] Second, acknowledging that TCM education has a special dimension, Chinese law recognises the legal status of apprenticeship[233] and encourages TCM doctors to inherit the experience of their veteran TCM colleagues.[234] Third, Chinese law makes it clear that TCM professionals should abide by their own TCM diagnosis and treatment principles, their own standards and guidelines.[235] In areas and activities that call for technical expertise, such as technical appraisal and authentication, TCM issues should be decided by TCM experts.[236] Therefore, we can confidently say that, in assessing medical or technical matters, Chinese law follows the "same school" rule and honours peer review. That means, the standard of care applicable to TCM practitioners is the TCM standard rather than

[232] Stipulations on Many Issues Surrounding Running Traditional Chinese Medicine Hospitals (1980, Ministry of Health), Article 5 (中医医院工作若干问题的规定(试行), 1980年, 卫生部,第5条).

[233] Regulation on Traditional Chinese Medicine of People's Republic of China (2003, State Council), Article 11 (中华人民共和国中医药条例, 2003年, 第11条).

[234] Regulation on Traditional Chinese Medicine of People's Republic of China (2003, State Council), Articles 16–19 (中华人民共和国中医药条例, 2003年, 第16-19条).

[235] Regulation on Traditional Chinese Medicine of People's Republic of China (2003, State Council), Article 12 (中华人民共和国中医药条例, 2003年, 第12条).

[236] Regulation on Traditional Chinese Medicine of People's Republic of China (2003, State Council), Article 30 (中华人民共和国中医药条例, 2003年, 第30条). However, complaints have been made by TCM orthopaedists and osteopaths, claiming that experts who authenticate "medical accident" in their field are dominated by Western medicine experts. That will place them in disadvantage because TCM and Western medicine differ on theories and practices of orthopaedics and osteopathy. *See*, Zhang Yong Chao 2005, 36–41.

the Western medicine standard. The argument that, in medical malpractice litigation, the standards for identifying malpractice will come from modern scientific medicine (Ruiping 2003, 215 and 219) is a misconception. This point has been made clearer in some Local Regulations. For example, *Beijing TCM Regulation* clarifies that technical authentication about TCM medical accidents should be made by a panel dominated by TCM experts.[237] Shandong Province has the same legal rule.[238]

However, in China the TCM standard of care, which is applicable to TCM practitioners, has a strong Western medicine involvement and modern science component. Chinese government never tires of efforts to promote "standardisation", "modernisation" and "scientificisation" of TCM. The "ideal" focus is always placed on combining "inheritance and innovation", and combining "traditional theories and methods" with "modern scientific means",[239] ignoring the difficulty of integrating the two fundamentally different medical cultures. In the context of diagnosis and treatment, I do not favour and advocate an "integrative" medicine. Modern medicine and CAMs are irreconcilable in both theory and practice. It is difficult, if not impossible, for a practitioner to have undivided loyalty to both medicines. I prefer to see that health care professionals show loyalty to their own "school of thought", acknowledge limitations of every "school", and if needed, make referrals to other "schools". I do not see much wisdom in the Chinese integrative approach, especially in the context of treatment. However, the Chinese way of integration is applaudable in that it strengthens the modern medicine knowledge base for TCM practitioners and, is, therefore, helpful in providing patients with full information disclosure. In the area of information disclosure, I prefer to see practitioners to have "integration" of knowledge about both modern medicine and CAMs.

10.4.2 TCM Practitioners and Informed Consent Law

As I explained earlier, TCM practitioners are subject to almost every piece of health care legislation. Together with Western medicine doctors, TCM doctors should comply with the same legal rules, including the informed consent rules. As I indicated in the account of "legal context", Chinese informed consent rules have different formulations, which appear in several pieces of legislation. They are: (1) "Doctors should truthfully explain the patients' conditions to the patients or their family members".[240] (2) Medical institution should respect the patient's right to be informed

[237] Beijing TCM Regulation (2001, Beijing), Article 30 (北京市发展中医条例, 2001年, 第30条).

[238] Shandong Province TCM Regulation (1999, Shandong Province), Article 33 (山东省中医条例, 1999年, 第33条).

[239] Regulation on Traditional Chinese Medicine of People's Republic of China (2003, State Council), Article 4, 9 and 22 (中华人民共和国中医药条例, 2003年, 第4, 9, 22条).

[240] Law on Practising Doctors of the People's Republic of China (1998), Article 26 (中华人民共和国执业医师法, 1998年, 第26条).

of *condition, diagnosis and treatment,* and, when administrating operations, special examination, and special treatment, medical institution should give the patient "necessary explanation".[241] (3) "In the activities of medical treatment, medical institutions and medical practitioners should truthfully inform patients of their conditions, treatment measures, medical risks and others".[242] (4) "Medical professional shall, during diagnosis and treatment, inform patients about their conditions and treatment measures. If surgery, special examination, or special treatment is required, medical professionals shall disclose to patients about medical risks, alternative treatment plans and other information in a timely manner, and obtain their consent in writing."[243] Among the four, the fourth version of the informed consent rule is the newest one and is formulated in the context of tort law. It will be the dominant version of Chinese informed consent rule.

TCM practitioners should disclose risks of TCM therapies. TCM treatments are not risk-free. A Chinese survey reveals that medical practitioners and patients have different degree of awareness about adverse reactions of TCM therapies. While 99% of medical professionals surveyed understand that TCM therapies may have adverse reactions, only 54.5% of patients surveyed were aware that TCM treatments may trigger adverse reactions (Yu Lei 2008, 30). Fortunately, a high percentage of both groups (83.2% for patients and 80.2% for medical professionals) realise the necessity of informed consent in the context of TCM (Yu Lei 2008, 30). Patients want to know about the treatment plan (77.2%), possible efficacy (72.3%), possible side effects and adverse reactions (52.5%) and contra-indications (49.5%) (Yu Lei 2008, 30). The risks of many TCM therapies are "unknown". For these therapies, TCM practitioners should inform patients of the fact that risks are "unknown", rather than claim that the therapies are "risk-free". Because in China TCM drugs are subjected to similarly rigorous regulation as conventional drugs, more information regarding the safety, efficacy and adverse reactions of TCM drugs would be revealed. In addition to risks of treatments, following Chinese informed consent rules, TCM practitioners should also inform their patients of alternative treatment options. Those alternative treatments include both TCM alternatives and Western medicine alternatives.

Information disclosure in the field of TCM is not free from barriers and challenges. Most TCM theories cannot be explained by modern scientific knowledge. The rationales for many TCM practices are not readily understandable for patients (Yang Li Xin and Wang Ling Fang 2007, 15–16). In a society where Western medicine dominates, TCM practitioners should be well-prepared to explain the difference between TCM and Western medicine in diagnosing and treating patients.

---

241 Rules for Implementing the Regulation on Medical Institutions (1994, Ministry of Health) Article 62 (医疗机构管理条例实施细则, 1994年, 卫生部, 第62条).

242 The Regulation on the Handling of Medical Accidents (2002, State Council), Article 11 (医疗事故处理条例, 2002年, 国务院, 第11条).

243 Tort Liability Law of People's Republic of China (2009, Standing Committee of NPC), Article 55 (1) (中华人民共和国侵权责任法, 2009年, 全国人大常委会, 第55(1)条).

Furthermore, some TCM recipes and prescriptions, which are, in most cases, family-based and experience-based, may be under legal protection as "business secret".[244] That poses another question of how to reconcile a patient's right to be informed and a "business secret" holder's right of intellectual property.

10.4.3 Western Medicine, Chinese Medicine and Disclosure of Alternatives

Thanks to the Western-medicine-oriented integration, TCM practitioners in China have a strong knowledge base of Western medicine. That is mainly due to the integrative nature of curriculum prepared for TCM students. Moreover, compared to CAM practitioners practising in Western countries, TCM practitioners in China enjoy a wider scope of practice, and they can use Western medicine diagnostic methods and administer Western medicine treatments. That lends weight to the argument that Western medicine alternative treatments should more readily fall within Chinese TCM practitioners' duty to inform about alternatives. For "dual" practitioners who have Western medicine degree and who used to practice Western medicine but choose to learn and practice TCM, patients' expectation that they know and will disclose both conventional medicine and TCM treatments would be more justifiable.

Compared to TCM practitioners who are exposed to a strongly Western-medicine-oriented integration, Western medicine practitioners in China have relatively weak knowledge about TCM. A TCM course is normally available for Western medicine students. That would give them familiarity with basic TCM theories and therapies. According to the law, General Practitioners and Village Doctors in China should possess basic TCM knowledge and know how to use basic TCM diagnosis and treatment methods to manage patients.[245] Understandably GPs and doctors in rural areas would have more access to, more frequent use of, and therefore more awareness of, TCM therapies than specialists and urban doctors.

Because the ready availability of TCM practitioners and TCM practice in Chinese society, Western medicine practitioners do not bother too much to learn and *practice* TCM or respond to patients' demand to practice TCM, especially after *Mao*'s political push became a history. However, because they are exposed to an integrative medical

---

[244] Chinese law is committed to protect "business secrets". "Business secrets" is defined as "the technical information and operational information which is not known to the public, which is capable of bringing economic benefits to the owners of the rights, which has practical applicability and which the owners of the rights have taken measures to keep secret". *See*, Law of the People's Republic of China for Countering Unfair Competition (1993, Standing Committee of NPC), Article 10 (中华人民共和国反不正当竞争法, 1993年, 全国人大常委会, 第10条).

[245] Regulation on Traditional Chinese Medicine of People's Republic of China (2003, State Council), Article 12 (中华人民共和国中医药条例, 2003年, 第12条).

Table 10.4 TCM/Dual/Western medicine practitioners and disclosure of alternatives in China

	Adoption (Integrative)	Disclosure of alternatives (Contextualised)
TCM practitioners	TCM + Western medicine	TCM + Western medicine
Dual practitioners	Western medicine + TCM	Western medicine + TCM
Western medicine practitioners	Western medicine + prepared Chinese medicine	Western medicine (+TCM?)

culture and they know that TCM has a stable and widespread presence in health care, Western medicine practitioners in China have less excuse than their counterparts in Western developed countries to avoid mentioning TCM when TCM therapies are necessary. Moreover, patients in China are more likely to raise questions about TCM treatments. Furthermore, thanks to the Western-medicine-oriented integrative culture, the profiles of many TCM treatments and drugs, for example, prepared Chinese medicine, are reformulated in modern science language and in Western medicine terms. That, to some extent, eradicates medical language barriers for Western medicine practitioners to understand and move close to TCM therapies. TCM therapies that have been rigorously tested under the Western medicine model, therefore have clear risk-benefit profiles, and are understandable and describable in the eyes of Western medicine practitioners, have more chances to fall within the ambit of Western medicine practitioners' duty to disclose. The integrative medical culture facilitates formation of a more "integrative" model of information disclosure (Table 10.4).

10.5 Conclusion

In addition to the approach of courts creatively and proactively expanding the scope of information disclosure, China witnessed another way of embracing disclosure of alternatives within a doctor's duty to inform – passing legislation. As a civil law jurisdiction, legislation plays a vital part in Chinese legal system. Partly because of its high authority, Chinese scholars, the medical profession and the public invest hope and confidence in the new-born Tort Law to improve the doctor-patient relationship and protect the patients' rights. However, those who are optimistic about the Tort's roles ignore the deficiencies and inconveniences that a Tort approach has. Tort law cannot provide the ideal context to protect patients' rights, especially the right of autonomy enshrined in the doctrine of informed consent.

Unlike other jurisdictions, where medical professions enjoy State-sanctioned self-regulation, China has a tradition of government involving in regulating medical professions. That provides a possible avenue for a government-appointed entity to actively and effectively scrutinise the health care, in a way that is distinct from the tort context. I would like to see China to learn from the New Zealand's Code experiences and construct a similar mechanism to fulfil the mission of protecting patients' rights. That can be done either by providing new legislation or by transforming existing legislation.

In China, health care is still very paternalistic. Many medical practitioners see the rule of informed consent as functional. They use "informed consent" as a shield to avoid legal liability rather than as a communicational tool. Chinese *Tort Liability Law* answers patients' expectation that they want to be fully informed before undergoing a procedure. As far as the disclosure of alternative treatments is concerned, Chinese Tort Law only envisages the following scenarios: (1) *non-surgical, conservative, non-invasive, or less invasive* treatments – alternatives to *invasive* treatments (surgery); (2) *riskless or less risky* treatments – alternatives to *risky* treatments; (3) *conventional, well-established* treatments – alternatives to *experimental* treatments; (4) *cheap* treatments – alternatives to *expensive* treatments. The last one reflects the reality that China has a fee-for-service health care, and doctors have a strong motive and financial incentive to pursue expansive procedures.

As I consistently argued, Chinese law needs to make distinctions between the context of a doctor recommending, adopting or administering a procedure and the context of a doctor disclosing information about procedures. A doctor is entitled to recommend and administer only well-established and conventional treatments. However, as witnessed by Japanese law, *emerging and minority* treatments that a treating doctor does not recommend or favour may fall within his duty to inform.

Chinese health care also has a dichotomy between conventional (Western) medicine and Traditional Chinese Medicine. TCM practitioners are incorporated at every level, both the legal level and the clinical level, of "mainstream" health care system. The "integrative" model is significantly Western-medicine-oriented. That provides two distinctions between Chinese TCM practitioners and their overseas counterparts. First, Chinese TCM practitioners have a stronger knowledge base about conventional (Western) medicine. Second, Chinese TCM practitioners enjoy a wider scope of practice. They are given latitude in using conventional medicine and TCM. That gives me confidence to argue that in China TCM practitioners should, and have competence to, disclose conventional medicine treatments when necessary. Conversely, in China Western medicine practitioners should inform patients of some, although not all, TCM treatments that have been subjected to rigorous testing, have some evidence base, and have been formulated in modern medicine terms. The Chinese integrative approach lends support to my argument that health practitioners should present patients with balanced information that overcomes the boundaries of "schools" of thought.

References

Beijing High Court. 2010. *The guiding rules about how to adjudicate cases of liability for medical damage* (November 18, 2010, Jing Gao Fa Fa [2010] No. 400). http://lawyer.fabao365.com/21692/article_101666. Accessed 20 Apr 2012 (北京市高级人民法院关于审理医疗损害赔偿纠纷案件若干问题的指导意见(试行)(2010年11月18日,京高法发[2010]第400号).

Chen, Hua. 2009. A reflection on informed consent from the different perspectives of Chinese and western cultures. *Medicine and Philosophy (Humanistic & Social Medicine Edition)* 30: 17–19 (陈化: "从中西文化差异审视知情同意", 载《医学与哲学(人文社会医学版)》2009 年第7期, 第17-19页).

Chen, Zhihua. 2010. *Liability for medical damage: Comments and cases*. Beijing: Law Press (陈志华:《医疗损害责任深度释解与实务指南》,法律出版社2010年版).

Chen, Ke Ji, and Yue Rong Jiang. 2009. Current status and problems in developing clinical guidelines for Chinese medicine and integrative medicine. *Journal of Chinese Integrative Medicine* 7: 301–305 (陈可冀, 蒋跃绒: "中医和中西医结合临床指南制定的现状与问题", 载《中西医结合学报》第7卷2009年第4期,第302-305页).

Dai, Qingkang. 2003. Informed consent in China: *Status Quo* and its future. *Medical Law International* 6: 53–71.

Devereux, J.A. 2007. *Australian medical Law*, 3rd ed. London/New York: Routledge-Cavendish.

Fan, Ruiping. 2003. Modern western science as a standard for traditional Chinese medicine: A critical appraisal. *The Journal of Law, Medicine & Ethics* 31: 213–221.

Fu, Zi Tang, et al. 2006. *Empirical analysis on adjudication of medical lawsuits*. Beijing: People's Court Press (付子堂 等著:《医疗纠纷案件审理之实证分析》, 人民法院出版社2006年版).

Gao, Shengping. 2010. *China's Tort Liability Law: Issues, statutory provisions in other jurisdictions and leading cases*. Beijing: Peking University Press (高圣平:《〈中华人民共和国侵权责任法〉立法争点、立法例及经典案例》,北京大学出版社2010年版).

Harris, Dean M., and Wu Chien-Chang. 2005. Medical malpractice in the People's Republic of China: The 2002 regulation on the handling of medical accidents. *The Journal of Law, Medicine & Ethics* 33: 456–477.

He, Xian Zhong. 2004. Leader of abolishing TCM: Yu Yun Xiu and his conducts. *Nature Dialectics* 26: 72–76 (郝先中: "废止中医派的领袖——余云岫其人其事",载《自然辩证法通讯》第26卷2004年第6期,第72-76页).

Hesketh, Therese, and Wei Xing Zhu. 1997. Health in China: Traditional Chinese medicine: One country, two systems. *British Medical Journal* 315: 115–117.

Ho, Christina S. 2010. Health reform and *de facto* federalism in China. *China: An International Journal* 8: 33–62.

Huang, Sheng-Li, and Xiao-Yan Ding. 2011. Violence against Chinese health-care workers. *The Lancet* 377: 1747.

Ji, Tao. 2010. Who exercises the right of informed consent in the therapeutic context? *Zhe Jiang Social Science* 2: 10–13 (季涛: "谁是医疗关系中知情同意权的主体?", 载《浙江社会科学》2010年第2期, 第10-13页).

Jiang, Chun Ling. 2006. On the patient's right to informed consent: Cases survey and thinking. *Nanjing University Law Review* (Autumn) 113 (姜春玲: "论患者的知情同意权 ——判例调查基础上的理论与立法检讨", 载《南京大学法律评论》2006年秋季号, 第113页).

Krause, Joan H. 1999. Reconceptualizing informed consent in an era of health care cost containment. *Iowa Law Review* 85: 261–386.

Lachlan, Mc.Murtrie. 2006. Setting the legal standard of care for treatment and evidence-based medicine: A case study of antenatal corticosteroids. *Journal of Law and Medicine* 14: 220–227.

Lei, Yi, and Ming Wu. 2010. Survey on medical staffs' perception of the doctor-patient relationship: A case study of a public hospital in Beijing. *Practical Journal of Cardiac Cerebral Pneumal and Vascular Disease* 18: 1055–1057 (雷祎,吴明: "北京市某三甲医院医务人员对医患关系的认知及其影响因素研究",载《实用心脑肺血管病杂志》2010年第8期,第1055-1057页).

Li, Xiao Yun. 2010. Analysis of reasons for choosing caesarean section and responding measures. *Contemporary Medicine* 16: 103–104 (李晓芸: "社会性因素剖宫产术原因分析及预防对策", 载《当代医学》2010年第9期, 第103-104页).

Li, Jian Sheng, and Xue Qing Yu. 2010. Current situation and thinking on the development of TCM clinical treatment guidelines. *CJTCMP* 25: 647–650 (李建生,余学庆: "中医临床治疗指南制定的现状与思考", 载《中华中医药杂志》第25卷2010年第5期, 第647-650页).

Liang, Hui Xing. 2010. On the "medical damage liability" of the Tort Liability Law. *Studies in Law and Business* 6: 35–37 (梁慧星: "论《侵权责任法》中的医疗损害责任", 载《法商研究》2010年第6期, 第35-37页).

Liao, Huan Guo. 2010. How to establish medical fault: Understanding and applying medical damage liability law. *Politics and Law* 5: 18–27 (廖焕国: "论医疗过错的认定———以医疗损害侵权责任的理解与适用为视点", 载《政治与法律》2010年第5期, 第18-27页).

Liao, Tian Ming, et al. 2010. Survey and reflections on medical authentication in medical malpractice cases. *Journal of He Tian Normal College* 2: 2–3 (廖天明等: "医疗损害赔偿案件中医疗鉴定问题的调研思考", 载《和田师范专科学校学报》(汉文综合版)2010年第2期, 第2-3页).

Lin, Wen Xue. 2010. Exploration of some issues regarding medical damage liability of 'Tort Liability Law'. *Journal of Law Application* 7: 21–24 (林文学:"《侵权责任法》医疗损害责任规定若干问题探析",载《法律适用》2010年第7期,第21-24页).

Liu, Xue Ying, Yue Ning Deng, and Zhong Jian Li. 2008. Investigation and analysis of violation of doctors' rights in five cities and An-san, Tie-ling of Liao Xi. *Chinese Medical Ethics* 21: 87–89 (刘雪莹,邓悦宁,李中建: "辽西五市和鞍山铁岭两市医生遭遇侵权现状的调查与分析", 载《中国医学伦理学》2008年第4期,第87-89页).

Ministry of Health (People's Republic of China). 2010. *Letter regarding recommended "medical informed consent forms"*. http://www.moh.gov.cn/publicfiles/business/htmlfiles/mohyzs/s3586/201003/46248.htm. Accessed 2 Oct 2010 (卫生部医政司: "关于推荐使用《医疗知情同意书》的函(卫医政疗便函〔2010〕42号)").

Montgomery, Jonathan. 2003. *Health care law*, 2nd ed. New York: Oxford University Press.

Nie, Jing Bao. 2002. Is informed consent not applicable in China? Intellectual flaws of the "cultural difference argument". *Medicine and Philosophy* 23: 18–22 (聂精保: "知情同意在中国不适用吗———"文化差异论"的认知错误", 载《医学与哲学》2002年第6期,第18-22页).

People's Hospital of Peking University. 2010. *Compilation of medical informed consent forms*. http://www.moh.gov.cn/publicfiles/business/htmlfiles/mohyzs/s3586/201003/46248.htm. Accessed 2 Oct 2010 (北京大学人民医院: "医疗知情同意书汇编").

Project Group of "Study on Judicial Interpretation of Tort Liability Law". 2010. *Suggestion and discussion draft of judicial interpretation of Tort Liability Law of People's Republic of China*. http://www.civillaw.com.cn/article/default.asp?id=49876. Accessed 12 July 2010 (中国人民大学民商事法律科学研究中心"侵权责任法司法解释研究"课题组:"中华人民共和国侵权责任法司法解释草案建议稿(草案)").

Qian, Hua. 2008. The difficulty of combining TCM and Western medicine and solutions. *Chinese Journal of Information on TCM* 15: 1–2 (钱华: "中西医结合的难点和方法思考", 载《中国中医药信息杂志》第15卷2008年第2期, 第1-2页).

State Council. 2012. *Plans and implementing measures on deepening the health care system reform in the period of "twelve five year"* (Guo Fa (2012) No. 11, March 14, 2012). http://www.gov.cn/zwgk/2012-03/21/content_2096671.htm. Accessed 4 May 2012 ("十二五"期间深化医药卫生体制改革规划暨实施方案 (国务院, 国发〔2012〕11号, 2012年3月14日)).

Su, Yin Li, and Le Zhi Li. 2008. Progress research on attitudes to the patient's right of informed consent among the patients, their relatives and medical staffs. *Medicine and Philosophy (Humanistic & Social Medicine Edition)* 29: 28–29 (苏银利,李乐之:"医患不同角色群体对患者知情同意权的态度研究进展",载《医学与哲学(人文社会医学版)》2008年第29卷第3期, 第28-29页).

Sun, Ze Ting, et al. 2006. The present situation of and thinking on combining traditional Chinese medicine and western medicine. *Medicine and Philosophy* 27: 77–79 (孙泽庭,聂正怀,邓崇平: "中西医结合的现状与思考", 载《医学与哲学》第27 卷2006年第3期, 第77-79页).

Tai, Michael Cheng-tek, and Tsung-po Tsai. 2003. Who makes the decision? Patient's autonomy vs paternalism in a confucian society. *Croatian Medical Journal* 44: 558–561.

The Chief Official of the First Civil Court of the SPC. 2004. *Answers by to Reporters' questions on how to apply laws in adjudicating medical lawsuits*. http://www.cmda.gov.cn/yishiweiquan/weiquanzhishi/2009-02-25/5311.html. Accessed 19 Sept 2010. (最高人民法院民一庭负责人就审理医疗纠纷案件的法律适用问题答记者问).

The Lancet. 2010. Chinese doctors are under threat. *The Lancet* 376: 657.

The Lancet. 2012. Ending violence against doctors in China. *The Lancet* 379: 1764.

The Legislative Affairs Commission of the Standing Committee of the National People's Congress. 2010. *Explanations about the Tort Liability Law of People's Republic of China*. Beijing: Peking University Press (全国人大常委会法制工作委员会民法室:《〈中华人民共和国侵权责任法〉条文说明、立法理由及相关规定》,北京大学出版社2010年版).

The Supreme People's Court of China. 2012. *Interpretation on how to apply laws in adjudicating cases of liability for medical damage* (Discussion Paper). http://www.ahyllaw.com/display.asp?id=1238. Accessed 20 Apr 2012 (最高院关于审理医疗损害责任纠纷案件适用法律若干问题的解释(征求意见稿)).

Wang, Yue. 2010. Exploration on issues regarding medical damage compensation. *Chinese Journal of Forensic Sciences* 2: 34–37 (王岳: "对医疗损害责任相关问题的探讨", 载《中国司法鉴定》2010 年第2 期, 第34-37页).

Wang, Yi Feng, and Yi Ping Xu. 2009. Survey on implementation of the informed consent rule in hospitals. *Hospital Administration Journal of Chinese People's Liberation Army* 16: 52–54 (王译锋,徐懿萍: "医院实施知情同意调查", 载《解放军医院管理杂志》2009年第1期,第52-54页).

Wen, Xiang. 2004. The *traditional Chinese medicine regulation* by Nanjing Guo Min Government. *Min Guo Dang An* 4: 82–86 (文 庠: "南京国民政府《中医条例》述评", 载《民国档案》2004年第4期, 第82-86页).

Wen, Chao Ying, Xiu Hua Pi, and Wen Zhong Dong. 2007. The reasons for disharmony of doctor – patient relationship. *Medicine and Philosophy (Humanistic & Social Medicine Edition)* 28: 24–26 (温超英、皮秀华、董文忠:"医患关系不和谐的原因",载《医学与哲学》2007年第5期,第24-26页).

Wu, Xi, et al. 2010. Characteristics of "acupuncture clinical practice guidelines" and their implementing principles and methods. *Guiding Journal of Traditional Chinese Medicine and Pharmacy* 16: 1–4 (吴曦 等: "'针灸临床实践指南'的特点及制定的原则与方法探讨", 载《中医药导报》2010年第16卷第6期, 第1-4页).

Xia, Yun. 2007. *Medical malpractice law: Reflections on Japanese law*. Beijing: Law Press (夏芸著:《医疗事故赔偿法——来自日本法的启示》,法律出版社2007年版).

Xia, Yun. 2009. Japanese reform of medical malpractice lawsuits and evaluation of appraisal conclusions. *Evidence Science* 17: 261–282 (夏芸:"日本医疗诉讼改革及对鉴定结论的评价", 载《证据科学》2009年第17卷第3期,第261-282页).

Xia, Yun. 2011. Rethinking the theory of "medical level" and the test for medical negligence. *Oriental Law* 5: 29–40 (夏芸:"再考 '医疗水平论'及医疗过失判断标准",载《东方法学》2011年第5期,第29-40页).

Xu, Xin, and Rong Rong Lu. 2008. Violence and mistrust: Research on violence in medical treatment in transforming China (2000~2006). *Law and Social Development* 1: 82–101 (徐昕、卢荣荣: "暴力与不信任———转型中国的医疗暴力研究: 2000~2006", 载《法制与社会发展》2008年第1期,第82-101页).

Yang, Li Xin. 2009a. Study on the concept of medical damage liability. *Politics and Law* 3: 75–82 (杨立新: "医疗损害责任概念研究", 载《政治与法律》2009 年第3 期, 第75-82页).

Yang, Li Xin. 2009b. On the principle and system of imputation for medical damage liability. *Journal of China University of Political Science and Law* 10: 62–72 (杨立新: "论医疗损害责任的归责原则及体系", 载《中国政法大学学报》2009 年第2 期, 第62-72页).

Yang, Li Xin. 2009c. Proof and burden of proof of medical negligence. *Journal of Law* 6: 1–6 (杨立新: "论医疗过失的证明及举证责任", 载《法学杂志》2009年第6期, 第1-6页).

Yang, Li Xin. 2010. The reform of liability for damages caused by medical treatment in the Tort Liability Law: Its success and shortage. *Journal of Renmin University of China* 4: 9–16 (杨立新: "《侵权责任法》改革医疗损害责任制度的成功与不足", 载《中国人民大学学报》2010年第4期, 第9-16页).

Yang, Li Xin, and Ling Fang Wang. 2007. TCM practitioners' duty to inform and liability for breach of the duty. *Journal of Gansu Institute of Political Science and Law* 95: 13–16 (杨立新, 王玲芳: "试论中医师的告知义务及违反告知义务的责任", 载《甘肃政法学院学报》总第95期, 第13-16页).

Yang, Hui, et al. 2003. Why are doctors not happy? *Hospital Management Forum* 2: 18–20 (杨辉等:"医生为什么不满意?",载《医院管理论坛》2003年第2期,第18-20页).

Yang, Yi, et al. 2010. Facing up to the threat in China. *The Lancet* 376: 1823–1824.

Yu, Lei. 2008. Thought on the application of informed consent in traditional Chinese medicine clinical diagnosis and treatment. *Medicine and Philosophy (Humanistic & Social Medicine Edition)* 29: 30–31 (俞蕾: "知情同意在中医药临床诊疗中的应用思考",载《医学与哲学(人文社会医学版)》 2008年第29卷第3期,第30-31页).

Yu, Mingshui. 2010. *Litigation for compensation for medical damage*. Beijing: Law Press (余明永:《医疗损害赔偿纠纷》,法律出版社2010年版).

Zhang, Yong Chao. 2005. Embarrassment in authenticating TCM orthopaedics and osteopathy medical accidents. *Ji Yuan Ling Dao Jue Ce Can Kao* 6: 36–41 (张永超: "中医正骨医疗事故鉴定的尴尬", 载《医院领导决策参考》2005年第6期, 第36-41页).

Zhang, Ao Hui, and Yu Zheng Dong. 2010. Analysis on the reasons for difficulties in enforcing informed consent. *Chinese Medical Ethics* 23: 30–31 (张奥会,董玉整: "患者知情同意落实难问题之原因分析", 载《中国医学伦理学》2010年第2期, 第30-31页).

Zhang, Gui Qing, and Jin Li Han. 2008. Comparison of the preoperative psychological condition of the patients who made informed consent themselves and those whose family members did instead. *Chinese Mental Health Journal* 22: 383–386 (张桂青,韩金丽: "本人知情同意与家属知情同意情况下患者术前心理状况的比较", 载《中国心理卫生杂志》2008年第5期,第383-386页).

Zhang, Ying Tao, and Fu Chuan Sun. 2004. Localization of informed consent in China: The trend of informed consent in the context of Chinese culture. *Medicine and Philosophy* 25: 12–15 (张英涛,孙福川: "论知情同意的中国本土化———中国文化视野中的知情同意走向",载《医学与哲学》2004年第25卷第9期, 第12-15页).

Zhao, Xiju. 2008. *Study on medical law*. Beijing: Law Press (赵西巨著:《医事法研究》,法律出版社2008年版).

Zhao, Xiju. 2009. Adoption and disclosure of emerging therapies. *Oriental Law* 6: 119–133 (赵西巨: "医生对新疗法的使用与告知",载《东方法学》2009年第6期,第119-133页).

Chapter 11
Conclusion

Abstract The book makes a distinction between diagnosis/treatment and information disclosure, and distinguish the balanced, unbiased, and contextualised "disclosure" of alternative treatment options from the "selection" of treatment and the "recommendation" of treatment. The book finds that the threshold for a treatment option falling within a practitioner's duty to inform may be lower than that required to satisfy the *Bolam* test or the "two schools of thought" doctrine. The book examines that the common law jurisdictions differ in the extent to which they recognise a *legal* duty to inform about alternatives. The book concludes that, compared to the approaches of either heavily relying on tort law or relying exclusively on professional regulation, the New Zealand's Code (of Patients' Rights) approach has the merit of combining the authority, stability, and proactive character of legislation, with the flexible and embracing nature of professional regulation, at the same time avoiding the inconveniences of medical negligence lawsuits.

The doctrine of "informed consent" has many elements, such as a doctor's duty of *information disclosure*, a patient's *competency* in decision-making, and a patient's *understanding* of information. This book concentrated on the component of "information disclosure". A healthcare professional's duty of this kind is subject to many *exceptions*, such as waiver, therapeutic privileges and emergency circumstances. These exceptions were beyond the scope of this book. A wide range of *information* may fall within a healthcare professional's duty to inform, such as the risk-benefit profile of the proposed course of action, the availability and profiles of *alternatives*, and other categories of information. The focus of this book was on the duty to inform about "alternatives".

The scope of the duty to inform about "alternatives" requires *distinct* examination. There is a significant gap between theoretical pronouncements regarding informed consent and the way the doctrine functions in practice. The problem of theory-practice "gap" is acute in the context of disclosure about alternatives. Moreover, even in a jurisdiction which, in theory, recognises a doctor's duty to

X. Zhao, *The Duty of Medical Practitioners and CAM/TCM Practitioners to Inform Competent Adult Patients about Alternatives*,
DOI 10.1007/978-3-642-31647-0_11, © Springer-Verlag Berlin Heidelberg 2013

inform about alternative treatment options, in reality the obligation to disclose information about treatment alternatives may be conflated with the obligation to disclose information about risks. As I demonstrate in the book, some jurisdictions are silent on the legal duty of disclosure of *alternatives* and focus only on the failure to disclose a *risk* that subsequently materialised. The vast majority of cases focus on both the failure to disclose risks *and* the failure to disclose alternatives. They may also involve allegations of medical negligence in performing the procedure. Few cases address the significance of the failure to disclose treatment alternatives *alone*.

This book investigates whether there is a duty to inform about alternatives and the ambit of such a duty (or what "alternatives" may fall within its scope). Both issues are complex. It is difficult to formulate generalised principles and rules which are universally applicable to disclosure of every category of "alternative". Seeking patients' "informed consent" is a very contextualised and individualised process. The diversity of jurisdictions this book examined, the wide range of alternatives that have the potential to fall within the scope of the duty to inform, and the discrepancies between the *legal* duty to inform about alternatives and the *professional/ethical* duty to do so further complicate the attempt to formulate general rules. Despite that, I still make attempts to collate the collective wisdom of the different jurisdictions and try my best to formulate a general line of thinking before special attention is paid to the duty to inform about specific categories of alternative and the distinctions that exist between those jurisdictions.

The rationale underlying the doctrine of informed consent is to honour a patient's right to autonomy and self-determination. Were this a philosophy book, there would be a need to examine the philosophical basis for this right, or at the very least demand. But as it is a law book, one can simply proceed on the basis that this emphasis on patient autonomy and self-determination has become very widespread indeed since the mid-twentieth century. It has a variety of philosophical or ethical underpinnings, not all of which are consistent with one another. What is striking, and significant, is the ubiquity of such notions, and the challenge they present to traditional medical practices.

To protect a competent patient's interest in autonomous decision-making, and self-determination, the tort of battery has been considered to provide a better context than the tort of negligence. Without the need to prove causation and show actual damage, battery is conceptually more attractive. However, most jurisdictions prefer to examine a doctor's duty to inform within the framework of negligence. Traditionally, medical negligence law is more doctor-friendly. Courts pay a very high degree of respect to medical judgment, professional opinions and medical expert evidence in setting the standard of care for healthcare professionals and in finding negligence. The shift from the doctor-oriented standard of information disclosure to the patient-oriented standard reflects the law's rethinking about the appropriateness of locating a doctor's duty to inform within negligence law and the acknowledgment that the duty to inform has distinct aspects.

The patient-oriented standard of information disclosure is more appropriate than the doctor-oriented standard. To demonstrate the distinct profile of the information disclosure issue, I review relevant case law and establish that, under the patient-oriented standard of information disclosure and the "materiality" test, the "information" prong, such as that concerning the gravity, likelihood of the potential risks of treatments, and existence/availability of treatment options, is subject to medical judgment, but the "materiality" prong, i.e. whether or not a reasonable person in the patient's position would attach significance to the undisclosed information, falls within human/layperson knowledge.

The information/materiality dichotomy reflects the phenomenon that "[a] patient requires medical and scientific information in order to make a decision, but the critical choice is based upon considerations arising out of the patient's circumstances in life, including personal philosophy, domestic and economic situation and, for instance, ambitions (Downie et al. 2002, 138)." It recognises the significance and diversity of patients' lifestyles and values in making medical decisions. Because information disclosure involves less medical judgment, the judicial approach of adopting a more interventionist attitude towards medical practice in this context is expected, justified and even required. The judiciary can ask healthcare professionals to transcend the boundaries of professional opinion and give more patient-centred information.

Theoretically, the move from disclosure of risks to disclosure of alternatives is not difficult. Explicitly holding that the duty to disclose attaches both to risks and alternative treatment options, or adopting more encompassing words such as "material information", are two ways in which the disclosure of alternatives may be accommodated within the duty to inform. In the landmark informed consent cases, several judges contemplated disclosure of alternative treatment options as a component of the duty to inform. However, extending the scope of this duty to encompass disclosure of alternatives is not easy. Normally a case comes before a court only after an undisclosed risk has materialised. As a consequence the focus of common law is almost always on non-disclosure of "risks", and not all common law jurisdictions have recognized a *legal* duty to inform about *alternatives*.

There are three ways to overcome the deficiencies that result from piecemeal common law development. The first, as witnessed by English law, is to keep the focus on disclosure of "risks", but highlight the need to disclose "comparative risks" of alternative procedures. Secondly, as Canadian case law has shown, the courts can proactively translate academic aspirations towards disclosure of alternative treatment options into binding legal rules. Thirdly, as illustrated by New Zealand law, legislation can proactively create a statutory and encompassing duty to inform, including the duty to inform about alternatives.

To highlight the controversy surrounding the duty to inform about alternatives, I reveal a line of authorities which confine the duty to disclose to the proposed or recommended procedure. According to this line of thought, the duty to disclose does not attach to non-recommended procedures. This approach has the problem of confusing the context of selection/recommendation of the proposed treatment with that of disclosure of treatment options. It demonstrates the need to place the issue of alternatives disclosure in a clear and wider context.

To illustrate the correct place for "disclosure" of alternatives in health care, I identify and distinguish four aspects of health care: *disclosure, selection, recommendation* and *performance* of procedures. They have distinct rationales and focuses. First, actual, technical *performance* or provision of a procedure is distinct from disclosure of divergent procedures. This distinction helps to answer the question of whether a patient has a right to require or demand treatments. It also helps to solve the conflicts that exist between resource-sensitive provision of service and autonomy-honouring information disclosure.

Second, disclosure of treatment options is different from *selection* of treatments. The "two schools of thought" doctrine and the *Bolam* test exemplify the judiciary's respect for divergent medical opinions. The law accords considerable latitude to healthcare professionals in selecting procedures for patients. However, the law expects health care professionals to present patients with contextualised information that overcomes the constraints and boundaries that result from a health care professional's favouring a particular line or "school" of medical opinion.

Third, disclosure of treatment options should not be confused with a doctor's *recommendation* of a particular treatment option. The *laissez-faire* approach of a doctor merely setting out a menu of treatment options without any recommendation is a misreading of the relationship between information disclosure and recommendation. The requirement of unbiased disclosure of treatment options does not prevent a doctor from making personalised recommendation about preferred treatments. Arguably the law should give a doctor's genuine recommendation, even persuasion, more allowance than a doctor's selection of treatment options because recommendation involves more subjective and personalised professional judgments. However, the recommendation should be made in a context. Contextualised information disclosure should precede a doctor's recommendation.

The model I construct in Chap. 3, which attempts to contextualise *disclosure* of treatment options, helps to clarify the relationship between information disclosure and other aspects of health care, such as selection, recommendation and performance of treatments. It mirrors the general distinction drawn between the context of information disclosure and that of diagnosis/treatment. It avoids confusing other aspects of health care with disclosure of alternatives. It gives "disclosure" of alternatives a clear place in the process of delivering health care. Balanced, unbiased and contextualised disclosure of divergent treatment options should precede selecting, recommending and performing a particular treatment that a doctor personally prefers. A doctor needs to avoid or overcome preferences and personal opinions when presenting information about treatment options. In reality, the biggest enemy to full disclosure of treatment options is a doctor's preference for one "school" of thought rather than another "school". Patients are likely to be exposed to fragmented and biased information. The law needs to respond to this.

Divorced from a narrow school of medical opinion and driven by patients' needs, a doctor's duty to inform about alternatives would be very encompassing and unpredictable, however. The law's focus on "reasonable" patients puts some boundaries around the duty to inform. In addition, to alleviate the fear associated with contextualised disclosure of alternatives, I single out four factors that help indicate which alternatives fall within the scope of the duty to inform. First, the existence and availability of treatment options is subject to medical knowledge and medical judgment.

A doctor may abuse the "knowledge" qualification by deliberately claiming that he does not know treatment options that he should know. To avoid this happening, "knowledge" needs to be construed as including not only actual knowledge but also constructive knowledge, knowledge that the practitioner can reasonably be expected to possess.

Second, in a real-life scenario, the menu of treatment options is subject to consideration of a particular patient's conditions and stage of illness. For a particular patient who has particular conditions and is at a particular stage of illness, the number of treatment options available may not be prohibitively large. Third, a doctor only needs to disclose information about alternatives to which a reasonable person in the patient's position would have attached importance or significance. Fourth, if the duty to inform about alternatives is explored in the tort context, the issue of "causation" always forms a formidable barrier to success.

I prefer to formulate the term "alternatives" in a wide fashion. It can be categorised into four groups: (1) available treatment options; (2) legally, financially or geographically unavailable treatment options; (3) alternative providers; (4) choices between conventional medicine and CAM. First, the majority of "alternatives" are "treatment options". Second, treatment options, which are medically available, may in fact be unavailable because of non-medical (legal, financial and geographical) factors. That raises the issue of whether to disclose legally, financially or geographically unavailable treatment options. Third, a doctor's inexperience in performing a complex procedure might expose the patient to additional risks, leading to the notion that a patient has a right to be informed of the option of having the procedure performed by alternative (more experienced) practitioners or in a better-equipped and better-staffed institution. Fourth, with the increasing prevalence of CAM, there is a pressing issue of whether a practitioner has a duty to inform about alternative therapies that are beyond the scope of their variety of "medicine". My book focuses on "treatment options". Therefore, I concentrate on the first, the second, and the fourth categories of alternatives rather than the third.

As far as disclosure of "available treatment options" is concerned, there are at least three indications that the law reinforces conservative and conventional treatment options. First, it has been held that if a surgery is "elective", a doctor should inform patients of the "elective" nature of the surgery and the availability of conservative, non-surgical treatment options. Second, if a procedure is "experimental", a doctor should reveal to patients the "experimental" nature of the proposed procedure and the conventional treatment options. Third, a doctor may need to make the patient aware that the conservative option of "doing nothing" is an alternative to a surgical option. A key issue is whether a doctor has a duty to inform patients about non-conventional or emerging treatment options.

A doctor may sometimes have a duty to inform about non-conventional, not-well-established, and emerging treatment options. In order to determine the kinds of non-conventional treatment options that may fall within a doctor's duty to inform, I examine the threshold for "a school of thought" or "a body of professional opinion" benefiting from the "two schools of thought" doctrine, or the *Bolam* test. I find that, to qualify as a school of thought under both theories, a line of thought should pass both a qualitative threshold, such as being "reputable", "respected", "respectable", or "responsible", and a quantitative threshold, such as being supported by a "considerable number" within the profession. The "two schools of thought" doctrine, or the *Bolam* test, still favours more conventional and well-established treatment options, although these do not need to reach the standard of support by a "majority".

On the basis of the distinction drawn between the selection of treatment and the disclosure of options, especially the patient-oriented nature of information disclosure standard, I argue that the range of treatment options that fall within the duty to inform may be wider than the range of treatments that satisfy the threshold for the "two schools of thought" doctrine or the *Bolam* test. Or, to put this another way, the threshold for a treatment option falling within a doctor's duty to disclose may be lower than that required to fall within the "two schools of thought" doctrine or the *Bolam* test.

In the case of disclosure about treatment, the scope of the duty to inform is driven by the patient's needs and wishes, rather than by medical opinion. If warranted, a doctor may need to mention less mature, or less time-honoured, and even controversial treatment options. A school of medical opinion attracting only a small minority of followers may have to be disclosed. A doctor's duty to inform should not be confined only to conventional, standard and well-established treatment options. As shown in this book, Canadian, New Zealand and Japanese case law have embraced the notion that a doctor's duty to inform may be extended to encompass "minority" or emerging treatment options.

In the context of *adopting* emerging treatment options, the law gives doctors some leeway in trying innovative or new therapies. An English case reveals that some courts show readiness to loosen the thresholds for the *Bolam* test and characterise an emerging line of medical opinion as "a responsible body of medical opinion" when the patient's prognosis is dire, there is no available alternative and the patient or her family express strong wishes to pursue the emerging option. Even if the doctor-friendly *Bolam* test or the "two schools of thought" doctrine is not available for doctors who pursue emerging options, the standard "reasonable doctor" test or the ordinary risk-benefit analysis still can justify a doctor's decision to opt for emerging treatments. Finally, having patients involved in making informed decision about participating in experimental treatments has the potential to help doctors avoid liability. All of these create room for a doctor adopting emerging treatment options.

Doctors have latitude in deciding whether to adopt emerging treatment options. For those who *opt against* adopting an emerging treatment option, information about that may still fall within the duty to *disclose*. More and more doctors *opting for* an emerging treatment would facilitate the formation and development of a "school" of professional opinion. As I showed when examining Japanese law, the fact that an emerging procedure is favoured by another school of medical opinion, that it is available from other practitioners or in other institutions, that the efficacy and safety of the procedure is becoming more established, that there are indications of a patient's desire to know about the procedure, that the procedure has fallen within a doctor's knowledge, and that the patient is a candidate for the procedure, may all point towards a positive duty for the doctor to provide information about the alternative procedure, even though it is non-conventional and not-widely-accepted, and the treating doctor personally holds negative attitudes towards it, and therefore decides not to recommend and administer it.

I devoted a separate chapter to the issue of whether alternative treatment options that are not readily available in the public-funded health care system should fall within the duty to inform. I gave an affirmative answer. This conclusion was supported by the distinction made between the provision of services and the disclosure of treatment options.

In the context of a doctor providing services, the cost-containment culture may produce two bodies of medical opinion: a resource-conscious body of opinion and a resource-blind body of opinion. The law should honour and promote the resource-conscious body of opinion, and allow, accommodate, even require considerations of limited resources in defining the standard of care for healthcare professionals. Honouring a patient's right to autonomy cannot always be manifested in the context of providing services, but it can be done in the context of information disclosure. A patient has no right to be provided with resource-blind treatments. However, he deserves a right to be informed of both cost-effective and other treatment options.

I responded to a few objections to expanding the duty to inform to cover financially unavailable treatment options. The first and the most frequently raised is that the combination of explicit rationing and honesty in presenting information about the treatments available would be distressing to both patients and doctors. However, these concerns seem to be detached from patients' expectations. A survey reveals that the vast majority of patients are pleased with being exposed to a full story and do not want to be kept in ignorance about treatment options unavailable in publicly-funded health care.

Second, there is concern that honest presentation of treatment options would undermine and disrupt rationing. However, the concern does not reflect the reality and the case law. The judiciary pays high deference to the decision-making of rationing bodies. Third, resource-blind information disclosure would be time-consuming. This is challenged by a survey, which reveals that concern about "time available" is the least cited explanation for withholding information about treatment options.

There is an approach, popular in the medical profession, for dealing with the disclosure of financially unavailable treatment options. That is to tailor the extent of disclosure to a few specified circumstances, such as whether or not the patient is wealthy, well-educated, well-informed, had raised questions about the availability of treatments, or might even cause trouble. I characterise this approach as "reactive", "sensitive" and "discriminatory". Although this approach has some merits, it is built on paternalistic assumptions and contradicts the preference of the majority of patients. It reinforces rather than redresses social inequalities. The duty to inform about financially unavailable treatment options should be proactive and patient preference-dependant rather than reactive and patient-status-dependant.

The last specific category of "alternative" which I explore in a separate chapter concerns choices between conventional medicine and CAM. It is still questionable whether or not the court's initiative to require healthcare professionals to disclose unbiased and contextualised information about alternative treatment options will extend *beyond conventional medicine* to contexts involving both conventional medicine and CAM. With regard to CAM, contextualised information disclosure would mean that the scope of a health practitioner's duty to inform about alternatives would not be confined to the alternative treatment options of the practitioner's own approach to "medicine". That would mean that conventional medicine practitioners would have a duty to inform about CAM therapies and, conversely, CAM practitioners would have a duty to disclose conventional medicine treatment options.

The current law involving CAM and conventional medicine disclosure seems to be conventional-medicine-reinforcing. CAM and conventional medicine do not have equal status. The requirement for full disclosure is one-way. CAM practitioners and dual practitioners are required to disclose a full range of treatment options, including the availability of conventional medicine treatments. However, conventional medicine practitioners do not have a comparable duty to inform about CAMs. Little law supports the argument that an orthodox practitioner similarly has a duty to inform about CAM therapies. New Zealand law adopts a very liberal approach to the issue of disclosing alternatives. However, even in New Zealand, the law's call for contextualised information disclosure ends at the boundaries of conventional medicine. It has not yet extended to the realm of CAM therapies.

The requirement that a CAM practitioner disclose the possibility of conventional medical treatments is consistent with this book's theme that contextualised information disclosure is better than preference-adulterated information disclosure. However, I have a deep concern about some CAM practitioners' ability to meet this duty. I invest hope in rigorous professional regulation to increase CAM practitioners' awareness and knowledge about conventional medicine.

People always show understandable caution in suggesting that conventional medicine practitioners have a duty to inform about CAM therapies. That is due to concerns that CAMs do not have a strong evidence base and that conventional medicine practitioners do not have a knowledge base about CAMs. Both concerns are subject to challenge. First, different CAMs have support of different levels of evidence. Some CAM therapies have a convincing and encouraging evidence base. Second, more and more conventional medicine students and practitioners are exposed to CAMs in the course of their education. That should increase their awareness and knowledge about CAMs. If a CAM has a clear and competitive risk-benefit profile, it already falls within a doctor's actual knowledge or constructive knowledge, and it is understandable and explainable in conventional medicine terminology, I do not think there is a need to discriminate against CAM when formulating rules regarding disclosure of alternatives.

CAM practitioners have a narrow scope of practice. I mean that they cannot practise *conventional medicine*. But they are required to disclose conventional medicine treatments even if they cannot offer them. Conventional medicine practitioners enjoy a wide scope of practice. They have latitude in deciding whether or not to adopt *CAMs*. But they are not required to disclose available CAM options.

On the one hand, a liberal scope of practice increases the presence and availability of CAMs in the conventional medicine world. Adopting a particular CAM to treat a particular condition has the possibility of becoming "a responsible body of medical opinion" in the orthodox world. On the other hand, a doctor has a liberty not to opt for a CAM, based on his personal opinions. However, a doctor's duty to disclose CAMs cannot be excused by the fact that the doctor does not decide to offer or administer the CAM.

In a context involving both conventional medicine and CAM, promoting unbiased and balanced information integration is particularly important. This is because of the hostility between the two categories of medical culture with each claiming supremacy over the other, and the patients being at risk of exposure to biased information. Patients need integrated, contextualised and balanced information rather than fragmented, unbalanced and isolated information.

Compared to their CAM counterparts in conventional-medicine-dominated jurisdictions, *TCM practitioners* in China have three advantages. First, they are accorded equal legal status to conventional (Western) medicine practitioners. They are embraced into health care legally, politically and administratively. Second, they have wide scopes of practice. They are required to make a Western medicine diagnosis along with a TCM diagnosis. They also have freedom in choosing to offer, or not offer, Western medicine treatments. Third, Chinese TCM practitioners have a strong knowledge base about Western medicine. They are exposed to a heavy component of Western medicine in their education and a strong Western-medicine-oriented culture. Based on these, I have more confidence in saying that, in China, conventional (Western) medicine treatment options should fall within a TCM practitioner's duty to inform about alternatives.

There are also some differences between Chinese *conventional (Western) medicine practitioners* and most other conventional medicine practitioners. First, all Western medicine practitioners in China have been subjected to TCM education. They all have knowledge, although weak, about TCM. Second, many TCM products have been exposed to a Western medicine research and manufacturing model and are readily available in the Western medical world. Third, Chinese patients are more familiar with, feel more comfortable with, and have more awareness of TCM options. Questions about TCM treatments are likely to be more frequently raised by Chinese patients. All of these give me confidence to assert that, in China, we cannot confine the scope of Western medicine practitioners' duty to inform only to Western medicine treatment options.

When drawing distinctions among jurisdictions, I chose England, Canada, Australia, New Zealand and China as examples. Among them, New Zealand is the most liberal jurisdiction in the sense that it not only happily embraces disclosure of alternatives in a health practitioner's duty to inform, by way of legislation, but also offers a potentially wide range of alternatives that may fall within the scope of the duty to inform.

All the common law jurisdictions I compared share very demanding professional regulation on information disclosure, in that, in these jurisdictions, health care professionals have a *professional and ethical* duty to disclose alternative treatment options. However, they differ in the extent to which they recognised a *legal* duty to disclose alternatives.

The discrepancies in recognising a *legal* duty to disclose alternatives are due to the fact that the common law is characterised by piecemeal development and is basically reactive in nature. All landmark informed consent cases concerned non-disclosure of "*risk*". The focus of informed consent in the common law is still on "*risks* of proposed treatment" rather than "*alternative* treatment options". That is also partly because claims of non-disclosure of "alternatives" are almost always intertwined with those of non-disclosure of "risks". Materialisation of risks motivates the lawsuit. Claims of non-disclosure of "alternatives" lack a sufficient and distinct presence in legal proceedings. So the common law in this area remains poorly developed.

There is a line of authorities in Canada which recognise a doctor's *legal* duty to inform about alternative treatment options. That duty even covers disclosure of "minority" treatment options. Canadian courts overcome the reactive nature of the common law by proactively citing academic comments and translating academic wisdom into common law rules.

The English law still focuses on a doctor's duty to disclose the "risks" attaching to the proposed procedure, but contemplates that disclosure of "comparative risks" of alternative procedures is warranted when the alternatives have more attractive risk-benefit profiles than the treatment proposed, such as when they are non-invasive and less risky than the proposed procedure.

There is no Australian case law that I have been able to locate, which warmly embraces the notion that a doctor's legal duty to inform encompasses disclosure of alternatives, although Australian case law has made a great contribution to informed consent law by formulating and offering a very encompassing test for "risk" disclosure (the *Rogers* test). As I noted in my book, Australia does not lack academic commentaries which argue that the *Rogers* test should be equally applicable to the disclosure of alternative treatment options. Some judges are also open-minded towards this expansive approach. What remains to be seen is whether Australian courts will follow Canadian courts and proactively transform those ideas into legal principles.

New Zealand offers the most encompassing range of alternatives that may fall within the duty to disclose. A healthcare professional's duty to inform may cover a variety of treatment options, including minority treatment options. Providers are required to inform patients of alternative management options, including the option of seeking private treatment and the option of having the procedure performed by alternative providers. The Health and Disability Commissioner has hinted that information about treatment options available overseas may also fall within a reasonable patient's expectation. New Zealand is leading other common law jurisdictions in recognising a *legal* duty to inform about some categories of alternative, especially minority treatment options, financially unavailable treatment options, and alternative providers.

Another advantage that New Zealand patients have is that, under New Zealand's Code of Patients' Rights, the Commissioner does not consider causation and damage when deciding whether or not to intervene. Breach of the duty to inform itself justifies the Commissioner's responses, to protect patients' rights, although these responses are at a low-level. In medical negligence cases concerning non-disclosure of "alternatives", causation is especially pivotal in determining prospects for success. The absence of consideration of "causation" and other elements of the tort of negligence in the New Zealand's Code approach potentially and significantly liberates the scope of a doctor's duty to inform.

There are three main avenues for responding to concerns about the non-disclosure of information: the common law (torts), professional regulation and legislation. Compared to professional self-regulation, legislation is sometimes more effective in combating doctors' preferences and affording patients more balanced information about treatments. An example arose in the USA. Although the period between the 1950s and the 1970s witnessed the development of newer, less disfiguring treatment options (such as lumpectomies and radiation therapy) which were equally effective for many breast cancer patients, many surgeons in the 1970s still routinely continued to perform radical mastectomies, often without disclosing those new treatments (Krause 1999, 379). Due to their own personal considerations, many surgeons had strong personal preferences for invasive procedures over the less invasive alternatives. To guarantee breast cancer patients access to complete information about treatment alternatives, many states in USA enacted breast cancer informed consent statutes, which required doctors to provide breast cancer patients with information about medically viable treatment alternatives (Krause 1999, 379). This approach of enacting statutes to protect a vulnerable group of patients, coupled with disciplinary reactions to breach of the legal duty, proved to be very effective and efficient in forcing "recalcitrant physicians to disclose information when they would prefer to keep silent" (Krause 1999, 383).

The tort system, involving civil actions for damages, is not always the most appropriate mechanism to respond to every aspect of information disclosure. Because the law of informed consent has been annexed to the law of negligence, there are many barriers to recovery in an informed consent tort action, such as proving breach of the standard of care, causation and compensable harm. This limitation ignores the primary rationale for the development of the doctrine – respect for individual autonomy.

Proving elements of a tort action based on failure to inform is particularly problematic in the context of alleging failure to disclose *alternatives*. For example, in a case involving the nondisclosure of treatment options, the "harm" may be far less tangible. If the non-disclosed treatment option has fewer risks or a better outcome than the proposed treatment, the patient may not have too much difficulty benefiting from the traditional tort action. However, if the non-disclosed treatment option is more risky than the proposed one, yet had a lower risk of certain side effects that were particularly important to the particular patient, it would be more difficult to ascertain the "injury" that the patient had sustained. The requirement that the risk must materialise makes little, if any, sense in cases of nondisclosure of alternatives. If the only injury sustained is to the patient's dignity or the patient's right of autonomy, the negligence theory does not provide the best context to protect the patient's dignitary interests.

The law needs to protect the decision-making "process" itself and the patient's right of self-determination. Where non-disclosure of treatment alternatives leads to physical harm, it often can be characterised as a typical "risk disclosure" case. Where no physical injury has occurred, which is particularly true in the context of nondisclosure of *alternatives*, it may be necessary to design other means of protecting a patient's "dignitary" or "process" right.

Some people want the tort law to accommodate this by awarding some nominal amount of damages for patients when failure to disclose information did not result in physical injuries. China's *Tort Liability Law* offers an example. Chinese law attempts to accommodate the need to protect a patient's right to be informed in the framework of tort law. However, it ignores the fact that bringing a tort suit is time-consuming, slow and expensive. It is necessary to identify a means of protecting patient informational rights that does not rely so heavily on expansion of the over-burdened tort system. Professional regulation and professional discipline provide a better mechanism to resolve violations of the patient's right to information in the absence of causation and tangible harm.

If the purpose pursued is to deter non-disclosure rather than to award large monetary settlements to patients who have suffered purely dignitary harms, the professional regulation and professional discipline system is a better way to induce doctors to comply with their informed consent obligations. It has the virtue of relieving the plaintiff-patient of the often decisive burdens of proof required in a negligence suit. Its focus is squarely on the question of whether the doctor has lived up to his or her professional role as a source of information – the essence of the informed consent obligation. It can supplement the tort role. Pure rights violations would be handled through the professional regulation and disciplinary scheme, while violations accompanied by physical harm would remain actionable in tort. This approach has the advantage of providing some degree of legitimacy for rights claims while avoiding additional strains on the tort system. Moreover, compared to tort actions, a professional disciplinary scheme provides a more timely resolution to the patient's day-to-day informational concerns.

As has already been stressed, the common law develops in a piecemeal fashion and has a reactive nature. Tort law is characterised as formal and deterrent, but is often burdensome and inconvenient. Professional regulation offers convenience and a timely response, but lacks authority and independence. New Zealand's Code, and related Commissioner and Tribunal jurisdictions, offers a good model of combining the authority and stability of legislation, the convenience of a low-level resolution mechanism and the flexibility of professional regulation. Dynamic interpretation of the Code by an independent Commissioner overcomes the inflexibility and unresponsiveness that are associated with statute law. Compared to the approaches of either heavily relying on tort law, or relying exclusively on professional regulation in dealing with disclosure of alternative treatment options, New Zealand's Code approach is the preferred option.

Although there are differences among jurisdictions I examined, there are many similarities among them in the area of informed consent and information disclosure. That is one of the reasons why I decide to adopt a collective approach to the issue of disclosure of alternatives in the first half of the book. The notion of a patient's autonomy and the principle of informed consent have been well established in many civilised societies in the past decades. Even China and Japan, which have a different culture from that of "Western" countries, have moved to acknowledge, promote and protect the idea that an *individual* patient has a right of self-determination. That explains why China and Japan present legal landscapes that are very similar to that of major common law jurisdictions, with regard to information disclosure, including disclosure of alternatives.

Finally, I conclude my book by noting that the more open and honest doctors are towards their patients, the less likely these patients will pursue litigation and make complaints. The extent and quality of communication between patient and doctor have an impact on patients' decisions whether to sue or complain. In the context of disclosure of alternatives, doctors should be honest with available alternatives, no matter whether or not they conform to their own preferences or "school of thought".

References

Downie, Jocelyn, Timothy Caulfield, and Colleen Flood. 2002. *Canadian health law and policy*, 2nd ed. Markham: LexisNexis Butterworths.

Krause, Joan H. 1999. Reconceptualizing informed consent in an era of health care cost containment. *Iowa Law Review* 85: 261–386.

Appendices

Appendix 1: Treatment Options and Recommendation

Available options	Considerations and qualifications
1. Doing nothing	(1) The defendant, "acting competently and regarding the case with which she was presented as one which was *causing considerable distress to her patient*, would [not] have done more than *merely mention* the possibility of a non-medical and non-surgical responses"(emphasis added); (2) The defendant "would have had regard to the failure of such responses to alleviate [the patient's] symptoms in the past."
2. Pesaries	(1) The use of pessaries "would have been short lived and they would not have avoided the need for surgery"; (2) Pessaries can interfere with sexual intercourse, and so age is important; they are "generally used for patients in two categories, elderly women, and women who have medical disorders which make them unfit for surgery"; (3) "Patient's past medical history meant that it was unlikely that pessaries would succeed in alleviating her condition"; (4) In the court's conclusion, "[the defendant], acting competently and having regard to her own views, would have explained the use of pessaries to [the patient], but *would not have said anything which would have encouraged* [the patient] to try them." (emphasis added)
3. Anterior repair	(1) The defendant herself was doubtful whether the option of the anterior repair would have *sufficiently* dealt with the patient's condition; (2) An expert testified that "[a]n anterior repair alone traditionally was used to relieve stress incontinence and to deal with a solitary bladder prolapse with no other prolapse. Here there was descent of the uterus, … An anterior repair would probably not have solved the problem";

(continued)

X. Zhao, *The Duty of Medical Practitioners and CAM/TCM Practitioners to Inform Competent Adult Patients about Alternatives*,
DOI 10.1007/978-3-642-31647-0,

(continued)

Available options	Considerations and qualifications
	(3) In the court's judgment, the defendant, "acting competently and having regard to her own views, would have held out to [the patient] the option of an anterior repair, with the *qualification* that, in [her] opinion, such an operation would not have led to a resolution of her patient's problems". (emphasis added)
4. The ManchesteFothergill Procedure	(1) The Manchester-Fothergill procedure involves the amputation of the cervix *when the cervix is elongated and there is minimum uterine descent*;
	(2) It was doubtful whether it would have successfully alleviated the patient's condition;
	(3) The operation is not one which is frequently performed, "it is not part of [the defendant's] own repertoire", it was "a somewhat dated procedure";
	(4) In the court's opinion, the defendant "acting competently and have regard to her own views and experience, would have held out to [the patient] the possibility of having the Manchester procedure, but *without recommending* it and with the *qualification* that such a procedure would have to be performed by some other surgeon". (emphasis added)
5. A vaginal hysterectomy without McCall's procedure	(1) A vaginal hysterectomy without the McCall's procedure does *not involve the use of Ethibond or other non-absorbable sutures*;
	(2) The experts were sharply divided on whether it was incumbent on the defendant to tell the patient that the McCall's procedure *would entail the use of non-absorbable sutures* and to advise her as to the accompanying risks;
	(3) The use of four non-absorbable sutures was inherent in the adoption of the McCall's procedure;
	(4) The use of such sutures carries risks of suture erosion;
	(5) The risk rate of suture erosion "would not have been known in the United Kingdom in 1999";
	(6) The defendant "was not in breach of duty in failing to deal with the subject of non-absorbable sutures in her discussion with [the patient]".
	(All 5 available options: should be disclosed, but not recommended)

Source: SEM v The Mid Yorkshire Hospitals NHS Trust (2005) EWHC B3 (QB), at [41]–[47]

Appendix 2: Treatment Options and Physical Conditions

Here I cite prostate cancer, which is typical of having a wide and growing range of treatment options, as an example to illustrate the close relationship between the stages of illness and available treatment options. The source of information is NICE (UK) Guideline on prostate cancer. Prostate cancer is a heavily lifestyle-involved illness. The Guideline recommends that men with prostate cancer should be offered individualised information tailored to their own needs. Healthcare professionals should adequately inform men with prostate cancer and their partners or carers about the effects of prostate cancer and the treatment options on their sexual function, physical appearance, continence and other aspects of masculinity. Healthcare professionals should support men and their partners or carers in making treatment decisions, taking into account the effects on quality of life as well as survival.

Prostate cancer and treatment options

Types/stages	Treatment options	Conditions
Localised prostate cancer	Watchful waiting	Low-risk men; Intermediate risk men; High-risk men; most suitable for *older men, or those with significant co-morbidities who are thought unlikely to have significant cancer progression during the likely natural life span*
	Active surveillance	Low-risk men; Intermediate risk men; suitable for *younger, fitter men who are fit for radical treatment in the event of disease progression*; *particularly suitable for* a subgroup of men with low-risk localised prostate cancer who have clinical stage T1c, a Gleason score 3 + 3, a number of biopsy cores with <10 mm of any core involved
	Radical prostatectomy	Low-risk men; Intermediate risk men; High-risk men; typically only offered to *fitter men without co-morbidities* and is uncommon over the age of 70
	External beam radiotherapy	Low-risk men; Intermediate risk men; High-risk men
	Brachytherapy (a form of radiotherapy)	Low-risk men; Intermediate risk men; *not possible in men with enlarged prostate*
	Cryotherapy	Low-risk men; Intermediate risk men; High-risk men (in the context of *clinical trials*)
	High intensity focused ultrasound (HIFU)	Low-risk men; Intermediate risk men; High-risk men (in the context of *clinical trials*)
Biochemical relapse after radical treatment	Local salvage therapy	
	Systemic therapy (such as hormonal therapy)	Hormonal therapy is routinely recommended for men who have symptomatic local disease progression, or any proven metastases, or a PSA doubling time of <3 months
Locally advanced prostate cancer	Neoadjuvant hormonal therapy	T3a – T4 prostate cancer; men receiving radical radiotherapy
	Adjuvant hormonal therapy	T3a – T4 prostate cancer; recommended for a minimum of 2 years in men receiving radical radiotherapy for locally advanced prostate cancer who have a Gleason score of ≥8
Metastatic prostate cancer	Hormonal therapy (first line)	
	Chemotherapy	For hormone refractory disease
	Corticosteroids	For hormone refractory disease
	Palliative care	

Source: NICE (UK) *Prostate Cancer: Diagnosis and Treatment – Full Guideline* (February 2008)

Localised prostate cancer

	Low-risk men (PSA ≤10 ng/ml and Gleason score ≤6 and T1-T2a)	**Intermediate risk men** (PSA 10–20 ng/ml or Gleason score 7 or T2b-c)	**High risk men** (PSA ≥20 ng/ml or Gleason score ≥8 or T3-T4)
Watchful waiting	Treatment option	Treatment option	Treatment option
Active surveillance	*Preferred* treatment option	Treatment option	
Radical prostatectomy	Treatment option	*Preferred* treatment option	*Preferred* treatment option
External beam radiotherapy	Treatment option	*Preferred* treatment option	*Preferred* treatment option
Brachytherapy	Treatment option	Treatment option	
Cryotherapy	Treatment option *in the context of clinical trials*	Treatment option *in the context of clinical trials*	Treatment option *in the context of clinical trials*
HIFU	Treatment option *in the context of clinical trials*	Treatment option *in the context of clinical trials*	Treatment option *in the context of clinical trials*

Source: NICE (UK) *Prostate Cancer: Diagnosis and Treatment – Full Guideline* (February 2008)

*Appendix 3: Chinese Legal System**

Chinese law is one of the oldest legal traditions in the world. For most of its history, China's legal system has been based on the Confucian philosophy of social control through moral education, as well as the Legalist emphasis on codified law and criminal sanction. In the late Qing dynasty there was a concerted effort to establish legal codes mainly by importing German codes with slight modifications. Following the Revolution of 1911 which resulted in Imperial China coming to an end with the overthrow of the Qing dynasty, the Republic of China continued the effort to formulate a largely German-style legal code. Sadly, the People's Republic of China (PRC), which was established in 1949, abolished all the laws of the predecessor state, the Republic of China. This left a substantial legal vacuum. There was a period in which Chinese law was heavily influenced by the legal system of the then Soviet Union. Recurring political turmoil, including Cultural Revolution, prevented any substantial development of the legal system for the first three decades of the PRC, but with the start of the post-Mao era of economic reform in 1979, a number of positive changes began to occur. The 1982 Constitution recognised the idea of individual rights and the notion of "rule of law".[1] Significant amounts of legislation emerged and the

*Written by Xiju Zhao.

[1] The current constitution, created in 1982, has some general principles, including that no organization or individual is above the law. *See*, The Constitution of the People's Republic of China (Amended in 2004), Article 5 ("All state organs, the armed forces, all political parties and public organizations and all enterprises and institutions must abide by the Constitution and the law"; "No organization or individual is privileged to be beyond the Constitution or the law".). Passage of the Administrative Litigation Law of 1987 created legal recourse for individuals from arbitrary government actions. This avenue was previously unavailable.

institutions of the legal system – in particular, courts, judges, and lawyers – received more attention. From 1980s, Chinese law developed steadily and rapidly.

Chinese law[2] has a tradition of civil law. The Chinese legal system is in form much closer to the legal systems of continental Europe than to the common law, although it is very open-minded towards ideas from common law jurisdictions. The sources of Chinese law include the PRC Constitution, written laws, regulations, directives and local laws, laws of Special Administrative Regions and laws resulting from international treaties entered into by the PRC government. Court case verdicts do not constitute binding precedents, although they are used for the purposes of judicial reference and guidance.

At the national level, according to China's Constitution, the National People's Congress (NPC) is the highest organ of state power.[3] It is the highest legislative authority, and functions as Parliament. Its permanent body is the Standing Committee of the National People's Congress. The National People's Congress and its Standing Committee exercise the legislative power of the state.[4] The State Council, or the Central People's Government, is the executive body of the highest organ of state power.[5] It is the highest organ of state administration. It can be described as China's cabinet or executive branch. It can adopt administrative measures, enact administrative rules and regulations and issue decisions and orders in accordance with the Constitution and the law.[6] The people's courts are the judicial organs of the state.[7] There are four levels of courts in China: the Supreme People's Court (SPC, the highest judicial organ) at the centre, the Higher Level People's

[2] When I mention Chinese law, it means law from the mainland China. Hong Kong and Macau are outside of the legal jurisdiction of the People's Republic of China, except on constitutional issues. After the transfers of sovereignty, Hong Kong and Macau keep their English Common Law and Portuguese legal systems respectively, with their own courts of final appeal. Taiwan has a civil law tradition.

[3] The Constitution of the People's Republic of China (Amended in 2004), Article 57 (中华人民共和国宪法, 2004年修正, 第57条).

[4] The Constitution of the People's Republic of China (Amended in 2004), Article 58 (中华人民共和国宪法, 2004年修正, 第58条). The National People's Congress can (1) amend the Constitution; (2) supervise the enforcement of the Constitution; (3) enact and amend basic laws governing criminal offences, civil affairs, the state organs and other matters. The Standing Committee can (1) interpret the Constitution and supervise its enforcement; (2) enact and amend laws, with the exception of those which should be enacted by the National People's Congress; (3) partially supplement and amend, when the National People's Congress is not in session, laws enacted by the National People's Congress provided that the basic principles of these laws are not contravened; (4) interpret laws. *See*, The Constitution of the People's Republic of China (Amended in 2004), Articles 62, 67 (中华人民共和国宪法, 2004年修正, 第62, 67条). Because the NPC has thousands of members and meets infrequently, its Standing Committee has significant power as a practical matter.

[5] The Constitution of the People's Republic of China (Amended in 2004), Article 85 (中华人民共和国宪法, 2004年修正, 第85条).

[6] The Constitution of the People's Republic of China (Amended in 2004), Article 89 (1) (中华人民共和国宪法, 2004年修正, 第89(1) 条).

[7] The Constitution of the People's Republic of China (Amended in 2004), Article 123 (中华人民共和国宪法, 2004年修正, 第123条).

Courts at the provincial level, and the Intermediate Level and Basic Level People's Courts further down at the local level. The people's procuratorates (state organs for legal supervision)[8] have a similar structure, with the Supreme People's Procuratorate being the highest procuratorial organ.[9] The Supreme People's Court has the power to give general *interpretation* on the application of laws in *judicial* proceedings ("judicial interpretation"("司法解释"("*Si Fa Jie Shi*"))). Both the State Council and the Supreme People's Court are subordinate to the NPC. Chinese legal system places the NPC and its Standing Committee, as the representatives of the people, above the other branches.

China is a civil law jurisdiction. Legislation plays a pivotal role in Chinese legal system. To maintain consistency of the law, there is a need for the "Law" on *legislation*. China's written law has a hierarchy: (1) Constitution; (2) Law (法律 ("*Fa Lü*"))[10]; (3) Administrative Regulation (行政法规("*Xing Zheng Fa Gui*")); (4) Local Regulation (地方性法规("*Di Fang Xing Fa Gui*")), Autonomy Regulation (自治条例("*Zi Zhi Tiao Li*")) and Separate Regulation (单行条例("*Dan Xing Tiao Li*")); (5) Rule (规章("*Gui Zhang*")).

The National People's Congress enacts and amends basic criminal, civil and state structure laws and other *basic laws*.[11] The basic civil system should have "laws".[12] If no law has been enacted on a matter that should have law, the National People's Congress and its Standing Committee are entitled to make the decision to authorize that the State Council may, according to the actual needs, formulate the administrative regulations first, waiting for the conditions being ripe for enacting a law on an authorized legislative matter.[13] The *State Council* formulates *administrative regulations* in accordance with the Constitution and laws.[14] China does not adopt the system of federalism. Laws and regulations promulgated by NPC and State Council apply uniformly to all mainland China. The people's congresses and their standing committees of *provinces, autonomous regions, municipalities directly under the Central Government and larger cities* may formulate *local regulations* in accordance with the specific conditions and actual needs of their respective

[8] Procuratorates are judicial bodies that have responsibility for supervising the courts and public security agencies, as well as for pursuing criminal prosecutions.

[9] The Constitution of the People's Republic of China (Amended in 2004), Articles 129, 132 (中华人民共和国宪法, 2004年修正, 第129, 132条).

[10] It needs to be noted that, unlike the ordinary meaning of the term "law", which includes all types of binding legal authority at any level of government, Chinese characters (法律("*Fa Lü*")), which are translated into "law", generally confine the term "law" to enactments of specified legislative bodies (the NPC or its Standing Committee). In the context of Chinese law, "laws" have a higher legal status than other forms of legislations, such as regulations.

[11] Law of the People's Republic of China on Legislation (2000), Article 7 (中华人民共和国立法法, 2000年, 第条).

[12] Law of the People's Republic of China on Legislation (2000), Article 8 (中华人民共和国立法法, 2000年, 第8条).

[13] Law of the People's Republic of China on Legislation (2000), Articles 9–11 (中华人民共和国立法法, 2000年, 第9–11条).

[14] Law of the People's Republic of China on Legislation (2000), Article 56 (中华人民共和国立法法, 2000年, 第56条).

administrative areas.[15] The people's congresses of *national autonomous areas* are entitled to formulate the *autonomy regulation* and *separate regulation* according to the local national political, economic and culture characteristics.[16] The State Council's ministries, commissions, the People's Bank of China, the National Audit Office, the organs directly under the State Council with administrative functions, and the governments of provinces, autonomous regions, municipalities directly under the Central Government and larger cities may formulate the *rules*.[17]

A general principle is that the inferior law should not be in conflict with the provisions of the superior law.[18] First, the Constitution is the pinnacle of legal authority. The Constitution states its own supremacy.[19] The Constitution's supremacy is reiterated in the *Law on Legislation*.[20] Second, the force of *laws* is superior to that of *administrative regulations, local regulations and rules*, and the force of *administrative regulations* is superior to that of *local regulations and rules*.[21] Third, *local regulations* have priority over *rules* of local governments at the same level or the lower levels.[22] Therefore, the basic principle is that legislative enactments of higher legal authority supersede enactments of lower legal authority.

Moreover, there are two other principles of legal interpretation. One is that if the *special* provisions and the *general* provisions of laws, administrative regulations, local regulations, autonomy regulation, separate regulation and rules formulated *by the same organ* are inconsistent, the special provisions apply.[23] That dictates that specific provisions preempt more general provisions, assuming that both the specific and general provisions were issued by the same level of authority. Another principle of legal interpretation is that if the *new* and *old* provisions are inconsistent, the new

[15] Law of the People's Republic of China on Legislation (2000), Article 63 (中华人民共和国立法法, 2000年, 第63条).

[16] Law of the People's Republic of China on Legislation (2000), Articles66 (中华人民共和国立法法, 2000年, 第66条).

[17] Law of the People's Republic of China on Legislation (2000), Articles 71–73 (中华人民共和国立法法, 2000年, 第71–73条).

[18] Law of the People's Republic of China on Legislation (2000), Articles 87 ("If a law, administrative regulations, local regulations, autonomy regulation, separate regulation or rules has any of the following circumstances, the relevant organ changes or revokes it in accordance with the limits of power specified in Article 88 of this Law: 1. In excess of the limit of competence; 2. The inferior law violates the provisions of the superior law…") (中华人民共和国立法法, 2000年, 第87条)

[19] The Constitution of the People's Republic of China (Amended in 2004), Article 5 (中华人民共和国宪法, 2004年修正, 第5条) ("No laws or administrative or local rules and regulations may contravene the Constitution.").

[20] Law of the People's Republic of China on Legislation (2000), Article 78 (中华人民共和国立法法, 2000年, 第78条) ("The Constitution has the supreme force of law, and all laws, administrative regulations, local regulations, autonomy regulation, separate regulation and rules may not contradict the Constitution.").

[21] Law of the People's Republic of China on Legislation (2000), Article 79 (中华人民共和国立法法, 2000年, 第79条).

[22] Law of the People's Republic of China on Legislation (2000), Article 80 (中华人民共和国立法法, 2000年, 第80条).

[23] Law of the People's Republic of China on Legislation (2000), Article 83 (中华人民共和国立法法, 2000年, 第83条).

provisions prevail.[24] Again, application of the principle that the new provisions have priority over the old provisions has a prerequisite: both the new and old provisions should be issued by the same level of authority.

*Appendix 4: Chinese Medical Negligence Law: From 1986 to 2009**

1 The 1986 General Principles of Civil Law

The *General Principles of the Civil Law* (GPCL)[25] provides general guidance on civil liability. It is readily applicable in the context of personal injury and medical malpractice. The GPCL is civil law, dealing with civil relationships (property relationships and personal relationships) between civil subjects with equal status, that is, between citizens, between legal persons and between citizens and legal persons,[26] rather than between citizens/legal persons and governments/states. That makes it distinct from administrative or public law and criminal law. It serves as a forerunner in the field of civil law legislation, waiting for the emergence of a comprehensive and detailed Civil Code. The GPCL envisages two main types of civil liability: civil liability for breach of contract,[27] and civil liability for infringement of rights.[28]

The GPCL aims to protect a wide range of *civil rights*,[29] including *personal rights*. A person's "rights of life and health"[30] is one of the personal rights. A doctor's negligent conduct may cause personal injury and infringe a patient's "rights of life and health", therefore falling within the scope of GPCL. Pursuant to the GPCL provisions, a doctor's medical liability is fault-based.[31] The GPCL imposes an obli-

---

*Written by Xiju Zhao.

[24] Law of the People's Republic of China on Legislation (2000), Article 83 (中华人民共和国立法法, 2000年, 第83条).

[25] General Principles of the Civil Law of the People's Republic of China (1986, NPC) (中华人民共和国民法通则, 1986年, 全国人大).

[26] General Principles of the Civil Law of the People's Republic of China (1986, NPC), Article 2 (中华人民共和国民法通则, 1986年, 全国人大, 第2条).

[27] General Principles of the Civil Law of the People's Republic of China (1986, NPC), Articles 111–116 (中华人民共和国民法通则, 1986年, 全国人大, 第111–116条).

[28] General Principles of the Civil Law of the People's Republic of China (1986, NPC), Articles 117–133 (中华人民共和国民法通则, 1986年, 全国人大, 第117–133条).

[29] There are four categories of rights: Property Ownership and Related Property Rights (Articles 71–83); Creditors' Rights (Articles 84–93); Intellectual Property Rights (Articles 94–97); Personal Rights (Articles 98–105).

[30] General Principles of the Civil Law of the People's Republic of China (1986, NPC), Article 98 ("Citizens shall enjoy the rights of life and health.") (中华人民共和国民法通则, 1986年, 全国人大, 第98条).

[31] General Principles of the Civil Law of the People's Republic of China (1986, NPC), Article 106 (unless the law stipulates that civil liability shall still be borne even in the absence of fault, tort liability is fault-based) (中华人民共和国民法通则, 1986年, 全国人大, 第106条).

gation to pay monetary damages if the doctor "infringes upon a citizen's person and causes him physical injury".[32] Compensation for medical injury (personal injury) may include the incurred medical expenses, lost income, living subsidies for those disabled, and if the victim dies, compensation must cover the funeral expenses and the living expenses for the dependants of the deceased.[33]

2 From the 1987 Regulation to the 2002 Regulation

As mentioned above, the GPCL has a wide applicability. It already provides civil remedies for infringement of a citizen's rights of life and health. It can apply comfortably to the context of medical negligence. However, the advent of a medical-profession-protective regulation complicated the situation. In 1987 the State Council promulgated the *Regulation on Dealing with Medical Accidents* (hereafter "the 1987 *Regulation*").[34] Most legal scholars who were familiar with civil liability theories felt uncomfortable about the *Regulation* because it did not strictly follow the basic theories of fault-based liability.

The 1987 version of medical accidents regulation defined "medical accidents" (医疗事故 ("*Yi Liao Shi Gu*")) as an event that, during the process of diagnosis, treatment or nursing, due to his or her negligence, a health professional "directly caused" a patient's "death, disability or tissue-organ functional impairment".[35] It set "direct causation" and "death, disability or tissue-organ functional impairment" as the thresholds for compensation. A medical "error" (diagnosis, treatment or nursing error) cannot constitute "medical accident" if that error does not cause a patient's death, disability or functional impairment.[36] The 1987 *Regulation* contemplated only two categories of medical accidents: medical accidents caused by a health professional's failure to follow professional guidance and custom ("*Ze Ren Shi Gu*", 责任事故), and medical accidents caused by a health professional's "technical negligence" ("*Ji Shu Shi Gu*", 技术事故).[37]

In addition to the narrowness of the definition of medical accident, the 1987 *Regulation* also suffered from other flaws, such as unfair limitations on compensation,

---

[32] General Principles of the Civil Law of the People's Republic of China (1986, NPC), Article 119 (中华人民共和国民法通则, 1986年, 全国人大, 第119条).

[33] General Principles of the Civil Law of the People's Republic of China (1986, NPC), Article 119 (中华人民共和国民法通则, 1986年, 全国人大, 第119条).

[34] Regulation on Dealing with Medical Accidents (1987, State Council) (医疗事故处理办法, 1987年, 国务院).

[35] Regulation on Dealing with Medical Accidents (1987, State Council), Article 2 (医疗事故处理办法, 1987年, 国务院, 第2条).

[36] Regulation on Dealing with Medical Accidents (1987, State Council), Article 3 (1) (医疗事故处理办法, 1987年, 国务院, 第3(1)条).

[37] Regulation on Dealing with Medical Accidents (1987, State Council), Article 5 (医疗事故处理办法, 1987年, 国务院, 第5条).

weaknesses in the system for expert authentication, and conflicts and lack of integration with other laws.[38] First, the financial remedy to the injured patient was limited to a low, "one-time economic compensation" paid by a health care facility.[39] Second, under the 1987 *Regulation*, "technical authentication committees" provided medical expertise for the resolution of medical accidents.[40] However, the credibility of authentication committees was undermined by a lack of transparency, monopoly, and protectionism. Third, the *Regulation* did not fit comfortably with other laws or regulations that were potentially applicable to the context of medical injury,[41] including the GPCL. The State Council intended its *Regulation* to preempt the more general GPCL and procedural laws, even though the GPCL and procedural laws had been enacted by a higher level of authority.

Due to the above-mentioned deficiencies of the *Regulation* that were widely and well recognized among Chinese legal scholars, the 1987 *Regulation* was doomed to have a short life. In 2002, the State Council adopted a new Regulation, called the *Regulation on the Handling of Medical Accidents* (hereafter "the 2002 *Regulation*").[42] The 2002 *Regulation* was designed to remedy the perceived deficiencies in the 1987 *Regulation*.

The 2002 *Regulation* was a little bit ambitious. It inherited the two functions that the previous *Regulation* intended to serve: both as professional regulation/disputes resolution scheme, and as medical injury compensation scheme. It not only contains many mechanisms of quality control of health care, but also tries to deal with the

---

[38] *See*, Dean M. Harris and Chien-Chang Wu "Medical malpractice in the People's Republic of China: the 2002 Regulation on the Handling of Medical Accidents" (2005) 33 Journal of Law, Medicine & Ethics 456, 460–463.

[39] Regulation on Dealing with Medical Accidents (1987, State Council), Article 18 (医疗事故处理办法, 1987年, 国务院, 第18条).

[40] Regulation on Dealing with Medical Accidents (1987, State Council), Articles 12–17 (医疗事故处理办法, 1987年, 国务院, 第12–17条).

[41] Those other laws included Civil Procedure Law, Criminal Law, Criminal Procedure Law, Administrative Procedure Law, State Compensation Law, Consumer Rights and Interests Protection Law, and even judicial interpretations by the Supreme People's Court.

[42] The Regulation on the Handling of Medical Accidents (2002, State Council) (医疗事故处理条例, 2002年, 国务院). Not long after the adoption of the 1987 *Regulation*, there were requests for its revision. In 1996, the Ministry of Health began work on a revision of the 1987 regulation. Based on opinions collected from a symposium on the 1987 regulation in January 2000, the original draft was later revised up to nine times. In 2001, the State Council reported the draft to the NPC. Considering that the issue was too urgent and too complex, pursuant to the Legislation Law of 2000, the NPC authorized the State Council to adopt a new regulation on medical accidents. The State Council further revised the draft more than 20 times. Finally, on April 4, 2002, the *Regulation on the Handling of Medical Accidents* was adopted by the State Council and it went into effect on September 1, 2002. *See*, Dean M. Harris and Chien-Chang Wu "Medical malpractice in the People's Republic of China: the 2002 Regulation on the Handling of Medical Accidents" (2005) 33 Journal of Law, Medicine & Ethics 456, 463.

issue of compensation for patient's injuries caused by medical negligence. It is actually a mixture of administrative/public law and civil/private law.

First, the 2002 *Regulation* looks like a law regulating professional behaviour, promoting quality of care and resolving disputes. It gives the issue of "prevention and handling of medical accidents" one separate chapter. That includes requirements that medical institutions and health professionals should abide by legal, professional, and ethical standards.[43] The *Regulation* requires medical institutions, such as hospitals, to establish a system of *quality control*.[44] It imposes the *reporting* obligations on health professionals, medical institutions, and administrative department of health.[45] The Regulation also imposes on medical institutions and healthcare professionals requirements with regard to the maintenance, preservation, and disclosure of *medical records*.[46] Furthermore, it makes three avenues of *dispute resolution* available to both parties of the doctor-patient relationship: negotiation, mediation, and civil litigation.[47] The availability of civil litigation does not depend on the exhaustion of two other low-level options. However, the option of mediation conducted by administrative department of health is available only after *a finding* has been made that a medical accident has occurred.[48] The department of health only mediates on the issue of compensation, not the issue of whether or not there was a medical accident. The courts also can conduct mediation.[49]

Second, the *Regulation* is also expected to play a role as a medical accident compensation law. The 2002 *Regulation* reaffirmed its commitment to a fault-based liability rather than a no-fault one. It reformulated the definition of "medical accidents" (医疗事故 ("*Yi Liao Shi Gu*")) as "accidents that have *caused personal injury* to the patients *negligently* by the *medical institutions or the staff members* thereof in the *activities of medical treatment* by violating the *laws, regulations, ministerial rules* concerning medical treatment and health or the *standards or conventions of*

[43] The Regulation on the Handling of Medical Accidents (2002, State Council), Articles 5–6 (医疗事故处理条例, 2002年, 国务院, 第5–6条). Hospitals have an affirmative obligation to educate their staff members about legal requirements, standards of medical care, and professional ethics.

[44] The Regulation on the Handling of Medical Accidents (2002, State Council), Article 7 (医疗事故处理条例, 2002年, 国务院, 第7条).

[45] The Regulation on the Handling of Medical Accidents (2002, State Council), Articles 13–14 (医疗事故处理条例, 2002年, 国务院, 第13–14条).

[46] The Regulation on the Handling of Medical Accidents (2002, State Council), Articles 8–10 (医疗事故处理条例, 2002年, 国务院, 第8–10条).

[47] The Regulation on the Handling of Medical Accidents (2002, State Council), Articles 46–48 (医疗事故处理条例, 2002年, 国务院, 第46–48条).

[48] The Regulation on the Handling of Medical Accidents (2002, State Council), Article 48 (医疗事故处理条例, 2002年, 国务院, 第48条).

[49] The Regulation on the Handling of Medical Accidents (2002, State Council), Article 44 (医疗事故处理条例, 2002年, 国务院, 第44条).

medical treatment and nursing".[50] As I highlighted above, the definition of "medical accidents" share some elements of medical negligence, such as the existence of negligence, personal injury and causation. However, compared to the common law, the Chinese notion of "medical accidents" has at least two distinct elements. First, it makes enterprise or vicarious liability readily available by involving medical institutions as a party bearing liability.[51] Second, it treats laws, professional standards and medical custom as *conclusive* evidence in establishing "medical accidents".

The scope of "medical accident" seems to be smaller than that of "medical negligence". Although medical accident shall be medical negligence, not all medical negligence can be medical accidents. The 2002 *Regulation* abandoned the practice of categorising medical accidents into only two types as it did in the 1987 *Regulation*. It broadened the ambit of "medical accidents" by loosening the threshold for personal injury from "death, disability or functional impairment" to "death, disability, functional impairment, and obvious injury".[52] It expanded the scope of compensation and gave an explicit and exhaustive list of recoverable damages.[53] In determining the amount of compensation, three elements shall be taken into account: (1) the grade of the medical accident; (2) the contribution of the negligent medical act to the consequences of the injury; and (3) the relationship between the injury and the patient's existing conditions.[54]

---

[50] The Regulation on the Handling of Medical Accidents (2002, State Council), Article 2 (医疗事故处理条例, 2002年, 国务院, 第2条) (emphasis added). According to Article 33, it excludes: (1) unfavourable consequences resulting from emergent medical measures taken for rescuing the life of the critically ill patient; (2) unexpected consequences resulting in the process of medical treatment from the unusual state of illness or the special physique of the patient; (3) unfavourable consequences that cannot be predicted or prevented under the existing technical and medical conditions; (4) unfavourable consequences caused by faultless blood transfusions; (5) unfavourable consequences caused by the delay of medical treatment because of the patient's fault; (6) unfavourable consequences caused by force majeure.

[51] The obligation to pay compensation rests with the medical institution, such as hospital, rather than with individual doctors. Under Article 52 of the 2002 Regulation, "compensatory expenses for medical accidents … shall be paid by the *medical institution* that is held to be responsible for the accident." (emphasis added)

[52] The Regulation on the Handling of Medical Accidents (2002, State Council), Article 4 (医疗事故处理条例, 2002年, 国务院, 第4条). The 1987 *Regulation* classified medical accidents into three categories on the basis of severity: (1) Grade 1: death; (2) Grade 2: serious disability or serious functional impairment; (3) Grade 3: disability or functional impairment (Article 6). The 2002 *Regulation* broadened the Grades from 3 to 4: (1) Grade 1: death or serious disability; (2) Grade 2: middle-level disability or serious functional impairment; (3) Grade 3: mitigated disability or general functional impairment; (4) "obvious injury" (Article 4).

[53] The Regulation on the Handling of Medical Accidents (2002, State Council), Article 50 (医疗事故处理条例, 2002年, 国务院, 第50条).

[54] The Regulation on the Handling of Medical Accidents (2002, State Council), Article 49 (医疗事故处理条例, 2002年, 国务院, 第49条).

Overall, the coverage of the 2002 *Regulation* is very comprehensive. It ambitiously combines professional regulation, quality assurance, dispute resolution and injury compensation into one piece of legislation. It has the elements of administrative law, civil law and procedural law. While nobody is unhappy with the *Regulation*'s effort to regulate the medical profession's conduct and promote the quality of health care, many scholars expressed unease about the *Regulation*'s capacity to deal with civil liability, especially when the *Regulation*'s stipulations about injury compensation are inconsistent with the general civil law principles.

3 From the 2002 Regulation to the 2009 Law

The 2002 *Regulation* was expected to remedy the deficiencies of the 1987 *Regulation*. The 2002 *Regulation* did make some progresses, for example, by broadening the scope of medical accidents, authorizing more adequate recovery of compensation, strengthening the system of quality improvement, increasing the credibility of technical authentication, and offering more flexible options of dispute resolution. However, several weaknesses from which the 1987 *Regulation* suffered remain unresolved. There are still continuing concerns about the *Regulation*'s inconsistency with basic legal principles, especially in the arena of medical negligence law. I will provide two examples to illustrate the conflicts between the *Regulation* and other sources of law.

(a) The GPCL v. the Regulation

As the basic civil law, the GPCL is applicable to the context of medical liability. As the specialised law dealing specifically with medical accidents, the *Regulation* also has a component of medical injury compensation law. The problem and disputes originate from the fact that the two pieces of legislation have different thresholds for compensation and different rules regarding the amount of compensation. The GPCL is more generous than the *Regulation* in both respects. The *Regulation* is more doctor-protective.

First, GPCL has a lower threshold for compensation than the *Regulation*. In the context of GPCL, if infringement of a patient's personal right (right of life and health) caused *personal injury*, civil remedies, including compensation, will be available. However, in the context of "medical accidents", the lowest threshold is *"obvious" injury*.[55] It seems that the *Regulation* omits to consider and compensate personal injuries that are not "obvious". It explicitly denied compensation

[55] The Regulation on the Handling of Medical Accidents (2002, State Council), Article 4 (医疗事故处理条例, 2002年, 国务院, 第4条).

for medical negligence that does not constitute "medical accident".[56] Moreover, the *Regulation* does not govern the context of "illegally practising medicine" (非法行医 ("*Fei Fa Xing Yi*")), even if illegal medical practices cause personal injuries to the patients.[57] Furthermore, Article 33 of the *Regulation* excludes some unexpected or unavoidable consequences from the definition of "medical accidents". Second, the GPCL promises more generous and extensive compensation for personal injury than the *Regulation*. The *Regulation* provides for both economic and non-economic damages, such as lost wages, disability living support, disability equipment, support for dependents, funeral expense, and spiritual injury, but formulates them in a restrictive fashion.[58]

The coexistence of the GPCL and the *Regulation* and their inconsistencies in substantive clauses actually create a two-layered scheme of medical injury compensation. The *Regulation* has a higher threshold for compensation, but authorizes a lower level of compensation for medical accidents. That produces anomalies and bizarreness. Patients suffering similar medical injuries might be awarded higher amounts of damages under the GPCL than they could receive under the *Regulation*. Medical injuries that do not cross the thresholds or are excluded from the *Regulation* may fall within the ambit of the GPCL, therefore exposing medical professionals to greater liability. Less serious medical injuries may have a higher level of compensation under the GPCL than more serious medical injuries under the *Regulation*.

Understandably State Council, Ministry of Health, and medical practitioners prefer the *Regulation*, adopting one of the principles of Chinese legal interpretation, namely that specific provisions preempt more general provisions, as a

---

[56] The Regulation on the Handling of Medical Accidents (2002, State Council), Article 49(2) ("If a medical accident is defied, the medical institution is not responsible for making any compensation.") (医疗事故处理条例, 2002年, 国务院, 第49(2)条). This exclusion clause was later reinterpreted that it is only applicable within the context of the *Regulation on the Handling of Medical Accidents*. If medical negligence did not constitute "medical accident", medical institution shall not compensate for it *according to the Regulation*. That does not mean medical institution shall not compensate for medical negligence according to *other sources of law*, such as GPCL. *See*, Answers by the Chief Official of the First Civil Court of the SPC to Reporters' Questions on How to Apply Laws in Adjudicating Medical Lawsuits (最高人民法院民一庭负责人就审理医疗纠纷案件的法律适用问题答记者问), http://www.cmda.gov.cn/yishiweiquan/weiquanzhishi/2009-02-25/5311.html (accessed 19 September 2010).

[57] The Regulation on the Handling of Medical Accidents (2002, State Council), Article 61 ("Illegal medical practices that cause personal injuries to the patients shall not be deemed as medical accidents; if the provisions of the criminal law have been violated, the offender shall be subject to taking criminal liabilities; if any compensations are involved, the victim therefrom shall institute actions directly at the people's court.")(医疗事故处理条例, 2002年, 国务院, 第61条).

[58] For example, living expenses for disabled dependents of an injured patient can only be paid for 20 years, if the disabled dependent is more than 16 years old. *See*, The Regulation on the Handling of Medical Accidents (2002, State Council), Article 50 (医疗事故处理条例, 2002年, 国务院, 第50条).

justification.[59] On the other side, patients and their advocates want to circumvent the more medical-profession-protective *Regulation* and pursue remedies from the more generous GPCL, arguing for the application of another principle of legal interpretation, namely enactments of a higher legal authority supersede enactments of a lower legal authority.

Confusion compelled the Supreme People's Court (SPC) to clarify the situation. Answering the question delivered by Tian Jin High People's Court about how to apply laws in a medical malpractice case, the SPC, in its 1992 Reply (judicial interpretation), affirmed the applicability and priority of the GPCL in adjudicating medical malpractice cases.[60] Regrettably the SPC's 1992 Reply did not solve the conflicts between the GPCL and the then 1987 *Regulation*, claiming that both the GPCL and the 1987 *Regulation* share the same "basic spirit".

On January 6, 2003, the SPC proactively released a Notice regarding adjudicating *medical malpractice cases* to Local High People's Courts and Military Courts (hereinafter "the 2003 Notice").[61] As far as laws applicable for medical malpractice cases, the 2003 Notice suggested a compromised approach: for medical negligence which constitutes "medical accident", the 2002 *Regulation* should be applied; for medical negligence which does not constitute "medical accident" or medical compensation disputes not caused by "medical accident", the GPCL is still open to apply. The 2003 Notice actually divided medical lawsuits into two categories: medical accident cases and non-medical-accident cases. The two contexts have two different applicable rules.

Soon after, on December 4, 2003, the SPC released an Interpretation regarding how to apply law in adjudicating *personal injury cases* (hereinafter "the 2003 Interpretation").[62] The 2003 Interpretation does not mention the *Regulation* on

---

[59] This argument is very weak. As I mentioned before, according to Article 83 of Law of the People's Republic of China on Legislation (2000), application of the principle that special provisions have priority over old provisions has a precondition: both the special and general provisions should be issued by *the same level of authority* (the same organ). Obviously, the GPCL and the *Regulation* are formulated by different organs (NPC and State Council respectively). The general principle that legislations of higher authority prevail over legislations of lower authority should apply.

[60] Supreme People's Court's Reply to Tian Jin High People's Court Regarding How to Apply Laws in Adjudicating the Medical Accident Compensation Case of *Li Xin-rong v. The Affiliated Hospital of Tian Jin No. 2 Medical College* (1992, SPC) (最高人民法院关于李荣诉天津市第二医学院附属医院医疗事故赔偿一案如何适用法律问题的复函, 1992年, 最高人民法院). Although the SPC acknowledged the applicability of both the GPCL and the 1987 *Regulation*, in formulating the reply, the SPC put the GPCL on the head of the list of laws that are applicable in the medical malpractice cases.

[61] Notice of the Supreme People's Court on Trying Civil Cases on Medical Disputes by Referring to the "Regulation on Handling Medical Accidents" (No. 20 [2003] of the Supreme People's Court) (最高人民法院关于参照《医疗事故处理条例》审理医疗纠纷民事案件的通知, 2003年, 最高人民法院).

[62] The Interpretation of the Supreme People's Court Concerning Some Issues on the Application of Law for the Trial of Cases on Compensation for Personal Injury (2003, SPC) (最高人民法院关于审理人身损害赔偿案件适用法律若干问题的解释, 2003年, 最高人民法院).

medical accidents. The focus of this piece of Judicial Interpretation is on how to apply GPCL and Civil Procedural Law. The 2003 Interpretation follows GPCL and details how to determine compensation for personal injury caused by infringements of a person's life, health and body.[63] It aroused the hope that GPCL would be more readily available for medical malpractice cases.

However, subsequently, a Newsletter released by the chief official of the First Civil Court of the SPC[64] revealed that the SPC still favors the two-layer approach it previously adopted. On the one hand, the Newsletter made it clear that fairness and justice dictate that compensation liability should attach to all medical negligence, not just medical accidents. On the other hand, the Newsletter acknowledged the position that as a "special" legislation, the 2002 *Regulation* should have priority over the GPCL in dealing with *medical accidents cases*. It maintained the dichotomy drawn between the cases of medical accidents and non-medical-accident cases. The GPCL and the 2003 Interpretation shall apply to non-medical-accident cases or cases of personal injury, and the 2002 *Regulation* and 2003 Notice shall apply to the special context of medical accidents. Envisaging that patients may prefer to institute legal proceedings under the more patient-friendly "non-medical-accident" cause of action rather than the "medical accident" lawsuit, the Newsletter gave medical institutions an opportunity to rebut the "name" of "general medical lawsuit". When a medical institution establishes that the lawsuit concerned is not a non-medical-accident case, and authentication established that the patient's injury was caused by "medical accident", the court should apply the 2002 *Regulation*, and the victim cannot pursue GPCL. According to the Newsletter, the level of Chinese economic development, medical institutions' level of affordability and promoting medical progress justify awarding the low-level of compensation for medical accidents. Responding to the concerns that medical malpractice law may hinder medical progress, the Newsletter invested hope in developing medical insurance to help medical institutions to disseminate risks.

(b) Technical Authentication v. Forensic Examination

Another area that illustrates the inconsistency between the *Regulation* and other sources of law is about technical authentication. The *Regulation* creates a medical accident *technical authentication* system. The *Regulation* sets forth detailed procedures for the operation of technical authentications by panels of medical experts,

[63] The Interpretation of the Supreme People's Court Concerning Some Issues on the Application of Law for the Trial of Cases on Compensation for Personal Injury (2003, SPC), Articles 1, 17–35 (最高人民法院关于审理人身损害赔偿案件适用法律若干问题的解释, 2003年, 最高人民法院, 第1, 17–35条).

[64] Answers by the Chief Official of the First Civil Court of the SPC to Reporters' Questions on How to Apply Laws in Adjudicating Medical Lawsuits (最高人民法院民一庭负责人就审理医疗纠纷案件的法律适用问题答记者问), http://www.cmda.gov.cn/yishiweiquan/weiquanzhishi/2009-02-25/5311.html (accessed 19 September 2010).

who are selected from a pool of medical experts maintained by medical societies.[65] The panel of medical experts (three or more) is selected by the parties from the pool.[66] The conclusions reached by the majority of the panel will be expressed in the form of a letter of authentication. The letter is required to touch on the following issues: (1) the breach of the duty issue – whether the medical conduct violated any legal requirements or medical norms; (2) the causation issue – whether there exists a causal connection between the medical conduct and the injury; (3) the degree of contribution by medical conduct to the injury; (4) the severity or grade of injury.[67]

The medical expert authentication system was originally intended to provide the courts with professional expertise that they need. However, great concerns have been raised about the impartiality and credibility of the system. There are continuing concerns about bias, professional protectionism, and departmental protectionism in the selection and operation of authentication committees under the 2002 *Regulation*.[68] Conclusions of technical authentications are reached *collegially*.[69] The collegial decision-making process may avoid individual responsibility and mask protectionism.[70] The authentication committee consists of medical professionals and forensic medicine professionals.[71] The result of authentication represents "medical" voices. There are no layperson representatives in the panel. The system is criticised as just shifting from the old model of *fathers* (administrative departments of health) judging the conduct of their *sons* (medical practitioners) to the current model of *brothers* (medical professionals) judging the conduct of their *brothers* (medical professionals).[72]

---

[65] The Regulation on the Handling of Medical Accidents (2002, State Council), Articles 20–34 (医疗事故处理条例, 2002年, 国务院, 第20–34条).

[66] The Regulation on the Handling of Medical Accidents (2002, State Council), Articles 23–24 (医疗事故处理条例, 2002年, 国务院, 第23–24条).

[67] The Regulation on the Handling of Medical Accidents (2002, State Council), Article 31 (医疗事故处理条例, 2002年, 国务院, 第31条).

[68] Local medical associations are in charge of arranging authentications, and most of the experts in local databanks have local connections. The Chinese Medical Association may arrange authentications in certain cases. However, according to its charter, one of the goals of the Chinese Medical Association is to serve health professionals and protect their lawful rights and interests. The close relationship between medical associations and health departments is also a cause for concern.

[69] The Regulation on the Handling of Medical Accidents (2002, State Council), Article 25 (医疗事故处理条例, 2002年, 国务院, 第25条). Conclusions are reached by majority rule.

[70] Since no individual signature was required on the authentication reports, it was difficult to hold responsible or cross-examine any individual member of a committee for the quality of their work in performing authentications.

[71] The Regulation on the Handling of Medical Accidents (2002, State Council), Article 24 (医疗事故处理条例, 2002年, 国务院, 第24条).

[72] You Zhong Hua "Problems and Suggestions regarding Current Medical Accident Technical Authentication Law" (2004) 11 Journal of Law and Medicine 11, 11 (尤中华: "当前医疗事故技术鉴定中的问题及建议", 载《法律与医学杂志》2004 年第1 期, 第11页). *Compare*, Li Yi "Comparative Study on the Rate of Medical Accidents Authenticated in Guang Dong Province (2001–2003)" (2006) 37 Guang Zhou Medicine 54, 55 (李益: "广东省2001~2003年医疗事故技术鉴定事故比率的对比研究" 载《广州医药》2006年第3期, 第55页) (defending the fairness of technical authentication system).

It is questionable that members of those authentication committees could fairly scrutinize the medical practices of their colleagues and subordinates.

Dissatisfaction with the technical authentication system motivates plaintiff-patients to circumvent it and pursue alternatives. That raises the issue of the nature of conclusion of technical authentication. Does it have a monopoly status? Is it conclusive? Can courts seek other forms of expert opinion? It seemed that the Ministry of Health claimed that authentication committees are the only "legal" entities for conducting technical authentications. However, while some courts treated authentication committees in that way, other courts preferred to assign *forensic medical experts* to conduct independent examinations, and made decisions according to forensic medical reports. In this respect, the SPC still maintains the distinction it drew in the context of determining applicable laws, that is, distinction between cases of medical accidents and non-medical-accident cases. According to the 2003 Notice, for medical accidents, courts should request medical associations to organize medical accidents technical authentications; otherwise, courts should follow the *Management Regulation on Entrusting External Forensic Examination by People's Courts*.[73] Again, the SPC created a two-layer authentication scheme for medical malpractice cases. On the one hand, the SPC requires courts to follow the procedure of *technical authentication* when they deal with *medical accidents*. On the other hand, for *non-medical-accident* cases, the courts have the freedom to organize *forensic examination*.

With regard to applications for and conclusions of technical authentications or forensic examinations, the Notice requires courts to follow the SPC's rules regarding evidence in civil litigation.[74] That means conclusions of technical authentications or forensic examinations will be treated as one form of "evidence". While courts are likely to defer to the opinion of the panel on matters of professional expertise, the conclusion of the expert panel is not technically binding on the court. The courts are reluctant to give absolute deference to the letter of authentication.

In conclusion, the SPC's approach of drawing dichotomy between the cases of medical accidents and non-medical-accident cases and subjecting them to different legal contexts does not resolve the problem of inconsistency between GPCL and the *Regulation*, although the SPC's efforts may ease the potential conflicts between them.

---

[73] Notice of the Supreme People's Court on Trying Civil Cases on Medical Disputes by Referring to the "Regulation on Handling Medical Accidents" (No. 20 [2003] of the Supreme People's Court), Article 2 (1) (最高人民法院关于参照《医疗事故处理条例》审理医疗纠纷民事案件的通知, 2003年, 最高人民法院, 第2 (1)条)("In adjudication of civil cases … when it comes to forensic examination of medical accidents, the conduct of those examinations shall be handed over to medical societies as stipulated in the 2002 regulation. When it comes to non-medical-accident cases, forensic examination shall be conducted according to the Regulation on the Management of Forensic Examinations Entrusted by People's Courts to External Entities").

[74] Notice of the Supreme People's Court on Trying Civil Cases on Medical Disputes by Referring to the "Regulation on Handling Medical Accidents" (No. 20 [2003] of the Supreme People's Court), Article 2 (2) (最高人民法院关于参照《医疗事故处理条例》审理医疗纠纷民事案件的通知, 2003年, 最高人民法院, 第2 (2)条).

There is still a widespread public dissatisfaction with the two-layer approach. The SPC's approach actually strengthened the inconsistencies between two groups of applicable law. The approach created *three dichotomies or distinctions, i.e.* distinctions between two causes of action, two groups of applicable laws and two systems of authentication. The *Regulation* was formulated by State Council and Ministry of Health. The SPC did not have audacity to ignore it or challenge it. In the area of medical injury compensation, the SPC may feel that it has no other choice but to embrace it.[75] Can NPC's new legislation change the situation?

After nearly eight years of consultation, debate and revision,[76] on December 26, 2009, the Standing Committee of NPC promulgated China's *Tort Liability Law* (hereafter "the Tort Law").[77] The Tort Law, together with Chinese Contract Law (1999), Chinese Property Law (2007), and several other branches of civil law, will be part of the Chinese Civil Code. The adoption of the Tort Law solidifies the foundation of China's Civil Code. Before the Tort Law, China has already developed a tort law system. One of the Tort Law's missions was to consolidate the provisions and principles scattered throughout more than 40 different pieces of legislation in a single piece of legislation.[78]

The Tort Law has a broad ambit, covering a wide range of subject matter. It contains 12 Chapters and 92 separate provisions. It protects "civil rights and interests".[79] It specifically lists 18 categories of "civil rights and interests".[80] The extremely

---

[75] It was said that, before the *Regulation* was adopted by the State Council, the then Chinese Premier of State Council, Zhu Rongji, asked the SPC if they would support the *Regulation*. The SPC said "yes". *See*, Professor Yang Li Xin *Opinions on Tort Liability Law*, at http://www.civillaw.com.cn/article/default.asp?id=45436 (last accessed 20 April, 2010) (杨立新: "对侵权责任法讨论的意见", 载中国民商法网, 2010年4月20日访问).

[76] It will become effective on July 1, 2010. China has experienced a significant increase in the number of tort-related cases in recent years, with courts reportedly hearing 980,000 new tort cases in 2007 and more than a million in 2008, with a significant increase expected for 2009. China's effort to craft a comprehensive tort liability law began in 2002, when the first draft was reviewed by the National People's Congress (NPC). The Tort Law was revised and submitted to the NPC again in December 2008 and finally in the fall of 2009.

[77] Tort Liability Law of People's Republic of China (2009, Standing Committee of NPC) (中华人民共和国侵权责任法, 2009年, 全国人大常委会).

[78] For example, Chapter 5 of the Tort Law discusses liability for defective products. The principles are consistent with the provisions of China's *GPCL, the Law on Protection of Consumer Rights and Interests (Consumer Rights Protection Law)* (1993), *the Product Quality Law* (1993, revised 2000), and *the Food Safety Law* (2009), and relevant interpretations of the Supreme People's Court.

[79] Tort Liability Law of People's Republic of China (2009, Standing Committee of NPC), Article 2 (中华人民共和国侵权责任法, 2009年, 全国人大常委会, 第2条).

[80] Those civil rights and interests include the right to life, the right to health, rights associated with names, reputation rights, honorary rights, the right to one's image, the right to privacy, the right to marital autonomy, the right to guardianship, ownership rights, usufruct, collateral rights (security interests), copyrights, patent rights, exclusive rights to use trademarks, discovery rights, equity rights and inheritance rights, and other personal and property rights and interests. *See*, Tort Liability Law of People's Republic of China (2009, Standing Committee of NPC), Article 2 (中华人民共和国侵权责任法, 2009年, 全国人大常委会, 第2条).

broad list is non-exhaustive. Damage compensation is not the sole way of consuming tort liability. The Tort Liability Law contemplates seven other remedies that may be used, either independently or jointly.[81] In addition to general provisions, it encompasses seven special torts liabilities: product liability (Articles 41–47), liability for automobile accidents (Articles 48–53), liability for medical malpractice (Articles 54–64), liability for environmental damage (Articles 65–68), liability for hazardous products and activities (Articles 69–77), liability caused by persons who raise animals (Articles 78–84), and liability for damages caused by the collapse of structures or buildings (Articles 85–91). It also addresses Internet service provider liability (Article 36); liability for operators of public accommodations and facilities such as hotels, malls and banks (Article 37); and liability for injuries as a result of the acts or omissions of educational institutions (Articles 38–40). It embraces notions such as joint and several liability (Articles 9–14), punitive damages (Article 47), compensation for mental distress (Article 22), and comparative negligence (Article 26).

The Tort Law gives Medical Damage Liability one separate chapter (Chapter 7) and 11 separate Articles (Articles 54–64). It provides new and uniform guidance on Chinese medical negligence law. The Tort law does not echo the concept of "medical accident". It follows the GPCL's principle that compensation liability for injury should be attached to a person's fault and negligent act. If a patient is injured during diagnosis and medical treatment and such injury is caused by the fault of a medical institution and its medical staff members, the medical institution shall be liable for compensation.[82] It does not set additional thresholds for compensation. In determining the amount of compensation, the Tort Law does not distinguish medical negligence from other torts. All torts shall follow the same rules regarding methods of assuming liability and damage compensation.[83] The Tort Law adopts the GPCL & the 2003 Interpretation's level of compensation.

After the Tort Law came into being, there are still disagreements about the fate of the 2002 *Regulation*. Some scholars still prefer to save and keep the *Regulation*, arguing that the Tort Law cannot trump or replace the *Regulation* because they are dealing with different issues. As I noted before, the *Regulation* actually has two components: one being the rules for preventing medical accidents, promoting quality of health care, and resolving disputes; another being the rules regarding medical

---

[81] Possible remedies include: (1) Requiring an individual or company to cease infringement (as of civil rights); (2) Eliminating the risk caused by a person's tortious conduct; (3) Removing the obstacle to the exercise of rights created by such conduct; (4) Returning property to the victim of a tort; (5) Restoring the state of affairs to what it was prior to commission of the tort; (6) Compensating the victim of the tort for damages suffered; (7) Making an apology; (8) Eliminating adverse effects; Restoring the injured party's reputation. *See*, Tort Liability Law of People's Republic of China (2009, Standing Committee of NPC), Article 15 (中华人民共和国侵权责任法, 2009年, 全国人大常委会, 第15条).

[82] Tort Liability Law of People's Republic of China (2009, Standing Committee of NPC), Article 54 (中华人民共和国侵权责任法, 2009年, 全国人大常委会, 第54条).

[83] Tort Liability Law of People's Republic of China (2009, Standing Committee of NPC), Articles 15–25 (中华人民共和国侵权责任法, 2009年, 全国人大常委会, 第15–25条).

accidents compensation. I would like to argue for saving and reinforcing the first component of the *Regulation* and transforming the *Regulation* into a law of professional regulation and complaint-resolution. Compensation is not the only way of responding to adverse events in health care.[84] In addition to accountability and sanction, communication, correction and restoration should also be the focus of legislation. The *Regulation* has the potential of becoming a good source of law targeting professional regulation and complaint resolution, thereby making contribution to a constructive doctor-patient relationship.

As to the second component of the *Regulation* – medical accident and compensation law – or the civil law component, I would like to see the *Regulation* withdrawn. In the context of medical injury liability, even before the advent of the Tort Law, the 2002 *Regulation* had already been "marginalized" by the courts because many courts preferred to apply the GPCL and the 2003 SPC Interpretation in adjudicating medical negligence disputes.[85] In the era of the Tort Law, the room for the *Regulation* becomes smaller, especially in the area of compensation for patients' injury. The Tort Law is a NPC legislation, and the *Regulation* is a State Council legislation. Both cover medical negligence law. The argument that the *Regulation* still survives the passage of the Tort Law is very weak. According to Chinese Legislation Law, the basic principle is that the force of NPC laws is superior to that of administrative regulations.[86] If the inferior law is in conflict with the superior law, the inferior law shall be changed or revoked.[87] The principle that special provisions have priority over general provisions only applies if both provisions are formulated by the same organ.[88] The "basic civil system" should have "laws" rather than administrative regulations.[89] Even if NPC can authorise State Council to formulate civil law rules, when NPC has enacted law on the authorised matter, the authorisation is terminated.[90]

It will be for the Supreme People's Court's Judicial Interpretation to help to clarify some unresolved issues in the Tort Law, including the relationship between

---

[84] *See*, Joanna Manning "New Zealand's Remedial Responses to Adverse Events in Healthcare" (2008) 16 Torts Law Journal 120, 120–155.

[85] Liao Tian Ming et.al. "Survey and Reflections on Medical Authentication in Medical Malpractice Cases" (2010) 64 Journal of He Tian Normal College 2, 2 (廖天明等: "医疗损害赔偿案件中医疗鉴定问题的调研思考", 载《和田师范专科学校学报》(汉文综合版)2010 年第2 期, 第2页) (revealing that more courts prefer *forensic* authentication rather than *technical* authentication of the *Regulation*).

[86] Law of the People's Republic of China on Legislation (2000), Article 79 (中华人民共和国立法法, 2000年, 第79条).

[87] Law of the People's Republic of China on Legislation (2000), Article 87 (中华人民共和国立法法, 2000年, 第87条).

[88] Law of the People's Republic of China on Legislation (2000), Article 83 (中华人民共和国立法法, 2000年, 第83条).

[89] Law of the People's Republic of China on Legislation (2000), Article 8 (中华人民共和国立法法, 2000年, 第8条).

[90] Law of the People's Republic of China on Legislation (2000), Articles 9–11 (中华人民共和国立法法, 2000年, 第9–11条).

the Tort Law and the 2002 *Regulation*. On June 30, 2010, just before the effective date (July 1, 2010) of the Tort Law, the first Judicial Interpretation regarding the new Tort Law[91] (hereafter "the 2010 Notice") surfaced. Pursuant to Article 3 of the 2010 Notice, People's Courts may, responding to the parties' application or on their initiative, decide to organize "medical damage authentication", when they apply the Tort Liability Law to adjudicate civil lawsuits. In doing this, the courts should "follow the *Decision of the Standing Committee of the National People's Congress on the Administration of Judicial Authentication*,[92] *Management Regulation on Entrusting External Forensic Examination by People's Courts*,[93] and stipulations of relevant national department".

Some explanation about the Notice is required. First, the Notice does not mention the "*medical accident* technical authentication" (医疗事故技术鉴定("*Yi Liao Shi Gu Ji Shu Jian Ding*")); it adopts a new term "medical damage authentication" (医疗损害鉴定 ("*Yi Liao Sun Hai Jian Ding*")). The new term is consistent with the Tort Liability Law. Second, when there is a need for authentication, the Notice accords high priority to *forensic* authentication or examination. Third, in the context of authentication, the Notice does not exclude absolutely the relevance of the 2002 *Regulation*. Although the list of applicable rules for authentication is headed by *forensic* authentication rules, it is open and not exhaustive. The 2002 State Council Regulation on medical accidents and the procedure of *technical* authentication may fall within the term "stipulations of relevant national department".

On the one hand, the Notice indicates that the SPC is not ready to absolutely say "no" to the 2002 *Regulation*. On the other hand, the significance and relevance of the *Regulation* in the courts' adjudication of medical negligence disputes are further diluted. It should be noted that, although the 2002 *Regulation* suffers from many flaws, such as high threshold for compensation, low level of compensation, and low credibility of the technical authentication procedure, it has some merits. As far as technical authentication is concerned, the *Regulation* rightly involves medical professionals in the process of establishing the standard of care, breach of standard, and causation. What the law needs to do is to enhance the credibility of the process of authentication, such as adding layperson voices to the authentication committee's conclusions and strengthening the external scrutiny over the process and its results, rather than abandoning the process. The forensic authentication and technical authentication should not compete and replace each other. They should complement

[91] Notice of Supreme People's Court on Several Questions Regarding How to Apply The Tort Liability Law of People's Republic of China (No. (2010) 23, 2010, SPC) (最高人民法院关于适用《中华人民共和国侵权责任法》若干问题的通知, 法发〔2010〕23号, 2001年, 最高人民法院).

[92] Decision of the Standing Committee of the National People's Congress on the Administration of Judicial Authentication (2005, Standing Committee of NPC) (全国人民代表大会常务委员会关于司法鉴定管理问题的决定, 2005年, 全国人大常委会).

[93] Management Regulation on Entrusting External Forensic Examination by People's Courts (2002, SPC) (人民法院对外委托司法鉴定管理规定, 2002年, 最高人民法院).

each other. The forensic medicine experts do not have the ability to provide all kinds of expertise and knowledge that the courts need. For example, in establishing the standard of care and negligence, the law needs to consider a reasonable doctor's conduct, medical profession's practices and follow the "same school" rule. That cannot be done well without the involvement of clinical professionals. The form of technical authentication conducted by medical associations still enjoys popularity and recognition among medical profession. 92.5% of hospitals surveyed and 84.1% of healthcare professionals surveyed believe the fairness and authoritativeness of medical accidents technical authentication organised by medical associations.[94]

---

[94] Fu Zi Tang et al. *Empirical Analysis on Adjudication of Medical Lawsuits* (People's Court Press, Beijing, 2006) 31 (付子堂 等著:《医疗纠纷案件审理之实证分析》, 人民法院出版社2006年版, 第31页).

The manufacturer's authorised representative in the EU is Springer Nature Customer Service Centre GmbH, Europaplatz 3, 69115 Heidelberg, Germany. If you have any concerns regarding our products, please contact ProductSafety@springernature.com

Printed and bound by CPI Group (UK) Ltd, Croydon, CR0 4YY
30/09/2026
02225645-0019